ANNALS OF THE NEW YORK ACADEMY OF SCIENCES

Volume 291

THE ROOTS OF AMERICAN PSYCHOLOGY: HISTORICAL INFLUENCES AND IMPLICATIONS FOR THE FUTURE

Edited by R. W. Rieber and Kurt Salzinger

The New York Academy of Sciences
New York, New York
1977

Library of Congress Cataloging in Publication Data

Main entry under title:

The roots of American psychology.

(Annals of The New York Academy of Sciences; v. 291)
"This series of papers is the result of a conference . . . held by The New York Academy of Sciences on April 28, 29, and 30, 1976."
1. Psychology–United States–Congresses. 2. Psychology–United States–History–Congresses. I. Rieber, Robert W. II. Salzinger, Kurt, III. New York Academy of Sciences. IV. Series: New York Academy of Sciences. Annals; v. 291. [DNLM: 1. Psychology–History–United States–Congresses. W1 AN626Y1 v. 291 / BF108.U5 R783 1976] Q11.N5 vol. 291 [BF108.U5] 508'.1s [150'.973]

ISBN 0-89072-037-1   77-5594

CCP
Printed in the United States of America
ISBN 0-89072-037-1

ANNALS OF THE NEW YORK ACADEMY OF SCIENCES

VOLUME 291

April 18, 1977

THE ROOTS OF AMERICAN PSYCHOLOGY: HISTORICAL INFLUENCES AND IMPLICATIONS FOR THE FUTURE*

Conference Organizers
R. W. RIEBER, KURT SALZINGER, and THOM VERHAVE

CONTENTS

*This series of papers is the result of a conference entitled The Roots of American Psychology: Historical Influences and Implications for the Future, held by The New York Academy of Sciences on April 28, 29, and 30, 1976.

Part III. Nineteenth and Twentieth Century Trends in the Psychology of the Self

Part IV. Socioeconomic and Political Factors in the Development of American Psychology

Part V. Historical Aspects of the Psychology of Language and Cognition

Part VI. Psychological Systems: Past, Present and Future

Financial assistance was received from:
- THE AMERICAN COUNCIL OF LEARNED SOCIETIES

INTRODUCTION:
HOW DEEP THE ROOTS?

R. W. Rieber

*John Jay College of Criminal Justice
City University of New York
New York, New York 10019*

Kurt Salzinger

*Biometrics Research Unit
New York State Psychiatric Institute
New York, New York 10032*

*Polytechnic Institute of New York
Brooklyn, New York 11201*

It has not been long since psychologists conceived of the subject of their history in the classical know-nothing style of "just one damned thing after another," or viewed the behavior of their antecedents merely as challenges to their ability to invalidate whatever they did. It is therefore refreshing to be able to introduce a series of papers here that consist of sophisticated historical analyses equal in quality to those performed with respect to any other science. It is fitting that we should be reviewing the history of American psychology in this, the Bicentennial of the United States of America, since historical examination profits much from the throwing of the widest nets.

In addition to the close inspection of the past of American psychology and its extra-American sources, we were able to assemble a number of distinguished psychologists who truly can be described as having *made* history. These papers by Inhelder, Murray, Piaget, and Skinner also provided the conference, and now the Annal, with a focus on those psychologists who can best make clear their own profound influence upon the course of history and the current status of psychology.

We are also able to present to the reader a true rendition of the discussions that took place in response to the papers, since all were tape-recorded and transcribed. Although we, with the speakers, have changed the wording in a number of instances, we did so only for the sake of clarity in communication and always retained both the tone and the content of each remark.

This conference received aid from a number of sources, and we would like to thank them all. First, we would like to thank Thom Verhave, who was, along with us, an organizer and speaker for this conference. We also benefited from Florence Denmark's advice both in her capacity as adviser of the Psychology Section and as representative of the Conference Committee of the New York Academy.

The conference which is the basis of this annal received the generous support of the American Council of Learned Societies and thus made it possible for us to have speakers from around the world. We thank the Council. We are grateful also to the Psychology Department of John Jay College, CUNY, for its support. As usual in our experience, the Academy staff was most helpful on each step of the many tasks involved in the planning of the conference and now in the preparing of the Annal: We wish to thank Ellen Marks, Ann Collins, Bill Boland, and Beatrice Radin, as well as their assistants, whose help was both formidable and gracious.

THE INFLUENCE OF GESTALT PSYCHOLOGY IN AMERICA

Mary Henle

Graduate Faculty
New School for Social Research
New York, New York 10013

In America, Gestalt psychology has always been a minority movement. A brief look at its history, both here and in Germany, will help us to understand why. It is well known that it began around 1910, when Wertheimer made his fateful stopover in Frankfurt to test his hypotheses about stroboscopic movement. Like the man who came to dinner, he remained for several years. Here he found Köhler and Koffka, and the three of them collaborated in what was to become Gestalt psychology.

The publication launching the new movement was Wertheimer's paper of 1912.[1] In 1911 Koffka left for Giessen, and work, particularly in perception, was soon coming out of his laboratory. In 1913 Köhler was appointed director of the Anthropoid Station of the Prussian Academy of Sciences on the island of Tenerife; because of World War I, he was unable to return to Germany until 1920. By 1914 a few significant titles had been added to the literature of Gestalt psychology. But then Wertheimer and Koffka were engaged in war work. Only Köhler, in the isolation of Spanish Africa, was able to continue his psychological research.

In 1920 Köhler became acting director, and soon afterwards, director of the Psychological Institute of the University of Berlin. Wertheimer was already there, as was Kurt Lewin, whose work bears a significant relationship to Gestalt psychology. From 1920 until the coming of the Nazis to power, Gestalt psychology flourished. Graduate students were coming to the Institute from a number of countries; the *Psychologische Forschung*, the journal of the Gestalt psychologists, was founded, and work was progressing in many directions.

In 1922 Koffka introduced Gestalt psychology to America with his paper "Perception, an introduction to the Gestalt-Theorie."[2] Two years later he came to the United States, settling in 1927 at Smith College, Northampton, Mass.

Wertheimer moved his family out of Germany before Hitler came to power: he was quick to realize what was happening. Köhler remained for some two years of courageous struggle with the Nazi authorities, who harassed his students, dismissed his assistants, made appointments to the Institute without consulting him.

By the end of World War II, the first generation of young Gestalt psychologists was essentially wiped out: for example, von Lauenstein was lost in the war, von Restorff died in Germany, Duncker in America, to name Köhler's chief assistants. The others were scattered; a few migrated to America, England, the Scandinavian countries, Israel; Zeigarnik returned to the Soviet Union. Some went into practical work. For example, Paul Koseleff, one of the Nazis' first targets at the Institute, became a psychoanalyst in Denmark; I recently learned that Krolik, whose perceptual experiments are among the most beautiful I know, became a school psychologist; Erich Goldmeier, who did excellent work on similarity and on

3

memory change, practiced medicine in America. Others found positions in school, not university, teaching.

Could a second generation be started in America? Koffka, it will be recalled, was a professor at Smith College, an undergraduate institution; somehow he managed to give one Ph.D., to Molly Harrower. Köhler went to Swarthmore, another undergraduate college in Swarthmore, Pa.; and when Wertheimer arrived at the New School for Social Research, it was not yet giving degrees; only at the very end of his life were a few graduate students working with him for the Ph.D.

But it was not only the lack of graduate students that stood in the way of a new generation of Gestalt psychologists. Behaviorism was and—however modified —has remained the dominant psychology in America. Köhler relates an amusing anecdote:

> In 1925, soon after my first arrival in this country, I had a curious experience. When once talking with a graduate student of psychology who was, of course, a behaviorist, I remarked that McDougall's psychology of striving seemed to me to be associated with certain philosophical theses which I found it hard to accept; but that he might nevertheless be right in insisting that, as a matter of simple observation, people do this or that in order to reach certain goals. Did not the student himself sometimes go to a post office in order to buy stamps? And did he not just now prepare himself for certain examinations to be held next Thursday? The answer was prompt: "I never do such things," said the student. There is nothing like a solid scientific conviction.[3]

Even when, years later, behaviorists became interested in cognitive problems, it was still a cognitive behaviorism; and the differences that distinguished Gestalt psychology from behaviorism remained. New developments were more closely related to behaviorism than to Gestalt psychology. As one example, the use of computer models of thinking still involves machine theory, no matter how sophisticated the machine. Machine theories of neural functioning have consistently been criticized by Gestalt psychologists.

Thus the Gestalt immigrants found themselves in an intellectual atmosphere dominated by behaviorism and its relatives; they were mainly without graduate students; and several of them died too soon to have much influence on the psychology of their new country. It is scarcely surprising that a new generation of Gestalt psychologists did not grow up in America.

And it was hardly likely that Gestalt psychology would be understood, even when it was listened to politely, or with respect. Misunderstandings may be seen as both cause and effect of the less than overwhelming influence which Gestalt psychology had in America. I would like to discuss a few of these.

The interesting thing about these misunderstandings is that, except for the first I will mention (which I have only recently begun to take as something other than a bad joke), they are not new. Gestalt psychologists have repeatedly spoken to these issues, but without effect. This problem of the persistence of misunderstandings is one which I hope will interest some future historian of ideas, and one which the cognitive psychologist should not neglect.

1. The most grotesque current misunderstanding of Gestalt psychology is that it has some relation to gestalt therapy. I will not discuss this distortion of history and of ideas, but will merely state that there is nothing in common between these two developments.

2. Gestalt psychologists, because of their opposition to certain empiristic hypotheses, have repeatedly been called nativists: for example, by Piaget in the 1930s, by Boring in the 1940s, by Allport and Tolman in the 1950s, by the Mandlers in the 1960s. Here is a quotation from R. L. Gregory in 1970:[4] "To the Gestalt

writers, these Organising Principles were innate, inherited." Another perceptionist, writing in 1975, remarks: "By and large, the Gestalt psychologists were nativists."[5] Considering the Gestalt psychologists' answer to the question of why units are perceived as units, he says:

> First, regarding the perception of the natural environment, evolutionary change has guaranteed that the brain will operate on the basis of laws that work, that is, that generally yield veridical perception. . . . Proximity and similarity evolved as laws of neural organization because of the nature of the environment in which animals evolved. In some other environment, different laws of organization would have evolved.

This last quotation is particularly interesting because it spells out exactly the *opposite* of what Gestalt psychologists say about evolution and thus about nativism. In the 1920s Köhler had already made his position clear.[6] He left no room for doubt about what he thought evolution can do and what it can*not* do in 1950;[7] and his last book, *The Task of Gestalt Psychology*,[8] contains perhaps the clearest statement of all. Gestalt psychologists are not nativists. I have no hope of being understood where the others were not, but I feel the obligation once more to state the position.

Nativism refers, of course, to explanations in terms of inherited mechanisms; we may consider in particular inherited features of the nervous system, though other parts of the anatomy are, of course, relevant. The nervous system exhibits certain histological structures because the organism is equipped with particular chromosomes—products of evolution. Thus a nativistic explanation, say of perceptual facts, makes these facts the contribution of evolution.

In his examination of this theory, Köhler shows that evolutionary theory does *not* permit such an explanation. Although we most often think of evolution as a theory of change or of variance, it contains, as an essential part, a principle of invariance. If organisms develop from inorganic nature, they must have something in common with this nature: factors that apply to inanimate nature apply also to the organisms that develop from it. The alternative is vitalism or emergent evolution, which scientists have for the most part rejected.

What is it that organisms share with inorganic nature? General principles (like conservation of energy), forces, elementary processes such as electric currents. Thus electric currents occur in the brains of organisms as well as in streaks of lightning. Since they are found throughout nature, they must be independent of the genetic equipment of any species or any individual. Surely nobody would maintain that electric or chemical processes corresponding to perception are inherited. As Köhler puts it, the principle of invariance states that "no essentially new kind of action appears in living systems."[7] It is only constraints that are contributed by evolution—in our case, anatomical structures in the nervous system and elsewhere that exclude certain possibilities of action. But actions themselves owe nothing to evolution. "Any action in any organism involves the operation of factors which are entirely independent of evolution," writes Köhler.[7] A nativistic interpretation can therefore not account for the facts of perception.

I started with a quotation that attributes to Gestalt psychologists the view that the laws of neural organization are a product of evolution. But evolution cannot possibly be responsible for such laws, since actions as such are independent of evolution. It is precisely the Gestalt psychologists who have pointed this out.

There is another, perhaps surprising, consequence of this application of the principle of invariance in evolution to psychological problems. It forces us to reject certain empiristic interpretations as well. We do not learn to see, learn to think, learn to learn, nor are motives learned in the usual meanings of these expressions. For again, these are all forms of action. Thus they involve the operation of factors that the organism shares with inanimate nature, with all species, and with all individuals—factors that must therefore be independent of the individual experiences of anybody.

This is, of course, *not* to deny a role to learning in all these cases. Each one exhibits important influences of experience. It is just that the *processes* themselves are no more learned than they are inherited.

To return to the main point, Gestalt psychologists are not nativists. They do not accept the nativism-empiricism dichotomy; there is a third class of factors, invariant dynamics, that applies to all of nature. In Köhler's words, "An enormous part of the business of living can never, as such, have been affected by the changes introduced during evolution."[8] He continues:

> Why so much talk about inheritance, and so much about learning—but hardly ever a word about invariant dynamics? It is this invariant dynamics, however constrained by histological devices, which keeps organisms and their nervous systems going.

I do not know why we find it so difficult to break out of the nativism-empiricism dichotomy. Are we unable to think in terms of trichotomies? If we are, we will continue to misinterpret Gestalt psychology and—more serious—our explanations will not do justice to our subject matter.

3. The criticism that Gestalt psychologists have neglected the role of past experiences in psychological processes likewise has a long history, and, once again, clarifications of their position do not seem to help. We still find statements like the following:

> A further feature of the theory was an almost complete denial of learning as important for perception.[9]
> The Gestalt psychologists did not absolutely deny that past experience affects perception.[10]
> As a matter of fact, the dialogue between the behaviorists and the Gestalt psychologists seems to have centered upon the relative importance of past experience and innate organizing properties of the brain.[11]

That Gestalt psychologists reject certain kinds of empiristic explanations has just been indicated. That they do not confine the issue to nativism vs. empiricism has been sufficiently discussed. But that they deny an important role of past experience in perception, thinking, motivation, and so on, is far from the case. The question they ask is: *How* does past experience operate in these connections, what role does it play? Space does not permit me to do more than refer you to the sources, which would be a valuable exercise also for the writers I have been quoting.

4. Isomorphism has come in for its share of misunderstandings. This is the hypothesis that there is a structural similarity between percepts and corresponding brain events. Here is an example of a recent version of isomorphism by a critic of Gestalt psychology:

> ... When viewing a circle, there was supposed to be a circular brain trace; for a sphere a spherical brain trace, and presumably for a house a corresponding house-shaped trace ....
> ... There is far more to perception than the recognition of shape. How does the 'isomorphism' idea cope with other perceptual features? Consider colour: are we supposed to believe that when we see a green traffic light, part of our brain turns green?[9]

This same author asserts that "Gestalt writers did tend to say that there are pictures inside the brain,"[12] and elsewhere he asks: If pictures, why not melodies? Another writer refers to the "picture-in-the-head Gestalt school," adding:

> This need not be a literal representation such that an actual recognizable picture of objects may be found in the brain if we know how to look for it . . . .
> . . . Köhler . . . was the first to assert that there is a one-to-one topological correspondence between what goes on in experience and what goes on in the brain. This is like saying that there is a picture in the head which is in topological correspondence with the picture in the mind . . . .[11]

Gestalt psychologists do not know anything about pictures in the brain. Köhler, in particular, has taken pains to explicate the functional—not geometrical—meaning of isomorphism. One formulation of his is particularly relevant to the current interpretations I have quoted: "Certainly, the processes in our brain do not represent a geometrical picture of spatial visual experience."[13] Let us take an example from the same source. What is the functional meaning of "between"? "In cases of dynamic self-distribution . . . a local process of the functional context is 'functionally between' two other processes whenever mutual influence of these two is mediated by an alteration of the third." He offers an analogy:

> I tell Mr. A a story which is meant for Mr. F, whom for some reason I cannot address directly. Mr. A is in the same situation and hands the story down to Mr. B. Mr. B talks with C, C with D, D with E and, at last, E with F. Thus A, B, C, D, and E are "functionally between" me and F in this case of an influence. At the same time F may be nearer to me geometrically than D; for example, he may even be "geometrically" between me and D. Still, functionally, the opposite is true.[13]

Other specific relations have likewise been analyzed.

Qualities, such as color, are not dealt with by isomorphism, which is a structural principle, since qualities do not possess structure. It is obvious that the brain does not turn green when we see that color: colors do not exist in the physical world. Presumably chemical reactions correspond to them, since these exhibit the required variety (cf. Köhler's *The Place of Value in a World of Facts*[14]).

Isomorphism has proved to be a powerful heuristic, leading Köhler first to the investigation of figural aftereffects, then to the demonstration of steady cortical currents hypothesized as corresponding to such effects and to the perception of segregated forms in general. Naturally, the theory of cortical currents has come under attack, notably by Lashley and by Sperry, with their co-workers. Why does everybody quote these criticisms, and why does nobody read Köhler's replies?[15-17] One of the current texts I have been using, after summarizing the work of Lashley and of Sperry, does, in fact, include the sentence: "There are, however, certain questions that can be raised concerning these experiments."[5] What these questions are is never indicated. Another recent writer simply dismisses the theory of figural aftereffects as "no longer accepted," presumably because of Sperry's work.[11] It is interesting to note that the latest reference to Köhler's work in this volume is to a monograph of 1944, although the text was published thirty years later. Still another well-informed writer refers to the objections to the satiation theory already mentioned, omits Köhler's replies, and concludes (a bit more mildly than the others quoted): "While it cannot yet be discarded in its entirety, it is now evident that it cannot be retained intact, either as to substance or promise."[18] Köhler himself has discussed unsolved problems in the field of figural aftereffects and has refined his concepts.[17] But these considerations seem to have escaped the attention of the textbook writers on perception.

It may be noted that the particular authors cited have been chosen, with one exception, not to be representative, but to be better informed than the average about the work of Gestalt psychology.

In the case of all the problems I have been discussing, why is one position so systematically ignored, or so consistently misinterpreted? We are concerned with developing a science, not with winning a debate. Can we afford to ignore or to misinterpret the hypotheses of one group of scientists, particularly ones who have made such important contributions?

I turn now to some of these contributions.

It seems to be pretty generally agreed that Gestalt psychology transformed the study of perception. In 1912, when Wertheimer's paper on stroboscopic motion appeared, the center of investigation was sensation; what we now call perception was accounted for, in one way or another, by the intervention of higher mental processes. A survey of some of the theories on the German scene can be found in Köhler's critical article of 1913.[19] In America, Titchener was at his height; his context theory is formally similar to theories criticized by Köhler. While such theories are even now not extinct, the focus today is on the study of the objects and events of our phenomenal world. Both by their criticisms of the older views and by their demonstrations and experiments, Gestalt psychologists were most influential in effecting this change of direction. Beginning with stroboscopic movement—which Wertheimer refused to call by its then customary name, "apparent movement," because that term accorded it less reality than other movement from which it was phenomenally indistinguishable, Wertheimer and Koffka undertook their perceptual investigations. Köhler was meanwhile studying various perceptual functions in chimpanzees and in hens, now criticizing by empirical methods the theories which made of size constancy "apparent size," of color constancy "memory color." Once more, it was the phenomenal object, not sensations transformed by learning or other processes, with which his work was concerned. I think nobody will deny that it was mainly the Gestalt psychologists who turned the psychology of perception in this new direction. Gibson, as one example, assessing Koffka's *Principles of Gestalt Psychology*[20] thirty-five years after its publication, comments: "His book, more than any other book of its time, set the psychology of perception on the course it is now following."[21]

Likewise in thinking, Gestalt psychology provided a fresh start. The old psychology of images was already beginning to give way to other approaches, but Wertheimer's first use of the Gestalt principle in connection with the number concepts of "primitive peoples" represented a more radical departure.[22] Köhler's work, published as *The Mentality of Apes*,[23] is an acknowledged turning point in the psychology of thinking. Departing from most paradigms then in use, Köhler gave his chimpanzees the opportunity to behave intelligently, and they did. But their curiously foolish errors were also illuminating. The concept of *insight* was introduced and its role in thinking and learning was progressively clarified after this early work. Insight has never been very popular among American psychologists, who even now tend to use protective quotation marks around the word, as if they suspected something mysterious about it. Duncker's work on problem-solving is still widely known, and his term "functional fixedness" has become part of our psychological vocabulary.[24] Wertheimer's major contribution to the psychology of the thought processes, *Productive Thinking*.[25] has not yet had the influence it deserves; but it may still have an effect on theory if we ever have the courage to turn our attention from how computers solve problems and look to human thinking at its best.

I will return to theoretical and research contributions of the Gestalt psychologists, but may I first mention another kind of contribution. Since Gestalt theory did not fit the intellectual habits of American psychologists, attempts have repeatedly been made to reinterpret findings of this group in more familiar terms. Thus, issues for controversy were provided which, in turn, inspired new research. For example, the finding that animals and human beings often solve problems suddenly, often without previous fruitless efforts to reach the goal, did not fit the generally held theories of learning as an incremental process. There followed the long controversy over continuity in learning, and the result was much new research. Köhler's work on the nature of associations initiated a controversy, with Postman defending the traditional associationistic position and Asch continuing with experiments in the Gestalt tradition. We have thus acquired much new knowledge about the nature of associations. Attempts were made to reinterpret the Restorff effect (or isolation effect) in terms of association theory, and again new research was produced. Asch's work on the formation of impressions of personality, interpreted by him in organizational terms, led to a good deal of research that attempted to return it to the traditional fold. A very large body of research has grown out of attempts to reinterpret figural aftereffects.

Some of this research is difficult to evaluate at the present time. But however the issues are resolved—if they are resolved—controversy gives rise to new research. The supplying of issues for controversy is thus in itself an important contribution of Gestalt psychology. Controversy is good for psychology.

Some of the directions in which the Gestalt psychologists took their work were left strictly alone by American psychology. This is true of problems as diverse as values and cortical currents. Value seemed to many Americans best ignored in the interests of a value-free science, this despite Köhler's analysis of the concept within the framework of natural science. For very different reasons, cortical currents were mainly ignored, except that the effort was made to show that they did not really correspond to perceptions anyhow: technological advance had made it possible to stimulate the single cell, and attention was shifted away from more molar cortical events. In this case, physiologists will surely some day take up the problems if we do not; in the case of value we seem to be leaving the task of analysis to philosophers. There are further examples of work that has been ignored. I wonder how many psychologists know that Gestalt psychologists have put forth a theory of recall and one of attention.

I think we must say, in short, that outside of the field of perception and perhaps of thinking, the contributions of Gestalt psychology have been insufficiently utilized. I wonder if it is too optimistic to think that there is change in the air. That cognitive psychology has returned to prominence is well known. Even behaviorism can no longer turn its back on cognitive problems. But concern with cognition is one thing; *how* cognitive problems are dealt with is another. Cognitive behaviorism and computer simulation are still a long way from Gestalt psychology. Still, the stage may be set for a return to some of the conceptions of the Gestalt group.

A promising development is Jenkins's contextualism, as put forth in a paper entitled "Remember that old theory of memory? Well, forget it!"[26] Jenkins describes the associationistic assumptions from which he started, remarking: "This view is so pervasive in American psychology that it is almost coextensive with being an experimentalist." But his own research forced him to what he calls a contextual position. "This means not only that the analysis of memory must deal with contextual variables, but also . . . that what memory is depends on context." There is no reference in this paper to Gestalt psychology, and the experimental paradigms illustrated differ considerably from those typically employed by the Gestalt investigators. But that Jenkins's own findings led him to abandon the atomism and the mechanistic assumptions of his earlier approach is an event of no little importance. Both atomism and mechanism have consistently been the targets of Gestalt psychological criticism.

Another small indication of change is what today is being called interactionism in personality and social psychology. After a critique of the situationism of behavior theorists, Bowers defines his own position: "Interactionism argues that situations are as much a function of the person as the person's behavior is a function of the situation."[27] Of course there is nothing new in this statement, and it took the Swedish psychologist Bo Ekehammar to point out that it has a history.[28] Certainly the most relevant previous formulation is that of Kurt Lewin, who, forty or more years earlier, not only stated the relationship quoted above, but worked out concepts for person and environment that seem to be lacking in contemporary interactionism.[29] Still, here is a small step toward where we were forty years ago.

Was Gestalt psychology ahead of its time—as some of these examples might suggest—or simply uncongenial to the American intellectual scene? Can we today make better use of the contributions of Gestalt theory than we have done in the past? Before trying to answer these questions, I would like to take another brief look back into history.

Gestalt psychology arose, not only as a protest against the traditional psychologies of the time, but also as a response to a much more general intellectual situation. This was called the crisis of science; the German phrase, *die Krise der Wissenschaft,* is more exact, since it was not only the sciences, but academic knowledge in general that was involved. The academic disciplines could no longer take for granted the respect they had previously enjoyed. Why the crisis of confidence? Because scholars seemed to be unable to contribute to matters of human concern, and indeed seemed to be uninterested in them. Science, by its very nature, seemed to exclude meanings and values and thus to exempt itself from pressing human problems.

In psychology, one solution to the crisis of science was to develop an understanding psychology that gave up scientific explanation and hoped, through understanding, to find an avenue to real life human concerns.

The solution of Gestalt psychology was different. Rather than abandon the scientific method, it undertook to reexamine it. It discovered that certain assumptions being made about this method were not a necessary part of it, that science did not require the atomistic and mechanistic approach prevailing in psychology. Problems excluded by these assumptions might be dealt with if psychology concerned itself with molar events, employed more natural methods of analysis, and adopted the scientific stance of field theory.

It seems to me that we are again in a crisis of science, at least in psychology. To a large extent, we see the massive problems facing us today as human problems, and as psychologists we are able to do little about them. There is, it is true, one big difference from that earlier crisis of science: we want to help. The cry for relevance comes from within psychology itself. We have developed new fields of psychology in the face of our crisis: environmental psychology, community psychology, the psychology of aging, population psychology. It is my impression that we have not learned how to formulate problems well out of practical necessity, and that our new "relevant" psychologies are as much an expression of our own concern as areas of scientific achievement.

One solution to that earlier crisis is with us again. With the apparent failure of scientific psychology to solve human problems, we find advocates of an understanding approach to these problems. Occasionally such an author presents his program with a knowledge of that earlier history (e.g. Giorgi); more often, not. I hear from students today a question that was simply not expressed in the university a decade ago: must psychology be a science? The understanding approach abandons or supplements the rational methods of natural science. It does not necessarily imply irrationalism, but today irrationalism is often one of its ingredients.

What is missing in our contemporary crisis of science is a radical reexamination of the scientific method. A reexamination of research paradigms—yes: field research vs. experimental research, multivariate vs. conventional analyses. We no longer want to deceive our subjects; indeed, we don't like to call them subjects, but rather research participants. We hear a great deal about paradigms these days. More important, there is discussion of outmoded philosophies of science on which we have relied: positivism, operationalism, and so on. But in a positive direction, what shall we do?

Here is my suggestion. It has been the theme of this paper that, except for the field of perception and, to a lesser extent, that of thinking, Gestalt psychology has not been given a real hearing. It has been misunderstood, its findings reinterpreted as if nothing new had happened, parts of it have been ignored.

In this present crisis of science, let us see how far the scientific method will take us in psychology. But let us examine the method we use. It would be reasonable to start in the direction of Gestalt psychology's reexamination of science— which, if I am correctly interpreting the contemporary scene, has yet to be followed up. Perhaps terminology will have to be changed; doubtless, specific concepts require modification. Surely they will be refined with further work. But this is still a direction that deserves to be explored by more than a few people. If such a revised psychological science is really tried and fails, I see two other courses open to us: a different kind of reexamination of science; or failing that, we may be forced to agree with such thinkers as Sigmund Koch that a coherent discipline of psychology is not possible.[30]

REFERENCES

1. WERTHEIMER, M. 1912. Experimentelle Studien über das Sehen von Bewegung. Zeitschrift Psychologie 61: 161-265. (Translation in Classics in Psychology. 1961. T. Shipley, Ed. Philosophical Library. New York, N.Y.
2. KOFFKA, K. 1922. Perception, an introduction to the Gestalt-Theorie. Psychological Bulletin. 19: 531-585.
3. KÖHLER, W. 1953. The scientists from Europe and their new environment. In The Cultural Migration: The European Scholar in America. F.L. Neumann et al., Eds. University of Pennsylvania Press. Philadelphia, Pa.
4. GREGORY, R. L. 1970. The Intelligent Eye. McGraw-Hill Book Co. New York, N.Y.
5. ROCK, I. 1975. An Introduction to Perception. Macmillan Co. New York, N.Y.
6. KÖHLER, W. 1929. Gestalt Psychology. Horace Liveright. New York, N.Y.
7. KÖHLER, W. 1950. Psychology and evolution. Acta Psychologica 7: 288-297.
8. KÖHLER, W. 1969. The Task of Gestalt Psychology. Princeton University Press, Princeton, N.J.
9. GREGORY, R. L. 1973. The confounded eye. In Illusion in Nature and Art. R.L. Gregory and E.H. Gombrich, Eds. Gerald Duckworth & Co. Ltd. London, England.
10. EPSTEIN, W. 1967. Varieties of Perceptual Experience. McGraw-Hill Book Co. New York, N.Y.
11. KAUFMAN, L. 1974. Sight and Mind. An Introduction to Visual Perception. Oxford University Press. New York, N.Y.
12. GREGORY, R.L. 1966. Eye and Brain. World University Library. McGraw-Hill Book Co. New York, N.Y.
13. KÖHLER, W. 1930. The new psychology and physics. Yale Rev. 19: 560-576. (Re-

printed in Selected Papers, W. Köhler, 1971. M. Henle, Ed. Liveright Publishing Corp. New York, N.Y.)

14. KÖHLER, W. 1938. The Place of Value in a World of Facts. Liveright Publishing Corp. New York, N.Y.

15. KÖHLER, W. 1959. Psychologie und Naturwissenschaft. Proc. 15th Inter. Congr. Psychology. Brussels, Belgium. 1957. North-Holland Publishing Co. Amsterdam, Holland. (Translation in Selected Papers, W. Köhler. 1971. M. Henle, Ed. Liveright Publishing Corp. New York, N.Y.)

16. KÖHLER, W. 1958. The present situation in brain physiology. Am. Psychol. 13: 150-154.

17. KÖHLER, W. 1965. Unsolved problems in the field of figural after-effects. Psychol. Record 15: 63-83.

18. HOCHBERG, J. 1971. Perception. I. Color and shape. *In* Woodworth & Schlosberg's Experimental Psychology. 3rd edit. J.W. Kling & L.A. Riggs *et al.,* Eds. Holt, Rinehart & Winston, Inc. New York, N.Y.

19. KÖHLER, W. 1913. Über unbemerkte Empfindungen und Urteilstäuschungen. Zeitschrift Psychologie 66: 51-80. (Translation in Selected Papers, W. Köhler. 1971. M. Henle, Ed. Liveright Publishing Corp. New York, N.Y.)

20. KOFFKA, K. 1935. Principles of Gestalt Psychology. Harcourt, Brace & Co. New York, N.Y.

21. GIBSON, J.J. 1971. The legacies of Koffka's *Principles*. J. Hist. Behavioral Sciences 7: 3-9.

22. WERTHEIMER, M. 1912. Über das Denken der Naturvölker. I: Zahlen und Zahlgebilde. Zeitschrift Psychologie. 60: 321-378. (Abridged translation in A Sourcebook of Gestalt Psychology. 1938. W.D. Ellis, Ed. Harcourt, Brace & Co. New York, N.Y.)

23. KÖHLER, W. 1925. The Mentality of Apes. (Translated by E. Winter.) Harcourt, Brace & Co. New York, N.Y.

24. DUNCKER, K. 1945. On problem-solving. (Translated by L.S. Lees.) Psychol. Monogr. 58(5), Whole no. 270.

25. WERTHEIMER, M. 1945. Productive Thinking. Harper & Brothers. New York, N.Y. (Enlarged edit. 1959. Michael Wertheimer, Ed.)

26. JENKINS, J.J. 1974. Remember that old theory of memory? Well, forget it! Am. Psychol. 29: 785-795.

27. BOWERS, K.S. 1973. Situationism in psychology: An analysis and a critique. Psychol. Rev. 80: 307-336.

28. EKEHAMMAR, B. 1974. Interactionism in personality from a historical perspective. Psychol. Bull. 81: 1026-1048.

29. LEWIN, K. 1935. A Dynamic Theory of Personality. (Translated by D.K. Adams & K.E. Zener.) McGraw-Hill Book Co. New York, N.Y.

30. KOCH, S. 1971. Reflections on the state of psychology. Social Res. 38: 669-709.

WILHELM WUNDT AND EARLY AMERICAN PSYCHOLOGY: A CLASH OF TWO CULTURES

Arthur L. Blumenthal

Department of Psychology and Social Relations
Harvard University
Cambridge, Massachusetts 02138

INTRODUCTION

At any moment in the course of a day, you or I could find ourselves in a situation something like the following: engaging a friend in conversation while, at the same time, dodging traffic on a street corner, struggling to remember items on a shopping list, being distracted by nude figures on a magazine cover, and scratching an itch. If we should pause to reflect, we might wonder how we remain so well coordinated, indeed how we even survive, given all the events that flow in and around us, pushing, pulling, and invading our lives.

Most people do manage, somehow, to survive such tumultuous situations with scarcely even a moment's appreciation of their accomplishment. But attempts to explain that ability might well destroy many a psychological theory. Yet it is only in the rather recent history of American psychology that interest in this human capacity for complex, real time, information processing took firm root. And now the above episode of the human psyche's survival would be explained by references to short-term memory, to scanning mechanisms, to buffers, to executive subroutines, or to automatic pattern-recognition schemes. Today a large number of American psychologists labor over these notions by experimentally assaulting our senses, by systematically distracting our attention, by overloading our memory stores, until at some point we break down—or suffer a loss of will— as subjects in their experiments.

In another time, another place, another culture, far removed from us today, an earlier generation of psychologists, many of them Americans, crowded into a few lecture halls and laboratories in several German universities to study essentially the same questions of human information processing. Of course, the technical vocabulary of that day was wholly different. Then, explanations were given in terms of memory afterimages, apperception, levels of consciousness, volitional processes, attention waves, and the like. The center of this earlier research was the Psychological Institute in Leipzig University, which was under the direction of its founder, Wilhelm Wundt.

Quite literally, Wundt trained the first generation of American experimental psychologists; hence he may be counted as one of the major roots of American psychology. Yet in spite of this rather considerable contribution, it would appear today, in retrospect, that very little of Wundt's actual system of psychology ever survived the return passage back across the Atlantic with those young Americans who traveled abroad around the turn of the century. But replicas of his laboratory apparatus and imitations of his laboratory procedures formed nearly all of the first American psychological laboratories.

In this paper I wish to outline some of the historical causes of this situation as well as explanations of what I feel has been a continuing lack of understanding of the early German-American interactions in the development of academic psychology. First I must say something more about Wundt's psychology, although because of space limits, I must be brief.

WUNDT'S PSYCHOLOGY

When describing his psychological system, Wundt said it belonged to the school of thought known as "Voluntarism." This meant that volitional processes were, for him, fundamental. Wundt was also an ardent opponent of any mind-body dualism, equally as much as are 20th century behaviorists. When he mentioned psychophysical parallelism, it referred to the different methodologies of physiologists and psychologists, or to their different levels of explanation of one and the same phenomenon.

Wundt was open to any method, however, for unraveling psychological processes—any method, that is, except casual introspection. This is not to say that Wundt himself did not introspect when speculating and theorizing about psychological processes. This he did just as many behaviorists, Gestaltists, functionalists, and others do when generalizing and developing their own theoretical positions. The point is that Wundt opposed the use for experimental purposes of the procedure where subjects are required to give verbal descriptions (protocols) of their inner experience.[20, 21] That technique was indeed used by the psychologists at Würzburg and by Titchener and his students at Cornell University.

Wundt was distinguished initially by his development of a psychological laboratory consisting of a large array of apparatus. In general, those instruments were used either for the controlled delivery of specific stimuli or for the objective measurement of reactions—often in the form of reaction times. It was his plan to infer characteristics of mental processes from these measures. In one well known effort, he attempted to relate specific emotional states, according to his speculative theory of emotion, to specific physiological response patterns. The effort was only partially successful.

Even though Wundt continually related his work to various philosophical systems, his strong technical emphasis on laboratory apparatus was uncongenial to James, Külpe, and perhaps to some others. James even described it as "boring." From the outset, however, Wundt restricted his experimental techniques to those situations where stimuli could be controlled and reactions objectively measured. Other psychological questions (those of the "higher" mental processes) were consigned to *Völkerpsychologie* (cultural psychology) to be studied historically, developmentally, and through naturalistic observation.

If psychology is to become science, Wundt argued, it will be through the establishment of some general laws. And so he saw his work as fundamentally the search for those laws. By the turn of the century he had produced six laws or principles—three concerning what many of us now call human information-processing, and three parallel laws concerning human development.[17] The best way to summarize Wundt's psychology in the briefest possible manner may be to cite these six generalizations.

The first is the one Wundt was best known for. This is "the principle of creative synthesis" (sometimes called "the principle of psychic resultants"). It describes the central constructive activity of the cortex in the forming of immediate experience; it is the assembly, selection, construction, and integration of thoughts, sensations, memories, affects, and actions. The synthesis ensures that the events of immediate experience will be organized into coherent wholes. These organizations can occur in any number of ways, depending on the needs, purposes, and values on the individual. And further, the synthesis creates properties or qualities that are not found in the separate elements that go into mental creations.

Second is "the principle of psychic relations." The significance of any mental event is dependent upon its context. Each experience depends not only on integration and construction but also on the comparison and relation of that experience to its context.

The third principle is "psychological contrast," which is an expansion of the second principle. Simply stated, antithetical experiences intensify each other. After a period of pain, a slight pleasure will loom large; a sweet substance tastes much sweeter if eaten after a sour substance, and so on.

Then the second set of three principles, those concerned with development, begin with "the principle of mental growth," which refers to the progressive integration or summation of experiences over longer intervals of time. Concept formation is the best example. Such formations are the basic mechanism of the continuity of experience and action. Without them, individual creative syntheses would remain separate from each other so that life would be disorganized and chaotic.

The second developmental principle is "the principle of heterogeneity of ends." It says that sequences of voluntary activity can be understood only in terms of the ends or goals toward which they are directed, but when those goals are attained, new and unforeseen results are always produced. That is, while we are always propelled by purposes and goals, we can never fully anticipate what the consequences of our actions will be.

Finally, Wundt's third principle of development is "the principle of development toward opposites." It is analogous to the principle of contrast for information processing. It states that men's emotions, behaviors, and experiences, when viewed developmentally, fluctuate between opposing tendencies. A long period of one type of activity or experience builds up a pressure to seek some opposite form of experience or action. These fluctuations, Wundt observed, are found not only in the life and experience of the individual, but also in the pattern of human history. Moods, styles, and social systems all reflect these cyclic patterns.

It was the characteristic of Wundt's writing that he amassed so much material, ostensibly illustrating these six generalizations, that it seems few have ever been able to read through it all. Let me summarize by quoting Charles Hubbard Judd, who may have read it all and who was, I believe, one of the more dedicated and consistent of Wundt's American students. Judd concludes that Wundt's psychology was "functional and synthetic, never atomistic and structural."[8]

I want now, in the remainder of this paper, to turn to the historical issues which at the outset I had promised to discuss.

THE LEIBNIZIAN AND THE LOCKEAN TRADITIONS

G. S. Brett, often called the most erudite among historians of psychology, makes a useful distinction between two contesting views of man.[5] One is within the German philosophical tradition that received inspiration from Gottfried Leibniz and that developed throughout the 18th and 19th centuries. The other is a tradition that is associated more with England and the philosophy of John Locke; it developed over the same two centuries. The names of Locke and Leibniz are only very general guide posts for two cultural trends that we must observe if we are to understand the history of psychology.

Wundt viewed his psychology as preserving and extending the best of the Leibnizian tradition, including the thought of Spinoza, Wolff, Mendelsohn, Kant,

Hegel, Schelling, Schopenhauer, and Fichte. Specifically, it includes Leibniz' notions of volition, of levels of consciousness, and of holistic orientations in psychology. It includes Spinoza's assertion that volition, or desiring and striving, is the supreme human faculty. Following them, Christian Wolff contributed an analysis of the differences between empiricist and rationalist psychology, and he speculated upon the possibility of introducing experimentation into psychology. And then came Moses Mendelsohn, who expanded the notion of volitional processes by introducing a psychology of feelings and emotions. Kant developed the notion of volitional apperception, which we find as the source of Wundt's creative synthesis. In Hegel we find sources for Wundt's developmental laws as well as certain tendencies toward holism. Schelling contributed more on the theory of feelings and emotion. In Schopenhauer and Fichte we find further sources of Wundt's voluntarism. To say the least, Wundt was not unmindful of these historical antecedents. Most of his texts have a history-of-philosophy orientation.

Recall, now, the Lockean tradition. Because of our nations's history, language, and cultural forms, we Americans have for the most part felt more comfortable with this stream of thought. Among the English thinkers we regard Adam Smith, Hartley, Hume, and Mill as our own. They are so familiar as to need no introduction. Closely related to this English tradition were streams of thought in France carried forward by Diderot, Montesquieu, Condillac, Condercet, and Rousseau.

Locke had taught that there is nothing in our mental processes but the product of sensation, and this had prompted Leibniz to reply that there is nothing, of course, except the mental processes themselves. Leibniz thereby charged Locke with ignoring those central processes which, as Leibniz felt, are directive in the formation of experience. Among the followers of these two men this difference of view has continued down to the present.

Both Locke and Leibniz stood on the threshold of the burst of 18th century intellectual activity known as the "Enlightenment." But the Anglo-French Enlightenment was especially concerned to make a break with the mystical past and, inspired by Newton's physics, to reorient philosophy on a basis of physical science. For psychology this meant the control of man by his environment, and it meant models of man that are based on machines or systems of Newtonian mechanics. There was also a spirited optimism found among the philosophers of this group regarding the future of man; it shows in their many programs and projects for utopian societies.[1]

YANKEE PSYCHOLOGY

Early American thought is an offshoot of the Anglo-French Enlightenment. Locke's philosophy spread rapidly throughout the colonies and became a gospel for American academic institutions and eventually for American politics.[12] Locke's political philosophy spelled out the argument that should a king's rule become tyrannical and inimical to the welfare of his subjects, then those subjects would be justified in rebelling.

American society at its outset, however, was guided more by the practical necessities of survival. It was a new country without an established intellectual tradition of its own and remote from European educational centers. Little wonder that this society would quite generally celebrate the yeoman's life and be suspicious of the obscurities of philosophical systems. The pioneer's glorification of the ordinary man gave him special faculties that pedantic philosophers were thought to lack.

But there is one other striking and informative example of the acceptance of a European philosopher in America. The case I have in mind occurs in the 19th century; it is that of Herbert Spencer, the ex-civil engineer and self-made, self-educated British philosopher. In comparison with other philosophical systems, Spencer's has a rather home-spun, cracker-barrel quality. But it was more than his style, or lack of it, that brought him unparalleled success in America. According to the historian Hofstadter, of all 19th century philosophers Spencer was closest to the spirit of the earlier Anglo-French Enlightenment of the 18th century. Yet Spencer was also armed with the Darwinian theory of evolution.

Again, his philosophy was utopian. He saw evolution as moving toward the greatest perfection and the most complete happiness. But then we find that this final reward was offered in return for acceptance of the social and political conditions of the early industrial society in which Spencer lived. Biology was used by Spencer as an argument in support of conservative laissez-faire economics. Spencer's sociological writings give arguments against all state aid to the poor, sanitary supervision, regulations on housing, and protection from medical quacks. As he explained, "The whole effort of nature is to get rid of [the poor and unfit], to clear the world of them, and make room for the better."[13]

Spencer made one celebrated visit to America in 1882, and it is likely that no other foreign intellectual has received a more lavish reception here. No less than Andrew Carnegie greeted Spencer at shipside in New York and hailed him as something of a Messiah.[7] In the universities such men as William James were using Spencer's *Principles of Psychology* in their classes. And some of his writings, which had not sold well in Europe, were being serialized in popular American magazines.

Hofstadter has described this period in American history, a time of rapid expansion and industrialization, as "a vast human caricature of the Darwinian struggle for existence and the survival of the fittest."[7] Spencer supplied that society with its gospel in the form of social Darwinism. But as Hofstadter recounts, Spencer fell from American popularity as suddenly as he had arrived when it became obvious to influential Americans that evolution was not proceeding in the directions they wanted. So Spencer's philosophy was soon replaced by pragmatism, a wholly American prescription, which allows men to manipulate and reorient the environment according to their needs and desires.

THE CLASH OF CULTURES

Toward the end of the 19th century the practical necessities of American life began to include greater demands for higher education. At that time the German universities were growing more rapidly than any others in the world, and one could then find certain types of scientific and medical training only in Germany. So American curiosity about things German was now growing. In the case of psychology, this meant curiosity about Wilhelm Wundt.

James was an early follower of Wundt and was hopeful of bringing the new German psychology to America. But alas, the scholarly relations between Wundt and James had no chance of success, and the sarcastic comments they soon directed toward each other are still quoted in textbooks. James, it seems, had absolutely no appetite for the German philosophical and analytical mind.

Many American students who went to study in Wundt's laboratory had similar difficulties. The problems they faced are easy to understand. Imagine the twenty-year-old American with only a year or two of college German and an introductory philosophy course behind him struggling to understand Wundt's lectures. Many survived, it seems, because although Wundt did not speak English, he understood spoken English, and so the Americans were not compelled to answer in German. But at one point, according to George Tawney, Wundt was on the verge of banning American students from his program because they didn't understand German well enough.[14]

Wundt's first American student, G. Stanley Hall, dropped out after one semester. Later Hall brought out a book titled *Founders of Modern Psychology* (1912), which was widely read in America. His chapter on Wundt is a disaster of error and misinterpretation that did not go unnoticed by Wundt.[4] Wundt's second American student, James McKeen Cattell, stuck it out. But Cattell characterized himself as having no taste for philosophy, as being an apparatus man, and as having no interest in theorizing.[12] It was Cattell whom Wundt singled out with that phrase so often repeated in American historical accounts, "*ganz Amerikanisch*," or "typically American." The long string of American students continued to file through Leipzig, some being more, some less, successful.

But when these young psychologists returned to America and established themselves in their new laboratories, they often adapted their apparatus and techniques for the testing of the "sensations" and "associations" of the Lockean tradition. Titchener at Cornell, who was trained more in England than in Germany, is a good example. And Titchener specifically stated that his psychology followed the British tradition.[12] Some other German-trained psychologists in America turned toward the pattern of behaviorism, in particular, Münsterberg (a native German), at Harvard. But just as bad from Wundt's point of view, Cattell at Columbia, Münsterberg at Harvard, and Judd at Chicago steered their research toward applied, industrial, and educational psychology; Hall at Clark was already heavily involved in applied psychology. Scripture at Yale eventually moved into speech therapy. Witmer at Penn turned to clinical psychology. Others turned to the development of various psychomotor tests. Against this trend, Wundt argued that applied psychology should not be housed in universities, and he tried to hold his students close to his own ideal of theoretical or "pure" science.[19]

With the approach of the World War the schism between Wundt and many of his American counterparts grew to a hopeless breach. His former students in America were now feeling embarrassment over his politics. In 1914, along with 92 other German professors, Wundt signed a manifesto condeming England and France for the international tensions. Then came Wundt's book *Nations and their philosophies*,[15] in which English and, by implication, American morality is examined unfavorably. And finally there appeared a pamphlet by Wundt titled *Concerning True War*,[18] containing similar sentiments.

Let us look briefly at what Wundt said in these writings. The English and Americans, he felt, view the existence of man as a sum of commercial transactions which everyone makes as favorable for himself as possible. And so he found material values to be wholly dominant in our society, with all other aspects of life subordinate. The primary goals of our sciences, he claimed, are useful inventions and physical comforts, rather than the deepening of man's understanding of himself and of nature.

In describing what he found to be a shallowness of British ethical theories (such as Spencer's) and what he found to be a simplistic-naïve realism in British philosophy, he used as epithets the words "egotistic utilitarianism," "materialism," "positivism," and "pragmatism." In regard to political freedom, he claimed that the Anglo-American societies had little to do with true invidualism. Rather, they led only to a leveling of life and a lack of diversity, where small but powerful economic interests are the chief agents in the formation of public opinion.

Wundt, it seems, feared the trends in the mass democratic civilization of the

West. But it was not the fear of a defender of a landed aristocracy; it was the fear of an intellectual fighting for a cultural heritage that he had dedicated his life to preserving and extending, and that was now slipping away. His Leibnizian tradition, which he felt offered a higher view of man because of its emphasis on volition and intellect,[16] was now under severe threat from foreign forces.[11]

Among the reactions in Germany that followed upon the loss of the war was a public clamor to abandon the older German professors and to convert German universities into centers for applied subjects and practical training. The German psychological laboratories then went into decline under the pressure of this and other social-economic upheavals. The American laboratories, originally inspired by Wundt, grew and flourished; but Wundt was rarely ever read again. At about the time of Wundt's death in 1920, caricatured accounts of him and of his psychology were beginning to appear, some from those writers who were eager to supersede him, some from those in America who were seeking additional justifications for divergent trends that were occupying the newer psychology in this country. These descriptions of Wundt were often motivated not out of serious interest in accurate historical portrayal, but rather out of our usual presentist motives of justifying our own condition. It is only in the past few years that corrections in these accounts have begun to appear.[2,3,9,10]

Knight Dunlap, an early American behaviorist, who once had failed an attempt to learn German and who professed a lack of ability to understand German philosophy, included the following prophetic comment in his autobiography of 1932:

> The astonishing thing clearly seen in retrospect is that where we apparently have made our greatest breaks with the past, we have actually honored historical consistency the most. In casting overboard the most confusing accumulations of theory and interpretation (for which we may hold the Germans largely responsible), we have based our progress more solidly upon the methods and practical aims of the German laboratories. If we consider the long line of researches upon reaction-times, perception of space and time, memory and learning, and all the other studies of performance initiated a generation ago, we realize that our reconstructions and reformulations are but preparation for the more vigorous attack on these problems . . . we are but the more honoring the sturdy pioneers who filed the claims on the territories we now occupy.[6]

REFERENCES

1. BECKER, C. L. 1932. The Heavenly City of the Eighteenth-Century Philosophers. Yale University Press. New Haven, Conn.
2. BLUMENTHAL, A. L. 1970. Language and Psychology: Historical Aspects of Psycholinguistics. John Wiley. New York, N. Y.
3. BLUMENTHAL, A. L. 1975. A reappraisal of Wilhelm Wundt. Amer. Psychol. 30: 1081-1086.
4. BORING, E. G. 1950. A History of Experimental Psychology. Appleton-Century-Crofts. New York, N. Y.
5. BRETT, G. S. 1912. A History of Psychology. Vol. 2. Allen. London, England.
6. DUNLAP, K. 1932. In A History of Psychology in Autobiography. C. Murchison, Ed. Vol. 2: 35-61. Clark University Press. Worcester, Mass.
7. HOFSTADTER, R. 1944. Social Darwinism in American Thought. University of Pennsylvania Press. Philadelphia, Pa.
8. JUDD, C. H. 1932. In A History of Psychology in Autobiography. C. Murchison, Ed. Vol. 2: 207-235. Clark University Press. Worcester, Mass.
9. KLEIN, D. B. 1970. A History of Scientific Psychology. Basic Books. New York, N. Y.
10. MISCHEL, T. 1970. Wundt and the conceptual foundations of psychology. Philos. & Phenomenol. Res. 31: 1-26.

11. RINGER, F. K. 1969. The Decline of the German Mandarins: The German Academic Community, 1890-1933. Harvard University Press. Cambridge, Mass.
12. ROBACK, A. A. 1964. A History of American Psychology. 2nd edit. Collier. New York, N. Y.
13. SPENCER, H. 1864. Social Statics. Appleton. New York, N. Y.
14. TAWNEY, G. 1921. In memory of Wilhelm Wundt. Psychol. Rev. 28: 178-181.
15. WUNDT, W. 1914. Die Nationen und ihre Philosophie. Kröner. Leipzig, Germany.
16. WUNDT, W. 1917. Liebnitz. Kröner. Leipzig, Germany.
17. WUNDT, W. 1897. Outlines of Psychology. (Transl. by C. H. Judd.) Engelmann. Leipzig, Germany.
18. WUNDT, W. 1914. Ueber den wahrhaften Krieg. Kröner. Leipzig, Germany.
19. WUNDT, W. 1910. Ueber rein und angewandte Psychologie. Psychol. Stud. 5: 1-47.
20. WUNDT, W. 1888. Selbstbeobachtung und innere Wahrnehmung. Philos. Stud. 4: 292-309.
21. WUNDT, W. 1907. Ueber Ausfrageexperimente und ueber Methoden zur Psychologie des Denkens. Psychol. Stud. 3: 301-360.

THE VICISSITUDES OF FECHNERIAN PSYCHOPHYSICS IN AMERICA

Helmut E. Adler

Department of Psychology
Yeshiva University
New York, New York 10033

Parallelismus strictus existet inter animam et corpus,
ita ut ex uno, rite cognito, alterum construi possit.

(A strict parellism exists between mind and body in such a way
that from one, properly understood, the other can be constructed.)*

At the beginning of scientific psychology stands the figure of Gustav Theodor Fechner (1801-1887), the romantic mystic, who almost inadvertently shaped the future course of psychology by being the first to successfully apply quantitative thinking to the study of sensations. As the above quotation from Fechner's "Premises"[1] (his *Habitilationsschrift* in 1823) indicates, the problem of the relationship of body and mind had occupied his thinking for many years prior to the "proper understanding" that came to him during the morning of October 22, 1850 and that resulted in the publication of his *Elemente der Psychophysik*[2] ten years later.

Fechner's nature combined two contradictory elements. On the one hand, he was a romantic idealist, given to wideranging speculative thinking, under the influence of the nature philosophy of Oken[3] and the idealism of Fichte,[4] Schelling,[5] and Hegel.[6] On the other hand, he was a careful, painstaking, if somewhat plodding, scientist, in the tradition of E.H.Weber and L.H.F. von Helmholtz. Stimulated by Herbart's attempt at a mathematical psychology[7] but vigorously rejecting Herbart's approach, he formulated his own solution, founded on "the basis of material phenomena that underlie the psychical, because they allow a direct mathematical approach and definite measurement, as is not true with respect to the psychical." (Zend-Avesta, 1851).[8]

In his search for a quantitative solution to the "functionally dependent relations of body and soul or, more generally, of the material and the mental, of the physical and the psychological worlds,"[2] he provided the basis of a new psychology that was able to move away from mental philosophy, much as the physical sciences had earlier separated from natural philosophy. Quantification made it possible to apply the scientific method, with its emphasis on measurement and experimentation, to mental phenomena.[9] Fechner was the first to clarify the nature of such measurement and to standardize the methods by which such measurements were to be made.

Fechner did not attain his ultimate goal, the refutation of a materialistic world view, but his psychophysics carried the seeds of an entirely new approach to what was then called the study of mind. As Boring[10] has put it: "That had to happen before anything else could take place in respect to scales and measure-

---

*G.T. Fechner. Premissae ad theoriam organismi generalem. Leipzig, 1823. Quoted by M.E. Marshall.[1]

Gustav Theodor Fechner

ment in the psychological sphere." Although there had been a great deal of psychological thinking prior to this innovation, it had not led to a scientific psychology. Eighteenth century mental philosophers had recognized the need for mental measurement but lacked the methods to translate their convictions into practice.[9, 11] Sensory phenomena had been studied by physiologists and physicists, but that alone would not have led to an independent science. One does not classify E.H.Weber, Helmholtz, Mach, or Aubert primarily among psychologists, even though they made highly significant contributions to psychology. The essential idea that the mind—consciousness—could be measured, was missing. As a consequence of Fechner's contribution, psychology advanced from a prescience to a science. This change was such an important landmark that it is proper to divide the history of psychology into a pre-Fechnerian and a post-Fechnerian period, just as biology can be divided into a pre-Darwinian and a post-Darwinian phase, and physics has its pre-Einsteinian and post-Einsteinian conception of the physical world.

Fechner's methods were quickly accepted by leading European scientists. Wundt taught the first course in "Psychology as a Natural Science" at Heidelberg in 1862, while still a *Privatdozent*.[12] Mach lectured on psychophysics in Vienna in 1863, although he already considered "Fechner's theory of formulae of measurement . . . erroneous."[13] American psychologists also picked up the new psychophysical methods and began experimentation. Charles S. Peirce,[14] best known as the founder of pragmatism, but also accomplished in chemistry, physics, and astronomy, as well as psychology, called for American scientists to follow the lead of Fechner and Wundt. He published, in 1877, what is probably the first psychophysical experiment carried out in this country.[15] It independently reported the discovery of what is now called the Bezold-Brücke effect, the change of apparent hue as a function of luminance of light from a monochromatic source, after Bezold, but before Brücke. The first American textbook incorporating a full account of psychophysics was published by G.T.Ladd in 1887.[16] Ladd never had any formal instruction in psychology. His discovery of these new quantitative methods was an exciting personal experience and well worth the six years he invested in the compilation of *Elements of Physiological Psychology*.[17] The efforts of these self-starters were soon augmented by the arrival of the first generation of European-trained psychologists. It was the age of the founding of laboratories at American universities: G.S. Hall (Wundt's first American student) at Johns Hopkins in 1884, James McK. Cattell at Pennsylvania in 1887, E.B. Titchener at Cornell in 1892. They brought with them not only the laboratory skills of the "new" psychology, but also knowlege of the controversies that had developed with regard to Fechner's philosophy and the interpretation of his measurements. Fechnerian psychophysics began to undergo the first of its many transformations. It was its fate to undergo many more changes. Because of this fact, it has frequently been the case that writers have lost sight of Fechner's lasting achievement, the successful introduction of measurement that irreversibly set the future course of psychology in the direction of a quantitative science.

QUANTITATIVE PSYCHOLOGY

In its wider sense, psychophysics was not only to be concerned with sense perception, but also with the "intensity of attention, clearness of consciousness, and so forth . . . . " (Ref.2, Vol. I, p.48), in fact, with any psychological process. The means of measurement and the operations of measuring were to be found in procedures setting up an equivalence between a physical magnitude and a psychological unit of measurement.[2] As Fechner points out, even physical measurement is in its "most general and ultimate sense" derived from "the fact that an equal number of equally strong psychical impressions are due to an equal number of equally large physical causes." (Ref.2, Vol. I, p.51)

Fechner understood the essential nature of measurement as "the assignment of numerals to objects or events according to rule—and rule."[18] The manipulation of numbers thus obtained, according to the formal model of mathematics, leads directly to the specification of relationships that cannot be directly observed. It is widely believed, for example, that the origins of geometry were connected to the need to fix land boundaries in Egypt after the annual Nile floods, and that mathematical analysis began with the need to predict astronomical events connected with the seasonal changes of the sun and the planets.

It was Fechner's goal to set up the proper operations by which numerical values could be assigned to psychological variables. He accomplished this task by first defining the concept of sensitivity, deriving from it the notion of the threshold, and devising or standardizing the procedures by which the threshold was to be found. He ended by constructing his famous psychological scale: "The magnitude of the sensation is not proportional to the absolute value of the stimulus magnitude, but rather to the logarithm of the stimulus magnitude, when the latter is expressed in terms of its threshold value, i.e., that magnitude considered as a unit at which the sensation appears and disappears. In short, it is proportional to the logarithm of the fundamental stimulus value." (Ref. 2, Vol. II, p. 13)

EARLY CRITICS OF PSYCHOPHYSICS

If, as Estes *et al.*[19] claim, the success of a theory should be judged by the number of fruitful inquiries to which it gives rise, psychophysics has achieved a very high rank on any scale. But when it first came upon the scene, it met some determined opposition. The foremost American critic also happened to be the most highly regarded American psychologist, William James. He was well acquainted with Fechner's work, but he was not impressed, as we may gather from a letter to G. Stanley Hall, written in 1880, in which James comments regarding Fechner: ". . . I have always thought his psychophysics as moonshiny as any of his other writings."[20] A decade later, in his *Principles of Psychology*,[21] he expressed his opinion publicly that this "dreadful literature" of psychophysics, the outcome of which was "just *nothing*," could hardly "have arisen in a country whose natives could be *bored*." (Ref. 21, vol. I, p. 192f.) And in perhaps the best-known passage he praises Fencher, "that dear old man," and dismisses his work that he feared "could saddle our Science forever with his patient whimseys, and, in a world so full of more nutritious objects of attention, compel all future students to plough through the difficulties, not only of his own works, but of the still drier ones written in his refutation." (Ref. 21, Vol. I, p.549)

As Boring[22] has pointed out, James could not appreciate Fechner's psychophysics because James approached psychology as a phenomenalist and was thus a forerunner of those present trends in psychology that stress richness, wholeness, and understanding, at the expense of precision and quantitative relationships. But interestingly enough, Fechner's own philosophy was essentially in agreement with James' point of view. Wertheimer[23] cites Fechner's attempt at relating mind and body as a synthesis between richness and precision in the handling of psychological issues. And James himself, as Marylin Marshall[24] points out, eventually discovered a close elective affinity with Fechner's philosophy, though not with his psychophysics.

Other critical voices were raised with respect to Fechner's fundamental assumptions; his methods were seen to be in need of modification. Joseph Jastrow, a student of Peirce and the first American Ph.D. in psychology, published his critique in 1888.[25] James McK. Cattell,[26] in collaboration with G.S.Fullerton, a philosopher, published a revision of psychophysical methodology that introduced a functional point of view in 1892. Instead of accepting the threshold as a fact to be described, they saw it in terms of a subject's success or failure to discriminate a given stimulus difference. Also in 1892, at the First Annual Meeting of the American Psychological Association (at a time when annual dues were $3), Hugo Münsterberg, then on his first visit to join James at Harvard, decried the tendency of experimental psychology merely to accumulate figures.[27]

E.B.Titchener[28] provided an unparalleled thorough and erudite review and a searching critique of the whole field in his *Experimental Psychology*, summarizing a literature that had already become unwieldy. Who cannot sympathize when we read: "There has been a strong tendency in the past few years toward the multiplication of psychological journals. Indeed, the number of serial publications is now so large and specialized, that they will hardly be found all together in a single

William James

institutional library,—to say nothing of a private library." (Ref.28, Vol.II, Part II, p.418) After declining to accept the contention that sensations had a measurable magnitude, the so-called quantity objection, admitting the equality of just noticeable differences only in a modified way, and rejecting the psychophysical interpretation of Weber's Law, what did Titchener find was left of Fechner's system? In the first place, Fechner "paved the way for experimental psychology." Second, we owe him the comprehensive development of the methods of just noticeable differences, the method of right and wrong cases (constant stimuli), and the method of average error. In third place, Fechner developed the concept of the difference threshold. Fourth, Fechner collected valuable data under the guidance of his own theory and carried out by the methods that he had developed. Finally, he should receive sole credit for the concept of mental measurement. Titchener's evaluation closes what might be called the classical period of psychophysics, but further changes were to come as innovative ideas permeated psychology.

PSYCHOPHYSICS ADAPTS TO NEW TRENDS

The new trends influencing psychophysics were probability theory and behaviorism. Fechner himself had made use of the normal probability integral, or Gaussian distribution, as he called it, in developing the method of right and wrong cases. Cattell,[29] in 1893, had attempted a statistical approach to discrimination. But it remained for L.L. Thurstone[30] to develop fully the potentialities of a probability approach to psychological scaling. His "Law of comparative judgment" was constructed on the assumption that a given stimulus did not correspond to a single point on a psychological dimension, but instead corresponded to a distribution centered around a point. Distances between points on a continuum could be scaled in terms of the probability of the differences between the two distributions. He distinguished five cases, of which Case V, assuming equal dispersions, has been found to be the most useful. Thurstone's scaling has been applied to physical stimuli to only a limited extent, but found its widest application in attitude scaling.

Another attempt to incorporate probability principles was due to Crozier.[31] His basic assumption was that the population of excitatory neurons varied in threshold according to a normal probability distribution. The importance of his theory lay in the fact that the resulting functions became independent of the particular sense organ being stimulated.

The impact of behaviorism is best exemplified by the writings of G. Bergmann and K.W.Spence,[32] and of C.H.Graham.[33,34] According to the former, the process of psychophysical measurement becomes the verbal discrimination of human observers or their motor responses in accordance with verbal instructions. Observers may use numerals in their response, but these are not the same as physical measurements. Psychophysical measurement becomes a technique in its own right that cannot be subsumed under any customary classifications of physical measurement.

According to Graham, one seeks to establish specific explicitly stated relations between a stimulus, a response, and whatever hypothesized variables become logically necessary. On the one hand there are the physical changes in the environment, on the other hand, the behavioral manifestations of the organism as a function of these stimuli. Responses are often restricted to such statements as "Yes," "No," or "Equal." "From such a relation it is possible to obtain a new datum, a value of the stimulus variable that corresponds to a particular probability of response occurence—for example, the 50% value .... and so derive ... perceptual functions ... functions obtained from a sequence of experiments concerned with finding thresholds under many different conditions." (Ref.34, pp.67-68) Under this approach the threshold becomes a dependent variable of behavior, unlike the classical sensory concept with its intervening variable connotation. Another consequence is the evaporation of any differences between "sensory" and "perceptual" phenomena.

THE NATURE OF THE PSYCHOPHYSICAL LAW

Fechnerian scaling was based on indirect methods, ultimately on discrimination. His famous logarithmic law depended on integration of just noticeable differences (JNDs). It assumed that all JNDs are equal in subjective magnitude. In contrast to this approach, there are the so-called direct methods of scaling that result, in many cases, in a different kind of mathematical function, the power law.

Direct scaling has a respectable history. It goes back to Plateau's attempt, in 1852, to equate intervals of lightness. This blind Belgian physicist had asked eight artists to paint a gray that appeared half-way between a white and a black surface.[35] This is the method of bisection. Other well-known direct methods are the category rating scale, where subjects are given some number of categories prior to the experiment and instructed to assign stimuli, one at a time, to one of the categories. A third type of direct scaling involves the setting of one stimulus so that it stands in direct ratio to another stimulus. Merkel,[36] in 1888, asked subjects to set a variable stimulus so that the sensation it produced was judged to be twice as great as the comparison stimulus. Fullerton and Cattell[26] had used a similar procedure, asking their subjects for both multiples and fractions of a standard. Richardson and Ross[37] were the first to use direct assignment of numerals to classify the loudness of tones, a method now designated as magnitude estimation.

S.S.Stevens and his collaborators determined the shape of many sensory functions by this method, leading him to propose the power law as the general psychophysical functions[38] and to repeal Fechner's law.[39] Briefly stated, the power law describes the relationship

$$\log \psi = \beta \log \phi + k' \text{, or}$$
$$\psi = k \phi^{\beta},$$

where ψ = psychological magnitude, ϕ = stimulus intensity, $\log k = k'$ = constant, and the exponent β is specific to a particular sense modality. Expressed in words, it states that "equal stimulus ratios produce equal sensation ratios." This law holds for prothetic continua, such as loudness, that have purely quantitative changes, but not for metathetic continua that undergo qualitative as well as quantitative changes, such as pitch. Contrast this function with Fechner's logarithmic law, the *Massformel*,

$$\psi = k \log (\phi / b),$$

where ψ = sensation magnitude, ϕ = stimulus magnitude, b = threshold stimulus magnitude, and k = constant. Fechner's law can be expressed in words as "equal stimulus ratios produce equal sensation intervals."

The internal consistency of Stevens' sensory scales has been supported by cross-modality matching. In this procedure, stimuli in one dimension (for example, luminance) are adjusted by a subject so that their magnitudes appear to match those in another continuum, such as loudness. Predictions can now be made of the slope of one of the functions from knowledge of the slope of the other.

Stevens' Law as a statement of empirical relationships has been widely accepted, but his assumption that he was measuring sensations directly has been questioned (e.g., by MacKay,[40] Savage[41] Treisman[42]). The application of his methods to the study of sensory processes has been very productive.[43] Direct scaling also has been generalized successfully to such social variables as status, the seriousness of offenses, and the severity of recommended punishment[44-46]. It might be added that Fechner had anticipated the usefulness of measurement and scaling in this area and cited as his example the logarithmic relation between "*fortune physique*" and "*fortune morale*", of money and its subjective value, that Bernoulli had put forward in 1738.[2,47]

S.S. Stevens

Stevens' is by no means the only alternative method of scaling that has been advanced in recent years. Norman Anderson's functional measurement[48,49] proposes two laws. A number of physical stimuli S impinge on the organism and are converted by a valuation operation or psychophysical law into psychological stimuli s. The psychological stimuli are combined according to an integration function or psychological law to yield an implicit response r, which is then transformed into the overt, observable response R. The psychophysical law therefore becomes the function that relates the physical stimulus to its subjective counterpart, whereas the psychological law relates the subjective stimulus values to the response via the nonobservable covert response. To a Fechnerian there are strong echoes of outer and inner psychophysics in this theory. Compare Fechner's formulation: "By its nature, psychophysics may be divided into an outer and an inner part, depending on whether consideration is focused on the relation of the psychical to the body's external aspects, or on those internal functions with which the psychic are closely related." (Ref. 2, Vol.1, p.9)

RECENT DEVELOPMENTS

At first glance, animal psychophysics seems a paradox. Animals (apart from a few chimpanzees) cannot tell us about their sensations. To an objective psychologist this fact is an advantage, of course. But does a mind-body problem exist for animals? Fechner would have smiled. He was sure that not only animals but even plants and the whole nature shared in the world soul.[50]

Ratliff and Blough's adaptation of the tracking technique to obtain sensory thresholds[51, 52] has been applied to a wide variety of psychophysical measurements in animals. Adler,[53] for example, measured dark adaptation and spectral sensitivity of starlings and robins in order to define the limits of their sensory capacity for the purpose of evaluating the validity of theories of animal navigation. Sommers and Herrnstein[54] have tested a procedure that yielded magnitude-estimation data for pigeons' judgment of luminance. Signal-detection theory has been applied to pigeon data by Wright.[55]

The same theory of signal detection has done away with the concept of the threshold, so dear to Fechner.[56, 57] This theory treats separately the measure of sensitivity and the decision criterion of the observer. It assumes a continuum of sensory excitation and derives its quantitative data from judgments generated under the control of such factors as instructions and values and costs, or the observer's motivation. Since these conditions may vary, there is no fixed threshold. The threshold has also not fared well in the hands of the neural quantum theorists.[58, 59] Whereas the previously described theory took account of noise—i.e., stimulation extraneous to the particular stimulus value being tested—the theory of the neural quantum attempts to do away with noise entirely. Under these conditions momentary, random fluctuations in neural sensitivity affect the stimulus magnitude necessary to activate a given neural unit, resulting in a discontinuous psychophysical function. No threshold in Fechner's sense exists. It is of historical interest that attacks on the threshold concept can already be found in Jastrow's critique of 1888.[25] In a different vein, the extension of the ideas of relativistic physics to psychophysics has led to the suggestion that the notion of an unchanging physical world may also have to be replaced by one in which reality itself depends, at least in part, on the observer, according to Rosen.[60] Acceptance of this position would help to account for deviations from Weber's Law, as Rosen argues, and by extension, could also be applied to the logarithmic law and the power law.

All of the theories of scaling and psychological measurement so far discussed have shared the notion of some unit of measurement that was applied to the data. In a reversal of this position, Coombs[61, 62] advocates a procedure by which data define the measurement. It is an axiomatic theory, placing mathematical terms, such as the real numbers, in correspondence with properties of empirical observations. (For a detailed exposition, see Krantz et al.;[63, 64] for an application to psychophysical measurement see Falmagne.[65])

CONCLUSION

Where do these developments leave Fechner? They leave his contributions undiminished. He still deserves the credit for being the first to introduce measurement into psychology and thereby radically changing its direction. The exact nature of the functions is immaterial in this context, as far as the judgment of history is concerned.

Yet Fechner is not cited frequently in today's psychological literature. His name rarely appears in our introductory textbooks. There is a reason for this lack of interest. It was James who made the distinction between the tough- and the tender-minded. The tender-minded are in the majority at the present time. It looks as if William James will have had the last laugh. Most of America's Psychologists did not put up with an old man's patient whimsies. But for the minority of America's psychologists who seriously try to advance psychology as a science, there remains a great debt. Fechner's insights had fallen on fertile soil. A viable and lively branch of psychology had taken root in America. Psychology had become an experimental science.

REFERENCES

1. FECHNER, G. T. 1823. Premissae ad theoriam organismi generalem. Leipzig, Germany See MARSHALL, M.E. 1974. G.T. Fechner: Premises toward a general theory of organisms (1823). J. Hist. Behav. Sci. 10: 438-447.
2. FECHNER, G.T. 1860. Elemente der Psychophysik. Vols. 1 and 2. Breitkopf & Härtel, Leipzig, Germany. (Vol. 1 trans. by H.E. Adler, D.H. Howes & E.G. Boring, Eds., 1966, as Elements of Psychophysics. Holt, Rinehart & Winston, Inc. New York, N.Y.)
3. OKEN, L. 1809. Lehrbuch der Naturphilosophie. Jena, Germany.
4. EVERETT, C.C. 1892. Fichte's Science of Knowledge. S.C. Griggs & Co. Chicago, Ill.
5. ROBINSON, D.N. 1976. An Intellectual History of Psychology. Ch. 10. Macmillan Publishing Co. New York, N.Y.
6. STACE, W.T. 1955. The Philosophy of Hegel: A Systematic Exposition. Dover Publications. New York, N.Y. (First published in 1924.)
7. HERBART, J.F. 1891. A Text-Book in Psychology: An Attempt to Found the Science of Psychology on Experience, Metaphysics, and Mathematics. Trans. by Margaret K. Smith. D. Appleton. New York, N.Y. (First published in German, 1816) Excerpted In History of Psychology: A Source Book in Systematic Psychology. 1968. W. Sahakian, Ed. F.E. Peacock Publishers. Itasca, Ill.
8. FECHNER, G.T. 1851. Zend-Avesta, oder über die Dinge des Himmels und des Jenseits, vom Standpunkt der Naturbetrachtung. L. Voss. Leipzig, Germany.
9. ZUPAN, M.L. 1976. The conceptual development of quantification in experimental psychology. J. Hist. Behav. Sci. 12: 145-158.
10. BORING, E.G. 1961. Fechner: Inadvertent founder of psychophysics. Psychometrika 26: 3-8. (Reprinted In E.G. BORING. History, Psychology and Science: Selected Papers. 1963. R.I. Watson & D.T. Campbell, Eds. John Wiley & Sons, Inc. New York, N.Y.)
11. RAMUL, K. 1960. The problem of measurement in the psychology of the eighteenth century. Amer. Psychol. 15: 256-265.
12. BRINGMANN, W.G., W.D.G. BALANCE & R.B. EVANS. 1975. Wilhelm Wundt 1832-1920: A brief biographical sketch. J. Hist. Behav. Sci. 11: 287-297.
13. MACH, E. 1959. The Analysis of Sensations. Trans. by C.M. Williams. Dover Publications. New York, N.Y. (First published in 1886)
14. CADWALLADER, T.C. 1974. Charles S. Peirce (1839-1914): The first American experimental psychologist. J. Hist. Behav. Sci. 10: 291-298.
15. PEIRCE, C.S. 1877. Note on the sensation of color. Amer. J. Sci. 3rd Ser. 13: 247-251.
16. LADD, G.T. 1887. Elements of Physiological Psychology. Charles Scribner's Sons. New York, N.Y.
17. MILLS, E.S. 1974. George Trumbull Ladd: The great textbook writer. J. Hist. Behav. Sci. 10: 299-303.
18. STEVENS, S.S. 1959. Measurement, psychophysics, and utility. In Measurement: Definition and Theories. C. W. Churchman & P. Ratoosh, Eds.: 18-63. John Willey & Sons, Inc. New York, N.Y.
19. ESTES, W.K., S. KOCH, K. MACCORQUODALE, P.E. MEEHL, C.G. MUELLER, W.N. SCHOENFELD & W.S. VERPLANCK. 1954. Modern Learning Theory. Appleton-Century-Crofts. New York, N.Y.
20. JAMES, H., Ed. 1920. The Letters of William James. Vol. II: 18-19. The Atlantic Monthly Press. Boston, Mass.

21. JAMES, W. 1890. The Principles of Psychology. 2 vols. Henry Holt. New York, N.Y.
22. BORING, E.G. 1942. Human nature vs. sensation: William James and the psychology of the present. Amer. J. Psychol. 55: 310-327. (Reprinted *In* E.G. BORING. Psychologist at Large. Basic Books, New York, 1961.)
23. WERTHEIMER, M. 1972. Fundamental Issues in Psychology. Holt, Rinehart & Winston. New York, N.Y.
24. MARSHALL, M.E. 1974. William James, Gustav Fechner, and the question of dogs and cats in the library. J. Hist. Behav. Sci. 10: 304-312.
25. JASTROW, J. 1888. Critique of psychophysic methods. Amer. J. Psychol. 1: 271-309.
26. FULLERTON, G.S. & J. McK. CATTELL. 1892. On the perception of small differences. Univ. Penna. Phil. Ser. No. 2.
27. SOKAL, M.M. 1973. APA's first publication: Proc. Amer. Psychol. Ass. 1892-1893. Amer. Psychol. 28: 277-292.
28. TITCHENER, E.B. 1905. Experimental Psychology. Vol. II. Part II. Macmillan. New York, N.Y.
29. CATTELL, J. McK. 1893. On errors of observation. Amer. J. Psychol. 5: 285-293.
30. THURSTONE, L.L. 1927. A law of comparative judgment. Psychol. Rev. 34: 273-286.
31. CROZIER, W.J. 1940. On the law for minimal discrimination of intensities: IV. Δ I as a function of intensity. Proc. Nat. Acad. Sci. 26: 382-389.
32. BERGMANN, G. & K.W. SPENCE. 1944. The logic of psychophysical measurement. Psychol. Rev. 51: 1-24.
33. GRAHAM, C.H. 1950. Behavior, perception and the psychophysical methods. Psychol. Rev. 57: 108-120.
34. GRAHAM, C.H. 1958. Sensation and perception in an objective psychology. Psychol. Rev. 65: 65-76.
35. PLATEAU, J.A.F. 1872. Sur la mesure des sensations physiques, et sur la loi qui lie l'intensité de ces sensations a l'intensité de la cause excitante. Bull. de l'académie Royale de Belgique 33: 376-388.
36. MERKEL, J. 1888. Die Abhängigkeit zwischen Reiz und Empfindung. Philos. Studien. 4: 541-594.
37. RICHARDSON, L.F. & J.S. ROSS. 1930. Loudness and telephone currents. J. Gen. Psychol. 2: 288-306.
38. STEVENS, S.S. 1957. On the psychophysical law. Psychol. Rev. 64: 153-181.
39. STEVENS, S.S. 1961. To honor Fechner and repeal his law. Science 133: 80-86.
40. MACKAY, D.M. 1963. Psychophysics of perceived intensity: A theoretical basis for Fechner's and Stevens' laws. Science 139: 1213-1216.
41. SAVAGE, C.W. 1966. Introspectionist and behaviorist interpretations of ratio scales of perceptual magnitudes. Psychol. Mono. 80: No. 19 (Whole no. 627).
42. TREISMAN, M. 1964. Sensory scaling and the psychophysical law. Quart. J. Exp. Psychol. 16: 11-22.
43. MARKS, L.E. 1974. Sensory Processes. Academic Press. New York, N.Y.
44. STEVENS, S.S. 1966. A metric for social consensus. Science 151: 530-541.
45. STEVENS, S.S. 1972. Psychophysics and social scaling. General Learning Press. Morristown, N.Y.
46. EKMAN, G. & L. SJÖBERG. 1965. Scaling. Ann. Rev. Psychol. 16: 451-474.
47. BERNOULLI, D. 1954. Exposition of a new theory on the measurement of risk. Econometrica 22: 23-25. (Originally published in 1738.)
48. ANDERSON, N.H. 1970. Functional measurement and psychophysical judgment. Psychol. Rev. 77: 153-170.
49. ANDERSON, N.H. 1975. On the role of context effects in psychophysical judgment. Psychol. Rev. 82: 462-482.
50. WOODWARD, W.R. 1972. Fechner's panpsychism: A scientific solution to the mind-body problem. J. Hist. Behav. Sci. 8: 367-386.
51. RATLIFF, F. & D.S. BLOUGH. 1954. Behavioral studies of visual processes in the pigeon. USN, ONR. Technical Report, Proj. NR 140-072.
52. BLOUGH, D.S. 1958. A method for obtaining psychophysical thresholds from the pigeon. J. Exp. Anal. Behav. 1: 31-43.
53. ADLER, H.E. 1963. Psychophysical limits of celestial navigation hypotheses. Ergeb. Biol. 26: 235-252.
54. HERRNSTEIN, R.J. & P. VAN SOMMERS. 1962. Method for sensory scaling with animals. Science 135: 40-41.
55. WRIGHT, A.A. 1974. Psychometric and psychophysical theory within a framework of response bias. Psychol. Rev. 81: 322-347.
56. SWETS, J.A. 1961. Detection theory and psychophysics: A review. Psychometrika 26: 49-63.

57. GREEN, D.M. & J.A. SWETS. 1966. Signal Detection Theory and Psychophysics. John Wiley & Sons, Inc. New York, N.Y.
58. CORSO, J.F. 1956. The neural quantum theory of sensory discrimination. Psychol. Bull. **53:** 371-393.
59. CORSO, J.F. 1963. A theoretico-historical review of the threshold concept. Psychol. Bull. **60:** 356-370.
60. ROSEN, S.M. 1976. Toward relativization of psychophysical "relativity." Percept. Mot. Skills. **42:** 843-850.
61. COOMBS, C.H. 1950. Psychological scaling without a unit of measurement. Psychol. Rev. **57:** 145-158.
62. COOMBS, C.H. 1960. A theory of data. Psychol. Rev. **67:** 143-159.
63. KRANTZ, D.H., R.D. LUCE, P. SUPPES & A. TVERSKY. 1971. Foundations of Measurement. Academic Press. New York, N.Y.
64. KRANTZ, D.H., R.C. ATKINSON, R.D. LUCE, & P. SUPPES. 1974. Contemporary Developments in Mathematical Psychology. Freeman. San Francisco, Calif.
65. FALMAGNE, J.-C. 1976. Random conjoint measurement and loudness summation. Psychol. Rev. **83:** 65-79.

WILLIAM STERN AND AMERICAN PSYCHOLOGY:
A PRELIMINARY ANALYSIS OF
CONTRIBUTIONS AND CONTEXTS*

Francis P. Hardesty

Department of Psychology
The City College
City University of New York
New York, New York 10031

In assessing the prominent influence upon his biosocial approach to the origins and structure of personality and perception, Gardner Murphy recently had this to say about the role of William Stern:

> . . . in the early 1930s . . . when I was groping around for the rudiments of a conception of personality, I stumbled upon Stern's work. I think I probably encountered it first in Gordon Allport's writings and our conversations. I was quite electrified by the idea of a personalistic approach to each event, making a higher order integration so [one] did not have to talk about, let's say perception, but a personal process which was expressed through the act of perceiving. Of course, he had documented this with regards to studies of testimony and other fields showing that each person's testimony expressed his full individuality. . . . But an equally important thing was the chance to meet Stern. One of the great events of my professional life was meeting Stern and Wertheimer at the King's Crown Hotel in New York. . . . Sitting in and talking very vigorously was Wertheimer, of course, pleading all the time for *Gestalt*, and Stern saying there is just as much *Ungestalt* as there is *Gestalt*. . . . That was a very memorable occasion.[1]

For the historian, these remarks acquire significance in view of Murphy's position in the range and scope of what contemporary psychology has become and in view of the fact that in a sample of American psychologists Murphy is ranked second to Freud as the individual most influential in leading them into their specialty.[2] Allport's designation of himself as a student of Stern is well known,[3] and his promotion, critique, and modification of Stern's overall psychological views are well documented.[4-7] Perhaps less known is Wolman's observation[8] that Kurt Lewin adopted the philosophical outlook of Stern, and that it came to provide the underlay of Lewin's approach to psychology. With respect to Watson's 1974 compilation of bibliographical references for 538 eminent contributors to psychology,[9] we are told that of the original 1,040 individual names submitted to the international panel of judges selected by Watson and Boring, William Stern obtained a recognition rating of 26 points out of a possible 27, placing him in the group of the 76 most significant psychologists in the world between the years 1600 and 1967.[10]

Today these observations are likely to meet with a decidedly different set of impressions regarding William Stern's relation to the contemporary status of psychology. At one level, such is a predictable function of the extent to which attention has been concentrated in the rapid development of one or another subspecializations of our discipline over the last few years. For example, experimental and physiological psychologists are likely to recall the name of Stern in con-

*Supported in part by a Fulbright–Hays Research Award for the academic year 1973-74 at the University of Heidelberg, Heidelberg, Germany.

33

nection with his invention of the tone-variator[11] and with a series of studies, done early in his career, determining limens for the various sensory modalities under conditions of continuous change.[12-15] Investigators versed in psychometry tend to associate Stern with the early phases of the testing movement, with his introduction of the concept of IQ to the literature of measurement,[16,17] or with his later construction of the Cloud Pictures.[18,19] Workers pursuing the more interdisciplinary aspects of psychology are likely to recall Stern's part in securing forensic psychology in the first years of this century.[20-22] For developmentalists and those concentrating in experimental psycholinguistics, familiar notes may be rung by Stern's systematic use of observational methods, of thematic materials,[23] his early use of descriptive statistics in analyses of the emergence of language,[24] and the psychological development of the young child.[25]

Fragmented impressions of Stern's contributions to contemporary psychology may also be traced to the way our histories have been compiled. To date the bulk of these tend to be of the immanent or problem-centered variety. Contextural approaches have been few, and handling of the transcendental type even more rare.[a] There are valid reasons for this state of affairs, inasmuch as each variety of historiography yields material contributive to our grasp of the historical process and to how things come to attain the status they do. The fact remains, however, that most historical portrayals of contemporary psychology consist of a focus on a progression of concepts, immanently generated by the findings of the laboratory, modified and improved through steady transmission from one generation of investigators to the next. Neglected in these treatments are two major considerations: one is the fact that modern psychology has evolved into a field comprised of much more than basic science and researchers; the other is the consideration that psychology, as we know it today, is a structural convergence not only of influences from within, but of forces stemming from without and external to it.[33,34]

In this connection it is to be noted that a hundred years have ensued since Wundt completed the first edition of his principles of physiological psychology[35] and made his historic move from Zurich to Leipzig. Development of the field since that time has been steady, but hardly simple or programmatically straightforward. On the path to achieving the status as a science, a specialization, and an applied discipline it enjoys today, psychology has been attended by many fits and starts, crises, and deviations. Psychology, like any other form of science, has been and continues to be shaped by a dynamic interplay of internal and external forces distributed over time and location.

In this context and viewed as a form of institutionalized behavior, contemporary psychology can be seen as consisting of three interrelated aspects: first, as an enterprise in the pursuit of basic knowledge; then as a set of roles for which persons are educated; and finally, as a cluster of expert skills to be used in the resolving of societal problems.[b] Contemporary struggles in finding appropriate institutionalization of the activities of psychologists today can thus be seen as evolving from that of the professor-scholar-scientist role that became insitutionalized toward the end of the last century. Treated within this frame, preliminary analysis indicates that the contributions of the multifaceted William Stern categorize him as a highly salient figure centrally located in a series of role transformations leading away from the original one as a professor-scholar-scientist to current problems in finding appropriate institutionalization of the activities of psychologists as scientist-professional and flexible problem solvers.

Chronologically, the career of William Stern can be marked off in four major periods. *The Berlin years* coincide with the completion of his doctorate in philosophy at Friedrich Wilhelm University in 1893, the first four years of independent postdoctoral research and his early publications.[c] *The Breslau years*, running from 1897 to 1916, include activities associated with his initial position there as *Privatdozent* in philosophy, psychology, and pedagogy, and with his advancement in 1907 to associate professor. The third period, *the Hamburg years*, spans the interval 1916 to 1933 and covers Stern's activities and influence first with his acceptance of a professorship in that city-state's Program of General Lectures (*Allgemeines Vorlesungswesen*) and then with implementation of his first full-fledged University *Ordinariat* following the founding of the University of Hamburg in 1919. *The years of emigration* mark off Stern's fourth and final period. These include a brief residence in the Netherlands followed by his acceptance of a position in 1934 as lecturer and then professor at Duke University in Durham, North Carolina. There, in Durham, coronary occlusion suddenly and apparently without prior warning[3] closed the life of William Stern and his career of 45 years on the night of March 27, 1938.

Since the present paper centers on the second of these periods, the Breslau years, it seems worth while to remind ourselves what the social landscape looked like at that time. Such a backdrop is not only significant for furnishing a general frame within which William Stern was to set aspirations for himself and the new psychology, it is also a setting that proffers striking parallels to features attending our world today.

The year 1900, plus and minus ten years, was a time of remarkable unrest and social upheaval, of sporadic breakdowns and progressive reorderings affecting almost every facet of what previously had been well-settled institutions constituting western societies.[d] It was an era that found the major powers of Europe sidestepping confrontations between themselves at home but involved in skirmishes in Africa, Asia, the Carribbean, and the Pacific; a time when England's poor labored long hours for desperate wages and lived in impoverished circumstances; a time when a prominent judge, destined later to become President of the United States, would advance the concept that many more workers would have to be killed before disturbances attending the Pullman strikes would subside; a time when Emile Zola would be led to accuse French authorities of inflicting one of the greatest inequities of the century in the case of Alfred Dreyfus; a time when no less than a half dozen heads of state were to be murdered and the governments of western societies were to be terrorized by assassins.[34]

The era spanning the turn of the century was to witness worker movements seek an international mould, and women to militantly demand the elimination of inequities associated with the status of sex;[e] the mission of universities was to be reformed, educational systems vastly revised and extended, and legal definitions of the mentally ill, retarded, and handicapped accommodated to fit advances in medicine and psychiatry. The social and behavioral sciences were to be put on their feet, and the older physical and natural sciences were to be confronted with paradigmatic changes ushering in their own version of the *Age of Uncertainty*. For psychology, it was the era of rapid proliferation of its great schools, the search for comprehensive systems, of the discovery of the individual, and of securing the establishment of the psychologies of child, educational, industrial, social behavior, and other applications of psychology to the host of pressing problems.[34]

Against this background, William Stern in 1897 satisfied the requirements for inauguration into the faculty of the University of Breslau at the invitation of Hermann Ebbinghaus. His *Habilitationsschrift*[46] on theoretical and experimental aspects of the apperception of change was enlarged to appear in book form the following year under the title of *Psychologie der Veraenderungsauffassung*.[15]

In November of his first year in Breslau, Stern, along with eight other university colleagues in psychology, medicine, law, and education, founded a professional organization which in 1899 became a new section of the German Society for Psychological Research, complementing those already existing in Berlin and Munich. Meeting regularly and sponsoring programs of select public lectures, this organization was to grow rapidly, expanding to well over a hundred members in the next few years. Occurring frequently in the schedule of lectures, Stern's addresses give early glimpses of what later were to become his more articulated perspectives regarding the inadequacies of the "constancy hypothesis" and associationist viewpoints,[f] the limitations of the doctrine of specific neural energies,[48,49] and a deep-going appreciation for the significance underlying the interrelated psychophysics and more philosophical treatises of Gustav Fechner.[50] One set of these lectures[51] to find its way into the literature of the time was an interpretive overview of developments in the physical and natural sciences during the nineteenth century and the meaning these held for the emerging new psychology and for philosophy.

But it was another series of works appearing over the first years of this century that was to bring William Stern to early international distinction and to the first of two honorary doctorates conferred upon him by American institutions of higher learning.[g] Gordon Allport dubbed this phase of Stern's Breslau years " . . . a period of true genius [in which he] manifested his orginality to its fullest extent." (Ref. 4, p. 273) The estimate is not without merit, since during this time, Stern released a series of trail-blazing publications and activity reshaping the then virgin terrain of forensic, child, differential, and applied psychology. With them came fresh methods and new perspectives making transparent the relevance principles that derived from the laboratory had and continue to have for the disciplines of law, education, medicine, and the psychology of personality.

Stern's first monograph on the psychology of testimony,[20] an item of renewed interest today, appeared in 1902. Other investigations in this area quickly followed, and the first journalistic effort he was to edit, *Beitraege zur Psychologie der Aussage,*[22] was established in 1903. *Die Kindersprache,*[24] one of several works developed in collaboration with his wife[h] based on her carefully kept diaries of their three young children, was published in 1907. This well-known classic systematically traced phases in the emergence of language from early vocalization to articulation of the child's first sentences. It was followed the next year by *Erinnerung, Aussage und Luege in der ersten Kindheit,*[23] a less quantitatively approached and more anecdotal monograph. Representing extension of the psychology of testimonials to the verbal behaviors of the young child, the latter monograph demonstrated the theoretical and practical implications that the covergence of maturational limits and experience impose on the individual's remembrance and verbal reconstructions, and their relationship to fabrication and falsehood in childhood. The views underlying these works, along with an earlier monograph[55] assaying tactual sensations and the unconventional but well-organized processes whereby America's Helen Keller acquired language, were subsequently extended to investigations of other varieties of perception and expression in childhood.

Activities of Stern and the small psychology seminary in Breslau resulted in still other works of major importance. One appeared in 1912[16] and was translated into English two years later by Guy Whipple of Cornell University under the title of *Psychological Methods for Testing Intelligence*.[17] It was in the first German edition of this volume that Stern introduced the concept of *Intelligenzquotient*, together with its abbreviation as *IQ*, and discussed its usefulness in a re-analysis of data originally reported by Chotzen and others. *Die Psychologie der fruehen Kindheit*[25] was issued in 1914 as a text systematically detailing the principles governing psychological processes and individual psychological development through the preschool years. The third and sixth German editions of this work appeared in English in 1924 and 1930, respectively, as *The Psychology of Early Childhood*, translated by Anna Barwell.[56] The two foregoing treatises were subject to repeated revisions and translation into other foreign languages.

Two additional influential volumes to flow from Stern's pen during his Breslau years deserve special mention. Both appeared before the midpoint of his Breslau years was reached, and both had much to do with furnishing the explicit theoretical orientation and methodological scaffolding of what came before and especially after their appearance. Issued in 1900, *Ueber die Psychologie der Individuellen Differenzen*[57] created a systematic framework calling for the emancipation from the general field of psychology that branch we today more commonly term *differential psychology*. As will be seen later, this work was intended to be programmatic; it was completely rewritten in 1911,[58] revised and extended again in 1921.

The second work of this period was of a different order and appeared in 1906 a year before Stern's elevation to the associate professorship in Breslau. It was the first segment[59] of his *Person und Sache* (Person and Thing), elaborating the basic tenets and derivatives of his philosophical view of how the world works, his *critical personalism* and method of radical synthesis. The second and third segments[60] of this three-volume work, dealing with the nature of the human personality and the philosophy of values, were to be completed during the first phase of his Hamburg years.

Joining this manifold of publications and activity during his years in Breslau, William Stern was also to issue three calls[i] for programmatic inquiry which were to have substantial effects on the psychological communities of the period and the evolving structure of psychology. One of these is to be found in his previously mentioned monograph[57] of 1900 dealing with the psychology of individual differences. Its opening line—"Individuality, the problem of the twentieth century!"—constituted a call for the turning of experimental inquiry from its pursuit of the tenet that every person is like all other persons, to the additional observation that in some ways every person is simultaneously like *some* other persons and yet like *no* other person. In Stern's approach to the problem, several features are outstanding when the three editions of this work are taken together. One relates to the fact that the test is defined not so much as a clinical device to be used by the practitioner, but more as another variety of experimental procedure to be used in the empirical search for psychological invariants underlying the puzzle of differential individual reality. Striking too, in terms of today's perspectives, is the systematic character in which individual differences are conceptualized, not as a matter of heredity versus environment, but as moments in inner-structuring and of individuation as a matter of convergence between the two. Another striking feature is to be found in the extent to which an international perspective permeates the bases from which the call is made and the programmatics constructed. For example, of the studies cited in the first edition of the work, far more originate from outside than from within the German language community.

Another call, contributive to the shape the new psychology was to take, was Stern's 1903 appeal for the programmatic development of psychology as an applied discipline capable of serving in the practical affairs of the world. Contained in an article[63] leading off the first issue of his *Beitraege*, Stern envisioned as basic to applied psychology the blending of the twin constructs *Psychodiagnostik* and *Psychotechnik*, the latter more than ten years before Hugo Muensterberg[k] at Harvard University was to adopt it and bring it to fame. In the proposal Stern also called for the establishment of a centralized agency and outlined the advantages a clearing-house would have for the collection and organization of scientific information to serve as a basis for consultantships and special-topic workshops. The idea did not go unheeded. In 1906, two years after the formal founding of the German Society for Experimental Psychology, the Institute for Applied Psychology and Cumulative Psychological Research was organized in Wilmersdorf-Berlin under the administration of Stern, Otto Lipmann, and an advisory board comprised of G. E. Mueller, Ernst Meumann, Friedrich Schumann, and Robert Sommer.[l] The next year Stern and Lipmann were to begin their coeditorship of a new journal, *Die Zeitschrift fuer Angewandte Psychologie und Sammelforschung*, as a function of the new Institute and as an official organ of the German Society. Succeeding the earlier *Beitraege*, the new journal and its soon-to-follow special one-volume supplements (*Beihefte*) were to represent a major broadening of publication outlet for ideas, discussion of issues, and reserach reports relevant to applications of psychology for the next quarter of a century.

In a brief survey[67] addressed to an international audience concerning the status of the field in Germany if 1923, Stern was to note that psychology:

> . . . has entered into closer contact with practical life. Education and industry, technics and the court of justice, as well as many other branches of culture, have felt the need of bringing their problems . . . before the consideration of the psychologist. . . . When the present reviewer, two decades ago, advanced the concept of *applied psychology*, *psychotechnic*, and *psychognostic* [sic] for the first time, it was simply a question of proposing a program for the future. Today, applied psychology has become a vital fact . . . and its indispensibility is established beyond a doubt . . . [its] rapid development . . . is due in no small degree to the pressure of the times and to the vital changes in the life of the country. The war made certain demands which had to be satisfied immediately; the badly shattered industrial life was glad to grasp the help which was offered from entirely new quarters; post-war educational reform likewise demanded a new psychological orientation. (Ref. 67, pp. 227-228)

Supplementing his early appeals to secure the psychologies of differential and applied, William Stern was to advance yet another. Issued as his involvements with research into child life and psychometry acquired momentum, this call came in the form of a two-pronged affair. Both aspects centered on pressing needs to expand empirical knowledge in new directions if psychology, as a theoretical and practical enterprise, was to exercise its part in restructuring older educational practices. Published in 1910 in a German journal devoted to the welfare, education, and study of youth,[68] this appeal of Stern was translated into English by Lucy Day of Cornell University to appear the following year in the *Journal of Educational Psychology*.[69] In it, Stern directed attention to the surging new data-base concentrated on subnormal and normal functioning and, in turn, called for the extension of such to include systematic inquiry into the relatively neglected area of "giftedness" as the next step in the coordinate continuum of investigations. The call, in more overarching and urgent terms, was reinforced in 1916 in a subsequent brochure[70] outlining the general study of youth as a compelling cultural requirement in the context of problems generated by modern society. Prepared as a kind of position paper, the latter represented a statement preliminary to Stern's acceptance of the professorial post in the Hamburg *Vorlesungswesen* made vacant the year before by the death of Ernst Meumann.

If pathfinding was characteristic of his Breslau years, then constructive implementation and consolidation of these was the outstanding feature of William Stern's span of years in Hamburg. The three calls for programmatic inquiry and the thematics of all of the aforementioned major publications were to be carried over to find their concrete integration.

Details with respect to the growth and development of the Hamburg Laboratory and Psychological Institute[71-74] as well as interpretive overviews of these and Stern's other activities[27, 75, 76] may be found in the literature. It must suffice here to note that changing distributions of a social, economic, and political order attending the war and its immediate aftermath fostered a fast interlacing of the mission of the Laboratory with the pressing needs of Hamburg's system of public schools, its child and juvenile centers, its vocational and counseling authorities, and that city-state's courts and law enforcement agencies. By 1922, in addition to pursuit of general psychology with its theoretical and experimental components, the program of Stern's institute had taken on a rather stable structure of research commitments, course offerings, and services embracing two other integral divisions: child psychology, ranging accross the psychologies of early and middle childhood, development, and assessment; and industrial psychology, centering on the construction of procedures and apparatus for vocational counseling, selection, and evaluation of man-machine interface.

In many ways representing a unique innovation in the setting and traditions of German universities of the time,[m] the program forged by Stern and his coworkers was to expand still further not only to become an important center in northern Germany, but also to achieve international distinction for its investigations into the invariant characteristics of the psychological worlds of the child and adolescent, the conditions affecting human behavior and development, and the measurement and identification of giftedness. By 1931, for example, before transcending economic and political crises were to penetrate and contribute to decline of its structure, operations of the Psychological Institute were housed in spacious quarters consisting of some 41 rooms, making its physical plant one of the largest in Germany at that time. To the established research and instructional concentrations in general psychology, child and adolescent psychology, and industrial psychology, a fourth had been integrated focused on psychological aspects of legal proceedings, criminology, and forensics. In addition to routine publication outlets, two periodic supplements to his journal for applied psychology, *Hamburger Arbeiten zur Begabungsforschung* and *Hamburger Untersuchungen zur Sozial- und Jugendpsychologie*, were available for reports of the Institute's projects. The research and curriculum of the institute encompassed a wide range of topics, interlacing psychology not only as a science and applied discipline, but as an interdisciplinary partner in the concerns of the schools of law and medicine of Hamburg University, and von Uexkuell's Institute for Environmental Research (*Umweltforschung*).

In April 1933, political turns and abrupt legislative decisions of the new central government in Berlin suddenly were to bring down the psychological insitute that William Stern and his coworkers had built over a period of 17 years.[n] A number of Stern's associates and students were known and eventually became more familiar to American psychology. Among these were Curt Bondy, Ernst Cassirer, Fritz Heider, Betty Katzenstein, Heinrich Kluever, Martha Muchow, Martin Scheerer, and Heinz Werner.

Pulling this matrix of observations together, William Stern emerges as a highly significant but often neglected figure whose activities and contributions represent an early expression of the shape psychology in its more institutionalized forms has taken today. For Stern, psychology held an undisputedly secure place not only among the sciences as an instrument for the generation of knowledge and the enlightenment of man, but as an institution fully capable of confronting the problems of modern society and contributing its share to the resolution of the latter as these affect the behavior of the individual. His work, particularly that prior to his years of emigration, attests to his overriding conviction that a fundamental unity underlies the field of psychology in all of its diverse aspects. With a variety of syntheses, manifest early and typical of him throughout his career, Stern advocated and brought about an early fusion of experimental and applied components of psychology, its theory and practice. In a similar vein, his final major publication, *General Psychology from a Personalistic Viewpoint*,[82, 83] represented an attempt to transform his more speculative views of how the world works, his *critical personalism*, into tenents and terms scientifically acceptable to a rapidly advancing objective psychology.[27]

It is sometimes said that the paths beaten by our pioneers cannot be expected to bear the burden of today's traffic. It likewise seems to be true that, in the rush of things, original trail-markings become blurred or looked upon as irrelevant. It is ironic that many of our histories report Stern's invention of the IQ as if this were his most outstanding contribution. Stern did not consider it so. Rather, while defending its heuristic use, he regarded the index of limited value in the appraisal of individual intelligence if used without reference to a given person's situation and assessment of other facets of personality.[27] He was amazed that the concept spread so rapidly,[84] and he expressed early misgivings about its indiscriminate application in massive selection procedures as was done in the United States.[85] As if to remind his audience of his other contributions, Stern inserted the note into an invited address[86] before a group in New York City five months before his death stating that he was happy to find that William Healy[87] and Frederick Bartlett[88] had put to fruitful use methods first applied by him.

More substantial influences of Stern's work, modified and made over, are still to be found in many areas of today's psychology. Reference to its impact on the psychologies of Gordon Allport and Gardner Murphy has already been made. But the perspective of Stern, taking as it did its point of departure from empirical analyses into the structure and functions of language, established a vital link in the European conceptual posture extending from Rousseau and Pestalozzi through Preyer to today's flourishing Geneva School.[34] Stern's constructs and portrayal of phases in the development of cognitive and other psychological functioning of the preschool child furnished an arrangement of conceptual blocks and empirical findings upon which Piaget was to build his early work.[89] Limitations of time do not permit tracing of other aspects of Stern's influence: his polemics with the other schools and systems of the day;[o] his contributions regarding the interplay between sensorimotor, affective functioning, and higher units in cognition; his contribution to the contemporary, widely accepted concept of the functional autonomy of motives; or applications of his continuum of saliency and embeddedness to treatments involving the measurement of evoked social attitudes.[94, 95]

In general, William Stern's greatest contributions and most identifiable influence on American psychology were his charting of new paths when he contributed to perspectives, methods, and the shape contemporary psychology has taken. Those years, however, were not only his years. They were the years of reformulation shared by many during a time of great social change when the European-American interchange of ideas in psychology was at its zenith, less unilateral than is today the case, when reciprocity of vision, concepts, and ideas was part and parcel of the relationship.

It is perhaps in this broader context that meaning is to be found in Fritz Heider's assertion that it is difficult to determine how far current trends that are in line with Stern's conceptions " . . . stem from his work and how far he should be thought of as merely anticipating independent developments." (Ref. 96, p. 264) With the observations of the present paper in hand, one can go a step further with Heider and agree, as Robert MacLeod would have,[97] that," For psychologists who feel the need to go beyond a fragmented view of human nature, Stern's personalism, centered as it is in the concrete unity of the person, will always have a special attraction. It may be that, as he himself felt, this will be the most lasting part of his work." (Ref. 96, p. 264)

ACKNOWLEDGMENTS

The assistance of Dr. Horst Gundlach (University of Heidelberg), Diplom Psych. Matthias Burisch (University of Hamburg) and of Mr. Donald Petty and Ms. Carolyn Snyder (The City College, City University of New York) in gathering some of the data forming the basis for this paper is most greatefully acknowledged. Encouragement by the CUNY Committee for Transnational Research and Exchange in Psychology, especially that of Dr. Morey Wantman, is also appreciated.

NOTES

a. Approaches to the history of psychology can be conceptualized along a continuum running from the *immanent* to the *transcendental*.[26,27] The approach of Boring[28] illustrates the former, that of Holzkamp,[29] the latter. Intermediately dispersed between these two anchorages, the *problem-centered*, and *contextural*, and the *historical psychology* approaches hold successive positions along the same continuum. Examples of these are to be found in the works of Pongratz,[30] Van Hoorn,[31] and Van den Berg,[32] respectively.

b. For description and discussion of these differentiations, see the recent elaborate analysis by Tyler,[36] also Hardesty.[27]

c. Centering on the use of analogy in conventional thinking, Stern's inaugural dissertation[37] was successfully defended on April 12, 1893 against challenges by Franz Eulenburg, Arthur Wreschner, and a doctoral candidate in mathematics named Zermelo. Moritz Lazarus provided a short preface for the extended version published in book form[38] later the same year. The series of independent investigations eventually leading to the experimental base for Stern's *Habilitation* as well as the construction of the tone variator bearing his name were understaken under the aegis of Hermann Eibbinghaus and Arthur Koenig at the university in Berlin. The studies continued under the sponsorship of Carl Stumpf[39] after Ebbinghaus, in 1894, moved into the "chair" vacated by Theodor Lipps at the University of Breslau.

d. For a dramatic portrayal of these and other sociopolitical features of the period, see Tuchman.[40]

e. Other movements, of course, were also characteristic. One was the European youth movements of the time in France and especially in Germany. These broke over the turn of the century and were to take on a degree of institutionalized status in the ensuing decade and its aftermath.

Following on the heels of a generation of unprecedented industrialization, urban concentration, unparalleled material prosperity and realignments affecting the full scope of its vital social institutions, Germany of the 1890s had obtained a place in the sun. Pulling together a wide range of materials[41-44] dealing with the effects on youth of the time, George Rosen[45] tells the story most poignantly: "But . . . large numbers of German youth saw nothing admirable in a society that was being overwhelmed by tides of commercialism and uniformity. For them there was no brave new world. . . . What they saw was a brassy, tarnished society, in which moral bankruptcy and social fraud were rampant. They were . . . disillusioned by the world of their elders, whose values, traditions, and institutions appeared threadbare and irrelevant . . . they saw parental religion largely a sham, politics trivial . . . economic activity deceitful . . . education stereotyped and lifeless, art trashy and sentimental, literature commercialized, family life repressive and insincere, and the relations between the sexes, marital or extramarital, shot through with hypocrisy. The times were ripe for revolt. . . . By 1900 all over . . . northern Germany one could find tanned, travel-stained young men, and later girls, in nondescript clothes . . . on their backs a few simple belongings in knapsacks, and on the shoulders of at least a few lutes and guitars that they played while wandering. . . . They developed a headquarters for each group . . . embellished with their own hand made furniture, carvings, paintings and leatherwork . . . their credo was goallessness." (Ref. 45, pp. 7-9)

Numerous treatises on the movement frequently focus on it as a significant forerunner to the rise of National Socialism. The movement, however, embraced a full spectrum of political orientations, right and left. Such analyses often fail to take as a point of departure the changing constituencies of the movement, and the fact that the social time-frames for the 1890s, 1900s, 1910s as well as those of the 1920s are different.[34]

f. Stern's break with elementarism and the mechanistic views underlying associationism occurred in advance of his Breslau years. A humorful man, his stance toward the limited use of associationism in describing the inner-structuring of psychological events was also given expression much later in the 1913 version[47] of his *Psychologen-Leid*. Set to the melody of the student song *Crambambuli*, its fifth stanza reads as follows, adapted from the translation by Mrs. James Burt Miner whose husband was a member of the Psychology Department at the University of Minnesota at that time:

> Associationism—truly 'tis a word of magic!
> Twill, if you please, with greatest ease
> Break every problem's seals.
> And many seek with it alone to conjure
> A counterfeit so true that it
> The mind's real form reveals.
> Ideas check or aid each other
> They jostle, crowd and squeeze one another.
> And lo! A psychologic hash
> Comes from this clash. (Ref. 47, p. 414)

g. Both were honorary doctorates of laws. The first was conferred in September 1909 in the course of the now-celebrated conference at Clark University in Worcester, Mass. commemorating the 20th anniversary of the university.[52] The other honorary degree was awarded by Wittenberg College, Springfield, Ohio during proceedings of the International Symposium on Feelings and Emotions[53] convened there in October 1927 on the occasion of the opening of its new psychology laboratories.

h. As Klaus Eyferth has noted,[54] details with respect to the life and background of Clara Stern née Joseephy are still to be compiled. Apart from several brief encyclopedic entries, little is actually known. Indications are that she gained a degree of recognition in her own right. The aforementioned publications represent one, if not the first, of several husband-wife teams wherein coauthorships were shared.

i. Other calls, less explicit and programmatic, issued by Stern are beyond the scope of this paper. One relates to the cultural crisis shared by many members of the central European academic communities of the time. The background and course of the crisis has been described in detail and analyzed by Fritz Ringer.[61] In a paper published in 1915,[62] Stern underscored the concern of his colleagues in his assertion that unless a new *Weltanschauung* could be found, society ran the risk of not mastering its technology and of losing its humanity.

j. For example, of the 196 bibliographical items listed, 69.4% are publications in English,

French Italian, and other languages. With respect to investigators whose works and conceptions are cited in five or more instances in the text, the following researchers appear: James M. Baldwin (United States), Alfred Binet (France), Theodore Flournoy (Switzerland), James McKeen Cattell (United States), Francis Galton (United Kingdom), and Joseph Jastrow (United States).

k. The relationship between Muensterberg and Stern is worthy of treatment unable to be given here. For example, Muensterberg's failure to integrate his psychological and philosophical perspectives is mentioned in several instances by Stern[39,64] as being pivotal in the latter's decision to achieve a full synthesis. Apart from this, a long-term academic and personal correspondence existed between the two.

l. All members of the advisory board were, at the same time, members of the executive committee of the German Society for Experimental Psychology. Mueller (University of Goettingen) was president (*Vorsitzender*) of the German Society; Sommer (University of Giessen) its vice-president (*stellvertretender Vorsitzender*); and Schumann (University of Berlin), its recording secretary.[66]

m. Centers with programs in applied psychology and psychotechnics were generally housed in the non-university-affiliated institutes of technology and special professional schools, the *Technische-* and *Handelshochschule*. The offerings at the Universities of Berlin, Hamburg, and Leipzig were exceptions.[77]

n. On April 7, 1933, two weeks after a new enabling act had empowered the National Socialist regime to govern for the next four years without a constitution, the Law for the Restoration of the Professional Civil Service[78] came into effect. Its provisions included the mandated dismissal and forced retirement of all tenured and nontenured members of the civil service system for higher education on grounds of any one of the following pretexts: insufficient qualifications; non-aryan status; political unrealiability; administrative simplification. The law required full enforcement of its main provisions by the end of September 1933. However, by April 1935, it had run through more than a dozen modifying decrees.[79]

   The law of April 7 immediately barred Stern and many of his associates from conducting courses and the business of the institute. Stern's long-standing services to the university no longer mattered. His writings were removed from libraries and his students were warned that he was a *Schaedling*.[80] Stern's several editorships were terminated later that year, and Felix Krueger replaced him as president of the German Society for Psychology. The "chair" Stern occupied in the University of Hamburg was subsequently dismantled, and its moneys later were used for the creation of an *Ordinariat* in art history.[81]

o. "Polemics" is perhaps too harsh a term for Stern's view. Scattered throughout his publications, Stern's principal critique of other systems was that they each represented perspectives that were necessary but not sufficient. With respect to the Berlin *Gestalt* School, the core of Stern's critique hinged on its overemphasis on salient components in experience and other factors reflected in his dictum "no *Gestalt* without a *Gestalter*."[90] Of the four methods advocated by Watson's behaviorism, Stern exercised three: observation, objective tests, and verbal report (*Aussage*). Even in relation to applications of psychoanalytic conceptions where Stern's stance was often most severe,[56,91] exceptions are to be found. Alfred Adler, for example, acknowledged that the system he found most in sympathy with his own was Stern's personalism. As early as 1914, Adler noted that " . . . Stern, in a different way, has arrived at results similar to mine" (Ref. 92, p. 1). Adler elaborated the point again in 1931.[93]

REFERENCES

1. EVANS, R. 1966. Dr. Gardner Murphy Speaks. Part II. NSF Notable Contributors to the Psychology of Personality Series. University Houston. Houston, Texas. (Film sound track.)
2. CLARK, K. E. 1957. America's Psychologists: A Survey of a Growing Profession. American Psychological Association. Washington, D. C.
3. ALLPORT, G. W. 1938. William Stern: 1871-1938. Am. J. Psychol. 51: 770-774.
4. ALLPORT, G. W. 1968. The personalistic psychology of William Stern. *In* The Person in Psychology: Selected Essays. G. W. Allport, Ed.: 271-297. Beacon Press. Boston, Mass.
5. ALLPORT, G. W. 1937. The personalistic psychology of William Stern. Character and Personality 5: 231-246.
6. ALLPORT, G. W. 1937. Personality: A Psychological Interpretation. Henry Holt & Co. New York, N. Y.

7. ALLPORT, G. W. 1961. Pattern and Growth in Personality. Holt, Rinehart and Winston. New York, N. Y.
8. WOLMAN, B. 1960. Contemporary Theories and Systems in Psychology. Harper & Row. New York, N. Y.
9. WATSON, R. I., Ed. 1974. Eminent Contributors to Psychology Vol. I. A Bibliography of Primary References. Springer Publishing Co. New York, N. Y.
10. ANNIN, E. L., E. G. BORING, & R. I. WATSON. 1968. Important psychologists, 1600-1967. J. Hist. Behav. Sci. 4: 303-315.
11. STERN, L. W. 1902. Der Tonvariator. Z. Psychol. 30: 422–432.
12. STERN, L. W. 1894. Die Wahrnehmung von Helligkeitsveraenderungen. Z. Psychol. 7: 249-278; 395-397.
13. STERN, L. W. 1896. Die Wahrnehmungen von Tonveraenderungen. Z. Psychol. 11: 1-30.
14. STERN, L. W. 1899. Die Wahrnehmung von Tonveraenderungen. Z. Psychol. 21: 360-387; 22: 1-12.
15. STERN, L. W. 1898. Psychologie der Veraenderungsauffassung. Preuss & Juenger. Breslau, Germany. 2nd edit., 1906.
16. STERN, L. W. 1912. Die psychologischen Methoden der Intelligenzpruefung. *In* Bericht ueber den V. Kongress fuer experimentelle Psychologie. F. Schumann, Ed. 1-102. J. A. Barth. Leipzig, Germany.
17. STERN, L. W. 1914. The Psychological Methods of Testing Intelligence. Translated by G. M. Whipple. Warwick and York, Inc. Baltimore, Md.
18. STERN, W. 1937. Cloud pictures: A new method for testing imagination. Character and Personality 6: 132-146.
19. STERN, W. 1938. General Psychology from the Personalistic Standpoint. Macmillan. New York, N. Y.
20. STERN, L. W. 1902. Zur Psychologie der Aussage. Z. Ges. Strafswiss. 22.
21. STERN, L. W. 1904. Die Aussage als geistige Leistung und als Verhoersprodukt. J. A. Barth. Leipzig, Germany.
22. STERN, L. W., Ed. 1903-1906. Beitraege Zur Psychologie der Aussage mit besonderer Beruecksichtigung von Problemen der Rechtspflege, Paedagogik, Psychiatrie, und Geschichtsforschung. J. A. Barth. Leipzig, Germany.
23. STERN, C. & W. STERN. 1908. Erinnerung, Aussage und Luege in der ersten Kindheit. J. A. Barth. Leipzig, Germany. 2nd edit., 1920; 3rd edit., 1922; 4th edit., 1931.
24. STERN, C. & W. STERN. 1907. Die Kindersprache: Eine psychologische und sprach-theoretische Untersuchung. Leipzig, Germany. 2nd edit., 1920; 3rd edit., 1922; 4th edit., 1928, 1965, 1975.
25. STERN, W. 1914. Psychologie der fruehen Kindheit bis zum sechsten Lebensjahre. Quelle & Meyer. Leipzig, Germany. 2nd edit., 1921; 3rd rev. edit., 1923; 4th edit., 1927; 5th edit., 1928; 6th rev. edit., 1930; 7th edit., 1952; 8th edit., 1965; 9th edit., 1967; 10th edit., 1971.
26. VAN HOORN, W. 1972. Personal communication.
27. HARDESTY, F. 1976. Louis William Stern: A new view of the Hamburg years. Ann. N.Y. Acad. Sci. 270: 30-44.
28. BORING, E. G. 1950. A History of Experimental Psychology. Appleton-Century-Crofts. New York, N. Y.
29. HOLZKAMP, K. 1973. Sinnliche Erkenntnis: Historischer Ursprung und gesellschaftliche Funktion der Wahrnehmung. Athenaeum Fischer. Frankfurt am Main, Germany.
30. PONGRATZ, L. J. 1967. Problemgeschichte der Psychologie. Francke. Bern, Switerland.
31. VAN HOORN, W. 1972. As Images Unwind: Ancient and Modern Theories of Perception. University Press Amsterdam. Amsterdam, The Netherlands.
32. VAN DEN BERG, J. H. 1974. Divided Existence and Complex Society: An Historical Approach. Duquesne University Press. Pittsburgh, Penn.
33. HARDESTY, F. & K. EYFERTH, Eds. 1965. Forderungen an die Psychologie. Verlag Hans Huber. Bern, Switzerland and Stuttgart, Germany.
34. HARDESTY, F. 1976. Early European contributions to the history and status of contemporary developmental psychology: Overview, contexts and selections. *In* The Developing Individual in a Changing World. K. Riegel and J. Meacham, Eds. Mouton. The Hague, the Netherlands.
35. WUNDT, W. 1874. Grundzuege der physiologischen Psychologie. Engelmann. Leipzig, Germany.

36. TYLER, F. B. 1970. Shaping of the science. Am. Psychol. **25:** 219-226.
37. STERN, L. W. 1893. Die Analogie im volkstuemlichen Denken: Inaugural-Dissertation. Philosophisch historischer Verlag. Berlin, Germany.
38. STERN, L. W. 1893. Die Analogie im volkstuemlichen Denken: Eine psychologischen Untersuchung. Philosophisch historischer Verlag. Berlin, Germany.
39. STERN, W. 1927. William Stern. *In* Philosophie der Gegenwart in Selbstdarstellungen. R. Schmidt, Ed. Vol. 6: 129-184. Felix Meiner. Leipzig, Germany.
40. TUCHMAN, B. 1966. The Proud Tower: A Portrait of the World before the War. 1890-1914. Macmillan. New York, N.Y.
41. BECKER, H. 1946. German Youth: Bond or Free. New York, N. Y.
42. LUEKENS, C. 1925. Die deutsche Jugendbewegung. Frankfurter Societaets-Drukerei. Frankfurt a. M., Germany.
43. SCHELSKY, H. 1957. Die skeptische Generation: Eine Soziologie der deutschen Jugend. E. Diederich. Duesseldorf-Koeln, Federal Republic of Germany.
44. SCHMIDT, R. C. 1946. German Youth Movements: A Typological Study. University of Wisconsin. Madison, Wis. Unpublished doctoral dissertation.
45. ROSEN, G. 1970. The revolt of youth: some historical comparisons. *In* The Psychopathology of Adolescence. J. Zubin and A. M. Freedman, Eds. : 1-14. Grune & Stratton. New York, N. Y.
46. STERN, L. W. 1897. Theorie der Veraenderungsauffassung. Pruess Juenger. Breslau, Germany.
47. STERN, W. 1914. The psychologist's song. J. Ed. Psychol. **5:** 413-416.
48. STERN, L. W. 1899. Das Dogma von die specifischen Sinnesenergie. Z. Paedagog. Psychol. **1:** 48-49.
49. STERN, L. W. 1899. Psychophysica rediviva. Z. Paedagog. Psychol. **1:** 278-280.
50. STERN, L. W. 1901. Fechner als Philosoph und Psycho-Physiker. Z. Paedagog. Psychol. Pathologie. **3:** 405-407.
51. STERN, L. W. 1900. Die psychologische Arbeit des 19. Jahrhunderts, in besondere in Deutschland. Z. Paedagog. Psychol. Pathol. **2:** 329-353; 413-436.
52. CLARK UNIVERSITY. 1910. Lectures and Addresses Delivered before the Departments of Psychology and Pedagogy in Celebration of the Twentieth Anniversary of the Opening of Clark University. Clark University Press. Worcester, Mass.
53. REYMERT, J., Ed. 1928. Feelings and Emotions: The Wittenberg Symposium. Clark University Press. Worcester, Mass.
54. EYFERTH, K. 1977. The Contributions of Clara and William Stern. *In* The developing Individual in a Changing World. K. Riegel and J. Meacham, Eds. Mouton. The Hague, The Netherlands. In press.
55. STERN, L. W. 1905. Helen Keller: Die Entwicklung und Erziehung einer Taubstumm-blinden als psychologisches, paedagogisches und sprachtheoretisches Problem. Reuther & Richard. Berlin, Germany.
56. STERN, W. 1924. The Psychology of Early Childhood up to the Sixth Year of Age. Translated by A. Barwell. Henry Holt & Co. New York, N. Y. 2nd rev. edit., 1930.
57. STERN, L. W. 1900. Ueber Psychologie der Individuellen Differenzen, J. A. Barth. Leipzig, Germany.
58. STERN, W. 1911. Die Differentielle Psychologie in Ihren Methodischen Grundlagen. J. A. Barth. Leipzig, Germany. 2nd edit., 1921.
59. STERN, W. 1906. Person und Sache. Vol. 1. Ableitung und Grundlehre. J. A. Barth. Leipzig, Germany.
60. STERN, W. 1917; 1924. Person und Sache. Vol. 2. Die Menschliche Persoenlichkeit. Vol. 3. Wertphilosophie. J. A. Barth. Leipzig, Germany.
61. RINGER, F. 1969. The Decline of the German Mandarins: The German Academic Community, 1890-1933. Harvard University Press. Cambridge, Mass.
62. STERN, W. 1915. Vorgedanken zur Weltanschauung. J. A. Barth. Leipzig, Germany.
63. STERN, L. W. 1903. Angewandte Psychologie. Beitraege zur Psychologie der Aussage. **1:** 4-45.
64. STERN, W. 1917. Hugo Muensterberg: In memoriam. J. Appl. Psychol. **1:** 186-188.
65. STERN, W. & O. LIPMANN. 1908. Nachrichten aus dem Institut fuer angewandte Psychologie und psychologische Sammelforschung. Z. Angew. Psychol. **1:** 164-170.
66. SCHUMANN, F., Ed. 1907. Bericht ueber den II. Kongress fuer experimentelle Psychologie in Wuerzburg. von 18. bis. 21 April 1906. J. A. Barth. Leipzig, Germany.
67. STERN, W. 1923. Psychological science in Germany. Scand. Sci. Review. **2:** 225-229.
68. STERN, W. 1910. Das Uebernormale Kind. Z. Jugendwohlfahrt, Jugendbildung, Jugendkunde. **Feb.-Maerz:** 72-79; 160-167.

69. STERN, W. 1911. The supernormal child. J. Educ. Psychol. **2**: 143-148; 181-190.
70. STERN, W. 1916. Die Jugendkunde als Kulturforderung: Mit Besonderer Beruecksichtigung des Begabungsproblems. Quelle & Meyer. Leipzig, Germany.
71. STERN, W. 1922. Das Psychologische Laboratorium der Hamburgischen Universitaet. Z. Paed. Psychol. Exp. Paed. **23**: 161-196.
72. STERN, W. 1925. Aus dreijaehriger Arbeit des Hamburger Psychologischen Laboratoriums. Z. Paed. Psychol. Exp. Paed. **26**: 289-307.
73. STERN, W. 1931. Das Psychologische Institut der Hamburgischen Universitaet in seiner Gegenwaertigen Gestalt. Z. Angew. Psychol. **39**: 181-227.
74. STERN, W. 1933. Aus dem letzten Arbeiten des Psychologischen Instituts der Hamburgischen Universitaet 1931-33. Z. Angew. Psychol. **45**: 397-418.
75. HARDESTY, A. S. 1953. The Psychological Institute of the University of Hamburg: History, Contemporary Development, Outlook. Psychological Institute, University of Hamburg. Hamburg, Germany. Mimeographed.
76. BONDY, C. 1961. William Stern: Ein Bild des Psychologen und Hamburger Universitaetslehrers. Neues Hamburg. **14**: 41-43.
77. DORSCH, F. 1963. Geschichte und Probleme der Angewandten Psychologie. Verlag Hans Huber. Bern, Switzerland and Stuttgart, Germany.
78. REICHSMINISTERIUM DES INNERN (Hrsg.) 1933. Gesetz zur Wiederherstellung des Berufsbeamtentums vom 7. April 1933. Reichsgesetzblatt **34**: 175-177. Reichsdruckerei. Berlin, Germany.
79. HARTSHORNE, E. Y. 1937. The German Universities and National Socialism. Harvard Univ. Press. Cambridge, Mass.
80. BONDY, C. 1973. Festvortrag zum 100. Geburtstag von William Louis Stern. Paper presented Oct. 29, 1971. Kokoschka Hall. University of Hamburg. Hamburg, Federal Republic of Germany. Mimeographed.
81. UNIVERSITAET HAMBURG (Hrgs.) Universitaet Hamburg 1919-1969. Selbstverlag der Universitaet Hamburg. Hamburg, Federal Republic of Germany.
82. STERN, W. 1935. Allgemeine Psychologie auf personalistischer Grundlage. Martinus Nijhoff. The Hague, The Netherlands. 2nd edit., 1950.
83. STERN, W. 1938. General Psychology from the Personalistic Standpoint. Translated by H. D. Spoerl. Macmillan Co. New York, New York.
84. STERN, W. 1930. Eindruecke von der amerikanischen Psychologie Z. Paed. Psychol. Exp. Paedagog, **31**: 43-51; 65-72.
85. STERN, W. 1925. Theory of constancy of intelligence. Translated by H. Kluever. Psychol. Clinic. **16**: 110-118.
86. STERN, W. 1939. The psychology of testimony. J. Abnorm. Soc. Psychol. **34**: 3-20.
87. HEALY, W. & G. M. FERNALD. 1911. Tests for practical mental classification. Psychol. Monographs. **8**: Whole No. 54.
88. BARTLETT, F. C. 1932. Remembering. Cambridge Univ. Press. Cambridge, England.
89. INHELDER, B. Personal communication.
90. STERN, W. 1927. Personalistischer Psychologie. *In* Einfuehrung in die Neuere Psychologie. E. Saupe, Ed.: 187-197. A. W. Zickfeldt. Osterwieck-Hartz, Germany.
91. STERN, W. 1914. Die Anwendung der Psychoanalyse auf Kindheit und Jugend: Ein Protest. Z. Angew. Psychol. **8**: 71-101.
92. ADLER, A. 1914. Die Individualpsychologie, Ihre Voraussetzungen und Ergebnisse. Scientia. **16**: 74-87.
93. ADLER, A. 1931. Der nervoese Charakter. *In* Festschrift William Stern zum 60. Geburtstag am 29. April 1931. Mitarbeitern am Psychologischen Institut Hamburg (Hrgs.) Beihefte Z. Angew. Psychol. **59**: 1-14.
94. HARTLEY, E. L. 1946. Problems in Prejudice. King's Crown Press. New York, N.Y.
95. HARTLEY, E. L. & R. E. HARTLEY. 1952. Fundamentals of Social Psychology. Alfred A. Knopf, Inc. New York, N. Y.
96. HEIDER, F. 1968. William Stern. *In* International Encyclopedia of the Social Sciences. D. L. Sills, Ed. **15**: 262-265. Crowell Collier & Macmillan, Inc. New York, N. Y.
97. MACLEOD, R. B. 1938. William Stern (1871-1938). Psychol. Review. **45**: 347-353.

FRANCIS GALTON AND AMERICAN PSYCHOLOGY

Solomon Diamond

California State University, Los Angeles
Los Angeles, California 90032

Karl Pearson has told us that Galton's motto was *Whenever you can, count.*[40] He followed it with extraordinary persistence. For example, having had his portrait painted at 60 and again at 81, he could report that each artist had touched the brush to canvas about 20,000 times, although the first used slow, methodical strokes, and the second (in the impressionist era) made flurries of quick dabs.[29] The habit of counting repetitive acts is also a conspicuous behavior of many American psychologists. I have been told that at a round table of distinguished persons, one of our present conferees skilfully increased the rate of finger-wagging by a long-winded participant, by reinforcing each such gesture with a nod of his head. This is not in itself proof of Galton's enduring influence, but it does illustrate the fact that American psychology is largely imbued with the essence of Galtonism: the conviction that any significant problem can be stated in terms which make it accessible to quantitative study.

That conviction was the foundation for each of Galton's many important contributions. Some that have had very wide application in the work of other psychologists are these:

(1) The method of word association,[19] which first opened the way to quantitative analysis of the higher thought processes and individual dynamics.

(2) The introduction of test batteries,[24] to arrive at a many-sided assessment of abilities for a given person.

(3) Systematic use of the questionnaire,[20] out of which all inventory-type tests were developed.

(4) Use of the normal distribution for purposes of classification,[15] which has been a boon to the sophisticated, as well as devising the system of scoring by percentile ranks,[25] which has made it possible for us to communicate with the unsophisticated.

(5) The method of twin comparison,[18] which, aside from its special application to the problem of nature vs. nurture, is notable as the first use of a control group in psychological research, since Galton compared results based on pairs of identical twins with those based on fraternal twins.

(6) Finally, and most important in this abbreviated list, the concepts of regression[26] and correlation,[27] which opened up new possibilities for the analysis of complex phenomena which, like heredity, are dependent on multiple influences.

In early textbooks and manuals of experimental psychology Galton's name is cited most often in connection with Galton's whistle, Galton's bar, or Galton's weights. These products of his anthropometric research were to be found in almost every laboratory in which students were trained in the psychophysical methods. His more important innovations in experimental design and statistical analysis of data were assimilated more slowly, but without them it would have been a far more difficult task to give psychology its new direction, that is, to change it from a normative science, which had been conceived as the propaedeutic

47

basis for philosophy, into a functional science of behavior, independent of philosophy.

Cattell was the most important conduit of Galton's influence on American psychology. His fellow psychologists ranked him second in importance only to William James.[8] When Galton died, only five months after the passing of James, Cattell wrote that these were the two greatest men he had known.[10] In later years he said flatly that Galton was the greatest man he ever knew.[12, 13] Rating scientists for distinction was a serious matter to Cattell, and he would not have made such a judgment without due deliberation.

Since Cattell had both G. Stanley Hall and Wundt as his formal teachers, we cannot assess his relationship to Galton without reviewing the full course of his university studies. In 1880 Cattell, not yet 20, heard Lotze at Göttingen.[45] After an interlude of study at Paris and Geneva, he spent a semester at Leipzig, where he heard both Wundt and Heinze. After this double exposure to the new psychology, he planned to continue his work under Lotze,[44] but this plan was upset by Lotze's unexpected death. In 1882, Cattell enrolled at Johns Hopkins University, Baltimore, Md., and won a scholarship with an essay on Lotze's philosophy. There were no psychology courses during the first semester, and his principal interests then were team sports and personal experimentation with drugs. Then Hall was brought in, and Cattell enrolled in his laboratory course along with John Dewey, Joseph Jastrow, and E. M. Hartwell. Except for Cattell, they were all to complete doctorates at Johns Hopkins. In Hall's laboratory, Cattell performed the pioneer experiment on the time required to recognize letters. The next year Cattell left Johns Hopkins because of what he perceived, probably correctly, as double-dealing on Hall's part.[43] He returned to Leipzig and Wundt, *faute de mieux*.

The results of the experiment performed at Johns Hopkins are included in Cattell's first article in the *Philosophische Studien*.[5] The clue to the fact that it was not performed at Leipzig is in the initials of the observers who participated. They include J.D. for Dewey, E.H. for Hartwell, and G.H. for Hall. One can only speculate as to what extent Cattell's resentment toward Hall, to what extent Wundt's jealousy of other laboratories, contributed to the failure to mention where the experiment had been performed.

Cattell was justly proud of this experiment, but he is not strictly accurate in the claim that it was the first to be concerned with individual differences, and to make no appeal to introspection. This point is not trivial, because it is so often said that interest in individual differences was an autocthonous development of American soil. In 1879 Obersteiner, a collaborator of Exner at Vienna, published an account of reaction-time experiments in which he emphasized the importance of differences between individuals.[39] He found no difference between the sexes, said that members of the serving class are less consistent in performance, and that extremely long times are an indication of mental derangement. Since this article appeared in English, it might well have been known to Cattell, and was almost certainly known to Hall, before Cattell did his experiment. Furthermore, in 1883 Galton's friend Romanes reported an experiment in which the subjects were allowed 20 seconds to read a short printed paragraph and were then required to write down all they could remember.[42] Although all the subjects were "accustomed to much reading," they showed "a positively astonishing difference . . . with respect to the rate at which they were able to read." Romanes also remarked that the swifter readers generally retained more of the content than the slow readers. Even at this early date, therefore, Cattell and America had no monopoly on psychological research in individual differences, or on using objective criteria of performance.

At Leipzig, Cattell broke precedent by rejecting the introspective problem which Wundt assigned to him, and he was permitted to continue work on his own problem. This time he used far more elegant apparatus of his own design—the gravity tachistoscope and the voice-key—and the work was carried on in his own rooms "in part because Wundt would not allow the testing in his laboratory of individuals who could not profit from introspection."[40]

After Leipzig, Cattell spent the greater part of two years in England. He participated in a stillborn effort to establish a psychological laboratory at Cambridge,[46] but worked chiefly at Galton's laboratory, which had originally been established at the International Health Exhibition. Cattell states that he helped set it up in its new quarters at the South Kensington Museum of Science and that he and Galton "began in cooperation the preparation of a book of instructions for a laboratory course in psychology."[12] It was an ideal learning situation. The famous article "Mental Tests and Measurements" was the outgrowth of this experience, and the recommendation in it that all students should take a battery of anthropometric tests followed a line of thought which Galton had initiated much earlier.[16] The battery of tests described was an amplified version of the Galton program, which had been fitted to a level of public tolerance. But the most important outcome was the fact that Walker points out, that Cattell's psychology courses were the first "to make consistent and systematic use of statistical methods."[51] It was a sharp turn from the Leipzig orientation, for, as Walker also states, "It does not appear that Wundt himself was committed to a belief in the statistical treatment of the results of experimentation." It was from Galton that Cattell acquired that faith which caused it to be said, supposedly first by Titchener, that "Cattell's god is Probable Error."[52]

Galton was a figure with whom Cattell could readily identify. Both men had a flair for mechanical invention, and they also shared an obvious pride of membership in that natural aristocracy of talent which even Thomas Jefferson[37] recognized as deserving of recognition. By calling Galton the greatest man he ever knew, Cattell, who was probably conscious of the many points of resemblance, was not lowering his own stature. His career might have been quite different had it not happened that, as Lyman Wells put it, his "formative years brought him into contact with another exceptional man through whom his interests were fixed upon the quantitative properties of the human mind."[52] It is clear that Cattell profited from his contact with Galton immeasurably more than from his contact with Wundt, and American psychology profited as a result.

Joseph Jastrow was another conduit of Galton's influence.[36] He inherited no silver spoon, and had no opportunity to study abroad. While still a student he began earning money by writing papers of a popular scientific character. Thus he was launched on his career as a popularizer of scientific psychology, whose own contributions were of secondary importance. The titles of some of his early papers show the Galton influence already at work: Some peculiarities in the age statistics of the United States[30]—Composite portraiture[31]—The longevity of great men[32]—The dreams of the blind[33]—Eye-mindedness and ear-mindedness.[34]

In 1888, Cattell returned from England to a chair at the University of Pennsylvania, Jastrow received an appointment at Wisconsin, and Hall and Sanford went from Johns Hopkins to newly founded Clark University. Almost overnight America had four active psychology laboratories in place of one.

With a means of livelihood at last assured, Jastrow took leave the following spring for his first trip abroad. Characteristically, on his return he published a series of articles on "Aspects of Modern Psychology."[35] He said of Galton's work that it "could not readily be classified in the psychological activity of any country," but formed "a unique chapter of science, interesting no one more deeply than the students of scientific psychology." He described American psychology as characterized by "a readiness to introduce innovations whenever circumstances will allow, and . . . utilizing the freedom . . . of intellectual and educational youthfulness." With hindsight we may read these statements to mean that Galton was laying down new lines for psychology, and only the Americans were free enough from the restraints of traditional university disciplines to follow in the path he indicated.

Jastrow was active in the AAAS, and he was asked to organize the psychology exhibit for the World's Columbian Exposition, which opened in Chicago in 1893. Galton's influence was dominant in shaping the result, which Jastrow later described as "the first attempt to introduce tests to the American public."[37] The Official Directory[54] informed all visitors that "any one who wishes can have, by the payment of a small fee, various tests applied and can be measured and recorded upon cards which are given to the person, while the record is made upon the charts and tables hanging on the walls of the laboratory." It was as if Galton's anthropometric laboratory had been transported to Chicago. Popplestone[41] points out that the lack of any historical record of the public response compels us to wonder if the affair may not have been a dud, perhaps because it was located in a remote corner of the vast Exposition grounds. Whatever the public response may have been, this mobilization of all the current techniques of testing surely stimulated additional interest among psychologists themselves.

Even before the Exposition opened, Titchener[49] deplored the manner in which the exhibit confused anthropometrics with psychology, using the very argument which had driven Cattell to experiment in his own rooms: that a psychological experiment presupposes introspectively practiced observers. "It is one of the commonest errors," he wrote, "that since we are all using our minds, in some way or another, everyone is qualified to take part in psychological experimentation. As well maintain, that because we eat bread, we are all qualified to bake it." His protest was futile. Soon most of the new psychology laboratories, though they might be headed by Wundt's former students, were busy with anthropometrics. Titchener[50] in desperation wrote to Galton to solicit aid to repulse the invasion. "You would speak with authority," he wrote, "as you could not be suspected of wanting to undervalue Anthropometry. Unless some sort of protest is made, the American laboratories will all run over into anthropometrical statistics: which are, of course, valuable—but not psychology." The appeal is testimony to the high prestige that Galton enjoyed, but he must have been amused to be thus solicited to assist in throttling his own creation to defend the purity of experimental psychology.

Madison Bentley, then a student at Cornell, later said of this period that among the "adventitious" factors that shaped the careers of young psychologists might be the "worship of a Wundt or a Galton."[1] Among the partisans of Galton we must count Terman and Thorndike. Terman wrote in his autobiography: "Of the founders of modern psychology, my greatest admiration is for Galton."[47] Thorndike wrote: "Excellent work can surely be done by men with widely different notions of what psychology should be, the best work of all perhaps being done by men like Galton, who gave little or no thought to what it is or should be."[48]

The case of Woodworth is most interesting.[53] If we say, with Boring,[4] that "it is almost true that American psychology was personified in the person of Cattell," we may add that it is equally true that his student Woodworth personified the shift of orientation without which such a statement could not approach validity. Woodworth's undergraduate teacher in philosophy directed him to study science, as a preparation for philosophy; when later he abandoned philosophy in favor of a career in psychology, he spent more than five years of apprenticeship as a physiologist, to complete the preparation; yet he found in Cattell, whose attention went to the probable error and not to the brain, "the chief of all (his) teachers in giving shape to (his) psychological thought and work." This epitomizes the development of American psychology during the last quarter of the nineteenth century. Having begun the study of psychology as a propaedeutic to philosophy, it was soon caught up in the fascination of research on the physiology of brain, nerves, sense organs, and muscle, but then transferred its principal energies to the study of behavior, including especially the quantitative study of competence in all its manifestations. Psychology was able to pass through the two earlier phases because of the fluidity of the new universities, one consequence of which was that instruction in "mental science" passed from the hands of the college presidents, who almost invariably had theological training, into the hands of specialists. If we wish to claim the third phase as distinctively American, we shall have to give Galton a posthumous grant of American citizenship. We must ask whether the swift progress of individual psychology in the United States is not to be explained by the absence of the restraints on such development which were imposed by the more rigid university structure in Europe, at least as much as by the presence of stronger motivating forces in that direction.

In 1904, when the world met at St. Louis, psychology had another chance to speak to the nation. On that occasion Cattell not only rejected mentalism, in his statement that "it is no more necessary for the subject to be a psychologist than it is for the vivisected frog to be a physiologist," but he also rejected all limiting definitions for the new science, declaring that psychology consists of what psychologists wish to do "*qua* psychologists."[9] It was the first time that psychology had been defined broadly enough to include Cattell's true mentor, Galton.

By the time of the entry of the United States into World War I, the study of individual differences accounted for well over half of all work reported at meetings of the APA,[11] if we omit papers of historical and philosophical nature, which had by then declined from the largest to the smallest category. American psychologists had developed the skills which they put to work in the war effort.

In 1929, Cattell presided over the International Congress at New Haven, Conn. It was neither in his nature nor in the American character to acknowledge the full extent of our indebtedness to foreign mentors. "Wundt and Galton," he said, "are the foreign psychologists whom we most honor, but it may be that if neither of them had lived psychology in America would be much what it is."[13] Boring[2] concurred in part, writing that "it is an open question as to how much [Galton] influenced Cattell and the American tradition of individual psychology and the mental tests." In the revised edition of his history[3] this passage is omitted, and we read instead: "Perhaps it is true that America, while giving homage to Wundt, has overlooked Galton, to whom it owes a greater debt." Let us consider some of the reasons why we have been so much more ready to give homage to one than to the other.

The rise of American psychology was linked with the reform of American higher education, which was signaled in 1869 by the election of a chemist, Charles Eliot, as president of Harvard University. The theological domination of the colleges was to give way to an industrial-scientific orientation. The German universities were taken as models. Their great strength was in their laboratories, which had originated with Liebig's chemical laboratory at Giessen in 1824, and had subsequently provided the basis for Germany's world leadership in physiology. For a young man seeking a job in the expanding system of American universities, experience in a German laboratory was like money in the bank. Students of chemistry and physiology flocked to Germany. Psychologists were a miniscule group, but when they heard of a psychology laboratory at Leipzig, it became their Mecca. Even those who disliked what they found there were victims of the cognitive dissonance effect. After a young man spends several years of effort to earn a degree in a foreign country, all the while yearning for a sweetheart back home, and then returns triumphantly to a prestigious job and chances of advancement, he is unlikely to say that another course of study might have been more satisfying. Wundt was more than a prophet: he really led his American students into the promised land. Galton, on the other hand, was a man who lacked university status in a country which lacked a psychology laboratory, and where the leading universities were still primarily devoted to educating country divines who might make a hobby of science. Americans might read his books and articles with excitement, but there was no economic inducement to acclaim him as a leader.

It is universally agreed that all Galton's work in psychology radiated from one dominant concern: to learn how we might best manipulate the forces of evolution to mankind's advantage. While philosophers battled over the ethical implications of natural selection, or attempted to subordinate it to a cosmic drive toward higher forms of existence, Galton the pragmatist turned his attention to the phenomenon of variation, as providing the means by which we might accelerate the process. The anthropometric laboratory he set up at great personal expense was a device to tease the public into providing the data he needed for his research. His interest in individual differences was therefore derivative, not primary, but the resulting anthropometric work attracted the interest of psychologists. His ideas about evolution were more correct than Spencer's, and his ideas on the mechanism of heredity were more correct than Darwin's, but they had little following. It was Spencer who was almost universally regarded as the grand theorist of evolution. The American historian Fiske[14] had ranked Spencer's achievement with that of Newton, and the British zoologist Mitchell[38] compared him to Descartes and declared that his writings "may be regarded as the *Principes de la Philosophie* of the 19th century."

Galton's influence derived wholly from his genius in quantitative investigation. He arrived at the concepts of regression and correlation because they were peculiarly appropriate to the study of heredity, and thus also to the study of any complex phenomenon that is influenced in its quantitative manifestation by a large number of causal factors. Indeed, it has proved even more valuable for econometrics than for anthropometrics. No rival claims of priority, no record of independent discovery by others, dims the brilliance of this discovery. For Cattell to have said that American psychology might have been much the same without Galton is an understandable expression of vanity, but it is difficult to see how a historian can concur in that judgment. As we have seen, Boring did retreat from it.

The principlal focus of this paper has been on Galton's positive contributions. There was also a negative aspect, of which we are all aware. Galton's advocacy of eugenics provided racists with a rationale for genocide which has been extensively exploited in the United States. When, however, we assess the degree of his culpability on this issue, we should not attribute to him opinions that were not his own. His views, as he himself remarked,[28] were often misrepresented. I shall discuss briefly some aspects of his thinking which are usually overlooked.

(1) It was not in Galton's manner of thinking to condemn a whole race as inferior. Once, after hearing a paper about the "dealings of colonists with aborig-

ines," he said in discussion (which was reported in the third person) that "ethnologists were apt to look upon race as something more definite than it really was. He presumed it meant no more than the average of the characteristics of all the persons who were supposed to belong to the race, and this average was continually varying."[21] He went on to indicate regret that Englishmen did not, like the ancient Romans, live more closely with the populations of the subject colonies, and make them more welcome in England. The notion of racial "purity" had no place in Galton's scheme of eugenics.

(2) Galton was always more interested (as Pearson[40] points out with obvious regret) in raising high intelligence rather than in eliminating low intelligence, which he was much more willing to leave to the slow processes of natural selection. He never subscribed to the theory of degeneration, which was so popular late in the nineteenth century, and which was the basis of the direction which the eugenic movement took after Galton's death.

(3) He always insisted that the great need was for research, to acquire a knowledge of heredity which would be a sufficient basis for wise eugenic practices (or, as we would now say, for informed genetic counseling). He fully recognized the danger of even well-intentioned programs based on inadequate knowledge. He said, for example, in 1884: "Our present ignorance of the conditions by which the level of humanity may be raised is so gross, that I believe if we had some dictator of the Spartan type, who exercised absolute power over marriages . . . and who acted with the best intentions, he might perhaps do even more harm than good to the race."[23]

(4) Finally, Galton was fully aware of the need for attention to environmental influences, both in research on heredity and in efforts to improve society. The conclusion of his study of twins, in which he defined the nature-nurture issue, was stated thus: "Nature prevails enormously over nurture when the differences in nurture do not exceed what is commonly to be found among persons of the same rank of society and in the same country."[18] He perfectly appreciated the statistical fact that more genetic gold can be mined from the great masses of the disadvantaged than from the thin layer of those who have risen to distinction.[26] That is why he could claim that "the sterling values of nurture, including all kinds of sanitary improvements," were "powerful auxiliaries" to his cause.[17] He also emphasized that "it cannot be too strongly hammered into popular recognition that a well-developed human being, capable in mind and body, is an expensive animal to rear."[28] To rear, be it noted, not to breed.

On the occasion of the conference on which this volume is based, it is especially fitting to recall one more expression of Galton's recognition of the power of environment: "The most likely nest . . . for self-reliant natures is to be found in States founded and maintained by emigrants."[22] Surely this is one reason why American psychology displayed what Jastrow called "a readiness to introduce innovations." Galton's innovative methods for the study of human capacities were accepted as a part of psychology, and they helped to give American psychology its distinctive character. It seems quite unlikely that the same development could have taken place in anything like the same time span without Galton's influence.

REFERENCES

1. BENTLEY, M. 1936. *In* History of Psychology in Autobiography. C. Murchison, Ed. Vol. 3: 53-67. Clark University Press. Worcester, Mass.
2. BORING, E.G. 1929. A History of Experimental Psychology. D. Appleton-Century Co. New York, N.Y.

3. BORING, E.G. 1950. A History of Experimental Psychology. 2nd edit. Appleton-Century-Crofts. New York, N.Y.
4. BORING, E.G. 1950. The influence of evolutionary theory upon American psychological thought. *In* Evolutionary Thought in America. S. Persons, Ed. : 267-298.
5. CATTELL, J. McK. 1885. Ueber die Zeit der Erkennung und Bennenung von Schriftzeichen, Bildern und Farben. Philosophische Studien 2: 635-650.
6. CATTELL, J. McK. 1886. Psychometrische Untersuchungen. I. Apparate und Methoden. Philosophische Studien 3: 305-335.
7. CATTELL, J. McK. 1890. Mental tests and measurements. Mind 15: 373-380.
8. CATTELL, J. McK. 1903. Statistics of American psychologists. Amer. J. Psychol. 14: 310-328.
9. CATTELL, J. McK. 1904. The conceptions and methods of psychology. Popular Science Monthly 66: 176-186.
10. CATTELL, J. McK. 1911. Francis Galton. Popular Science Monthly 78: 309-311.
11. CATTELL, J. McK. 1917. Our psychological association and research. Science 45: 275-284.
12. CATTELL, J. McK. 1928. Early psychological laboratories. *In* Feelings and Emotions, the Wittenberg Symposium. M.L. Reymert, Ed. : 427-433. Clark University Press. Worcester, Mass.
13. CATTELL, J. McK. 1929. Psychology in America. Address of the president of the Ninth Int. Congr. of Psychology. Science Press. New York, N.Y.
14. FISKE, J. 1874. Outlines of Cosmic Philosophy. 2 vols. Macmillan & Co. London, England.
15. GALTON, F. 1869. Hereditary Genius. Macmillan & Co. London, England.
16. GALTON, F. 1874. Proposal to apply for anthropological statistics from schools. J. Anthropol. Inst. 3: 308-311.
17. GALTON, F. 1873. Hereditary improvement. Fraser's Mag. NS 7: 116-130.
18. GALTON, F. 1876. The history of twins, as a criterion of the relative powers of nature and nurture. J. Anthropol. Inst. 5: 391-406.
19. GALTON, F. 1879. Psychometric experiments. Brain 2: 149-162.
20. GALTON, F. 1880. Statistics of mental imagery. Mind 5: 301-318.
21. GALTON, F. 1882. J. Anthropol. Inst. 11: 352-353.
22. GALTON, F. 1883. Inquiries into Human Faculty and its Development: 82 Macmillan & Co. New York. N.Y.
23. GALTON, F. 1884. Record of Family Faculties. Macmillan & Co. London, England.
24. GALTON, F. 1885. On the anthropometric laboratory of the late International Health Exhibition. J. Anthropol. Inst. 14: 205-219.
25. GALTON, F. 1885. Some results of the anthropometric laboratory. J. Anthropol. Inst. 14: 275-287.
26. GALTON, F. 1885. Types and their inheritance. Science 6: 268-274.
27. GALTON, F. 1888. Co-relations and their measurement, chiefly from anthropometric data. Proc. Roy. Soc. 45: 135-145.
28. GALTON, F. 1903. The Daily Chronicle (London). July 29. *Excerpts in* K. Pearson. 1930. The Life, Letters and Labours of Francis Galton. The University Press. Cambridge, England. Vol. IIIA: 252-253.
29. GALTON, F. 1905. Number of strokes of the brush in a picture. Nature 72: 198.
30. JASTROW, J. 1885. Science 5: 461-464.
31. JASTROW, J. 1885. Science 6: 165-168.
32. JASTROW, J. 1886. Science 8: 294-296.
33. JASTROW, J. 1888. New Princeton Rev. 5: 18-24.
34. JASTROW, J. 1888. Popular Science Monthly 33: 597-608.
35. JASTROW, J. 1890. Aspects of modern psychology. *In* Epitomes of Three Sciences. H. Oldenberg, J. Jastrow and C.H. Cornill. :59-100. The Open Court Publishing Co. Chigaco, Ill.
36. JASTROW, J. 1930. *In* History of Psychology in Autobiography. C. Murchison. Ed. : 2: 297-331. Clark University Press. Worcester, Mass.
37. JEFFERSON, T. 1925. Letter dated Oct. 28, 1818. *In* Correspondence of John Adams and Thomas Jefferson. P. Wilstach, Ed. The Bobbs-Merrill Co. Indianapolis, Ind.
38. MITCHELL, P.C. 1910. Evolution. *In* Encyclopedia Brittanica. 11th edit. 10: 22-37. The University Press. Cambridge, England.
39. OBERSTEINER, H. 1879. Experimental researches on attention. Brain 1: 439-453.
40. PEARSON, K. 1914-1930. The Life, Letters and Labours of Francis Galton. 3 vols. in 4. The University Press. Cambridge, England.
41. POPPLESTONE, J.A. 1976. The psychological exhibit at the Chicago World's Fair of

1893. Paper presented at the meeting of the Western Psychol. Assoc. Los Angeles, Calif. April, 1976.

42. ROMANES, G.J. 1883. Mental Evolution in Animals. Kegan Paul & Co. London, England.

43. ROSS, D. 1972. G. Stanley Hall: The Psychologist as Prophet. Chicago University Press. Chicago, Ill.

44. SOKAL, M.M. 1969. Influences on a young psychologist: James McKeen Cattell, 1880-1890. Paper presented at mtg. of the History of Science Society. Washington, D.C., December, 1969.

45. SOKAL, M.M. 1971. The unpublished autobiography of James McKeen Cattell. Amer. Psychol. 26: 626-635.

46. SOKAL, M.M. 1972. Psychology at Victorian Cambridge—the unofficial laboratory of 1887-1888. Proc. Amer. Phil. Soc. 116: 145-147.

47. TERMAN, L.M. 1932. In History of Psychology in Autobiography. C. Murchison, Ed.: 2: 297-331. Clark University Press, Worcester, Mass.

48. THORNDIKE, E.L. 1936. In History of Psychology in Autobiography. C. Murchison, Ed.: 3: 263-270. Clark University Press. Worcester, Mass.

49. TITCHENER, E.B. 1893. Anthropometry and experimental psychology. Phil. Rev. 2: 187-192.

50. TITCHENER, E.B. 1898. Letter to Francis Galton, dated 18 IV 1898. Copy in Archives of the History of American Psychology, The University of Akron. Akron, Ohio.

51. WALKER, H.M. 1929. Studies in the History of Statistical Method. Williams & Wilkins Co. Baltimore, Md.

52. WELLS, F.L. 1944. James McKeen Cattell: 1860-1944. Amer. J. Psychol. 57: 270-275.

53. WOODWORTH, R.S. 1932. In History of Psychology in Autobiography. C. Murchison, Ed.: 2: 359-380. Clark University Press. Worcester, Mass.

54. WORLD'S COLUMBIAN EXPOSITION. 1893. Official Directory. Chicago, Ill.

THE EUROPEAN ROOTS OF AMERICAN PSYCHOLOGY: QUESTIONS OF IMPORT

Wolfgang G. Bringmann*

Department of Psychology
University of Windsor
Windsor, Ontario, Canada N9B 3P4

During the past ten years, genealogy has become the third most popular American hobby, close on the heels of stamp and coin collecting. It has been suggested that the tracing of one's ancestral history is one of the most fascinating types of detective work.[1] It is an interest most commonly found in mature individuals who are emotionally aware that personal death is not only inevitable, but is, in fact, approaching. Of course, anyone who has dabbled in genealogy knows that it is a strenuous, time-consuming, and quite expensive endeavor.[2] The completion of a first-rate family history requires all one's leisure time, day in and day out, for several years. It involves a thorough search of records and interviews with older persons, as well as visits to court houses, archives, and cemeteries in all corners of the country or countries from which one's ancestors came. Researching one's family tree is a most rewarding experience, especially if one can document an old family tradition or discover an interesting new fact. At times, disappointments must be swallowed. After many months of labor, one may discover a direct blood relationship with the "Jukes" or "Kalikaks," and one may be tempted to abandon the search.[3] However, tracing a relationship to an eminent person, even a notorious but successful criminal, may be gratifying. Perhaps the greatest gain in researching one's genealogy is the realization that one's forefathers were real people. They may not have accomplished all they set out to do, but they had feelings and hopes, and, in the richness of their records, their lives speak to us.

I think it is quite appropriate that we, as psychologists, should turn our attention to the "European Roots of American Psychology," especially during this Bicentennial year. Traditionally, histories of psychology, like Boring's massive *History of Experimental Psychology*[5] or Roback's *History of American Psychology*,[6] have included a discussion of the intellectual family tree of psychology in the United States. Unfortunately, all too often such treatises have largely reflected the beliefs of these authors that contemporary psychology is primarily a behavioral science.[7] The importance of psychological ancestors, whose accomplishments were in scientifically less respectable fields, such as phrenology, graphology, or parapsychology, has either been denied or at least substantially overlooked. Autobiographies of eminent psychologists, like the classical collections by Schmidt[8] and Murchison[9] or the new series by Pongratz *et al.*[10] and Pongratz[11] usually contain a wealth of important information useful in tracing intellectual genealogies. These very personal documents, however, also may suffer from a tendency to magnify, minimize, or even totally omit the influence of significant teachers and associates.

*Present address: Department of Psychology, University of South Alabama, Mobile, Ala. 36608.

Specific intellectual genealogies of the "master and pupil" type exist for psychologists from several countries.[12, 13] Weigel and Gottesfurcht[14] have shown, in their recent article in the American Psychologist, that it is not too difficult to trace the origin of a fairly typical university psychology department to Wilhelm Wundt (1832-1920) and his student, Hugo Münsterberg (1863-1916). All of these personalistic methods, however, are only a first step in tracing an intellectual genealogy. These leads must be validated by in-depth studies of the works of eminent contributors to psychology and related fields.[15] Citation analysis is a valuable tool, and computers can be utilized to sift and analyze the vast amount of data for trends of intellectual influences.

I shall address my remarks to each of the five important ancestors of contemporary American psychology, which have just been discussed here. For the sake of continuity, I shall proceed chronologically, beginning with Fechner and ending with Dr. Henle's paper on the impact of Gestalt psychology.

GUSTAV THEODOR FECHNER

What has struck me most about Fechner's influence upon American psychology is that it has come relatively late, that it has been mediated largely through the writings of others, rather than Fechner's own works, and that his reception by contemporaries was somewhat less positive than one would assume from a reading of most histories of psychology.[16]

Fechner's psychophysical writings, which appeared during the last third of his life, are by far the best known part of his extensive works, although they comprise, at most, only about 10-15% of his total output. As far as his *Psychophysik*[17] is concerned, most psychologists remember only his three scaling methods (method of just noticeable differences, method of right and wrong cases, and method of average error). They have probably forgotten or never known that he developed his procedures in an attempt to document his philosophical beliefs about the unity of mind and body. Even his contributions to psychological measurement were not received in America with unanimous enthusiasm. You have already heard at this conference that James considered Fechner's "Psychophysics" as "moonshiny"[18] in 1880. A decade later he was even more critical of Fechner and the entire branch of psychology inspired by him.[19]

> Fechner himself indeed was a German Gelehrter of the ideal type . . . but it would be terrible if even such a dear old man as this would saddle our Science forever with his patient whimsies, and, in a world so full of more nutritious objects of attention, compel all future students to plough through the difficulties . . . of his own works. . . . Those who desire this dreadful literature can find it; it has disciplinary value; but I will not even enumerate it in a footnote.

American psychologists know little about Fechner's interest in parapsychological phenomena between 1868 and 1879, which was concurrent with his research in psychophysics and experimental aesthetics. G. Stanley Hall (1844-1924), who met Fechner repeatedly, while studying in Leipzig, talked with him at length about these varied interests and apparently considered him quite mad.[20]

> Fechner is a curiosity. His eyelids are strangely fringed and he has a number of holes, square and round, cut, Heaven knows why, in the iris of each eye—and is altogether a bundle of oddities in person and manner. He has forgotten all the details of his *Psychophysik*; and is chiefly interested in theorizing how knots can be tied in endless strings and how words can be written on the inner side of two slates sealed together . . . [he] wants me to go to Zöllner and talk to him about American spiritualism, but I have not been. Fechner is tedious enough . . . .

Hall, of course, is referring to Fechner's adventures with the notorious American medium Henry Slade, who began his stormy career in Europe in 1876 with a series of successful seances in London, which attracted believers, sceptics, and the simply curious *en masse*. Slade was a master of "slate writing," also called "spirit writing," in which a medium produces mysterious messages without any contact with the writing materials. He was in fact making an excellent income from the substantial fees that he charged for participation in his seances, until he was unmasked in September, 1876. At that time, two British scientists discovered, during one of the seances, that the message was already on the tablet before the "spirit writing" was to have taken place. Slade was convicted of vagrancy and sentenced to three months at hard labor for a violation of witchcraft statutes, but his sentences was set aside on the understanding that he leave the country forthwith. He found shelter with the astrophysicist, *Friedrich Zöllner* (1834-1882), of Leipzig University. Zöllner was a friend of Fechner. There is no doubt that Fechner believed that parapsychological phenomena were real and were supported by a respectable amount of evidence.[21] This view, however, was not derived from his own very limited and somewhat disappointing experiences with several clairvoyants, but rested instead on the favorable testimony of scientists like the mathematician, Wilhelm Weber (1804-1891), whom he had come to respect as a highly competent researcher in the past.[22] It is not known why Boring, as well as all other historians of psychology, omitted this episode from Fechner's portrait. His interest in paranormal phenomena was quite well known in the nineteenth century.[23] Perhaps this is an example of a reputable psychologist's life being edited to conform with our scientific biases.

Fechner's mystical speculations about the relationship between body and soul and, especially, about survival after death have attracted considerable attention from philosophers and theologians. His *Little Book on Life after Death* was translated into English as early as 1882, has been repeatedly republished, and, until the recent (1960) excellent translation of the first volume of Fechner's *Elemente der Psychophysik*[24] was the only one of Fechner's vast works that was available in English. Many contributions of interest and relevance to modern psychology have failed to attract the attention of American psychologists. For example, Fechner was a very funny opponent of naïve materialism and "scientism," so prevalent among physicians and natural scientists of his period. If he were alive today, he might well have joined the Szasz crusade against the medical model of psychopathology. During his prolonged illness (1840-1843), he clearly used behavioristic treatment procedures of his own design to control his severe depression and to overcome a very serious formal thought disorder. Even a glance at his *Introduction to Aesthetics*[25] will show his superb understanding of the role that learning principles play in the development of our artistic taste. Finally, it seems worth noting that Ellenberger[26] has acknowledged Fechner to be one of the major precursors of psychoanalytic theory:

> It was from Fechner's philosophy of nature that Freud borrowed several basic concepts that he incorporated into his metapsychology. Fechner's influence on psychoanalysis is evidenced by the fact that Freud quoted him in the *Interpretation of dreams, The Wit and the Unconscious,* and *Beyond the Pleasure Principle* .... A large part of the theoretical framework of psychoanalysis would hardly have come into being without the speculations of the man whom Freud called the great Fechner.

FRANCIS GALTON

In contrast to Dr. Diamond, it is my opinion, shared also by other contemporary historians of psychology, that Galton's contributions to psychology at large, and to American psychology in particular, were quite modest. It has become a custom among psychologists, and eminent psychologists are no exception, to link their own achievements to some outstanding predecessor, regardless of how tenuous such a relationship may be. This, in my view, is exactly what happened in the case of Cattell and Galton. Cattell was apparently quite interested in the study of individual differences before he ever met Galton. At least we are told that he carried out research on individual differences at Johns Hopkins University and that he continued to work in this general problem area in his own rooms at Leipzig University.[27]

Although Galton carried out a number of experimental studies on psychological topics and even developed and maintained a laboratory for some years, his impact on the laboratory movement in American psychology has been minimal. In the first place, his laboratory was an anthropometric, and not a psychological, one.[28] Undoubtedly some of the same equipment would be found in both. In Galton's laboratory, however, the collection of physical and mental measurements from the public was carried out without the guidance of theories or hypotheses. The only outcome of subjecting more than 10,000 persons to laborious anthropometric procedures was a book containing the complete records of 400 people. Galton did collect data in his laboratory, but, as we know today, this is only a minor step in productive research.

The opportunity to acquaint himself with the laboratory method in science was certainly available to Galton. Although his own medical training at Birmingham Hospital and King's College was a practical one in the tradition of English medicine, he was later admitted to the famous chemical laboratory of Giessen University in Germany. In this respect, his background is very similar to that of other English and American scholars for whom, as Dr. Diamond has indicated, "experience in a German laboratory was like money in the bank."[29] The Giessen laboratory had been established as early as 1824 by Justus von Liebig (1803-1873). Galton's account of his experiences in Giessen come from letters to his father in 1840.[30]

> Wm. Miller is going to Giessen . . . to Liebig's Laboratory - Liebig is the 1st Chemist (in organic chemistry) in the world. In his Laboratory there is every opportunity for getting on . . . Liebig's assistance will of course be invaluable to me in after life; and as his immediate pupil, more especially as I am a foreigner and come with an introduction from Daniell, I shall have every opportunity of acquiring his friendship.

The realities of studying at a provincial university in a small town in Germany differed substantially from Galton's daydreams. It took him little time to discover this.[30]

> I arrived yesterday at Giessen in the afternoon. I find that Liebig's laboratory is under different arrangements to those which Mr. Daniell, Mr. Miller and I myself expected. The plan . . . is as follows: A number of men (30 at present), who have long studied practical chemistry, wish individually to examine certain organic substances . . . . These men go to Liebig who gives his opinion as to how they are set to work . . . he experimentalizes . . . Liebig looks up the men once or twice a day, telling them how to go on etc. etc. Their investigations are all published with the name of the experimentalizer attached. Liebig therefore presupposes delicacy of manipulation and professes to teach the *application* of it to particular cases. It is the first part that I wish to practise and, not having done so sufficiently, of course instruction in the after part is useless. Under these circumstances and with the advice of Mr. Miller I have determined not to enter the chemistry class, but shall work at learning German instead.

Liebig's laboratory was apparently organized much like laboratories today. Students who had acquired some basic knowledge in the field learned by conducting experiments. Closely supervised by Liebig, their work was eventually published. All this, of course, would have been arduous and would have required a working knowledge of German. Galton does not seem to have been in the mood to acquire the necessary prerequisites of laboratory skills through readily available private tutoring, nor willing to spend the time to learn German.[30]

> Being thoroughly ennuied at Giessen and having nothing to do from morning to night, I have determined to make a bolt down the Danube and to see Constantinople and Athens. I have made all the calculations of time and cost and they are very favorable. I do not wait for an answer before I start, lst that I have not time and 2ndly as you promised me a good summer's tour to Sweden and Norway, of course you can have no objection to a comparatively civilized trip.

Galton, unconvincingly, tries to rationalize his quick decision.[30]

> My conscience being thus pacified, I will tell you something of Giessen.—It is a scrubby, abominably paved little town—cram full of students, noisy, smoky and dirty. Of these students, by far the best are the Chemicals, they being all first rate men, who write books and so forth; they are one shade less dirty than the others, that is to say they are the colour of umber, the others being Bt. Sienna.

Without waiting for his father's answer—he thanks him in advance for his "kind consent"—Galton set out in late summer on a trip through Austria, Greece, and Turkey, conveniently misplacing his chemical testbooks in the Frankfurt train station at the beginning of his journey. He returned to England in the fall in time to become a student of mathematics at Trinity College, Cambridge.[30] His friend William Allen Miller, who had first directed Galton's interest to Giessen, was more patient. He completed his study in Giessen and became a Professor of Chemistry at Kings College in London.[30]

In summary, Galton ignored his chance to learn about laboratory research in Germany, unlike other foreign scholars who studied there and afterwards became leaders of important research centers in their own countries. It seems that his personality, combined with his independent financial position, kept him from working seriously at anything; this same personality pattern was traceable throughout his life. Galton had little influence on the development of psychology in America, precisely because he was a stranger to the much-respected and admired laboratory procedures that were the mainstay of the science of his time and have been, rightly or wrongly, emulated by modern psychology. He seems to have been a superior "idea man" who could invent a variety of scientific projects at the drop of a hat, but who lacked the perseverance to follow through on any one topic. He impresses us today more as a gifted amateur in psychology, than as a scientist of the calibre of Wundt, Helmholtz, Müller, and others, who left their indelible stamp on modern American psychology.

WILHELM WUNDT

Most psychologists know that Wilhelm Wundt established the first real psychological laboratory in the world at Leipzig University, Germany, in 1879. Beginning with only a handful of "faithful" students in a single room, his institute became the model for the many teaching and research laboratories that have been developed in the United States for the behavioral sciences.[31] I shall chronicle the prehistory of Wundt's own experience with the laboratory method in science.[32]

Unlike Galton's famous teacher, Liebig, Wundt did not carry out experiments under his school desk. In fact, his classical education at the Heidelberg Lyceum included only a total of six hours of instruction in "natural science," in which he was merely expected to memorize a few major principles and facts from physics and chemistry. His first year at Tübingen University was equally disappointing. As a premedical student, he enrolled in the required courses in botany, chemistry, physics, and anatomy, but soon lost interest, when instruction again primarily centered on books. For example, his botany teacher would occasionally pass around a few plant specimens to the class, and the experiments of his chemistry-physics professor never quite seem to have worked out.

Unimpressed with his classes, Wundt devoted most of his time enjoying the extracurricular life of a University student. He became a member of an elite dueling fraternity and concentrated his efforts on concerts and plays and reading the latest novels in the library. His first year in Tübingen was his last. Returning to Heidelberg in August, 1852, by train and riverboat, the young Wundt had adequate time to worry about his future. He realized that he had learned little so far. He knew that he would have to begin again, if he ever wanted to become successful.[32]

> My mother, a minister's widow, was extremely limited in her funds, and it had been decided in the family council that I was to complete the study of medicine within a period of four years. Of this period one year was already gone, during which the budget had been substantially reduced. Thus, only three years remained during which the greatest economy had to be used to make up for what had been neglected.

Wundt emerged from these gloomy thoughts with the conviction that he could complete his medical training in the three remaining years, but he knew that he would have to improve his study methods to make the best use of his time.

Wundt immediately enrolled in the chemical course of *Robert Bunsen* (1811-1899), who had founded one of the earliest laboratories in 1840 at Marburg University, and who impressed the young Wundt deeply, because he accompanied his lectures "with demonstrations of marvelous perfection." Under his influence, Wundt carried out his first research project. He deprived himself, insofar as possible, of all salt intake. The dependent variable was the change in salt concentration of his urine. Wundt has stated that he enjoyed this "rather unimportant" experiment more than any other later work, because it was published soon afterwards and was even quoted in the scientific literature.

Still, Bunsen was not perfect, as Wundt was to discover, when he entered his laboratory as a practicum student, apparently in the hope of making chemistry his life's work.[32]

> I was all the more disappointed, since the impression, which I received here, contrasted as sharply as possible with the lectures. Bunsen, who was still busy obtaining his first primitive equipment for his laboratory and his own research, paid little attention to beginners. He merely turned them over to his assistants, who themselves were novices in their positions.

Without delay, Wundt resigned from Bunsen's Institute and entered, instead, the private laboratory of a young chemistry instructor who impressed him strongly with his interest and devotion to his students and their work.

In 1854, Wundt carried out his first independent research, in which he examined the effects of severing the *vagus* and *recurrens* nerves upon respiration. Although queasy about vivisectioning, his mother served as his assistant, and the kitchen of their home was his laboratory.

After receiving his M.D. degree in the fall of 1855 *summa cum laude* at the age of 23, Wundt accepted an appointment as assistant to his former teacher, *Ewald Hasse* (1810-1902), in the gynecological department of the university hospital in Heidelberg. Despite his demanding schedule, which occupied him around the clock, Wundt managed to perform an ambitious study on touch sensitivity in hysterical patients.

After the completion of this internship, Wundt studied physiology in the laboratories of *Johannes Müller* (1801-1858) and *Emil Du-Bois Reymond* (1818-1896) at Berlin University for one semester. Again he was disappointed by the actual conditions of a world-famous research institute.[32] Du-Bois Reymond's laboratory consisted of a small room for himself and a hallway for his students. Müller, the director of the Institute, worked during the winter in the decrepit old anatomy building and, during the summer, sweated in a few ramshackle rooms on the top floor of the main university building. Müller had only four students, and Wundt was the sole student of Du-Bois Reymond.

Wundt's next involvement with a laboratory was in the summer of 1857. He offered his first course in Experimental Physiology, in his mother's kitchen, to four students and he planned to cover the whole field in six weekly lectures with laboratory experiments and demonstrations. He became seriously ill, however, and was prevented from completing this course.

During his convalescence in Switzerland, Wundt applied for an appointment as laboratory assistant to *Hermann von Helmholtz* (1821-1894) in the newly established physiological institute of Heidelberg University.[34] He got the job. Much like Bunsen, Helmholtz seems to have turned over his laboratory to his young assistant, who provided most of the instruction for the beginning medical students working in the lab. Wundt faithfully carried out these responsibilities, and to the full satisfaction of the exacting Helmholtz. During nearly seven years in this position, he also utilized the laboratory to perform much research of his own.

Bored with routine duties, Wundt resigned in the spring of 1865 and quickly established a laboratory of his own in his apartment in Heidelberg. He maintained this research facility out of his own pocket for about ten years. It seems to have been relatively large and well equipped, for he was able to use it for instructional purposes in addition to his personal research.

Obviously Wundt was not a novice to the laboratory method of teaching and research when he established the Psychological Institute in Leipzig. He had thirty years of experience in several laboratories, first as a student, then as an assistant, and finally as an independent teacher and researcher. His facilities had ranged from a corner in his mother's kitchen to larger but old-fashioned and poorly equipped facilities in Berlin and Heidelberg. He learned early that laboratory research can be quite expensive, but he was still willing to utilize his slender resources in the support of his own independent research and teaching facilities. Wundt had discovered the importance of high-level, individualized instruction, along with the fact that laboratory directors, as a rule, were seldom personally interested in the work of their students, instead delegating supervision to relatively inexperienced assistants. He had learned that even primitive research facilities can be used to produce significant experimental work. Finally, he knew, from his own experience, that the presentation of research findings at scientific meetings, as well as the publication of results, are an integral part of any laboratory venture.

While there were important parallels, the differences in approach to experimental psychology between Wundt and Galton are significant and readily discernible. Both were poorly prepared for laboratory instruction, did rather poorly in their premedical studies, and were repeatedly disappointed by the university establishment of their time. Yet, while Wundt persevered and labored for nearly thirty years to improve the quality of laboratory teaching and research, despite many handicaps, Galton surrendered to his *"Wanderlust"* and, throughout his life, treated research as well as laboratory work as a hobby. Without Wundt's laboratory, American psychology as we know it would not exist. It is noteworthy that the German Democratic Republic has invited the International Union of Scientific Psychologists to meet at Karl Marx University in Leipzig in the summer of 1980, in recognition of the one hundredth anniversary of the founding of Wundt's laboratory. It seems appropriate to celebrate the centennial of the first psychologist, and it is hoped that similar Centennial activities will occur in the United States.

WILLIAM STERN

Another example of the tendency to adopt primarily methodological and technological contributions from foreign sources is the popularity of the IQ concept, which was initially proposed by *William Stern* (1871-1938).[36]

> To be sure there has been and there still is exaggerated faith in the power of numbers. For example, an "intelligence quotient" may be of provisional value as a first crude approximation when the mental level of an individual is sought; but whoever imagines that in determining this quantity he has summed up "the intelligence of an individual once and for all, so that he may dispense with the more qualitative studies, leaves off where psychology should begin.

His comments about the proper use of intelligence tests are still worth listening to, after nearly thirty years.[36]

> The excessive enthusiasm with which these methods were at first greeted has now given place to a more reserved and critical approach. This is only to be welcomed. For a time there was seen in intelligence testing a universal method that could accomplish anything and supersede all other methods of appraisal in education, psychiatry and vocational selection. This was a mistake which impeded the legitimate application of these tests. We know the value and significance of intelligence tests when they are constructed as elastic *partial* methods in many-sided diagnostic investigations, and when applied as auxiliary methods in making intensive psychological analyses.

It is at least feasible that, if American psychology had paid attention to this very professional advice about the proper use of intelligence testing, a great deal of justifiable disillusionment and resentment of the public towards psychology and psychologists could have been avoided.

GESTALT PSYCHOLOGY

Turning to the topic of Gestalt Psychology and its influence on American Psychology, there is little that I can add to the eloquent paper of Dr. Henle. It seems to me possible that the strong theoretical orientation and relative lack of a special technology, which has characterized Gestalt psychology, may in part account for the limited impact of this orientation in modern psychology. Although most Gestalt psychologists were refugees from Nazi Germany, it could also be, ironically, that their contributions to American psychology were largely overlooked because of their often very German outlook, as well as the complexity of their terminology. I disagree with Dr. Henle's comments about the relationship between Gestalt Psychology and Gestalt Therapy, to some degree. *Kurt Lewin* (1890-1947) has been credited with being one of the important originators of the T-Group, or sensitivity group, approach, which, in turn, has exerted strong influence on the methods of Gestalt Therapy.

CONCLUSION

Reviewing this conference, I have been impressed with how selectively Americans have adopted contributions from Europe. In general, methods and techniques that fit the natural science model of psychology have been much preferred to theories and philosophical speculations. This one-sided stress on the tangible has, in my opinion, produced a great deal of dissatisfaction with psychology and has encouraged the search for a people-oriented, humanistic psychology in contemporary America. If we had brought the fuller range of psychological accomplishments of Fechner, Wundt, Stern, and Gestalt psychologists to North America, it is possible that a broader and less rigorous psychology might have developed. Of course, in that case, we might perhaps face an experimental and not a humanistic revolution in our field today!

REFERENCES

1. DOANE, G. H. 1960. Searching for Your Ancestors. 3rd edit. University of Minnesota Press. Minneapolis, Minn.
2. WILLIAM, E. 1961. Know Your Ancestors: a Guide to Genealogical Research. Tuttle. Rutland, Vt.
3. VON BRANDT, A. 1959. Werkzeug des Historikers. 5th edit. Kohlhammer. Stuttgart, Germany.
4. SCHETELICH, E., Ed. 1971. Taschenbuch Archivwesen der DDR. Staatsverlag. Berlin, DDR.
5. BORING, E.G. A History of American Psychology. 2nd edit. Appleton-Century-Crofts. New York, N.Y.
6. ROBACK, A. A History of American Psychology. Library Publishers. New York, N.Y.
7. BERELSON, B. & G. STEINER. 1964. Human Behavior. Harcourt, Brace, & World. New York, N.Y.
8. SCHMIDT, R., Ed. 1921-1929 Die deutsche Philosophie der Gregenwart in Selbstdarstellungen. Meiner. Leipzig, Germany.
9. MURCHISON, C., Ed. 1930-1936. A History of Psychology in Autobiography. Clark University Press. Worcester, Mass.
10. PONGRATZ, L. W. TRAXEL & E. WEHNER., Eds. 1972. Psychologie in Selbstdarstellungen. Huber. Bern, Switzerland.
11. PONGRATZ, L., 1967. Problemgeschichte der Psychologie. Franke. München, Germany.
12. BORING, M. & E.G. BORING. 1948. Master and pupils among the American Psychologists. Am. J. Psychol. 61: 527-534.
13. WESLEY, F. 1965. Master and pupils among the German psychologists. J. Hist. Beh. Sci. 1: 252-255.
14. WEIGEL, H. & L. GOTTESFURCHT. 1972. Faculty genealogies. Am. Psychol. 27: 981-983.
15. BRINGMANN, W. 1975. Design questions in archival research. J. Hist. Behav. Sci. 11: 23-26.
16. BRINGMANN, W. & W. BALANCE. 1976. Gustav Theodor Fechner (1801-1887): Columbus of the new psychology. In press.
17. FECHNER, G.T. 1860. Elemente der Psychophysik. 2 vols. Breitkopf & Härtel. Leipzig, Germany.
18. ADLER, H. This volume.
19. JAMES, W. 1890. Principles of Psychology. 2 vols. Holt. New York, N.Y.
20. PERRY, R.B. 1935. The Thought and Character of William James. 2 vols. Little, Brown & Co. Boston, Mass.
21. BRINGMANN, W. & W. BALANCE. 1976. Der Psychologe, der sich selbst geheilt hat. Psychologie Heute 3: 43-48.

22. FECHNER, G.T. 1879. Die Tagesansicht gegenüber der Nachtansicht. Breitkopf & Härtel, Leipzig, Germany.
23. LASSWITZ, K. 1896. G. T. Fechner. Frommann. Stuttgart, Germany.
24. FECHNER, G.T. 1836. Das Büchlein vom Leben nach dem Tode. Grimmer. Dresden, Germany.
25. FECHNER, G.T. 1876. Vorschule der Aesthetik. 2 vols. Breitkopf & Härtel. Leipzig, Germany.
26. ELLENBERGER, H. 1970. The Discovery of the Unconscious. Basic Books. New York, N.Y.
27. DIAMOND, S. This volume.
28. WATSON, R. 1963. The Great Psychologists. Lippincott. Philadelphia, Pa.
29. VON DECHEND, H. 1963. Justus von Liebig. Verlag Chemie. Weinheim, Germany.
30. PEARSON, K. 1914-1924. The Life, Letters and Labours of Francis Galton. 3 vols. Cambridge University Press. Cambridge, England.
31. BRINGMANN, W. & W. BALANCE. Wilhelm Wundts Lehr-und Wanderjahre. Psychologie Heute 2: 12-18, 74-77.
32. BRINGMANN, W. & BRINGMANN, N. 1976. The foundations of Wilhelm Wundt's Leipzig Laboratory. Psychol. Beitr. In press.
33. BRINGMANN, W., W. BALANCE & R. EVANS. 1975. Wilhelm Wundt 1832-1920: a brief biographical sketch. J. Hist. Behav. Sci., 11: 287-397.
34. BRINGMANN, W., G. BRINGMANN & D. COTTRELL. Helmholtz und Wundt an der Heidelberger Universität 1858-1871. Heidelberger Jahrb. In press.
35. BRINGMANN, W. 1975. 1865, 1875, 1879 or when did Wundt establish his first laboratory? Paper read at Ann. Mtg. SEPA. Atlanta, Ga.
36. STERN, W. 1938. General Psychology. Macmillan. New York, N.Y.

DISCUSSION

Julian Jaynes, *Moderator*

Department of Psychology
Princeton University
Princeton, New Jersey 08540

QUESTION: I'd like to ask Mary Henle why she didn't mention one other misunderstanding, one that seems to me so prevalent in current Gestalt psychology or past Gestalt psychology, and that is the identification of Gestalt psychology with the School of Gestalt Qualität of Graz. In other words, the notion that Gestalt theories say that the whole is more than the sum of its parts, rather than that the whole is totally different from the sum of its parts.

DR. HENLE: I should indeed have mentioned it, and I'm afraid I ran out of time. And I should have mentioned it all the more because that kind of theory is still with us today.

DR. WOODWARD: Dr. Blumenthal made the comment that introspection was not used by Wundt. That's very interesting to me, and I'd like to hear some comment from you on how it entered American psychology, if not from Wundt via Titchener.

DR. BLUMENTHAL: The basis of Wundt's "new" psychology, as I read it, was his move away from casual introspection and toward the introduction of experimental technique. He argued at length against introspection, at least against what we mean by that term today. Like most of us, however, Wundt often produced speculations, conjectures, opinions, and personal impressions—but those should be kept separate from his laboratory procedures, at least for the purposes of today's discussion.

I think an American myth arose that says nothing but simplistic introspection existed in pre-Watsonian psychology. At times that myth was used to help launch the behaviorist movement, and the speculative passages in Wundt were then highlighted or put forth as representing the whole of his work. And his phrase "experimental self-observation" was seen as no different from "casual introspection." Also, the fact that one's subject matter is mental processes, as it is for many modern cognitive psychologists, means to many people that you must be some kind of armchair introspectionist—but it doesn't have to mean that, as Wundt often pointed out.

Wundt criticized the Würzburgers, especially Bühler, at some length for their regression to a form of pre-Wundtian introspective psychology. This was the whole point of his methodological criticisms in the papers of 1907 and 1908. And finally, there is considerable distance between Wundt and Titchener, which is obvious if you read them in the original. I suspect it was not Titchener's true style to be a tough-minded experimentalist. He was partly shaped by his strong philosophical training at Oxford. And I'd say that when he was at Cornell he looked much more like Külpe (at Würzburg) than like Wundt.

DR. WOODWARD: That's helpful to me, and I think that Külpe might be a key figure here, since Titchener followed him very closely.

DR. LAZAR: I was hoping you'd comment about Titchener's influence on Americans. I imagine he was the single person who did the most to give a particular kind of psychology to Americans.

DR. BLUMENTHAL: That's the standard line according to E.G. Boring.

DR. LAZAR: I was always interested in the differences between Titchener and Wundt.

DR. BLUMENTHAL: E. G. Boring was the student and disciple of Titchener, so Titchener plays a very large role in his history. Münsterburg, by contrast, gets little space in Boring's *History*. Yet Müsterburg was very prolific and just as antagonistic toward Wundt; they disagreed about applied psychology and about Münsterburg's materialism.

I think you will find a much better characterization of Wundt in the writings of Charles Hubbard Judd. J. R. Angel, in his APA address of 1904, titled "The Province of Functional Psychology, paraphrases notions in Wundt's outlines of psychology. Let's see, I forgot your question.

DR. LAZAR: The point was that it's been thought that Titchener was Wundt's mouthpiece here, and there are certainly a lot of differences. It would be interesting to explore this question.

DR. BLUMENTHAL: One ironic case is Ladd at Yale, who never went to Germany, but his *Principles of Physiological Psychology* seems to be a condensation of Wundt's *Physiological Psychology*. Ladd was a voluntarist and a functionalist and was generally ignored by Münsterburg, by Hall, by Titchener and others, so Ladd had less impact on American psychology. But he gives a good presentation of Wundtian ideas, though he did not study with Wundt.

Titchener may be the biggest reason why we have the distorted interpretations of Wundt. But Titchener was also very isolated.

DR. CADWALADER: I'd like to comment on Dr. Blumenthal's statement, quite literally, that Wundt trained the first generation of American experimental psychologists. I'd like to suggest here, as I have elsewhere, that the first generation of American psychologists were Pierce, James, and Ladd. Now certainly, Ladd—

DR. BLUMENTHAL: You left out "experimental."

DR. CADWALADER: Well, O.K., I'll get to that. Ladd certainly was not an experimentalist in the sense of a laboratory man, and certainly James was involved in only two experiments, only one of which was published. Therefore, you might argue that James is not an experimentalist. I would submit here, as elsewhere, that Pierce is the first American experimental psychologist; his first experiment was published in 1877, and he continued his experimentation in visual processes to perhaps the end of the century.

Now it's true that Wundt certainly influenced Pierce, and it was Pierce who was the first American to be influenced by Wundt. Pierce later says that he read Wundt as early as 1862, and we know that he was in correspondence with Wundt at least as early as 1869. So, I would like to suggest that it is the second generation that Wundt trained, although he certainly influenced even the first generation.

DR. BLUMENTHAL: By the first generation I mean the men who established the laboratories and who established academic psychology in the sense of all the laboratories in and around universities.

DR. CADWALADER: O.K. If you define it that way—

DR. JAYNES: How close were the relations of Stern and Lewin?

DR. HARDESTY: The relationship goes back to at least 1913, when Lewin was still a student. The relationship that shows most is in conjunction with Stern's philosophy of critical personalism, less so with Stern's psychology. But the general concept of the person that Lewin used, particularly in relation to the definition of the behavioral situation—that is basically Stern. I would exclude the idea of group dynamics; that happens much later. Stern included in the 1930, if not an earlier, edition of his *Psychology of Early Childhood*, Lewin's article illustrating the use of film for the study of expressive movements of children. There may be a more formal relationship. I have not gone into this.

DR. RIEGEL: Would you give us your opinion about the relationship between Stern and Cassirer.

DR. HARDESTY: Cassirer was invited to become a faculty member at the University of Hamburg in 1919. In point of fact, Stern was instrumental in bringing about the invitation. The relation between Stern and Cassirer was one of long standing. I do not know all of the personal aspects of it, but at the time it was clear that the University of Hamburg was going to be created with Stern the only professor there representing philosophy and psychology. He quickly got Cassirer, and they shared the same office from 1919 or so right up to 1933. From the early 1920s on, Stern shared the codirectorship of the Department of Philosophy with Cassirer. In addition to this, Stern retained the directorship of the Psychological Laboratory, later named the Psychological Institute.

Cassirer and Stern lived about five blocks from each other. This was also the case with respect to Heinz Werner, Fritz Heider, Martha Muchow, and others. The Hamburg Institute was a very intimate one.

DR. HENLE: I'd just like to know more specifically the conceptual, not the geographical, relation between Lewin and Stern.

DR. HARDESTY: That is a big question.

DR. HENLE: Well, answer a little of it.

DR. HARDESTY: The conceptual relation certainly has a phenomenological aspect that they definitely shared.

DR. HENLE: But you said all of Lewin's personality theory, which, by the way, I don't believe he had—

DR. HARDESTY: I didn't say that. I said that Wolman has made the observation, on the basis of his analysis, that Stern's philosophical outlook provided the underlay for Lewin's approach to psychology.

DR. HENLE: I hope Ben Wolman is here, because I think he is dead wrong on that.

DR. RIEBER: I'd like to make two comments. First, about Dr. Bringmann's discussion. You cannot have it both ways. That is, you cannot accuse Francis Galton of not having the influence because he wasn't a good enough laboratory scientist, as you put it, and then, on the other hand, say that Gestalt psychology did not have an influence because it wasn't applied enough. Certainly Wundt's Psychology was not applied in the first place; application wasn't his intention. It was a laboratory approach without any applications, and therefore should have the same effect that Gestalt psychology allegedly had, as you put it.

I think you were a bit too polemical in your talk, and I think you've been terribly unfair to Sir Francis and much too enthusiastic about Professor Dr. Wundt.

The other comment was directed toward Dr. Woodward's comment about introspection and how it was introduced into American psychology. I think that it would be profitable to differentiate between introspection as used as a laboratory technique, and introspection as an empirical phenomenological event. The latter was introduced at the very beginning of American psychology in the 18th century and worked its way through, as it were, into the Transcendentalist movement in the 19th century, and so on. So it has its roots in the Scottish-English philosophers, then the Transcendentalists, and finally, experimental introspection comes in at the end of the 19th century. Hickock, in America, is allegedly the first person to have used the term *instrospection*, in the 1850s.

DR. ADLER: I'd like to comment on two points of Dr. Bringmann's, whose work on Wundt I appreciate very much, incidentally. The first one has to do with Fechner's influence on Freud. I had to skip this because of time limitations. Freud acknowledged his debt to Fechner in "The Interpretation of Dreams," and Freud was not a person given to a lot of footnotes and acknowledgments, in connection with the notion of the unconscious, which he felt that Fechner contributed to the scientific community. The notion of the unconscious is not something that I dealt with in my approach to Fechner's psychophysical measurement. A second acknowledgment of Fechner comes in his "Project for a Scientific Psychology," where Freud attempted to incorporate the logarithmic law into his system. Of course, this attempt was not something that led to anything important, except in terms of Freud's own thinking.

The second point I want to make regards Fechner's philosophy. Dr. Bringmann pointed out that Fechner's philosophy was a very mystical and very nonmaterialistic kind of philosophy, which, oddly enough, nevertheless led to this rather realistic employment of psychological measurement.

What I want to point out is that Fechner's philosophy was quite well known in America and was appreciated. For example, I could cite that his philosophical writings, such as his book on Life After Death, were published here in 1906, whereas the Elements wasn't published until 1966.

DR. HARDESTY: (In response to an inaudible question): This is a descriptive kind of thing. The impression I have is that toward the last half of the nineteenth century, philosophy in Germany had collapsed, had been absolutely "bombed out." For example, Stern actually talks about this in his autobiography and about what it was like at the University of Berlin as a young student. Edward von Hartmann was unknown among university circles, and there were no lectures on his works. Lectures were not offered on Fechner's metaphysics. The things that Stern thought were so significant were absent. The way I read this involves going back and looking at the funding phenomenon from 1848, perhaps even before then. The impression I have of the period, particularly after 1871—and this is an hypothesis—is that science had such a tremendous privileged position that the humanities were in total disarray.

The youth movement that I mentioned was an alienation phenomenon hinging in part on the enormous number of students coming into university situations which were not designed to accommodate such numbers. Students then began to become much more receptive, so to speak, to some kind of revolt. There is one article after another breaking over the turn of the century, dealing with the cultural crisis, written by outstanding members of the academic community of the time. Georg Simmel is but one example; there are many others. Even Wundt gets into the picture in 1913 with a today much-overlooked monograph dealing with psychology and its struggle for existence. In it, Wundt does not stress the relationship of psychology to the natural and physical sciences. Rather, he asserts that special chairs in philosophy should be created for individuals trained in empirical methods, objective methodology, and so on. But to map out the many trends and patterns with all the twists and turns of the period is a jungle as far as I can see, as an American looking at it.

DR. RIEGEL: I was very much impressed by the different ways in which history can be written. But before I make my comments, I would like to indicate that I hope that after my statement, the members of this distinguished panel will be still my friends. First, I think we have seen that history can be written in a *resentful manner*; namely, by pointing out that what some historical figures have done has never been properly recognized. In order that their contributions can be recognized, some major revisions of our interpretation of their work are necessary. A modification of this approach I will call the *negative view*. In this case, the historians seem to have correctly represented a particular scientist in the historical context, but basically this scientist aimed at something quite different, which was not recognized by his contemporaries. And so we have to start all over again and try to find the real McCoy, for example, the real Wundt.

Now, this leaves out—I think—the most important aspect, namely, the *constructive aspect* of the historical interpretation, the interpretation that as we advance in science, we move forward in history. If we adopt this type of interpretation we do not necessarily try to set matters straight and correct historical injustice. After all, history in the more general and also in the political sense doesn't really care if one or the other historical figure is properly historically represented in the textbooks of history. What matters is the historical unfolding of the ideas and whether they are fitting appropriately into particular slots of historical movements. This requires us to construct history and to learn by interpreting psychology, i.e., what our directions and intentions ought to be. I found that this constructive aspect was barely represented by the panel.

DR. MAX GARFINKEL: (*University of Montreal; Montreal, Canada*): The Panel members addressed themselves to the question of European influence on the "great man" theory of history, and I wonder if you would look at the same subject matter from a history-of-science perspective that Thomas Kuhn talks about when he tells us that we move from one paradigm to another; I was trying to figure out whether you considered European psychology as basically all functioning within one paradigm, with different theories and methods, but a kind of consensus about the image of the subject matter, or whether you saw each particular person there working within a different paradigm.

DR. ADLER: Very briefly, I think that there is a paradigm involved, and it is the change from a qualitative to a quantitative approach to mental philosophy, as it used to be called. That, of course, is built on the model of the natural sciences, and I think that is the important change that was taking place, all the changes that followed really depended on that one basic idea.

DR. JAYNES: Would Dr. Henle agree?

DR. HENLE: I would just like to say that it has not really been established that the concept of paradigm applies to psychology, and just to give you one very good reference I'd like to refer to Professor Jaynes's article on Routes of Science. I mean, why do we automatically apply to psychology something that Kuhn applies so very well to physics?

DR. EVANS: I have a comment, maybe a couple of brief comments, on Dr. Blumenthal's paper, particularly on the topic of who is the more appropriate or most appropriate interpreter of Wundt. There's been a lot of talk and a lot of papers on this recently. I think the crux of the problem comes down to which Wundt are you talking about. William James, for instance, was very early stimulated by Wundt, but he was stimulated by the Wundt of the 1860s, who was a very different kind of Wundt, writing a medical student type of psychology in those days.

Titchener, when he arrived in Leipzig in the 1890s, was very much interested in Wundt, the systematist. The psychology had changed tremendously between the 1860s and 1890s, and the kind of psychology that completely turned Titchener on in the 1890s was ignored or completely disliked by James. By the time Judd appeared, he found a very different kind of Wundt again. You find a Wundt in Judd's time dealing with the higher mental processes, the ethnic psychology— again, a very different sort of psychology. I can see how Judd could describe the Wundt that he knew as something of a functionalist type of worker. Titchener would describe a very different kind of person because he knew a different sort of person.

I think you have here not one proper interpreter and one improper interpreter, but different people seeing an individual at a different time.

My second comment is on this matter of introspection. I really can't accept the idea that Wundt did not use introspection. It is true that Wundt did attack the use of one concept of introspection, but the kind of introspection that Wundt was attacking was the Cartesian type of introspection, the turning the mind's eye inward in describing the processes of mind. Surely what Wundt was doing was introspection within the definitions of the description of experience, and as a matter of fact, this attack on Würzburgers, in my opinion, at least, was made because the Würzburgers were not playing according to the rules of proper introspection.

DR. BLUMENTAL: I'm happy to answer that. In his "attack," the *rules* that Wundt explicity referred to were "reliability of measurements," "replicability of experiments," and "quantifiability of data"—call that proper introspection, if you want to. Let me talk about introspection first because there is such a bugaboo in the American psychological tradition about the word *introspection*. The charge of introspection that is inappropriately leveled at Wundt by most critics today concerns the Cartesian introspection. The distinction of types is not made. But I would ask to see a place or passage in Wundt's writings where he favors any kind of introspection over more solid laboratory data based on experimental procedures. True, there are speculative and theoretical passages. Is that what you have in mind? Or do you mean having subjects give verbal descriptions of their own uncontrolled experiences? The latter was not typical of Wundt. I find that reaction time was his most often-used dependent variable. Is that to be called introspective? He used the kind of reaction-time tests that are used by Sternberg, Sperling, or Shepard today. You might call their work introspective because it concerns mental processes, imagery, and consciousness. Shepard's work on the rotation of mental images is perhaps even a little more mentalistic, or "introspectionist," than Wundt's—Wundt never got to be that clever in the use of reaction-time techniques.

The disagreement with the Würzburgers was strictly over the fact that they had people give descriptions of their experience (à la Descartes) and that these descriptions were uncontrolled. They were not replicable. They were idiosyncratic. They simply weren't "laboratory" experiments. So, I don't know if that satisfies you, but I simply don't find old-fashioned introspection, either the Cartesian kind or the Würzburg kind, as being seriously promoted in Wundt's work. You do find plenty of reaction times, the Donder's substractive procedures, judgments, and discriminations. In Wundt's lab, introspection often came in the form of a key press, a response to some array of stimuli.

One other thing on Wundt's work: the more I look at it, the more historical consistency I find in it, and I think you'll see Titchener and other early American psychologists describing this same characteristic; namely, that the whole system is there in germinal form in 1862. His first, and basic principle of *creative synthesis* is there in 1862, and then soon after he founds his lab, it appears in his system of philosophy and in his two-volume *Logic,* which are not books on logic and philosophy as much as they are psychology texts where you find his psychological theories repeated. The later changes that came along were an evolutionary development, like the development of the theory of feeling and affect. But the *basic* Wundtian psychology seems to me rather consistent. And I think Titchener agreed on that point.

DR. EVANS: I guess my difficulty with your handling of introspection is that it's true, you're emphasizing the reaction-time experiments, which were quite important. But how, for instance, could Wundt describe a sensory experience in terms of qualities and intensities and not be using a verbal report, as introspection?

DR. DIAMOND: I think, as a first hasty answer to this challenge, that one has to point to the work Wundt did or to the discussions Wundt uses, which are really quite basic, on the levels of attention and on the formation of rhythms in perception. I just heard someone say "reaction time." No, it is not reaction time. It is introspective data on how series of sounds are formed into rhythm, or how perceptual phenomena fall into the two or three levels of attention. This is basic to his system and cannot be done without introspection.

DR. BLUMENTHAL: Well, that was the data that was gathered by Dietze, his student, in one of the early experimental projects.

DR. DIAMOND: No, I think Wundt's discussion of levels of attention goes back beyond that time into an earlier period, back as far as the—

DR. BLUMENTHAL: Yes, I agree, and those earlier discussions included his so-called "complication" experiment, which was a reaction-time experiment and which was his initial laboratory discovery of certain operational characteristics of attention. His early discussions of "creative synthesis" were also about attention, but the important thing here is that there were early laboratory procedures and reliable data, coming from Wundt, that bore directly on the process of attention. By the way, modern cognitive psychology, from that of Broadbent onwards, has determined similar levels of attention, and it has done so with Wundtian-style reaction times and not with introspection.

DR. LAZAR: The point I want to make in the context of the discussion turns on whether Galton was an experimentalist or not and what kinds of laboratories there were back in the last part of the eighteenth century. I think the point that is the most influential to me, that Bringmann made, is that Galton perhaps was not a long-time, hard-nosed experimentalist, but on the other hand, I think we can't forget that experimental laboratories in his day were very much home-made.

Hitzig, for example, did it in Fitch's room, I think. When you describe the way that Mueller's laboratory—and even Wundt's laboratory—has been described by people who are less pompous than Galton, it was a very small place, lacked equipment, and so on; so I'm suggesting two points: one, that Galton's kinds of experimenting were no more homemade than the rest of the psychological kinds of experimenting that were going on. The second point is that Galton didn't have to worry about tenure and could work out long-term experimental plans; in fact, he had the proper experimental strategy: starting with observations on humans, taking the first kinds of gross data which would then lead to more precise experimenting, or, in fact, too precise experimenting.

People like Wundt had a lot of this background behind them and were able to ask more precise experimental questions.

DR. DIAMOND: It would take quite a long discussion to deal with Galton's work as a founder of experimental method. That was not the task, I think, that any of us had, but only to speak of influences on American psychology. But I think one of the striking examples of it, which is not well known, is his work with the sweet pea, which was done at the same time that Mendel did his work. The point is this: he didn't do an experiment by himself. He collected sweet peas and he distributed them to friends in, I think, eleven different parts of the island, and instructed them all about how to plant them and how to raise them, and then to send back the sizes, and so on.

I mentioned, in connection with the twins, that the twin experiment used the first control group in psychological experimentation. For here was very careful experimental control which, you might say, is anticipating the agricultural work of the Rothamsted station now in England. He was an extremely sophisticated experimenter and well in advance of anything then taking place at the universities. The fact that he was wealthy—well, he just poured his wealth into this.

As I tried to point out, he was not interested in individual variations. He was interested in heredity. The data that he gathered, that he just teased out of the public with an anthropological laboratory, he used to create the best theory of heredity that existed in his time. He really drew very sound conclusions from it— on the subject he was really interested in.

He didn't regard himself as a psychologist, and nobody else did. The question is, though, what about his influence on American psychology? His influence on American psychology has been because of his genius in devising experimental procedures that we have continued to use.

DR. JAYNES: As to twin studies, do you know this thing of St. Augustine, disproving astrology because twins could be brought up in different ways? I think maybe that takes precedence. I think we have one comment here.

UNIDENTIFIED SPEAKER: I want to make a general comment as to Dr. Bringmann's very provocative critique and then illustrate it specifically addressing myself to Dr. Henle's presentation on Gestalt psychology. What I felt, listening to Dr. Bringmann, is that, as we look into his type of perspective at the people who went before us, we do have the right to choose and pick what may be useful, and it's not only in music that we can take certain elements and recombine them and come up with something creative, but I hope that it also applies to psychology. And so I think that American psychology has done quite well in this respect in picking and choosing and making of it something of its own, because, after all, we need to be comfortable with what we believe in; and I think that as Dr. Diamond said, one of the great things about the American non-tradition is that we could be free to choose and not have that many constraints.

In that regard, I wanted also to reassure Dr. Henle that at least Gestalt psychology is well and alive in Brooklyn. The point that I want to make as a cognitive psychologist in the educational setting is that we do apply it. We may adulterate it a little bit to suit our purposes, but it is being applied and is very helpful.

NINETEENTH CENTURY INSTITUTIONAL MENTAL CARE

Norman Dain

*Department of History
Rutgers University
Newark, New Jersey 07102*

There is considerable disagreement today about how to evaluate mental hospitals, past and present. This discussion occurs within a broader context of dissatisfaction with most institutions in our society that only occasionally reaches the point where a significant body of critics calls for the virtually total abolition of the institution concerned. In the case of mental hospitals, this point has been reached and surpassed: reformers, influencing Congress, state legislatures, and substantial portions of the mental health establishment, have been able to go beyond discussion in order to effect a major decline in the role that mental hospitals play in the treatment of mental disorders. The hospital population has diminished by about half within the past decade, mental hospitals have been on the defensive, and community mental health programs are seen as the preferred alternative to hospitalization. It would be hard to find another major public institution in the United States that has experienced such radical devaluation.

Demands for both sweeping changes in the hospitals and the virtual elimination of hospitalization as the method of choice in dealing with mental disorders are not new. What is new is that reformers managed to win over by the late 1960s more than a few persons in the mental health professions, more than a few educated laymen, and more than a few officials and politicians—and enough of them all to accomplish extensive change and to create the possibility, if not the reality, of substantial improvement in the lives of the mentally ill. Historically, such reform impulses have emerged when some articulate and significant group concluded that mental hospitals were neither therapeutic nor humane and that new, more effective therapeutic techniques or approaches could be implemented. Successes in the past, such as they were, were fitful, as evidenced by the recurrent need for reforms, radical or otherwise; it remains to be seen whether contemporary reforms will last any longer.

Perhaps more than any previous reform movement the present one has looked to the past, usually the nineteenth century, when the mental hospital became established as an accepted, if not always acceptable, repository for mental patients. Among both reformers and radicals of our day and some historians as well, history has had an instrumental function: to justify present programs. Such a tendency can skew a reading of the past: to gain a better understanding of both nineteenth-century and twentieth-century mental hospitals, a broader, less single-minded perspective than that expressed by persons disputing the pros and cons of mental hospitals today is necessary. It is simply not enough to deny that these hospitals performed or were intended to perform any function except to imprison the insane, to put an undesirable and troublesome element in society out of the way. That is a simplistic picture, obscuring a more complex reality. The hospitals were never unipurpose institutions, nor were all of them the same;

any or all or some of them might do better in fulfilling some objective than others, or in serving the interests of one group rather than another. They also changed through time. Like many other institutions, so complex a one as a mental hospital was not likely to achieve all its goals or even any one goal except partially; that is, there are degrees of success and failure. Finally, there is the important question of whether there were any real alternatives to hospitals in the nineteenth century.

What I would like to do here is to touch on and raise questions about various classes of persons intimately involved with the nineteenth-century mental hospitals and about the various functions that the hospitals served for them and in such a way as to tie them to the existing hospital system.

First, there were the patients, an important if not always the central concern of those who have controlled the fortunes of mental institutions. Persons considered insane or lunatic, to use nineteenth-century terms, probably fared better inside than outside those hospitals. This was expecially so for the indigent who were institutionalized early in the history of the founding of a public hospital, that is, while a hopeful attitude toward therapy prevailed, a situation generally found before the Civil War. Treatment varied according to class and social status, but the evidence we have indicates that home care was less satisfactory than hospital care for all classes. Generally better than care in private homes, much more so than that in jails and almshouses or for those insane persons wandering about on their own, the hospitals still left a great deal to be desired. As public hospitals, usually within a decade after opening, became overcrowded, there appeared a growing gap between the ideal, known as moral treatment—a humane, therapeutic, psychologically oriented system similar to the milieu therapy or therapeutic environment of our own day—and the actual treatment received. By the late nineteenth century the gap no longer existed, not because the ideal was achieved but because it was abandoned. As the aim of cure through humane care gave way to hopelessness and a belief that the only realistic goal was custodial care, goals and practices came into close accord, to the detriment of the patients whose needs then tended to be subordinated to the interests of the institution.

During the first half of the nineteenth century, the heyday of moral treatment and the time when Dorothea Dix, Horace Mann, and others campaigned for state-supported hospitalization of the neglected insane, it was the relatively small, corporate, nonprofit hospitals catering to the upper and middle classes and claiming unprecedented cures that set the tone and served as models for the public hospitals the reformers succeeded in establishing. Eventually these state institutions housed the overwhelming majority of the mentally ill, and after the Civil War it was the conditions and morale there that characterized the whole field. The chronic overcrowding in state hospitals and their increasing size, along with prejudice against the foreign born and the poor, white and black, together with the inability of medical superintendents to maintain high rates of cures under the best of conditions, set the scene for a decline in the quality of hospital care. Custodialism became not only the fact but the aim of many hospitals for the lower classes. Nevertheless, it would be unfair and a distortion of the evidence not to recognize that at different times and even in particular hospitals there were superintendents and staff members who were hopeful, humane, and relatively effective. A general tendency is just that, a tendency and not an iron law: among the three hundred hospitals in operation at the turn of the nineteenth century there was variety in treatment and in attitudes, and some patients, even if a small number, did believe they were treated well and benefited from their stay in a mental hospital. The large majority, however, lived dull, hopeless lives where decent care was at a premium, and an undetermined but all too large number suffered inhuman physical conditions coupled at times with overtly brutal treatment.

This deterioration applied to patients with money as well as to the indigent, for in the absence of efficacious therapeutic methods the condition of the upper-class patient, while generally better than that of the nonpaying patients, also fluctuated as custodialism and pessimism pervaded the entire world of the mentally ill and their caretakers. Mental disorder in a sense declassed all its sufferers. Even if they could pay for more luxurious accommodations or go to a private asylum, well-to-do patients could be troublesome and helpless and could therefore be mistreated and neglected, especially if they had no relatives or friends keeping a close watch over their welfare. It is essential to keep in mind that when effective therapeutic techniques specific for mental illness were wanting, good treatment included not only a satisfactory physical setting but a sympathetic and hopeful attitude on the part of the hospital staff. Although wealth could buy the former, it could not usually secure the latter in the face of pessimism in the medical profession and among the general public. What was probably more true of the better corporate and private hospitals than of the public hospitals was that the general environment, being more comfortable and pleasant than in most public hospitals, did not impede spontaneous recoveries, which conditions in many public hospitals were likely to do.

The doubtful contribution of mental hospitals to the welfare of patients affected no other group so immediately and deeply than their relatives. Surely the hospital's ability to restore patients to health was the primary concern of most relatives, but lacking that ability, or at least having it to a very modest degree, hospitals did perform a vital function for families of patients: their existence obviated the responsibility for home care. The importance of this function can hardly be overestimated, albeit many who write about the role of mental hospitals today do not discuss this question except perhaps to sneer at hospitals for catering to the "convenience" of relatives. To care for a clinically depressed parent, spouse, son, or daughter, or one who is suicidal or highly excited over an extended period, is virtually beyond the psychological capacity of most people, no matter how devoted or well-meaning. This is especially so where there are other family obligations and where financial resources are limited, conditions that apply to most people. And if humane means of controlling excited patients, meant, according to the moral treatment model, the prohibition of straitjackets, hand restraints, strong rooms, padded cells, or whipping, then the proper management of excited patients required having on hand at least several trained attendants to persuade, restrain, or distract them, something almost impossible to provide in a private home. The public was also informed that mental patients needed to develop good work habits through farming, gardening, hand crafts, and had to be stimulated intellectually through hearing lectures, attending classes, and having at their disposal collections of books and natural history specimens, all planned to be therapeutic. Not many families could create on a systematic basis such conditions; nor could they provide all sorts of other activities and entertainment to help overcome depression.

There were also in the nineteenth century, before the advent of modern psychological theory, hospital superintendents—the psychiatrists of the time—who considered the family setting pathological and believed that patients needed to be removed from the so-called unhealthy associations of the home in order to recover. Given the widely accepted medical model of mental illness—the view that the etiology of mental illness was somatic and susceptible to treatment by physicians—where better to place them than under the care of concerned medical specialists in institutions designed for their care? Experience in England with boarding patients in physicians' homes had been bad and had resulted in the for-profit proprietary institutions, where patients were often mistreated.

In an increasingly urbanized society the insane were troublesome and difficult, even for the best and most affluent of families, and once hospitals arose there seemed to be little choice but to send them there, however difficult a decision; for the lower classes hospitals seemed preferable to almshouses and prisons. This was true even later, when hope for cures had declined and moral treatment faded away.

For example, Clifford Beers, future author of *A Mind That Found Itself* and the founder of the modern mental health movement, experienced indifferent to bad and even cruel treatment in several hospitals. His brother, George Beers, his guardian and head of the Beers family, responded to his complaints by transferring him to other hospitals. What else could he do? The family had tried. In the early stages of Clifford Beers' illness, after a suicide attempt, he had been kept at home, but seemed only to sink deeper into an illness that forced the family to face the need to hospitalize him, despite their deep love for him and the pain of the decision at a time when there was still considerable stigma attached to being a mental patient. They did not know how to help him and were afraid that he would try again to kill himself. Even so, they later sent him to live with an attendant's family for several months, only to resort again to hospital care when his condition worsened. Beers himself did not, in his depressed stage, want to stay at home; his delusions had made him too suspicious and fearful of his family. While living in the attendant's home he was not only terrified that his hostility toward other people might lead him to violence but found being in the "sane" world disturbing because of the constant reminder both of his inability to function there and of the difference between himself and other people. These feelings that Beers had raises another point—one not usually considered by historians— the security that an institutional setting could offer persons who had difficulty functioning in a competitive, individualistic, complex world.

The key individual to whom relatives entrusted their hospitalized loved ones was the medical superintendent, whose interests were initially closely tied to that of the patients. In eighteenth-century hospitals physicians often did not direct the care of mental patients beyond dispensing medication, but by the mid-nineteenth century, they controlled virtually all aspects of patient care in the mental hospital, and in the small institutions of pre-Civil War days their high status within the medical profession as well as in society at large depended primarily upon their success in running a therapeutic and humane institution. But the pessimism about cure that began to permeate the medical profession after the war, consequent in part to the decline in reported recovery rates, operated to create a distinction between the interests of the superintendent and his patients. It was now possible to preside over an exclusively custodial institution with minimum facilities for even the basic needs of patients and still be considered a successful superintendent. If a superintendent's colleagues, public officals, and the general public accepted custody as a valid or the only realistic goal, then not only did recovery rates no longer function as a criterion of success but, not uncommonly, the very objective of humane care would go by the boards as well.

Cost per patient, always important and thought to depend increasingly on the size of hospitals, became the most widely used yardstick by which to judge medical superintendents, though in fact there were no automatic economies of size in hospitals, or for that matter in the manufacturing establishments that set the example for efficiency in late nineteenth-century American society. But if large hospitals were not always cheaper places to care for patients than small ones, they had other advantages for those in charge. Just as an oversized manufacturing company might be technically less efficient than its smaller competitors but have more economic and political influence and therefore might be able to amass greater profits, so the supervision of a large mental hospital could give its director more power, both within the hospital and outside it, in dealing with public officials, the general public, and medical colleagues.

The superintendents needed all the bureaucratic power they could get, for their position was, in reality, shaky. With the lapse into custodialism and the loss of the innovative and pioneering spirit that characterized the moral treatment era, the superintendent's standing in the medical profession declined from that of highly esteemed practitioner to that of isolated custodian and administrator, at the same time as general medicine was winning more respect for new discoveries and clinical advances. Especially disturbing to superintendents in many states was the use of hospitals for political patronage, a situation that threatened the tenure of medical superintendents and, more often, meant periodic turnover of staffs. Also endangering the authority of superintendents was the growth of state bureaucracies in the form of boards of charity designed to oversee the mental hospitals and other state social services and the ever-present problem of charges of abuse and unjustified commitment made by former patients.

The single-minded devotion to the interests of patients so characteristic of many men among the first two generations of medical superintendents was replaced by single-minded dedication to order and economy, and the staunch, proud founding fathers of the psychiatric profession by fearful, time-serving men adept at trimming their sails to the winds of political and bureaucratic expediency. The new men saw themselves as an embattled group whose primary task was the smooth administration of largely custodial institutions, a task to be accomplished usually with inadequate funds and requiring self-defense in face of an almost contemptuous medical profession ignorant of their specialty and of scandal-seeking newspapers and a gullible public ready to believe almost any charge of atrocities made by former patients seeking, in superintendents' eyes, to prove their sanity by slandering mental hospitals. Worst of all, superintendents' authoritarian power within the hospital was counterpoised by their impotence as physicians to effect significant improvements in therapy and to guarantee humane care of their patients.

In the early small hospitals, prior to 1850 the superintendents usually knew and personally treated all their patients; with the growth of large institutions (400-600 patients) and then mammoth ones with patients numbering in the thousands, superintendents and members of the medical staff, always in short supply, had to leave the actual daily care of patients to attendants, whom patients, according to the glimpses we have of their attitudes, held responsible for much that was unpleasant or cruel in hospital life. With rare exceptions, attendants, who usually came from the badly educated lower classes and many from the lowest strata among them, received no formal instruction on the nature of mental disorders and how to cope with them; they learned what they could on the job. At some institutions former patients became attendants, and there were instances where criminals were also employed. There was little that superintendents could do to keep good attendants, nor indeed was there much point in discharging bad ones, since they would most likely be replaced by equally unsuitable persons.

If patients were confined to wards and hospital grounds in a boring routine, the attendants' lives were only slightly less restricted, and their rewards meager. They were poorly paid, worked long hours—ten to twelve hours a day six days a week was not uncommon—and often had to live on hospital grounds. Not only their pay but their status was low. Just as the patient often considered the attendant his jailor, so did the public. The consequence for patients subject to the power of such caretakers would frequently be mistreatment either through neglect or through actual overt acts of hostility.

Not only did attendants come to their work with all the prejudices of their class and of their day, but, of equal if not greater importance, the needs of patient and attendant tended to be in sharp conflict. This was particularly true as hospitals grew bigger, overcrowding and understaffing became chronic, and custodial care became the norm, the last a condition that attendants could not but approve and encourage. They must care for ten to twenty or more patients each, some of them highly disturbed, incontinent, and, in most places, without occupation or diversion. Understandably, the attendants' full time would be devoted to preventing disorder among patients with nothing to do all day but sit around and, in the attendants' view, create trouble or threaten to disobey some administrative ruling considered essential for keeping order. The overworked attendants would often resort to mechanical restraints in order to run a tight ship, and patients would take out their frustrations upon attendants as well as other patients.

Even with the best of intentions, attendants usually lost hope, in view of the prevalent belief in the late nineteenth century that hospitalized mental patients were for the most part incurable. Indeed, there was a tendency to hold them responsible for their disorder and to see them as representing constitutionally inferior types bereft of the bodily and psychological strength to recover. In terms of Social Darwinism and theories of degeneration so influential in scientific, medical, and intellectual circles, the insane were misfits, the inferior throwbacks of the human race. Although these so-called scientific ideas met resistance, they had their enthusiastic adherents among medical superintendents and did cast a pall over efforts of concerned attendants, as well as physicians, to care for mental patients and help them to recover.

The attendants who did try nevertheless to do so found themselves working against a bureaucracy resistant to change and oriented to standardized procedures for the sake of "efficiency," that is, the administrator's convenience, and not the efficiency that would help restore patients to mental health or provide them with humane living conditions. The logical result of this situation was for attendants to avoid doing any more work than necessary and to try to arrange their work so that patients lockstepped in a routine that left little chance for the unexpected or for excitement, change, or disruptive activity.

The good patient was docile, quiet, and no trouble. Attendants in the affluent, corporate hospitals did live a better life and receive better pay and some rewards from relatives for considerate care of patients, but even in such institutions the large proportion of incurable patients that accumulated over the years helped to create a hopeless attitude.

Another group involved in this system of institutional care was public officials, the men who had to vote for, appropriate, and oversee the expenditure of funds for mental hospitals. Early in the nineteenth century they, like the general public, only slowly showed an interest in hospital care of the insane, but they were educable, and eventually reformers were able to persuade them to support the construction of institutions practicing moral treatment. Before then most hospitals in the north were corporate or private institutions, whereas in the south

state-supported facilities predominated; after 1840 the northern states started
to build public institutions on a fairly large scale, a practice imitated in the mid-
west and then in the newly settled west. By the last decades of the century, state
hospitals held the vast majority of all institutionalized mental patients, north
and south. Obviously, state officials had to become deeply concerned with institutions that consumed a large part of the public moneys, and when the optimism
that helped launch the hospital construction boom in the 1840s was replaced
later by pessimism, their concern became more material than humanitarian, especially when the prewar social reform movements had died out and ruling elites
and elected officials were no longer as closely allied to reformers as they had
been in outlook, background, and personal ties.

Unfortunately, the prewar reformers' contention that one hospital per state
would handle the problem (provided patients were received shortly after the onset of the disorder when they were supposedly highly curable) grossly underestimated its extent, the discovery of which created a new situation. The faith
that America could become something of a utopia assumed that no significant
proportion of the population would require public assistance. Physicians wrote
about the health of Americans as if in time disease would virtually disappear,
as would other conditions that created dependence. The sad awakening after the
Civil War involved awareness not only of the large numbers of mental patients
requiring hospitalization, but also that the aged were being sent to mental hospitals in increasing numbers and that there were mentally handicapped persons
awaiting public assistance, not to mention the masses of the poor needing charity
and the prisons crowded with criminals. From the view that the nonproductive
elements in society would be insignificant and therefore not a serious drain upon
the economy, many came to fear that the reverse was true, that the number of
persons requiring public support would bankrupt American society, a fear that
contributed toward public officials' retreat from the position that the community should provide therapeutic and humane care for all mental patients; it was
too expensive and its value was dubious. In brief, so long as it appeared that the
numbers of the insane were small and they could be easily cured, the ideal of
therapeutic and humane treatment could be espoused and supported by those in
control of the public purse; when the enormity of the problem became apparent,
the ideal was easy to abandon. Public officials began to worry more about costs
and to see hospitals, particularly the big ones, as offering opportunities for
patronage through appointments to boards of trustees, superintendencies, and
various staff positions. There was money to be made out of them, too, through
constructing, outfitting, and then supplying them, prizes shared in and competed
for by public officials, trustees, local entrepreneurs, and even hospital staff members. And this is not to speak of the jobs and business accruing to the many communities in which a hospital was the largest establishment.

The people whom politicians placed in charge of the expanding state services,
including boards of mental hospitals, tended to look at their jobs as essentially
bureaucratic and fiscal, with little attention to or interest in the hospitals' therapeutic functions or in supporting the research in which neuropsychiatrists, who
by the turn of the century were coming into control of the better hospitals, had
become interested. Members of state boards or of other agencies that were supposed to oversee the care of mental patients rarely sought money from legislatures for research into the causes and treatment of, for example, dementia
praecox (or schizophrenia), then as now a major mental illness.

The system of hospital care was not a closed one in that there were always
people trying to break into it and sometimes succeeding in improving the condi-

tion of mental patients; although the system became resistant to change, it was not immune to it. But most reformers, with a few exceptions for a short time, did not want to intervene in order to eliminate the hospitals and substitute something else for the concept of institutionalization, which early nineteenth-century reformers had promoted as an enlightened mode of psychiatric treatment. This initial movement was sparked by reform-minded physicians and laymen anxious to apply the latest psychiatric ideas from Europe—that is, moral treatment—to the problems of the care of the mentally ill in the United States. The small hospitals in bucolic settings with a physician-in-chief and a staff who were in daily, intimate contact with patients and who tried to create a family atmosphere furnished the models for social reformers like Dix, who wanted the same conditions for the medically indigent masses of the insane without hospital care. She and her colleagues persuaded state governments to take responsibility for such care, but the focus was on building hospitals, albeit on a proper standard. After the Civil War, reformers' interests shifted from hospital building to hospital watching; the quality of treatment became the primary object of concern. Hospital superintendents, previously their chief allies and considered part of the reform movment but now seen as the primary obstacles to change within hospitals, became the chief targets of reformers. Among critics of superintendents were practitioners of the new medical specialty of neurology who claimed greater knowledge and skill in dealing with mental illness.

In 1881 a number of them, together with interested laymen, formed an organization designed to combat what they considered to be a brutal and unenlightened hospital system and especially the ignorant, unscientific superintendents in its charge. These neurologists rejected the value of hospital treatment and urged the public instead to bring their mentally ill relatives to neurologists' offices for treatment. The most famous American neurologist, S. Weir Mitchell, insisted that hospitals be completely avoided except by patients too poor to afford private-office treatment and a few very deteriorated cases. For various reasons this movement petered out, and not least because by the early twentieth century neurologists had succeeded in dominating the practice of psychiatry, including hospital psychiatry. They became the chiefs of many of the more progressive mental hospitals and abandoned their opposition to institutionalizing mental patients, except for Mitchell, who remained steadfast in his position. In effect, then, by the close of the nineteenth century most of the physician-reformers were coming back into the fold in that they envisaged reform as the improvement, not the abandonment, of mental hospitals. It remained for a talented former mental patient, Clifford Beers, to launch a spectacular new movement for change, and in alliance with prominent social reformers of the Progressive Era, but he, too, and in close liaison with the neuropsychiatrists, never questioned the medical model of mental illness or the need for mental hospitals. His crusade was to humanize the institutions, to make them therapeutic, and to investigate through scientific research the causes, cures, and prevention of mental illness.

What can one conclude about the mental hospital of the nineteenth century? It changed through time, and in failing to realize the optimism and hope of its early years, it shared the fate of other institutions established to deal with social and clinical problems. Its continued existence can be attributed to the inability to find an acceptable substitute, and to the goal displacement that seems to take over in large institutions, especially in those like mental hospitals whose original aims have become ambiguous or not fulfillable. As the needs of the institution *qua* institution took precedence over the needs of the persons the institution was created to care for, the possibility of a return to a therapeutic environment became ever more remote without new scientific and medical discoveries or a galvanizing social force from outside trying to break a system that had various things to offer to the different groups locked within it. Without some recognition of this process, the tenacious survival of mental hospitals despite the almost constant attack they underwent from the 1870s to our own time becomes an inexplicable mystery.

ISAAC RAY AND MENTAL HYGIENE IN AMERICA

Jacques M. Quen

Section on the History of Psychiatry and the Behavioral Sciences
Department of Psychiatry
New York Hospital-Cornell Medical Center
New York, N.Y. 10021

Isaac Ray was one of the "original thirteen" founders of the Association of Medical Superintendents of American Institutions for the Insane (AMSAII), now the American Psychiatric Association (APA). Besides founding this oldest of the American medical specialty organizations, Ray was, effectively, the founder of legal psychiatry as an area of special study. In 1952 the American Psychiatric Association established the Isaac Ray Award, to be given annually to the person deemed "most worthy by reason of his contribution to the improvement of the relations of law and psychiatry." A friend and supporter of Dorothea L. Dix, Ray was, himself, a social reformer.

Born in Beverly, Mass., in 1807, Isaac Ray was the first child of a widower Yankee sea-captain and his second wife. Isaac was followed by Lydia, Mary Ann, and Albert, in that order. The eight-week-old infant, Albert, died when Isaac was almost seven years old. Eight months later, Isaac Ray had a second tragedy to cope with, the death of his father. We know little else of his early years other than that he attended Phillips Academy at Andover, Mass., where he roomed with Robert Rantoul, Jr., who later became a notable social reformer and the successor to Daniel Webster in the U.S. Senate.

Isaac Ray entered Bowdoin College in Brunswick, Maine, in 1822, at the age of fifteen. This was during Bowdoin's remarkable decade, when it was the Yale of Maine. Its student body included Henry Wadsworth Longfellow, Nathaniel Hawthorne, William Pitt Fessenden, Franklin Pierce (our fourteenth president), and Luther V. Bell. Bell later became the Superintendent of the McLean Asylum and one of Ray's fellow founders of the AMSAII.

Ray dropped out of Bowdoin in 1824, perhaps due to ill health; however, he began the study of medicine in that same year, under the guidance of Dr. Samuel Hart of Beverly. In 1827, Ray received his medical degree from the Medical School of Maine at Bowdoin College. His dissertation, "Remarks on pathological anatomy,"[1] was remarkably knowledgeable about the currents of medical researches in Europe. The dissertation can also be read as an article of faith in the scientific method and a rejection of vitalism.

Isaac Ray said of his first effort to establish himself in private practice: "At the tender age of 20, being a member of the medical profession in regular standing, I offered my services as practitioner of medicine and surgery to the people of Portland, [Maine] in 1827. They manifested no vehement desire to avail themselves of this privilege, and thinking my services might be better appreciated somewhere else, I removed in 1829 to Eastport, where I resided till 1841."[2] Two years after his move to Eastport, Isaac Ray married Abigail May Frothingham of Portland.

In 1838, he published *A Treatise on the Medical Jurisprudence of Insanity*. It made little stir here in America, but separate editions were published in 1839 in Edinburgh and in London. In 1843, Daniel M'Naghten's defense attorney based the bulk of his case on this American physician's book. "It is safe to say that never since, in an English or an American courtroom, has a scientific work by a psychiatrist been treated with such respect."[3]

Although Benjamin Rush's *Medical Inquiries and Observations Upon Diseases of the Mind* (1812) was our first major psychiatric publication, it consisted of Rush's own clinical experiences and thinking about insanity. It was, in fact, a presentation of one man's "observations and inquiries." Ray's *Treatise* was the first systematic exposition of Western World medical thinking about insanity written in the United States. About a third of the book is devoted to "such legal consequences as seem warranted by a humane and enlightened consideration of all the facts."[4] The remainder of the 25 chapters are devoted largely to clinical discussion and speculations on etiology and pathology. It was the definitive American psychiatric text and the definitive work on the medical jurisprudence of insanity for more than a generation. It became relied on enough to warrant several American editions, the fifth and last in 1871. Winfred Overholser, the late Superintendent of St. Elizabeth's Hospital, remarked, in 1962, "We have not even yet fully caught up with the reforms he advocated." (Ref. 4, p vii., reprint edit.)

In 1841, Ray was appointed Superintendent of the Maine Insane Hospital in Augusta. Four years later he resigned his position to become superintendent of the yet-to-be-built Butler Hospital, which opened in 1847. He used the intervening time to study the asylums in Europe.[5] Shortly after his return, the Rays' 14-year-old daughter, Abby, died of a consumptive disease. Their son, Benjamin Lincoln, now their only child, became a physician and worked with his father at the hospital. In 1867, Ray reluctantly retired because of ill health and moved to Philadelphia.

Isaac Ray's retirement years were remarkably active and productive. He soon became a controversial public figure in social reform and in hospital reform. Unfortunately, in 1879, Benjamin Lincoln Ray died of an unspecified "brain disease." The Rays were grief-stricken. One friend described Mrs. Ray as appearing crushed and resigned. "[O]ne feels as if in such entire surrender her life must go before too long. In Dr. Ray one sees more of a struggle . . . . his talk was as earnest and clear as ever, yet with all its naturalness, I felt the hidden agony."[6] Almost a year later, Isaac Ray wrote to his old and good friend, Dorothea L. Dix: "My poor brain is so torpid and my ribs so full of rheumatism, that I shrink from writing, even a letter. I sleep well and eat well, but I am good for little else. I can walk one square with much discomfort, and two causes distress. I have not written a line except as a letter since Lincoln died, and the sofa and easy-chair now furnish about all the day-comfort [sic] I have."[7]

Isaac Ray died quietly in his sleep on March 31, 1881, of tuberculosis, at the age of 74. Mrs. Ray survived him by four years. The bulk of their estate was left to Butler Hospital. They are buried, alongside Benjamin Lincoln Ray, in the Swan Point Cemetery, in Providence, R.I., adjacent to the hospital.

I have presented a brief summary of Isaac Ray's life, but I have not mentioned that, in 1863, he published a book titled *Mental Hygiene*.[8] The book was written during the latter years of Ray's tenure as Superintendent of Butler Hospital. As such, it was the product of a mature and experienced psychiatrist, in contrast to the *Treatise*, which was written by a young general practitioner who had had no significant experience with the insane or with the law. At the time he wrote *Mental Hygiene*, the term was a relatively new one. It had appeared for the first time in American medical literature in 1843.[9]

It will be helpful to define mental hygiene. Few, probably, would hesitate to accept the *Oxford English Dictionary* definition of hygiene: "that department of knowledge or practice which relates to the maintenance of health; a system of principles or rules for preserving or promoting health."[10] It would seem to be a short and equally acceptable step from the dictionary definition of hygiene to a definition of mental hygiene by inserting the word "mental" before the word "health." It is here, however, that difficulties become apparent. When we ask for a definition of mental hygiene, we are predicating a dualistic nature to man, and requiring clear distinction between the mental and physical hygienes or healths. Should a well-balanced diet be part of mental hygiene? or should that more properly be considered physical hygiene? Certainly inadequate nutrition yields physical conditions that impair mental functioning (e.g. beri-beri, pellagra, and some forms of cretinism). Where shall we assign physical conditions related to emotional etiologies? Is preventive psychosomatic medicine properly part of mental or of physical hygiene? To complicate the problem of defining mental hygiene, Albert Deutsch, in his excellent review of its history, suggests that mental hygiene in the twentieth century is "indelibly associated with *organized* [emphasis in original] efforts to promote mental health, more specifically, with the mental hygiene movement."[11] The definition used in this paper will be implicit and not incompatible with the definition used by Isaac Ray, which will be presented later, nor with the previously referred-to dictionary definition of hygiene.

It will be useful to note some of the antecedent "principles or rules for preserving or promoting [mental] health." Since antiquity, the concept of moderation, or the Greek "Golden Mean," has been basic to almost all systems of hygiene or medicine. In the 1769 edition of William Buchan's *Domestic Medicine*, the discussions of the causes of hysteria, hypochondriasis, madness, and melancholy, implicate various excesses.[12] William Falconer's prize-winning *Dissertation on the Influence of the Passions Upon Disorders of the Body* (1788) discusses phrenitis, hypochondriasis, melancholia, hysteria, and mania, and takes essentially the same position.[13] In America, at the beginning of the nineteenth century, Benjamin Rush and David Hosack do likewise.[14, 15]

In 1832, a young Connecticut physician, Amariah Brigham, published a book that was critical of child-education practices, with their overemphasis on the early development of the intellect and their neglect of the physical aspects and physical well-being of the child.[16] The book was characterized by Albert Deutsch as "the most popular of works on psychosomatic medicine in the first half of the nineteenth century" and as "a pioneer American work in that aspect of mental hygiene known as child guidance." (Ref. 11, p. 327) Hunter and MacAlpine describe it as "a guide to mental hygiene with the stress on social influences."[17] In 1835, Brigham extended his mental hygiene efforts in *Observations on the Influence of Religion Upon the Health and Physical Welfare of Mankind*, in which one of his major conclusions was that "numerous meetings for religious purposes, night meetings, camp meetings, protracted meetings, &c., injure the health—cause insanity, and other diseases, and ought to be abandoned . . . ."[18]

Brigham was a strict dualist, convinced that the mind itself could not be diseased, "for that which is capable of disease and decay may die,"[19] but that mental illness was a disease solely of the brain. "The phrase *derangement of mind*, conveys an erroneous idea; for such derangement is only a symptom of disease in the head, and is not the primary affection. It is true that moral and mental causes may produce insanity, but they produce it by first occasioning either functional or organic disease of the brain." (Ref. 19, p. 20)

In 1840, Brigham became Superintendent of the Hartford Retreat, resigning after two years to become the first Superintendent of the State Lunatic Asylum at Utica, N.Y. It was here that he founded and published the *American Journal of Insanity* (AJI) which eventually became the official organ of the APA and in 1922 was renamed the *American Journal of Psychiatry*.

In 1843 Dr. William Sweetser published a book titled *Mental Hygiene*.[9] In his introduction, Sweetser said: "The mutual relationship and constant interchange of influence subsisting between our mental and corporeal natures can hardly have escaped even the most careless observation. The functions of either being disturbed, more or less derangement will almost necessarily be reflected to those of the other. What frame so hardy as to escape the agitations and afflictions of the mind? and what mind so firm as to remain unharmed amid the sufferings and infirmities of the body?" (Ref. 9, pp. ix-x) Like Brigham, but without mentioning him, Sweetser believed that the timing of formal schooling in relation to the development of the brain of the child was particularly important because "Premature and forced exertions of the mental faculties must always be at the risk of the physical constitution." (Ref. 9, p. 52)

In 1859, Dr. George Cook, founder of the private asylum Brigham Hall, in Canandaigua, N.Y., published a two-article series in the AJI titled "Mental Hygiene."[20] In explicit disagreement with Amariah Brigham who believed in a faculty psychology and a phrenological organization of the brain, Cook asserts, "We believe that the mind is a unit, that it has capacities and powers far beyond our present conception, that it is through the brain and nervous system that it manifests itself and is developed: we do not believe that it is made up of isolated faculties, one or more of which may be impaired or destroyed, leaving the remainder or that it is not influenced or modified by its material associations." (Ref. 20, p. 274)

In agreement with Brigham and Sweetser, Cook suggests that "Any tendency to undue nervous [system] development should attract the attention, and instead of being cherished by parental pride as a mark of precocity and promise, should give rise to a watchful anxiety; and especial care should be taken to retard the early growth of this dangerous element." (Ref. 20, p. 275) Cook is quite concerned with the mental hygiene of children. Allowing for the differences in vocabulary and style, many of his comments have a definite contemporary quality. "Children should be early impressed by the routine of daily life that there is a place for them in the home-circle, ever vacant in their absence. . . . " (Ref. 20, p. 275) He criticized parents "who, while professing to be guided by faith in truth and goodness, resort to deception and falsehood, too thinly veiled to deceive the quick perceptions of childhood." (Ref. 20. p. 280) And, finally, "We would have the thoughtful reader consider well the blighting effects of parental hypocrisy, spreading out into an unconscious social hypocrisy, which pervades many homes." (Ref. 20, p. 281)

Four years after the publication of Cook's articles, and four years before resigning from the Superintendency of Butler Hospital, Isaac Ray published *Mental Hygiene*. He had been thinking about the book long before it appeared, as evidenced in a letter he wrote to Edward Jarvis in 1855, inquiring "Do you know of anything lately published on the general subject of mental dietetics, within a year or two past? I except a translation of a little German book, which I have seen. To be guilty of a pun, I think of dieting for a book of that sort."[21] The German book was probably Ernst von Feuchtersleben's *Zur Diätetik der Seele* which had been translated into English as *The Hygiene of the Mind*.[22] What delayed the writing of the book and what made Ray abandon the phrase "mental dietetics" is unknown.

During the four years that followed the appearance of Cook's articles, how-ever, the materialist-spiritualist, mind-brain controversy had not diminished. Ray entered the arena and threw down the gauntlet in the opening pages of his book by stating, "The efficiency of the mental powers is determined in a high degree by the hygienic condition of the bodily organs, especially the brain . . . . the spiritual element of the mind has seemed to place it beyond the accidents of health and disease . . . . If the mind may be diseased, then it may perish, and so our hopes of immortality be utterly destroyed. This startling conclusion has been sufficient to deter the mass of mankind from admitting very heartily the facts which physiological and pathological inquiries have contributed to this sub-ject . . . . Thus they completely missed the principle which is the foundation of all true mental hygiene, viz that the manifestations of the mind and the organic condition of the brain are more or less affected by each other." (Ref. 21, pp. 1-2) This is an obvious, though unacknowledge, reference to Brigham's thesis in his *Remarks on the Influence of Mental Cultivation Upon Health.* (Ref. 19, p. 20)

Ray does explicitly recognize the limitations of the knowledge of his time when he points out that "the conditions of this relation,—the parts respectively borne by the bodily and the spiritual element in the production of the mental manifestations,—of course, are but imperfectly understood." (Ref. 8, p. 2) He proceeds to raise a question that parallels one often raised in our contemporary nature-nurture controversies: "Is the *development* of the mind a result exclusive-ly spiritual, or exclusively cerebral? . . . It may be doubted if it is quite correct to consider the individual as composed of two things essentially distinct both in origin and nature, instead of considering him as a being endowed with various powers which, though each serving a special purpose, form an harmonious whole —a single, individual man." (Ref. 8, p. 6) Ray derives from this "the general principle that whatever improves the physical qualities of the brain also improves, in some way or other, the qualities of the mind; and that judicious exercise of the mind is followed by the same result [in the brain]." (Ref. 8, p. 8)

This 1863 belief finds a 1974 confirmation in a review article in *Science* on research in environmental enrichment and its effects on brain chemistry and anatomy. "Many scientists have believed for some time that very early exper-iences are critical in intellectual and emotional development, but only within the last decade has it been demonstrated that the actual structure and chemistry of brain tissue are affected by differential rearing."[23] The conditions of rearing lab-oratory animals in an enriched environment includes raising them in groups with many playthings that are changed daily. "Berkeley scientists found that, com-pared with 'impoverished' rats, enriched rats had a heavier cerebral cortex, which is an area of the brain associated with intellectual functioning and infor-mation processing, and greater thickness of cortical tissue."[23] The "enrichment" is essentially psychological, and, as Isaac Ray postulated, exercise of the mind is followed by improvement in the physical qualities of the brain.

Ray offered, as a definition of mental hygiene, "the art of preserving the health of the mind against all the incidents and influences calculated to deterio-rate its qualities, impair its energies, or derange its movements. The management of the bodily powers in regard to exercise, rest, food, clothing, and climate; the laws of breeding, the government of the passions, the sympathy with current emotions and opinions, the discipline of the intellect,—all come within the province of mental hygiene." (Ref. 8, p. 15) Ray adds that the brain "being the instrument of the mind, its condition must necessarily affect the mental man-ifestations, and therefore, it may not be improper to speak of mental disorders as if the brain were the only agency concerned in them."

Ray proposes two requisites for a sound and vigorous mind: first, a brain free from hereditary or congenital "tendencies to disease or deterioration, and [second,] a healthy condition of the other bodily organs." (Ref. 8, p. 17) The first requirement, Ray would achieve by applying the "laws of breeding" to humans, or what later would be called eugenics. However, Ray's conception was not aimed toward some goal of monolithic perfection. In fact, he considered that such a goal was doomed to failure. "The fleet Arabian cannot be considered as nearer the point of equine perfection than the immense English dray-horse; nor would anyone but a Smithfield drover contend that a Berkshire or a Suffolk [pig] was a worthier specimen of the porcine race than the wild boar of the forest . . . . the general rule is that each special excellence is obtained at the expense of some other. So well is this now understood, that nobody attempts to obtain in one breed the excellences of all. Now what we seek for as the proper result and aim of mental cultivation is, not a particular endowment that may be transmitted from one generation to another, but a large range of capacity, great facility of achievment, and great power of endurance." (Ref. 8, pp. 13-14) Ray, in effect, was striving for the elimination of hereditary pathology, and here too, there is an appreciation of the integrated relationship of the psychological and the physical.

To illustrate his point about hereditary or congenital diseases, Ray speculated that "A complete history of the inmates of our jails and prisons, embracing all their antecedents, would show, in regard to a large proportion of them, that the active element was not immoral training, nor extraordinary temptations, but defective cerebral endowment . . . . They enter upon life with a cerebral organization deficient in those qualities necessary for the manifestation of the higher mental functions. Many of them are bad subjects from the cradle, and their whole life is a series of aggressions on their fellow-men. Whether they finish their career in a hospital or a prison, is a point oftener decided by adventitious circumstances than any definite, well-settled principles. The frequency of insanity among convicts in prison is, probably, not so much owing to the immediate circumstances of their position, as to this latent element of mischief in their mental constitution, which, no doubt, is rendered more active by confinement." (Ref. 8, pp. 21-22) Compare this with a mid-twentieth century statement by Bernard Diamond, professor of law and psychiatry: "The widespread electroencephalographic testing of habitual criminal offenders, sociopaths, and those with character disorders has revealed what many of us had long suspected: That [sic] many of these unfortunate individuals are suffering from an organic, neuro-physiological disease of the brain, which completely dominates their behavior."[24]

Further on in *Mental Hygiene*, in a somewhat different approach, Ray says: "In the *moral sense* or *faculty*, it is easy to recognize two different elements, viz the power to discern the distinction between right and wrong, virtue and vice, the honest and the base, and the disposition to pursue one and avoid the other. These elements, like those of the intellect, are unequally developed in different men, which inequality may be either congenital or produced in after life, by moral or physical causes. And thus though a person may act with perfect freedom of will, unconscious of any irresistible bias, yet it is obvious that his conduct is governed more by these variable conditions of his moral nature, than by any abstract notions formed by the intellect [emphasis in the original]." (Ref.8, pp. 61-62) How much like Freud that last sentence could sound. Let us, however, contrast these words with those of Bernard Diamond, who, a century after the publication of *Mental Hygiene*, speaking of criminals with brain disease, says, "Their appearance of normalcy, their apparent ability to exercise free will, choice, and decision (and somehow invariably choose the wrong instead of the right) is purely a facade, an artifact that conceals the extent to which they are victims of their own brain pathology." (Ref. 24, p. 198)

As Ray's definition indicated, he did not conceive of mental hygiene as involving simply a hereditarian approach. Mental hygiene problems required practical, multiple, and coordinated approaches. "But while we are bringing to bear upon [the poor and the criminal] all the kindly influences of learning and religion, let us not overlook those physical agencies which determine the efficiency of the brain as the material instrument of the mind. The tract and the missionary may do good service in the dwellings of the ignorant and depraved, but active ventilation, thorough sewerage, abundance of water, will be found, eventually, no less efficient in the work of reform and elevation. To check the increase of crime, improve, if you please, your penal legislation and penal discipline, but, above all things, improve the dwellings of the poor. Render industry and virtue as attractive as possible, but never cease, by all practicable means, to prevent the production of tubercle, rickets, scrofula, and all defective or unequal developments." (Ref. 8, p. 23) But that was more than a century ago, and now is merely history.

Like Brigham, Sweetser, and Cook, Ray had fairly definite views on child education practices and their relation to mental health. Like these others, Ray was critical of the social pressure to have children learn at a very young age and to be encouraged in intellectual or academic precocity. "There is another kind of cerebral labor in regard to which it is of the utmost importance that the theory and practice of the community should be correct,—I mean that which is imposed upon the young in the process of education, under the name of study . . . . Here, as in everything else, speed is the great test of merit. Lesson is piled upon lesson, the hours of study are increased, and the active, irritable brain of tender youth is habitually forced to the utmost power of effort." (Ref. 8, p. 117-118) "It is the law of the animal economy that the various organs do not arrive at their full maturity of vigor and power, until some time after the adult age has fairly commenced. To suppose the youthful brain to be capable of an amount of task-work which is considered an ample allowance to an adult brain, is simply absurd, and the attempt to carry this folly into effect must necessarily be dangerous to the health and efficiency of this organ." (Ref. 8, p. 121-122)

"The precise period at which school instruction should begin will vary a little, of course, in different children; but I feel quite safe in saying that it should seldom be until the sixth or seventh year. Not that the mind should be kept in a state of inactivity until this time, for that is impossible. It will necessarily be receiving impressions from the external world, and these will begin the work of stimulating and unfolding its various faculties. Instinctively the young child seeks for knowledge of some kind, and its spontaneous efforts may be safely allowed." (Ref. 8, pp. 135-136) Ray used practically the same words in an address he gave, in 1850, to a group of Rhode Island educators.[25]

It should be noted that these themes are not restricted to nineteenth century America. George Mora, in a recent publication, compared the thinking of the seventeenth century Italian philosopher, Giambattista Vico, and Jean Piaget, and found similar themes in the works of these two men.[26] Incidentally, Mora also refers to contemporary and, perhaps, characteristic American interest in accelerating infant preschool education. (Ref. 26, p. 376)

Ray's observation that the child will be "receiving impressions from the external world, and that these will begin the work of stimulating and unfolding its various faculties," certainly calls to mind much of the new and exciting work in ethology and the researches on the remarkable influence that the presence or absence of early sensory stimulation has on the subsequent anatomy and functional capacity of sensory and information processing areas of the brain.[23, 27, 28] The combination of nineteenth century conceptions regarding differential development of mental faculties with twentieth century laboratory findings leads me to speculate that we may soon be reading about epigenetic epistemology as a refinement and development of the current concept of genetic epistemology. But that is for some other discussion.

I should like to return to Ray's definition of mental hygiene, specifically the phrase "the sympathy with current emotions and opinions." Ray did not use the term "sympathy" in its current sense, but rather in its older meaning, such as the sympathetic vibrations of a violin string. In Ray's sense, sympathy refers to a compulsive, extrapersonal force to which the individual responds passively and, frequently, unconsciously, as a function of his own structure.

Ray said, "A principle more prompt and impulsive than the slow and cautious deductions of reason is required to meet all the exigencies of the social state; and its existence, in some of its forms at least, has long been recognized under the names of *sympathy* and *propensity to imitate*. It is in ceaseless operation wherever men are gathered together; but whether quietly and irresistibly upon scattered individuals, or with tremendous manifestations of its power upon large masses, few are aware of its nature—many not even of its existence—and fewer still apprehend the importance of rightly regulating its influence upon themselves. . . . Independent, self-originating movement is, probably, a far rarer thing than that which springs, more or less directly, from some outward source, which is to be found in the prevailing mental movements that, like the atmosphere about us, exert an increasing, unconscious, inevitable pressure . . . . By an irresistible and inevitable law, they impart their own moral complexion to whatever they involve in their progress . . . . We are instinctively impelled—some more, some less, strongly—to imitate whatever others are feeling and doing around us. The passion or emotion exhibited by one excites the same passion or emotion in others. . . . Whoever lives in close communion with one who is irascible, peevish, and overbearing, is liable to become equally irascible and peevish . . . . The sad, depressed, and sorrowing spirit will inevitably impart its leaden tinge to all who live within its shadow . . . . Over and above the appeal made by every example to the reasoning faculties, there is an instinctive tendency to admire what others admire, to seek distinction where it is sought by others, to fall into the same social routine which is followed in the community around us. In this process of assimilation the intellect is entirely passive, and the result is accomplished without calculation, almost unconsciously. The individual is transformed without being aware of the change." (Ref. 8. pp. 156-162) Space does not allow me to expand upon the parallels and associations to contemporary psychoanalytic psychologies, including those of Freud and Sullivan; however, the idea is much broader and extends to other behavioral disciplines and other cultures.

The 1911 edition of the *Encyclopedia Brittanica* article on "Imitation" says: "There is among the majority of adults a tendency to assimilate themselves either to their society or to those whom they especially admire or respect: this tendency to shun the eccentric is deeply rooted in human psychology. Moreover, even among highly developed persons the imitative impulse frequently overrides the reason, as when an audience, a crowd, or even practically a whole community is carried away by a panic for which no adequate ground has been given, or when a cough or a yawn is imitated by a company of people . . . . The universality of the imitative impulse has led many psychologists to regard it as an instinct (cf. William James), and in that large class of imitative actions which have no obvious ulterior purpose the impulse certainly appears to be instinctive in its character."[29] Later, during the period of the first World War, Trotter's book on the "herd instinct" appeared, based on the phenomena referred to by Ray and others.[30] In 1945, Trotter's work constituted a significant portion of the psychology presented in the textbook used in my college abnormal psychology course.[31] And today, we find the same phenomenon being studied in ethology and sociobiology, as, for instance, the cultural transmission of potato washing in Japanese macaque monkeys.[32] Contemporary studies of humans indicate that the same principle may be involved in the unconscious synchronization of biorhythms such as menstrual periodicity among cohabiting groups of women[33] or the synchronization of temperature cycles of men to those of the women they live with, when those women are not controlling their menstrual cycles with the "pill."[34-36]

Earlier, I referred to the materialist-spiritualist controversy that still raged at the time of the publication of Ray's *Mental Hygiene* and to his throwing down the gauntlet in the opening pages of his book. That gauntlet was picked up by his colleague, John P. Gray, editor of the AJI, who said in a review, "[Ray's] doctrine is that the mental phenomena have only one origin, the physical organization; whence it follows that there can be but one mode of treating them, which is from the side of natural laws. This is simply the doctrine of the old phrenologists, and is, we think, fairly exploded and obsolete .... Aside from the one fatal doctrine, so persistently urged ... we can only speak in terms of unqualified admiration of the whole book. As it is, we confess to a feeling of impatience that so much matter of the highest importance to the welfare of the community should be deprived of its practical value by the union with a false philosophy of a past age."[37]

It is ironic that only thirteen years after having published his antimaterialistic review of Ray's book, John P. Gray, in an address on mental hygiene to the International Medical Congress at Philadelphia (on the occasion of our nation's centennial celebration), said, "Indeed we must start with the proposition that what is now denominated Mental Hygiene is practically inseparable from Physical Hygiene."[38]

Since much has been written of Ray's interest in phrenology, it may be worth while to cite here what Ray said about phrenology in the early part of *Mental Hygiene*. "It was reserved for our own day, however, to see ... a complete and systematic body of doctrine, in which every portion of the cortical substance of the brain is assigned to some particular faculty, sentiment, or propensity, each of which is regarded as an original, innate independent power, exercised by its appropriate organ. In the localization of these organs the founders of Phrenology profess to have been guided solely by observation; but they also endeavor, in every instance, to show that the necessities of the human economy require such a power. In the latter branch of their system, they have been more fortunate, perhaps, than in the former. In a few instances, both the existence and the place of the organ have been established by abundant proof; but, with these exceptions, the evidence has not satisfied the deliberate and unbiassed judgement of scientific men. As a speculative theory, it unquestionably contains much truth, recognized as such, too, by many who have little sympathy with its anatomical doctrines. Its analysis of the mental phenomena is clear and precise, indicating— what metaphysical inquiries seldom have—a shrewd observation of springs of action, and a profound insight of the relations of man to the sphere in which he moves. Deficient as it is, as a theory of mind, it is nevertheless valuable as having indicated the true mode of investigation, and especially for the light it throws on the whole process of education and development." (Ref. 8, pp. 8-10)

This review of Isaac Ray and mental hygiene in nineteenth century America must, of necessity, remain incomplete. I have not touched upon his views on temperance and alcoholism,[39] exercise, sleep, diet, novels, the epidemic nature of suicide, and many other factors falling within his concept of mental hygiene. I hope that you will make the opportunity to read *Mental Hygiene*, as well as Ray's other publications. I should like to close with a paraphrase of a statement George Santayana made in *The Life of Reason or the Phases of Human Progress*. "Progress, far from consisting [merely] in change, depends [largely] on retentiveness. When change is absolute there remains no being to improve and no direction is set for possible improvement: and when experience is not retained . . . infancy is perpetual."[40]

REFERENCES

1. QUEN, J.M. 1964. Isaac Ray and his "Remarks on pathological anatomy." Bull. Hist. Med. 38: 113-126.
2. RAY, I. 23 March 1854, manuscript letter to Parker Cleaveland, Alumni Archives, Alumni Office, Bowdoin College, Brunswick, Maine.
3. DIAMOND, B. 1956. Isaac Ray and the trial of Daniel M'Naghten. Am. J. Psychiat. 112: 655.
4. RAY, I. 1838. A Treatise on the Medical Jurisprudence of Insanity. Charles C. Little and James Brown. Boston, Mass. Reprint edition. 1962. Winfred Overholser, Ed.: 8. The Belknap Press of Harvard University Press. Cambridge, Mass.
5. RAY, I. 1846. Observations on the principal hospitals for the insane in Great Britain, France, and Germany. AJI 2: 289-390.
6. KIRKBRIDE E. B. 1879. Manuscript letter to Dorothea L. Dix, Dec. 15. Dorothea L. Dix Collection. Houghton Library. Harvard University, Cambridge, Mass.
7. RAY, I. 1880. Manuscript letter to Dorothea L. Dix, Nov. 29. Dorothea L. Dix Collection. Houghton Library. Harvard University, Cambridge, Mass.
8. RAY, I. 1863. Mental Hygiene. Ticknor and Fields. Boston, Mass.
9. SWEETSER, W. 1843. Mental Hygiene, or an Examination of the Intellect and Passions, Designed to Illustrate Their Influence on Health and the Duration of Life. J. & H. G. Langley. New York, N.Y.
10. OXFORD ENGLISH DICTIONARY, Compact Edition. 1971.: 1358. Oxford University Press. New York, N.Y.
11. DEUTSCH, A. 1944. The history of mental hygiene. *In* One Hundred Years of American Psychiatry. J. K. Hall, *et al.*, Eds.: 332. Columbia University Press. New York, N.Y.
12. BUCHAN, W. 1769. Domestic Medicine; or, the Family Physician: Being an Attempt to Render the Medical Art More Generally Useful, by Shewing People What is in Their own Power Both With Respect to the Prevention and Cure of Diseases. Chiefly Calculated to Recommend a Proper Attention to Regimen and Simple Medicines: 508-509, 516. Balfour, Auld, and Smellie. Edinburgh, Scotland.
13. FALCONER, W. 1788. A Dissertation on the Influence of the Passions Upon Disorders of the Body: 42-45, 59-61, 70-83, and *passim*. C. Dilly and J. Phillips. London, England.
14. RUSH, B. 1812. Medical Inquiries and Observations Upon the Diseases of the Mind. Kimber and Richardson. Philadelphia, Pa.
15. HOSACK, D. 1838. Lectures on the Theory and Practice of Physic, Delivered in the College of Physicians and Surgeons of the University of the State of New York. Henry Ducachet, Ed. Herman Hooker. Philadelphia, Pa.
16. BRIGHAM, A. 1832. Remarks on the Influence of Mental Cultivation Upon Health. F. J. Huntington. Hartford, Conn.
17. HUNTER, R. & I. MACALPINE. 1863. Three Hundred Years of Psychiatry: 1535-1860. A History Presented in Selected English Texts: 822. Oxford University Press. London, England.
18. BRIGHAM, A. 1835. Observations on the Influence of Religion Upon the Health and Physical Welfare of Mankind: 331-332. Marsh, Capen & Lyon. Boston, Mass.
19. BRIGHAM, A. 1833. Remarks on the Influence of Mental Cultivation and Mental Excitement Upon Health: 20. 2nd edit. Marsh, Capen & Lyon. Boston, Mass.
20. COOK, G. 1859. Mental hygiene. AJI 15: 272-282, 353-365.
21. RAY, I. 1855. Manuscript letter to Edward Jarvis, Nov. 3. Edward Jarvis Collection, The Francis A. Countway Library of Medicine. Harvard University. Cambridge, Mass.

22. VON FEUCHTERSLEBEN, E. 1838. Zur Diätetik der Seele. Armbruster. Vienna. The Hygiene of the Mind. (Trans. by Aimé Ouvry.) 1852. Churchill. London, England.
23. WALLACE, P. 1974. Complex environments: effects on brain development. Science 185: 1035.
24. DIAMOND, B. 1962. From M'Naghten to Currens and beyond. Cal. Law Rev. 50: 198.
25. RAY, I. 1851. Education in its Relation to the Physical Health of the Brain. A Lecture Delivered Before the Rhode Island Institute of Instruction, Oct. 18, 1850. Ticknor, Reed, and Fields. Boston, Mass.
26. MORA, G. 1976. Vico, Piaget, and genetic epistemology. In Giambattista Vico's Science of Humanity. G. Tagliacozzo and D.P. Verene, Eds.: 365-392; 375, 376, 381, and passim.
27. VAN DER LOOS, H. & T.A. WOOLSEY. 1973. Somatosensory cortex: structural alterations following early injury to sense organs. Science 179: 395-397.
28. BLAKE, R. & H.V.B. HIRSCH. 1975. Deficits in binocular depth perception in cats after alternating monocular deprivation. Science 190: 1114-1116.
29. ENCYCLOPEDIA BRITANNICA. 1910. Eleventh edit., 14: 332. The Encyclopedia Britannica Co. New York, N.Y.
30. TROTTER, W. 1916. The Instincts of the Herd in Peace and War. T.F. Unwin. London, England.
31. HART, B. 1931. The Psychology of Insanity. 4th edit. The Macmillan Co. New York, N.Y.
32. WILSON, E.O. 1975. Sociobiology: The New Synthesis: 51. The Belknap Press of Harvard University Press. Cambridge, Mass.
33. MCCLINTOCK, M.K. 1971. Menstrual synchrony and suppression. Nature 229: 244-45.
34. MEDICAL TRIBUNE. 1976. Men's temperature changes equated to menstrual cycle. April 14: 9. Medical Tribune. New York, N.Y.
35. HENDERSON, M. 1975. The menstrual cycle and evidence for a male hormonal cycle. Health 25: 7.
36. AUSTRALIAN MED. ASS. GAZETTE. April 1, 1976.
37. GRAY, J.P. 1864. Mental Hygiene by I. Ray. AJI 20: 338-342.
38. GRAY, J.P. 1878. Mental hygiene. AJI 34: 307.
39. QUEN, J.M. 1967. Isaac Ray on drunkenness. Bull. Hist. Med. 41: 342-348.
40. SANTAYANA, G. 1905. The Life of Reason or the Phases of Human Progress. Vol. I. Introduction and Reason in Common Sense: 284. Charles Scribners Sons. New York, N.Y.

BENJAMIN RUSH AND MENTAL HEALTH*

Eric T. Carlson

*Section on the History of Psychiatry and the Behavioral Sciences
Department of Psychiatry
New York Hospital - Cornell Medical Center
New York, New York 10021*

Benjamin Rush discusses the problems with England and the need for naval action on the high seas in a letter he wrote to Thomas Jefferson on March 15, 1813. Although largely devoted to political affairs, as he approaches its end he shifts subjects and states: "I have lately published a volume of inquiries upon the diseases of the mind. They have been well received by the public. If you wish to look into them, I shall do myself the pleasure of sending you a copy of them. The few sands that remain in my glass urge me constantly to quicken my labors. My next work will be entitled, 'Hygiene, or Rules for the Preservation of Health accommodated to the climate, diet, manners, and habits of the people of the United States.' All the imperfections of both these publications must be ascribed to a conviction that my time in this world must necessarily be short."[1] Rush did not realize how little time he actually had, for within a month he was dead from an acute infection. He did not live to complete his book on hygiene on which he had been laboring for at least six years.

HAPPINESS AND HEALTH

Rush ends his letter with the following salutation: "From, dear sir, your sincere old friend of 1775." Rush here recalls the days of their meeting and the excitement of participating in the Second Continental Congress of 1775-1776. As is well known, Jefferson was largely responsible for drafting the Declaration of Independence, and Rush was proud to be able to affix his signature to it as a representative from the State of Pennsylvania. As a way of introducing Rush's concepts of health, let us begin by turning to the stirring words of Jefferson as given in his own draft: "We hold these truths to be self evident: that all men are created equal; that they are endowed by their Creator with inherent and unalienable rights: that among these are life, liberty, and the pursuit of happiness:."[2] It was God who made these rights inherent; He put them into nature; consequently, they became known as the natural rights of which five are most frequently mentioned: life, liberty, property, conscience, and happiness. The quest for happiness was an important preoccupation of the eighteenth century. As Alexander Pope (familiar to Rush) wrote in his *Essay on Man* (1732-1734), "Oh Happiness! Our Being's End and Aim! Good. Pleasure. Ease. Content. Whate'er thy Name!"[3] That happiness in itself is a complex concept may be illustrated by Jefferson's own words: "Our greatest happiness . . . is always the result of a good conscience, good health, occupation, and freedom in all just pursuits." "Be assiduous in learning, take much exercise for your health, and practice much virtue. Health, learning, and virtue will insure your happiness."[4]

*Background research for this study was supported in part by National Institutes of Health grant LM00919 from the National Library of Medicine.

Rush would certainly have agreed with their views, for he felt that health and virtue were both vital for man's proper functioning and therefore for his happiness. Rush, being medically orientated, quite naturally shifted to another of Pope's words, "pleasure," to be considered a vital ingredient of happiness and wrote, "I shall consider pleasure as a unit; in which I shall include all those sensations that are known by the names of agreeable, gay, delightful, joyful, and rapturous. They are all the effects of impressions acting with different degrees of force, and upon different parts of the body." He continues, "Pleasure is not only one of the ingredients of health; but its deficiency and its excess are frequent cause of disease."[5] †

To support his hypothesis that pleasure and disease are interrelated, Rush turns to two quite different sources. "It is no new opinion that pleasure and pain are related to each other. The fable of Socrates long ago taught the world that pleasure and pain, were originally sisters; that they met with different lots in life: the one being accepted everywhere; the other avoided and hated. Upon viewing this different reception of these two sisters in the world, the fable adds that Jupiter joined them together in such a manner, that whosoever embraced one, could not avoid embracing the other." (Ref. 5, p. 228)

THE ORIGIN OF EVIL AND SICKNESS

Rush goes on to his second point, "It will be necessary ... to remark, that since the loss of primeval innocence, pain appears to be the natural state of man." (Ref. 5, p. 183) Rush literally meant this; although he showed a great Enlightenment interest in science and naturalism and was liberal in many of his religious views, he never wavered from a fundamental belief that his world belonged to God. God created the world and makes it run, and man's salvation lies in God's grace through man's acceptance of Christ, was Rush's creed. Man's pride led to his disobedience to God and to the banishment from the Garden of Eden. (The name Eden comes from a Hebrew word meaning pleasure.) The male was condemned to "toil and sweat" while the female would experience pain in childbirth. Both were given the death sentence; they would return to their original Dust.

Rush incorporates biblical history into his Lectures on Pathology as follows: "The origin of sickness and death like the origin of evil must be sought for in the fall of man. It is true the execution of the death sentence which was pronounced upon him in consequence of his disobedience was suspended beyond the day in which it was denounced, but the causes which finally produced his death began to act on his system as soon as he lost the image of his Maker."[6]

Rush continues: "I shall divide evil into two kinds: *Physical* and *Moral*. *Physical* includes the evils which exist in the human body, and in the globe. *Moral* includes the evils which exist in the mind."[7]

The close connection between sin, vice, and disease follows easily from Rush's belief that God's solitary hand provides a comprehensible and unified quality to the world; "as one Sin [i.e., pride] introduced all the vanity and complications

†Rush's manuscript lectures on physiology to the medical students of the University of Pennsylvania are owned by the Library Company of Philadelphia and were used through the courtesy of Edwin Wolf II, Librarian. The portion on the faculties of the mind is at the College of Physicians of Philadelphia, where the late Walter B. McDaniel II was most helpful. Rush's various lectures on medicine, pathology, and therapeutics are also at the Library Company.

of Sin, so one disease, viz. debility, produced all the vanity and complication of diseases."[8] "The analogy of disease and evil you see is very *striking*. 1. One cause, viz. debility, has introduced all the diseases of the human body. In like manner one cause, viz. debility, in the will introduced all the moral evil into our world. 2. Both these effects innumerable. Who can number all the mortifications, diseases of the body, or all the vices of the mind in all their almost infinite variety of forms-degrees-and combinations?"[7]

Ultimately, the only solution for man's weakness (debility) comes from "good, in the form of power and love." The final good is brought to man from God through Christ in the form of the Holy Spirit. Late in his life Rush depended more heavily on heavenly salvation; in his earlier, more hopeful and vigorous years he shared both the scientific optimism of the Enlightenment and the newer religious millennialism[9] that anticipated rapid progress toward God by the increasing understanding and manipulation of nature. Rush fervently believed in this earthly salvation and saw his medical theory as a major contribution in that direction. Diseases could be treated successfully, but, more important, could be prevented through proper hygiene. Because our focus today is on the mental rather than the physical aspects of hygiene, we run the risk of some distortion. Rush saw both as whole, but his emphasis on an eighteenth century type of stimulus-response theory, that keeps the excitability and excitement in the body stable, brings us naturally into the sensory system. In his lectures on pleasures he discusses the proper uses of both the senses and the faculties of the mind in order to achieve not only pleasure but health.[10]

THE SENSES AND HEALTH

Rush follows the traditional number of senses, five in number, and discusses them in the following order: touch, taste, smell, vision, and sound. He remarks on their relationship to the body: "In a word, our bodies may be compared to a violin: The senses are its strings; everything beatiful and sublime in nature and art is its bow; the Creator is the hand that moves it; and pleasure, nearly constant pleasure, their necessary effect." (Ref. 5, p. 224) The senses follow the laws of sensation; some are increased by repetition, others are not. The sense of smell is of short duration, hearing lasts longer, whereas taste and seeing allow for the most complex and "durable pleasures." For Rush, the final purpose of the pleasures "must be obvious to you all. They prompt us to eat, to drink, and to propagate our species. They impel us to action and to rest. They allure us from our beds in the morning, and drive us to them in the evening. They invite us to explore the works of nature and art. They are the channels through which health is communicated to the body, and pleasure and activity to the mind; and they should be the avenues through which we should be conducted to the great and original fountain of more durable and substantial happiness." (Ref. 5, p. 236) There is the risk, however, that the senses may be subject to misuse through either overstimulating or understimulating the given sense.

Another danger lurking close by is the misuse of the sense either in terms of timing or in the disregard of the socially and morally appropriate ways of its utilization. To demonstrate these concepts, we shall select two senses: touch and taste. Touch subsumes motion and is used to illustrate the need for adequate stimulation. Touch includes sex (which also partakes of qualities of an appetite and a passion); here the risks are more complicated, being a blend of excessive and inappropriate use. Taste, in turn, presents a clear-cut example of overuse.

Rush believes that motion or exercise is essential to the pleasures and development of childhood. But there is something even more fundamental. "Man was formed to be active. The vigour of his mind, and the health of his body can be fully preserved by no other means than by labour of some sort. Hence, when we read the sentence which was pronounced upon man after the fall, 'That in the sweat of his brow he should eat bread all the days of his life.' We cannot help admiring the goodness of the Supreme Being, in connecting his punishment with what had now become the necessary means of preserving his health. Had God abandoned him to idleness, He would have entailed tenfold misery upon him."[11]

Rush lashes out at the vice of idleness, which, after all, was a portion of sloth, one of the seven cardinal sins, and at slavery, which was one of the social parameters that made idleness possible. He was particularly distressed to see the idleness of the American Indian males. Higher social class also brought its risks, and in one of his earliest publications, *Sermons to Gentlemen upon Temperance and Exercise* (1772), Rush discussed his view that the laborers of the world enjoyed better health. The idleness that wealth would bring should be counteracted by planned exercise, which would be either passive or active in nature. The passive ones include sailing (Rush even cites later the pleasures of balloon flights) riding in carriages, and, even better, the more vigorous effects of horseback riding. Health-promoting active exercises include walking, dancing, swimming, fencing, and a variety of others, including the currently fashionable custom of golf. Today we might consider sexual activity as a form of exercise, but Rush saw it differently.

We have spoken of two of the cardinal sins (pride and sloth); another is lust or lechery. Rush speaks "Of Lust" in his unpublished lectures: "This is an appetite so intimately connected with the passions, and with moral evil . . . ."[12] He often calls it a venereal desire or speaks of the "propagation of the species," which is used as a euphemism for sexual intercourse. It was implanted by God for just that purpose and therefore had to be both healthy and desirable. Nevertheless, the risks involved with it seem to be almost insurmountable to a modern reader. As Rush says: "Its excessive and unlawful gratification constitutes a disease of both the body and the mind."

Lust partakes of many roots, but when discussing pleasure, Rush puts it under the category of the sense of touch. He waxes almost poetic as he describes the gentle and artistic points of contact between the two sexes in the persons of Angelica and Medoro in the widely admired painting of his fellow Philadelphian, Benjamin West. This represents the lowest grade of sexual pleasure, kissing is more intense, while "propagation of the species" is the largest; Rush only lists these without elaborating.

To maintain mental health in this essential area of human behavior, it is vital to avoid excessive and inappropriate sexual activity. Rush has a number of suggestions. Most of these are various means of avoiding the stimulation of sexual desires. Because food is the basic source of energy for the body, Rush recommends a "low diet" to reduce sexual drive and even mentions the diet utilized personally and effectively by a Dr. [William (?)] Stark which consisted of bread and water. Idleness and a sedentary life also creates increased sexual temptation; Rush counsels the usefulness of work or, if this is not possible, constant exercise. He recommends horseback riding, which has been a traditional exercise since the time of Hippocrates. Women are seen as a source of dangerous appeal to the male sexual appetite. Loose and wanton women are to be avoided completely; if one must be with women, one should seek only "the company of chaste and modest women." But he continues, "The avoiding of all dalliance with the female sex is a powerful security against the dominion of this appetite." As an example he cites a man of Philadelphia "who assured me that he had gained a complete victory over his venereal disires by a strict attention to this directive. Such was his caution in avoiding everything that could excite them, that he never saluted a woman upon any occasion—nor ever took one of the sex by the hand. In the consequence of this means, in the course of seven years he assured me that he had never violated the 7th commandment by an unchaste wish or thought."[12] In a similar fashion, a clergyman whom Rush knew always avoided looking a woman in the face. Consequently, it also was essential that a man avoid all kinds of internal lascivious thoughts and all events that might provoke them, such as looking at obscene pictures, reading obscene books, and participating in obscene conversations that would inflame the imagination.

Matrimony is the solution par excellence for sexual desires, but even this step has dangers if one is tempted to be unfaithful. Rush is particularly revolted by what he calls the uncleanness of North American Indians; "They are . . . strangers to the obligations both of morality and decency, as far as they relate to the marriage bed."[13] The social setting of sexual release is therefore important to mental health. "The solitary vice of onanism," for example, seems to be dangerous in the extreme. Rush follows and abets the rising crescendo of concern in the 18th century with the dangers of masturbation. But excessive sexual outlets, promiscuity, and onanism, all ran the risk of producing a variety of disorders from impotence to tuberculosis to death.

It might seem that no sexual indulgence would be the safer course. Not so, although Rush is clearly ambiguous on this subject. In his *Disease of the Mind* he says: "When [the venereal desire is] restrained, it produces tremors, a flushing of the face, sighing, nocturnal pollutions, hysteria, hypochondriases, and in women the furor uterinus."[14] He presents no such clinical cases, however, and in the following quotation suggests that the lack of sexual outlet is no impediment to health and success. In his discussion of ways to avoid sexual responsiveness he advocates, "close application of the mind to business, or study of any kind, more especially to the mathematics. Sir Isaac Newton conquered this appetite by means of the latter study, and the late Dr. [John] Fothergill by constant application to business. Both these great and good men lived and died batchelors, and both declared, upon their death beds, that they never had known, in a single instance, a criminal connection with the female sex." (Ref. 14, p. 355)

We leave the topic of human sexual activity with the uneasy feeling that this is a dangerous performance at best and that Rush has not greatly assisted us by demonstrating what the tolerable limits might be. One of his precautions for avoiding the temptations of sex that we have not mentioned leads us into our next topic, that of the risks of alcohol and drunkenness.

Another of the seven sins is that of gluttony; an intemperance in the intake of food and drink, which Rush discusses under the sense of taste. He explores various aspects of eating and digestion in his lectures, but today we will focus only on his comments about drinking. His attention to this topic starts early in life. His *Sermons* of 1772 starts with "On Temperance in Eating" and then moves on to the second sermon, "On the Use and Abuse of Wine and Strong Drink" before ending on exercise. Even at this early date, he is fairly liberal in his view of the use of fermented beverages such as wine and beer; but he does advise that wine should really not be drunk until a person approaches his fortieth birthday. Later he says that fermented beverages contain so little spirits and are associated with other unpleasant side effects if taken in quantity that they rarely produce intoxication.

In 1784 Rush composed a little pamphlet entitled *An Enquiry into the Effects of Spirituous Liquors*, which was destined to be his most popular publication; by 1820 it had gone through nineteen separate printings, and the American Tract Society later reported they had printed 172,000 copies by 1850 (Ref. 1, p. 273). Ardent spirits are those that are obtained from the distillation of fermented liquors; their effects may be considered as acute or chronic. Rush presents a devastatingly accurate list of various behaviors seen as the drinker progressed from mild social intoxication to the point of drinking to unconsciousness. Chronic effects on the body range from a bulbous red nose to symptoms of liver disease to episodes of seizures. "Not less destructive are the effects of ardent spirits upon the human mind. They impair the memory, debilitate the understanding, and pervert the moral faculties. It was probably from observing these effects of intemperance in drinking upon the mind, that a law was formerly passed in Spain which excluded drunkards from being witnesses in a court of justice. But the demoralizing effects of distilled spirits do not stop here. They produce not only falsehood, but fraud, theft, uncleanliness, and murder. Like the demoniac mentioned in the New Testament, their name is 'Legion,' for they convey into the soul a host of vices and crimes."[15] Rush continues by illustrating how destructive drunkenness is to the family and society. His constant amalgam of physiology, social reform, and theology is well exemplified by the "Moral Thermometer" illustration which he published separately in 1789, but which came to be a standard addition to his ardent spirits pamphlet. On one scale he proceeds from the purity of water down to the fiendish ardent spirits of rum, gin, and brandy. As one goes down the graduations, parallel and comparative scales compare the results not only on health, but also on a series of resulting vices and punishments. The latter include idleness, fighting, fraud, murder, and suicide, with accompanying debt, hunger, jail and gallows. The worst vice of all that Rush identifies is chronic and heavy drinking, which is self-destructive and when it leads to death, he says, it is a form of self-murder or suicide.

The solution to the problem of these examples of boorish behavior, multiple diseases, and morally corrupting vices is, naturally, to avoid the use of ardent spirits. For this reason Rush was widely acclaimed by the temperance movement of the nineteenth century as their intellectual founder.

FACULTIES OF THE MIND AND HEALTH

We have seen in the above account the effects of alcohol on some of the faculties of the mind. These faculties, like the senses, are subject to neglect, over-stimulation and misuse. Rush's psychology is sensationalistic, but more basic to his theory are the "internal senses," which are made up of a series of interlocking faculties and their shared operations.[16] The principal operations are sensation, perception, association, judgment, reasoning, and volition. The misuse of one of them, association, may lead to madness. Rush cites book sellers as an example, for their minds have to shift quickly from one subject to another, depending on the demands of their customers (Ref. 14, p. 37) Based perhaps on an accurate observation of the flight of ideas of an excited person, Rush reasons from the symptom and supplies a cause. Strongly influenced by Scottish philosophers, Rush simplifies their complex faculty psychology to only nine fundamental functions. They may be divided into three groups: The intellectual faculties (understanding, memory, and imagination), the moral faculties (the moral sense, conscience, and the sense of deity), and the three remaining miscellaneous ones of will, the principle of faith, and the passions. Rush introduces this, his second class of pleasures, as follows: "In listening to the detail of the pleasures of the mind, I am about to deliver, I beg you to recollect, that they are all of a medicinal nature; and that they have often cured diseases which have baffled the most powerful remedies that have been taken from the vegetable and mineral kingdoms. They have, further, the great advantage over most of them, in being cheap, and at all times agreeable to sick people."

All the faculties of the mind play a role in the maintenance of mental health; we shall select only the passions to illustrate Rush's manner of thinking. Rush follows Thomas Reid in dividing the internal senses into those that are active and those that are passive. He recognizes that the division is limited in value, for some of the faculties variably partake of both qualities; the passions, however, are clearly active. "Passion is a generic word. I shall include in it propensities, affections, passions properly so called, and emotions. The *propensities* include the appetite for food and sexual appetite. The *affections* include domestic attachments, compassion, friendship, benevolence, etc. The *Passions* properly so called have for their objects *future* good, or *future* evil. They are accompanied with desire, or aversion. The former are chiefly love, hope, ambition, and avarice; the latter are hatred, malice, fear, envy and the like. Emotions are such vehement impressions of the objects of the passions upon the mind, as to produce bodily actions or motions. Joy, anger, terror and astonishment are all emotions. They are generally produced by present good or present evil." (Ref. 5, pp. 2:45-46, 238) These descriptions are basically ancient ones, coming through the intellectual traditions of Plato, Aristotle, and St. Thomas Acquinas. One should also note that they include the remainder of the cardinal sins: avarice, envy, and wrath. Four of these passions, according to Rush, are especially liable "to derangement, or to an unreasonable and morbid excess." (Ref. 14, p. 314.) These are: love, grief, fear, and anger. Let us look at two of these emotional states: love and anger.

Love, Rush asserts, "becomes a disease only when it is disappointed in its object." Apparently, excessive sexual excitement is possible, but not love. Love in its requited state is "an inexhaustible source of mental pleasure" and "creates a little heaven upon earth." (Ref. 5, p. 247) Unrequited love brings minor symptoms of distress, or if severe may lead to "dyspepsia, hysteria, hypochondriasis, fever, and madness." These may be prevented by psysical or psychological remedies. Rush suggests constant employment, the avoidance of the loved one, or counteracting the love with another passion, such as the admirable one of ambition. He also had found, in several clinical instances, success in Ovid's recommendation that the man find a new mistress in replacement of his unsuccessful love. If this is not possible, then a form of behavior therapy should be used. "Ovid, advises an unsuccessful lover to find out, and dwell upon all the bad qualities, and defects in person and accomplishments, of his mistress. 'If she have a bad voice (says he) press her to sing, if she touch a musical instrument clumsily, beg her to expose herself by playing upon one of them.' " (Ref. 14, pp. 315-316)

Turning to anger, Rush says: "This passion was implanted in the human mind for wise and useful purposes. Its exercises, within certain limits, are admitted in the scriptures. It is only when it ascends to rage and fury, or when it is protracted into malice and revenge, that it becomes a sin and a disease." (Ref. 14, p. 333.) A number of methods are available to prevent the development of abnormal anger.

When anger arises from envy or malice, Rush once thought that little could be done about these deep-seated vices beyond turning to religion. But a madman at the Pennsylvania Hospital taught him the idea of writing out one's angry thoughts and therefore emptying one's mind in a fashion analogous to vomiting an undigestible meal. In addition, a later reading of these words would likely lead to shame and disgust, thereby furthering the process of eliminating the anger. Rush also learned one other technic that he found useful. If the two hostile persons could meet frequently in convivial society, "it never fails to soften resentments, and sometimes to produce reconciliation, and friendship." (Ref. 14, pp. 342-343) Rush used a similar method with his friends John Adams and Thomas Jefferson. Because of political differences a rift had developed between them in the early 1790s. In late 1811 Rush decided to rectify this situation, although he had been working toward it for a long time. By the use of adroit letter-writing recalling the common bonds they shared in the spirit of 1776, and by what John Adams called the "teasing" of both himself and Jefferson, they recommenced their correspondence and friendship, which lasted until their mutual deaths on a celebrated day, July 4, 1826.

To return to anger proper, Rush makes his usual physical and psychological suggestions for its prevention and control. Once again the use of a low diet, such as the one of milk and vegetables that Dr. [John] Arbuthnot had recommended, is useful. But on the other hand, one should not allow oneself to get too hungry, for this raises irascibility! In a similar fashion, so do thirst and fatigue. Alcohol, both of the fermented and distilled varieties, should be avoided, because they predispose to anger even if taken in such small amounts that intoxication is not obvious. For psychological measures, Rush suggests avoiding speaking in a loud voice if one feels irritated, and using other passions to oppose the welling hostility. He then makes a classical allusion. "Thetys—eradicated the anger of her son Achilles, by exciting in his mind the passion of love." Reason plays its role, although Rush does not make it the overriding consideration. "The cultivation of the understanding has a great influence in destroying the predisposition to anger. Science of all kinds is useful for this purpose, but the mathematics possess this property in the most eminent degree. They produced that effect upon the temper of Sir Isaac Newton, of which the following instance is mentioned by one of his contemporaries. Upon seeing a large collection of papers on fire that contained the calculations of many years, in consequence of his little dog jumping upon his table and oversetting his candle upon them, he barely uttered the following words; 'O! Diamond! Diamond! little dost thou know the mischief thou hast done thy master.' " (Ref. 14, pp. 336-337)

CONCLUSION

"Republican theology" is the apt term Donald D'Elia has used to describe the intimate blend of religion and politics that characterizes the thought of Benjamin Rush.[17] With God at the center of Rush's personal world and the solitary creator of the universe, Rush found it very natural to reason by analogy in a fashion that today would be considered both simplistic and naïve. We have seen how evil is a unitary concept that may be refracted into a spectrum of sin, vice, and disease. Methods of prevention are applicable to one or all of these divisions, with minor variations, of course, in the techniques employed. How Christian thought parallels Rush's mental hygiene is well illustrated. The appearance of the seven cardinal sins is a remnant of this long tradition. They fit easily into Rush's scheme, but I wish to make it clear that Rush at no time is explicit in expressing his indebtedness to the individual sins. What are specifically formulated are the doctrines of the original sin of man and man's continuing culpability.

Was Rush not also influenced by medical writings in the field of illness prevention? The answer is yes, but we have purposefully avoided the details. Rush cites such famous writers as Jerome Cardan, Santorio Santorio, both Clément Joseph and Simon André Tissot, as well as Johann Georg Zimmermann. Important to all these writers is the medical concern with the so-called "six non-naturals."[18] They have their origins in the writings of the Roman physician, Galen, and continue well into the nineteenth century in a changed and diluted form. They include: 1) air, 2) food and drink, 3) sleep and wakefulness, 4) motion and rest, 5) evacuation and repletion, and 6) passions of the mind. The history of the application of these medical themes and their related theological precepts to mental health is still to be written. In these writings will be found various recommendations for applying regularity, temperance, harmony and balance, too much or too little, force and counterforce. It was in these ideas that Rush found optimism in his more enthusiastic days; a hope that later diminished, but never disappeared.

As previously stated, as Rush grew older he turned increasingly to his God. "Since the year 1790 I have taken no part in the disputes or parties of our country. My retirement from political pursuits and labors was founded upon a conviction that all I had done, or could do for my country would be fruitless, and that things would assume the same course in America, that they had done in Europe, and from similar causes, and that disorder would reign everywhere until the coming of the Messiah. This disorder is perhaps necessary to form a contrast to his divine and peaceful government. 'Offences must come.' Tyranny, anarchy, war, debt, standing armies &c are the natural consequences of liberty and power uncontrolled by the spirit of christianity. They must therefore exist, perhaps to furnish an opportunity of a display of divine power in destroying them." (Ref. 17, p. 102)

ACKNOWLEDGMENT

The author thanks Marilyn Kerr for her editorial assistance.

REFERENCES

1. BUTTERFIELD, L.H. Ed. 1951. Letters of Benjamin Rush. Vol. 2: 1188-1189. American Philosophical Society. Philadelphia, Pa.
2. PADOVER, S.K. Ed. 1939. Thomas Jefferson on Democracy: 13. New American Library. New York, N.Y.
3. HAZARD, P. 1954. European Thought in the 18th Century. Chap. 2. Happiness: 14-25. Hollis & Carter. London, England.
4. FOLEY, J.P. Ed. 1900. The Jeffersonian Cyclopedia: 3631-3632. Funk and Wagnalls Co. New York, N.Y.
5. CARLSON, E.T., J. L. WOLLOCK & P.S. NOEL, Eds. Benjamin Rush's Lectures on the Mind. Typewritten manuscript: Vol. 2: 185.
6. RUSH, B. Lectures on Pathology. (Manuscript Yi 2, 7396, F 16)
7. RUSH, B. On the Origin of Evil of Every Kind. (Manuscript Yi 2, 7397, F 36)
8. CORNER, G.W. Ed. 1948. The Autobiography of Benjamin Rush: 233. American Philosophical Society. Philadelphia, Pa.
9. TUVESON, E.L. 1968. Reemer Nation: The Idea of American's Millenial Role. University of Chicago Press. Chicago, Ill.
10. RUSH, B. 1811. Sixteen Introductory Lectures: 397-455. Bradford & Innskeep. Philadelphia, Pa.
11. RUNES, D.D., Ed. 1947. The Selected Writings of Benjamin Rush: 358. Philosophical Library. New York, N.Y.
12. RUSH, B. Lectures on the Practice of Medicine. (Manuscript Yi 2, 7394, F 13)
13. RUSH, B. 1806. Essays, Literary, Moral and Philosophical. 2nd edit.: 256. Thomas & William Bradford. Philadelphia, Pa.
14. RUSH, B. 1812. Medical Inquiries and Observations upon the Diseases of the Mind: 347. Kimber & Richardson. Philadelphia, Pa.
15. RUSH, B. 1805. Medical Inquiries and Observations. 2nd edit. Vol. 1: 346. J. Conrad & Co. Philadelphia, Pa.

16. NOEL, P.S. & E.T. CARLSON. 1973. The Faculty Psychology of Benjamin Rush. J.
     Hist. Behav. Sci. **IX** (4): 369-377.
17. D'ELIA, D.J. 1974. Benjamin Rush: Philosopher of the American Revolution. Trans.
     Am. Phil. Soc. **64,** Part 5.
18. RATHER, L.J. 1968. The "Six Things Non-Natural": A Note on the Origins and Fate
     of a Doctrine and a Phrase. Clio Medica **3:** 337-347.

FROM SPECULATION TO EMPIRICISM IN THE STUDY OF MENTAL DISORDER: RESEARCH AT THE NEW YORK STATE PSYCHIATRIC INSTITUTE IN THE FIRST HALF OF THE TWENTIETH CENTURY*

David Zubin and Joseph Zubin

Biometrics Research Unit
New York State Psychiatric Institute and Hospital
and Columbia University
New York, New York 10032

INTRODUCTION

From its inception in 1896, the New York State Psychiatric Institute (P.I.) has been devoted to the dual function, in varying degrees, of research and clinical work in the field of mental hygiene. Although the continuous history of psychological research at the Institute starts with the arrival of Carney Landis in 1930 when the Institute moved to its present quarters at the Columbia-Presbyterian Medical Center, there have been strong undercurrents of theoretical interest providing a basis for experimental investigation of the psychological factors involved in mental disorders during the entire history of the Institute, and these undercurrents occasionally surfaced in the form of specific programs. One such period came with the founding of the Institute when Ira Van Gieson, the director, and Boris Sidis, the psychologist on the staff, conducted their psychopathological researches. Another occurred ten years later when the Kent-Rosanoff team at the Kings Park State Hospital and F. Lyman Wells at P.I. made significant contributions to psychological testing through their work on the word-association technique. A third instance took place years later when David Wechsler advanced the testing of memory in his study of retention in Korsakoff psychosis. Soon after this, Nicholas Kopeloff refuted Henry Cotton's focal infection theory of mental disorder with a carefully controlled experiment that profoundly influenced later evaluation of therapy and the study of mental disorder in general.

One of the most important theoretical undercurrents during the early years of the Institute was an interest in observable phenomena which led to objective and thorough recording of patient behavior on a sound phenomenological basis, originally propounded by Adolf Meyer and nurtured by August Hoch, George

*This paper is based on the monograph "Seventy-Five Years of Research in the Behavioral and Social Sciences at the New York State Psychiatric Institute," written in conjunction with the 75th anniversary celebration of the Institute. Some sections of this paper are based to varying degrees on the annual reports of the New York State Psychiatric Institute and Hospital, which will not be specifically cited in the text. These reports have been issued over the years under the following titles: Annual Report of the Director of the Psychiatric Institute and Hospital to the Department of Mental Hygiene (1930-present); Annual Report of the Director of the Psychiatric Institute to the Commissioner, Department of Mental Hygiene (1927-1929); Annual Report of the Director of the Psychiatric Institute of the New York State Hospitals to the State Hospital Commission (1912-1926); Annual Report of the Director of the Psychiatric Institute of the New York State Hospitals to the State Commission in Lunacy (1908-1911); Annual Report of the Pathological Institute of the New York State Hospitals to the State Commission in Lunacy (1896-1907). All other sources are cited in the text and bibliography.

Kirby, and succeeding directors. This interest—although clinically oriented in that the treatment of individual patients was the primary objective—provided an indispensable theoretical prerequisite for modern quantitative evaluation procedures.

VAN GIESON'S PATHOLOGICAL INSTITUTE: THE "NEURON ENERGY" MODEL OF PSYCHOPATHOLOGY

The New York Pathological Institute (the original name of the N.Y.S. Psychiatric Institute) was founded in 1895 by the state legislature under a mandate from Carlos MacDonald, then the president of the State Commission in Lunacy, calling for a "laboratory . . . operating as a coordinating and processing center for the pathological work of the state hospitals (Ref. 1, p. 22). Dr. Ira Van Gieson came to the institute as its first director with a background in neuropathology, having been associated with the pathological laboratory at the Columbia College of Physicians and Surgeons. He designed a multidisciplinary research program for the institute that went far beyond Dr. MacDonald's original mandate and exceeded the bounds of his own area of specialization, a program coordinating work in fields as diverse as comparative neurology, psychopathology, psychology, bacteriology, and (physical) anthropology in the study of mental disorders.[2] Van Gieson found encouragement for his ambitious program for the institute in his association and friendship with Boris Sidis, a student of William James who was interested in hypnosis, and a dissociation theory of mental disorders that stemmed from Janet's work with double personalities.[3] Sidis elaborated this line of theoretical speculation to include the "moment consciousness" contributed by each neuron to a total mental state.

Together, Van Gieson and Sidis refined both the neurological and the psychological aspects of this speculative trend to provide an accounting for clinical observations of normal and abnormal behavior on the basis of a dynamic model of neurophysiology. In 1898 they formally presented their neurophysiological model to the profession in an article entitled "Neuron Energy".[4] Neurons, they claimed, must maintain a certain level of "dynamic energy" in order to conserve their position in a "neuron aggregate," and the position of this aggregate in an "associated cluster."† If the energy level in a particular neuron drops from the dynamic level to a level of "static energy," the neuron aggregates begin to dissociate from each other, and the individual neurons then tend to separate from their aggregates. With further loss of energy a lower level of static energy is reached, resulting in degeneration of the neuron. If the energy falls to the lowest organic level, then the neuron is destroyed.

The energy level of neurons is associated with the alternation of "sleeping" and "waking" states. Ultimately, this energy balance is dependent on the supply of food:

> If there be one all-important question in the production of insanity, it relates to the *balance between food supply of the nerve cells* and the *work* performed or *withdrawal of nervous energy* [italics his]. This is a practical question, because every one knows that if more energy is drawn off from the nerve cell than can be produced from its food supply, the result is bankruptcy of the nervous system. (Ref. 2, p. 82)

†A concept reminiscent of the "cell assembly" construct developed some 50 years later by Donald O. Hebb.

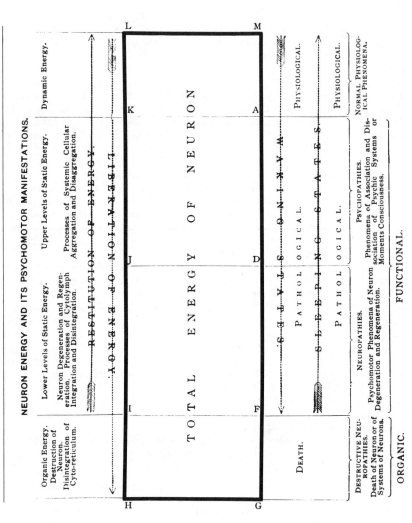

FIGURE 1. The neurophysiological model of Van Gieson and Sidis.[4]

The balance of food supply in the nerve cell and expenditure of energy is adversely affected by two factors. One is overexertion:

> Any one may see this in his daily walks of life in the man who overworks and overfatigues his nervous system. We see this bankruptcy of the nervous system everywhere about us in the endeavor to cheat time in the pressure of hurry and haste in the activity of large cities. People expend more energy from their nervous system than they supply through food and rest. (Ref. 2, p. 82)

The other factor affecting the food supply to nerve cells is summed up by Van Gieson under the rubric "poisons":

> the poison of syphilis and the chronic and persistent poisoning of the body by alcohol, both of which seem to operate largely by diminishing quantitatively or qualitatively the food supply of the body cells . . . cause degeneration of the nerve cells . . . . (Ref. 2, p. 119)

The hypothetical changes of neuron energy level and the resulting hypothetical dissociation, degeneration, and destruction of neurons and their aggregates correlate, in Van Gieson's theory, with clinically observed malfunction in various mental disorders. For example:

> The phenomena of psychopathic anaesthesia, aboulia, amnesia, psychopathic fixed ideas, recurrent dissociated moments, multiple personality—all form an inexhaustible mine for the study of the laws and relations of mental processes and the various types of mental activity, and we may arrive at the important generalization that functional psychosis is a disaggregation of psychophysiological constellations, a dissociation of moments-consciousness accompanied by a corresponding dissociation, or possibly retraction, of neuron systems. (Ref. 5, p. 10)

> Broadly speaking, psychopathies run parallel to the phenomena of retraction and expansion of aggregates of neurons, while neuropathies are concommitant with actual degeneration of the neuron, especially of its cytolymph. (Ref. 4, p.11)

The parallelism of mental and physical phenomena provided Van Gieson with his primary reason for establishing research laboratories in a variety of disciplines and insisting that their work be interrelated. He pointed out

> the incongruity of setting forth the claims of any of these departments of the institute investigating insanities as distinct, isolated methods of research. They must all be linked together and work hand in hand. A concrete example of this is the apportionment and yet linking together of the work in the departments of psychology and normal anatomy of the nervous system . . . . Working conjointly, the psychologist and the anatomist show, in an ideally scientific way, the states of the *parallelism* of the psysical process in the nerve cell and the corresponding psychic phenomena. [italics his] (Ref. 2, p. 74)

Van Gieson refers to the correlation between physical process and psychic phenomena as "states of parallelism" with deliberate intent. He notes a fundamental distinction—the unbridgeable gap between mental and neurological phenomena—that has been a perennial source of difficulty for psychology:

> The most perfect knowledge, even down to the understanding of the very molecules of the nerve cell, would not help the anatomist or the chemist to postulate the laws and phenomena of *thought* and *consciousness*, for these are not *products* of nerve cell activity. The brain does not secrete thought, as the kidneys secrete urine; thought is not a material thing; it can neither be weighed nor measured. A sensation of color, for instance, as experienced by the eye, has no material existence in the physical world. We can only speak of the phenomena of consciousness

as running parallel or being concomitant with the workings and metabolism of the nerve cell, lest we drop into the pitfall of the materialistic basis of consciousness, which has been utterly abandoned long ago. [italics his] (Ref. 2, p. 73)

It must be borne in mind that Van Gieson and Sidis postulated these neuro-physiological processes; they did not observe them. Nevertheless, they did consider their claims about retraction and degeneration of neurons, and about the integral importance of food supply to the neurons, to be empirical. Van Gieson and his colleagues adapted cell-staining techniques of others and elaborated some of their own so that they could study brain tissue from animals that had been subjected to trauma, food deprivation, and various poisons. They hoped to find the effects of fatigue in the arrangement of nerve cells, but all they were able to observe were gross lesions.

This was also true of their study of human brains. The only stage at which Sidis and Van Gieson could make an actual correlation between their neuro-physiological model and the clinical behavior of human beings was when actual "degeneration" of nervous tissue had taken place, as in general paresis:

> The earliest manifestations of general paresis, for instance, are those corresponding to the liberations or restitutions of the uppermost levels of static energy, but finally the process of liberation reaches such a depth that the disease becomes destructive. (Ref. 4, p. 13)

The particular fact that Van Gieson and Sidis were wrong in attributing the clinical manifestations of general paresis to the spontaneous loss of nerve cell energy rather than to the destruction of cells by the spirochete is less symptomatic of a general failure of their scientific method than of the limitation of the knowledge of the day; their dynamic model of neural processes was untestable in view of the technology they had available; thus they had no way of knowing whether their claims about general paresis, or any other clinical phenomena, were on the right track. Their model of neuron energy in effect provided metaphorical descriptions of clinical phenomena, rather than standing in an explanatory relationship to them.

That Boris Sidis and Ira Van Gieson were not alone in their attempt to provide a neuronic basis for behavior is clearly demonstrated by Freud's attempt in this direction about the same time in his famous "Project for a Scientific Psychology."[6] Apparently, the physicalism introduced by physiological psychology from Helmholtz to Wundt and their followers constituted a permeating feature of the zeitgeist, and Freud's exposure to this mode of thinking at the Physiological Institute at Vienna under the aegis of Ernst Brücke led him to develop the "Project." The underlying common denominator of this movement was the belief that only physical-chemical forces are active within the organism and that appeal to extraneous forces was unnecessary to explain behavior. The neurons were the units that carried these physical-chemical forces. Van Gieson and Sidis on the one hand, and Freud on the other seemed to be imbued with this belief, and their attempts at implementing it through theories of neuronic conduction reflect their varying approaches. But whereas Van Gieson and Sidis remained adamant in their pursuit, Freud gave up the idea when he found it impossible to explain psychopathology on this level. He resorted to a postulation of new forces beyond the physical-chemical inherent in matter, forces that could be of equal stature in producing attraction and repulsion tendencies in man parallel to the attraction and repulsion forces in inanimate matter. This eventually resulted in his anatomy of personality, i.e., the forces of the id, ego, and superego in relation to conscious and unconscious behavior. Although Van Gieson and Sidis remained stuck in their tracks in their common effort, Sidis did move on to such matters as hypnosis and dissociation after leaving P.I. and returning to Massachusetts.

The department of psychology and psychopathology was well outfitted with instruments—such as sphygmographs, cardiographs, pneumographs, chronographs, ergographs, and reaction-timers—for the purpose of measuring the psychophysical manifestations parallel to nerve-cell phenomena. Sidis seems to have been the main impetus behind the introduction of these experimental techniques, and in addition made use of psychological tests. For example, in a study of prison inmates he suggested that memory be tested by using recall of short series of numbers and letters, both written and spoken. This technique was not as popularly used then as now.

The Anthropology section, under the direction of Dr. Alois F. Hrdlicka, was well integrated into Van Gieson's overall plan for the coordination of research activities at his institute. The neuron energy model, in viewing mental abnormality as a function of cell deprivation and destruction, would predict concomitant deprivation of the "germ plasm" and, as a result, the passing on of mental abnormalities from one generation to another. Thus, Van Gieson's and Sidis' theory concurs with many of the notions of "degeneracy" attributed to mental abnormalities during the nineteenth century and earlier; in fact, it may be regarded as the most sophisticated attempt to integrate these notions into a scientific model. Van Gieson expressed his views of heredity and its relation to psychopathology as follows:

> We can now have some glimpse of how immutable are the laws of heredity. This material—the germ plasm—transmitted in equal amounts from both parents to the new individual, will surely pass on damages incurred by the ancestors. If a man exposes his germ plasm to the poisonous influences of alcohol, or still worse, syphilis, such damage is not confined to his individual life only but passes on to the next generation . . . . What are the agencies which damage the germ plasm and cause departures from its normal constitution? Precisely the same agencies, to a certain extent, which cause degenerations or induce disease processes in other cells of the body besides the germ cell. These agencies may be summed up under poisons and factors which depreciate the food supply of the body cells. (Ref. 2, pp. 84-85)

Slight damage to the germ plasm, according to Van Gieson, tends to be manifested in the most complex mental functions, rather than on a lower level:

> According to the degree of pathological changes in the germ plasm do the defects of development of the progeny pass successively from higher to lower and lower planes of organization in the nervous system so that all grades of degeneracy and mental instability may be witnessed down to the weak-minded imbeciles and idiots. (Ref. 2, p. 119)

This progression "from higher to lower . . . planes of organization" was associated, for Van Gieson, with the fact that some disorders seem to appear first in adolescence. He explained the association this way:

> During childhood such inherited incapacity of the energy of these higher parts of the nervous system does not always appear, unless the hereditary effects due to damage of the germ plasm be gross and severe, for at this period such higher centres are comparatively little used. During adolescence and later life, however, when these higher centres of the nervous system are called upon for the greatest and most extensive expenditure of their nervous energy they may fail. (Ref. 2, p. 120)

This progressive degeneration in the individual is paralleled by progressive degeneration through generations.

It becomes worse in the next generation for the reason that this unstable brain energy in the first generation is liable to cause the individual to commit excesses. ... Degeneration of the germ plasm once established tends to set up a vicious circle increasing the degeneration in each successive progeny. The third generation becomes still more unstable in the energy of the higher portions of the brain which hold the lower ones in check. It is from this or succeeding generations that are recruited the inmates of the prison, of the lunatic asylum, of the reformatory and of the hospital for the epileptic. (Ref. 2, pp. 120-1)

Among the roles that the Anthropology section was to fill were identifying degenerates in a population and tracing the progress of degeneracy in an individual and across generations. For the first role the section obtained a variety of instruments for measuring body proportions. Van Gieson indicated that because "the population is so heterogeneous" in this country, careful preparation involving the standardization of measurements on normal individuals would have to be done.

Some research in tracing progressive degeneration during adolescence was conducted by Hrdlicka at a boys' reform school. He tried to correlate various measures of physical growth with performance on sensory tests, with a particular eye to finding corresponding abnormalities of "phases of degeneracy" in both areas. Henry Lyle Winter[7] studied a group of inmates of Irish descent at the Kings County Penitentiary, comparing their social background with general clinical observations of behavior and anthropometrical measurements. He found "hereditary" factors such as lack of religiosity in the parents, social factors such as the parents[2] drinking habits, physical factors such as a slight or marked asymmetry in the head contour, and "psychical" factors such as a lack of "moral sense" and "remorse" in his subjects. All of his correlates seem to have been impressionistically formulated and determined, except, of course, for the anthropometry.

Van Gieson hoped that there would be a correlation between a history of degeneracy in the family of an individual and his prognosis:

... one prominent purpose of anthropology at the Institute is to ascertain the proportion of cases of insanity occurring in normal individuals, (i.e.) in individuals who have no hereditary predisposition toward insanity—and to compare this proportion with the other cases of insanity complicated with or resulting from hereditary predisposition. For in the former class of cases insanity is more or less of an accident, and in the great majority of cases recovery is to be expected; whereas in the latter class with predisposition recovery is much less liable to occur.[2] (p. 123)

It should be remembered that the hypothesis of damaged germ plasm antedated the rediscovery of Mendel at the turn of the century. Although much of Van Gieson's and Hrdlicka's theorizing now sounds quaint and out of date, they were right in step with the prevalent Lamarckian theories of degeneracy caused by injury to the germ plasm of the parents.

Some of the work on genetics emanating from the mental hospitals of New York a decade and more later, including publications from Manhattan State Hospital no doubt influenced by the Institute, have a more modern ring. Thus, Rosanoff (Kings Park State Hospital) on "The inheritance of the neuropathic condition"[8] and on "Dissimilar heredity in mental disease,"[9] Philip Smith (Manhattan State Hospital) on "Psychoses in twins,"[10] and H. H. Laughlin (Kings Park State Hospital) on "The diffusion of defective traits,"[11] constitute the beginnings of modern genetic research at P.I. and in the state hospitals system.

Van Gieson's plan for a "correlation of sciences" was ahead of its time in two senses. First, there was as yet no widespread support in the state hospital system and in the legislature for an institution devoted only to research supported by public funds; indeed, the development of this support was to take a full generation. Within a few years after his appointment, Van Gieson ran into heavy fire from the state hospital superintendents and from the State Commission in Lunacy, which had appointed him. They conceived of the Institute as a training center for state hospital physicians and as a central laboratory facility for pathological work. But Van Gieson was adamant in his refusal to modify the original plan. He did not want to dilute the energies of the Institute by trying to teach state hospital physicians, who, to his mind, were incompetent as scientists. He also felt that routine pathological work belonged in the state hospitals, leaving the Institute free for research. His program was defended by the neuropsychiatric research community outside the state hospital service, but in spite of this support, the political pressure emanating from the Commission in Lunacy and the legislature won out, and he was forced to resign. Schulman,[1] in a thorough and insightful review of this period of the Institute's history, points out that conservative opposition to Van Gieson's plans, rather than lack of faith in his abilities, was the reason for his removal:

> The burden of the Commission's, and ostensibly the Legislature's case against the Institute was not that its research program was poor, i.e., professionally illegitimate, but rather that such a research establishment had no place in a state hospital system which required specific services if it were to meet its obligations to the state's insane and taxpayers. (p. 25 fn)

Secondly, models of psychopathology and experimental techniques had not yet been developed to the point where experimental work in different disciplines could be coordinated on a sound empirical basis. Van Gieson and Sidis could only conjecture, as pointed out above, about the relation of hypothetical neuronic processes to clinical phenomena. Thus what has remained of Van Gieson's plan, in the passing of time, is his vision of coordinated research in a spectrum of physical, biological, and social-psychological disciplines, a vision which was to be gradually realized more than a generation later in the modern period of the Psychiatric Institute's development.

Some of the weaknesses in Van Gieson's background and approach were highlighted by the man to succeed him as director, Adolf Meyer. Meyer felt Van Gieson's basic flaw to be a lack of practical experience in clinical work, resulting in a tendency to hypothetical abstraction rather than to deal directly with the complex symptomatology at hand. He recounts his first encounter with Van Gieson in 1895:

> He showed me a little booklet in which he had noted 48 mainly neurological and biological problems to be worked out. And out of the elements he made, in a remarkably comprehensive manner, his picture of the Correlation of Sciences, in which there were unfortunately two fatal gaps: he had no place for man as we know man, i.e., not as a sum of elements but as a real specific unit; and he had no place for psychiatry as we know psychiatry at work. (p. 5)[12]

In his criticism of Van Gieson's approach, Meyer revealed the direction in which his own theoretical interests lay:

> By sparing ourselves the trouble of discussing plain facts in terms of brain-cells and hypothetical brain centers, unless we prove them or really further our activity by the hypothesis, we save ourselves time for a better functional analysis of the facts and the hearer unnecessary and harmful mystification.[13] (p. 327)

ADOLF MEYER AND THE RISE OF PSYCHOGENESIS

Reorganization of the Institute under Adolf Meyer marked the beginning of a primarily clinical phase in its history. Meyer stressed clinical work both because he felt it had been neglected ("the aim of the Institute lies chiefly in the raising of the standard of medical work in the state institutions") and because of his belief that progress in studying the cause and prevention of mental disorders would have to be based on a foundation of careful and thorough clinical observation. His interest in clinical work was such that he made the removal of the institute to Ward's Island, adjacent to Manhattan State Hospital, a condition for his acceptance of the directorship.

Meyer's thoroughgoing common sense attitude toward psychiatry and hospital administration bore fruit in major improvements in patient care and treatment. As such, this clinical aspect of his work as director of P.I. from 1901 to 1910 may be considered his main contribution to psychopathology and has been recognized as such. However, the fundamental importance of his thinking for the course of psychological and social research in psychopathology has generally been underestimated. Theodore Lidz[14] emphasized that because of Meyer's obscure writing style, his conceptions and theoretical orientation passed directly into practice through his teaching and "became so solidly incorporated into the body of American psychiatry that they seemed self-evident (p. 321)." Nevertheless, a careful reading of his papers reveals his theoretical trend of thought—usually framed in terms of practical application and treatment—to be often strikingly original. Indeed, he should be considered one of the originators of the modern pluralistic perspective in which psychopathology is viewed through a wide-angled lens ranging from the ecological to the developmental, learning, genetic, internal environmental, and neurophsiological models. The attention he paid to these multiple insights into psychopathology is reflected in his mapping of the "psychobiological personality," an example of which is found in Figure 2, his well-known "life chart" technique for representing the developmental history of an individual, illustrated in Figure 3, and his use of the now standard geneological diagram for charting the family history of an individual, which he borrowed from Charles Davenport.

Walter Freeman expresses his evaluation of Meyer's position in the theoretical climate of psychopathology at the turn of the century in this way:

> Meyer was first an anatomist and pathologist and with this background he decried efforts of theorizers to explain mental disease on anemia or hyperemia of the brain; on changes, largely reversible, in the appearance of nerve cells in the cerebral cortex and elsewhere; and on hypothetical toxins, or deficiencies that could not be supported by any findings in chemistry, physics, or physiology. He was equally dubious of the formulations of Freud, Jung and others of the psychoanalytic school.[16]

Meyer seems in fact to have taken a "laissez faire" attitude toward psychodynamics, indicating that he was in sympathy with some general precepts of the trend, if not with many of the extreme formulations. This sympathy was particularly marked during the infancy of the psychoanalytic movement in the United States. A young colleague of his on Ward's Island commented:

> Although Meyer understood psychoanalytic theory he seemed never quite able to reconcile himself to some of its fundamentals, especially the examination of sexual aberrations and the early sexual trauma in the development of neuroses. So whereas Meyer never completely accepted Freud, he did not reject him. He credited psychoanalysis with focusing a new and searching light upon psychotic syndromes.

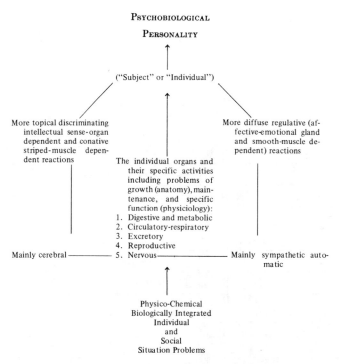

FIGURE 2. Adolf Meyer's schematic outline for his "psychobiological" concept of personality, reflecting an interest in ecological, internal environmental, and neurophysiological aspects of psychopathology.[15] (p. 270) (By permission of the Johns Hopkins University Press.)

> Meyer ... never used psychoanalysis as a therapeutic technique. He demanded that the staff at Ward's Island become familiar with the dynamic approach as an aid in interpretation and diagnosis.[17] (p. 84)

One result of Meyer's sympathy for psychodynamics was that he encouraged the invitation of Freud and Jung to the Centennial Celebration at Clark University in 1909, where they introduced their systems first-hand to American colleagues, an occasion at which Meyer presented his own differing "psychobiological" outlook on psychopathology. The next year Meyer contrasted his own views on schizophrenia with those of Freud and Jung:

> We find here two tendencies,—the one of Freud and Jung, which emphasizes *concrete* experiences and reactive complexes thereto, and the less specific attempt to formulate the loss of balance attempted by me, on ground of habit deterioration and tantrums or more lasting reactions biologically unfavorable to restitution to a normal attitude, sometimes with evidence of short-circuits, but always with more or less characteristic mechanisms which may ultimately deserve differentiating instead of our having to bring the after all heterogeneous mass into too large a disease unit. The two viewpoints form no contrast; the concept of complexes really furnishes the most fruitful material and issues of research, while in other cases the habit conflicts offer a better formulation of the broad lines and possibly the only material accessible.[18] (p. 280).

Heredity: Paternal Uncle Alcoholic. Maternal Grandfather Insane. One Brother Had Two Depressions.

Year:		Birthday: Jan. 11, 1895.	Yr.
1896		Youngest of 17. Mother — second wife. Learned to walk and talk in the first year.	1
1897	Cholera Infantum		2
1898	Bronchopneumonia		3
1899	Croup	Well developed; large for his age.	4
1900	Usual exanthemata		5
1901			6
1902		Began school.	7
1903		Open disposition; friendly, but quiet.	8
1904		Preferred staying at home to playing with others.	9
1905			10
1906	Autoerotism continued to present (1916)		11
1907	Malaria	No worries.	12
1908		Only close companion a cousin of own age — very wild boy. Intimacy continued to present time (1916).	13
1909		Dredge-hand in boat of brother-in-law. Left school (7th grade).	14
1910		Industrious, saving money.	15
1911		Bought boat. Crabbing, dredging oysters. { Summers at home. Winters in Balto. with brother.	16
1912		Quarrels with brothers; thought he was abused, being the youngest.	17
1913	Illicit relations. Neisser infection.	Went with girls often, but no serious love affairs.	18
1914	Autoerotism increased		19
1915	Depression	Feb. — Refused admission to lodge; kidney trouble. Depressed; stopped work; worried over illness. At home.	20
1916		Worked 6 weeks. Unconscious in boat (Aug.). Peculiar words and behavior. Reproached sisters for immorality. Hears voices; uneasy; frightened; then dull. At home.	21
1917		Development of semi-stupor and indifference. Entered Clinic.	22

FIGURE 3. Meyer's developmental interests: the life chart of a case of schizophrenia.[15] (p. 54) (By permission of the Johns Hopkins University Press.)

Meyer's "psycho-biological" approach has special importance for modern psychological research in that it contains the seeds of a behavioral model:

Without disputing the views that mental disorders are essentially physical disorders, I maintained that many of the most potent factors leading to dementia praecox cannot be expressed in any other terms than terms of *conduct and behavior*, and that by singling out the fundamental determining elements of mental life, the habits‡ of conduct and of adjustment, a sane and useful psychology could be shaped. That disorders like those constituting the prodromal stage of dementia praecox could be best expressed in terms of habit disorders . . . has been shown more and more by a careful study of these cases. With this principle as a foundation, the way was opened to a broader conception of dynamic psychology, i.e. a broader valuation of mental events and their possible role in the explanation of mental upsets. . . . Mind, like every other function, can demoralize and undermine itself and its organ, and the entire biological economy. . . .[19] (p. 4) [italics his]

He carried through with this awareness of what psychology could contribute to the study of psychopathology be requesting, in the annual report for 1901-2, "an additional department of psychology in order to make accessible the methods of modern psychology." This request did not materialize, however, as a concrete program during his tenure as director of the Institute.

Much of his interest in the social aspects of mental disorders stems from the influence that Jane Adams and Julia Lathrop exerted on him while he was still at Kankakee State Hospital near Chicago, Ill. They first came into close contact when he slipped on the ice and broke his leg near Hull House, in Chicago, and was invited to stay there while recovering. Meyer apparently had a close relationship with Julia Lathrop; Mrs. Meyer and he were so taken with her that they named their daughter after her. Mrs. Meyer herself pioneered in the field of psychiatric social work and helped her husband in his study of families. She would make home visits, gathering the background information necessary for Meyer's comprehensive case studies. Thus Meyer and his wife introduced the home environment as an etiological factor in the study of mental disorder.

Adolf Meyer's role as an early proponent of a "dynamic psychology," favoring attention to the content of symptoms, is not as generally recognized as his clinical work. Although, as pointed out, he was not a Freudian and did not accept much of psychodynamic interpretation uncritically—his own "psychobiological" concept viewed psychological reactions as merely the most complex type of biological, i.e., physiological reaction—he did establish two conditions that promoted the development of psychodynamic theory by others. Firstly, he insisted on a break with existing classifications of disorder based on notions of "exhaustion" and "autointoxication," turning rather to a careful analysis of the history and symptom picture of each patient as an individual.

The old-fashioned symptomatology dealt with psychology in a manner which did not inspire the physician to expect from psychopathology anything beyond the definition of some terms like illusion, hallucination, delirium, compulsion and perhaps depression, excitement and dementia. Misconceptions about psychology, together with the ease with which impersonal physical explanations, such as degeneracy and auto-intoxication, could be put forth as the "facts" supposed to underlie what would [otherwise] involve one in tedious observations and difficulties of explanation, and perhaps in investigation of the private life of families [i.e. Meyer's approach], had led to the widely spread dogma that mental disorders were "physical" disorders.[19] (p. 3) [parenthetical inserts ours—DZ & JZ]

‡Lidz[14] notes that " 'habit' for Meyer had the broad connotation of organized patterns of behavior and thinking, much as Pierce used the word." (32 fn)

This essentially phenomenological method produced detailed and accurate case studies that provided the raw material for psychodynamic interpretation. Secondly, he accepted psychogenesis in principle as a valid explanation for disordered behavior.

> Psychogenic disorders are those which depend on conditions or events which can only be described satisfactorily in terms of psycho-biology; actions, emotional reactions and attitudes, and intellectual or "thought" constellations,—and their conflicts and abnormal combinations or atavistic or fundamentally or directly abnormal reactions, with their effect on the general mental balance. Every mental activity or reaction leaves its engram and has a certain dynamic value in the after-life of the individual and his general economy.[18] (pp. 227-8)

Meyer credited Kraepelin for providing the initial impetus for this theoretical development through his "fundamental shaking up of tradition, the declaration of independence and the right of seeing things according to their medical importance."[13] (p. 333) But on the other hand, he became increasingly critical of Kraepelin's formulations, because he

> "found that the symptoms manifested by many so-called "functional" patients fitted into neither of the great groups of non-organic mental disorders, dementia praecox and manic-depressive insanity, that Kraepelin kept shuffling and reshuffling in his efforts to establish them as definitely separate entities. . . . Meyer reiterated that a full collection . . . of "all the facts" in the life history of a patient should always be assembled. He and his assistants found that the data corresponded so remotely with Kraepelin's elaborate descriptions that he felt obliged to acknowledge this insufficiency.[17] (pp. 83-94)

During the first decade of the century other physicians destined to play an important role in the development of psychodynamics at P.I. began to form a collaborative group. C. Macfie Campbell, who had studied with Kraepelin, and in addition was interested in symbolic interpretation of clinical data, first came to P.I. in 1904 for a few years to work with Meyer, and then returned as Associate in Clinical Psychiatry in 1908. George H. Kirby came to Manhattan State Hospital at about the same time, and soon became Director of Clinical Psychiatry there. August Hoch during this time was at the Bloomingdale Hospital, where he had developed an early interest in psychogenic interpretation and in psychoanalysis. In the 1907 annual report of the Bloomingdale Hospital he wrote that

> mental disorder is nothing more than the becoming dominant of such conflicts in various forms of peculiar abnormal reactions and faulty attempts at adjustment. These manifest themselves in delusions, hallucinations, peculiar acts, and the like. In each case, therefore, a careful psycho-analysis is necessary . . . [leading to] an understanding of the actual struggles and difficulties which are hidden under the perplexing array of mental symptoms.[20] (p. 386)

A colleague of Hoch[17] reports that his interests along these lines went back to his work at the McLean Hospital from 1897 to 1907.

Meyer and Hoch formed the nucleus of a group at Ward's Island, which, beginning about 1908, comprised the first state hospital center using psychoanalysis "day in and day out to clarify the psychiatric syndromes of committed patients . . . at a time when the two leading clinics of Germany . . . had ignored Freud's work.[17] (p. 81)

C.P. Obernodorf, a resident at Manhattan State Hospital during the formative period of this group, stressed the strong influence of close interaction among the members of the group on the development of their thought.

The presence of many younger men, with their enthusiasm and varied interests in psychoanalysis, living together on Ward's Island afforded mutual help in the professional conversation at meal time and after-hour discussions. The interchange of experience fostered a communal striving to learn the essentials of the psychogenesis of schizophenic, depressive, and above all, the mixed forms of neurotic illness. . . . These zealous endeavors were reflected in case presentations at the State Inter-hospital Conferences (and at meetings of the Ward's Island Psychiatric Society) . . . . Interest in psychoanalysis at Manhattan State did not represent a strife against authority . . . but conformity to it.[17] (p. 89)

The minutes of one such meeting, containing formal presentations and informal commentary, illustrate the cooperation and sense of purpose among the members of the group. At the quarterly conference of state hospital superintendents in January, 1909[21] Campbell gave a paper entitled "Psychological Mechanisms with Special Regard to Wish Fulfillments." In it he concluded that:

We are now ready to pay more attention to what the hallucinations and delusions really are and what they mean . . . we wish to have the actual description of the odd behavior, which we know prognostically to be ominous, and to find out from what chain of circumstances this behavior was derived; we are no longer satisfied with "a priori" statement that such reactions are meaningless, are due to the mere disordered activity of the nervous structures, and therefore not susceptible of psychological analysis. . . . Thanks to the teaching of Meyer we now approach our cases freed from the incubus of this assumption, willing to accept the facts in their entirety. (p. 22) One of the factors, which make such an analysis difficult, is the fact that, when the mind is not playing its normal directing role in the adjustments of practical life, thought at a lower level tends to be less clear, to identify objects on account of superficial resemblances, to represent in a plastic and symbolic manner what would have more direct and logical form. (p. 12)

Meyer, in the ensuing discussion, cited the papers as an example of "determining the actual difficulties and tangles of the patient's mental working and effecting a setting aright of the otherwise unguided mental drift." (p. 24) Meyer's comment exemplifies his habit of always couching his words in strictly practical terms of diagnosis and treatment, although underlying this the theoretical trend of his thought is evident. Kirby, who was also present, observed that:

Cases analyzed in this way are far more interesting and instructive than if dealt with in the usual formal descriptive manner. It is a safe and practical plan of work because we are getting at the real difficulties and conflicts which the patient has had to meet and over which he has apparently gone to pieces. To understand the mechanism by which these painful experiences become moving forces in the individual's life and give form and color to the psychosis is a most welcome addition to our knowledge. We cannot deny that psychogenetic factors play an important role in the etiology of mental disorders and as such they deserve our closest attention. (p. 26)

Hoch was not present, although he frequently attended these meetings. During the discussion of Campbell's paper a member of the staff directed the attention of the participants to the work that Hoch was doing along those lines at the Bloomingdale Hospital.

The effect that these men were having in establishing a climate in which psychodynamics could flourish is evidenced by the remarks of other physicians at staff meetings. For example, M. J. Karpas of Manhattan State Hospital summed up his review of a case of "dementia praecox" at a meeting of the Ward's Island Psychiatric Society in 1909:[22]

What does the record of this case teach us? First the importance of psychogenic factors in functional psychoses. Second, that psychotic and neurotic symptoms are governed by complexes which originate from definite undercurrents of patients' mental lives. Third, the profound teachings and methods of Freud, Jung and Bleuler should receive our serious attention for we are indebted to them for the true progress of psychopathology (p. 527).

These four men—Meyer, Hoch, Kirby, and Campbell—set the stage for the development of psychodynamics at P.I., but their major achievements in this area, except for Kirby, were destined to be carried out elsewhere. Meyer left in 1910 to become founding director of the Phipps Clinic at the Johns Hopkins University Medical School in Baltimore. Campbell left a year later, to eventually become medical director of the Boston Psychopathic Hospital. August Hoch, who had been able to associate with this group from his position at Bloomingdale Hospital for years, replaced Meyer as director of P.I. His own contributions at P.I. were to be cut short by early retirement in 1917 because of ill health.

In January, 1913 Hoch brought John T. MacCurdy to the Institute staff. His acute interest in symbolic interpretation is shown by summary comments in a paper published in 1914 entitled "A Psychological Feature of the Preciptitating Causes in the Psychoses and its Relation to Art"[23]

> In attempting recently to analyze the precipitating causes of the functional psychoses, we have been struck by the frequency in which an incident apparently innocuous from a moral standpoint has been the occasion of a mental breakdown where the utterances of the patient have shown an outcropping of infantile, i.e., unconscious tendencies. The inner meaning of these precipitating causes has been determined or presumed as follows: We know that with great frequency the content of a psychosis represents a reaction to the precipitating cause. In this way, therefore, we can often see the hidden meaning of the precipitating factor—the patient, in a sense, explains it himself. Again, there are certain symbols which repeat themselves so often that, where patients are not accessible for a complete psychoanalysis, we can take their meaning for granted, for the sake of theoretic study. When these occur as precipitating causes, we assume that the latent content of the symbol is responsible for the upset, and proceed to verify that assumption by examination of the utterances in the psychosis. (p. 298)

MacCurdy's research depended on close association with his mentor Hoch, and in general, MacCurdy's psychodynamic speculations were based on the excellent data provided by experienced clinicians, especially Hoch and Meyer.

> Both of these pre-eminent psychiatrists had the same point of view in clinical research: that it must begin with painstaking record of what patients say and do, regardless of the pertinence of these observations for any particular theory, and, further, that the descriptions of mental symptoms must be put into terms of common speech, so far as is possible, because technical labels tend to obscure individual differences of reactions. . . . Every worker in the Institute was trained to follow these rules.[24] (p. ix)

MacCurdy left the Institute for military service at the time Hoch retired, but he did not give up the research he and Hoch had conducted during their years of association at P.I. Upon being discharged from military service in the spring of 1919, he went immediately to visit Hoch, then in retirement in California, to continue their cooperative efforts. This cooperation lasted until September, 1919 when Hoch died, but MacCurdy continued their research, which ultimately culminated in his book, *The Psychology of Emotion*,[24] a classic of Psychodynamics. This work was published in 1925, long after MacCurdy's and Hoch's formal association with P.I. ended, and yet much of the theory, as well as the research and the phenomenological base from which it sprang, are an integral part of the history of P.I.

MacCurdy's association with P.I. and his dependence on the clinical work of Hoch, Meyer, and others parallels Karl Jaspers' work at the Heidelberg Clinic at the time Franz Nissl, with others, created a "community of living research" in which "phenomenology and the psychology of meaningful connections came into being."[25] (p. xii). Both MacCurdy and Jaspers, each in his own setting, were brilliant psychodynamic theoreticians who, either by choice or by force of circumstance, depended on the excellent phenomenological material provided by others, and did not spend many years developing their own clinical experience.

ADOLF MEYER'S PHENOMENOLOGICAL METHOD AND THE STANDARIZATION OF PSYCHIATRIC ASSESSMENT

The Psychiatric Institute has made major contributions—through the early work of men like Meyer, Hoch, Kirby, Cheney, and Lewis—to the development of today's standarized quantitative methods of evaluation. Although the efforts of these early workers in providing detailed guides for evaluation and diagnosis were primarily clinical in their orientation, they must be recognized for providing the indispensable basis of phenomenological material and categorization necessary for later formal attempts at standarization.

Even during his earliest experiences in mental hospitals before the turn of the century, Adolf Meyer was dissatisfied with the haphazard way in which notes were taken and diagnoses made, and particularly with the custom of relying on unobservable internal physical phenomena presumed to be the etiological factors instead of paying strict attention to the observable facts of each case.§ By the time he was appointed director of P.I., he had begun to work out methods for achieving greater thoroughness and objectivity in the reporting of clinical observations. In 1904 he indicated that a systematization of the phenomenological base for psychiatric evaluation was necessary before formal standardization of techniques could be achieved.

> The feeling that the old method of case books was inadequate had already led to a reform in the shape of a system of blanks a few years ago. I think you all agree with the statement that the blanks alone are far from bringing the real salvation. They foster the appearance of completeness, but when you wish to use the results for any specific purpose, you are bound to find many important individual traits of the case rubbed off, and the rest forced into a rigid vocabulary, as rigid as the blank itself. . . . The failure of the older plans led me to recommend the later plan of having the records written out, provided with summarizing headings and underscoring, and to urge that the results of the work shall be submitted to staff meetings for mutual criticism and correction.[26] (p. 122).

It should be pointed out that Pinel was the first in modern times to take careful notes on patient behavior—often written on whatever paper was available at the moment, such as the backs of envelopes—but it wasn't until Meyer came on the scene that systematic case notes were introduced.

Kirby[27] reports that at about this time Meyer "prepared a set of clinical guides or outlines" (p. 5) which were distributed to state hospital physicians in typewritten form. These guides, later printed privately in 1908, represent the first

---

§ The same tendency was evident in experimental psychology when hypothetical physiological processes were invoked as an explanation for behavior, leading Skinner to refer to CNS (Central Nervous System) as the "Conceptual Nervous System."

step toward standardizing and objectifying diagnostic procedures in the state hospital system. It was also adopted at many other hospitals throughout the country, indicating that it ranked among the first standarized diagnostic guides in use.

Meyer's concern for objectivity is shown by the opening remarks of his *Guide*.[28]

> The examination consists of a series of tests of efficiency of the various organs and functions, and the coordination of the results for the determination of the types and nature of disorders. . . . The direct findings must be given in exact terms of test and reaction, and in the mental examination, to quite an extent, with the verbatim account of question (or prompting) and answer. A stenographic record is frequently essential. (p. 139)

The guide is divided into a physical examination aimed at uncovering the somatic components of the patient's disorder, and an examination of the mental condition of the patient. The physical examination consists of psychophysical tests for the functioning of the sensory organs, and motor tests for coordination and presence of tremors, paralysis, and other somatic disfunctions, in addition to tests and observation of the various organ groups.

The mental examination is composed of: 1) general observations on the patient's adaptation to his environment; 2) samples of his "spontaneous drift of mental activity and utterances;" 3) observation of "special moods and emotional traits," especially affective and delusional or hallucinatory states, topics of rumination, and substitutions; 4) a set of mental status tests; 5) an evaluation of the patient's insight into his condition; and 6) observation of "the evolution of symptoms" over a period of days or weeks.

> Of particular interest are the psychological tests, constituting a special inquiry into the condition of the sensorium . . . as shown in the grasp on the past and present, and including tests for orientation as to place, time, and persons; memory of recent and remote events; retentions; fund of information; counting and calculating; reading; enunciation, writing. (p. 142)

Diagnosis and prognosis are based on an analysis of the physical and mental symptom picture in terms of a set of reaction types: 1) "reactions of organic disorders"; 2) "delirous states with dreamlike imaginative experiences, hallucinations. . ."; 3) "affective oscillations"; 4) "paranoic developments"; 5) "substitutive disorders of the types of hysteria . . . and psychasthenia"; and 6) "types of defect and deterioration."

During August Hoch's tenure as director of the Institute he edited materials for a guide specifically for the evaluation of personality to supplement Meyer's general guide to psychopathology, and together with George Amsden of the Bloomingdale Hospital he published "A Guide to the Descriptive Study of the Personality" in 1913.[29] The guide is set up as a questionnaire, although Hoch preferred it to be considered "a guide to be modified in individual cases," especially in light of the difficulties met in sizing up affective reactions. A preliminary set of questions aims at an estimate of intelligence and judgment, at the general output of energy in the individual, and at his estimate of himself, i.e., such traits as "self-reliance, self-depreciation, conceit, or self-pity." The body of the guide contains questions relating to the following:

1. "Adaptability toward the environment" in terms of ease of social relationships; aggressiveness; openness to others; exaggeration of traits such as order, and demand for truthfulness; assertiveness; and hold on reality.

2. "Mood," especially degree of affect, manic or depressive behavior, willingness to overcome despondency, anxiety, reaction to irritants.

3. "Traits related to the sexual instinct," such as ability to hold friends, relationships with family members, and attitudes and behavior towards the opposite sex, as well as an assessment of overt sexual behavior and preoccupation with sex-related ideas.

4. "General interests," including hobbies, fads, interest in work, and religiosity.

A final section inquires into pathological traits such as "tendencies to hallucinate without definite psychosis . . . nocturnal enuresis, tics, etc."

The guides by Meyer and Hoch were revised and combined into a new edition by George Kirby in 1921[27] during his tenure as director. Kirby included the contents of the anamnesis which had been developed by Meyer[30] specifying details of family and personal history, including intellectual, social, and sexual development. Otherwise, he followed closely the content of Meyer's and Hoch's guides. This work was in turn revised by Clarence O. Cheney[31] in 1934 and 1938 while he was director of the Institute, and then again by Nolan D.C. Lewis[32] in 1943 during his tenure as director.

The successive steps of reediting did not obliterate the foundations provided by Meyer and Hoch, and in fact the continuity through successive editions has demonstrated the soundness of the original guides. Changes tended to add to, rather than to alter the original material. The continuity of Meyer's and Hoch's influence through successive editions of the Guides was paralleled by the establishment as a tradition of their standards of phenomenological excellence in record-taking at P.I. An ongoing study by Kuriansky et al.,[33] using P.I. patient records, has shown this. In her study Kuriansky sampled patient records from the 1930s and 1940s and submitted them—with indications of the original diagnosis deleted—to a group of psychiatrists for rediagnosis. As part of the study Kuriansky asked the psychiatrists to evaluate their confidence in the quality of the records as a basis for rediagnosis, with most of them expressing satisfaction with the adequacy and completeness of the records. Kuriansky reports that earlier records, taken when Meyer, Hoch, and Kirby were exerting their influence directly, were fairly constant in their format and exemplary in the completeness of their content.

The Lewis edition of the Guides in 1943[32] took an important step forward in the trend toward standarization. Joseph Zubin, then Associate Research Psychologist in the Psychology Department, collaborated with Lewis and provided psychometric methods for the evaluation of intelligence and personality, many of which were developed by researchers who had been formerly associated with the Institute. Grace Kent's "Emergency Battery of One-Minute Tests" was adopted for a quick evaluation of intelligence, as well as her "Opposites Test," for testing the ability to maintain an associative trend. F. Lyman Wells' "Absurdity Test" was incorporated for evaluating syllogistic thinking. Items from David Wechsler's Wechsler-Bellevue Test were adopted for detecting impairment of judgment in psychopathic personalities (see the next section for a discussion of their researches). Thus early research opportunities afforded by the Psychiatric Institute and the State Hospitals System paid dividends in later cross-fertilization when these individuals moved elsewhere.

The cooperation of psychology with psychiatry in extending the mental status schedule provided one of the inputs to the psychological testing on the Columbia-Greystone Topectomy Project (1947-1956).[34-36] Although the Mental Status Schedule was oriented primarily toward diagnosis, whereas the psychologists on the Topectomy project were primarily interested in determining brain function as affected by psychosurgery, the content of the mental status schedule and its trend toward standardization were nevertheless important prerequisites for the later psychological study of brain function.

Zubin also became interested in the possibility of systematizing the results of the Mental Status Examination by providing a schedule for recording the findings. Unfortunately this was 1944, during World War II, and he had to leave for military service before he could develop the schedule further. Although it was used for a while, the lack of manpower soon resulted in its being shelved.

It was revived in 1960, after the Biometrics Research Unit was established, in the form of a Ward Behavior Rating Scale[37] prepared by Eugene Burdock, Anne Hardesty, Gad Hakerem, and Joseph Zubin. Subsequently, urged on by Zubin and with the help of an NIMH grant to the Unit, a systematic approach was started by Burdock and Hardesty in the development of a structured interview for assessing the psychopathology of mental patients.[38] This differed from the rating scales already available insofar as it involved direct systematic interviewing with regard to specific assessable behaviors that could be noted as present or absent, rather than on overall global judgments based on prior knowledge of the patient. Subsequently, Robert L. Spitzer joined this team as a research fellow and eventually Jean Endicott joined Spitzer in the newly formed Evaluation Section of the Biometrics Research Unit, which devoted itself to the preparation of a series of systematic objective interviews and rating scales.[38] At a later date, Gurland and Sharpe formed a section on Diagnosis and Psychopathology and further adapted the available instruments and developed new ones for international comparisons in the bilateral study of diagnosis in the US and UK.[38]

Thus modern research in the quantitative and objective evaluation of the mental status of patients has roots going back to the efforts of Meyer and Hoch to standardize diagnostic procedure just after the turn of the century, efforts that were aimed at eradicating the nineteenth century legacy of diagnostic procedures based on subjective impressions and recorded in terms of fancied neurological dysfunction and degeneration. We have not yet made much progress in uncovering etiology, but we have at least systematized the descriptive approach to psychopathology by providing interview tools that are reliable and valid.

QUANTITATIVE APPROACHES TO THE STUDY
OF WORD ASSOCIATION AND MEMORY

The three decades from 1902, when Meyer became director, until 1930, when the institute was restructured to include a broad-spectrum research program, were a period of primary preoccupation with clinical work and teaching at P.I. The lack of a permanent research staff in the social and behavioral sciences, due largely to the lack of funding, prevented the development of a substantial program of research. In spite of this, P.I. continued to be involved in research advances through the influence of staff members on research conducted elsewhere in the state hospitals system, and by providing a suitable environment for outside scientists to conduct research. A discussion of the important research projects carried out in connection with P.I. during this period will exemplify how P.I. continued to exert an influence on research interests.

Meyer's work in psychodynamics brought his attention to the early work done by Jung and others with the word association technique. Lief[39] reports:

> In his work at the Institute he used with success some of Jung's word-association tests for a glimpse into undercurrents. They showed peculiarities of interest and

emotional trends. He acknowledged this technique as a great step forward achieving systematic objectivity in the quest for determining factors of psychic life. (pp. 229-30).

Meyer himself does not report any of his work with association tests, but the comments of doctors in the state hospital system show that Meyer's interest was strong, and that he was having a definite effect on the employment of this technique: "In the United States the pioneers in this field have been Meyer and Hoch. . . . It is with much hesitation and a keen appreciation of our small experience in the practical use of the association tests that, at the suggestion of Dr. Meyer, we have approached the subject.[40] (p. 31)

Meyer presided at an interhospital staff meeting at the Kings Park State Hospital in April, 1908 at which Grace Kent and Aaron Rosanoff presented preliminary results of their quantitatively-oriented association studies.[41] Their main finding was a purely quantitative one: schizophrenics tended to use the same reaction word for different stimulus words more often than did the manic-depressives. Their conclusion was that the schizophrenics were adopting a strategy of least effort. Meyer was mildly critical of this preliminary study: "The simple form of numerical test seem to be open to a good many accidents. I should strongly suggest a combination of the numerical and the dynamic, the quantitative and the qualitative investigations." (p. 567)

This is in fact exactly what Kent and Rosanoff subsequently did. In the main report of their association studies, "A study of Association in Insanity"[42] published in July and October, 1910 they successfully integrated quantitative and qualitative techniques. A carefully selected list of stimulus words was standardized by determining the range of responses that a normal "control" population would make to it. The test was then administered to mental patients to determine, in an objective and quantitative way, deviation in the content of their responses from the normal population. This study was to become a classic in the field of psychological testing.

August Hoch, the new director at P.I., carried forward Meyer's underlying interest in psychological research. During his tenure at the Bloomingdale Hospital he had experimented with the association test as a clinical tool. He succeeded in 1910 in getting the funds with which to start a "psychological department" at P.I. and to bring F. Lyman Wells, an experimental psychologist, from the McLean Hospital. Wells concurred with Hoch's interest in using experimental psychological methodology as an aid to clinical investigation:

> The proper starting point for experimental investigations in psychopathology is the psychotic symptom itself. Problems must be chosen, first, with reference to actual clinical groups and the pictures that form them; secondarily, to the convenience of the experimental method, and as little as possible with reference to preconceived psychological systems. The nature of such problems can be known in one way only—by actual knowledge of the cases that present them.[43] (p. 405).

There were, in addition, much deeper intellectual ties between the two men. Wells was one of the early proponents of the psychodynamic approach to psychopathology. He participated in the Clark University centennial celebration in 1909 in which Freud, Jung, and Meyer presented their views; later he wrote critical and expository reviews of the psychoanalytic literature for the *Psychological Bulletin*, as well as original articles, in which a major current was his desire to see psychodynamic formulations submitted to more vigorous experimental validation. David Shakow[44] comments that Wells' "considerable role in introducing and reconciling psychoanalysis to academic psychology has largely remained unappreciated and unrecognized." (p. 48). Wells thus came to P.I. with a background and interests promising meaningful collaboration with Hoch and other staff members interested in psychodynamics.

In a paper[43] read before the Ward's Island Psychiatric Society¶ Wells surveyed the field of psychological research to give a picture of what he thought his department should be engaged in. Among the experimental approaches he mentioned is the association test, used for "the discovery of certain associational trends which may be indicative of a given disease condition" and as an aid in psychoanalysis. Measurement of the psychogalvanic reflex would allow a study of "involuntary responses to given suggestions" in "cases who come under observation totally inaccessible, mute, irresponsive, furnishing absolutely no clue as to their mental content." The study of writing speed and pressure, the speed of tapping, and ability of the "eye to follow a rhythmically moving object, as on a pedulum" may help distinguish "the retardation of the manic-depressive condition and the blocking . . . of dementia praecox."

Wells felt the study of memory to be of paramount importance in psychopathology. He differentiated study of the sense modalities of the stimuli; the study of memory for "the occurrence or non-occurrence of a series of single events;" logical memory, associative memory, and recognition memory; and the study of retentiveness, i.e., the time elapsing between stimulus and reproduction. Experiments along these lines would, he felt, be valuable in the study and diagnosis of senility, "manic cases," "dementia praecox," the Korsakoff syndrome, and general paralysis. In particular, he anticipated the potential of memory testing for differentiating between arteriosclerosis on the one hand and general paralysis and senile dementia on the other.

Wells' own work during his short association with the Psychiatric Institute continued his evaluations of the association reaction test begun at the McLean Hospital. He rejected the philological approach to classifying responses, as exemplified by the work of Jung and Riklin, an approach which grouped "the reactions in a series of logical categories, based largely upon grammatical conception," because it was "very unwieldy, very subjective, and its interpretation more than ambiguous." In the analysis of association reactions he noticed two kinds of phenomena that, to him, provided an objective classification: 1) "a tendency to react with either supra-ordinate (the non-specific of Kent and Rosanoff) or else with contrast association" and 2) "the extent to which the reactions are influenced by the individual's special experience or judgment." A further step toward objectivity was provided, in his opinion, by Kent and Rosanoff's technique of comparing the frequency of specific response-words to a standardized control population, rather than attempting to classify the responses of the individual.

In his work at the Psychiatric Institute Wells was able to ascertain "the existence of definite types of association reactions in different individuals" which he hoped would lead to a delineation of different personality types. He was also concerned with the effect of practice on association reactions. In working with students of R.S. Woodworth of Columbia University he applied association tests, a tapping speed test, and sensory and memory tests to the study of "manic-depression insanity."

The fate of the two research psychologists in the State Hospitals system during this period seems to indicate that the climate was not yet ready for a permanent research facility. Grace Kent resigned from the staff of the Kings Park State Hospital in November, 1910, just after the publishing of her classic study on

¶ Composed primarily of the staffs of P.I. and Manhattan State Hospital, New York, N.Y.

word association, to join the staff of the government hospital in Washington, D.C. Wells, appointed to P.I. the same month that Kent left Kings Park, resigned the following July because of "ill health," and returned to the McLean Hospital.

Several years after Well's departure the Institute again briefly became the focus of psychological research when David Wechsler, the now famous author of the Wechsler Intelligence Test, then a graduate student under Professor Woodworth at Columbia University, came to conduct his Master's essay research under the clinical supervision of August Hoch, who had previously brought F. Lyman Wells to the Institute. Wechsler's study was an investigation of memory in five alcoholic Korsakoff cases and one general paretic. This was one of the first quantitative psychological studies at P.I. and the first investigation of the Korsakoff syndrome in the English literature. He tested four hypotheses about the amnestic syndrome, so prominent in Korsakoff cases: (1) defective perception, (2) failure to link new associations with old ones, (3) rapid fading of newly formed associations and (4) inability of reproduction. Wechler concluded that the third hypothesis was most tenable as an explanation of the memory defect— inability to form durable new associations. This research concluded in the publication, in 1917, of "A Study of Retention in Korsakoff Psychosis,"[45] reprinted in the collected papers of P.I. Unfortunately, the initial report of this study was buried in the state hospital reports, so that when interest in memory studies following ECT arose, this earlier study was not available as a guide for investigation.

In the early 1920s Gardner Murphy made use of the patients and the nursing staff at Manhattan State Hospital for a word association study of schizophrenics, manic depressives, and normals in which he worked closely with F. L. Wells, who had returned to the Boston Psychopathic Hospital. He used both the traditional classification of responses according to logical type and the methodology of Kent and Rosanoff, and concluded in agreement with Kent and Rosanoff that there is a gradual transition rather than an abrupt change from the normal state to pathological states, and that "types of word association, as such, are but little related to the fundamental attitudes and adaptations to life underlying the mental disorders which are here compared."[46] (p. 571)

THE KOPELOFF EXPERIMENTS

Popular attention was given in the early 1920s to the focal infection hypothesis of Henry Cotton, [47,48] which held that the sources of mental disorder were to be found in the toxins produced by such foci of infection as infected tonsils, adenoids, colons, dental carries, and so on. Surgical removal of these sources of infection was proposed as a means of eliminating mental disorders. Nicholas Kopeloff, the Associate Bateriologist at P.I., and Clarence O. Cheney and George Kirby of the clinical service tested this hypothesis in a series of studies[49, 50] which proved to be an important forerunner of subsequent work in the evaluation of therapy. They removed the foci of infection in some 60 patients and compared the improvement rate of this group with that of a suitable control group after a year's follow-up. The improvement rates did not differ (for the "dementia praecox" cases, $p = .50$; for the manic depressive cases, $p = .82$; and for the total sample, $p = .66$‖). The only difference noted was in the higher mortality rate of the operated group.

The importance of this experiment goes far beyond its refutation of the focal infection theory. As one of the earliest controlled experiments in psychiatry, it

‖Computed by J. Zubin.

served and has continued to serve as a paradigm for research into the causes of mental disorder, as well as for the evaluation of therapy. Just one example of the influence of this experiment is to be found in a proposal for the evaluation of psychoanalysis made by C.O. Cheney and Carney Landis.[51] They planned to select a group of patients for psychoanalysis and to match this group with controls who would receive identical treatment, except for the psychoanalytic therapy. Cheney and Landis give credit to the earlier Kopeloff experiments for this controlled approach.

> Several years ago the Psychiatric Institute conducted an investigation of the scientific therapeutic merits of the elimination of foci of infection as they bore on remission and recovery from mental disease. These studies . . . might well serve as patterns for a similar investigation of the therapeutic value of psychoanalysis. [p. 1162]

CARNEY LANDIS' DEPARTMENT OF PSYCHOLOGY IN THE NEW PSYCHIATRIC INSTITUTE

The dream of an autonomous institute uniting research and teaching functions in the study of mental disorders had long been nurtured by scientists within the Psychiatric Institute and without. In 1920 the first legislative overtures were made. In 1923 the passage of a $50 million bond issue for state institutions made funds available for a new building. In the years that followed, a happy cooperative effort conceived by Dr. Thomas Salmon between the State Hospital Commission and the administrative board of the Columbia-Presbyterian Medical Center was set up, resulting in a restructured and expanded Psychiatric Institute which was completed at its present site on Washington Heights in 1929. The plans of the new Institute included a department of clinical and research psychology, specifying laboratories on the 13th floor.

It is not clear who may have been the moving force behind the inclusion of a psychology department in the plans for the new institute. Certainly the establishment of psychological research departments at other institutions, such as St. Elizabeth's Hospital in Washington, D.C., Worcester State Hospital, Mclean Hospital, and the Institute for Juvenile Research in Chicago, was indicative of a developing "zeitgeist" in which the techniques of experimental psychology were increasingly important for psychiatric research. Kirby, the director of the Institute, was asked by the State Hospital Commission to submit plans for the organization of the new institute in 1925. His annual report to the commission in 1926 includes plans for laboratory space for experimental psychology. Later reports mention clinical psychology as well. Given a mandate to expand the facilities and the research staff of the Institute, Kirby no doubt included psychology as a matter of course.

Once P.I. moved from Ward's Island to its newly built home at the Columbia-Presbyterian Medical Center the sporadic work in research psychology took on a more continuous character. Soon after the building opened, Carney Landis—who had noticed the availability of a research position at P.I. in an advertisement and, out of curiosity, had taken the civil service examination for it, which he passed, to his great surprise—was appointed Associate Research Scientist heading up the newly created Department of Research Psychology. Many of his colleagues in academic psychology, who were surprised by this move, tried to dissuade him by warning him of the political forces limiting the work in institutions and cautioning him that he was giving up what promised to be a brilliant career in physiological psychology. He took the job nonetheless. The premonitions of his colleagues proved to be false when he subsequently received academic recognition through a professorship in the Department of Psychology at Columbia University. In that position he was in charge of teaching in Abnormal Psychology, and was able to recruit many graduate students for his laboratory at P.I. and for dissertations in the field of psychopathology.

When Landis came to P.I. he had already demonstrated his research ability with such problems as facial expression in emotion and in examining delinquent behavior and in a keen analysis of the psychogalvanic reflex phenomenon. He gathered about him a coterie of enthusiastic young researchers including William A. Hunt, Joseph McVicker Hunt, Walter Shipley, Theodore Forbes, and Joseph Zubin and others who began to tackle the various aspects of psychopathology in a systematic manner.

An interesting struggle developed between the clinical service-minded staff, who were largely drawn from state hospital circles, and the newly appointed associate research staff, who were primarily raised in academic circles. The clinicians, being in command, expected that the researchers would turn their attention to burning clinical issues such as schizophrenia, while the academicians, unaccustomed to dictation, wanted to choose their own research areas without reference to local clinical needs. Furthermore, the clinical staff, influenced by such men as August Hoch, John MacCurdy, and MacFie Campbell, were under the spell of psychoanalysis, whereas Carney Landis as well as the other academically trained scientists were not infatuated with psychoanalysis to the same degree as their clinical peers. The struggle often erupted into open hostility. Landis reflected on this in an interview held many years later:[1]

> The scientific staff was unable to come to terms with what they might do for and with the clinical staff. Only Drs. Ferraro (neuropathology) and Kopeloff (bateriology) had come over from Ward's Island. The rest of us were new and had not worked with the clinicians. The fuss came with chemistry, internal medicine, and my department, experimental psychology. The clinicians wanted us to see patients and to give them the benefit of our knowledge. They wanted us to work for them at their direction and at their orders. We fought it out with them and there were bloody heads all around. (pp. 51-2)

Since the clinical staff had the upper hand, the scientists soon began to compromise lest their financial support for research be curtailed. Landis apparently was sufficiently flexible to accommodate himself to the clinical demands. He introduced a clinical psychologist—Dr. Zygmunt Piotrowsky—into the department in 1930 to take care of clinical testing and began to investigate schizophrenia and subsequently epilepsy and other clinical conditions as the need arose. In this work he was greatly helped by the close cooperation of Sigfried Katz, a fine-tuned clinician who had had some psychological training. This was especially fortunate because many of the problems undertaken in psysiological psychology would have been impossible to conduct without medical supervision. Landis often discussed the need for a medical degree in order to permit a free undertaking of studies involving drugs or other intradermal experiments. He realized, however, that the holder of a medical degree would run the risk of being railroaded into practice rather than research because of the great need for clinical service. He regarded the absence of a medical degree as a defense against being seduced.

One of the first problems that attracted his attention was that of the striking muscular behavior of the catatonic. He examined the effect of oxygen and carbon dioxide on catatonics, the stereotypy of their autonomic responses; he investigated whether their cataonic tonicity disappeared during sleep by photographing their posture while awake and while asleep, and was surprised to note that though manics were more active than catatonics in their motility, the difference, when measured, was much smaller than had been supposed. This led to a series of studies of muscle tonus in normals and patients which yielded no differences. This research in catatonia was a far cry from what the clinicians had expected—since it contributed little to methods for treatment—but it indicated how psychology can serve as the basic science for psychopathology even as physiology serves internal medicine.

Landis did not limit himself to the problems raised by clinicians and, intrigued by Bill Hunt's attempt at replicating Maranon's studies of induced emotion by injection of adrenaline, he continued together with Hunt to find that "the injection of sufficient amounts of adrenalin will reproduce roughly the organic picture usually characterized as emotion.[52] (p. 483.) The individual reactions varied widely, however, with some subjects reporting only organic effects, some reporting emotion-like states, and a few experiencing emotions that seemed satisfying and genuine.

The introduction of a children's ward into P.I. engendered research in child development, especially in the area of play techniques and in investigations of emotional behavior. No differences were found between mentally defective children at Letchworth Village and children at P.I. in emotional behavior through the use of Jersild's interviewing techniques.

Because of the use of hyperthermy in treatment of general paresis, psychological and neuromuscular tests were conducted with general paretics and measures of improvement on psychological tests were used in connection with the evaluation of outcome of treatment.

Soon after Hans Strauss described the Startle Pattern in Germany he was invited to come to P.I. to collaborate on further studies of this phenomenon by the use of ultrarapid moving-picture cameras. This classic work appeared in 1939 as the first published volume reporting the products of the laboratory.[53] In general, they found a consistent response pattern to a pistol shot in normals and patients, including eye-blink, distortion of facial features, forward movement of the head, and a variety of body movements.

Landis, Hunt, and Strauss wanted to determine to what extent this response was involuntary, because of a basic interest in the functioning of the central nervous system. In order to determine the effect of habituation on the startle pattern, they visited a firing range of the New York Police Department with their high-speed motion-picture equipment and tested a group of beginners and several experienced marksmen. Even those with frequent gun-firing experience showed eyelid, head movement, and facial distortion responses, although some denied it until shown the films. This experiment established the startle pattern as an involuntary response.

In the work with mental patients, no qualitative differences from normals in the startle pattern were found, although the quantitative degree of reaction was somewhat greater, especially in the feebleminded. This difference was attributed to the possibility that the normals were more aware of what was going on, thereby reducing the element of surprise. In epileptics, however, they found a drastic reduction in response level. Out of 109 patients tested at the Craig Colony, 30 showed no reaction at all, not even eyeblink. A more careful analysis of higher-speed film revealed that some of these epileptics were making an almost imperceptible partial blink, but this only served to confirm the qualitative differential between the epileptics and other clinical categories tested, along with the normals.

The findings with epileptics were followed up by testing schizophrenics undergoing experimental convulsive treatment with metrazol, in order to study what happened during seizure. The startle pattern was completely eliminated during a seizure, and returned gradaully five to ten minutes after it was over. Other experiments were conducted with deaf subjects, normals given adrenalin injections, and hypnotized subjects. The deaf and those under hyponosis showed a sharp reduction in response.

These findings were used, especially by Strauss, to construct hypotheses about possible neurological processing. No great advance was made in the formulation of a neurophysiological model, but on the other hand, these experiments represented a methodological breakthrough in drawing attention for the first time to the relevance of autonomic responses in the microscopic interval of milliseconds after stimulation.

Another area that occupied the attention of the Department was the general area of physiological psychology, including electrical phenomena of the skin, thyroid gland action, and electrical processes of the cochlea and auditory nerve, in which Landis and Forbes made basic progress; but there was no payoff for psychopathology. Even the auditory threshold failed to differentiate schizophrenics from normals.

Another area that began to flourish in the 30s was that of personality inventories. Together with Page, Benton, and Zubin, considerable effort was expended on developing inventories that would help in screening the mentally ill from the well by self-reporting questionnaires. Although this work did not pay off with psychotics, it did form the basis for screening techniques subsequently used in World War II by Walter Shipley in the Navy and by J. Zubin in the Merchant Marine Service. Zubin, with the help of the War Shipping Administration, developed a screening inventory for merchant seamen which proved very effective in eliminating the unfit sailors from the hazardous duties of the merchant marine during the war. Shipley adopted this technique in the development of his Navy Personal Inventory II, which was widely used during World War II. Both the late Walter Hunter and Clarence Graham regarded it as an important contribution from the OSRD committee. Some basic developments in methods for determining similarities in patterns of response arose from this work and culminated in a method for measuring likemindedness.

Another area in which the department pioneered was that of psychosexual development. This work, beginning in 1934 with a study of 700 psychotic women by Frances Strakosch Alexander,[54] was followed in the early forties by studies of neurotic women and physically handicapped women with Agnes Landis[55] and Majorie Bolles,[56] respectively, as coinvestigators. Interviewing techniques were developed by them, before Kinsey, for obtaining relevant psychosexual information. It was found that the mentally ill did not differ strikingly from the well in early psychosexual development. Despite this, adult patients did exhibit greater deviation from normals in sexual behavior and adjustment.

These studies of psychosexual development were anticipated by the work of C. E. Gibbs[57], who studied the physical and behavioral pathology relating to sex and development in schizophrenic and manic-depressive patients at P.I. in the early 1920s. His research, in its concentration on the distribution of pubic and mammary hair, seems to have been based in part on the by then rapidly failing degeneracy hypothesis, and thus did not attract attention. He did use a control group in the investigation, and employed quantitative techniques to analyze the data.

Hardly had a new treatment been introduced when the Department of Research Psychology would begin to evaluate it. First came the treatments for general paresis in 1934 when electropyrexia, electropyrexia followed by tryparsamide combined with mercury, and tryparsamide combined with fever treatment were compared, and the second type of treatment found to be superior on the basis of psychological test improvement; following this came evaluations of child therapy, psychotherapy, psychoanalysis, experimental neuroses in children suffering from diffuse difficulties, insulin therapy, metrazol therapy, ECT, psychosurgery, antihistamine, and, finally drug therapy. All treatments were subjected to the crucible of objective evaluation by this department. One of the most noteworthy studies in the evaluation area was the pioneer study on the evaluation of psychotherapy conducted by Landis, in which he reviewed the literature on outcome of this treatment against the outcome of psychotherapy at P.I.[58] His findings, which were subsequently confirmed by Eysenck, by Zubin, and others, led to the conclusion that when control studies are considered, the efficacy of psychotherapy remains undemonstrated.

When psychoanalysis became popular enough to require attention, Dr. Landis turned attention to this treatment. In order to be able to assess it properly he underwent a didactic psychoanalysis himself, and in 1940 reported his experience in the series of reports in the Journal of Abnormal Psychology[59] in which several other eminent psychologists participated. His critical assessment was one of the first to subject the psychoanalytic process to objective scrutiny.

Then followed a series of studies in the epidemiology of the mental disorders which was reported in a volume with James D. Page entitled "Modern Society and Mental Disease."[60] In this book a survey was made of the ecological factors that influenced the distribution of the various mental disorders throughout populations and became a classic in this field.

Among the psychological techniques that the department developed for diagnosis, prognosis, and evaluation of treatment in addition to the previously described personality inventories were sorting tests for investigating thought disorder, handwriting analysis, and the Rorschach technique and other projective techniques. Joseph McVicker Hunt spent the year 1934 as a postdoctoral student investigating thought processes in psychotic patients. When the late Kurt Goldstein arrived at P.I., a whole series of sorting tests were devised or adapted to investigate sorting behavior in schizophrenics as contrasted with general paretics and brain-injured cases. One outcome was a series of scales developed by Zubin for classifying sorting behavior which proved to be prognostic of outcome in insulin therapy. Zygmunt Piotrowski introduced the Rorschach technique and developed it over the course of the years. He found it to be prognostic of outcome in insulin treatment and developed organic indicators as well as a whole series of new scoring methods, especially for movement responses. A series of scales of evaluating handwriting was developed by Thea Stein Lewinson and Zubin. The effect of ECT on memory was investigated by Zubin and colleagues and resulted in the finding that whereas ECT temporarily wipes out recall memory, recognition memory is relatively unscathed, although a new phenomenon does appear—that of loss of familiarity. Three weeks after the end of therapy these aberrations were found to disappear.

During the World War II period, research practically came to a standstill, except for the studies in ECT memory loss and personality inventories. Some work was also done on test pilots in the measurement of muscular rigidity at critical points during flight and regarding emotional difficulties interfering with learning. Most of the younger men had joined the armed forces and Landis seized this opportunity to write a textbook of Abnormal Psychology,[61] together with Marjorie Bolles, who served as research assistant for many years. The textbooks of abnormal psychology that were available previously consisted primarily of case histories and descriptive approaches. The only numbers to be found were at the top of the page. Landis and Bolles wrote one of the first texts to include substantive experimental data, and it soon became a classic. Zubin became interested in the work on will by Narziss Ach and devoted some months to translating Ach's "Analyse des Willens" into English. This, however, was interrupted by military service.

With the coming of the age of psychosurgery, the department threw itself into the evaluation of this method by joining forces with Fred Mettler and his Columbia-Greystone Associates in the classic topectomy studies[34-36] (the word topectomy was coined by this group to replace the earlier bastard word areaectomy). Fortunately, a group of graduate students freshly returned from the War was available to undertake the task of determining the effect of topectomy on behavior, and the classic series of chapters on psychology in the book "Selective Partial Ablation of the Frontal Cortex"[34] consists of their dissertations. This was one of the first collaborative studies in psychopathology and set the pattern of interdisciplinary research in psychiatry by combining the efforts of the following disciplines in an attack on a common problem: neurology, psychiatry, statistics, neurosurgery, anatomy, general medicine, psychology, otolaryngology, internal medicine, neurophysiology, neuropathology, and physiology. The results of this investigation and of the two succeeding projects advanced knowledge of brain function dramatically. Although the efficacy of psychosurgery for unselected schizophrenics proved to be doubtful, and although some of the findings regarding the influence of topectomy on behavior have since been challenged, the impact of these studies, in which psychology at P.I. played a crucial role, was quite impressive, especially as techniques of surgery and evaluation alongside physiological as well as psychological techniques became more refined. The failure of psychosurgery as a general therapeutic technique for schizophrenia raised doubts about the efficacy of the other somatic therapies as well, and led to a survey of the literature on all the therapies in 1957.[62] The results of this survey, conducted by Virginia Staudt, serving as a postdoctoral student with Zubin, led to the conclusion that as far as immediate outcome of treatment was concerned, each therapy seemed successful, but in five-year followup, none of the therapies seemed to be more efficacious than spontaneous improvement in "untreated" patients.

One of the outcomes of the Columbia Greystone studies was an interest in developing more objective indicators of brain function than was afforded by the clinical tests. The finding that critical flicker fusion (CFF) was influenced by surgical operations on the frontal lobe led Landis to hope that CFF might turn out to be a good indicator of brain function, and he spent almost a decade tracking down the various parameters influencing this function. Unfortunately, this project proved to be rather disappointing in his estimation, and his younger colleagues later demonstrated, using signal detection theory, that the CFF differential between patients and normals was not a difference in sensory sensitivity, but in the criterion adopted by the subjects for deciding whether the light is flickering or fused. While this finding does not eliminate the usefulness of CFF as a clinical testing device, the interpretation of the results is completely altered.

One of the last achievements of Dr. Landis was his book, published posthumously in 1964, on the Varieties of Psychopathologic Experience,[63] which attempted to present in casuistic fashion the feelings, attitudes, emotions, and thinking of the mentally disturbed from their own point of view. From a collection of 200 autobiographical books and as many journal articles, Landis drew a series of introspective descriptions characteristic of a wide range of psycho-pathological experience. These he analyzed into their underlying dimensions, and developed a systematic view for the subjective experience of mental illness.

The course of development of the Psychology Department at P.I., both in style and in the content of research, was guided for more than three decades by Carney Landis. A student and colleague of his during much of this period, William Hunt, has paid close attention to the course of Landis' career[64,65] and aptly summarizes his guidance of the department.[66]

> How best can Carney Landis' contribution to the Psychiatric Institute be sum-marized? I think by pointing out that his absence of any limiting theoretical bias, his diverse and wide range of research interest, and his continued fascination with and receptivity to the new and novel provided a broad base of intellectual stimula-tion that enthused his own laboratory, attracted collaborators from without, and encouraged and stimulated work in other departments beside his own. True inter-disciplinary research most often arises from the simple overflow of creative energy from some investigator whose mind cannot be contained within the narrow boundaries of a single discipline. Landis' could not. Moreover, his tremendous energy assured on the administrative side an expansionist philosophy that guaran-teed the continued growth and development (and the feeding) of a sound and adequate research laboratory for psychology. In matters of budget and facilities he was often like an angry mother hen, and equally dangerous, a trait that some-times did not endear him to colleagues in other departments who had their own chicks to protect. Yet, if Landis believed in another man's work, be he brother psychologist or not, he could marshal this same manipulative energy in support of the other fellow. His sense of empire lay in the behavioral sciences in general and not in psychology alone.
> But a laboratory ultimately must be justified by its productivity, and this one was, and the craftsmanship assured the quality of this productivity and guaranteed its respect. So psychology grew and flourished and the Institute benefitted and grew with it. Landis' diversity of interest combined with his insistence on quality gave his laboratory an air of unorthodox orthodoxy that was both exciting and supportive. It was always fun to be there." (p. 425-6)

CONCLUSION

Carney Landis died in 1962, leaving behind him a legacy of careful attention to detail in the empirical investigation of psychophysiological phenomena. He also had wide-ranging interests, as evidenced by his pre-Kinsey work on psycho-sexuality with Agnes Landis and Marjorie Bolles, the didactic analysis he under-went in order to better approach psychoanalytic methodology, and his late work on the phenomenology of mental disorder. But the main thrust of his career was in the elaboration of empiricist methodology. The pendulum had come full swing from the early days of the "Pathological Institute" under Van Gieson, when the late nineteenth century spirit of mentalism and speculation held sway. Van Gieson did use careful methods in the pathology laboratory to the extent that materials and techniques of the day permitted, but his main interests while at P.I. were centered on developing a detailed speculative scheme linking ab-normal behavior in a pre-Kraepelinian categorization to the hypothetical retrac-tion and degeneration of neuron aggregates. The stress here is on "speculative." Van Gieson had neither the laboratory technology nor the clinical observational framework to provide any kind of empirical base for his speculations.

Succeeding generations of scientists at P.I. made advances in these areas. Meyer along with his colleagues and followers established and improved the ob-servational basis for description and diagnosis of mental disorders, in addition to introducing psychodynamic principles into observation and theory. Objective techniques for psychological testing were developed by the Kent-Rosanoff team, by F.L. Wells, and by David Wechsler under the aegis of Hoch and then Kirby at P.I. Kopeloff introduced modern concepts of hypothesis testing to P.I. in his refutation of the "focal infection" theory. In the following decades the empiricism characteristic of Carney Landis' laboratory placed theorizing at the sidelines.

Out of this transition from speculation to empiricism has developed a new synthesis characterized by the conscious construction of scientific models, which are, in a sense, theoretical speculation grounded in empirical investigation. In the forties Franz Kallmann joined the staff at P.I., bringing with him genetic models pertaining to mental disorder, as well as the latest data-gathering techniques for testing these models. Kallmann found a welcome haven in the psychology depart-ment until he was able to establish his own department of Medical Genetics. In the fifties and sixties the developing Biometrics Research Unit brought to P.I. a consciously multidisciplinary approach based on etiological models ranging from the genetic, neurophysiological, and internal environment approaches on the one hand, to developmental, learning theoretic, and ecological approaches on the other. The elaboration of these models had consequences for both clinical descrip-tive practices and for experimental design. In order to evaluate the models rigorously, the need arose for more careful description of psychopathology along the lines that Adolf Meyer had laid down. This need was satisfied by the provision of systematic, structured interview and rating techniques developed by the Bio-metrics staff. On the other hand, the research programs designed to test hypo-theses growing out of these models individually and out of their interactions constitute the main work of the staff. Research interests at P.I. have proliferated, so that now there are a number of new departments taking a variety of approaches to the description and etiology of mental disorders.

If Van Gieson were alive today he might well be regarded as a prophet whose time has come. The modern structure of P.I. and its research interests bear a striking resemblance to the multidisciplinary play Van Gieson developed with Boris Sidis for his Pathological Institute at the turn of the century. The essential differences lie not in the collaboration of sciences, but in the modern spirit of constructing scientific models and empirical techniques for evaluating them.

ACKNOWLEDGMENTS

The authors wish to express their gratitude to Dr. Lawrence Kolb, former director of the New York State Psychiatric Institute, for his initial support and encouragement of their project, and to Mr. James Montgomery and staff of the Institute library for their tireless efforts in making available a wealth of material relevant to the history of the Institute, as well as for their friendly support and encouragement.

REFERENCES

1. SCHULMAN, J. 1969. Remaking an Organization. State University of New York Press. Albany, N.Y.
2. VAN GIESON, I. 1898. Correlation of sciences in the investigation of nervous and mental diseases. Arch. Neuropath. Psychopath. 1: 25-262.
3. ROBACK, A. A. 1952. History of American Psychology. Library Publishers. New York, N.Y.
4. VAN GIESON, I. & B. SIDIS. 1898. Neuron energy. Arch. Neuropath. Psychopath. 1: 1-24.

5. SIDIS, B. 1902. Psychopathological Researches. Studies in Mental Dissociation. Stechert. New York, N.Y.
6. FREUD, S. 1971. Project for a scientific psychology. Discussed in R. Lowry. The Evolution of Psychological Theory. 1650 to the Present: 137-143. Aldine-Atherton. Chicago, Ill.
7. WINTER, H. L. 1897. Notes on criminal anthropology and bio-sociology. Being a study of 73 Irish and Irish-American criminals made at the Kings Co. Penitentiary, Brooklyn, N.Y. State. Hosp. Bull. 2: 462-498.
8. ROSANOFF, A. J. 1912. On the inheritance of the neuropathic condition. State Hosp. Bull. n.s. 5: 278-292.
9. ROSANOFF, A. J. 1913. Dissimilar heredity in mental disease. State Hosp. Bull. n.s. 6: 379-380.
10. SMITH, P. 1912. Psychoses in twins. N.Y. Med. J. 96: 1268-1272.
11. LAUGHLIN, H. H. 1913. The diffusion of defective traits. State Hosp. Bull. n.s. 6: 378.
12. MEYER, A. 1928-29. Thirty-five years of psychiatry in the United States and our present outlook. Am. J. Psychiatry. 85: 1-31.
13. MEYER, A. 1907. Modern psychiatry: Its possibilities and responsibilities. Speech delivered at the N.Y. Academy of Medicine. In Collected Papers of Adolf Meyer. 1951. E. Winters, Ed.: 149-172. The Johns Hopkins University Press. Baltimore, Md.
14. LIDZ, T. 1966. Adolf Meyer and the development of American psychiatry. Am. J. Psychiatry 123: 320-332.
15. WINTERS, E., Ed. 1951. The Collected Papers of Adolf Meyer. Vol. 3. Johns Hopkins University Press. Baltimore, Md.
16. FREEMAN, W. 1968. The Psychiatrist. Personalities and Patterns. Grune & Stratton. New York, N.Y.
17. OBERNDORF, C. P. 1953. A History of Psychoanalysis in America. Grune & Stratton. New York, N.Y.
18. MEYER, A. 1911. The nature and conception of Dementia Praecox. J. Ab. Psychology 5: 274-296.
19. MEYER, A. 1906-1907. Annual Report of the Pathological Institute of the New York State Hospitals to the State Commission in Lunacy for the Year 1906-1907.
20. RUSSELL, W. L. 1945. The New York Hospital. A History of the Psychiatric Service, 1771-1936. Columbia University Press. New York, N.Y.
21. 1909. Minutes of the quarterly conference . . . of state hospital superintendents . . . January 26, 1909. State Hosp. Bull. n.s. 2(1): 3-55.
22. 1909. (minutes of the monthly) meeting of the Ward's Island Psychiatrical Society, March 16, 1909. State Hosp. Bull. n.s. 2(2): 506-528.
23. MACCURDY, J. T. 1915. Psychological feature of the precipitating causes in the psychoses and its relation to art. State Hosp. Bull. n.s. 7: 514-537.
24. MACCURDY, J. T. 1925. The Psychology of Emotion. Harcourt, Brace. New York, N.Y.
25. JASPERS, K. 1963. General Psychopathology. University of Chicago Press. Chicago, Ill.
26. MEYER, A. 1904. Discussion of cooperation between the State Hospitals and the Institute. 16th Annual Report of the State Commission in Lunacy 32-48.
27. KIRBY, G. 1921. Guides of History Taking and Clinical Examination of Psychiatric Cases. State Hospitals Press. Utica, N.Y.
28. MEYER, A. & G. KIRBY. 1918. Notes of Clinics in Psychopathology. Privately printed. Reprinted in The Collected Papers of Adolf Meyer. 1951. Vol. 3. E. Winter, Ed.: 139-148. Johns Hopkins University Press. Baltimore, Md.
29. HOCH, A. & G. AMSDEN. 1913. A guide to the descriptive study of personality. State Hosp. Bull. n.s. 6: 344-355.
30. MEYER, A. 1918. Outlines of Examinations. Privately printed. Reprinted in The Collected Papers of Adolf Meyer. 1951 E. Winter, Ed. Vol. 3: 224-258. Johns Hopkins University Press. Baltimore, Md.
31. CHENEY, C. O., Ed. 1934 & 1938. Outlines for Psychiatric Examinations. New York State Department of Mental Hygiene. Albany, N.Y.
32. LEWIS, N. D. C., Ed. 1943. Outlines for Psychiatric Examinations. New York State Department of Mental Hygiene. Albany, N.Y.
33. KURIANSKY, J. B., W. E. DEMING & B. J. GURLAND. 1974. On trends in the diagnosis of schizophrenia. Am. J. Psychiatry 131(4): 402-408.
34. METTLER, F. A., Ed. 1949. Columbia Greystone Associates. Selective Partial Ablation of the Frontal Cortex. Paul B. Hoeber. New York, N.Y.
35. METTLER, F. A., Ed. 1952. Columbia Greystone Associates, Second Group. Psychosurgical Problems. Blakiston. New York, N.Y.

36. LEWIS, N. D. C., C. LANDIS & H. E. KING, Eds. 1956. Studies in Topectomy. Grune & Stratton. New York, N.Y.
37. BURDOCK, E.I., A. S. HARDESTY, G. HAKEREM & J. ZUBIN. 1960. A ward behavior rating scale for mental hospital patients. J. Clin. Psychol. 16: 246-247.
38. ZUBIN, J. 1969. Cross-national study of diagnosis of mental disorders: methodology and planning. Am. J. Psychiatry 125(10) (Suppl.): 12-20.
39. LIEF, A., Ed. 1948. The Commonsense Psychiatry of Dr. Adolf Meyer. Fifty-two Selected Papers. McGraw Hill. New York, N.Y.
40. GILLESPIE, E. & R. CHAPMAN. 1910. A study of dementia praecox and allied conditions by means of psychoanalysis and association tests. State Hosp. Bull. n.s. 3(1): 30-47.
41. KENT, G. H. 1909. Preliminary report of application of Sommer's Association Test. State Hosp. Bull. n.s. 1: 552-567.
42. KENT, G. H. & A.J. ROSANOFF. 1910. A study of association in insanity. Am. J. Insanity 67: 37-96, 317-390.
43. WELLS, F. L. 1910. The experimental method in psychopathology. State Hosp. Bull. n.s. 3: 403-416.
44. SHAKOW, D. 1973. The Contributions of the Worcester State Hospital and Post-Hall Clark to Psychoanalysis. U.S. Department of Health, Education, and Welfare. Washington, D.C.
45. WECHSLER, D. 1917. A study of retention in Korsakoff Psychosis. Psychiatric Bull. 2: 403-451.
46. MURPHY, G. 1923. Types of word-association in dementia praecox, manic-depressives, and normal persons. Am. J. Psychiatry n.s. 2: 539-571.
47. COTTON, H. A. 1921. The Defective Delinquent and the Insane, Princeton University Press. Princeton, N.J.
48. COTTON, H. A. 1922. The etiology and treatment of the so-called functional psychoses. Am. J. Psychiatry 2: 157-210.
49. KOPELOFF, N. & C. O. CHENEY. 1922. Studies in focal infection: Its presence and elimination in the functional psychoses. Am. J. Psychiatry 2: 139-156.
50. KOPELOFF, N. & H. G. KIRBY. 1923. Focal infection and mental disease. Am. J. Psychiatry 3: 149-198.
51. CHENEY, C. O. & C. LANDIS. 1935. A program for the determination of the therapeutic effectiveness of the psychoanalytic method. Am. J. Psychiatry 91: 1161-1165.
52. LANDIS, C. & W. A. HUNT. 1932. Adrenalin and emotion. Psychological Rev. 39: 467-485.
53. LANDIS, C. & W. A. HUNT, (with a chapter by) H. STRAUSS. 1939. The Startle Pattern. Farrar & Rinehart. New York, N.Y.
54. STRAKOSCH, F. M. 1934. Factors in the Sex Life of Seven Hundred Psychopathic Women. State Hospitals Press. Utica, N.Y.
55. LANDIS, C., et al. 1940. Sex in Development, Paul B. Hoeber. New York, N.Y.
56. LANDIS, C. & M. M. BOLLES. 1942. Personality and Sexuality of the Physically Handicapped Woman. Paul B. Hoeber. New York, N.Y.
57. GIBBS, C. E. 1924. Sexual behavior and secondary sexual hair in female patients with manic depressive psychoses, and the relation of these factors to dementia praecox. Am. J. Psychiatry 4: 41-56.
58. LANDIS, C. 1937. A statistica evaluation of psychotherapeutic methods. Chapter in Concepts and Problems of Psychotherapy. L. E. Hinsie. Columbia University Press. New York, N.Y.
59. LANDIS, C. 1940. Psychoanalytic phenomena. J. Ab. Soc. Psychology 35(1): 17-28.
60. LANDIS, C. & J. D. PAGE. 1938. Modern Society and Mental Disease. Farrar & Rinehart. New York, N.Y.
61. LANDIS, C. & M. M. BOLLES. 1946. Textbook of Abnormal Psychology. Macmillan. New York, N.Y.
62. STAUDT, V. & J. ZUBIN. 1957. A biometric evaluation of the somatotherapies in schizophrenia. Psychological Bull. 54: 171-196.
63. LANDIS, C. 1964. Varieties of Psychopathological Experience. F. A. Mettler, Ed. Holt, Rinehart & Winston. New York, N.Y.
64. HUNT, W. A. 1962. Carney Landis: 1897-1962. Am. J. Psychology 75: 506-509.
65. HUNT, W. A. 1962. In memoriam . . . Carney Landis (1897-1962). Am. J. Psychiatry 119: 390-392.
66. HUNT, W. A. 1972. The development of psychology at the Psychiatric Institute: an historical survey. Psychiatric Q. 46: 423-431.

DISCUSSION

Virginia Staudt Sexton, *Moderator*

Herbert Lehman College
City University of New York
The Bronx, New York 10468

DR. ZUBIN: I'd like to direct a question to Dr. Dain. He has pointed out that there was a time when even the well-to-do resorted to state hospitals as places for admitting their sick relatives.

But this was not always true. There were periods when only the poor entered the hospital, followed by periods when the trend was reversed. Are there any factors you can point to that determined the shift in attitude toward mental hospitals?

DR. DAIN: No, I can't do it. The first hospitals, say, Eastern State Hospital—that's what it's called now—was in Virginia, opened in 1773. It was the only one in Virginia, and if you were sending anyone to an institution, that was the only place you could send him or her. And so you had people there of some means. In the North, the first hospitals that were essentially therapeutic (Pennsylvania Hospital and subsequently Retreat, Bloomingdale Friends' Hospital). Now those were corporate, nonprofit hospitals, and the well-to-do middle classes went there, with some of the poor also accepted as patients.

In the 1830s and '40s and subsequently, a division occurred. The corporate, nonprofit hospital, as well as private hospitals, tended to take the middle- and upper-class patients, and the poor were taken out of them and sent to the newly established state hospitals. When I say "nonprofit corporate hospitals," one should understand that in their early years these hospitals were always somewhat subsidized. Bloomingdale, for example, was subsidized by the state, and as such, it had to take some public patients. But the middle-class, upper-class patients and relatives objected, and there was also overcrowding; so a division occurred. By the '40s and '50s it was very clear that the public hospitals took the lower-middle class and the poor, and the corporate hospitals essentially took the upper-middle class and the well-to-do, and that kind of division has existed to the present. From the eighteenth to the twentieth century, there have been ups and downs in the public regard for mental hospitals. There have been periods of time when all hospitals were regarded more highly than others. This would include corporate as well as state hospitals.

In the earliest period, let's say of optimism, the first half of the nineteenth century, many people viewed hospitals positively, and so you'll find that when a state opens up a new hospital, the middle-class and upper-class patients send them patients, especially if they are geographically far away from corporation, private hospitals. In time, sometimes the minute it's opened, sometimes ten years later, state hospitals become overcrowded, and so people start taking the upper-class patients out of these state hospitals and sending them to the Hartford Retreat (Institute of Living), Bloomingdale, and other upper-class institutions.

DR. QUEN: I think that there's another aspect. You've emphasized that the wealthy and the middle-class people were getting annoyed at the proximity to the poor, and to some extent that probably was true, though the therapeutic approach was that the patient would do well when maintained in the style of living that he was accustomed to; so that the poor had rather spartan quarters, and the wealthy, if they wanted to, could have a servant with them.

But another apsect of it is that at that time the State subsidized the poor, and it was understood in the nonprofit hospitals that they would take all patients, and they were set up for doing that. With the advent of the state hospitals in states where there were also private hospitals, you get legislatures beginning to require that patients be transferred to the state hospitals unless it really was a lot cheaper to stay at the nonstate hospitals, and what that did was set up an inevitable move toward a separation of standards, and I think that this is an important factor in their development. What has not been adequately researched in the development of the state hospital is the effect of cumulative legislative decisions that have had derivative consequences.

For instance, in the early nineteenth century, while it was requested or even mandated that the insane in the almshouses or the jails be sent to the hospitals, it was done so that it cost the county aldermen money, and very often they would not send the patients to the hospitals because it was cheaper for the town treasury not to do so.

Then when you get into the twentieth century, in the time of Adolph Meyer, Meyer and the reforming neuropsychiatrists felt that the psychopathic hospital was really going to be the answer and very much like what the community psychiatrists are talking about today. Have it in the middle of the community. Have the people in. Treat them quickly, get them out, a great move. But Adolph Meyer's concept included a place for the state hospital, and that is, if the patient didn't respond or wasn't curable, he was sent to the state hospital.

What happens, then, to the morale of the patients and their families, and to the professional staff of the state hospital, when they know they're at the end of the road for the incurable? And what happens in the legislature, where it's important to get money budgeted that will draw taxpayers' support? What happened was that at Worcester State Hospital, for instance, in the 1920s, they moved to a discharge rate of about four percent, and in the early nineteenth century, when Woodward was there, approximately 50% of their discharged patients never were rehospitalized, and they had higher than a 50% discharge rate. The interesting thing is that today, I think, at Psychiatric Institute or at the State Hospitals in New York, at any rate (Dr. Zubin can correct me), I think that for every 100 admissions, 60 are readmissions, and this is to some degree a function of pressures that historians have not paid attention to, that have to do with nonpsychological, nonacademic, nonclinical factors, but have to do with hard economics.

DR. ADLER: I have a question for Dr. Quen. You mentioned Isaac Ray's interest in the imitational process, and I wonder whether you would comment on a couple of questions I have on that. First of all, does Ray use the term "imitation," instinctive imitation as you used it, as a kind of faculty, a faculty of imitation that he was thinking of? In what respect can you actually equate that with the modern approach to imitational learning such as things that you quoted about the monkey, Japanese monkeys, and other modern approaches, which are essentially a kind of a learning situation rather than instinctive approach?

DR. QUEN: He speaks of the propensity to imitation and of sympathy. I can't find it at the moment. I would say that if he were pressed, he might have called them a faculty, but in fact, in the book where he did call other mental traits faculties, he did not use the term faculty for imitation. I think he thought of that as an instinct in the biological sense.

His concept was broader, I believe, than the conscious cognitive processes.

Yes, I think that we could say that to *some* degree the Japanese macaque, in what has now become a cultural trait of the colony, which they didn't have before they started washing their potatoes, is close to a conscious process. I think that he was referring to a broader spectrum. I thought, for instance, when I read these pages, about how clinical psychologists and psychotherapists in practice will limit the number of depressed patients they treat, because if they treat too many, they themselves tend to get depressed.

I was fascinated by the work on biorhythm, which is really quite unconscious and, I think, technically is a biological learning but not learning in the way we think of it. I think that he included that kind of process. I omitted from my presentation that there is a line of development from earlier times and this is not original with Ray. He was presenting this, I think, in a somewhat different light. William James was impressed, as I mentioned, with the propensity of imitation. Of course, Trotter, in the early twentieth century, with his herd instinct, was a significant figure in psychology, though now you can't find Trotter's name in any of the contemporary psychology books.

But we do have the phenomenon. It's been reported recently, for instance, about men whose normal temperature cycle is about 16 days, when living alone. When they lived with women, not on the pill (that is, women who have normal menstrual, biologically determined menstrual cycles) as couples, the male temperature cycles will take on a 26-32-day periodicity that parallels that of the woman, except for one hormonal phase of it. When the woman goes on the pill, the man reverts to a 16-day cycle. Now this, I think, is biological learning, and I think it falls somewhere within what Ray was talking about.

DR. RIEBER: There's a very interesting problem that I didn't mention in my paper in relationship to Ray's and Upham's ideas, and it has a bearing on this, so I might just mention it. Upham never mentions Ray and Ray never mentions Upham. This is rather strange, and Jacques Quen spoke of this to me some time ago. Both Ray and Upham were at Bowdoin College at the same time, and they certainly must have known about each other's work. Ray was stressing the medical model for mental pathology, whereas Upham was stressing the "moral-mental" model.

Now, there's no necessary incompatibility with these two approaches except in terms of stressing one more than the other. Upham, it appears, tried to have the best of both possible worlds. He did admit that there was the possibility for mental disease to be a by-product of brain damage or some derangement of the brain, but at the same time he stressed the secret dynamics of the mind that had nothing to do with brain pathology but had more to do with mental and moral problems.

It looks to me as if Ray was really much more interested in stressing "instinctual imitation," which is a term compatible with a medical model and plays down the other approach that Upham advocated.

DR. QUEN: The medical model has become what I think Dr. Zubin refers to as a "buzzword," and I believe that it might give it a somewhat different light and be closer to what Ray had in mind if we were to refer to it as a biological model. But I do wonder, did Upham mention the propensity to imitation or sympathy?

DR. RIEBER: Upham allows for everything. "Whatever exists can go wrong," was his approach. I don't remember ever reading that phrase, but I would imagine that if you were hard pressed to make a case, it was compatible with his system. The point is that Upham stressed the holistic approach to the operations of the mind and the disorders of the mind. He didn't have a narrow concept of mental illness; on the contrary, he had a global concept of it. On the other hand, I get the feeling that Ray was really advocating, at that point in time, a much more biological concept of mind. Ray was, in other words, supporting a medical model, whereas Upham was advocating the "psychomoral" model.

THE TEMPORALIZATION OF EGO AND SOCIETY DURING
THE NINETEENTH CENTURY: A VIEW FROM THE TOP

Thom Verhave

*Department of Psychology
Queens College
City University of New York
Flushing, New York 11367*

Willem van Hoorn

*Psychological Institute
The University of Leiden
Leiden, The Netherlands*

> . . . if we do not know our environment, we
> shall mistake our dreams for a part of it, and
> so spoil our science by making it fantastic, and
> our dreams by making them obligatory.
>
> George Santayana, 1910

Let us state our *central* theme by way of six quotations presented in historical order from Pascal (c. 1650) to George Herbert Mead (c. 1927).

1) Blaise Pascal, c. 1650: *The Religious Soul in Conflict*
. . . man knows that he is wretched. He is therefore wretched, because he is so; but he is really great because he knows it.
This twofold nature of man is so evident that some* have thought that we had two souls. A single subject seemed to them incapable of such sudden variations from unmeasured presumption to a dreadful dejection of heart.[1]

2) George Berkeley, 1710: *The Soul Beyond Time*
But, besides all that endless variety of ideas or objects of knowledge, there is likewise something which knows or perceives them and exercises diverse operations, as willing, imagining, remembering, about them. This perceiving, active being is what I call "mind," "spirit." "soul," or "myself," By which words I do not denote any one of my ideas, but a thing entirely distinct from them, wherein they exist or, which is the same thing, whereby they are perceived . . .
We have shown that the soul is indivisible, incorporeal, unextended, and it is consequently incorruptible. Nothing can be plainer than that the motions, changes, decays, and dissolutions which we hourly see befall natural bodies . . . cannot possibly affect an active simple, uncompounded substance; such a being therefore is indissoluble by the force of nature; that is to say, the soul of man is naturally immortal.[2]

3) Adam Smith, 1759: *The Socialization of the Self*
Was it possible that a human creature could grow up to manhood in some solitary place without any communication with his own species, he could no more think of his own character, of the propriety or demerit of his own sentiments and con-

*This allusion seems to have been to Manichaeism.

duct, of the beauty or deformity of his own mind, than of the beauty or deformity of his own face. All these are objects which he cannot easily see, which naturally he does not look at; and with regard to which he is provided with no mirror which can present them to his view. Bring him into society, and he is immediately provided with the mirror which he wanted before. It is placed in the countenance and behavior of those he lives with, which always mark when they enter into, and when they disapprove of his sentiments . . . †[3]

4) John Stuart Mill, 1840: *The Temporalization of the Self*

. . . that entire unfixedness in the social position of individuals—that treading upon the heels of one another—that habitual dissatisfaction of each with the position he occupies, and eager desire to push himself into the next above it—has not this become, and is it not becoming more and more, an English characteristic? In England, as well as in America, it appears to foreigners . . . as if every body had but one wish—to improve his condition, never to enjoy it; as if no Englishman cared to cultivate either the pleasures or the virtues corresponding to his station in society, but solely to get out of it as quickly as possible; or if that cannot be done, and until it is done, to *seem* to have got out of it. 'The hypocrisy of luxury', as M. de Tocqueville calls the maintaining an appearance beyond one's real expenditure, he considers as a democratic peculiarity.‡

. . . the mobility and fluctuating nature of individual relations—the absence of permanent ties, local or personal; how often has this been commented on as one of the organic changes by which the ancient structure of English society is becoming dissolved?

. . . it may now be said, that in all the relations of life, except those to which law and religion have given perpetuity, change has become the general rule, and constancy the exception.[4]

5) William James, 1890: *A Plurality of Social Selves*

Properly speaking, a man has as many social selves as there are individuals who recognize him and carry an image of him in their mind.[5]

6) George Herbert Mead, c. 1927: *Towards the Reintegration of Self and Society*

A multiple personality is in a certain sense normal . . . There is usually an organization of the whole self with reference to the community to which we belong, and the situation in which we find ourselves. What the society is, whether we are living with people of the present, people of our own imaginations, people of the past, varies, of course, with different individuals. Normally, within the sort of community as a whole to which we belong, there is a unified self, but that may be broken up.[6]

Soul, self, social mobility, social self, multiple personality, dissolution, fragmentation: these are some of the key concepts in the above quotations.§ Arranged in chronological succession they are symptomatic of a complex set of interacting historical processes. Their beginnings can be traced to the breaking up of the static medieval world order of the eleventh century.[9] It was between about 1050-1200 A.D. that the modern individual emerged.[10] From then on, the more or less fixed relationship between "self and society" was to begin a series of escalating transformations.[11]

---

†Daniel Defoe's *Robinson Crusoe* was published in 1719.

‡A. de Tocqueville (1805-1859). As we have said, in order to understand the beginning of the temporalization process, it is necessary to return to the observations of contemporary social analysts such as De Tocqueville, J.S. Mill, Veblen, and G.H. Mead. De Tocqueville's classic work *Democracy in America*, which appeared in French in 1835, is a gold mine.

§For a summing-up of the processes indicated, see Van den Berg (1963), *passim*; especially pp. 152-153.[7] See also chapter 4 in M.D. Altschule's recent sourcebook.[8]

Now that we have given a preliminary indication of the central theme, let us state an ambitious question. Given the current manifold ambiguity of the words "Ego" and "Self" and their verbal kin, what *related* social and economic processes can be uncovered as the derivatives of these words (such as "self-control"[12]) enter the vocabularies of the theologies, philosophies, anthropologies, psychologies, psychiatries, and sociologies since the beginning of the nineteenth century? By 1800, "heresy," ecclesiastical as well as secular, was already well enough advanced to make all these specialities themselves "multiparadigmatic."[13] When Benjamin Rush, c. 1810, addressed his medical students "on the Utility of a Knowledge of the Faculties and Operations of the Human Mind . . ." he said: "I am aware, Gentlemen, that the science which I am now recommending to you is an unpopular one; and that it is often treated as chimerical and uncertain. While it bore the name of metaphysics, and consisted of words without ideas, of definitions of nonentities, and of controversies about the ubiquity and other properties of spirit and space, it deserved no quarter from the rational part of mankind . . ."[14]

To return to our central question, a matrix of eight sets of five terms each can provide a useful hint at what is involved in our question about related historical process (TABLE 1). Each of the rows indicates a *separately distinguishable* historical process, of which changes in vocabulary are so often indicative. Note that many of these processes are out-of-phase with each other.

In J.H. Van den Berg's pioneering work *Divided Existence and Complex Society* (1963), the historical emergence of individuals with "plural selves" and the consequent development of a psychiatric and psychological analysis of "states of double consciousness" and "multiple personalities" is described as a result of a "splitting, alienating and pluralizing process".[7] The beginning of that process he locates in the eighteenth century, coincident with the onset of the Industrial Revolution (c. 1760). In this essay we are placing the same developments in a somewhat different context.¶

We view the processes of our matrix as a form of "temporalizing" as that term was employed by A.O. Lovejoy in his classic study of the demise of *The Great Chain of Being*.[15] When something starts to disintegrate, that "thing" or "substance" was either in actual fact—or was merely imagined to be—fixed, solid, unchanging, indivisible, incorruptible, immutable, eternal, immortal, or at least more or less stable. Such a "thing" was Descartes' and Bishop Berkeley's Soul or Self, as was indicated in one of the opening quotations.

When a once indivisible soul, that long cherished "enduring substance" of the Eleatic ontology or of the Christian Faith, when such an "abiding essence" breaks into fragments like another Humpty Dumpty, the impact is bound to reverberate . . . The transition, from a once static "thing" into a dynamic or temporal process was to be a painful one. According to M. Eliade, the development of the notion of an "abiding essence" was a defensive maneuver against "time" as the unfolding present: dealth, destruction, history, change.[16] A similar view can be found in the works of A.O. Lovejoy: "A great part of the history of Western, as of Eastern, philosophy . . . has been a persistent flight from the temporal to the eternal, the quest of an object on which the reason or the imagination might fix itself with the sense of having attained to something that is not merely perduring but immutable, because the very notions of "before" and "after" are inapplicable to it."[17] It is in this context that we want to place the

¶Van den Berg seems to bemoan "The World We Have Lost," to use Peter Lasslett's title. By contrast, the events of the nineteenth century can be viewed as a necessary stage in the loosening of a once fixed social order. The transient phase which the *entire* world is now going through may yet be succeeded by a more humane democracy based on a cybernetically regulated economy.

TABLE 1

RELATED HISTORICAL PROCESSES

	Duality or Unity		Disintegration		Reintegration
Political— Theological— Philosophical Context	God/Person substance soul true self	King/Subject spirit mind autonomy	Society/Self ego consciousness social self	Individuation/ Socialization self-scrutiny mental process attitude	Culture/ Personality personal identity behavior role
Socio- psychological Interphase	alienation	duplicity	dissociation	anomie	unconscious
Socio- economic Context	hierarchy urbanization handicraft	aristocracy stratification manufacture	social mobility secularization division of labor	democratization industrialization assembly line	meritocracy professional- ization neutralized labor

"disintegration or pluralization of the ego."[7] Temporalization is a subjection to time; the ego like the Chain of Being is *temporalized*.[15] (See the matrix.)

The Chain consisted of a fixed hierarchy of created forms ordered according to a scale of perfection. It ranged from primary matter by way of mortal and immortal beings to the most perfect one, such as the Neoplatonic One or God. The disintegration and temporalization of that once mighty cosmic Chain would, in the nineteenth century, result in the Theory of Evolution.

It is during the same period (1740-1800) that Lovejoy placed the temporalization of the Chain of Being** that two other interrelated developments take place. There is an increasing temporalization of labor: beginning with crafts and continuing with manufacture and on to industrial production and a full-blown division of labor. This was already commented upon by Adam Smith in 1776. There is also the emergence of a psychology of *disturbed* consciousness, which shows itself in two different ways. In the lower classes there is an alienation of labor of which alcoholism and other acts of "dissociation" are symptomatic. In the more well-to-do classes, Veblen's emerging "Leisure class," one can detect the beginnings of fashionable diseases such as George Cheyne's "English Malady" (1733), which will develop into the full-blown neurotic syndromes of the nineteenth century.[7] It is in this context that the temporalizing of self and society needs to be placed.

The word "temporal," according to the Random House dictionary, can mean (1) of, or pertaining to time; (2) ... wordly, ... ; (3) temporary, transitory ... ; (4) ... pertaining to ... a temporal adverb or to the tenses of a verb; (5) secular, lay, civil, as opposed to ecclesiastical. All of the above meanings of "temporal" are clearly appropriate to the dissolution of the Christian Soul and its transformation into a mere "fluid self," recently identified with the "Human Potential Movement": "Our current inability to sustain relationships or responsibilities is the result of a largely unnoticed, but nevertheless remarkable transformation in our sense of self stemming from that philosophy."[18] As we showed at the beginning of this essay, the "mobility and fluctuating nature of individual relations," "the absence of permanent ties, local or personal," was already commented upon by J.S. Mill in 1840. It had also been observed a hundred years earlier by George Cheyne. The English Malady was caused by "The Moisture of our Air, the Variableness of our Weather, . . . the Rankness and Fertility of our Soil, the Richness and Heaviness of our Food, the Wealth and Abundance of the Inhabitants . . . the Inactivity and sedentary Occupations of the better Sort (among whom this Evil mostly rages) and the Humour of living in great, populous and

---

**Although temporalization of the Chain takes placed during the period indicated, there is as yet, *no theory of evolution*!

consequently unhealthy Towns." These conditions, he thought, " . . . have brought forth a class and Set of Distempers, with atrocious and frightful symptoms, scarcely known to our Ancestors. . . ."[19]

By 1770, treatment of disorders of the "nervous kind" had become a lucrative and apparently much abused part of medical practice. There is, observed John Gregory in 1770 in his *Observations on the duties and Offices of a Physician . . .*, a

> numerous class of patients who put a physician's good nature and patience to a very severe trial; these I mean who suffer under nervous complaints. Although the fears of these patients are generally groundless, yet their sufferings are real . . . Disorders in the imagination may be as properly the object of a physician's attention as a disorder of the body . . . It is not unusual to find physicians treating these complaints with the most barbarous neglect, or mortifying ridicule, when the patients can ill afford to fee them; while at the same time, among patients of higher rank, they foster them with the utmost care and apparent sympathy: there being no diseases, in the stile of the trade, so lucrative as those of the nervous kind.[20]

Some physicians were soon to follow up John Gregory's assertion that "imaginary distress" was the proper object of a physician's attention. System-builders, such as Erasmus Darwin, would attempt (c. 1794) to formulate an integrated system of medicine.[21] Others such as David Hartley, themselves victims of England's most fashionable disease, would attempt to work through their own problems and conflicts by writing massive volumes filled with "observations on Man, His Frame, His Duty and His Expectations" (1749).[22]

As the quotations from G. Cheyne, John Gregory, and J.S. Mill might indicate, our present social and "clinical" problems date back to an initial spurt in the growth of population during the first half of the eighteenth century. This spurt is related to the Agricultural Revolution of the late seventeenth and early eighteenth centuries, which was due to technical improvements and the cultivation of new crops.[23] These developments, in turn, interact with the beginning of the Industrial Revolution, which brings with it the division of labor and the expansion of towns and cities. All this will lead to the eventual decay of our modern cities, a host of social and public health problems and the ecological crisis, to use one more cliché.

The "social fluidity" commented upon by G. Cheyne and J.S. Mill has now still further penetrated many other aspects of modern culture and society. By now, religious institutions just barely, and legal institutions with great difficulty, provide the "constancy" J.S. Mill still gave them credit for in 1840. All of the aforesaid implies the concept of institutional lag dealt with in our other paper (this volume). It is perhaps significant that J.S. Mill does *not* mention the nuclear family as a stabilizing institution. It could be that he still took the wholesomeness of the family as much for granted as Thomas Upham did.[24] The family as a possible source of alienation, in the sense of the 19th century, was perhaps still "unthinkable" for him. Today it is a rather overworked cliché. The early history of the realization of the family as a source of individual and social pathology would be an important field of investigation, of more importance than the currently fashionable subtopic of "The History of Childhood".

Since the days of the Albigenses and the Averroists of the thirteenth century, each successive step on the way from the "indivisible soul of yore" to the plural self of today has been fought by a conservative opposition. The historical record shows that all those defensive counterreactions against the successive phases and diverse manifestations of the manifold temporalizing process have so far been *a waste of time.* As Harry Stack Sullivan pointed out, c. 1930, "Change has to be accepted as one of the given characteristics of reality. Attitudes intolerant to the new or the old are morbid, and only a broad tolerance fits one to deal with people as they are . . . our growing appreciation of the nature of man and the social processes manifested in and through him must make us even more skeptical toward any finality in human formulations, and increasingly cautious about emotional extravagance in regard to beliefs and customs."[25] This does not mean that such reactionary movements already well and alive during the eighteenth and nineteenth centuries, are now extinct. The neo-Thomists, for example, still favor a corporatist state, if necessary encompassed by a new Chain of Being. Those who imagine themselves to be Cartesians are still in search of the Holy Grail of the Unified Self. Hegelians, although imbued with ideas of organic growth and development, seek to shake off the insecurities of temporal change by inventing imposing "whole" and "totalities."

Within the context of the temporalization of the soul, the persistence of historically older conceptions, arguments, and assumptions can easily be demonstrated. Often the "logic" of such distinct and identifiable religious or philosophical sects, schools, or subcultures can also be observed to remain the same even as their "logos" or style of argumentation adjusts itself to new onslaughts.

In the eighteenth century, the most widely known reaction to David Hume's introspective claim to be empty of self was that of Thomas Reid and the "Scottish Philosophy." As a remnant of the old Colonial Regime, it was to remain influential in the USA until about 1890.†† This is nicely demonstrated by Prof. R.W. Rieber's paper on Thomas Upham.[24]

Prof. Woodward's paper on "Lotze, the Self and American Psychology" demonstrates that the secularization of the Ego transformed it into a plurality of social roles without even giving the appearance of anything "substantial."[26]

The nineteenth century had no such apt term as "future shock," which has only recently become popular.[27] By 1867, Americans already were complaining about the fast-changing times and speculating about the psychological consequences. "We live in an age of intense mental activity and everincreasing cerebral strain," wrote Edward L. Youmans in his *Observations on the Scientific Study of Human Nature.* "Steam and electricity," he continued, "are tasked to bring daily tidings of what is happening all over the world, and impressions pour in upon the brain at a rate with which nothing in the past is comparable. The fierce competitions of business, fashion, study, and political ambition, are at work to sap the vigour and rack the integrity of the mental fabric, and there can be no doubt that there is, in consequence, an immense amount of latent brain disease, productive of much secret suffering and slight aberrations of conduct, and which is liable, in any sudden stress of circumstances, to break out into permanent mental derangement. The price we pay for our high-pressure civilization is a fearful increase of cerebral exhaustion and disorder, and an augmenting ratio of shattered intellects."[28]

Two other related words, however, are closely connected to our central theme: "historicism" and "crisis." Both, like "pessimism" and "nihilism," became fashionable during the nineteenth century. Historicism today has more or less lost its nineteenth century polemical connotations. It refers to the now general recognition that all things human, values as well as institutions, are subject to historical change. Comparative Mythology and Religion, Folklore, Ethnology, Comparative Linguistics, and "Völker Psychologie," all are devel-

††This, of course, would indicate *a discontinuity* in the history of American psychology.

opments of the first half of the nineteenth century. The development of the social sciences since the days of Vico can be viewed as a process of temporalization that runs parallel with the temporalization of the Great Chain of Being. By the time of William James' *Principles of Psychology* (1890), the once substantial and unitary ego has turned into a "spiritual," a "material," and a "social" self. After James, the social self was to "disintegrate" still further into a multitude of "social roles" and "attitudes." The word "crisis" came to have its first more or less technical meaning among nineteenth century economists interested in what is now referred to as "the business cycle."

In addition to the temporalization of both Species and Society, Substance, a traditional bulwark of metaphysics since the day of Parmenides, disintegrated too. Separated from the Scholastic version of Form, Soul as a Cartesian substance became consciousness, then a stream of mental processes, next conduct, and finally, behavior. During the same period "Psychology" changed from a term mainly associated with questions about the immortality of the soul into a still unstable science, continually rearguing its elusive object, scope, and method. The shift from substance to conscious processes, itself a partial consequence of the religious wars and the revival of skepticism of the 16th century, makes the still-puzzling problem of Personal Identity a central and recurring theme of Theology, Philosophy, Psychology, and Psychiatry.

It might be noted in passing that matter, that other Cartesian substance, is also temporalized. The mere mention of the names of Ernst Mach and Albert Einstein is sufficient to make the point.[29]

Still other aspects of the Microcosm are temporalized all at an accelerated pace during the nineteenth century. As the medieval feudal and political hierarchy breaks up, the status of the individual with respect to society becomes unstable and problematic. This produces social phenomena not unlike those which occurred during the disintegration of the Roman Empire.[30] This time, however, they occur within the *novel context* of increasingly more secularized and industrialized separate nation states and their more "primitive" colonies. Individualism, nihilism, anomie, dissociation, are tell-tale products of that nineteenth century which has bequeathed us all its unsolved problems and still unresolved conflicts.[31]

Psychologists, of whatever persuasion, will do well to keep in mind Freud's recognition of the limitations of psychotherapy. In a letter to James J. Putnam, he wrote:

> I believe that your complaint that we are not able to compensate our neurotic patients for giving up their illness is quite justified. But it seems to me that this is not the fault of therapy but rather of social institutions. What would you have us do when a woman complains about her thwarted life, when, with youth gone, she notices that she has been deprived of the joy of loving for merely conventional reasons? She is quite right and we stand helpless before her . . . . But the recognition of our therapeutic limitations reinforces our determination to change other social factors so that men and women shall not longer be forced into hopeless situations.[32]

That, however, raises political and economic issues which *historians* of psychology have avoided for too long.

A SUMMING UP

That all is flux has remained the enduring insight of Heraclitus. Change, function, and process became the central themes of nineteenth century philosophy, biology, psychology, and physics. It would appear that the one thing that has remained invariant in the social, political, and cultural flux since the days of Petrarch has itself been a process: the temporalizing of all things human.

As an antidote to the "metaphysical pathos,"[15] so easily aroused by words such as "flux" and "disintegration," it must be pointed out that the word "crisis" (from Greek "Krisis," to divide or separate) unlike its relative "schism" (from Greek "schizein," to split or cleave) implies *a crucial turning point* as in a disease. The modern, postcolonial, increasingly more closely integrated, and obviously economically interdependent world may yet achieve a measure of economic, political, social, and thus also psychological stability in the cybernetic sense of that ancient concept.‡‡ If it does so, and it may not, developments in psychology and related sciences after the start of the Industrial Revolution will be viewed as the natural creative consequences of an unstable *transient* period which lasted two hundred, perhaps even four hundred years. To see things "sub specie temporalis," however, is as Spinoza would have acknowledged, "as difficult as it is rare".

REFERENCES

1. PASCAL, B. 1670. Pensées (nos. 416 and 417). 1941 edit.: 131, 132. Random House (Modern Library). New York, N.Y.
2. BERKELEY, G. 1710. A Treatise concerning the Principles of Human Knowledge, wherein the chief causes of error and difficulty in the sciences, with the grounds of skepticism, atheism, and irreligion, are inquired into. 1965 edit. C.M. Turbayne, Ed.: 24-95. Bobbs-Merrill. Indianapolis, Ind.
3. SMITH, A. 1759. The Theory of Moral Sentiments; or An Essay towards An Analysis of the Principles by which Men Naturally judge concerning the Conduct and Character, first of their Neighbours, and afterwards of Themselves, to which is added, A Dissertation on the Origin of languages. 6th edit. 1777. J. Beatty and C. Jackson, Eds.: 180-181. Dublin, Ireland.
4. MILL, J.S. 1840 An Appraisal of Volume II of Democracy in America. *In* A. de Tocqueville. Democracy in America. 1961 edit. Vol. 2: XLIV-XLV. Schocken Books. New York, N.Y.
5. JAMES, W. 1890. The Principles of Psychology. Vol. 2: 294. Henry Holt & Co. New York, N.Y.
6. MEAD, G.H. 1934. Mind, Self and Society from the Standpoint of a Social Behaviorist: 142-143. The University of Chicago Press. Chicago, Ill.
7. VAN DEN BERG, J.H. 1963. Leven in Meervoud. Een metabletisch onderzoek. Callenbach. Nijkerk, The Netherlands. Engl. edit. 1974. Divided Existence and Complex Society. Duquesne University Press. Pittsburgh, Pa.
8. ALTSCHULE, M.D. 1976. The Development of Traditional Psychopathology. A. Sourcebook. John Wiley & Sons. New York, N.Y.
9. BRANDT, W.J. 1966. The Shape of Medieval History. Studies in Modes of Perception. Yale University Press. New Haven, Conn.
10. MORRIS, C. 1972. The Discovery of the Individual. 1050-1200. Harper and Row. New York, N.Y.
11. BENTON, J.F. 1970. Self and Society in Medieval France. The Memoirs of Abbot Guibert of Nogent (1064?-1125). Harper and Row. New York, N.Y.
12. KLAUSNER, S.Z., Ed. 1965. The Quest for Self-Control. Classical Philosophies and Scientific Research. The Free Press. New York, N.Y.
13. LAKATOS, I. & A. MUSGRAVE, eds. 1970. Criticism and the Growth of Knowledge. Cambridge University Press. London, England.
14. RUSH, B. 1811. On the Utility of a Knowledge of the Faculties and Operations of the Human Mind, to a Physician: 271. Bredford & Innskeep. Philadelphia, Pa.
15. LOVEJOY, A.O. 1936. The Great Chain of Being. A Study of the History of an Idea. Harvard University Press. Cambridge, Mass.
16. ELIADE, M. 1949. Cosmos and History. (Le mythe de l'éternel retour). 1959 edit. Harper and Row. New York, N.Y.

‡‡Compare terms such as constancy, equilibrium, harmony, balance.

17. LOVEJOY, A.O. 1961. The Reason, the Understanding and Time: 75-76. Johns Hopkins Press. Baltimore, Md.
18. KILPATRICK, W. 1975. Identity and Intimacy: 3. Dell Publishing Co. New York, N.Y.
19. CHEYNE, G. 1733. The English Malady: or, a Treatise of Nervous Diseases of All Kinds; as Spleen, Vapours, Lowness of spirits, Hypochondriacal, and hysterical distempers, etc. . . . 1739 edit.: I-II. Strahan & Leake. London, England.
20. HUNTER, R. & I. MACALPINE, Eds. 1963. Three Hundred Years of Psychiatry. 1535-1860. A History presented in selected English Texts: 438. Oxford University Press. London, England.
21. VERHAVE, T. & P.R. BINDLER. 1974. A Man of Knowledge Revisited: A Preface to the New Edition of Zoonomia. AMS Press. New York, N.Y.
22. VERHAVE, T. 1973. David Hartley: The Mind's Road to God. An Introduction to the New Edition of Hartley's Theory of The Human Mind. AMS Press. New York, N.Y.
23. BUER, M.C. 1926. Health, Wealth and Population in the early days of the Industrial Revolution. George Routledge & Sons. London, England.
24. RIEBER, R.W. This volume.
25. SULLIVAN, H. 1972. Personal Psychopathology: 9. Norton. New York, N.Y.
26. WOODWARD, W.R. 1976. Lotze, the Self, and American Psychology. This volume.
27. TOFFLER, A. 1970. Future Shock. Random House. New York, N.Y.
28. YOUMANS, E.L., Ed. 1867. The Culture Demanded by Modern Life: 402-403. D. Appleton. New York, N.Y.
29. TOULMIN, S. & J. GOODFIELD, e.g. 1965. The discovery of time: 266. Harper and Row. New York, N.Y.
30. DODDS, E.R. 1965. Pagan and Christian in an Age of Anxiety. Some Aspects of Religious Experience from Marcus Aurelius to Constantine. Norton. New York, N.Y.
31. ELLENBERGER, H.F. 1970. The Discovery of the Unconscious. The History and Evolution of Dynamic Psychiatry. Basic Books. New York, N.Y. See also WALLACE, A.R. 1898. The Wonderful Century, its Successes and Failures. 1903 edit. Dodd and Mead. New York, N.Y.
32. HALE, N.C. 1971. James Jackson Putnam and Psychoanalysis: Letters Between Putnam and Freud: 90-91. Harvard University Press. Cambridge, Mass.

DEVELOPMENTAL PSYCHOLOGY AND THE SELF

John M. Broughton

Department of Psychology
Wayne State University
Detroit, Michigan 48202

Klaus F. Riegel

Department of Psychology
University of Michigan
Ann Arbor, Michigan 48104

To dress correctly for the Bicentennial, psychologists are required to sport the tasteful color combination of pride and optimism. The arrival of the "Self" would rudely shatter the atmosphere, for this unwelcome guest wears a tattered and outré costume. She used to be the life and soul of the party; now people whisper behind her back. "She's charming on the surface, but after a while you find there's no substance to her." If two of the early presidents of the A.P.A., Mary Whiton Calkins and James Mark Baldwin, proclaimed psychology as "the science of selves," so much the worse for the A.P.A.

Like its political past, America's developmental interpretations of the Self are founded upon distinctly different intellectual traditions originating in seventeenth and eighteenth century Europe. The British empiricism of Locke and Hume, which was most significant for experimental psychology and the study of individual differences, also exerted a formative influence upon the psychology of the Self as expressed by American functionalists, most notably Allport. In this tradition, the Self was conceived as arising from experience through a clustering of impressions.

The idea of such an empirical Self constituted an intellectual reaction to the rational Self of Descartes. The Self seen from this latter perspective represents the core that makes any knowledge of the person possible at all; the concrete experiences appear as mere symptoms documenting and demonstrating what is known to begin with. The autonomous Self, although in a more moderate form, entered into the logical *a-priorism* of Kant, and through Kant influenced American developmental interpretations.

Both orientations, British empiricism and Continental rationalism, remained individual-centered (or rather, "Self-centered"). The social determinants were treated as only secondary. Moreover, both orientations were a-developmental and a-historical. Thus, viewing the Self in its intimate interdependence with social conditions appears to be one of the most original contributions of American sociologists, most conspicuously, the symbolic interactionists. This idea also had its predecessors: proponents of idealistic and materialistic dialecticism like Hegel, Marx, and Engels. Departing from these philosophical orientations, however, symbolic interactionism stripped the dialectics of its concrete historical basis, thus making its interpretation more congruent with the synchronic viewpoints of traditional philosophy and sciences, most notably with the theories of Self originating from British empiricism and Continental rationalism. It remains an important and uncompleted task to elucidate the historical and developmental aspects of the study of Self.

Instead of the more usual focus on Freudian and neo-Freudian concepts of the Ego which has been well handled by Loevinger, Rapaport, and others,[1] we will explore the evolution of some other conceptions of Self: the more distinctly American approaches of functionalism, symbolic interactionism, and cognitive-developmentalism. First, we will discuss skeptical empiricist critiques of the idea that there is a substantial "Soul." The view that the Self is no more than a Self-Concept is examined to see if it results in a substantially different interpretation. Other reflexive views, which introduce into the Self its extrinsic social relations, are then dealt with, comparing the different approaches of Laing, Goffman, and the Baldwin/Mead tandem. Baldwin's work is the fulcrum upon which we find balanced the symbolic interactionist tradition on the one hand, and the cognitive-developmental tradition on the other. The post-Kantian concerns of developmental theories (Baldwin, Piaget, and Kohlberg) then raise the issues of subject/object relation, intersubjectivity and self-consciousness in all their complexity. However, these theories leave us the "prisoners of form,"[2] still without the needed understanding of practical and historical aspects of the Self. Finally, the "double interaction" paradigm of Rubinstein is discussed, as a potential contribution to such an understanding. Throughout, we will be reminded that concepts of Self dialectically condition and are conditioned by concepts of experience, consciousness, and knowledge.[3]

SUBSTANCE AND ANTISUBSTANCE

Behaviorists like Skinner have rejected the "Self" of everyday language because this concept is imbedded in an approach that

> . . . is a vestige of animism, a doctrine which in its crudest form held that the body was moved by one or more indwelling spirits.[4]

To criticize such a crude "thingification" of the Self is, of course, correct. Although in everyday metaphorical parlance we often speak as though we have an "inner man," such a homuncular conception begs the question: What is the Self of the little man? This leads to an infinite regress.

However, that notion of the Self is somewhat of a straw man. In addressing the homunculus notion, one runs the risk of confusing a Medieval or Enlightenment spiritualism with a pre-Socratic animism, and thereby choosing the wrong opponent (after the fashion of Muhammad Ali).

Furthermore, such a criticism does not even serve the purpose of distinguishing behaviorists from humanists. Humanistic psychologists (like Bugental and Allport, for example), *also* vilify any crass reification of the organism's activity, and find it in the interests of scientific humanism to dispense with the Self or Ego as such.[5] In this case, therefore, Skinner's *ignoratio elenchii* serves incidentally to bind him to the Humanists, rather than separate him from them. For both, activity preserves the integrity of the organism, and it is this observable organism that is active, not some introspected Agent, or homunculus.

Others[6] have disposed of the Self by simply arguing that emphasis on the individual ignores the essentially social and interactive nature of man. The creed of this point of view is that nothing is separated and isolated; everything is given in relation. This position is often supported by appeal to the situational variability of human behavior, and a downplaying of theories that reify substantial "traits."[7]

These objections, however, leave the Cartesian concept of Self as Substance less impaired than might be imagined. The substantial Soul of Descartes is conceived as an immaterial thinking thing, and is not a minature person or a collection of traits. Neither is it a material object, although admittedly Substance is conceived metaphorically on the model of material reality, and as though it occupied a location internal to the person. The substantial Self is the law-like essence or "nature" of the individual, which is independent, immutable, indivisible, and self-intuiting. Like an explanatory "law of the person," it binds together at a deeper level all the variable particular instances or relations of the manifest person. This allows us to say that these are variations of *something*, or relations of *something* to its social context, rather than instances of different things.

The essential attribute of this *thing* was thought. However, Hume's critique, like William James' after him, intelligently questioned whether one needed to assume that thought was an attribute of some*thing*. From his standpoint, the Self was never given to us as a whole. Certainty attached instead to the individual data of sense experience,[8] and the soul was merely an illusory belief, or an idle metaphysical speculation. Or in the spirit of James,[9] if thinking is the essential thing, why not just confine the Self to the present, passing Thought? To para-phrase that scholarly denizen of the Big Apple, Woody Allen, to attempt an empirical study of the Soul is like trying to get a plumber on weekends.

Hume's empiricist interpretation, and James' elaboration of its psychological component, made Self an empirical "me," placing it entirely within experience, and opening the way to a *psychological* approach to self-conception. This self-conception is not Descartes' inner intuition of the certainty of Self, but is a Self-Concept—a cognitive induction from the regular features of self-experience. In the empiricist view, this induced concept is an abstraction, and as such does not claim to point to anything "real" beyond itself.

A modern example of this approach is the work of Bugental and Zelen in 1950.[10] They studied individuals' self-concepts simply by asking them to give answers to the question "Who Are You?" Under this kind of interpretation, and using this now-popular[11] kind of method, the developmental psychologist usually charts the quantitative age-related regularities in such self-descriptions, not claiming to distinguish development from change,[12] and usually preferring a *description* of ontogenesis rather than an explanation. This description can deal with changes in the content and organization of the self-concept, with its increasing complexity or efficiency, for example, but does not look for *developments* in the *form* of the Self-Concept. All people at all times have a self-concept of basically the same kind.

The functionalist perspective on Self receives its clearest formulation in the work of Gordon Allport[5] carried out (perhaps not entirely by coincidence) in William James Hall at Harvard. Allport's "Proprium" is an empirical self, comprising the unique attitudes, values, and self-perceptions which are of persistent importance to the individual. At its center is a dynamic "self-image" of the individual's "present abilities, status and roles: and what he would like to become, his aspirations for himself"[14] (p. 47). The difference between actual present self and future ego-ideal generates a "propriate striving" of the individual, a specific kind of competence motivation which Allport compares to the "self-actualisation" of Goldstein and Maslow. The process of striving by the organism is supposed to maintain the integrity of its boundaries and the internal consistency of the individual's "personality."

The integration of past, present, and future plays a significant role, because the fact that our concerns extend into the future, and (as Hume admitted) (Frondizi,[8] p. 121 ff.), the fact that we can extend our personal identity backwards beyond our memory, are both indicative of some persistent Self over and above a bundle of perceptions. A similar function is served covertly by the emphasis on life crises and struggling.

But does this persistence over time not embarrass the Self-Concept or Self-Image theorist, who appears, in the true spirit of positivism, to want to follow Hume's or James' critique of metaphysical Substance? Ironically, the Self-Concept has taken on many of the characteristics of substantiality that had suffered under the cutting edge of Hume's skepticism and James' pragmatism. The Self-Concept or Proprium is typically attributed stability and permanence, is resistant to change, expresses the "essence" which the person strives to realize, and takes on a central dynamic role, like an Agent, in the individual's life. Although Allport denies it (Evans,[13] p. 42), the idea of Self-Concept even appears to presuppose Cartesian self-knowledge as privileged access to private mental events, expressing the absolute independence central to the concept of Self as Substance. Finally, in this tradition, self-conception is construed as *a* self-concept, or *a* proprium, suggesting a unitary entity. Hume was always embarrassed by the fact that his view indicated the Self was a *bundle* of perceptions (Frondizi,[8] p. 121 fn.), and not just *perceptions per se*.

Recently, American humanistic psychologists like Bugental,[5] and Bohart[6] have seen the apparent fixity of the Self-Concept as a problem for the man-in-the-street, *for the individual self-conceivers,* who simply make a mistake in thinking that way instead of in terms of a process or a flux of particulars. If this were the case, we might legitimately ask, as Hume did, for a psychological account of how people come to such an illusory belief.[14] But is it not also a problem *for the theory*, encumbered by a confused theoretical construct which, while ushering one metaphysical mistress out of the front door (for reasons of purity) allows another to illicitly sneak in the back? This Marx Brothers routine reflects genuine *conceptual* problems inherent in the concept of the Self-Concept, such as the following.

1) How does one know which of one's characteristics are *unique?* Does this not imply knowledge of other selves, also?

2) Even given this, how does one know that these characteristics are properties of *the same self*, rather than, say, a "fruit salad" from several people?

3) Even given that these are properties of the same self, how do I know that it is *my* self, and that these properties pertain exclusively to *me?* (One interesting alternative would be that this "thing" is a *"selves-concept,"* representing *general* characteristics of the human self, pertaining to all individuals. This would take advantage of the broader meaning of "concept." The empiricist view limits "conceiving" to a quasivisual process of concrete perception.[15]

4) Does the Self-Concept not imply a self-conceiver or a Self conceived? (The hyphen always splits the Self into two parts. Thus, in the ideology of Self-Control,[4] there must be a "Master-Self" and a "Slave-Self.")

5) If the Self-Concept does not imply a Self, is the Self-concept true of anything, or is it just a set of "attributions" or guesses?

6) If the typifications of oneself are at all veridical, how is it that one can take an objective stance towards oneself? (This again would appear to assume that reflection is reducible to a visual "self-seeing" that is purely receptive and does not transform the Self observed in any way.)

7) Why should we assume that impressions or self-perceptions are absolute givens, when we deny this privilege to the substantial self?

8) How can we claim that a self-concept or proprium is an *empirically discovered* clustering of properties, when the self-report techniques used to tap Self-Concept *assume* that there must be such a constellation of attitudes, for example, in the very question "Who Are You?" It is hard to see what form an empirical disconfirmation of the existence of a Self-Concept or Proprium would take. Allport's Jamesian criterion, that some values and self-perceptions are "warm"[13] (p. 42), or *more important* to the individual than others, seems weak and debatable as evidence. Similarly, the holistic notion of the integrity of the organism, which is basic to the functionalist approach, appears less of a product of factual observation than a precept necessitated by the assumption that experience is essentially fragmentary.

THE INTERSUBJECTIVE SELF

Hidden behind these issues is a deeper assumption. The theories of the empirical self we have been discussing concern the individual's description of *what* he or she is. This, however, assumes that the individual already knows somehow *that* he or she is. Descartes and Kant have in common this rationalist concern with the logically prior self-experience that tells me that I *exist*. R.D. Laing[16] therefore took everyone by surprise when he suggested that not only do people not take this for granted, but that it is the ontological question of the Self's existence that underlies personality development and pathology. This would have been no more than an interesting curiosity, again confirming the eccentricity of the British, if it were not for the following fact. Laing argued that the assertion of the Self's existence, which had previously been confined to the shady and speculative realms of metaphysics, was now found to be very relevant indeed in the emergence of personality. In addition, Laing's empirical documentation of behavior, albeit clinical, was enough to pique the interest of even the diehard positivist. Evidence of human self-consciousness was thereby shown to be independent of introspection, a position argued theoretically by Kant long before, in opposition to Descartes. Yet, Laing appeared to take sides *with* the sceptics, being as virulent an opponent as they of the substantial interpretation of the Subject. He thus backed Hume's critique, while avoiding the narrowness of Hume's view that Existence implied Essence.

Because of this peculiar combination of stances, it has been tempting to regard Laing as a theoretical chameleon, and to assimilate those parts of the mixture that resonated with traditions outside European existentialism and phenomenology. The symbolic interactionism of Mead, Baldwin, and Cooley, developed in the first third of this century, fills such a role neatly, since, like the Laingian view, it stresses interpersonal relations as the matrix from which the Self develops.[17]

Although symbolic interactionism is often considered an alternative paradigm to functionalism in the social sciences, it has much in common with Dewey's original emphasis on the situational context.[18] Self is not a simple biological individual or an essence, but is part of a dialectically elaborated social polarity. Self and Other develop *pari passu,* through a process of interpersonal interaction at the symbolic or ideational level. One reacts to the other as someone similar to oneself, takes the role of the other, and is thus able to respond covertly to oneself as an object. One has a "generalized self"—the imaginations that others have of the self which are introjected. Similarly, the other is a function of the ideas that the self has of the other.[19] The development of the self therefore follows the development of role-taking, which, in turn, is dependent on the give-and-take of social experience. Communication is made the point of interpenetration of individual and society, and it takes place either through a shared language (Mead) or through acts of social imitation (Baldwin).

This view has in common with the Self-Concept approach that it places the Self within consciousness—as a reflexive self-*concept* or interpretation. The Self-Concept tradition has in common with other approaches its attempt to render a "nonegological" conception of consciousness (to borrow a phrase from Gurwitsch.[20]) The entity "Self" is reduced to a reflexive *relation*, to a hyphen, as in Self-Concept, Self-Realization, Self-Regulation, Self-Control, and so on. Symbolic interactionism also reduces substance to relation, although it differs in that the relation of self to itself is now *through another self.* The experience of oneself is dependent upon experiencing the world as containing other selves. The concepts of self and of other selves develop together. This reflective consciousness peculiar to humans is *intersubjective,* and involves the taking of another's role; it is no longer the activity of an individual alone.

This approach therefore has the advantage of exposing the fictitious quality of an absolutely subjective and private personal experience and the spatialization of Self that occurs when one views it as "inner" rather than "outer." Cooperative expressions of reflection, like science, become understandable. We are, however, left with some familiar problems and some new ones.[21]

1) How do we reintroduce the subject/object relation into this approach which so much emphasizes the subject/subject relation? Whereas the Cartesian model led to a privately subjective and idealistic notion of experience, symbolic interactionism appears to lead to a *publicly* subjective and idealistic interpretation. Social reality, and even nonsocial reality, are not distinguished from social consciousness. The possibility of "false consciousness" is thereby eliminated, and objectivity becomes absorbed in intersubjectivity (Lichtman[21]).

2) Similarly, on the subject side, we again have the problem of distinguishing the Self from a personification of the Self, for as Harry Stack Sullivan says,

> . . . the relation of personifications to that which is personified is always complex and sometimes multiple; and that personifications are not adequate descriptions of that which is personified.[7] (p. 167)

In the symbolic interactionist's view, is the individual's personification veridical? Does it represent a *perception of* the self, or is it a mere *attribution of characteristics to* the self, of dubious and inestimable objectivity?

3) Again, restricting the Self to a perceived or imagined "me" means that the Self is treated as "an object which is in most respects like all other objects."[22] This raises the possibility of taking the role of objects, and makes the Self hard to differentiate from nonconscious and nonself-conscious things. The subjectivity of the Self is thus removed.

4) Why is intersubjectivity *necessary* for reflection? Is self-consciousness not possible without role-taking? The "outer" now appears to receive undue stress at the expense of the "inner," in reaction against the old "inner" substantial Self. Reflection as role-taking is simply substituted for, and not integrated with, individual self-reflection.

5) This raises the question of how someone knows when he or she is conscious of himself or herself, and when conscious of another self? Said slightly differently, how do I know when I am reflecting on *my* thoughts, and when on *your* thoughts or *our* thoughts, or even *someone else's* thoughts?

6) As Dewey has pointed out,[23] the upshot of this is that making Self a shared meaning, without sufficient attention to the *differentiation* of Self and Other, leaves the Self to be absorbed into the larger whole of a Social Self. We cannot then account for the psychic sense of individuality. Dewey further argues that symbolic interactionism does not demonstrate the *origins* of individual and society, only their reciprocal relations to each other, taking their existence for granted to start with. Self is therefore fragmented in a similar way to the empiricist fragmentation mentioned above, the discrete units now being roles indeterminate as to the subjects filling them or taking them.

The apparent consequences just outlined bear a marked resemblance to the loss of Self in other sociological accounts, especially those that emphasize the liberal virtue of "flexibility." For example, Parsons *et al.*[24] reduce personality to an anonymous role cluster, at the center of which is no one. Such a role cluster can vary in its complexity and in the degree and efficiency of its organization.[15] Goffman also uses the concept of "role" in his reduction of Self to its extrinsic relational properties.[25] The Self for Goffman is no more than a series of "presentations" or false facades, approximating the "false" or "disembodied" Self of Laing. Whereas Laing argues that this division of the "me" from the "I" is a pathology of the Self, for Goffman there is no distinction between this inauthentic, alienated Self and a normal or real Self.[26]

Goffman's "masks" are presented in a semideliberate fashion, in order that the reaction of the other can be predicted and controlled. The Self is thus defined as free agent by its ability to act on the other to act on the Self.[27] Thus the Self-as-Role corresponds to the Self-as-Idea (Self-Concept), in the sense that the former is something one chooses rather than being the *chooser*, while the latter is something one thinks, rather than being the *thinker*.

SELF AS DEVELOPMENT

Despite the similarities between this approach and symbolic interactionism, the latter differs in that one *takes* the role of the "generalized other," a universal subjective point of view, rather than (in the dramaturgical metaphor) *playing* a specific role or part. Prediction or control of the specific content of the concrete other's reactions is not the main purpose in such role-taking.

A certain idealism is suggested by this concentration on the general form of the role, rather than its content, and on the theoretical intent or meaning of thought rather than on the practical intent of action or manipulation. It is not surprising, then, that symbolic interactionism finds its roots largely in Hegel's dialectic of reason, or that it receives its most trenchant criticisms at the hands of neo-Marxist thinkers.[28] The mutual role-taking described is Hegelian in the sense that it not only comprises a synchronic social dialectic, but also, by the contradictions that it raises, opens up the possibility of a diachronic perspective as well. The Self can not only *change content* over time, or become more efficiently organized, but can rise to a qualitatively superior level through the radical reconstruction of its underlying assumptions—through a development in *form*. It becomes more certain of its existence as it becomes progressively differentiated from the Other.

Unlike Goffman, Mead and Baldwin see social knowledge as a developmental process of this kind, although their emphasis is on the diachronic as *development* more than as *history*. Modern developmental theorists like Werner, Piaget, and particularly Kohlberg are the contemporary heirs of this tradition.[29] Such theorists follow Hegel's assumption that the real is rational consciousness, and that development *is* the development of thought. Development is in fact taken as the defining quality of life and of the human Self. It is not simply contingent, therefore, that in Werner, Piaget, and Kohlberg, "Development" and the "Self" find themselves together. It is logically inherent in the organismic model that the Self is that which undergoes organic differentiation and reintegration through successive transformations or "sublations," the differentiations representing decreased egocentrism and increased self-knowledge (Blasi,[21]). As MacMurray[17] points out, "The answer to Hume's scepticism about the form of the material was the construction of the form of the organic." (p. 82)

Both Self and Development then are species-defining properties, a consequence of the fusion of Hegelian with Darwinian thought that the work of Mead, Baldwin, and Dewey represents.[30] Evolutionary theory emphasized the biological aspect of neo-Hegelian concepts, shifting the center of gravity away from cultural-historical world views toward the adaptive cognitive development of the biological individual, despite the fact that evolution occurs primarily at the *population* genetic level. The cognitive-developmental theories have thus strongly resisted the reduction of Self to its extrinsic relations, aligning themselves very much with Kierkegaard, who

> . . . argued that the most important dialectical process is manifested in the subjective, personal development of individual existence. Kierkegaard denied that there are dialectical processes in history or nature, but held that such processes are dominant in the life-histories of individuals.[31]

The invariant logical sequence of stages in cognitive-developmental theories removes one possible source of relativism. However, subordinating the dialectics of history, nature, or social context does not necessarily preserve the Self as entity. Self-as-Organism is a precarious identity-in-difference. Self and Development are in constant tension, since the Self is viewed as existing only in its own self-negation—in its Becoming rather than its Being.

A somewhat illusory impression of stability is afforded by the assumption that there is a "final stage." This is the *telos* of the Self fully differentiated from the Other, but in the sense of a universal transcendent, or self-conscious Self, aware of its own subjectivity, not a particular individual with unique concrete personality content.[32] While the idea of a *telos* does not imply vitalism, it effectively defines the way in which we understand the course of development that culminates in the "logic" of the final stage. However, as Piaget in particular admits[32] (p. 33f), Godel's theorem demonstrates that there is no way that the logic of any system can substantiate that there is no logic more comprehensive than its own. . . . "Final" stages must therefore always stand as provisional. There is always the possibility that a further development might reflexively bring into question even the concept of "stage" itself.[23] There are already murmurings about the self-transcendence of Piaget's final stage, particualrly with respect to the limitations of a formal logic as the ultimate definition of intelligence. Similarly, Kohlberg metaphorically refers to a mystical-religious "stage 7" modeled after Baldwin and Spinoza, that surpasses his "final" 6th stage of principled moral judgment. Habermas, on the other hand, has made specific theoretical proposals for a seventh stage that lies still within the realm of normative ethics and metaethics.[34]

Keeping in mind, then, the provisional nature of Piaget and Kohlberg's "final" stages, we can still ask how they characterize the mature and fully-differentiated Self. Without going into the details of their theories, we can

TABLE 1

PIAGET'S ERAS AND STAGES OF LOGICAL AND COGNITIVE DEVELOPMENT*

Era I (age 0–2) The Era of Sensorimotor Intelligence

Stage 1.   Reflex action.
Stage 2.   Coordination of reflexes and sensorimotor repetition (primary circular reaction).
Stage 3.   Activities to make interesting events in the environment reappear (secondary circular reaction).
Stage 4.   Means/ends behavior and search for absent objects.
Stage 5.   Experimental search for new means (tertiary circular reaction).
Stage 6.   Use of imagery in insightful invention of new means and in recall of absent objects and events.

Era II (age 2–5) Symbolic, Intuitive, or Prelogical Thought

Inference is carried on through images and symbols which do not maintain logical relations or invariances with one another. "Magical thinking" in the sense of (1) confusion of apparent or imagined events with real events and objects and (2) confusion of perceptual appearances of qualitative and quantitative change with actual change.

Era III (age 6–10) Concrete Operational Thought

Inferences carried on through system of classes, relations, and quantities maintaining logically invariant properties and which *refer to concrete objects*. These include such logical processes as (1) inclusion of lower-order classes in higher-order classes; (2) transitive seriation (recognition that if a > b and b > c, then a > c); (3) logical addition and multiplication of classes and quantities; (4) conservation of number, class membership, length, and mass under apparent change.
Substage 1.   Formation of stable categorical classes.
Substage 2.   Formation of quantitative and numerical relations of invariance.

Era IV (age 11 to adulthood) Formal-Operational Thought

Inferences through logical operations upon propositions or "operations upon operations." Reasoning about reasoning. Construction of systems of all possible relations or implications. Hypothetico-deductive isolation of variables and testing of hypotheses.
Substage 1.   Formation of the inverse of the reciprocal. Capacity to form negative classes (for example, the class of all not-crows) and to see relations as simultaneously reciprocal (for example, to understand that liquid in a U-shaped tube holds an equal level because of counterbalanced pressures).
Substage 2.   Capacity to order triads of propositions or relations (for example, to understand that if Bob is taller than Joe and Joe is shorter than Dick, then Joe is the shortest of the three).
Substage 3.   True formal thought. Construction of all possible combinations of relations, systematic isolation of variables, and deductive hypothesis-testing.

*From Kohlberg & Gilligan.[42]

summarize by saying that their final stages share a structure of possibilities, generated through reflection, among which determinate choices are made (TABLES 1 & 2).[35] For Piaget, the theoretic Self chooses through an act of scientific judgment and empirical method.[36] For Kohlberg, the moral Self chooses in an act of Will, and through a method of ethics (akin to Kant's categorical imperative). These mature structures are not just the most "complex," or "flexible." To say that would be to borrow again the functionalist or system-theory notions of the adaptive organization of content. The consequence of using such concepts is a return to a relativistic position, in which what counts is an ability to accommodate to specific situations, and in which what counts as "flexibility" or "complexity" varies with the cultural or historical context. Also, "complexity" and "flexibility" are, by virtue of their very generality, leveling concepts that apply equally to all domains. Their use can therefore obscure the qualitative difference between logic and morality. By contrast, the final stages

TABLE 2
DEFINITION OF MORAL STAGES*

Preconventional Level

At this level the child is responsive to cultural rules and labels of good and bad, right or wrong, but interprets these labels in terms of either the physical or the hedonistic consequences of action (punishment, reward, exchange of favors), or in terms of the physical power of those who enunciate the rules and labels. The level is divided into the following two stages.

Stage 1: *The punishment and obedience orientation*. The physical consequences of action determine its goodness or badness, regardless of the human meaning or value of these consequences. Avoidance of punishment and unquestioning deference to power are valued in their own right, not in terms of respect for an underlying moral order supported by punishment and authority (the latter being stage 4).

Stage 2: *The instrumental relativist orientation*. Right action consists of that which instrumentally satisfies one's own needs and occasionally the needs of others. Human relations are viewed in terms like those of the market place. Elements of fairness, of reciprocity, and of equal sharing are present, but they are always interpreted in a physical pragmatic way. Reciprocity is a matter of "you scratch my back and I'll scratch yours," not of loyalty, gratitude, or justice.

Conventional level

At this level, maintaining the expectations of the individual's family, group, or nation is perceived as valuable in its own right, regardless of immediate and obvious consequences. The attitude is not only one of *conformity* to personal expectations and social order, but of loyalty to it, of actively *maintaining*, supporting, and justifying the order, and of identifying with the persons or group involved in it. At this level, there are the following two stages:

Stage 3: *The interpersonal concordance or "good boy—nice girl" orientation*. Good behavior is that which pleases or helps others and is approved by them. There is much conformity to stereotypical images of what is majority or "natural" behavior. Behavior is frequently judged by intention—"he means well" becomes important for the fist time. One earns approval by being "nice."

Stage 4: *The "law and order" orientation'* There is orientation toward authority, fixed rules, and the maintenance of the social order. Right behavior consists of doing one's duty, showing respect for authority, and maintaining the given social order for it's own sake.

Postconventional, autonomous, or principled level

At this level, there is a clear effort to define moral values and principles which have validity and application apart from the authority of the groups or persons holding these principles, and apart from the individual's own identification with these groups. This level again has two stages:

Stage 5: *The social-contract legalistic orientation*, generally with utilitarian overtones. Right action tends to be defined in terms of general individual rights, and standards that have been critically examined and agreed upon by the whole society. There is a clear awareness of the relativism of personal values and opinions and a corresponding emphasis upon procedural rules for reaching consensus. Aside from what is constitutionally and democratically agreed upon, the right is a matter of personal "values" and "opinion." The result is an emphasis upon the "legal point of view," but with an emphasis upon the possibility of changing law in terms of rational considerations of social utility (rather than freezing it in terms of stage 4 "law and order"). Outside the legal realm, free agreement and contract is the binding element of obligation. This is the "official" morality of the American government and constitution.

Stage 6: *The universal ethical principle orientation*. Right is defined by the decision of conscience in accord with self-chosen *ethical principles* appealing to logical comprehensiveness, universality, and consistency. These principles are abstract and ethical (the Golden Rule, the categorical imperative); they are not concrete moral rules like the Ten Commandments. At heart, these are universal principles of *justice*, of the *reciprocity* and *equality* of human *rights*, and of respect for the dignity of human beings as *individual persons*.

*From Kohlberg.[54]

of Piaget's and Kohlberg's schemes represent respectively the most *logical* and the most *moral* cognitive structures. That is, formal operations generate universally true judgments of logic and scientific reasoning, while stage 6 generates moral judgments of universal ethical validity.[37] It is logical *necessity* within formal operational structures, and the *prescriptivity* of principled moral judgments that make the judgments fit for all, and so represent the *universality* of the human Self.[38]

Something else that these final stages share, then, is their explicit claim to unify experience in a self-consistent structure of logical or moral judgement. Cognitive logic and morality are therefore different forms of rationality which are sources of consistency making the person a person—any unification of experience must carry with it a corresponding unity of self.

Each affords a "unity of apperception" in Kant's terms, which means that ideas are known *as thought by me*. Self-consciousness is therefore *implicit* in the structural consistency of cognition. The unity is not reified, and the whole is no more real than the parts. The final stage is no more real than the special cases of it which comprise the lower stages. So Platonism is avoided.

The Self in this Kantian paradigm is not substantial, but *formal*. It is a judging attitude, or Self-as-Perspective. It corresponds to a postcritical conception of knowledge in which it is realized that the forms of experience cannot be derived from the experienced objects, but involve *a priori* constructions of the subject.[39]

RESIDUAL PROBLEMS

With respect to conceptions of self, we are now left with at least four major questions. First, Kohlberg's "stage 6" does not define a concrete Self-as-*Agent*, even though morality involves practical interests. It is still an intellectual Self rather than an acting one—it is the transcendent Subject of ideas about practice, a generator of possible actions among which choices can be made. Its practical qualities stop short at the point of putting its choices into effect. Its domain is still the reflective or contemplative one of reasoning and justification, which are necessary but not sufficient conditions for concrete moral decisions.[40] This moral Self is therefore akin to Piaget's operational Subject. One question left is: how do we integrate these two theoretical, thinking Selves so that we have a single Subject instead of a double one?[44] Kohlberg, in Kantian fashion, has suggested a hierarchical relationship in which logical development is necessary but not sufficient for moral development (TABLE 3). The hypothesis leads to different empirical predictions from those generated by the "complexity" hypothesis, as well as being logically incompatible with it. It also appears to differ from Piaget's recent[43] statement, according to which social ideals are derivative of formal operational thought.

Second, even if we could answer the first question, how would we reconcile a single theoretical Self-as-Subject with the Self-as-*Agent*, the Self with *practical* intentions which *acts* concretely to *alter* the world? Kant's indication, followed specifically by MacMurray on a philosophical level, and by Kohlberg on the levels of theoretical and empirical psychology, is that the theoretical is necessary but not sufficient for the practical. This logically follows from Piaget's argument that in ontogenesis, *logos* derives from *praxis* by successive "reflective abstractions."[44] The latter "de-centrate" the individual by selecting out those aspects of its own, practical or sensorimotor experience which are legitimately general to all others (i.e., "universalisable,") thus constructing the norms of objective

TABLE 3
RELATIONS BETWEEN PIAGET LOGICAL STAGES AND
KOHLBERG MORAL STAGES*

Logical Stage	Moral Stage
Symbolic, intuitive thought	*Stage 0:* The good is what I want and like.
Concrete operations, Substage 1	*Stage 1:* Punishment-obedience orienta-
Categorical classification	tion
Concrete operations, Substage 2	*Stage 2:* Instrumental hedonism and
Reversible concrete thought	concrete reciprocity.
Formal operations, Substage 1	*Stage 3:* Orientation to interpersonal
Relations involving the inverse of	relations of mutuality.
the reciprocal	
Formal operations, Substage 2	*Stage 4:* Maintenance of social order,
	fixed rules, and authority.
Formal operations, Substage 3	*Stage 5A:* Social contract, utilitarian
	low-making perspective.
	Stage 5B: Higher law and conscience
	orientation.
	Stage 6: Universal ethical principle
	orientation.

*All relations are that attainment of the logical stages is necessary, but not sufficient, for attainment of the moral stage. From Kohlberg and Gilligan.[42]

thought. The difficulty here (which Baldwin called one of the "embarrassments of thought") is that de-centration appears to require that objectivity be attained at the expense of concrete subjectivity. This has led Turner to suggest that Piaget's abstract epistemic Subject, which is merely the structuring mechanisms "of the average subject" (Piaget,[32] p. 69), should be allowed a dialectical "re-centration" which returns the definition of selfhood to the individual conscious psyche. Otherwise, the Self threatens to be "truncated" or reduced to a purely objective meaning.[45] A parallel critique applies to Kohlberg's fully differentiated moral Self, which takes as the end of value a public "Other."[46] The role taken at stage 6 is not the concrete subjective point of view of the individual concerned, but the objective aspects of all singular points of view.

There are thus two issues here, closely intertwined: the relation of form and content, and the relation of judgment and action. If the former is not taken into account, the latter cannot either. Actions based on an objectification of Self and Others cannot entirely escape conformism. Thus, synchronically speaking, Piaget's formal operational subject can become the "prisoner of form"[2] in adhering too strictly to scientific *method* as the source of decision, rather than his or her own intelligent judgment. By the latter is meant the choice of a concrete subject, a choice that might intelligently employ methods other than that of the physical sciences. Diachronically speaking, we might also remark that forms cannot generate forms,[2] and so movement from one stage to another, from a lower level of Self-hood to a higher, must involve putting ideas into practice (or more precisely, must not involve inhibiting the action potential of ideas).

A third problem of interest, given that we could reconcile Self-as-Subject and Self-as-Agent, is that we would still be left with the paradox of self-consciousness *in the theory.* How is the *possibility of cognitive-developmental theories* to be explained?[47] The latter pretend to give a genetic account of thought *as a whole,* and therefore must reflexively include the possibility of themselves, presumably in the Hegelian fashion of postulating their own approach as the *telos* of the development of knowledge. However, even an active Kantian Self is a fixed speculative principle of knowing, or of willing, and seems to lack that very self-developing quality that the theory says gave rise to it. In the postcritical cognitive developmental tradition, we say that we have become aware of the self-formative character of our own consciousness, that *as theorists* we reflectively understand our selves as subjects, whose subjectivity has developed in correspondence with the progressive elaboration of objective knowledge. If we assume this, then the course of ego development can no longer be said to be fulfilled with the differentiation of a "complete" Kantian transcendental Subject or Free Will, as Piaget and Kohlberg appear to claim it can. Piaget's theory cannot reflexively account for its own existence, or Piaget's own theoretical reflectivity, and we all know that charity must begin at home.

One possibility here is to argue that further levels of reflectivity "beyond formal operations" must be added, in which the Self moves beyond simple self-consciousness to consciousness of the process of its own self-formation. Here we would need an account of the emergence of a methodological perspective— a developmental epistemology in addition to a developmental logic, or a developmental metaethics in addition to a developmental normative ethics.[48]

These alternatives, however, would still leave us trapped with the "monad" conception of the forms of experience as generating further, more reflective forms *within* the individual. Developing self-consciousness would now just be the *object* of consciousness, and vicious circles start to gnash their teeth.

We now move into our fourth and final problem. This is the fact that, like Mannheim's intellectual,[49] the Self of the Kantian cognitive-developmentalists claims to take an ideal position, *above and beyond* all perspectives, and free of interest.[50] Yet if *interest* is not admitted, fully differentiated structures of reasoning become neutral "methods" or "techniques" that can be used just as effectively in alienation and rationalization as in their opposites. This is reflected in the fact that Piaget does not entertain the active questioning of the assumptions of the scientific method (Broughton,[38] pp. 29-39). (Kohlberg also appears relatively uncritical of social scientific methodology.[46])

It has not been demonstrated that objectivity would be possible without the admission of specific interests.[47,49] With the reintroduction of interests, imbedded in particular cultural-historical traditions, development can no longer be seen naturalistically as only "adaptation to the environment," or knowledge as only the key to evolutionary self-preservation through "equilibration." Nature and culture are not completely continuous with each other. The inevitable role of action, history, and sociocultural context in the development of knowledge and the Self would therefore appear to require acknowledgment not only within the structure of developmental theories, but equally within the American functionalist and symbolic interactionist traditions.

Cognitive-developmentalists do not deny the presence or impact of the social environment, although its signficance does tend to be relegated to the role of encouraging or holding back "natural" developmental potentials of the individual. Regarding historical factors, the embryological metaphor of "recapitulation," handed down to developmental psychology from Haeckel and von Baer via Hobhouse and G. Stanley Hall, draws attention to the formal *parallels* between historical change and individual development. This avoids the need to *imbed* the latter in the former.[51] It also suggests formal parallels between psychology and biology, without attending to the need to also explicate the relationship of psychic and biological individuality.

DIALECTICAL PARADIGMS

All the different interpretations so far reviewed have at least two qualities in common; they place exceptional emphasis upon the individual, and they de-emphasize sociocultural contexts and historical changes. For British empiricism it was the sensory impressions of the individual upon which the Self was built, but the process of building it was not elaborated in the form of a systematic developmental interpretation, nor was the changing historical context considered as an influential condition for this development. Rather, the formation of complex ideas, including that of the Self, was analyzed in a principled manner, looking at some of its regularities but without tracing the details of the developmental and historical processes.

For the Continental rationalists, even more so, the Self existed within a developmental and historical vacuum. It was regarded as the prerequisite for knowing and consciousness, neither of which, it was argued, demanded any explanation for their development or their existence in historical context. On the contrary, the Self provided such an explanation and was the only source for it.

Also, the movement represented by symbolic interactionism tended to see the relationships between social conditions and the experiencing Self in a principled or synchronic manner. Undoubtedly, Mead paid some attention to differences in the relationship between the *I* and the *me's* under various developmental and historical conditions (as did Locke, Hume, and Kant), but he did not explicitly propose a theory of these changes. This is especially true for the *I* which appears from nowhere almost in a miraculous fashion. It represents the inner, energizing core of the individual, but it is not developing; it remains unchanged, unpredictable. Unlike the *me's*, who originate and develop through their dynamic interactions between the *I* and the social conditions, the *I* is not explained in this or any other manner.

In search of such an answer one might be tempted to lean on Piaget's paradigm of assimilation-accommodation, which in their mutual interaction bring about the operativity and development of the individual, the assimilation by incorporating the object for the sake of the subject, and the accommodation by producing changes in the subject in view of the object. Such a scheme, when extended, could possibly provide an explanation of the inner operations of the organism; that is, of the processes which, in conjunction with those proposed by the symbolic interactionists, would provide a comprehensive interpretation of the Self. Such an extension has not been proposed by Piaget, nor by the students of symbolic interactionism. It is implied, however, in dialectical interpretations proposed in Soviet psychology. In conclusion, we would like to draw your attention to these interpretive attempts.

The first period in the history of Soviet psychology—as described in a most insightful manner by Payne[3]—consisted mainly in the rejection of the former traditions, most of which were imported from continental Europe, in particular, from Germany.

This movement was not primarily concerned with the concept of the Self, but was directed against the introspectionism of early experimental psychology. Inasmuch as such psychology was built upon the classical mind-body dichotomy, the critique by Soviet psychologists was indirectly concerned with the concept of the Self. In this critique, the traditional Western view was rejected as either promoting a purely subjective-mentalistic or an objective-mechanistic interpretation without being able to bridge this gap and provide a comprehensive integration.

After this early stage of antisubjectivism, antiintrospectionism, and anti-idealism, the pendulum swung, indeed, toward mechanistic materialism. This movement therefore represents the other extreme of traditional, Western European thinking and should, from the Soviet point of view, be rejected as strongly as mental or idealistic subjectivism. Eventually, this was done, but in the late twenties mechanistic materialism represented the dominant trend in Soviet psychology and also characterized, for example, the early thinking of Pavlov (or at least the American interpretation of his work).

With the posthumous publication of the "Philosophical Notebooks" by Lenin in 1929,[52] this movement was severely criticized. As a consequence, focused attention was given to cultural and historical determinants of development, that is, to those aspects which play a decisive role in the Marxist's "Classics." Here they appear under the label of "historical dialecticism," as contrasted with "dialectical materialism." Vygotsky[53] was one of the most outspoken, though not wholeheartedly accepted, proponents of this movement.

With the prevalence of these two successive movements in Soviet psychology, the stage was set for a more embracing integration. This was achieved after the end of World War II and is most convincingly expressed in Rubinstein's double interaction theory.

Rubinstein's synthesis emphasizes the unity of consciousness and behavior. These terms do not denote separate systems; the former is not all internal nor the latter all external; both interpenetrate each other. Consciousness is not a passive contemplative state but an activity; behavior is not merely a movement, but is directed by internal organization. On the one hand, activity objectifies the inner-subjective world; on the other hand, the objective world is reflected in and by the subject. This distinction is very similar to Piaget's comparison of accomodation and assimilation, which produce the successful adaptation of the individual. Rubinstein refers to Marx. "By acting on the external world and changing it, he, at the same time, changes his own nature."

For Rubinstein the study of ontogenesis is not conceivable without the study of phylogenesis. Modifications in either case result in dialectical leaps that are brought about by changes in the structure of the organism. But as these structures change the functions also change, because structure and functions develop as a unit. At the beginning, the development of the organism is determined by the laws of biological evolution. With the phylogenetic emergence of psychic activities, however, development becomes codetermined by the laws of sociohistorical evolution. In particular, man, through his activities and labor, transforms his environment and creates new conditions for individual development. As stated by Payne,[3] man "creates himself by his own labor by transforming nature to transform himself." (p. 90)

When we focus on ontogenesis, the individual's development consists of the acquisition of human culture through his own activities. But this process has to be supplemented by the activities of others, by the activity of society. The activities have to permeate in both directions, from the individual to the culture and from the culture to the individual. The Self and knowledge of the Self are acquired through the individual's activities, but the activities of the society are of equal importance. The Self and knowledge are social in nature.

The dialectical interactions between the individual-psychological and cultural-sociological conditions are codetermined by a second system of interactions, that is, those between higher nervous activities and individual-psychological conditions. Rubinstein does not elaborate this interaction at length but refers to the work of Pavlov and his followers. With this renewed emphasis on the inner-biological basis, Rubinstein completes his synthesis. In the words of

Payne, "The relation of the psychic to the material world is fundamentally two-fold: to the inner matter of the brain (this relation constitutes the psychic in the quality of higher nervous activity) and to the outer matter of the external world in which relationship the psychic takes on the quality of ideal and subjective. The first quality Rubinstein calls the *ontological* aspect of the psychic; the second he calls *gnoseological* or theory-of-knowledge aspect."[3] (p. 98)

The notion of dialectical interactions penetrates all of Rubinstein's interpretations. It is most clearly revealed by the concept of "constitutive relationism," which he adopts from Hegel and Lenin. Lenin[52] emphasized that: "Every concrete thing, every concrete something, stands in multifarious and often contradictory relations to everything else: ergo it is itself and some other." (p. 124) In Payne's formulation,[3] ". . . every phenomenon or thing is determined and constituted by its relation to all the other phenomena of reality" (p. 99); consequently, individual-psychological states have a plurality of structures. There are several intrinsic structures, relating psychic activities to the brain, and several extrinsic structues relating them to the outer correlations both in the sociological and physical sense.

Rubinstein's interpretations lead to a reformulation of the mind-body problem. Traditionally the solution of this problem has been sought by determining the nature of both, the mind and the body, and then by investigating their interdependence. For Rubinstein the solution has to proceed in the reverse order. The relationship determines how we conceive of mind and how we conceive of body. Through the developmental interactions anchored in both inner and outer activities, the Self emerges. Thus, mind and body collapse upon the intersect of these two developmental processes. The Self produces these two interaction processes, and at the same time it is produced by them. Seen from a dialectical perspective—the Self orginates at the interaction of two developmental interaction systems; at the same time, it creates these two interaction systems. In other words, it is itself and some other.

ACKNOWLEDGMENTS

Thanks are due to the following for their contributions to the ideas discussed here: Augusto Blasi, Howard Gadlin, Emil Oestereicher, Edmund Sullivan, Michael Watts, and Robert Wozniak. Some unpublished notes by Lawrence Kohlberg were also of help. We are most grateful to Linda Lees for her help in preparing the manuscript. It should be noted that Riegel wrote the introduction and the final section on dialectics and Rubinstein, and Broughton contributed the sections on self-concept, symbolic interactionism, and cognitive-development. As Riegel pointed out at the conference (in true dialectical fashion!), the authors are not necessarily in agreement on all the issues discussed.

NOTES AND REFERENCES

1. RAPAPORT, D. 1959. A historical survey of psychoanalytic ego psychology. Psychological Issues 1: 5-17. LEITES, N. 1971. The New Ego. Science House. New York, N.Y. LOEVINGER, J. 1976. Ego Development. Jossey-Bass. San Francisco, Calif. YANKELOVICH, D. & W. BARRETT. 1970. Ego and Instinct. Random House. New York, N.Y.
2. OESTEREICHER, E. 1975. Form and praxis: a contribution to the theory of cultural forms. Unpublished. Richmond College, CUNY, New York, N.Y.
3. KURFISS, J. 1976. Developmental origins and psychological implications of "awareness." Paper presented at ann. mtg. Western Psychol Ass. April 8 Los Angeles, Calif. PAYNE, T.R. 1968. S. L. Rubinstein and the Philosophical Foundations of Soviet Psychology. D. Reidel. Dordrecht, The Netherlands.

4.   SKINNER, B.F. 1974. About Behaviorism: 184 ff. Random House. New York, N.Y.
5.   ALLPORT, G.W. 1955. Becoming: 36-39. Yale University Press. New Haven, Conn.
     BUGENTAL, J.F.T. 1971. The self . . . process or illusion? *In* Existential Humanistic
     Psychology. T.C. Greening, Ed. Brooks-Cole. Belmont, Calif.
6.   DUMONT, M.P. 1974. The Frankenstein factor. The Real Paper. June 12: 14.
     BOHART, A.C. 1976. Self-attribution and humanistic psychology. Paper presented
     at ann. mtg. of Western Psychol. Ass. April 8. Los Angeles, Calif. For a critical
     reply to Dumont, see BROUGHTON, J.M. 1974. Between the lines. The Real Paper,
     June 26: 2.
7.   SUZUKI, D.T. 1960. Lectures on Zen Buddhism. *In* Zen Buddhism and Psychoanalysis.
     E. Fromm, D.T. Suzuki, and R. DeMartino, Eds. Harper & Row. New York, N.Y.
     BOHART, A.C. See Ref. 6. SULLIVAN, N.S. 1953. The Interpersonal Theory of
     Psychiatry: 300f. Norton. New York, N.Y.
8.   CASSIRER, E. 1923. Substance and Function: 387 ff. Open Court. Chicago, Ill.
     FRONDIZI, R. 1953. The Nature of the Self. Southern Illinois University Press.
     Carbondale, Ill.
9.   JAMES, W. 1890. The Principles of Psychology. Vol. 1: 291-401. Henry Holt. New
     York, N.Y. HENRICH, D. 1969. Self-consciousness. Unpublished paper. University
     of Michigan. Ann Arbor, Mich.
10. BUGENTAL, J.F.T. & S. L. ZELEN. 1950. Investigation into the self-concept. J.
     Personality. 18: 483-498.
11. A review of Self-Concept research is presented in WYLIE, R.C. 1961. The Self-Concept.
     University of Nebraska Press. Lincoln, Nebraska. For a representative selection of
     work in the Self-Concept tradition, see the following. KUHN, M.H. & T. S. MC-
     PARTLAND. 1965. An empirical investigation of self attitudes. American Sociol.
     Rev. 19: 68-76. SCHLIEN, J. 1962. The self-concept in relation to behaviour.
     Religious Education, 10: Slll-S127. KATZ, P. & E. ZIGLER. 1967. Self-image dis-
     parity: a developmental approach. J. Personality and Social Psychol. 5(2): 186-195.
     GORDON, C. 1968. Self conceptions: configurations of content. *In* The Self in
     Social Interaction. C. Gordon & K.J. Gergen, Eds. John Wiley & Sons. New York,
     N.Y. GILL, M.P. & V.R. D'OYLEY. 1968. The construction of an objective measure
     of self concept. Paper read at the ann. mtg. Amer. Educa. Res. Ass. Chicago, Ill.
     GERGEN, K.J. 1971. The Concept of Self. Holt, Rinehart and Winston. New York,
     N.Y.
12. Regarding the distinction between development and change, see BLASI, A. 1976.
     Concept of development in personality theory. *In* Ego Development. J. Loevinger.
     29-53. Jossey-Bass. San Francisco, Calif.
13. ALLPORT, G.W. See Ref. 5. EVANS, R.I. 1971. Gordon Allport: The Man and His
     Ideas. E. P. Dutton. New York, N.Y. TARULE, J.M. 1976. The self-reflective capacity
     in adults. Unpublished qualifying paper, Graduate School of Education, Harvard
     Univ. Cambridge, Mass.
14. BROUGHTON, J.M. Epistemology as ideology: the cognitive development of subject/
     object concepts. *In* Dialectics as a Paradigm for the Social Sciences. A. Harris, Ed. To
     be published.
15. MACMURRAY, J. 1957. Self as Agent: 105/6. Faber and Faber, London, England.
16. LAING, R.D. 1960. The Divided Self. Tavistock. London, England.
17. MEAD, G.H. 1934. Mind, Self and Society. University of Chicago Press. Chicago, Ill.
     BALDWIN, J.M. 1897. Social and Ethical Interpretations. Macmillan. New York,
     N.Y. COOLEY, C.H. 1902. Human Nature and the Social Order. Charles Scribner's
     Sons. New York, N.Y. DENZIN, N.K. 1972. The genesis of self in early childhood.
     The Sociological Quarterly 13: 291-314. KOHLBERG, L. 1969. Stage and Sequence.
     In Handbook of Socialisation Theory and Research. D. Goslin, Ed. Rand McNally.
     Chicago, Ill. SELMAN, R. 1974. The development of conceptions of interpersonal
     relations. Mimeoed. Harvard/Judge Baker Social Reasoning Project. Boston, Mass.
     For Laing's most expressly interactionist position, see LAING, R.D. 1961. Self and
     Others. Tavistock Publications. London, England; LAING, R.D., H. PHILLIPSON &
     A.R. LEE. 1966. Interpersonal Perception. Springer. New York, N.Y. The method
     of existential dialectics is more fully explicated in ESTERSON, A. 1970. The Leaves
     of Spring. Tavistock Publications. London, England. Both Laing and Esterson explicitly
     acknowledge the influence of the Scottish philosopher MacMurray, whose interac-
     tionism is perhaps best expounded in MACMURRAY, J. 1961. Persons in Relation.
     Faber and Faber. London, England.
18. TIBBETTS, P. 1971. John Dewey and contemporary phenomenology on experience
     and the subject/object relation. Philosophy Today 15(4): 250-275.
19. Similar concepts arise in psychoanalytic theory. See LEITES, N.[1] Section 2.
20. GURWITSCH, A. 1966. A non-egological conception of consciousness. *In* Studies

in Phenomenology and Psychology. A. Gurwitsch, Ed. Northwestern Univ. Press. Evanston, Ill. For a critique of non-egological theories in general, see HENRICH, D. Ref. 9.

21. LICHTMAN, R. 1970. Symbolic interactionism and social reality: some Marxist queries. Berkeley Journal of Sociology 10: 75-94. BLASI, A. 1975. Role-taking and the development of social cognition. Paper presented at the annual meeting of the American Psychol. Ass. Chicago, Ill. August 28. McNALL, S. G. & J.C.M. JOHNSON, 1975. The new conservatives: ethnomethodologists, phenomenologists and symbolic interactionists. The Insurgent Sociologist. 5(4): 49-66.

22. KUHN, M.H. & T.S. McPARTLAND. See Ref. 11, p. 112. Regarding the loss of the subjective "I," see MOORE, J.S. 1933. The problem of self. Philosophical Review. 62: 487-499.

23. DEWEY, J. 1890. On some current conceptions of the term 'self'. Mind 15: 58-74. DEWEY, J. 1898. Social and Ethical Interpretations in Mental Development: review of book. Philosophical Rev. 7: 398-409.

24. PARSONS, T. & E. SHILS, Eds. 1951. Toward a General Theory of Action: 18. Harvard Univ. Press. Cambridge, Mass.

25. GOFFMAN, E. 1969. The Presentation of Self in Everyday Life. Penguin Press. London, England. Goffman's position is currently receiving a shot in the arm from Rom Harre—see HARRE, R. Some remarks on "rule" as a scientific concept. In Understanding Other Persons. T. Mischel, Ed. Blackwell. Oxford, England. For a brilliantly ironic critique of Parsons, Goffman, and others, see HELMER, J. 1970. The face of the man without qualities. Social Res. 37(4): 547-579. For further reflections on "role" see MEILAND, J. 1975. Styles of life: self, identity and roles. Unpublished. Univ. Michigan. Ann Arbor, Mich.

26. While Laing's symbolic interactionism has been assimilated to the Mead tradition, this more critical approach to alienation and ontological insecurity appears to have had little or no effect on developmental psychology, which has typically assumed that we know *that* we are, and gone on to ask *what* we are.

27. Compare HEGEL, G.W.F. 1975. Logic: xvii ff. Oxford Univ. Press. Oxford, England. Also SKINNER, B.F. Ref. 4.

28. JACOBY, R. 1975. Social Amnesia. Beacon Press. Boston, Mass. LICHTMAN, R.[21]

29. Baldwin was wont to lunch with Piaget's mentor Claparède in Paris. See KOHLBERG, L. Forthcoming. Baldwin's theory of moral development. To appear In Baldwin's Theory of Development: A Current Appraisal. D.J. Freeman-Moir, J.M. Broughton, and L. Kohlberg, Eds. Kohlberg's work is heavily indebted to Dewey and Baldwin, as Kohlberg himself states.[17] Selman[17] (op. cit.) and Loevinger[1] are also much influenced by Baldwin's work, although less directly.

30. See MOIR, J. 1975. A sense of the general. Unpublished doctoral dissertation. Harvard Univ. Cambridge, Mass.; NOVACK, G. 1975. Pragmatism and Marxism. Pathfinder Press. New York, N.Y. PIAGET, J. 1971. Biology and Knowledge. Univ. Chicago Press. Chicago, Ill.

31. STACK, G.A. 1971. On the notion of dialectics. Philosophy Today 15: 276-291. Related commentary is given in MARSTIN, R. 1974. Structuralism: limits and possibilities. Unpublished paper. Harvard University, Cambridge, Mass.; and RIEGEL, K.F. 1976. From traits and equilibrium toward developmental dialectics. Nebraska Symposium on Motivation. W. J. Arnold and J. K. Cole, Eds. Univ. Nebraska Press. Lincoln, Nebraska.

32. This abstract epistemic subject is characterized in PIAGET, J. 1970. Structuralism. Basic Books. New York, N.Y. Critical commentary appears in CASSEL, T.Z. 1972. A system of structured minds. Contemporary Psychology 17(12): 695-6; and TURNER, T. Piaget's structuralism. American Anthropol. 75: 351-373. See also KEGAN, R. 1976. Self and other: structural affect in ego transformation. Unpublished paper. Harvard Univ. Cambridge, Mass.

33. RIEGEL, K.F. 1973. Dialectical operations: the final period of cognitive development. Human Devel. 16: 346-380; FREEDLE, R. 1976. Logic, general systems and human development: preliminaries to developing a psycho-social linguistics. In Piaget and Beyond, Vol. 7. & G. Steiner, Ed. Kindler. Zurich, Switzerland.

34. KOHLBERG, L. 1973. Continuities and discontinuities in childhood and adult moral development revisited. In Lifespan Developmental Psychology—Personality and Socialisation. P. Baltes & W. K. Schair, Eds. Academic Press. New York, N.Y. HABERMAS, J. 1975. Moral development and ego identity. *Telos* 24: 41-55.

35. KURFISS, J. 1975. Late adolescent development: a structural-epistemological perspective. Unpublished doctoral dissertation. Univ. Washington. Seattle, Wash. See also ERIKSON, E. 1968. Identity: Youth and Crisis. Norton. New York, N.Y.; PERRY,

W. 1968. Forms of Intellectual and Ethical Development in the College Years. Holt, Rinehart and Winston. New York, N.Y.; LOEVINGER, J. & R. WESSLER. 1970. Measuring Ego Development. Vol I. Jossey-Bass. San Francisco, Calif. BLASI, A. 1976. Personal responsibility and ego development. In They Need Not Be Pawns: Toward Self-Direction in the Urban Classroom. R. DeCharms, Ed. Irvington Publishers. New York, N.Y. VAN DEN DAELE, L. 1975. Ego development in dialectical perspective. Human Develop. 18: 129-142.

36. BLASI, A. & E.C. HOEFFEL. 1974. Adolescence and formal operations. Human Develop. 17: 344-363.

37. KOHLBERG, L. 1975. Why stage 6 is best. In Collected Papers. Vol II. L. Kohlberg. Harvard Graduate School of Education, Cambridge, Mass.

38. BALDWIN, J.M. 1906-11. Thought and Things. Swann Sounenschein. London, England. 1975. Arno Press. New York, N.Y. BROUGHTON, J.M. 1974. The Development of natural epistemology in adolescence and early adulthood: ch. 5. Unpublished doctoral dissertation. Harvard Univ. Cambridge, Mass.

39. LONERGAN, B.J.F. 1968. The Subject: 22. Marquette Univ. Press. Milwaukee, Wis. MACMURRAY, J. [15]

40. BROUGHTON, J.M. The cognitive-developmental model of morality: a reply to Kurtines & Greif. Submitted for publication.

41. This is the question of the consistency of sources of consistency—i.e., the basic unity of the person which gives form to the logical and the moral (as well as the aesthetic, religious, epistemological, ontological, etc.) This question is that posed by Loevinger[1] and Blasi[12] as the matter of "ego development." It should be noted that Loevinger also includes aspects of motivation and action in her conception of the Ego, and so offers an alternative to the Kohlberg approach, which first differentiates cognition and action and then asks what the relation is between them.

42. KOHLBERG, L. & C. GILLIGAN. 1971. The adolescent as philosopher: the discovery of the self in a postconventional world. Daedalus 100(4): 1051-1086.

43. INHELDER, B. & J. PIAGET. 1958. The Growth of Logical Thinking from Childhood to Adolescence. Basic Books. New York, N.Y. See also BLASI, A. & E.C. HOFFEL.[36]

44. WARTOFSKY, M. 1971. From praxis to logos. In Cognitive Development and Genetic Epistemology. T. Mischel, Ed. Academic Press. New York, N.Y. FURTH, H. 1969. Piaget and Knowledge. Prentice-Hall. Englewood Cliffs, N. J.

45. LONERGAN, B.J.F.[39] BLASI, A.[12] BALDWIN, J.M.[38] Vol I, p. 269.

46. MORELLI, E.A. 1975. The sixth stage of moral development: a dialectical analysis: 24f. Unpublished. Univ. of Toronto. Toronto, Canada.

47. Cf. HABERMAS, J. 1971. Knowledge and Human Interests: Ch. I. Beacon Press. Boston, Mass. Also, see GADLIN, H. Toward a dialectical psychology: hermeneutic understanding and theoretical self-consciousness. To appear In Dialectics as a Paradigm for the Social Sciences. A. Harris, Ed.

48. BOYD, D. 1976. From conventional to principled morality. Unpublished doctoral dissertation. Harvard Univ. Cambridge, Mass.

49. KOLAKOWSKI, L. 1971. The epistemological significance of the aetiology of knowledge: a gloss on Mannheim. Triquarterly 22: 221-238.

50. KOLAKOWSKI, L. 1975. Very strong doubts about humanism. Paper presented at Univ. Michigan. Ann Arbor, Mich. Oct. 24.

51. TOULMIN, S. 1972. Human Understanding. Princeton University Press. Princeton, N.J.

52. LENIN, V.I. 1929. Philosophical Notebooks. In Collected Works: Vol 38. International Publishers. New York, N.Y.

53. VYGOTSKY, L.S. 1962. Thought and Language. M.I.T. Press. Cambridge, Mass.

54. KOHLBERG, L. 1971. From is to ought: how to commit the naturalistic fallacy and get away with it. In Cognitive Development and Genetic Epistemology. T. Mischel, Ed. Academic Press. New York, N.Y.

55. BUCK-MORSS, S. 1975. Socio-economic bias in Piaget's theory, and its implications for the cross-culture controversy. Human Devel. 18: 35-49.

LOTZE, THE SELF, AND AMERICAN PSYCHOLOGY*

William R. Woodward

Department of Psychology
University of New Hampshire
Durham, New Hampshire 03824

INTRODUCTION

What was the significance for psychology of the disintegration of the ego in nineteenth-century philosophy? I take this to be the issue raised by Dr. Verhave's paper, and it will be nicely exemplified by my remarks on the development of Lotze's concept of the self. First, I will discuss Lotze's concept of mind, or pure self, as it was formulated *vis à vis* the metaphysical psychologies of certain post-Kantians of the 1830s. Second, I will introduce Lotze's concept of the empirical self as found in his medical psychology and *Microcosmus*. And thirdly, I will examine the definitions of psychology and the self put forward in the 1880s and 1890s by the Americans Borden Parker Bowne, John Dewey, William James, James Mark Baldwin, and George Trumbull Ladd. My conclusion will be that there was an increasing emphasis on the empirical self in the new psychologies, despite certain parallels to the concepts of pure self in the earlier periods.

The problem of personal identity, of the temporal connection of mental states, arose with Hume's empirical concept of self. Does the flow of impressions and ideas require no subject to observe it? Does the passing thought, as William James proposed, provide knowledge of change in addition to change of knowledge?

Kant had a different solution. From Hume, Kant took the problem of the connection of states of consciousness in time. This was the counterpart of the other Humean problem of the connection of events in space and time, or causality. Kant's critical philosophy sought the conditions for this unity of the empirical ego in the transcendental concept of the pure ego. The three critiques of Kant drew out the implications of the two egos for practical and aesthetic philosophy, as well as for theoretical philosophy. Kant's best known disciples, Fichte, Schelling, and Hegel, developed these three approaches to the ego—through action, feelings, and reason—but it was Hermann Lotze who combined them into a single concept of self. In the words of John Theodore Merz, Lotze "stands, as it were, in the centre of the philosophical, and especially the psychological, thought of the century."[1]

LOTZE'S CONCEPT OF THE PURE SELF

Rudolph Hermann Lotze was a student of philosophy and medicine at Leipzig University in the 1830s, when Hegel's fame was at its height. He attended the lectures in philosophy of only one man, Christian Hermann Weisse. From

*The American psychologists discussed are directly conversant with Lotze's teachings or writings. I have excluded later psychologists influenced less directly if at all (M. Calkins, K. Dunlap, G. Allport) and philosophers who diverged from psychology (J. Royce, G. Santayana) despite their debts to Cotre.

Weisse, he absorbed the problem of German philosophy as it centered on the unification of the three critiques of Kant. This problem, as Weisse saw it, was the reworking of Hegel's dialectical system of necessity into a dialectical system of freedom. Kant had attempted to reconcile the realms of necessity and freedom in his third critique; however, Weisse's notion of their union was inspired by Schelling's treatise on freedom and later critique of Hegel. "True freedom," wrote Weisse, "i.e., the metaphysical category of freedom realized in the Creation, is found only where the creature itself achieves the principle of intelligence and will, and now for he first time attains the great alternative of spiritual good and evil (i.e., of the truly real good or evil)."[2] Thus, the first and third critiques, having to do with the principles of truth and beauty, were "sublated" into the principle of the second critique—the moral freedom to do good.

Unlike Hegel's absolute, Weisse's fundamental conception was both free and individual. He called it "Personality," and it was the result rather than the origin of the dialectic process; i.e., from being for itself, consciousness, and being in itself, world, came being in and for itself, consciousness of self and world. Weisse's motive was religious: by restoring the principle of moral freedom, he made a place in speculative theology for the Christian concept of sin. At the same time, he acknowledged that the principle of causality governs the natural world, a world created, or "specified," by God.[3]

Lotze accepted Weisse's objection to Hegel's Absolute: that it subordinated the value of the individual personality. But Lotze in turn shifted the issue of personality back to its original basis in Kant's transcendental psychology. Kant had sought to answer Hume's skepticism about personal identity by a deduction of the categories of pure understanding, e.g. substance and causality. In the transcendental logic of the first critique, Kant had essentially argued that we are conscious, that to be conscious we must be aware of objects, and that if we are conscious and aware of objects we are conscious of ourselves. The categories are immanent in our becoming aware of objects; this was the objective deduction. And they constitute the conditions upon which human thought depends; this was the subjective deduction.[4]

Lotze wrote his first book, *Metaphysik*, in 1841 when he was only twenty-four. Through a friendship with Ernst Friedrich Apelt, the student of Jakob Friedrich Fries, he had come under the influence of Fries' philosophy of nature and his "new critique of reason."[5] Lotze's return to Kant was inspired by Fries, who stood outside the Hegelian fold. But Lotze argued that Fries, by treating the forms of sensibility, understanding, and reason as faculties, had failed to reconcile his philosophy of nature with his philosophy of mind. Lotze wrote his metaphysics as a philosophy of being, nature, and mind in the Hegelian tradition, and his objective deduction of the categories treated consciousness as an example of the relation of one substance to another. In his own words, "one must first speak of the behavior of objective things toward one another, as it is determined by means of the lawfulness of cognition, and subordinate to this treatment the relation between us and things as a special case."[6]

Then Lotze turned to the realistic metaphysics of Johann Friedrich Herbart for his subjective deduction of the categories and intuitions of the mind. The foundation of Herbart's metaphysical psychology was the assumption that since every being is what it is, it cannot change. However, when one being is thought of in relation to another one, this "contingent view" gives the "objective appearance" of change.[7] Thus every sensation is supposed to point to a particular being in Herbart's monadology. By this regress to Leibnizian pluralism,

Lotze saw a way to circumvent the common view of the categories as "organs of reception." The subjectivity of the categories does not implicate a subject; this is "an old anthropomorphic error." And the forms of knowledge are not predicative determinations of things. Rather as Lotze put it, the "jerkings of the net" of the categories by the thing-in-itself give the objective appearance or "disturbance" between mind and being. "Disturbance" is Herbart's word, and whereas he used it for relations in the mind, Lotze meant by it the relations between mind and being.

The final portion of Lotze's metaphysical psychology is the ethical deduction. It comes from Kant's transcendental dialectic as reinterpreted by the right-wing Hegelians. The subjective and objective deductions do not solve the transcendental problem. They do not explain why we believe that reality is more than appearances. Why do we believe, for example, in a world, a self, and a God, when all of our sensory experience is conditioned and therefore incomplete. All consciousness testifies to such consciousness of wholes which precedes and conditions its parts. In Lotze's terms, purposes are realized by mechanical means. Lotze thus appropriated the principle of freedom from Weisse as a corrective to the dialectic necessity of Hegel. Being is not an Eleatic absolute, as with Hegel's monism and Herbert's pluralism, but a relation between what is and what ought to be. In other words, the world of things is founded on the world of action, and apodicticity is granted only to the Good.

I think it is important to immerse ourselves in this discussion of the 1830s over the metaphysical and ethical presuppositions of the forms of knowledge in order to appreciate the concept of self as it becomes more explicit later on. The self is not a prominent concept in this initial formulation of Lotze's psychology. The ingredients of his mature metaphysic of the soul are all here, nevertheless. The definition of substance as a relation, process, or event which gives the appearance of objectivity is applied consistently to bodies and souls. The Kantian admission that the categories are subjective, though only a special case of the objective relations, is grounded in a Herbartian monadology. Finally, the Hegelian view that metaphysics is not able to deduce the categories and that ethics must be invoked is a prelude to the empirical view that cognition is unable to fathom the world, and that feelings and will are the ultimate arbiters of value.

LOTZE'S CONCEPT OF THE EMPIRICAL SELF AND A MISUNDERSTANDING OF IT

We skip now to Lotze's medical psychology in 1852. The bulk of this book is taken up with the local sign theory of space perception.[8] However, it also contains the first statement of Lotze's view of the empirical ego. This ego is defined in a chapter on the consciousness of self; it is treated in conjunction with attention, since both are involved with inner perception. A theory of the consciousness of self, explains Lotze, must first tell where the content of our own ego comes from. Evidently it comes from the feelings of bodily movement, as did the content of the local sign. For example, the crushed worm differentiates its body from the rest of the world in just as emphatic a manner as when the educated mind distinguishes itself as ego from an external nonego. This insight that feelings are primary came to Lotze via Herbart and Weisse.[9] Both considered them to exemplify freedom in the judgment of value.

A theory of the consciousness of self must also describe this content of feelings. Taking the example of our own bodies, Lotze suggests that the specific character of the ego comes from the feelings of pleasure and pain, of our memories, and of our notion of our position in society. These natural conditions differentiate us from every other person. Here the issue is not the presuppositions of experience, as it was in his metaphysics. The ego, however, does rest on certain biological presuppositions, e.g. inborn talents, inclination, temperament, and phantasy. The empirical ego as thus defined is counter to the concept of self as unconditioned in Fichte and Hegel. Yet is is consistent with Lotze's definition of cognition, or pure ego, as the appearance of a relation between mind and body.

This juxtaposition of feelings, value, and consciousness was a new departure in medical psychology. Yet its philosophical lineage was clear: it came from Kant's third critique, the *Critique of Judgment*. Kant had there sought to join the theoretical judgment of truths with the practical judgment of goods in an aesthetic judgment which was both true and good. Thus Kant's judgment of the beautiful exemplified "free beauty," or beauty that is universally valid and independent of the observer. After Schelling pointed out that freedom is individual, and therefore aesthetic beauty depends on subjective criteria of feelings as well as objective criteria of form, Weisse transmitted this criticism of Kant and Hegel to Lotze. Indeed, it was Weisse's original rethinking of the defect of the concept of Identity in Schelling and of Absolute in Hegel that had led him to reformulate the logical unity as the multiplicity of God's creation. The union of abstract universal and concrete particular exemplified the beauty or value of the individual organism. In Lotze's essay on the concept of beauty in 1845 and his *Geschichte der Aesthetik* in 1867, he repeated the criticism of Kant for not giving the feelings their due emphasis in the aesthetic judgment. Agreeing that pleasantness was judged by sensibility, and goodness by reason, Lotze held that beauty and value are judged by subjective feelings of harmony between the observer and the object.[10, 11]

Lotze's theory of mental illness was also based on feelings as judgments of value that unite the sensible and intelligible worlds. Evidently he disagreed with Kant's claim that psychology could not become a science because its events had only the temporal dimension. Certainly the empirical ego was affected by the spatial conditions of the body. Citing from recent books on mental pathology by Jacobi, Ideler, Friedreich, Leubuscher, and Domrich, Lotze defined mental illness as a narrowing, or a widening, of the consciousness of self. This might come about through a disturbance of feelings, as in melancholy, or a disturbance of strivings, as in the monomanias (hyaromania, erotomania, nymphomania), or a disturbance of cognition, as in fixed ideas. Forensic psychology, dealing with responsibility in criminal cases, required a decision about whether the individual was capable of conceiving the external world correctly, of resisting the power of harmful drives, and of making value judgments by his feelings.

The concept of self was vastly enriched by Lotze's collection of empirical evidence for it in the medical literature. Moreover, his integration of the three critiques of Kant provided a comprehensive theory of mental health and disease. Little wonder that Lotze became known in American psychology for his concept of the ego. However, because they were unfamiliar with his earlier metaphysical critique of the absolute ego, the Americans were misled by his remarks on the self in his popular work Microcosmus of 1856. There he expressed his popular definition of the empirical ego as "the thinker of *our own* thoughts."[12] We differentiate this ego from the external world by our feelings, which come through experience. But we also have what we think is a "true ego" independent of experience—in our talents and temperament and the traits of our intellectual life. Lotze conveyed these two egos by the metaphor of the tree: the empirical ego is the foliage, with its changing colors; the true ego is the trunk and branches, which stay the same.

It is important to read between the lines of this popular exposition of the consciousness of self, for Lotze is here catering to what people want to believe rather than to what is justified belief. William James was unaware of these two cross-purposes in Lotze's exposition when he remarked that Lotze, "who in his early work, the *Medicinische Psychologie,* was (to my reading) a strong defender of the Soul-Substance theory, has written in ##243-245 of his *Metaphysik* the most beautiful criticism of this theory which exists."[13] Indeed, Lotze did write his scientific and popular accounts as if the soul were a substantial entity. Yet he generally prefaced his adoption of an occasionalist view of the soul in relation to the body with the proviso that this was only a shorthand or phenomenal description. His own critical philosophy, both in his metaphysics of 1841 and the first part of his medical psychology of 1852, had stated the presuppositions of such empirical concepts in terms of "apparent objectivity," "disturbance," and "relations."

The custom of beginning his psychology with a discussion of the use of the concept of soul in everyday language contributed to this misunderstanding. Lotze always mentioned three grounds for the existence of the soul, two of which he considered insufficient. Freedom is no argument for soul, since "it is indeed matter of universal and incessant experience that the changes of our mental states are dependent on external impressions and the reciprocal action between them and the material constituents of our bodies." Nor is the incomparability of mental and physical phenomena a justification for the existence of two kinds of being, but only for two different grounds of explanation. The decisive factor in guaranteeing the existence of soul is the unity of consciousness. Disregarding the supposed consciousness of unity, it is the mere fact of "our being able to appear to ourselves at all" that is convincing proof that manifold phenomena are united in a non-physical entity.

This phenomenal justification of the concept of soul underlies his concept of the empirical self. An ontological argument, however, is the basis of his concept of the pure self. Now we may examine the "beautiful criticism" of the soul theory in Lotze's *Metaphysik* to which William James referred.[14] Lotze considers first the necessity, then the meaning, of the unity of consciousness. We should not say "from two motions comes a third simple motion"; rather, "when two different impulses act simultaneously on one and the same material point, they coalesce at this point into a third simple motion *of this point.*" This mechanical analogy, when applied to the mind, requires us to assume a subject as the point whose states are combined. The meaning of the subjective unity produced had been misinterpreted by Lotze's mentor Fechner as a soul atom or soul substance.[15] In reply, Lotze quotes his own definition of substance: "it is not through a substance that things have being, but they have being when they are able to produce the appearance of a substance present in them." This central tenet of Lotze's ontology was construed by later psychologists in support of phenomenalism, since it was conveniently forgotten that things and souls are deduced by him from the spiritual principle of the Good.

This is, doubtless, confusing to the reader. Lotze seems to have asserted that the subject exists, only to recant and state that there is no substantial self. But this is not incompatible with a process philosophy. His subsequent critique of Kant's paralogism of pure reason concerning "personality" finally convinces us (as it did James) that his distinction is valid. Kant had proposed the analogy of a row of elastic balls, where one ball striking the next was similar to "substances such that the one communicates to the other representations together with the consciousness of them."[16] The last ball, or substance, would then be conscious of all the states of the substances before it. Lotze argues that this implied that consciousness has a substrate, whereas he would claim nothing of the sort. Kant had betrayed his prejudice that a person could *be* unity. Lotze insisted that the capacity of subject to know its identity, i.e., to act as a unity, entitled it to be called a substance without being one.

The concept of self, therefore, is anchored in Lotze's mature metaphysical psychology as it was in his youthful one. His view has not changed: the flow of subjective states is only the appearance of the motion of objective ones. So far, he is a realist and a pluralist. However, the phenomenal world of the empirical ego is viewed as the final outcome or meaning of a network of relations to the noumenal world. The noumenal world itself is not pluralistic, as was Herbart's system of real beings. It is monistic, in the sense of Hegel's "Absolute." Lotze attributes his conviction that a single principle will explain all the parts of the universe to Fichte.[17] Unlike Fichte, though, he feels that we can only approximate to an understanding of this principle from the variety of our phenomenal viewpoints. In a word, this principle is Personality, the spiritual source of all being.

Lotze's spiritual principle has been called the Truly Real by John Theodore Merz, to differentiate it from the Real World of consciousness. Lotze is no ordinary idealist. His ground for the essential realm is the worths of human thought and action, as realized in the unity of consciousness.[18] The very fact that we appear to ourselves is proof of the unity of feelings, ideas, and strivings. Lotze's psychology draws together these separate activities into a living, acting identity which is infinitely richer than the skeptical psychology of Hume. This conception of self was at the core of psychologies in America in the 1880s.

THE CONCEPT OF SELF IN AMERICAN PSYCHOLOGY

My objective in the remainder of this paper is to sketch the concepts of self in American psychology during the decade following Lotze's death in 1881. In this period, it was customary to write psychology as an empirical propadeutic to philosophy. The result was a proliferation of textbooks of psychology, reminiscent of the psychologies of the 1830s. The more theologically inclined men of this generation were unready to proceed through experiment. They were motivated by philosophical curiosity and evolutionary faith to find psychological answers to perennial questions of free will and the nature of personal identity. Although the training of these philosopher-psychologists would have had to include Spencer, Bain, Huxley, and Carpenter, it is perhaps not rash to suggest that the concepts of self put forward in America were equally indebted to German idealism and the Scottish school.

Borden Parker Bowne was a professor of philosophy at Boston University who wrote an *Introduction to Psychological Theory* in 1886.[19] His textbook is directed against materialists who claim that thoughts and feelings may exist without a subject. For him, psychology begins with the subject of mental life, the self. Although he had heard Lotze lecture, and his later philosophy called "personalism" has some affinity with Lotze's, he does not acknowledge Lotze's critique of the substantial soul. He is a Christian apologist, and his spiritualism is informed by the threefold unity of "the thought factor," the feelings, and will and action. Bowne rejected the attempt by Herbartians to deduce feelings from the relation of thoughts. Feelings have their source in bodily conditions and mental states, and they are prior to knowledges and action. This view of the empirical self is congruent with that of Lotze. Bowne emphasized the genetic aspect of consciousness. From feeling arises consciousness, which "depends on the distinction of subject and object." This distinction is acquired gradually, beginning with the child's experience of self and leading to the adult conception of self. Later self-consciousness is aware of its freedom to seek the ideal of harmony with the beautiful and the good. Bowne was closer to Weisse's speculative theology when he wrote that "as a result of our total experience, we posit God." He meant that the ideal of self was to unite the other ideals in that of revealed religion.

Another philosopher who schooled himself in psychology was John Dewey, whose textbooks for classroom instruction of psychology appeared in 1887.[20] In defining psychology as "the Science of the Facts or the Phenomena of Self," Dewey drew broadly from Herbartian psychologies, Scottish psychologies, and the French and English works; however, his main debt was to the German idealist tradition of Kant through Hegel. He explained that a soul, unlike a stone, exists for itself; it is aware of its changes. He classified the mental activities into three: knowledge was the objective side; feeling, the subjective side; and will, the relation between them. Differently put, knowledge was the universal; feeling, the particular; and will, their unity. Dewey confessed to a weakness for logical formulations, which he strove to overcome by applying them to educational psychology. For example, will is finally equated with self, since it is self realizing itself. "In moral matters," he wrote, "a man *is* what he would have himself be." Dewey referred to this capacity of the actual self to realize an ideal one as "Personality," and he couched it, like Weisse and Lotze, in terms of a "union of finite and infinite Personality" in the "specific acts" that form character.

Dewey, of course, was a disciple of G.S. Morris when he was at Hopkins, and of James at Harvard. Voluntarism was characteristic of both his mentors. It was also a step along the road to pragmatism. William James, as we observed above, accepted Lotze's critique of the substantial soul. His test of the presence of mentality was "the pursuance of future ends and the choice of means for their attainment."[21] James' point, and his originality, was his contention that consiousness is purposive in the absence of a substantial self. The fallacy of the psychologist, he claimed, is to make the distinction of self from thought the criterion of mental life. Sometimes we attend to self and sometimes not, but in either case consciousness is selective. For James, the self is an empirical concept. Rather than placing it at the end of his book, as others did, he lets it follow the early chapters on the physiology of the brain. This supports his assertion that the self is immediately given in consciousness; the thinker and the thought object are united in the passing thought. This allies him with the phenomenalism of Mach, Stumpf, Brentano, and Hodgson. And even if Milic Čapek is correct that the self reappeared in James' later philosophy, it was still an empirical self which steered clear of the nominalism of Hume and the transcendentalism of Kant.[22]

James may be compared with Fries, who also denied the transcendental self and admitted only the self-activity of the knowing mind. James' younger contemporary, James Mark Baldwin, also settled for an empirical account of the self.[23] Baldwin, however, stood in the Herbartian tradition, which derived the self from the interaction of presentations in the mind. He was critical of the claim of Spencer and Bain that we are immediately conscious of the change of presentations. First we must be conscious of the presentations themselves, then of their activity or change. In this criticism he followed Lotze, as well as the Herbartian textbooks of Waitz, Nahlowsky, and Volkmann. He did not, however, go so far as Lotze in endorsing the relational concept of self. Indeed, he avoided metaphysical conceptualizations of any kind. His emphasis was genetic and empirical. He wrote that "the identical experiences of inner causation lead us to apprehend the sameness of the *self*, a rational concept appearing early in life, and the basis of the developed exercises of knowledge." Because this "rational concept" of self is derived from presentations alone, the role of feelings is only secondary. In this he differs from Lotze, as well as from Bowne, Dewey, and James. In two books on mental development, however, Baldwin did develop a genetic theory of self based on imitation, suggestion, and pleasure and pain.[24]

Of all the American psychologists, George Trumbull Ladd at Yale was probably the closest to Lotze, both in his concept of self and his definition of psychology. Ladd was a Congregational minister before he learned psychology by translating six of Lotze's posthumously published lecture transcripts—on metaphysics, religious philosophy, practical philosophy, psychology, aesthetics, and logic—during the years 1884 through 1887. In 1888 he published a physiological psychology styled after Wundt's; however, his most original contribution to psychology was his *Psychology: Descriptive and Explanatory* in 1894.[25] Ladd's famous definition of psychology, much scoffed at by his undergraduates, was "the science which describes and explains the phenomena of consciousness, as such." By the tag "consciousness, as such," Ladd meant the thoughts, feelings, and desires treated as empirical facts rather than as faculties. He properly reserved the issue of the metaphysical status of the subject for his philosophy of mind. Nevertheless, he did devote a chapter to the knowledge of things and of self. Here he argues in the spirit of Lotze's medical psychology that external and internal perception are the source of our gradually perfected concept of self. Thus, local signs of external perception and bodily feelings of internal perception are stages along the way to self-knowledge.

CONCLUSION

For each of these representative American philosopher psychologists of the late nineteenth century, the empirical self provides a systematic definition of psychology. To a man, they defined psychology as the science of consciousness—including the three primary divisions of sensations, feelings, and desires. The significance of this systematic arrangement is that it preempted from epistemology, aesthetics, and ethics a new empirical domain. The facts of consciousness were viewed as propaedeutic to the rest of philosophy. These facts could be marshalled dialectically, as by Dewey, or genetically, as by Baldwin, or phenomenally, as by James. Regardless, the self was an empirical unity rather than an ontological one, as it had been for Hegel, Herbart, and Fries. And the three critiques of Kant taken together rather than separately became the starting point for the new psychology.

Hermann Lotze was widely read in the 1880s because he had successfully performed this amalgamation of the three critiques. He had converted the faculties into phenomena. And he had brought the phenomena into a scientific context by relating them to current research on outer and inner states of consciousness, e.g. spatial perception and mental disease. The fact that Lotze had come to his phenomenal description of the self by way of a detailed critique of the metaphysical concepts of self of his day was ignored by the American philosopher-psychologists, excepting Santayana.[26] Despite the methodological parallels between Hegel and Dewey, Herbart and Baldwin, and Fries and James, there is this fundamental difference—that the Germans were more interested in a metaphysical self and the Americans in an empirical one. Lotze's two concepts of self are historically important because they helped to alter the subject matter of psychology from the pure to the empirical ego.[27]

ACKNOWLEDGMENT

I am grateful to C. C. Gillispie, R. High, and J. J. Sullivan for helpful comments.

REFERENCES

1. MERZ, J.T. 1904-1912. A History of European Thought in the Nineteenth Century. Vol. 3 :264. W. Blackwood & Sons. London, England.
2. WEISSE, C. H. 1837. Die drei Grundfragen der gegenwärtigen Philosophic. In Zeitschrift für Philosophie und spekulative Theologie. I.H. Fichte, Ed. 1: 179-180.
3. WEISSE, C. H. 1835. Grundzüge der Metaphysik: 552-564. F. Perthes. Hamburg, Germany. 552-564.
4. SMITH, N. K. 1930. A Commentary to Kant's "Critique of Pure Reason." 2nd edit.: 234-284. Macmillan and Co., Ltd. London, England.
5. GRESKY, W. 1937. 21 Briefe von Hermann Lotze an Ernst Friedrich Apelt (1835-1841). In Blätter für Deutsche Philosophie 10: 319-337.
6. LOTZE, R. H. 1841. Metaphysik: 280, 304, 324. Weidmann. Leipzig, Germany.
7. HOFFDING, H. 1900. A History of Modern Philosophy. trans. by B. E. Meyer, Rpt. 1855: Vol. 2: 251-255. Dover. New York, N.Y.
8. LOTZE, R. H. 1852. Medicinische Psychologie :138, 493-500. Weidmann. Leipzig, Germany.
9. HERBART, J. F. 1829. Allgemeine Metaphysik. Vol. 2. A. W. Unzer. Königsberg, Germ. In Herbart's sämtliche Werke, K. Kehrbach and O. Flügel, Eds. 8: 198-244.
10. LOTZE, R. H. 1845. Ueber den Begriff der Schönheit. Göttinger Studien. Pt. 2. In Kleine Schriften von H. Lotze, Peipers, Ed. 1: 296-297.
11. LOTZE, R. H. 1868. Geschichte der Aesthetik in Deutschland.: 46-54, 65-68, 118-120, 193-195. J. G. Cotta. Munich, Germany.
12. LOTZE, R. H. 1856. Microcosmus. An Essay Concerning Man and his Relation to the World. Trans. by E. Hamilton and E. E. C. Jones. 1885. Vol. 1: 249, 253. T. & T. Clark. Edinburgh, Scotland.
13. JAMES, W. 1890. Principles of Psychology. H. Holt. Boston, Mass. Vol. 1: 349.
14. LOTZE, R. H. 1879. Metaphysic in Three Books: Ontology, Cosmology, and Psychology. B. Bosanquet, Ed. Vol. 2: 171, 174. 1st edit. 1887. Clarendon. Oxford, England. C.f. Ref. 13.
15. FECHNER, G. T. 1855. Ueber die physikalische und philosophische Atomenlehre. 2nd edit. 1864 :225-227. Hermann Mendelssohn. Leipizig, Germany.
16. KANT, I. 1781. Critique of Pure Reason. trans. by N.K. Smith. 1929. 342 (A 364), Macmillan and Co. London, England.
17. LOTZE, R. H. 1880. Philosophy in the Last Forty Years. Contemporary Review. 15: 134-155. In Kleine Schriften von H. Lotze, 3(2): 451-479.
18. BAMBERGER, F. 1924. Untersuchungen zur Entstehung den Wertproblems in der Philosophie des 19. Jahrhunderts I. Lotze. M. Niemeyer. Halle/Salle.
19. BOWNE, B. P. 1886. Introduction to Psychological Theory :186-197, 213-214, 204-206, 212, 249. Harper and Bros. New York, N.Y.
20. DEWEY, J. 1887. Psychology 1: 242-243, 411. Harper and Bros. New York, N.Y.
21. JAMES W. 1890. Principles of Psychology. Vol. 1: 1, 8; Vol. 2: 487, 523, 527. H. Holt. Boston, Mass.
22. CAPEK, M. 1953. The Reappearance of the Self in the Last Philosophy of William James. In Philosophical Review. 62: 541, 537, 543.
23. BALDWIN, J.M. 1889. Handbook of Psychology. Senses and Intellect; 324-325, 60, 62-63. H. Holt. New York, N.Y.
24. BALDWIN, J. M. 1895. Mental Development in the Child and the Race. Methods and Processes: 114-120, 316-331. Macmillan, New York, N.Y.

25. LADD, G. T. 1894. Psychology. Descriptive and Explanatory: 1, 4, 12, 519-531. C. Scribner's Sons. New York, N.Y.
26. SANTAYANA, G. 1889. Lotze's System of Philsophy. Diss. Harvard. Ed. with intro. and biblio. by P. G. Kuntz. Indiana Univ. Press. Bloomington, Ind.
27. WOODWARD, W. R. 1975. The Medical Realism of R. Hermann Lotze. Diss. Yale. Univ. Microfilms, No. 76-14, 576.

NINETEENTH AND TWENTIETH CENTURY TRENDS IN THE PSYCHOLOGY OF THE SELF

David L. Krantz, *Discussant*

Department of Psychology
Lake Forest College
Lake Forest, Illinois 60045

As I was listening to today's presentation, I began wondering about the nature of being a discussant. It is very curious, if you look back at your own graduate training, that you were seldom taught about acting as a professional. You were very good at reading, writing, and doing research, but where along the line did anybody ever teach you to be a discussant? This is my second discussant job. I had to learn what they did by observing other discussants. I noticed two important pieces of behavior. Discussants spend an enormous amount of time writing during a session. Also, contrary to the people who give the papers, the discussant is often the only one who talks extemporaneously. Both of these behaviors suggest that the discussant has never seen the papers before the session. So it seems that one important characteristic of the discussant is that he be capable of thinking on his feet, of "winging" it. There also seem to be some subtle norm constraints on the discussant's activity. Here are a few elements of a possible Discussant's Credo: be incisive but not hostile; be entertaining but not frivolous; be provocative but not seductive; be knowledgeable but not showy. But what seems to be a major role requirement is to find a hidden theme. In this role, I feel like a character at Borges' *Labyrinths*, trying to find a theme which may not exist in this maze of material, or like a child who is in the middle of an Easter egg hunt and has never been shown what an egg looks like. To be very honest, I am somewhat at a loss to find the theme. I know what the title of the symposium is, but it doesn't help much.

All I can do is respond as a member of the audience, except that I have the role of Discussant—by raising some of the issues and questions that struck me as I listened to the papers. Perhaps those questions will do the job of integration.

One major issue that seems common among the papers is the comparison of European psychology, predominantly Continental psychology and American psychology. American psychology comes across in both the presentations and in my own reading, as what one would call metaphysically naïve and yet glorying in its naïveté. There is a superb section in J. B. Watson's autobiography that underlines this perspective. He describes his philosophical training at Chicago, saying in essence, "I really never understood what they were talking about—it didn't make a hell of a lot of difference. It was sort of fun and I didn't care anyway." There is this certain quality to American psychology which raises a question for Mr. Woodward. In his paper he gave us a range of complex German metaphysics, which often sets me to wondering whether they're saying anything of importance or just using a lot of complex terminology. But what intrigues me most is why, out of this cafeteria of metaphysical possibilities in European psychology, do the Americans, who were at that time the consumers rather than the producers of their own unique psychology, choose a particularly American flavor in a metaphysically naïve and empirically oriented sense? I think that on some levels this is quite predictable, that Americans should choose empirical self in a quite denuded form whereas there is enormous metaphysical richness surrounding Lotze's view and the views of various other people like him. In a similar sense, in looking at the joint paper of Dr. Riegel's, I was again struck with the complexity of the metaphysics of people like Piaget, or, as Klaus didn't have the time to get into, the very complex metaphysics of Rubenstein. What emerges in the American version is, let's say, not metaphysically naïve but metaphysically blind or unconcerned confirmation. If this metaphysical denuding behavior of American psychology is consistent, and I have at least from the sense of the papers and much that I have heard so far that it is, I would be interested to see how Verhave's and Van Hoorn's theoretical model (see Part IV for Von Hoorn's paper), which is a fleshed version of sociology of knowledge via Mannheim and others, how that kind of model could take into account the resonance of American psychology with certain kinds of philosophical presuppositions or absence of them. Or does their model have the usual difficulty of sociology of knowledge of pointing to interesting correlations like "isn't it interesting that things look this way and we have corresponding changes in industrial production." For example, Dave Bakan (See Part IV for Bakan's paper), I think, made a reasonably interesting point about the experiment as a manipulation. I have seen Dave's argument before on this, and I think there is good reason to believe that in a sense the manipulative experiments have a relation to certain attitudinal factors in American society which, in turn, are perhaps related to certain industrial kinds of changes. Yet the argument is weakened by a lack of demonstrative causal connections.

What interests me (and Dr. Van Hoorn suggested it), yet it is not clear what it would look like, is that he talks about different kinds of historiography, historiography of pure psychology and historiography of applied, the practice of psychology. Each of these would represent a different kind of historiography, but unfortunately he did not go into what it would look like.

I think the applied kind of model explains most effectively the relations between social conditions and applications within industry, or the actual connections with social issues. But I don't think it works as well, nor is the historiography at all clear regarding the resonance between theoretical viewpoints and social conditions. It is not a total accident that behaviorism sank its roots very deeply into the United States. Or, as Mary Henle suggested (see Part I, for Henle's paper), in her paper on Gestalt psychology, this movement never really received the kind of play that it deserved in the United States. The question comes, why the differential reception of theoretical systems? Is it simply an accident, an accident that European movements imported into the United States seldom find fertile ground? For example, phenomenology did not receive a very large representation in the United States, nor did existential psychology. Or in a comparable way, the exporting of our psychologies of behaviorism and in part the colonization of Europe have found a similar unfertile ground on the other side of the ocean. I was wondering with Dr. Riegel's paper, and I recognize that he had to go very quickly over Rubenstein's theory, to what extent Rubenstein's position or the dialectical kind of argument could find fertile ground within the United States or in Western Europe. Again there is a sort of model sitting behind much of what I've been wondering, which is that the scientist is an intellectual in the very broad sense defined by Shils. He has a function and a set of constraints around him that are the restraints of the intellectual community, a set of boundaries that are defined by that community. Yet at the same time, he is also a member of a much larger social context. It is not at all clear which set of restraints and forces operate and what relation in terms of defining receptivity to theoretical models. What I was wondering was whether it would be possible for Verhave or Van Hoorn to talk about the cultural differences between intellectuals both as members of the intellectual community and as members of specific social contexts. For example, there seems to be implied in the Van Hoorn and Verhave papers what could be viewed as a controlled experiment, although a very weak kind of research. Thom was making the point that the changes in the concept of self and its fragmentation are correlated on some level to changing social and economic conditions and the fragmentation of society. If that argument holds any water, then we would theoretically look at cultures or other settings where fragmentation was less extensive. For example, it's fairly clear that the rational tradition of Continental philosophy is a whole different kettle of fish from the English or American systems. Now, how does one explain the differences between a very strong metaphysical stress of Continental philosophy in psychology as compared to American psychology in terms of how they deal with self? Do we say there are different economic and social positions that have changed and fragmented on different levels? Is there any way that we can empirically or observationally determine this? It seems to me there is implied in their model certain kinds of question which I think historiographically, or, if you want, sociologically, could be answered.

These questions are among many of the issues that were raised for me during the course of these papers. As I said, my role is simply to define rather than to develop something unique. I am as much a member of the audience as you; the kinds of questions that come from me arise out of my own concerns. I found in this labyrinth of papers the theme of a particularly unique quality that self-psychology took in the United States. The unifying question then becomes *is* there any uniform explanatory model for this observed difference between Continental and American psychology in terms of how they deal with the self concept? Does the Verhave and Van Hoorn thesis do this, or what will do it?

Now is the point at which I will leave it to your concern to raise whatever questions may have been elicited by the papers.

DISCUSSON

John A. Popplestone, *Moderator*

Department of Psychology
University of Akron
Akron, Ohio 44325

DR. POPPLESTONE: I have often repeated my observation that perhaps the unique attribute of human beings is not the opposable thumb, or the invagination of the cortex, or our belief in supernatural forces, but perhaps the more important and distinguishing factor about us as a species is our ability to take relatively simple things and then complicate them beyond all necessity or credibility. This ability to create complexities is probably best exemplified in psychologists among the scientists, and may well explain why we seem, still, after 100 years of claiming to be laboratory disciplined, to be actually preparadigmatic (as Edna Heidbreder has observed), and what few prescriptions (to use Watson's phrase) we have are very loosely defined and at the mercy of every innovative or complicating human.

A concept which richly illustrates this faces us in this session. Four highly intelligent, creative, well-respected psychologists are going to look at four faces of the word *ego*. (Note that I have been very careful to describe *ego* in the most parsimonious possible way.) And when these excellent, possibly overbold people have finished, a fifth bright, competent, psychologist is going to be faced with the task of the "Discussant," hopefully, to bring these four variations together and show us the theme which has been played in the four earlier variations.

Some of these participants are old friends from whom past experience indicates that we can expect a very high level of work. The others are new friends to me, and personal observation of the very recent past and reports from trusted observers indicate that here also we will receive a presentation of the highest order.

Unfortunately, one of the earlier scheduled participants, Wolfgang Bringmann, who was scheduled to be part of the panel, had to drop out by virtue of difficulties involved in the flooding of his house.

I would like to make two observations about our topic in nineteen and twentieth century trends in the psychology of the self. The first can be accomplished by presenting a sample from almost the nineteenth century. This is the 1901 definition of ego (and alter) prepared by James Mark Baldwin and G. F. Stout for the *Dictionary of Philosophy* and *Psychology:* "Ego and Alter—The object self, (the ego) of the individual consciousness, as distinguished in the same individual's thought from another, (the alter). The antithesis of ego and alter necessarily restricts the meaning of ego to the object-self, inasmuch as it is in relation to the alter, which is the object of thought. The interpretation of the ego/alter relation has been variously attempted: For the intuitive theory there is immediate apprehension of both the self and the other." I think that's quite clear.

Now I would like to contrast this with the 1958 definition of the ego in English and English, *Dictionary Psychological and Psychoanalytic Terms.* "The 'I', *self-person* or individual as distinguished from the others; that which is postulated as the 'center' to which a person's psychological activities and qualities are referred.' This meaning is often used by those who believe that the ego is un-knowable, that it is a mere formal or logical necessity." I think those two definitions certainly say something about the passage of time.

Secondly, I have been fascinated since correspondence and discussions of this session first began in July of 1975, to find the topics, the personnel, and the titles changing. I will not even guarantee that the accounts and titles in your program agree with those which the speaker has ready for us now.

DR. RIEBER: It seems to me that one must distinguish between an integrated ego and a disintegrated ego; we have to know one in order to know the other. This leads to my question to anyone who would like to answer it. What is the relationship between the individual phenomenological self, or ego, and the higher-order abstractions that we come up with in our psychological theories? There should be, if we are talking about something psychologically real, an intrinsic relationship between the two. On the other hand, I am not always sure we recognize that intrinsic relationship in our discussions as well as in our publications.

DR. VAN HOORN [See Van Hoorn's paper in Part IV]: I would like to react to your comments somewhat in opposition to Dr. Krantz. I was quite impressed by the array of cafeteria material and food items that have been presented here. I think the speaker, to a greater or lesser extent, gave you little menus and arranged meals in combination platters, or whatever it's called in various homes, and I think this is a necessary condition. There are some very basic issues that you might indeed call metaphysical that nevertheless can't be avoided, such as what is the role of the individual, what is the role of the society, and of the organism in a biological sense? Do we look at those entities in their relative significance but emphasizing their essentially stable units, or do we see them under the concept of changes?

I would, however, now agree with Dr. Krantz that what we should be aiming for is to find out how, for instance, different cultures select this emphasis, given one or the other. I think this is precisely what a historian should do. (I briefly mentioned that in my paper.) If the historian does so, he enters in what I would call essentially the constructive phase of historial interpretation that he creates himself by doing historical studies.

DR. WOODWARD: I think, when you ask the pointed question of what is the ego, we have to recapitulate the distinctions between the phenomenal or empirical one and the metaphysical one. I think it's useful to look at the parallel history of physics in the late nineteenth century and to see the models in physics changing from that of the corpuscular Newtonian world, changing also from the force fields of Faraday, of electromagnetism, to a new temporalized process, to use Thom's [Verhave] term. The discovery of the electron, you know, happened in the 1890's. This changed people's view of the atom. The atom was no longer a corpuscle. Energy was involved, and I think you have to think in terms of the spirit of the times of the 1890s to appreciate what was going on in psychology, and I think it's no accident that you have process-psychologies like Lotze's, James' phenomenalism, and the disintegration of the ego. There is a general feeling that there was a collapse of the metaphysical subject, and at least the only fruitful thing to look at was the change in energetic states, change in levels of consciousness, say. I think, also, that the Verhave, Van Hoorn papers brought out a new ingredient, which mine did not, namely, the input from medicine and the study of altered states of consciousness. The phenomena of hypnosis demonstrated that there were two cells rather than one, and this was something no philosopher had apparently thought of. It had to be dealt with in psychology.

DR. LEIF ANNENDALE: The question I have is that the panel was on nineteenth and twentieth century trends. There was no mention of psychoanalysis and its relationship to the concept of the self, and very little mention of the impact of phenomenology on knowledge of the self. Rather, the panel concerned itself, it seemed to me, with the very rationalistic view of the self and the development of the self. I said there was no discussion of psychoanalysis in relationship to the self and the ego and the importance of psychoanalysis and twentieth century understanding of the self, and also very little mention of phenomenology, particularly of the European school and its relationship to the concept of the self. I think these are two vital areas which I think are extremely important for our understanding of the contemporary knowledge and understanding of the self, but which have been excluded from the discussion. Would the panel make some comment on these contributions?

DR. VERHAVE: Since I am somewhat responsible for organizing this particular panel, let me answer that. The main reason is simply lack of time. Phenomenology is somewhat represented. I made reference in my paper to the book by J. H. Van Den Berg on *Divided Existence and Complex Society*. That book is written within the Dutch phenomenological position, so in that sense phenomenology was represented all through my paper, since it deals with the phenomenology of the self in the nineteenth century. The reason why psychoanalysis and phenomenology are not represented by a distinct paper is purely lack of time. I certainly agree with you that these are important traditions and I am sure that most of the panel members would do so too. In any full discussion of the entire history of the self, they could certainly not be left out.

DR. MARTIN HAGEN (New York University, *New York, N.Y.*): I am impressed by the fact that psychology seems still to be in the grip of the philosopher. The philosophers lost their clutch, more or less, on the natural sciences when Galileo dropped some objects from a tower and in a way advanced the cause of experimental science. Is it perhaps a little premature for us to be talking about psychology in terms of philosophical models? It may very well be that, since we have only something less than 100 years of experimentation to work with, we have a lack of really empirical evidence on which to base any models of things like ego. It may very well be, as Dr. Verhave suggested, that we may need another 200 years to change the subject of the program, but I wonder if one or more of the discussants would address himself or herself to the recognition that there are few facts in such things as perception, but that more of them have been developed. We are a fairly young science, that is the scientific part of it, and perhaps we need a little more of this evidence. I didn't hear anyone address themselves to any of the development in perception and related subjects as they might affect these models of, say, ego.

DR. RIEGEL: I am very pleased to reply, but I cannot disagree more with your comments. Certainly the philosophers have never lost the grip of psychology, including experimental psychology. It may be that the experimental psychologists aren't aware any more of what kind of philosophies they are using. Now, instead of giving you an example in the area of perception with which I am not very familiar, I would like to outline some ideas about memory research, particularly human memory research, that has been very deeply influenced by a distinct philosophical tradition.

If you start with the Ebbinghaus position that was mentioned on different occasions, a kind of a compartmentalization model of elemental associations emerges. This memory research has been biased by philosophical constraint; it has been looking at the human memorizer only in an idealized universal sense, not at the concrete human being. It has never happened to us, to many experimental and general psychologists, that memory must also change and that this change must be very significant.

Of course, there are the developmental psychologists. The developmental psychologists believe that they are sophisticated when they study memory functions at, let's say, 10, 12, 14, 16 years, maybe up to 80 or 90 years. But when they compare these groups in the typical cross-sectional manner in which 99% of these developmental studies are conducted, they do not study only differences in memories between ages, but between generations as well. They study how one memorizes at ten, how one memorizes at 20, at 30, and so on; but they forget that these different cross-sections are composed of different generations. Think of your mothers and grandmothers and how they were trained, for instance, in school. My grandmother had to rehearse, rehearse, rehearse from the Bible. I had to learn about two or three pages of poetry every week in school. Who is doing that today? If we believe that these changes have no influence on the memory of the children of the successive generations we are seriously mistaken.

Currently, the philosophical foundation of memory research is undergoing very radical changes. The example I gave you indicates the developmental interdependence of individual and cultural historical changes. It represents a dialectical concept. For all too long we have thought that memory is indicated by the precision with which we reproduce former material. The quality of memory was measured in terms of how precisely, in a one-to-one manner, we recall something an hour, two hours, or a week later. From a more enlightened viewpoint, this concept of memory is absurd.

Let us consider three events, A, B, and C, which are represented on a time line. If at point C we look back at A, A has been changed by the intervening B and by the process of recall at C itself. This is what memory researchers would call interference. But it is a temporary interference; you never enter into the same memory twice; what you recall is continuously changed. Traditionally, however, our philosophical foundation requires that we sudy the static conditions at point A, point B, and point C; that is, the extent to which A is exactly recapitulated at C. Such an approach is absurd. We have to see the dynamics of the memory, and for this purpose we would need a different philosophical model which, in this particular case, phenomenologists have offered. Thus, there is, and has always been, a very intimate and a very important integration of philosophical, social, historical, and experimental ideas. This topic, I think, needs to be explored much further.

DR. VERHAVE: I want to respond to the question from the audience and also to some of David Krantz's comments. In the first place, in answer to the question from the audience, I am now and started out as an experimental psychologist. I also grew up in Amsterdam and didn't really get to speak English until I was about 20 years old. In that sense I am a product of both a European and an American background at this point. Next, I want to make a comment about the statement that whereas physics has escaped from the clutches of philosophy, this is not true for psychology. I don't think physics has escaped from the clutches of philosophy, either. If you read contemporary physics, if you read through all the musings of Bohr and Heisenberg, as well as many contemporary English and American physicists, you'll begin to realize that they have no more escaped from these basic questions than psychologists have. That brings me to the presumed differences between European and Continental psychology. I think that they can be much overemphasized. The fact of the matter is that, for example, much of Skinner's behaviorism was strongly influenced by Ernst Mach, and Mach was about as Austrian as you can get. I'll simply leave it at that because I could mention many, many other examples.

DR. GERALD WEISS: I enjoyed these papers quite a bit, but I do experience the frustration of some people in the audience. I do not consider, as Dr. Riegel suggests, that what is the role of the individual is a philosophical question at all, or a metaphysical question at all. If we mean by it the empirical investigation, it's a scientific matter; if we mean what should the individual do, it's an ethical matter; none of this is, to me, a metaphysical question. A metaphysical question, to me, is: What does the individual do with the notion of particulars in philosophy; Is it necessary for us to have a more articulate conception of these disciplines? Must we ourselves have a view of the self in order to go back and do more than merely recount what a particular person, like Lotze, says about the self to be incisive?

DR. WOODWARD: I wish we could presuppose an introductory course on philosophy from each of you who were listening to these talks, because I think that the speakers presuppose at least that much in preparing their talks. As you indicated, it is a matter of universals and particulars, and I think that, reduced to its simplest outline, the discussion about the pure vs. the empirical self today is a question of whether you think that the self is a simple particular or whether you think you can form an abstract concept of it and insist on a universal, so you have a continuing debate between realists on the one hand and idealists on the other. I think the more interesting issue, though, in the late nineteenth century is the suggestion made by Riegel, I believe, that this subject/object distinction might be passé, that it might no longer be fruitful to look at the self in terms of subject and object, and this I think is where the originality comes in, in Lotze's work and in James' that followed him. To think of self in terms of our actions, in terms of a process, antedates John Watson, and I think that in that sense James and Lotze are behaviorists, if you will, and that we must revamp our our present metaphysical stance, the relation of concept of mind into the nineteenth century.

DR. RIEGEL: I would like to react briefly to Dr. Weiss' comments. I agree fully with him. It would be my tendency, however, to avoid any specific compartmentalization. This is metaphysics and this is something else. I agree essentially also with what Dr. Krantz pointed out, with the direction into which he wanted to push us, to recognize the underlying conditions that bring about this or that viewpoint and this or that society. Such an argument would go beyond metaphysics. Consider social, political, and economic issues. There is a difference between the people in England and the people on the European continent in the way they live, in what cooperation and competition means to them, in the sociopolitical structure from which history has emerged, and in the significance assigned to the efforts of individuals. These are the overriding issues that can give us answers, a direction, in terms of what these different metaphysically rigidified kinds of concepts, words, and terms mean. For this reason I find myself in agreement with Dr. Weiss that the whole range of phenomena should be inspected. My own inclination would be to move forcefully toward an analysis at the general, social, and political level.

THOMAS C. UPHAM AND THE MAKING OF AN INDIGENOUS AMERICAN PSYCHOLOGY

R. W. Rieber

*Department of Psychology
John Jay College of Criminal Justice
The City University of New York
New York, New York 10019*

INTRODUCTION

It was the great John Milton who made the Prince of Darkness say,

> *Receive thy new Possessor:
> one who brings
> A mind not to be chang'd
> by Place or Time.
> The mind is its own place,
> and in it self
> Can make a Heav'n of Hell,
> a Hell of Heav'n.*

Paradise Lost, Book I

This and similar views had a profound influence upon the seventeenth and eighteenth-century Puritan thinkers.

A leading figure at the twilight of this tradition was a nineteenth-century professor at a small but influential college in Maine. His name was Thomas Upham, and we will attempt to demonstrate that his academic mission was to produce an indigenous system of psychology for the nation.*

---

*Thomas Cogswell Upham was born at Deerfield, N.H. on January 20, 1799. His father was a congressional representative and a leading citizen of New Hampshire. Upham was educated at Exeter Academy and Dartmouth College, graduating from the latter in 1818. After attending three years of theological study at Andover Seminary he was selected by his professor, Moses Stuart, to assist him in Greek and Hebrew instruction at the seminary. Subsequently Upham became pastor at the Congregational Church at Rochester until 1824, at which time he was chosen for the professorship of Mental and Moral Philosophy at Bowdoin College, Maine. In 1825 Upham added to his duties at Bowdoin that of instructor in Hebrew. The result of Upham's earliest lectures was the first edition (1827) of his textbook *Elements of Intellectual Philosophy*.[1] In 1831 this was expanded into a more systematic work to two volumes, with the title changed to *Mental Philosophy*. Three years later appeared the *Treatise on the Will*, which completed his three-volume work on mental philosophy. He published a *Manual of Peace* for the Peace Society in 1836, and *Outlines of Imperfect and Disordered Mental Action* in 1840. In addition, Upham was the author of numerous books on the Christian life, such as *Principles of Interior or Hidden Life* (1844), *Religious Maxims* (1846), *The Life of Faith* (1857), and *Treatise on Divine Union* (1857). He retired from Bowdoin in 1867 after a career of more than four decades, and died in New York City on the night of March 21, 1872.[2] We have not yet had the opportunity of examining the Upham papers, which are supposed to be in the possession of Bowdoin College. An incomplete search for them was unsuccessful.

SOCIAL-POLITICAL BACKGROUND AND THE AMERICAN DREAM

Representing the culmination of the Puritan tradition in the field of mental and moral philosophy, Thomas C. Upham appears in retrospect as one of the principle founders of a truly indigenous American *system* of psychology. Nineteenth-century America positively accepted Upham for this role because the *system* presented in his textbooks was the one most compatible with the prevailing American social image. Additionally, in a negative sense, we can say that Upham's work synthesized the opposition to Kant and the rising transcendentalist schools, those bogeymen of the American intellectual establishment.

The seed of this *ganz Amerikanisch* psychology was planted by its adopted father, Jonathan Edwards, who, like Upham, was strongly motivated by pragmatic social and political considerations. It had been imported "with tax" from its English guardians such as Joseph Butler (1736),[3] Richard Baxter (1670),[4] John Wilkins (1675),[5] Isaac Watts (1741),[6] Philip Doddridge (1765),[7] John Mason (1745),[8] and others. This doctrine, seeking a "natural" method for the pursuit of salvation and self-knowledge, emphasized the teaching of proper moral action and the "cure of the soul." Although still couched in a theological framework, these can be seen as earlier versions of the twentieth-century concept of mental hygiene and psychotherapy.

The term "psychology" should be clear enough, but what exactly is meant when we say that Upham created one that was "indigenous" and "American"? Certainly we do *not* mean to imply that a completely original psychology was ever developed in America. What we do mean is that the unique combination of historical circumstances in this country had been gradually producing a characteristic systematization of the subject matter of psychology, with particular emphasis and omissions that were "different enough to make a difference." From the vantage point of the present this process might be compared to a certain selection of flowers still in the bud, out of a large and varied garden, which, not yet in bloom, may be difficult for us to identify; yet on closer examination we find that while none are really new, the composition of the bouquet is unique and especially suited to the occasion. Throughout the present paper we shall be using the word "tradition" to delineate particular historical contexts and processes out of which the ideas of present-day psychology have emerged. However, while it may be interesting and even necessary to know Reid[9, 9a] or Stewart[10, 11] or Hartley, it is not sufficient. We are interested in how these concepts become assimilated over a period of time. We also want to know how they help us better to understand the theories and methods of present-day psychology, as well as how they help us to pose and answer the most fruitful questions. Yet, at the same time we do not want to go to the other extreme by advocating a presentist or "whig conception" of history—that the significance of ideas in history is determined by the ideas that currently dominate—for this necessarily distorts the real nature of historical context.[12]

Whatever indigenous psychology there was in America, was at first eclectic and highly systematic in nature. This is particularly apparent at the point at which Upham's sytem emerged. It was a eclecticism perhaps best described by Morell (1846).[13]

> ... modern eclecticism ... is the summing up of the positive and negative results of all of the systems, and the complete separation of that which is valid truth in them all from that admixture of error in which it was before involved.

In this context Upham's contribution might be fairly described as a link from what one might call the cure of the soul through the hand of God, to the cure of the mind through the hand of science.†

As we have already suggested, the importance of Upham's mental philosophy comes not from any great originality or controversial ideas, but rather from the fact that it represents the mainstream, dead-center nineteenth-century American Protestant academic thinking on the subject. It was the most comprehensive publication of a truly indigenous *system* of American psychology, even though built upon the work of numerous predecessors. Upham's system held this position because it was the one most compatible with the emerging American social image. Not in its content, then, but as a system, Upham's was new and different, containing the essence of the American dream as we know it even today. Tarnished though this dream may be, it has not yet been replaced, perhaps because nearly all belligerents in our psychosocial controversies still subscribe to its premises. A view of this "dream" at a formative stage may help to give us a better perspective on psychology today, and more particularly, on the psychosocial distress of our times.

The image upheld in Upham's system could be instituted through the four great institutional pillars of society: church, school, family, and government.

1. Upham's moral system has some compatibility with that of Paley,‡ but is more eclectic, and less utilitarian, in the Lockean-sensationalist meaning of the term. The most important task of the church is to inculcate morality; sectarian differences are not very important and must be tolerated in a spirit of mutual respect. Questions of time and cosmos have been partitioned off into two subdivisions, historical criticism and science, respectively. As long as the church can invest these three functions—morality, history, and science—with a certain degree of sanctity, while in addition supporting the state that makes possible its own survival and proliferation, doctrinal differences are mere frills.

2. In Upham's view, education should cultivate all parts of the mind, reason, affections, imagination aesthetics, literary and scientific skills, and so on, in a unified scheme that is itself part of the natural order of things. The child's mind

---

†The term science refers to mental science, ie., psychology.

‡Paley (1830) advocated the Lockean notion of man's natural right to propserity. Some of his ideas were quite critical of the monarchy. For instance, he asked his readers to imagine a field of corn in which a flock of pigeons had settled:

> If (instead of each picking where and what it liked, taking just as much as it wanted, and no more) you should see ninety-nine of them gathering all they got, into a heap; reserving nothing for themselves, but the chaff and the refuse; keeping this heap for one, and that the weakest, perhaps worst, pigeon of the flock; sitting round, and looking on, all the winter, whilst this one was devouring, throwing about, and wasting it; and if a pigeon more hardy or hungry than the rest, touched a grain of the hoard, all the others instantly flying upon it, tearing it to pieces; if you should see this, you would see nothing more than what is everyday practised and established among men. Among men, you see the ninety-and-nine toiling and scraping together a heap of superfluities for one (and this one too, oftentimes the feeblest and worst of the whole set, a child, a woman, a madman, or a fool); getting nothing for themselves all the while, but a little of the coarsest of the provision, which their own industry produces; looking quietly on, while they see the fruits of all their labour spent of spoiled; and if one of the number take or touch a particle of the hoard, the others joining against him and hanging him for the theft.

King George III was not very pleased to read Paley's criticism of the monarchy. Paley knew that this passage might prevent his advancement in the church but he held his ground and said "Bishop or no bishop, it shall stand." See Smith.[14]

is to be institutionalized to the greatest possible extent, so that his life may follow the prescribed image.

3. The family could help in the task of creating a new society by giving emotional security, primary discipline, and moral training to the preschool child. One of Upham's earliest books, a collection of poems entitled *American Cottage Life* (1850) was specifically intended as family reading.

4. Upham believed in the importance of a government based on the interests of agrarian capitalism, § he saw a great compatibility between democracy and the free enterprise system, and encouraged public service, particularly in his *Manual of Peace*. Agrarian capitalism, as we now know, could survive only as long as it remained profitable; it was killed by the very financial system it supported. The type of morality, science, and history that Upham taught are the religious and intellectual counterparts of this financial system. The popularity of the self-made man in the nineteenth century would inevitably lead to a self-made American psychology.

Two aspects of this major trend in the Protestant tradition are especially important for the history of ideas, and germane to the present discussion; Natural Religion, and Millennialism. According to the first, God could be known not only through revelation (the Scriptures), but also through the accurate study of nature or creation reflecting its Creator. It was this very emphasis on nature, amounting in some cases to its actual or virtual deification, which would eventually drive God out of the picture.¶ According to the second of these doctrines, Millennialism, the will of God was expressed through the acts of man, and would lead through a steady, rapid, and rational progress to man's perfection. The cutting edge of psychological history is politics, and thus the psychopolitical concepts of "manifest destiny" and "might makes right" soon became the *de facto* theology of large modern states, and patriotism replaced the God which the study of nature was undermining. But for an interim period, which included Upham's lifetime, the new deity could still be called "God" and could still be more or less associated with genuine religious tradition. This combined essence of Natural Religion and Millennialism was expressed in the concept of "Natural History," and there was a Natural History approach to the study of man, as to any other part of nature.

In the realm of applied psychology, this Natural History approach was referred to as "cure of the soul." Natural Religion spurred the search for data: "the proper study of mankind is man." This new understanding of Natural History, with all its theological overtones, was to be applied toward the gradual improvement, or redemption, of mankind, in accordance with "God's plan of salvation." For in the light of the doctrine of original sin, "cure of the soul" takes on univeral proportions, since *everyone* is in need of the "cure." Thus humanity had come to be regarded primarily as "masses"—even individualism was becoming a mass individualism ‖ —and the most effective way to "cure" man was through the combined effort of perfected social and political institutions; Americans, and even Europeans, believed that only America offered the possibility for the construction of such a perfected society, and this is why the "American Dream" was being constructed with nineteenth-century psychology as one of its foundations:

§ See WAYLAND (1837)[55] for a discussion of this.

¶ The Darwinian revolution helped to achieve this in the latter part of the nineteenth century.

‖ As in the western rush for gold, equally in the phrenology movement, designed to foster individuality and self-improvement while at the same time appealing to the millions.

Rightly so, for how could such a dream materialize without applied knowledge of the faculties of the mind of man?

UPHAM'S SYSTEM OF A SOUND AND DISORDERED MIND

"Mental philosophy" grew out of an extended theological-psychological critique of Jonathan Edwards' *Freedom of the Will*. This effort had two immediate effects: First, the proliferation of threefold divisions of mental phenomena, (intellect-will-sentiment), which allowed for a distinction between desire (sentiment) and motives (will); and second, taking its cure from Anglo-Scottish sources,** a new division between mental and moral philosophy.

Upham's synthesis can be seen in better perspective if we compare it with the systems of two of his key predecessors, James Beattie and Thomas Brown. Beattie, today generally considered inferior to the other Scottish philosophers from a strictly philosophical point of view, nevertheless exerted a crucial influence on all the early American psychologists-philosophers, including Benjamin Rush, James Dana, Samuel West, Jonathan Edwards, Jr., John Witherspoon, Samuel Stanhope Smith, Levi Hedge, and Asa Burton,†† by consolidating, epitomizing, and popularizing the views of James Reid. Beattie's *Elements of Moral Science*, published in London in 1790-93, was soon reprinted at Philadelphia (1792-94). In this work of his later years, Beattie seems less concerned with polemics against Locke and Hartley, and more willing to incorporate some elements of their systems.

Beattie divides his moral science into psychology (or the study of the nature of mental faculties), and natural theology. The matter of psychology is further divided into perception and active faculties (or powers), the former including speech and language, the-five primary or external senses, consciousness, or the mind reflecting upon itself, memory and attention, imagination, dreaming, and the secondary or internal senses of feeling (emotion); and the latter, passions and affections (expressive emotions), and the will, as free agent. Under Natural Theology, Beattie treats of the existence and attributes (natural, intellectual, and moral) of God.

Thomas Brown‡‡ further emphasized those elements from Locke and Hartley, such as the Association of Ideas, which were not incompatible with the Scottish tradition. He felt that his predecessors Reid, Beattie, and Stewart[10, 11] had made the mind into a collection of faculties that too often seem to be separate entities in and of themselves; no sooner were certain affections of the mind classed together as belonging to the will, and certain others as belonging to the understanding, than the will and the understanding seemed to become two contending powers of the mind. Brown suggested, in contradistinction, that the phenomena of mind should not be regarded as anything other than mind itself in various states of thought and feeling. The will is not considered as a state of mind, and is simply implied within the system.

Brown (1820)[17] divided all mental phenomena into external states and internal states. The former include all variety of sensations, whereas the latter are of two kinds: intellectual (divided further into simple and relative "suggestion") and emotional, comprising passions and desires.

Upham,[18, 19] in keeping with his Calvinistic background, makes much more of the will than Brown or any of the Scottish school. According to Upham, volition

---

**Particularly Reid[9, 10] and Stewart.[10, 11]
††See Fay[15] and Roback[16] for information regarding these individuals.
‡‡Levi Hedge edited an American edition of Brown's *Lectures* in 1827.

is a state of mind, and the evidence of consciousness assures him that it is distinct from desire.

In the earliest version of his psychology, *Elements of Intellectual Philosopy*, Upham (1827, 1828)[1] is careful to avoid the construction of a dogmatic system, but the germ of his later system is present nevertheless. In the next version, *Elements of Mental Philosophy* (1831), the mental operations have been divided into two types, intellectual and sentient. Significantly, Upham from the start included material on pathology, or what he called disordered mental action, showing the influence of Benjamin Rush's *Diseases of the Mind* (1812), the first American textbook in psychiatry. An inadequate explanation of erratic mental action was the Achilles' heel of common-sense philosophy, which these Americans aimed to remedy.

A third volume of Upham's "System of Philosophy" appeared in 1834 under the title, *A Philosophical and Practical Treatise on the Will*. With this acknowledging the strong influence of Asa Burton (whose division was understanding, *taste,* and will), Upham had finally arrived at his threefold division of the mind. § §

A separate treatment of language is found in every edition; in the *Mental Philosophy* of 1836 it is appended to the first volume, after the section on intellect, but in the final system of 1869 it appears at the end of the last volume. All this suggests a lack of certainty in Upham's mind as to its proper place. He seems to have regarded language as a ubiquitous component of all mental operations, but not as a constituent of the mind itself.¶ ¶ "Every language," he writes, "is in some important sense a mirror of the mind. Something may be learned of the tendency of the mental operation not only from the form or structure of language in general, but even from the import of particular terms expressive of the three-fold view of the mind."[18] (p. 53)

By the last edition the system, unchanged in its essentials, had undergone considerable expansion. Under intellectual states of external origin, Upham deals with the five senses, habits of sensation and perception, conception, simplicity and "complexness" of mental states, abstraction, attention, and dreaming. Intellectual states of internal origin include consciousness, judgment, association, memory, reasoning, and imagination. The section concludes with the disordered intellectual actions, divided into "excited conceptions," or apparitions, and insanity proper. For Upham suggested various degrees of disturbance of the mind, from a very mild state, analogous to what we would now call a minor maladjustment, or mild neurosis, all the way up to various stages approaching full-blown psychosis.

Natural sensibilities again are divided into emotions and desires, the former section containing discussions of beauty, sublimity, and the ludicrous; the latter including instincts, appetites, propensities, affections malevolent and benevolent, love of the Supreme Being, and habits of the sensibilities. Under moral sensibilities or conscience, Upham discusses emotions of moral approval and disapproval, relation of the moral nature to reasoning, feelings of moral obligation, and moral education. The section concludes with a treatment of the

---

§ §Hence it is clear that the statement by Packard[2] (p. 9) to the effect that the tripartite division appeared to Upham in a flash of inspiration, is erroneous. James Dana (1770)[20] implied a three-part division to refute Edwards, and Asa Burton (1824),[21] without engaging in a direct polemic against Edwards, professed taste and not the will itself to be the real moral agent.

¶ ¶This provides an important contrast with Rush (1865),[22] which was the subject of a subsequent paper presented to the American Psychological Association meeting in Washington, D.C. September 1976.

sensibilities in a disordered state. (We see a general drift toward making morality and sentimentality the principle supports of society and religion).

The final division of Upham's system, the Will, was eventually transformed into two additional works, *Treatise on the Will* (1834) and *Outlines of Imperfect and Disordered Mental Action.* (1840).[19] Under "volitional states of the mind," Upham relates the intellect and sensibilities to the will, and distinguishes between desires and volitions. In another section he discusses "Laws of the Will," relating them to moral government, and "natures" and kinds of motives. A discussion of freedom of the will and power of the will, follow the latter, which concludes with constancy of character and discipline of the will. A concluding section on "disordered action" of the will is found in all editions except the last (1869), which refers the reader to the *Outline of Imperfect and Disordered Mental Action.* We shall discuss this book in more detail further on.

It is noteworthy that Upham uses the term "disordered mental action," as opposed to the "pathology" favored by some of his contemporaries such as Isaac Ray (who was, incidentally, a Bowdoin College graduate).‖‖ "Pathology" suggests a medical model, whereas Upham insists upon an integrated model that is not strictly medical, in order to avoid so much as a hint of materialism. He is, of course, aware of the importance of the mind-body connection, and admits that under certain circumstances insanity may have a physiological origin. Nevertheless, insanity is not exclusively a physical disease; the mind and the brain are not the same thing. And the mind's "secret impulses" are not physically caused. Upham recognizes the contribution of Cabanis, but warns against the latter's materialism and skepticism. A nice contrast might be made with Benjamin Rush's "Influences of Physical Causes upon the Moral Faculties." Rush's position is that although some moral problems may be treated through counseling and education, many are more properly treated by medical means. There is no real disagreement between the two; merely different areas of emphasis.

Upham's entire system is based upon the still-current notion that the study of the normal will aid in the understanding of the abnormal, and likewise the study of the abnormal will aid in the understanding of the normal. Indeed, this symmetry is worked out with such obsessive thoroughness as to raise the question "was there madness to his method, or method to his madness?" A little of both, we suspect. For the *Outlines* correspond exactly to the structure of his total system. He simply lifted the "disordered" sections of the system worked out in the three previous volumes and elaborated upon them while incorporating them into the *Outlines.* Sometimes one feels that this organization is too pat; everything fits. The structure of madness proceeds relentlessly from the structure of sanity, according to the external principle, "whatever exists, can go wrong." The study of insanity, Upham feels, " . . . ought not to be limited to anything short of the length and breadth and depth of the whole mind."[19] (p. 55)

The period following Upham saw the continuing integration of the findings of abnormal with those of general psychology; in other words, the ancient relationship between physiology and pathology was now being applied to the study of the mind. This set the stage for the new "mental physiology" of the late nine-

---

‖‖Worthy of further investigation is the question why Ray and Upham never referred to one another in their published writings. Ray was a life-long student of insanity, and published the first *Mental Hygiene* in 1863. Perhaps Ray did not want to make use of nonmedical models? Upham's silence is no less curious.

teenth century.*** There is also a parallel with the phrenology of Spurtzheim and Combe, in which phrenology becomes the model for the normal as well as the abnormal. These systems amount to what we might call a "divorce of convenience" or methodological monism; they deny neither mind nor body, but are centered on one or the other. Often pursued with lack of perspective, they prepared the way for the more radical monisms of extreme idealism and ultramaterialism.

It was no coincidence that the *Outlines* was published in the Harper's Family Library series (no. 100). The work was clearly intended as "mental hygiene" for the layman (though that term is from a later period). A similar work was "On Man's Power over Himself to Prevent or Control Insanity," of John Barlow, directed to the English public in the series "Small Books on Great Subjects" (1846) and subsequently reprinted in the United States. These authors could not, of course, give detailed prescriptions; they make general statements, leaving the reader to discover the application for himself. Nevertheless, it was their belief that the simple recognition of a problem was preventative in itself, because the will could then be directed to control the disorder.

The present study is a blend of living and dead history; in other words, its contents is not altogether irrelevant to, or markedly different from, current discussions of free will and related problems.††† It was the opinion of Howard (1958)[23] that Upham's *Treatise on the Will* represents a conservative, academic compromise, a halfway-house between the iron-block theology of Jonathan Edwards and the pluralistic indeterminism of William James—conservative in that Upham, like most of the educators and clergy of his time, tried to reconcile his mental philosophy of the free will with the prevailing Calvinistic theology: academic, in that it is the statement of free will *par excellence,* to which most pre-Civil War professors of mental and moral philosophy adhered, and moreover, a historical compromise, in that it tries to avoid the direct confrontation of absolute determinism and absolute indeterminism, which both Edwards and James considered unavoidable.

That Upham defended the cause of orthodoxy in his religions works, and frequently in moral terms even in the *Elements*, is true. Howard, while admitting this, nevertheless strongly denies that the elements were designed to refute the German metaphysics of Kant and his school. Further, he believes that the threefold division of mental powers is not an original discovery of Upham's, as would seem to be implied in Packard's account, since a threefold division (although different in substance) is an important feature of the *Critique of Pure Reason*. But Howard has perhaps delved too deeply into the philosophical aspects of the question, without paying sufficient attention to circumstantial or contextual matters which are more important from a historical standpoint. It may well be true that Upham offers us no real contradiction to Kant. Curtis demonstrated close links between Kant and the Puritan philosophy, concluding

---

***Previous efforts along these lines, but without a system, were made by John Haslam. A closer counterpart is Benjamin Rush, whose *Lectures on the Mind* correspond to his *Diseases of the Mind* in this way. The *Lectures* have been largely lost to history because they were never published; an annotated edition is currently being prepared by E.T. Carlson, J.L. Wollock, and P.S. Noel. During the later part of the nineteenth century, Carpenter (1874)[23] developed this trend with the concept of "unconscious cerebration." Maudsley had a similar approach in his Physiology and Pathology of the Mind (1867). Frederick Beasley of Philadelphia wrote a book in 1822 entitled *A Search for the Truth in the Science of the Human Mind*. In this book Beasley had a small section entitled "Alienation of the Mind."

†††Such as Skinner.[24]

that "If Edwards may be charged with making God selfish, the same count may be made against Kant in regard to man."[25] (p. 62) The historic fact remains, nevertheless, that Upham was hired by Bowdoin for the express purpose of combatting Kant's influence. (Ref. 2, p. 8; Ref. 26, p. 58) This is all the more striking when we consider that the new German philosophy was as yet (1824) scarcely known in this country. Obviously, the academic establishment perceived a serious threat from that quarter. Whether they judged him rightly or wrongly, Kant spelled infidelity and atheism to the guardians of America's morality. Upham's teacher, Moses Stewart, had made himself an excellent German scholar in order to keep abreast of the voluminous German theological literature. The fear was such that Stewart himself, certainly no Kantean, had undergone investigation by the trustees of Andover College in 1825. The committee claimed that "the unrestrained cultivation of German studies has evidently tended to chill the ardor of piety, to impair belief in the fundamentals of revealed religion, and even to induce for the time an approach to universal skepticism."[27] Fay comes closer to the truth in judging that Upham was an eclectic, who borrowed freely from the ancient writers and from the British, French, Germans, and Americans in the field of mental philosophy.[15]

In order to understand a philosopher's problems and to estimate his success in solving them, we need to know more than a little about the traditions which intersect in his work. It became generally accepted among the defenders of free will and the threefold division that any question about mental phenomena is a question of experience that must be referred to the psychology of consciousness. This gave to much of their work the character of what we would now call empirical psychology. Thus, while the immediate goal of these critiques of Edwards may have been to free the will from Calvinistic predestination, their remote effect was a "new science" of the mind. By Upham's time, the 1830s and 40s, this dispute over the will had already been well worked over, and was by no means unique to mental philosophy. Upham was indeed an eclectic; a positive virtue under the circumstances, which grew from a wish to avoid mere speculation as much as possible, to concentrate upon simple facts and the general laws which these facts demonstrated. In Upham's time, of course, moral and theological facts of life were as fundamental as pure mental phenomena in the scientific process; hence, it was not uncommon to explain mental phenomena by demonstrating moral rules. Upham, for example, argues that laws of the will are implied in moral government and the foresight of the deity. This double attention to empirical truth and moral sentiment led to a special relationship between mental and moral philosophy, described by President Samuel Stanhope Smith of Princeton. "Moral philosophy," Smith writes, "is an investigation of the constitution and laws of the mind, especially as it is endued with the power of voluntary action, and its susceptibility of the sentiments of duty and obligation. . . "[28] (p. 9)

John Gros[27] (p. 7) defined moral philosophy as "that science which gives rules for the direction of the will of man in his moral state or in his pursuit of happiness." A similar position was taken by Thomas Clap (1765),[30] President of Yale College. Two things are reflected here: First, that moral philosophy consists mostly of a system of rules for the formation of ethical judgments, directly related to the values of the culture, and second, that questions relating to consciousness and moral sensibilities will fall equally within the provinces of mental and moral philosophy. These have a common domain in man's consciousness and will, as the two faculties that direct and establish a moral nature. Hence it would be a mistake to consider Upham's system as belonging exclusively to either psychology or moral philosophy, even as those disciplines were then understood. In fact, its strength lies in its use of psychological evidence as well as philosophical argument to solve the perennial problem of freedom of the will versus determinism, and in so doing, to facilitate the moral execution of an "American Dream."

Upham was certainly not the last of the American psychologist-philosophers to tackle the free-will problem. But in those prebehaviorist days, the defenders of free will were able to find support in psychological evidence even though Edwards' purely speculative arguments against freedom had largely been granted. Introspective analysis revealed the difference between externally motivated will and internal spontaneous desire, whereas Edwards' refutation of free will rests on the denial of such distinction. In other words, it seemed to the mental philosophers that Edwards had overlooked certain facts about the mind and its operation which would reduce his argument to a philosophical fantasy.

The nature of Upham's compromise position will now be clear. While maintaining a version of Edwards' determinism of the will, he nevertheless supports the notion of mental freedom by appealing first to the significance of the moral fact of responsibility, and second to the evidence of consciousness. The evidence for free will is unique; it is empirical, and need not imply a universe of chance. In addition, Upham presents the thesis that if there is equally compelling evidence in support of determinism, then freedom and determinism must be compatible. The argument from consciousness, says Upham, is as decisive as it is plain and simple, and this may be why he does not discuss it in great detail.

Upham characteristically emphasizes the inductive (common sense) observational evidence for freedom. In this way he avoids any need to indicate a chance universe before accepting free will.

These are the most important features of Upham's compromise solution to the question of the freedom of the will. It is a fundamentally sentimental solution, resolving the conflict between intellect and will by raising sentiment to par with both.

UPHAM'S COMPETITORS

Prior to the time of Calvin the free will-determinism problem had not played a major role in Christian philosophy, largely because of the continued survival, in some measure at least, of a "negative theology." According to this approach, the determinism of the universe, which is God's free will, is of an entirely superior order and includes within it all the possibilities of a man's freedom. Man's freedom simply does not include the possibility of achieving a rational overview of this order as it is present to God, but only the signatures of its existence as revealed and as manifested to man. This negative theology was usurped by the arrogance of a rationalism incommensurate with its object. The advent of Romanticism in the late eighteenth century brought with it numerous attempts to redress this imbalance, including those of Reid and Stewart as well as Kant and the German school. The psychologist is particularly attracted to Upham's version because it turns from airy speculation to the empirical evidence of consciousness; the philosopher perceives that Upham is on the right track at least in recognizing the need to reinstate a balance between the two poles of freedom and necessity, neither of which could carry any real meaning without the other. If his philosophical arguments are "superficial and meager," as Orestes Brownson[31] (1842) asserted, if he glosses over the real difficulties of important philsophical problems, as the *North American Review* charged, it is because, still trapped within the confines of Lockean individualism, Upham did not see the deeper philosophical implications of the very existence of human consciousness, with its essentially active nature, and that all human knowledge, even knowledge of God, is ultimately an analogy to man. (Review 1840, p. 240)

Far from lessening Upham's importance for the history of American psychology, these shortcomings actually deepen our understanding of that history. Upham's psychological works, after all, were conceived as textbooks for use in a country that was self-consciously engaged in the task of constructing its national image in that most nationalistic of times. Textbooks were of fundamental significance toward that end; ordinary spellers, readers, grammars, and geographies expressed it so aggressively as, for example, to cause great consternation in Canada, where they were often the only ones available.[32] Upham's work expressed the national image in a far more sophisticated but no less deliberate manner. Like any philosopher, he formulated answers to universal questions according to the outlook of his time and place, and by thus linking those universals with that outlook, consolidated and intensified it further. It is of no concern to history whether his answers were correct or not, for Upham was clearly the choice of the establishment.

According to the *New York Review*, January, 1840:

> Professor Upham has brought together the leading views of the best writers on the most important topics of mental science, and exhibited them, as well as the conclusions which he himself adopts, with great good judgment, candor, clearness, and method. Mr. Upham is a calm and cautious thinker and writer; and we find no reason to differ from the substance of his views on almost all the subjects he has treated . . . of all the systematic treatises in use, we consider the volumes of Mr. Upham by far the best that we have. (*Review*, 1840)[50]

In the opinion of the *North American Review,* July, 1840.[51]

> Though we are not prepared to wish, that any [textbook] should take the place of Locke's "Essay," or Reid's "inquiry" in the lecture room, we suppose that they who are of a different mind may have to wait long before another appears of equal merit, on the whole, to the ones before us. . . . The method and diction are, in general, good; the questions come up in their natural order, and are discussed with regular fairness of mind; and pains are obviously taken throughout to simplify the study, and recommend it to the young." (*Review*, 1840)

Finally, George Peck, in a lengthy and enthusiastic article in the *Methodist Quarterly Review*, April, 1841, saw the following as the outstanding advantages of Upham's system:

1. It embraces a view of the whole mind.
2. The arrangement and classification is natural.
3. Terms are skillfully used.
4. Its style is transparent and based upon clear reasoning and rich illustration.
5. Other authors are given kind and courteous treatment.
6. The author fortifies his opinions with a course of consecutive and accumulative evidence.
7. The distinction between desire and volition is clearly established.
8. The existence of the moral sense, or conscience, is clearly demonstrated, and distinguished from reason.
9. Moral distinctions are shown to be the immutable foundation of virtue and obligation.
10. Freedom of will is supported on the solid foundation of its subjection to law.
11. It sheds light on the business of education, by showing that all the intellectual, sentiment, and voluntary powers are susceptible of cultivation.

12. It lays a philosophical basis for several of the leading truths of Christianity. (Peck, 1841)[33]

It is quite apparent that Upham's text had sold more copies than any of the competitors. Moreover, it is clear from the foregoing that these competitors, chiefly Neo-Kanteans and Hegelians (Transcendentalists), never came near achieving an upper hand in the academic establishment, the lifeline of the country's intellectual future. Coleridge, with his *Aids to Reflection* and *Biographia Literaria,* was the most important link to Kant in the English language. In the 1820s James Marsh, President of the University of Vermont, wrote to Coleridge: "The German philosopher Kant and his followers are very little known in this country and our young men who have visited Germany have paid little attention to that department of study while there . . . I am indebted to your writings for the ability to understand what I have read of [Kant's] works . . . " (Wellek, 1942[27]) Marsh set himself the task of adapting Coleridge to American needs, and brought out the *Aids to Reflection,* with his own introductory essay, in Burlington, Vt., in 1829.

The arrousal of this new interest, however, led to the introduction of Victor Cousin, through Caleb S. Henry, Professor of Philosophy at New York University, who brought the French philosopher's intuitive idealism to America in 1834 with his adaptation of *Elements of Psychology,* the first book in the English language to use the word psychology in its title. (Both Fay[15] and Roback[16] were apparently unaware of this fact, for they erroneously attributed this distinction to Frederick A. Rauch's *Psychology,*[34] first published in 1840).

Among the German group we should mention Frederick A. Rauch,[34] S.S. Schmucker,[35] Lawrence P. Hickok[36, 37] and Asa Mahan.[38]

Rauch was probably the first to bring Hegel's ideas to America. Emigrating to the United States from Heidelberg in the mid-1830s, he was well equipped to achieve the task he set out for himself. His textbook *Psychology, A View of the Human Soul, including Anthropology*[34] was first published in 1840, only one year before his death. In spite of this, it was well read and went through at least four reprintings in the 1850s. Rauch's objective was to unite German and American psychology into a unified approach to the study of the individual as an intricate part of the cosmos.

On the other hand, Schmucker and Mahan had no such intention; they expressed disappointment with the existing systems, both American and European, and set out to "roll their own." Although Schmucker and Mahan experienced some success, with their texts both going through several editions and printings, their impact upon American intellectual thought was at best marginal.

Hickok was the author of two books, *Empirical Psychology*[36] (1854) and *Rational Psychology*[37] (1855). His work was squarely in the German tradition founded by Christian Wolff in the eighteenth century. Fay pointed out that Hickok coined the term *introspection,* which was later in the century to become a household word for most psychologists.

There were many other books on mental philosophy published during this period. Next to Upham's *Elements,*[1, 18] the texts written by Francis Wayland[39] (1854), Leicester A. Sawyer[40] (1839), and Joseph Haven[41] (1859) were most influential.

These texts, although they competed on the market with those of Upham, did not represent competing schools of thought. For the most part they appeared in the late 1850s, many years after Upham's first edition. Haven's *Mental Philosophy*[41] was the most widely read and perhaps the best of the lot.

In reviewing this list of Upham's rivals, two facts chiefly emerge: They were too late, for Upham's reputation was already entrenched before anything else resembling a "system" appeared; and second, they were of distinctly foreign character, at a time when European immigration and, consequently, prejudices were on the rise in the United States. The reaction of the *New York Review* to Rauch's *Psychology*,[49] though benevolent, is typical.

> In the preface, the author informs us, that it was his wish to combine into one new and systematic whole, adapted to the state of this country, whatever is best in German and English philosophy. We do not think he has perfectly succeeded. The character of his work, as to form, method, development, mode of thought, and language, has a predominantly German cast. . . .

The review found a lack of sufficient development in some places, insufficient explanation in others, complaining that the important points are "not synthetically expressed, with that systematic order and connection, and with that fulness, precision and clearness," which are the requirements of a student text. In other words, Rauch was found wanting in precisely the virtues for which that same journal had praised Upham just six months earlier.

No, America was too intent upon building its own image to accept foreign philosophies. *"What shall be the type of our philosophy,"* thundered George Peck,[33] *"and whence shall we obtain it?"*

His review goes on to reject in turn the Anglo-Scottish schools, Cousin, Kant, Fichte, Hegel, and Coleridge, concluding, "It is daily becoming more evident that we cannot *import* a system of philosophy from the other side of the Atlantic which shall meet the necessities of American mind . . . Systems in order adequately to meet our wants, must grow up and be matured among ourselves."[33] (p. 263-268)

And Orestes Brownson[31] (p. 358) concurred, if somewhat more thoughtfully:

> The American philosopher . . . must not attempt a *new* system of philosophy; but must seek to continue uninterruptedly, by improving it, the philosophy the race has always embraced, and as modified by the faith and practice of his own nation. In other words, the American philosopher cannot transplant into his own country the philosophy of France or Germany, nor will it answer for him to seek to construct a philosophy for his countrymen from the French or German point of view. He must construct it from the English point of view, and continue English philosophy, as modified . . . by Jonathan Edwards, our only American metaphysician, and by our peculiar civil, political, social, and religious institutions. Our philosophy must be English philosophy Americanized, like the great mass of our population.

It should by now be apparent that Upham was the major force behind the creation of such a system, and its kinship with the parent tradition made it most acceptable to a nineteenth century English reviewer such as Robert Vaughn[42] (p. 93), who praised Upham as a "profound thinker."

Despite this evidence, Blakey[43] showed little appreciation for Upham's work. But Herbert W. Schneider[44] (p. 210) called Upham the first great American textbook writer in the field of mental philosophy, and J. W. Fay[15] (p. 107) ascribed to Upham anticipations of many ideas commonly supposed to be more recent, such as the distinction between introversion and extroversion, the emergence of suppressed desires in perverted forms, rationalization, and the James-Lang theory of emotion.

Francis Wayland[39] (p. 6), President of Brown University and one of the best known educators of the early nineteenth century, made the following comment suggested by Upham's work.

Locke compares the mind to a sheet of blank paper, Professor Upham to a stringed instrument which is silent until the hand of the artist sweeps over its chords. Both of these illustrations convey to us truth in respect to the relation existing between the mind and the material system which it inhabits. The mind is possessed of no innate ideas. Its first idea must come from without. In this respect it resembles a sheet of paper. In its present state it can originate no knowledge until called into action by impressions made by the senses. In this respect it resembles a stringed instrument. Here, however, the resemblance ceases. Were the paper capable not only of receiving the form of the letters written upon it, but also of combining at will into a drama of Shakespeare or the epic of Milton; or were the instrument capable not only of giving forth a scale of notes when it was struck, but also of combining them by its own power into the Messiah of Handel; then would they both more nearly resemble the spiritual essence which we call mind. . . . .

It is in the power of combining, generalizing, and reasoning, that the great differences of intellectual character consist. All men open their eyes upon the same world, but all men do not look upon the world to the same purpose.

CONCLUSION

Where does psychology stand at the present time? In a microscopic view one may say that the remnants of a nineteenth century political economy, as suggested at the opening of this paper, are still with us. Much of academic and applied psychology has taken on a corporate structure, closely resembling that of the business world. The Ivory Tower days are clearly no more, and it is not hard to understand how psychology has participated in the transformation that is turning the American Dream into a social, political, and economic nightmare. Psychology is an intricate part of the academic community, and we psychologists are being manipulated into the problem whether we like it or not; that aspect of the problem which manifests itself in the disintegration of American higher education. Outside the formal academic situation we see the problem expressed in the chaotic activities of various purveyors of mental hygiene and psychotherapy competing in the marketplace today like salesmen of soapsuds or potato chips.

A recent article by Christopher Lasch[45] beautifully exemplifies this situation by pointing out that psychotherapists and mental health workers exercise literally priestly functions in our society, and that psychotherapy has become the modern man's substitute for religion. Though somewhat simplistic in its expression, this idea has a great deal of validity, even if we cannot go so far as to agree with Lasch's conclusion that this "psychiatric priesthood" is actually running our society. While they do play a major role in hastening the onset of a nightmare, they are no different in this respect from any other professional group, all too eager to cooperate with those who really do run the society; namely, the politicians, corporate industry, and organized crime.

As to the assumption of a religious role by the mental health professions, to the extent that this is true, its origin can be clearly perceived in our exposition of the role that mental pathology played in the development of an indigenous American psychology, which had its origin in the Protestant religion.

Not the least of Upham's attractions was his ability to describe mental operations in a manner that was not esoteric, not abstract, but pragmatic. He thus gave America what it wanted: a means of applying knowledge of the faculties of the mind to the task of building the nation. Even today the persistence of this attitude is seen in the innumerable forms of applied psychology that infiltrate every institution in American life. And in the powerful and personal appeal of psychology to the American public, witness the popularity of subjects in any way connected with psychology: the mind of the criminal, of the animal, of the politician, of Patty Hearst. Perhaps this is because everyone seeks self-knowledge. And if someone packages it and puts it up for sale, the American public will buy it. From phrenology to psychoanalysis it has experienced its most dramatic successes, and its most overwhelming influences, in the marketplace of the mind.

What is happening today is not exactly what happened in the past. But just as the important events in the development of the human infant manifests itself throughout the rest of his life, so does the infancy of American psychology leaves its vestiges, dressed though they may be in the most sophisticated technological trappings and disguised in the latest professional jargon. But this may have its brighter side as well. Here are just four current examples, although many more might be given. Donald Campbell[46] (p. 1103, 1116), President of the American Psychological Association, recently wrote that present-day psychology and psychiatry are more hostile to religious morality than is scientifically justified. "I am indeed asserting a social functionality and psychological validity to concepts such as temptation and original sin due to human, carnal animal nature." This statement, although considerably weaker than the traditional doctrine of temptation and original sin as revealed Truth, is unquestionably a remnant of Jonathan Edwards' old Puritan psychology.

We have a second example in O.H. Mowrer[47] (p. 7), past President of the A.P.A., who wrote, "For twenty years I've had a growing conviction that the main reason mental illness has been such a mystery in our time is that we have so assiduously separated it from the realm of personal morality and immorality," a position quite compatible to that of the nineteenth century mental and moral philosophers.

Jacob Bronowski, with a naive optimism that would be ludicrous were it not so serious, gives us our third example. In his popular book and television series, *The Ascent of Man*, Bronowski predicted that the future science would be a science of morality, and only a science of morality would enable man to prevail. This is, of course, merely a variation of the theme of our nineteenth century moral science professors, though we do not know whether Bronowski was aware of the fact.

Our final example is taken from Erich Fromm.[48] In his book *The Sane Society*, Fromm comes to the conclusion that neurosis, in the final analysis, is moral failure, and that mental illness is primarily due to the failure of the development of a humanistic value system based upon *love*.

In concluding this essay we may well ask the question: "What can psychologists do about the problems mentioned in this paper?" The answer to this question is, of course, not easy. One is reminded of what Huxley said in his preface to *Brave New World*: "You pays your money and you takes your choice." It would appear that there are at least two possible choices today. The first is the highly materialistic dehumanizing trend to keep western man adjusted to an increasingly irresponsible life-style, discouraging all notion of person accountability. We would reject this in favor of a psychology of humanistic interdependence based on sincerity, respect, and responsibility. Surely the life of the mind should be our prime concern as autonomous individuals if we are to play our role in developing a society in which man may prevail.

SUMMARY

Thomas C. Upham represents the culmination of the Puritan tradition in the field of mental and moral philosophy, and appears therefore in retrospect as a principle founder of a truly indigenous American *system* of psychology. The choice of Upham was based upon the fact that his *system* was the one most compatible with the prevailing American social image; indeed, it was created to help mold that image. Upham was one in a line of natural successors to Jonathan Edwards, whose ideas in turn stem from the tradition of natural religion founded in England by Baxter, Wilkins, Watts, Doddridge, Mason, and others. His work synthesized the opposition to Kant and the rising transcendentalist schools.

Upham's entire system is based upon the still-current notion that the study of the normal will aid in understanding the abnormal, and likewise, the study of the abnormal will aid in the understanding of the normal.

The principle methods in this doctrine, is its pursuit of salvation and self-knowledge, were the teaching of proper moral action, and the "cure of the soul." The latter is in some measure an eighteenth century version of "mental hygiene" and psychotherapy.

The present study is a blend of living and dead history; in other words, its content is not altogether irrelevant to or markedly different from current discussions of free will and related problems.

Not in its content, then, but as a system, Upham's work was new and different, containing the essence of the American dream as we know it even today. Tarnished though this dream may be, it has not yet been replaced, perhaps because nearly all belligerents in our psychosocial controversies still subscribe to its premises. A view of this "dream" at a formative stage may help give us a better perspective of psychology today and more particularly of the psychosocial distress of our time.

REFERENCES

1. UPHAM, T.C. 1827. 2nd edit. 1828. Elements of Intellectual Philosophy. Shirley and Hyde. Portland, Me.
2. PACKARD, A.S. 1873. Address on the Life and Character of Thomas C. Upham. Joseph Griffin. Brunswick, Me.
3. BUTLER, J. 1736. The Analogy of Religion. Simmon. London, England.
4. BAXTER, R. 1670. The Life of Faith. Nevde Simmons. London, England.
5. WILKINS, J. 1675. Principles and Duties of Natural Religion. Chiswell. London, England.
6. WATTS, I. 1741. The Improvement of the Mind. Blackstone. London, England.
7. DODDRIDGE, P. 1765. A Course of Lectures. Rivington. London, England.
8. MASON, J. 1745. A Treatise on Self Knowledge. Pike. London, England.
9. REID, T. 1788. Essays on the Active Powers of the Human Mind. Creek. London, England.
9a. REID, T. 1795. Essays on the Intellectual Powers of Man. Dobson. London, England.
10. STEWART, D. 1792. Elements of the Philosophy of the Human Mind. Crutch. London, England.
11. STEWART, D. 1828. The Active Moral Powers. Wells & Lilly. Boston, Mass.
12. STOCKING, G.W. 1969. Race Culture & Evolution: 142. Free Press. New York, N.Y.
13. MORELL, J.D. 1846. Historical and Critical View of Speculative Philosophy in the Nineteenth Century. Pickering. London, England.
14. SMITH, W. 1956. Professors and Public Ethics: 58, 59. Cornell Univ. Press. Ithaca, N.Y.
15. FAY, J.W. 1939. American Psychology Before William James. Rutgers Univ. Press. New Brunswick, N.J.
16. ROBACK, A.A. 1964. History of American Psychology. New, revised edit. Collier. New York, N.Y.
17. BROWN, T. 1820. Lectures on the Philosophy of the Human Mind. London, England. 1824. John Grugg. Philadelphia, Pa.
18. UPHAM, T.C. 1869. Elements of Mental Philosophy. Harper. New York, N.Y.
19. UPHAM, T.C. 1840. Outlines of Imperfect and Disordered Mental Action. Harper. New York, N.Y.
20. DANA, J. 1770. An Examination of . . . Edwards' Enquiry on Freedom of Will. Kneeland. Boston, Mass.

21. BURTON, A. 1824. Essays on Some of the First Principles of Metaphysics, Ethics, and Theology. Mirror Office. Portland, Me.
22. RUSH, J. 1865. Brief Outline of an Analysis of the Human Intellect. J. B. Lippincott. Philadelphia, Pa.
23. HOWARD, V.A. 1958. The Academic Compromise on Free Will in Nineteenth-Century American Philosophy: a study of Thomas C. Upham's "A Philosophical and Practical Treatise on the Will." Ph.D. dissertation. University of Indiana. Bloomington, Ind.
24. SKINNER, B.F. 1971. Beyond Freedom and Dignity. Alfred A. Knopf. New York, N.Y.
25. CURTIS, M.M. 1906. Kantean elements in Jonathan Edwards. *In* Philosophische Abhandlungen, Max Heinze . . . gewidmet Berlin, Germany.
26. HATCH, L.C. 1929. The History of Bowdoin College. Loring, Short, and Harmon. Portland, Me.
27. WELLEK, R. 1942. The Minor Transcendentalists and German philosophy. New Engl. Quart. **15**: 652-80.
28. SMITH, S.S. 1812. Lectures on Moral and Political Philosophy. Fenton. Trenton, N.J.
29. GROS, J.D. 1795. Natural Principles of Rectitude. T. and J. Swords, New York, N.Y.
30. CLAP, T. 1765. An Essay on the Nature and Foundation of Moral Virtue and Obligation. Mecom. New Haven, Conn.
31. BROWNSON, A.O. 1842. Schmucker's Psychology. United States Magazine and Democratic Review **11**: 351-73.
32. WILSON, J.D. 1970. Common school texts in use in Canada prior to 1845. Papers of the Bibliographical Society of Canada **9**: 36-53.
33. PECK, G. 1841. Upham's mental philosophy. Methodist Quart. Rev. **23**: 276-81.
34. RAUCH, F.A. 1840. Psychology. Dodd. New York, N.Y.
35. SCHMUCKER, S.S. 1842 Psychology. Harper. 2nd edit. 1855. New York, N.Y.
36. HICKOK, L.P. 1854. Empirical Psychology. 2nd edit. 1871. Ivison, Blakeman, Taylor. New York, N.Y.
37. HICKOK, L.P. 1848. Rational Psychology. Derby, Miller, Auburn, N.Y.
38. MAHAN, A. 1845. A System of Intellectual Philosophy. 2nd edit. 1854. Sexton and Miles. New York, N.Y.
39. WAYLAND, F. 1854. Elements of Intellectual Philosophy. Phillips, Sampson. Boston, Mass.
40. SAWYER, L.A. 1839. Mental Philosophy. Durrie and Peck. New Haven, Conn.
41. HAVEN, J. 1857. Mental Philosophy. New edit. 1883. Gould and Lincoln. Boston, Mass.
42. VAUGHN, R. 1847. American Philosophy. British Quart. Rev. Feb.: 88-119.
43. BLAKEY, R. 1848. History of the Philosophy of Mind. Vol. **4**: 530. Trelawney, Saunders. London, England.
44. SCHNEIDER, H.W. 1963. History of American Philosophy. Columbia Univ. Press. New York, N.Y.
45. LASCH, C. 1976. Sacrificing Freud. New York Times Magazine. Feb. 22.
46. CAMPBELL, D. 1975. On the conflicts between biological and social evolution, and moral tradition. Amer. Psychol. **30**.
47. MOWRER, O.H. 1967. Morality and Mental Health. Rand, McNally. Chicago, Ill.
48. FROMM, E. 1955. The Sane Society. Holt, Rhinehart, Winston. New York, N.Y.
49. NEW YORK REVIEW. 1840. Review of Psychology, by F.A. RAUCH. **7**: 271-73.
50. NEW YORK REVIEW. 1840. Review of Elements of Mental Philosophy, by THOMAS C. UPHAM. **6**: 243.
51. NORTH AMERICAN REVIEW. 1840. Review of Elements of Mental Philosophy, by THOMAS C. UPHAM. **51**: 240.
52. PALEY, E. Ed. 1830. The Works of William Paley. Pickering. London, England.
53. CARPENTER, W.B. 1874. Mental Psysiology. Kegan Paul. London, England.
54. WELLEK, R. 1931. Immanuel Kant in England, 1793-1838. Princeton Univ. Press. Princeton, N.J.
55. WAYLAND, F. 1837. The Elements of Political Economy. Leavitt & Lord. New York, N.Y.

SOCIOECONOMIC FACTORS AND THE ROOTS OF AMERICAN PSYCHOLOGY: 1865-1914
AN EXPLORATORY ESSAY

Willem van Hoorn

Psychological Institute
The University of Leiden
Leiden, The Netherlands

Thom Verhave

Department of Psychology
Queens College
City University of New York
Flushing, New York 11367

FMC: Life had become a kind of hesitant choice between apathy and madness. Nothing else counted but that perpetual racket of those thousands and thousands of machines that the people obeyed to.

L.-F. Celine[33]

INTRODUCTION: THE SOCIOECONOMIC CONTEXT OF THE HISTORY OF PSYCHOLOGY

An overview of the recent historiographic literature on psychology (see Ref. 1) shows that socioeconomic factors have been somewhat overlooked as determinants of the emergence and development of psychology (and psychiatry) in the nineteenth and twentieth centuries. One of the main purposes of this paper is to indicate that America's change from a mainly agrarian society in 1850 to the world's leading industrial power in 1914 has been coresponsible for the emergence of the social and *behavioral* sciences. In this respect "the discipline of the machine" (Veblen's phrase)[8a] and its wide-spread effects on the life-style of the American people seems of fundamental significance.

As Marx, Veblen, Dewey, and Ogburn set forth, the natural sciences and technology are primarily concerned with the industrial forces of society, whereas the social sciences, including psychology, deal primarily with productive relations and the ideological superstructure built to maintain, justify, and rationalize them. By means of some concrete examples it will be shown that social science often lags behind the development of natural science and technology (*Nacheilung*). Sometimes, indeed, one gets the *impression* that the constant acceleration of the industrial forces in the second half of the nineteenth century forms the *premier raison d'être* of the social sciences. In view of the historical facts, we think one must distinguish between theoretical psychology, applied psychology, and the praxis of psychology. The latter may develop in social life quite independently of the former two.

The distinction between a university-based theoretical and applied science and a praxis of psychology based upon "the common sense and practical judgements of mankind" is shown by the following statement of E. L. Youmans in 1867:

> That there is a vast body of valid knowledge concerning the nature of man, which is reduced to application, and serves for the management of conduct, is shown in all the multifarious aspects of social activity: I simply hold that this knowledge, valuable as it is, is yet imperfect . . . and must grow into a higher state and a more scientific character; and that the organized culture of the present age is bound to help and not to hinder this tendency.[1a]

How true Youman's prediction was to become will become clear later on in this essay.*

The influence of industrial mechanization upon the praxis of psychology most certainly has to be taken into account. Phrenology, the mental test movement, Social Darwinism, the turn toward scientific management, and the outburst of Taylorism will be mainly regarded as developments in the praxis of psychology in a money-ridden, pragmatically oriented, industrializing society. As we have set forth in our other paper, alienation, anomie, dissociation, dissimulation, neurosis, and respression are the concomitants of urbanization, secularization, industrialization, stratification, and professionalization. It is a thesis well worth further investigation.[6] Instead of dealing with great men, great ideas, and great dates, this paper will concentrate upon movements, masses, and machines.

Short Overview of American Socioeconomics: 1865-1914

In America, the war of 1812 introduced the factory system. There is no doubt that the Civil War encouraged the Industrial Revolution in this country. It is the development of the Industrial Revolution which forms the outstanding feature of American economic life between 1860 and 1914. Until late in the seventies, agriculture was still the leading source of wealth, "but the Census of 1890 showed that manufacturing had forged to the front, and ten years later the value of manufactured products was more than double that of agricultural."[5] (See TABLE 1.)

A quick glance at TABLE 2 shows the economic changes taking place in the period under discussion.

In 1860, flour, cotton, and lumber form the three most valuable industries; in 1914 slaughtering and meat packing are no. 1, to be replaced in 1929 by motor vehicles. By this time flour has dropped back to the 15th position. Printing, which was no. 14 in 1860, moves to no. 10 in 1914 and no. 7 in 1929. Cotton, although it played a significant role during the Civil War, is constantly on the decline, from the second industry in 1860, to no. 6 in 1914, and to no. 11 in 1929. And so on; the reader can see for himself.

Without going into details, three main characteristics of the growth of American manufacturing may be mentioned: a relative scarcity of labor (an incentive for the inventive genius to develop labor-saving machinery), the prompt adoption of any power other than manual, and the freedom from tradition, which can hardly be overestimated. We shall come back later to the psychological problems caused by increasing mechanization. Before the Civil War, the North formed the industri-

---

*Unfortunately, the scope of this paper does not permit us to go into the intricate connections between industrialization, the helping services, and the health sciences in the U.S. (See Refs. 2-4)

TABLE 1

COMPARISON OF THE VALUE OF AGRICULTURAL AND MANUFACTURED PRODUCTS*

Value of Products	1889	1899	1909	1919
Agricultural	$2,460,107,000	$4,717,076,000	$8,498,311,000	$23,783,200,000
Manufactured (including those based on agriculture)	9,372,379,000	11,406,927,000	20,762,052,000	62,418,079,000

*From Ref. 5, p. 392.

TABLE 2

RANK OF LEADING INDUSTRIES, 1860, 1914, AND 1920*

Rank	1860 Industry	Value of Products (in thousands)	1914 Industry	Value of Products (in thousands)	1920 Industry	Value of Products (in thousands)
1	Flour and meal	$248,580	Slaughtering and meat packing	$1,651,965	Motor vehicles	$3,722,793
2	Cotton goods	115,726	Iron and steel, steelworks, and roll-mills	918,665	Meat packing, wholesale	3,434,634
3	Lumber planed and sawed	104,928	Flour-mill and gristmill products	877,680	Iron and steel, steelworks, and rolling mills	3,365,789
4	Boots and shoes	91,889	Foundry and machine-shop products	866,545	Foundry and machine-shop products	2,791,462
5	Iron founding and machinery	88,648	Lumber and timber products	715,310	Petroleum refining	2,639,665
6	Clothing, including furnishing	88,095	Cotton goods	676,569	Electric machinery	2,300,916
7	Leather, including morocco and patent leather	75,698	Cars and general shop construction and repairs by steam railroad companies	510,041	Printing and publishing, newspapers, and periodicals	1,738,299
8	Woolen goods, including yarn, etc.	65,706	Automobiles	503,230	Clothing, women's	1,709,581
9	Liquors	56,588	Boots and shoes	501,760	Motor vehicles, bodies and parts	1,537,930
10	Steam engines	46,757	Printing and publishing, newpapers, and periodicals	495,906	Bread and bakery products	1,526,111
11	Iron, cast	36,638	Bread and other products	491,893	Cotton goods	1,524,177
12	Iron, forged, rolled, and wrought	36,537	Clothing, women's	437,888	Lumber and timber products	1,273,472
13	Provisions (beef, pork, etc.)	31,986	Clothing men's	458,211	Car and general construction and repairs, steam railroads	1,184,435
14	Printing (book, job, etc.)	31,063	Smelting and refining copper	444,022	Cigars and cigarettes	1,066,909
15	Carriages	26,849	Liquors, malt	442,149	Flour and other grain-mill products	1,060,269

*Ref. 5, p. 395.

alized part of the country which favored protectionism; the cotton and flour producers in the South adhered to free trade. In addition, the South persisted in its economically lucrative slave trade, whereas the North was turning against the world's second oldest form of labor. Thus seen, many of the tensions leading to the Civil War were of economic origin.

In retrospect, the United States was in an extremely favorable situation to change from a mainly agrarian society in 1850 to the world's leading industrial nation around the turn of the century. Some of the main factors favoring this development were an abundance of raw materials, the availability of cheap water power, a rather favorable climate, geographical isolation, cheap immigrant and slave labor, oil as a source of energy since 1859, and the availability of sufficient capital for industrial investment. Add to this rosy picture the effects of the Homestead Act of 1862, which permitted anyone to take possession of 160 acres of public land simply by agreeing to work it. One had to produce a going crop within five years. The homesteaders did two things for America: they supplied the nation with cheap and good food, and they reinforced an important stable element in American society, the family. Just as an illustration with respect to the favorable food situation, one would like to mention that between 1867 and 1871 two million cattle were shipped out of McCoy's Chicago stockyards. Indeed, through full-blown mechanization, farming was turned into an industry, and this, incidentally, constitutes one of the main reasons for the emergence of new cities West of the Mississippi. Between 1860 and 1900 more than 400 million new acres came under cultivation, partly because of the effects of machines such as Cyrus McCormick's reaper.† All these changes meant a tremendous communications challenge. The railroad network grew enormously after George Stephenson's test of the *Rocket* locomotive in 1829. Telegraphic communications were successfully demonstrated in the U.S. in 1844. The telephone was patented by Alexander Graham Bell in 1876 and 1877. Commercial typewriters came into use ca. 1867; the teletypewriter, invented in 1904, used existing telephone circuits. In the 1880s, Hollerith introduced his business machines, which were used successfully in the Census of 1890. As we showed at the end of our other paper, by 1867, E. L. Youmans was speculating about the clinical consequences of this modern "high-pressure" civlilization![6]

Increase of Population and Anonymous Inventions

As a concomitant of all the agrarian improvements and immigration, the population rose from 17,000,000 in 1840 to 62,000,000 in 1890. The population explosion in this country began quite early. The total population doubled between 1840 and 1870; again between 1870 and 1900; and once more between 1900 and 1950. With regard to changes in population, immigration has, of course, been an all-pervasive characteristic of political, social, and economic life. In 1860 there were about 4,000,000 foreign-born settlers in the United States; between 1860 and 1920 almost 28,500,000 foreigners came to American shores. (See Figure 1.)

The incoming tide of labor corresponds quite closely with the periods of prosperity and depression. "Thus we find the peak years in 1873 with 459,803

---

†There are three phases in agrarian mechanization: reaping about 1850 (McCormick Reaper); reaping with hand-binding, about 1870 (Marsh Harvester); and automatic binding about 1880 (Appleby's Twine Binder). McCormick's Chicago factory put out 1500 machines in 1849, 4000 in 1856, 10,000 in 1874, and 80,000 in 1884, the year of McCormick's death.[8]

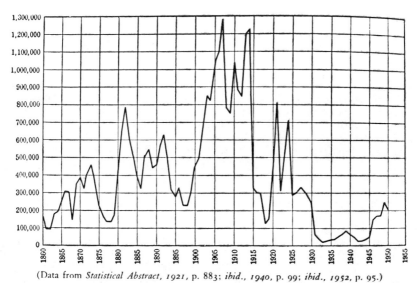

(Data from *Statistical Abstract, 1921*, p. 883; *ibid., 1940*, p. 99; *ibid., 1952*, p. 95.)

IMMIGRATION INTO THE UNITED STATES, 1860–1950.

FIGURE 1. Immigration into the United States. Data from Statistical Abstract, 1921 (p. 833); 1940 (p. 99); 1952 (p. 95).

arrivals: in 1882 with 788,922; in 1892 with 579,633; in 1907 with 1,285,349; and in 1914 with 1,218,420. While in actual numbers immigration increased in each decade up to the opening of the First World War, *emigration and the normal growth of population kept the proportion of foreign-born to the whole population at about 14 percent.* It was slightly under this in 1860, and slightly over in 1910" (Ref. 5, p. 474). The massive immigration from Europe and the overwhelming migration within the country are symptomatic of a general occidental alienation, anomie, and religious strife. Urbanization, secularization, and industrialization partly have to be paid for in dissociation and dissimilation of the people involved. Indeed, as we wrote elsewhere, the second half of the nineteenth century has bequeathed modern life with a host of unsolved socio-economic problems: a fair division of labor and national income among workers, the decay of city-life, the sprawl of suburbanization, the deterioration of the natural and social environment, and so on.[6]

After 1890 the source of immigration changes significantly. Until then, Great Britain, Ireland, and Germany contributed the greatest numbers. Between 1851 and 1860, for example, 88% of the immigrants came from these three countries. Between 1891 and 1910, this number shrank to 32%; during this period, southern and eastern European countries furnished over 50 percent. Leaving out the details, the main difference between the "old" and the "new" immigration came down to the relative supply of skilled or unskilled labor and the social consequences stemming from this difference. From 1882 to 1924 a number of immigration-restriction acts have been passed, which mainly favored the influx of skilled immigrants from northern European countries. The effectiveness of the various laws may be doubted. The proportion of arrivals excluded under the provisions of the various Immigration laws was actually negligible. The total number debarred in 1913, for example, was 20,000 or 1.4% of the total applicants for admission. Even the emergency act of 1921 proved to be ineffective; in consequence of increased immigration from Canada and Mexico (countries that were not included within the scope of the 1921 quota provisions), the total immigration from 1922-1924 was actually increasing, from approximately 300,000 in 1922 to 70,000 in 1924. The 1924 Johnson Act severely limited immigration; the years 1927 to 1935 saw more aliens leave the country than were admitted.‡ In the context of this paper, it is worth mentioning that the American Eugenic Society and leading psychologists were active in getting the Acts passed. The literacy test required by the 1917 Act was cooked up by psychologists, also.[7]

Leaving immigration and migration with their beneficial and disturbing effects aside, the overall American economic expansion between 1865 and 1914 has been heavily influenced by the fact that from the first phase of mechanization and industrialization on, the United States very soon reached the point where she began "to export towards herself." The ongoing Westward movement, the continuous increase in population, and the absence of tariff barriers between the states were of prime importance in this respect.

Looking at the economic expansion just mentioned from a sociopsychological standpoint, a few remarks are in order. First, the absence of a settled tradition, already mentioned. Social mobility in a buyers' market where several men, at least, could become kings, has played a crucial role. The educational process and its planning have to be viewed in this light. From the middle of the century on, there is a movement away from the religious and elitist-inspired education of the existing denominational colleges toward agricultural, technical, commercial, and architectural education, with all of its democratic implications. MIT was founded in 1861, the Business School of the University of Pennsylvania in 1881. The Morrill Land Grant Act was passed in 1862. E. L. Youmans' 1867 book clearly indicates the changing needs in education.[1a] Second, in studying the American Industrial Revolution one is struck by the fact that from mid-century on, America seems to be bewitched, if not bedeviled, by anonymous inventors. It would be misleading to think of the number of patents granted only, or just of the inventors still known by name, such as Pupin, Taylor, the Wright brothers, Lee de Forest, and Edison, Bell, and Westinghouse. According to Giedion toward the mid-nineteenth century the inventive urge "gained its hold over the broad masses, and perhaps nowhere more strongly than in the America of the 'sixties. Invention was in the normal course of things. Everyone invented, whoever owned an enterprise sought ways and means by which to make goods more speedily, more perfectly, and often of improved beauty. *Anonymously* and inconspicuously the old tools were transformed into modern instruments."[8] Significantly, the inventors already are, or quickly turn into, producers themselves, which tells us *something* about the rate of application of all those wonderful inventions. As Giedion makes clear, there is no simple correlation between the number of inventors and the *degree* of industrialization. As foreshadowed by the 'sixties, breadmaking and mass processing of meat would become two of America's leading industries. It was here that the assembly line originated and improved.

All the aforementioned factors do not sufficiently explain the course of the American Industrial Revolution. One key factor has still to be taken into account: the *concept of organization*. Improved organization of household management,

‡Partly due to the 1924 Act, and, of course, partly due to the socioeconomic situation of the depression years.

the farm, the factory, the state, and the federal government seems to be a royal road to understanding the Industrial Revolution in the United States.

INSTITUTIONAL LAG: MARX, VEBLEN, AND DEWEY

To follow up the relationship between psychology and the Industrial Revolution in America, the application of the idea of *institutional lag*, as originally put forward by Marx, Veblen, and Dewey, seems to be quite helpful. According to Marx, the natural sciences and technology are primarily concerned with the productive forces of society; the social sciences, however, deal primarily with productive relations and the ideological superstructure built to maintain and justify them. According to Marx, the productive relations almost invariably lag behind the development of the productive forces; thus one could maintain that the social sciences almost by necessity must lag behind the development of the natural sciences. Veblen, who far more clearly than most of his contemporaries perceived the decisiveness of the triumph of business civilization, has come to similar conclusions. Veblen points to the continuous clash between institutional norms and the almost self-perpetuating machine processes fed by the advance of technology. Social change, according to Veblen, mainly stems from science, applied science, and technology. Important social problems are due to the failure of institutions (education, religion, law, established labor relations, etc.), to keep pace with technical and technological change. As the "machine process" of industrial production reigns supreme, preindustrial concepts concerning private property rights and national sovereignty still dominate the social and political domain. Put in a somewhat simplified form, according to Marx and Veblen institutional lag is caused by a form of social friction stemming from the clash between the vested interests of the ruling class versus the not-yet recognized interests of those ruled.[8a]

As a cliché, it may be stated that Dewey's outlook on education strongly reflects the problems generated by the industrial revolution and the development of democracy.[9] Dewey's philosophy of education strongly reacts against the classical approach. According to Dewey, the exodus from the farm to the town and factory, the multiplication of machinery, and the growing complexity of urban life require a new curriculum. It is through practice that one must teach the arts and disciplines involved in living in an industrialized society.§ The essays collected by E. L. Youmans in 1867 in his *The Culture Demanded by Modern Life* nicely demonstrate the beginning of a Dewey-type Educational Philosophy. It must be noted that many of the authors (Tindall, Huxley, Faraday, Carpenter, Spencer, etc.) were Englishmen. Thus, one of the consequences of the rapid industrialization of American society was the reorganization of education. The growing need for skilled labor as well as for managers created the public school system from 1865 on. The demands imposed by processing large numbers of pupils would, in turn, lead to Age-Grade organization and eventually to standardized examinations.[10] Dewey's writings are a prolonged plea for practicality. The refutation of German-inspired idealistic epistemology became one of his life tasks. The general problem of institutional lag is clearly one of Dewey's concerns:

> Physical science has for the time being far outrun psychical. We have mastered the physical mechanism sufficiently to turn out possible goods; we have not

§In Joseph Ratner's apt title, "Intelligence in the Modern World," is the core of John Dewey's philosophy.

> gained a knowledge of the conditions through which possible values become actual in life, and so are still at the mercy of habit, of haphazard, and hence of force. . . . With tremendous increase in our ability to utilize nature for human use and satisfaction, we find the actual realization of ends, the enjoyment of values, growing unassured and precarious. At times it seems *as though we were caught in a contradiction*; the more we multiply means the less certain and general is the use we are able to make of them.[11]

Whether the late John Dewey would like it or not, this quotation could have come straight from Marx himself. Expressions like "physical science has outrun psychical" and "the more we multiply means the less *general* is the use we are able to make of them" indeed form actual illustrations of the perpetual contradiction between the state of development of the productive forces and the less developed or maladaptive social relations that accompany them.

What, then, does the idea of institutional lag contribute to the understanding of the relationship between American psychology and the American Industrial Revolution? From our present vantage point, we can see that the growing science and praxis of psychology in the second half of the nineteenth century have been codetermined by English, French, and German influences. These interact with genuine American economic requirements directly imposed by the machine process. Among the English influences are a Galtonian interest in individual differences, changing views on education brought about by England's own earlier Industrial Revolution, Spencerian evolutionism and its twin-sister Social Darwinism. By way of Karl Pearson (1857-1936), J. McKeen Cattell, and E. L. Thorndike, a Galtonian Social Darwinism will develop into the all-pervasive characteristic of American psychology until about 1960: the attempt at the quantification of behavior and mental abilities.

By 1867, the conservative American adaptation of the Scottish philosophy has become outdated to "modern" and "progressive" thinkers such as E. L. Youman.[1a] Wundt's American disciples form the remnant of the German ideological tradition in American psychology. They formed a *ganz un-Amerikanische* development indeed!

French influences, although important, have been lost sight of except for Binet. A more detailed study of the influence of French authors in the USA during the nineteenth century remains to be carried out.

A final point: the machine process has so deeply changed the meaning and significance of work (labor) that our modern life-style has been completely pervaded by it.¶ All the older relations implied by the words "work," "labor," "vocation," and "calling" have become irrelevant. This is true even of the specific nature of the tasks involved. The most important feature of an industrial society is the *mobility* of labor. The skilled crafts of the old guilds have become devalued, split up into endless sequences of industrial tasks. To understand the historical processes involved the classic Marxist formulations are perhaps especially helpful. According to Engels, the transition from prehuman existence to the human condition has been brought about by the process of work: "Work has produced man himself."[12] The work process, writes Marx, is typically human, "a process between man and nature, . . . in which man arranges, directs and controls his own action." "The work process . . . forms the eternal natural condition of human life; for this reason it is independent from any specific form of such life. It is common to all forms of society."[13]

¶ To indicate the overall pervasiveness of the phenomenon, we believe with Veblen that it is better to speak of the "machine process" than of "mechanization."

From here it is only one more step to formulate the general relationship between economic life and the societal superstructure built on it; the form of production of material life conditions all of the social, political, and cultural life processes. Who will now, in 1976, gainsay it?

SCIENTIFIC MANAGEMENT AND THE CHANGING SIGNIFICANCE OF LABOR

Earlier in this paper we made a distinction between theoretical, applied, and practical psychology. This section will show that scientific management and the operation of the assembly line form an unrecognized chapter in practical psychology. Mass immigration and the Westward movement of the frontier put America in a new labor situation. In a timespan of about 30-40 years a new development takes place, aptly characterized by Marx as the emergence of *labor sans phrase*, i.e., *the job*.‖ A "job" is the kind of work a worker can interrupt. He can go and work somewhere else. A job is the opposite of "calling." A job is the result of the triumph of the marketplace, without any connection to the ancient notions of original sin or a curse of paradise. A job has only one relation: to money. According to Marx: "Nowhere is man so indifferent towards labor as in the U.S.A. There is no other country where people know so well that work always produces the same result, viz. money."**

Between 1850 and 1880 the organization of labor and management becomes the effective characteristic of American economic life. By the end of the century labor has become organizing as well as organized.†† The development of the interrelationship between working men and women, natural resources, the machine process, and anonymous organizational forces enables us to see the place of labor in its proper perspective. In the end, through the combined effect of these influences labor appears to be *neutralized*. That is the moment, ca. 1880, at which scientific management got its impetus.

During the nineteenth century the smooth functioning of the machine became the paragon of human labor. The social problems of this situation would multiply a hundredfold. According to Mumford: "In creating the machine, we have set before ourselves a positively inhuman standard of perfection."[14] The first phase of the Industrial Revolution in the USA was governed by the demands of machinery rather than the needs of man. The enormous improvement in machinery and gadgetry, the studies made in the natural sciences, the growing knowledge of the mechanism of the body, all tended to focus on *man's likeness to the machine*. Scientific management as well as the nineteenth century public school system are the ideological expression of this tendency.

Psychogically viewed, scientific management focuses on the identification of human labor with machine labor; industrial psychology, mainly after World War I, pays attention to individual differences, thereby partly pulling the rug from under the basic tenets of scientific management. The mental test movement of the 1890s forms the intermediary stage between scientific management, which started about 1880, and an industrial psychology that jumps ahead from

‖The Marxian expression is: "Arbeit sans phrase," to be found in the *Grundrisse* of ca. 1857. See Marx, Karl, 1972. The *Grundrisse*. David McLellan, Ed. and transl.: 38-39. Harper Torchbooks. New York, N.Y.

**In this connection, it is interesting to note that the Dutch still say they "earn" (verdienen) their money, while the Americans say they "make" money.

††Giedion: "Before the turn of the century, the attention of industrialists was being claimed not so much by new inventions as by new *organization*." (Ref. 8, p. 96)

1910 on. Scientific management was "Wundtian"/"Newtonian" in orientation. Industrial psychology, by way of Cattell and Thorndike, owes its ideology to Galton.

Significantly, scientific management started with engineers, not with psychologists. Indeed, one can hardly think of anything more unpsychological than the basic aim of scientific management, viz. to arrive at "the one best way of doing the job." According to the scientific managers, just as the skater, swimmer, or golfer improves by expert teaching, so does the industrial worker. Taylor started scientific management studies at the Midvale Steel Company in 1881, but the roots of scientific management extend to at least the early 1870s, "if not to Wedgwood's Etruria and Watt's foundry in England of the late eighteenth century."[15] As far as human and animal motion is concerned, the period after 1850, when Helmholtz measured the rate of transmission of the nervous impulse quite accurately, and until Taylor's first studies of the early 1880s, is as yet unexplored. It may well be a gold mine of ideas for a better understanding of the emergence of scientific management as well as the new psychology. During the 1860s, De Jaager and Donders, at the University of Utrecht, were doing their famous reaction-time experiments.[16] In the late '60s the now obscure French physiologist E. J. Marey, totally preoccupied with movement in all its forms—in the blood stream, in the stimulated muscle, in the gait of the horse—attempted a graphic portrayal of movement.

"A dove harnessed to a registering device (FIGURE 2) transmits the curve of its wing beats to smoked cylinders. From these the form of the movement is plotted out point by point." (Ref. 8, p. 21)‡‡

And Taylor? Taylor devotes his time to building up the science of shoveling in a large steel plant. It has been noted many times that Taylor always picked the best workers for his experiments and fixed the task accordingly. Working in this fashion, he always approaches the limits of human elasticity. Taylor had three aims in mind: raising production, increasing wages, and reducing working hours. "In his famous experiments on shovelling, he tells his laborers in the yard of the Bethlehem Steel Company: 'Pete and Mike, you fellows understand your job all right, both of you fellows are first class men, but we want to pay you double wages." (Ref. 8, p. 117) And if you want to make double wages, you have to work more efficiently. Thus, the production process must be functionalized and standardized. The one best way of performing the job is determined by subdividing it into the smallest possible units of time and motion—the ultimate consequence of the division of labor. Then, these smallest time-motion units are recombined into "methods of least waste."

It is not too astonishing perhaps to recognize that during that very same period Ernst Mach and others were interested in reorganizing physics and the philosophy of science. The aim was to be the most economical description of the facts, and *to avoid all quantities not directly measurable.*

Scientific management *à la* Taylor is based on the presupposed *free* cooperation between management and workers. In *A Piece-Rate System* (1895), this is formulated as follows: workers are able and willing to produce more per hour if they are convinced that they will make more money in doing so. Employers are able to pay a higher wage per product if every man and machine delivers the utmost achievement. Thus seen, employer and worker have a common financial interest. According to Taylor, "What the workmen want from their em-

---

‡‡At the beginning of the '80s Marey began to use photography for the representation of movement, partly stimulated by the photographic studies of motion that Muybridge was performing in California.

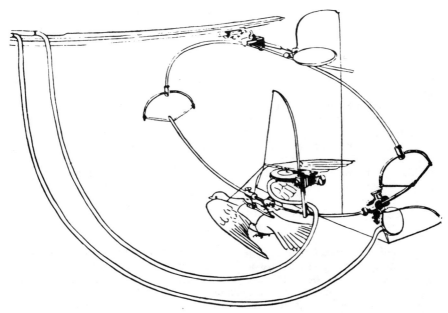

FIGURE 2. To trace the more extensive movements of a bird in flight, Marey (E. J. Marey, 1868, Recording Larger Movements–Flight) harnessed a piegeon to the arm of a merry-go-round. The wings, connected to pneumatic drums, record their trajectory on a cylinder.

ployers beyond anything else is high wages, and what employers want from their workman most of all is a low labor cost of manufacture."[17] This philosophy culminates into "Manager and workers must accept the philosophy that the interest of both and of society in the long run calls for ever greater output of want-satisfying commodities."[18]

During the 1930s, B.F. Skinner, whose philosophy of science was much indebted to Ernst Mach, was to rediscover Taylor's piece-rate system in the animal laboratory as "periodic reconditioning according to a fixed ratio."[19]

From *Shop Management* and *Scientific Management* we get the following picture. There must be a strict separation of brainwork (managing) and manual labor: "All possible brainwork should be removed from the shop and centered in the planning or laying-out department, leaving for the foreman, gangbosses, and workmen, work strictly executive in nature." One best way for every job: "Employees have to be scientifically placed on jobs where material and working conditions are scientifically selected so that standards can be met." With respect to training, Taylor wrote that: "Employees shall be scientifically and precisely trained to improve their skill in so performing a job that the standard of output can be met." All this rests upon the friendly cooperation of capital and labor: "An air of friendly and close cooperation will have to be cultivated between management and workers to insure the continuance of this psychological environment that will make possible the application of other principles." What good came of all this, asks the historian. Pay on a piecework basis became the most effective tool to increase productivity. By 1940, more than 90% of American industry had adopted the wage-incentive aspects of Taylor's blueprint of industrial utopia (Baritz).

It was Taylor's misfortune that his system was never accepted *in toto*. This partial application of scientific management in American industry has probably caused more evil than good, something clearly recognized by Taylor himself in his testimony before the 12th Special House Committee in 1912. Said Taylor: Scientific management involves a complete *mental revolution* on the part of the workman and on the part of the management; without this mental revolution on both sides scientific management does not exist: "That is the essence of scientific management, this great mental revolution."[20]

In summary, then, Taylor's practical engineers' psychology undoubtedly is part of the history of American psychology.§ § Taylorism did not bother itself with the negative mental and physical effects of scientific management. Despite Ricardo, Hegel, Marx, and Durkheim, the division of labor first had to be pushed to or beyond its limits before management would recognize its ultimate negative societal consequences.

MENTAL TESTS, EUGENICS, AND SOCIAL DARWINISM IN AMERICA CA. 1890

As indicated earlier in this paper, Galton's push towards the quantification of mental abilities, his plea for a eugenics policy, and his emphasis on individual differences have to be counted as an important contribution to American psychology. It is Wundt's and Galton's pupil, James McKeen Cattell, who forms the bridge between scientific management and industrial and military psychology. It is important to view Cattell's contributions of the '90s in the context of eugenic ideas and Social Darwinism. All three movements imply one basic question: what is the origin and social significance of human variability?

Social Darwinism, currently gaining popularity again as libertarianism, was also an important movement during the American Industrial Revolution. Herbert Spencer and William Graham Sumner were two of its most dedicated advocates.[21] Spencer, a fierce supporter of laissez-faire individualism, adhered to a contract theory of social order based on property values. He developed Social Darwinism as a theory relating environmental adaptation to the social order and individual morality. During the American Industrial Revolution he became the spokesman of rugged individualism, which nicely coincided with the theory of the survival of the fittest of the great entrepreneurs. Sumner helped to spread evolutionary accounts of the naturalistic emergence of biological and cultural phenomena, as already put forward by Spencer. In addition, Sumner was a fierce, conservative advocate of class stratification and "social immobility." The temporalization of society was anathema to him.

Social Darwinism, as we shall see, rests upon two principles: natural selection and Lamarckianism. Darwin himself had this to say about natural selection: "As many more individuals of each species are born than can possibly survive; and as, consequently, there is a frequently recurring struggle for existence, it follows that any being, if it vary however slightly in any manner profitable to itself, under the complex and sometimes varying conditions of life, will have a better chance of surviving, and thus be *naturally selected*. From the strong principle of inheritance, any selected variety will tend to propagate its new and modified form."[22] The general belief in the inheritance of acquired characteristics implied that, like miscegenation, "social mixing" was equally dangerous to the "better sort."

§ §For a management criticism of Taylor, see Peter Drucker, 1954, The Practice of Management, for example.

In Social Darwinism we have an emphasis on natural selection, rather than on variability. When we pass from the animal to the human sphere, one may ask how superior organisms develop. The answer can be stated in five propositions: (1) De-emphasize the problem of the source of variations by emphasizing natural selection; (2) regardless of the source of variations, the less fit varieties will be eliminated or subordinated, and the more fit will be maintained; (3) the foregoing presupposes *natural* inequalities among individuals, and this results in a stratified social organization, which is designated as "natural"; (4) if moral attributes are biological facts and if the measure of morality is the control of property, then it is "natural" that propertied individuals should exist at the expense of those without property; (5) the social structure must be stratified according to "natural" principles (Ref. 21, 14: 408). In sum, evolutionary processes, according to the gospel of Social Darwinism, become a conservative, reactionary social and political movement. If you are poor, it is your own fault. The poor, Spencer wrote, are unfit and should be eliminated. "The whole effort of nature is to get rid of such, to clear the world of them, and make room for better."[23] The nineteenth century is the age of the "poorhouse" mentality.

Eugenics fits in well with Social Darwinsim.¶ ¶ Galton: "Eugenics is the study of the agencies under social control, which may improve or impair the racial qualities of future generations either physically or mentally." In Galton's view, man must attempt to govern his own racial evolution: this means a restriction upon the very intimate human relationship of marriage. The differences between men are to no small extent the result of *inborn* differences. For this reason the study of individual differences is conceived as a study of *innate* individual differences. Much of Galton's statistical work seems to have been motivated by his concern to put eugenics on a firm scientific basis.[25] Like Spencer, Galton was greatly stimulated by Darwin's evolutionary theory. Under Darwin's influence, Galton fostered the idea of *consciously* influencing human evolution, something to be accomplished by the theory and practice of eugenics or race-improvement. In *Inquiries into Human Faculty and its Development,* 1883, Galton introduced the concept of eugenics for the first time. The book had "to touch on various topics more or less connected with that of the cultivation of race, or, as we might call it, with 'eugenic' questions."[24] According to Buss: "Thus, Galton's description and measurement of individual differences in mental ability, his genetic interpretation of such differences, and his statistical contributions were all based upon furthering the improvement of the race through encouraging the propagation of those individuals having desirable traits (positive eugenics) and discouraging those with undesirable traits (negative eugenics) (Ref. 24, p. 55). Unfortunately, one has to state here that it is perhaps only one more step from Galton's eugenics program to the Nazi's race theory and the elimination of the Jews as an inferior race; the Nordic Myth was a nineteenth century preliminary.

Fortunately, Galton's eugenics program has not been carried out. So far his eugenic certificates have not been issued. In Galton's eugenic *Walden Two, Kantsaywhere* (1911), the number of children a couple may have is strictly determined by their joint eugenics score. The insane or mentally defective were to be segregated for life, and, to no one's surprise, the power of the state was to put in the hands of a eugenic aristocracy. That overdoes the quest for nobility. Is it unclear why the succession of Platonic, Galtonian, and Tayloristic paradises always resemble the Fascist and Nazi totalitarian states so much?

Eugenics contrasts with euthenics, that "branch of applied science which

¶ ¶ "Eugenics" comes from the Greek *eugenes*—well born.

aims at the improvement of man by regulating his environment." That tradition can already be found among the French *philosophes*, most radically in Helvétius and in Robert Owen, more moderately in J. S. Mill, L. Ward, and outside the scope of this paper in J. B. Watson.

As far as Eugenics and Social Darwinism are concerned, the entire mythology that combined racism with Lamarckianism and Social Darwinism was also used to rationalize the supposed inferior position of women in a male-dominated industrial society.[26]

By 1890 we have two sets of opposed movements in psychology:

> (1) Taylorism, which would educate the worker through optimal training vs. Cattell, who would screen out the inferior of the big litter.
> (2) Euthenics vs. Social Darwinism/Eugenics.

It is clearly impossible to maintain the orthodox Marxist position which claims that the ideological superstructure invariably trails behind actual productive relationships.

In the title of his article published in *Mind* in 1890, Cattell coined the term "mental test."[27] In 1888, Cattell, as America's first professor of psychology, had developed a series of tests which he administered to his students at the University of Pennsylvania.∥∥ The tests of this series consisted of the determination of dynamometer pressure, sensation areas by means of the two-point threshold, just noticeable differences in weight, reaction time for sound, the memory span for letters, and several others. In an appendix to Cattell's paper, Galton described some other tests that also could have been used. From a historiographical standpoint, the most interesting thing about Cattell's interest in individual differences is that it forms an *original American* development in psychology. How do we have to understand this? As Watson (1963, p. 354) has made clear, Cattell's interest in individual differences dates back to the years 1882-1883. Thus Cattell was already interested in individual differences at least four years before he worked with Galton. From his theoretical interest in individual differences, Cattell went on to become the most vigorous promotor of applied psychology. Thorndike, who took his doctorate with Cattell in 1898, became America's undisputed leader in the mental test movement; Hollingworth (Ph.D., 1909),*** brought psychology to business and industry; Strong (Ph.D., 1911), is well known for his test of vocational interest and his work in industrial psychology. Poffenberger (Ph.D., 1912) used psychology in advertising and selling. These pupils of Cattell's contributed to the development of psychology in the USA during the first decades of this century. It is to industrial and applied psychology, that we shall now, finally, devote our attention.

INDUSTRIAL AND APPLIED PSYCHOLOGY

First, let us try to put things in order. In America, between 1840 and 1880 we see a development which results in the recognition of *neutralized labor* (*Arbeit sans phrase*). As was set forth earlier, by 1870 slaughtering and meat-packing were on their way to become the nation's leading industry. Due to the

---

∥∥We see no reason why one would call Cattell's professorship "the first . . . anywhere in the world" (Watson, 1963, 354); Lazarus, one of the founders of the *Zeitschrift für Völkerpsychologie* (1859), by that date was already professor of psychology at the University of Bern.

***See, for example, Hollingworth's Coca-Cola Co. study on the influence of caffein on mental and motor processes.[34]

immense growth of the population, the increased standard of living, the cultivation of new land and the greatly improved shipping facilities, slaughtering *had*
to be mechanized (meat for the millions). One of us worked during his high
school summer vacations in the heart of a meat-packing firm, the cutting hall.
Thus one learns from experience how complicated the hog is. Even in the 1950s
all the operations in the mass production of dressed meat had to be performed
by hand. A hundred years ago there was but one sollution to speed up the output: "to eliminate loss of time between each operation and the next, and to
reduce the energy expended by the worker on the manipulation of heavy car-
casses. In continuous flow, hanging from an endlessly moving chain at twenty-
four inch intervals, they now move in procession past a row of standing workers
each of whom performs a single operation." (Ref. 8, p. 94) Without doubt,
here we have *Arbeit sans phrase*. Here is the birth of the modern assembly line,
and perhaps most important of all, here is a new, qualitatively different form of
the *organization* of work. The date is 1870. Ten years later, Taylor starts his
time and motion studies. Both the organization of the assembly line and the new
forms of work resulting from scientific management studies are based on the
same principles of practical psychology. As so often happens, however, praxis
precedes analysis. To start with, practical psychology in the last quarter of the
nineteenth century tried, in vain, to fully adapt the worker to the discipline of
the machine, a failure marvelously ridiculed in Charles Chaplin's *Modern Times*.
In the 20th century industrial psychology tried to adapt the machine to the
worker. How much difference, however, does this make? The problem of neutralized labor is still very much with us.

Schematic overview of the Practical Tradition in American Psychology

1840-1880:   the emergence of neutralized labor
1865-1875:   the birth of the assembly line in slaughterhouses and classrooms
1880-1900:   scientific management comes of age.
1910-1920:   the growth of industrial and military psychology

As is clear from the above schematic overview, scientific management precedes industrial psychology by about a quarter of a century. It is possible,
it seems, for university professors to lag behind developments in material life
by such a stretch of time.

Narrowing down the discussion to industrial psychology as such, we pass
over in silence such impressionistic works as Scott's *Psychology of Advertising*.
We shall concentrate instead on Henry Ford and Hugo Münsterberg. It can be
shown that in the second decade of this century, both the business tycoon and
the professor were busy getting production raised and costs lowered. The tycoon
refused to use science and relied upon his horse sense; the urbane professor
tried—in vain, we think—to apply theoretical psychology to business problems.

In the second decade of this century, Henry Ford, after he had introduced
the Model T in 1908, thought that his old dream of mass production of the car
could be made a reality. To achieve this, a complete revolutionizing of the
manufacture of his product became necessary. In 1913 the first experiment with
an assembly line, the assembly of the fly-wheel of the magneto, was attempted.
But, before Ford could go into full assembly line production, the *labor problem*
had to be resolved first. In 1913 Ford required between 13,000 and 14,000
employees to run his plants, but, unfortunately, in the same year more than
50,000 workers would quit. This turnover problem had to be solved before
any technical innovation to speed up the production process could be installed.

It had always been Ford's policy to raise wages (production and sales is a tied knot) and reduce working hours. On January 5th, 1914, when Ford workers were being paid an average of $2.30 a day, the FMC announced that it would pay every man, even the janitors, a minimum of $5.00 per day.[28] At the same time, an eight-hour working day was introduced. The plan worked well. Ford was afraid that money made so easily would seduce his employees into evil ways. Thus a "Sociological Department" was set up to check upon the private lives of his employees. More than one hundred investigators regularly went into homes to see that everything was acceptable according to the department's norms. "No outside advice was sought in the creation of this department; company employees conceived and executed the plan." (Ref. 15, p. 33) From 1914 on it was possible to split the assembly of the engine into 84 different operations, taking a third of the former time. The chassis was first placed on a rails, operated by a rope and pulley. After some time, Henry Ford could rightly claim that the decision to pay $5.00 for an eight-hour day was "one of the finest cost-cutting moves we ever made." The Sociological Department, later called the Educational Department, told the *Ford Times* of 1916 that, "looked at from a cold-blooded point of view of business investment, the concern with human behavior was the very best investment the FMC has ever made." (Ref. 15, p. 33) Indeed, the quotation from the *Ford Times* exactly indicates what was going on at the time: psychologists and business men alike discovered the human element in carrying out a giant business enterprise. Ford's $5.00-a-day plan showed that you need neither psychologists, nor sociologists, but just horse sense, to ease labor tensions.

From 1913 on, the human factor begins to play its role in management. Obviously, good machinery was available to all. Thus, the difference between success and bankruptcy was the recognition of the human element. From now on the standard problem becomes the selection of workers half as good as the machines available.[15] At this point Hugo Münsterberg enters our story.

When Walter V. Bingham was elected secretary-treasurer of the APA at the 19th meeting, held at the University of Minnesota in 1910, he found in the record book the names of 222 members; about *170 of these were teaching psychology to college students.*[29] Hardly a handful were practicing clinical psychology in homes for the feeble-minded. Bingham remembers only one member in private practice without institutional affiliation. In 1950 the APA had 7,250 members. A *majority* of these were *practitioners* in industries, business offices, railways, hospitals, schools, clinics, welfare agencies, and the like.††† In 1910, Münsterberg began to think actively about the psychological problems of industry. In that year he sent out a circular to several hundred executives, asking what psychological traits they believed to be necessary in their employees.[30] The managers' response was encouraging, and thus Münsterberg sat down to formulate some simple principles of industrial psychology. In 1913 industrial psychology was formally launched with the publication of Münsterberg's *Psychology and Industrial Efficiency*. Let Münsterberg speak for himself. The psychology of industry was "a new science, which is to mediate between the modern laboratory psychology and the problems of economics: the psychological experiment is systematically to be placed at the service of commerce and industry." This description distinguishes between scientific management and industrial psychology; the former originated within the factory among some enlightened engineers. The latter developed some 25 years later

†††Bingham rightly distinguishes between psychology as a science, a technology, and a profession, a distinction of which the historiographical consequences still have to be drawn.

in the psychological laboratory. Münsterberg acknowledged the debt that his *nuova scienza* owed to scientific management. He thought Taylor's approach was inadequate, because of "helpless psychological dilettantism."‡‡‡ Keeping in mind that it was the managers desire to be able to select workers half as good as the machines available, Münsterberg claimed that psychology could detect for industry "those personalities which by their mental qualities are especially fit for a particular kind of economic work." Rather naively, Münsterberg also proclaimed that industrial psychology would cause "overflowing joy and perfect inner harmony" to radiate through the whole of society.[31] Neither Taylor nor Münsterberg seem to have understood that in a capitalistic society, labor and management necessarily have antagonistic interests.

In his *Business Psychology,* published in 1915, Münsterberg made clear that as far as *industrial conflict* is concerned, the psychologist has to act as *unbeteiligter Zuschauer.* The solution of social problems has to be left to others. Complete scientific detachment and the prediction and control of the workers' behavior should be the industrial psychologist's aim. John B. Watson's launching of an objective science of behavior during these same years can hardly be called a coincidence.

The development of industrial and military psychology from 1915 onward lies outside the scope of this paper. Hollingworth's and Poffenberger's *Applied Psychology* and the *Journal of Applied Psychology* both were published in 1917. The development of the army intelligence tests, of course, is of paramount significance. During America's active participation in World War I, the psychologists could show what psychology could do for the war effort. It is this accomplishment which turned the scale in favor of the application of psychology in business. After the war was over, no business manager or tycoon could still maintain that management could do without psychology. Because of the spectacular achievements accomplished during wartime, applied psychology had become a respected profession. Our final date to be mentioned is 1921. This is the year when Cattell (who else?) founded the *Psychological Corporation.* Its aim was to make the findings of applied psychology available to business and industry.

A SUMMING UP

In the introduction to this paper we wrote that the constant acceleration of the industrial forces in the second half of the nineteenth century was perhaps the main reason for the emergence of the social and behavioral sciences. Insofar as the development of American psychology is concerned, the statement is only partly true. Only when one distinguishes between the science of psychology, the application of psychology, and practical (nonacademic) psychology does the significance of this historiographical position become clear. Influenced by German, French, and English scholars, the science of psychology has grown, almost undisturbed by the changes in industrial life. Not so, practical psychology and applied psychology: until 1900 practical psychology has been heavily influenced by forces related to the Industrial Revolution. After 1910, applied psychology grows out of the intricate web of business, industrial, and commercial relations existing at that time. Why applied psychology has lagged so very far

‡‡‡It would be most interesting indeed to find out whether scientific management was adequate for the state of industrial problems between 1880 and 1910, while industry, business, and commerce had grown so complex that industrial psychology became a necessity from 1910 on.

behind the development of the industrial forces related to it still needs to be explained.

From least to most important, then, the roots of American psychology are at least fourfold: a German line, from Wundt and Mach to Titchener; a French line, from Cousin and others to Renouvier and James; another from Binet to Terman; an English line from Galton and Bain to Cattell and Thorndike. The genuine American contribution consists of the concept "that every meaningful human problem can be stated in terms which make it accessible to quantitative investigation." (S. Diamond)[32] This Newtonian idea was originally conceived by Galton, but only in Cattell's hands was it to become the definitive influence on the development of twentieth century American psychology.

NOTES AND REFERENCES

1. YOUNG, R. 1966. Scholarship and the history of the behavioral sciences. History of Science 5: 1-52. R. I. WATSON, 1967. Psychology: A Prescriptive science. Am. Psychol 22: 435-443. K. RIEGEL. 1972. Influence of economic and political ideologies on the development of developmental psychology. Psychol. Bull. 78: 129-141. J. SULLIVAN. 1973. Prolegomena to a textbook history of psychology. In Historical Conceptions of Psychology. M. Henle et al. Eds.: 29-47. Springer. New York, N.Y. W. WEIMER, 1974. History of psychology and its retrieval from historiography. Part I: The problematic nature of history; Part II: Some lessons for the methodology of scientific research. Sci. Studies 4: 235-258, 367-396. R. BUSS. 1975. The emerging field of the sociology of psychological knowledge. Am. Psychol. 30: 988-1002.

1a. YOUMANS, E.L. 1867. The Culture Demanded by Modern Life.: 411. D. Appleton, New York, N.Y.

2. COHEN, N.E. 1958. Social Work in the American Tradition. Holt, Rinehart and Winston. New York, N.Y.

3. LEVINE, M. & A. LEVINE. 1970. A Social History of Helping Services. Appleton-Century-Crofts. New York, N.Y.

4. ROSEN, G. 1975. Social science and health in the United States in the twentieth century. Paper presented at 7th meeting Cheiron, The International Society for the History of the Behavioral and Social Sciences. Carleton University. Ottawa, Can. June 5-8.

5. FAULKNER, H.U. 1964. American Economic History. 8th edit. Harper and Row. New York, N.Y.

6. VERHAVE, T. & W. VAN HOORN. 1976. The temporalization of the ego and society during the nineteenth century: a view from the top. This volume.

7. GOSSET, T. F. 1965. Race: The History of an Idea in America. Schocken Books. New York, N.Y. R. V. GUTHRIE. 1976. Even the Rat was White: A historical view of psychology. Harper and Row. New York, N.Y. L. J. KAMIN. 1974. On the Science and Politics of I.Q. John Wiley and Sons. New York, N.Y.

8. GIEDION, S. 1948. Mechanization Takes Command. 1969 edit. Norton. New York, N.Y.

8a. VEBLEN, T. 1923. The captain of industry. In Absentee Ownership and Business Enterprise in Recent Times. Ch. VI. New York, N.Y. Also T. Veblen. 1904. The discipline of the machine. In The theory of Business Enterprise. Ch. IX. New York, N.Y.

9. POUNDS, R. & J. BRYNER. 1973. The School in American Society. 3rd edit. Macmillan, New York, N.Y.

10. LEVINE, M. 1976. The academic achievement test. Its historical context and social functions. Am. Psychol. 31(3): 228-238.

11. DEWEY, J. 1910. The Influence of Darwin on Philosophy and Other Essays in Contemporary Thought: 71. Holt, Rinehart and Winston. New York, N.Y.

12. ENGELS, F. 1872. Die Dialektik der Natur. In Marx-Engels Werke. 1973 edit. 20: 444. Dietz Verlag. Berlin, Germany.

13. MARX, K. 1867. Das Kapital. In Marx-Engels Werke. 1973 edit. 23(part 1): 192. Dietz Verlag. Berlin, Germany.

14. MUMFORD, L. 1963. Technics and Civilization. 2nd edit. Harcourt Brace Jovanovich, New York, N.Y.

15. BARITZ, L. 1960. The Servants of Power. A History of the Use of Social Science in

American Industry: 28. Wesleyan University Press. Middletown, Conn. See also C. BABBAGE. 1832. On the Economy of Machinerie and Manufacture. Cambridge Univ. Press. Cambridge. England; 1835. 4th edit. Charles Knight. London. 1963. Augustus M. Kelley. New York, N.Y.

16. DE JAAGER, J. J. 1865. Reaction Times and Mental Processes. J.Brozek & M. Sibinga, Eds. and Transls. 1970. De Graaf. Nieuwkoop, The Netherlands. See also W. VAN HOORN. 1973. The quickest thought is the natural unit of time. Contemporary Psychol. **XVIII**(5): 288-289.

17. TAYLOR, F. 1903. Shop management. *In* Scientific Management. Harper & Bros. New York, N.Y. 1947 edit.: 22.

18. TAYLOR, F. 1911. The Principles of Scientific Management. Harper & Bros. New York, N.Y.

19. SKINNER, B.F. 1938. The Behavior of Organisms. Appleton-Century-Crofts. New York, N.Y.

20. TAYLOR, F. 1912 *In* Hearings before special committee of the House of Representatives to investigate Taylor's and other systems of Shop Management. 3 vols. Government Printing Office. Washington, D.C. 1947 edit.: 27. Our exposition of Taylor rests largely upon R. WESTERHOF. 1975. Frederick W. Taylor (his "method of bringing the workman and the science together"). Unpublished B. Sc. thesis. University of Leiden. Department of Psychology. Leiden, The Netherlands.

21. Social Darwinism. We have consulted the Social Darwinism article in the Int. Enc. Soc. Sciences by Tax and Krucoff, **14**: 402-406. See also R. HOFSTADTER. 1944. Social Darwinism in American Thought. 1959 edit. Beacon Press. Boston, Mass.

22. DARWIN, C. 1859. The Origin of Species. 1958 edit.: 29. Mentor Books. New York, N.Y. (Note also the expression "the strong principle of inheritance").

23. SPENCER, H. As quoted by Hofstadter (see Ref. 21). 1959 edit.: 41.

24. BUSS, A. 1976. Galton and the birth of differential psychology and eugenics: social, political, and economic forces. J. Hist. Behav. Sci. **12**: 47-58.

25. PEARSON, K. The Life, Letters and Labours of Francis Galton. Vol. I, 1914; vol. II, 1924; vol. IIIa and IIIb, 1930. Cambridge Univ. Press. Cambridge, England. See also R. S. COWAN. 1972. Francis Galton's statistical ideas: the influence of eugenics. Isis **63**: 509-528.

26. SHIELDS, S. 1975. Functionalism, Darwinism, and the psychology of women: a study in social myth. Am. Psychol. **30**: 739-754.

27. CATTELL, J. M. 1890. Mental tests and measurements. Mind **XV**: 373-381. For a treatment of Cattell and the attempt at quantification of human abilities: S. DIAMOND. 1976. Francis Galton and American psychology. This volume.

28. CRABB, R. 1970. Birth of a Giant. The men and incidents that gave America the motorcar. 2nd edit. Chilton Books. Philadelphia, Pa.

29. BINGHAM, W. 1950. Autobiography. *In* A History of Psychology in Autobiography. E. Boring *et al.*, Eds. Vol. 4; 1-27. Russell and Russell. New York, N.Y.

30. MUNSTERBERG, H. is treated in BARITZ, 1960 (see Ref. 15, pp. 35-40) and F. DORSCH, 1963. Geschichte und Probleme der Angewandten Psychologie. Huber. Bern, Switzerland.

31. MÜNSTERBERG, H. 1913. Psychology and Industrial Efficiency 3-7, 27, 116-117, 308-309. Houghton Mifflin. Boston, Mass. As there seems to be congeniality between Plato and Galton, so there is between Taylor and Münsterberg. In 1912 (see Ref. 20, p. 103), Taylor states: " ... after a long struggle, worker and employer regard one another as friends."

32. DIAMOND, S. 1976. Personal communication and this volume.

33. CELINE, L.–F. 1932. Voyage au Bout de la Nuit. Paris, France.

34. HOLLINGWORTH, H. 1912. The influence of caffein on mental and motor efficiency. Arch. Psychol. **22**:

POLITICAL FACTORS IN THE DEVELOPMENT
OF AMERICAN PSYCHOLOGY

David Bakan

Department of Psychology
York University
Downsview 463, Ontario, Canada

In recent weeks we have been seeing and hearing of students in Paris demonstrating against an effort on the part of the authorities to change the university curriculum. There is nothing new in this kind of thing. There have often been efforts, stemming from church, government, business, or the military to control the nature of the education of the young and the ideological cast of the academic institutions. And the American institutions of learning have not been immune from such pressures.

Modern academic psychology claims almost direct descent from the German university of the late nineteenth century, from the period in which sensitivity in Germany to the question of academic freedom and infringements upon academic freedom was unusually high. And psychology in America is generally under the impression that it, especially with its emphasis upon experimentation, is truly free from political and religious influences, or the like.

Psychologists have a vision of the development of science. They imagine it to be quite autonomous. The view is that the development of a science proceeds by each piece of research giving rise to the next piece of research; in turn, generating the next piece of research, and so on. The elaboration of this view would focus attention on the presumptive interplay of theory and data, how new data challenge theory, how theory gets modified, how new theory suggests what new data to collect, how the data are collected, and how the new data thus collected challenge theory,—and the renewal of the cycle.

When this view is incorporated into some history of science, where somehow the human identity of the major investigators presses upon one as important, that human identity is frequently squeezed into some narrow mold under rubrics such as "forerunner," "founder," "father of," or "follower of": whereas all of the other questions concerning the interactions of science and the two triads—thought-feeling-willing, on the one hand, and social-political-economic, on the other—are generally given only minor attention.

There is certain good reason for this autonomous vision of science, a reason that is particularly important when we consider the science of psychology. That good reason for maintaining the view of science as autonomous results from the gnawing underthought that if a science is not thus autonomous, it must necessarily be qualified in its authenticity. For characteristically science is viewed as having its authenticity at some level outside the reach of the unique thoughts, feelings, and wishes on the one hand, and the social, political and economic context on the other hand, associated with its investigators. For presumably the "truth" of a scientific proposition inheres in its match with that which it speaks of, and not its articulation with the psychological, social, political, or economic conditions of its investigators.

Indeed, there is often a kind of uncouthness and embarrassment associated with social science investigation. Social science investigation tends to indicate reasons for conduct other than those which participants would present to themselves or to others. We see this kind of seeming impropriety in writers as remote from each other as Jonathan Edwards, who argued that mean motives lurked behind seemingly altruistic motives, to Freud, who argued that the reasons for behavior were unconscious and/or lodged in childhood experiences, to Durkheim, who argued that human behavior was determined by "social facts" that only very sophisticated statistical demographic analysis might uncover. There is no way around it. An effort to understand the history of science in terms of reasons that may not have been apparent to investigators (or that they would not have wanted others to know about) is somehow less than polite.

It may be of some value for me to state my notion of science as simply as I can. For me, the major aim of science is to ascertain the nature of the circumstances that generate propositions. And the method of science is to study the propositions so generated.

I like this notion of science for several reasons. It allows the very study of science as an authentic part of the scientific enterprise, for certainly the scientific enterprise generates propositions. It allows that the circumstances studied by science have their own nature, as well as allowing that knowledge is contingent on the knowledge-getting process. It allows a place for the human sciences equal to that of the natural sciences. Although allowing for error, it does not fall into the quagmire of a total relativism. Finally, it allows the possibility that there are circumstances that do not or have not yet generated propositions, leaving the possibility that there is ultimate mystery in the universe.

Let me then enter upon this uncouth and impolite activity with respect to the development of American psychology. I will attempt to identify what appear to me to be some major contextual factors which have had an effect on the development of that science. My purpose is the same as the purpose of all intellectual enterprises: to contribute to emancipation. For, as I hope to indicate, the science of psychology has been under the influence of these factors in ways that are restrictive of development; and I hope that, by offering such consideration, to work toward the removal of such influences.

American psychology developed largely within the academy, the colleges and the universities. Up to, and for most of, the nineteenth century, the American academy was modest in size and was largely under the influence of the Protestant churches. Such psychology as was promoted under these auspices was closely related to the philosophy and the moral imperatives that the churches promoted. The explicit aim of the curriculum in psychology, where psychology was taught, was the development of such an understanding of psychological functions as would serve the promotion of moral virtues. It was a psychology of human conduct.

Things began to change dratiscally, however, from around the middle of the nineteenth century. Science came to be a significant presence in the academy. And the vocation of "scientist" came into being. It is a little hard now to imagine a world without scientists. Yet the word "scientist" did not even exist until it was coined by William Whewell in 1840. Science as a career, scientist-as-vocation, came into being as options for ambitious young men only very recently. Before that, science was largely avocational, as it was in the lives of Thomas Jefferson, Benjamin Franklin, and the like. Science as a self-conscious career activity came into being in the wake of industrialization following the middle of the century, the growing urbanization, and the great pressure on American agriculture to increase its productivity.

Perhaps one of the most important set of steps in the development of science was the promotion of scientific agriculture on the part of government to cope with the mounting food needs, and the milestone Morrill Act of 1862 establishing the land grant colleges.

Although there were some schools devoted to mechanical and agricultural arts, the land grant college gave new resources, dignity, and status to scientific activity. The creation of the land grant college led to a vision of an academy quite different from the academy of the church-related college.

The universities that were created or rejuvenated by, or redirected with, moneys from the great industrial fortunes, Vanderbilt University, Harvard University, and University of Chicago, Stanford University, Clark University, and others, came on the heels of the land grant colleges, all gracious to science.

Many of the old church-associated colleges were also transformed when the Carnegie Foundation offered to provide pensions for college teachers, but only if their colleges gave up their church affiliations. Thus Wesleyan, Drury, Drake, Brown, and others surrendered their church affiliations and bent toward the new scientific orientation in order for the teachers to receive the Carnegie foundation funds.

Thus science became entrenched in the academy. And with this there emerged what for want of a better term I will call the two-step vision of science. The two-step vision of scientific development is that knowledge is *first* developed by experiment and theory, and is only subsequently applied to concrete problems. The two-step notion is so firmly entrenched that one has difficulty imagining it to have been otherwise. Yet the two-step vision of science had difficulty in emerging. It deviated dramatically from the long-standing craft tradition in which theory and practice are so closely intertwined that the distinction is not even made. Indeed, it can be argued that modern technology owes more to the craft tradition than to science as we commonly understand it. Perhaps the single most important development to make modern technology possible was not what we would consider scientific advance at all. I am talking about the improvements in the late eighteenth and early nineteenth centuries in machine tools. As machine tools grew in their precision, it made possible the fabrication of parts that would fit and operate together without further adjustment. This opened the way for modern manufacture.

The method of assembly of standardized parts was pioneered by Eli Whitney —hardly a scientist in the modern sense—in the manufacture of guns in the early 19th century. Oliver Evans had created an extremely impressive fully automated flour mill in 1785, with conveyors, hoppers, and varieties of ingenious devices. Photography was developed without an understanding of the chemical processes involved. Craftsmen were cracking petroleum quite effectively before the researches on the effect of heat on hydrocarbons by Berthelot became known in 1867; the latter offering only an interpretation of what was common practice in the oil industry. A vast body of experience and observation for finding oil preceded the later more sophisticated science of geology.

The special modern case is electricity. It was largely in connection with the development of the use of electricity that the two-step vision received its greatest support, with the findings from the laboratory having played an extremely important role in the development of the large electric power plants and the distribution of electric power. As the two-step vision grew, so did the prestige of the academy. Industrial leaders became increasingly enthusiastic about the academy, and increasingly the control of the academy came into their hands. Subtle but profound changes took place in the academy following the Civil War. Most importantly, the authority of the professor in the field of human conduct became almost completely submerged to his role of monitor of, or even developer of, fact. Policy in the affairs of men were not his business any longer. That was to be left to the increasingly powerful people in the spheres of trade, manufacture, finance, and politics.

It is in this context that experimental psychology was introduced into the academy. It was clearly a form of psychology that was sufficiently remote from human conduct as not to be bothersome to the new economic and political powers. Science was rising in prestige, and the moral psychology was declining. Psychology announced itself vigorously as a laboratory science; and relentlessly stayed clear of all types of questions that might in any way be related to the more classical concerns of psychology of the nineteenth century. It dropped its role as authority on human conduct, freed itself from lingering moral surveillance, and could enjoy some of the advantages that its status as a science provided.

Let me skip quickly to World War II for appreciating the nature of the two-step notion of science. During World War II the evident value of the two-step vision of the nature of science took a giant step. Scientists of every kind participated in the war effort. They clearly demonstrated that talent and research could be transferred from the laboratory to conducting and winning a war, from step one to step two. The scientists made notable contributions such as penicillin, radar, and the proximity fuse, whereby bombs could be triggered by the proximity to the target instead of by the older, less reliable, timing devices. The most dramatic contribution was the atom bomb. Military and political leaders learned that scientists could not only solve problems that they provided, but could indeed come up with strategies and devices that they could not even imagine.

The atom bomb, in particular, provided a special lesson in connection with the two-step view: *Scientists could make contributions even if they did not know what they were working on*. The atom bomb was created by severe division of scientific labor, with each scientist knowing only enough to do his particular assignment. Division of labor had become commonplace in manufacturing. Now it was evident that division of labor could also be useful in scientific research. The scientist's way of working, devoting attention only to what appeared as intrinsic, was no handicap to the achievement of the ends of the military and the political leaders. Quite the contrary. It gave even greater prerogative in the fulfillment of military and political objectives. Ironically, at the same time, the scientists experienced themselves as having received an increase in autonomy.

Following the war, severe anxiety arose with respect to the scientific enterprise. The world had certainly been impressed with the power of science. This led to efforts to bring the scientist, his knowledge, his thoughts, his loyalties under control. Those seemingly abstruse and remote details with which the scientist occupied himself had extraordinary consequences even for the very safety of the nation. Loyalty oaths were required. There was close surveillance of the habits and attitudes of the scientists. There was fear and suspicion of any deviance from totoal personal conformity on the part of scientists. The rising tendency on the part of the scientists to participate in policy decisions was severely opposed. In 1954 Robert Oppenheimer, who had directed the Los Alamos Laboratory during the war, was deprived of his security clearance and was barred from access to classified material. The death penalty for peacetime espionage was introduced.

On the other hand, pressures toward granting yet greater autonomy to scientists also mounted. With Sputnik and the explosion of an atomic bomb by Russia, it became clear that the recruitment and functioning of scientists was not to be trifled with, and that the harassment of scientists would only restrict scientific recruitment and productivity. Thus the two-step notion was vigorously revived. Basic research had strategic advantages. The nation could develop and stockpile scientific research and talent. The transferability from step one to step two had been more than adequately demonstrated; and there was a firm belief that scientific research and talent would be available when and if needed for applied purposes. Basic research was to science what flight hours were in keeping pilots prepared. The scientists, on their part, could devote themselves to their problems quite unharrassed by the extremes of McCarthyism and even its less fanatical versions. Scientists would devote themselves to the production of fact-modules, fact-bricks, and they needed not concern themselves with the utilization of such fact-bricks. They were quite convinced that whatever they developed would work toward the common welfare, and they did not have to concern themselves with that in a direct manner.

American psychology again rode in on the support of so-called basic research after World War II, much as it had come in on the support of science in the late nineteenth and early twentieth centuries. Between World War I and World War II psychology had established a strong experimental laboratory tradition. The recruits to psychology prior to World War II had come largely from rural areas, heavily conditioned by the successes of the mechanization of American agriculture. They were people who were heavily cathected on apparatus, and thus the laboratory was very congenial. The *Popular Mechanics* mentality of metal- and wood-working, work with electricity, motors, and gears were congruent with the experimental, behavioristic ideology. And these psychologists from their rural backgrounds were comfortable with animals. The possiblity of vertical social mobility into the ever-widening vocation of scientist attracted increasing numbers of young men to the sciences, laboratory experimental psychology among them. With the decline in the possibility of hard-working and able young men becoming successful without access to capital, science was left as one of the important avenues still available for "rising to the top," as Andrew Carnegie put it. Hardly insignificant was the fact that the experimental psychological enterprise, combined with its behavioristic ideology, served the egalitarian spirit, not only with respect to personal rise, but also because of the seeming "fairness" associated with attending only to current behavior for subjects and investigators alike. The observation of behavior was a game anyone could play. It was not dependent on any richness of cultural background, social class, or special education. In the experimental laboratory the psychologists found that they could do a great deal with even the very limited capital equipment that they could scrounge, make out of common hardware, or buy with small sums of money that they could extract from their respective university administrations, and using volunteer subjects from among their students or animals that they could raise in the attic or basement of some old university building. With the kind of support they received in the decades after World War II, it became possible to acquire equipment of sophistication and complexity that had never before been possible.

The feeling of autonomy experienced by the scientist doing supported "basic research" was great. However, the basic fact-module orientation increasingly became the norm. Fact-module studies tended to win financial support. Smaller and narrower was better. Applications for grants for research were reviewed to eliminate "vague" proposals and those proposals which were not likely to produce fact-modules in a relatively short period of time. The mechanisms of support called for repeated review and repeated applications for further support.

The internal condition of the university worked equally to support the narrow-scope, fact-module orientation called basic research. Rapid publication of the findings of fact-modules and the bringing in of support funds to the university were rewarded. Administrators came to be extremely tolerant of neglect of the teaching enterprise and offered little or no objection to the narrowing of curricula to the teaching of fact-modules.

The selection of persons to occupy vacant posts came ever more strongly into the hands of existing faculty members themselves. Thus, one of the consequences with respect to the staffing of academic posts was an extreme form of ideological vetting and the filling of academic posts with persons who would be sympathetic to the basic experimental ideology.

Within psychology, the characteristic and uncriticized parametric theory of the nature of human functioning articulated with the fact-module approach. The parametric theory asserts that all human functioning is the result of a set of identifiable variables. Research, then, is simply the work of identifying and studying the patterns of covariation among these parameters. Statistical methods, envisioned as somewhow being capable of identifying the effect of variables over the noise, as it were, of other variables—that noise to be wiped out eventually by further research, presumably—became the methods of choice in psychological research. No examination of the parametric theory was ever seriously made. And the patent inadequacies of the statistical methods, even to serve the parametric theory, were regularly overlooked. What was more important was that the parametric theory appeared to be a ticket into the larger supported fraternity of scientists.

While this was going on inside the university, there was a lush growth of psychology taking place outside of the academy. It was largely Freudian. A good deal of it was expressed in fiction and other arts, and in some political thought.

Consider the role of fiction in western urban industrial society. One of its main functions is to come to the ideological rescue of the individual against the depersonalizing forces of the social, political, and economic milieu. Urban-industrial fiction regularly emphasizes the unique, the personal, and intimate nature of man, while the society stresses his parameters, his sex, age, vocation, marital status, and then his measurements on psychological variables, courtesy of the psychologist. In fiction, personality is more important than role. Indeed, a ubiquitous theme to be found in modern fiction is precisely the struggle—and often the victory—of the personal against the socially prescribed, parametrically expected role for the individual.

From the time of Freud's visit to the United States in 1909, American writers drew on his contributions in the fashioning of fiction. They liked ideas like repression-as-the-cause-of-neurosis, and that healing consists in overcoming oppression. They fully accepted the idea that the inner and psychic life of the individual was more vast and more complicated than had ever been previously imagined. Thus, largely through the efforts of writers of fiction, the image of psychology in the mind of the American public was more Freudian than like the thing developed in the academy. The American academic psychologist rejected this Freudian "underground" psychology. He was not uncognizant of its presence. There even were some occasional academic efforts to tame some of the ideas and observations of psychoanalysis by subjecting them to experimental study. Nor was there any great acceptance of psychoanalysis by the medical profession. The medical profession severely restricted the use of psychoanalysis in therapy to members of the medical profession, while at the same time keeping the development within medicine extremely restricted.

Virtually no funds were ever made available for psychological research that would be consonant with this psychology of the underground. Within the universities battles were fought repeatedly between students—that is, undergraduate students who could yet be forgiven for indiscretion—whose view of psychology was informed by the underground, and their experimentally, behavioristically minded psychology teachers. Every introductory course in psychology was a battleground. Indeed, one of the major aims of the introductory course was to impress students with the possibility of a so-called "scientific" psychology and to derogate the ever-present enemy, the psychology of the underground. The selection of students for taking advanced work, for admission to graduate schools, the selection of faculty, were all determined in large part on the basis of such "confession." "Wise" and career-oriented young people learned to overcome the error of their youth, which had been influenced by the underground. Those who persisted in any interest in the underground were relentlessly weeded out.

Outside the academy, however, especially after World War II, there was a growing need for a professional class to cope with people who were not successful in adjusting to the claims of urban-industrial society. That was largely an unmet need. Psychiatrists were certainly not numerous, and prior to World War II clinical psychology hardly existed at all as a profession. The difficulty, of course, has been that in the area of mental treatment, those most in need of service are characteristically those least capable of paying for such services.

A turning point took place after World War II in connection with the servicing of war veterans. There arose a substantial attempt to develop and supply psychological services out of public funds. Government offered funds to psychology departments to train a cadre of clinical psychologists, some percentage of which, it was presumed, would work in veteran's hospitals and the like. Psychology departments accepted the funds for the support of clinical training, but, characteristically, with great ambivalence. The clinical concept had prevailed almost exclusively in the underground. There was virtually no tradition of education in clinical psychology, with the exception of psychometrics, some child clinical psychology, and educational psychology. The departments of psychology, suddenly experiencing an embarrassment of riches and ideological compromise, sought to keep the new enterprise of clinical psychology as second class, and subject to the ideological control of the experimental psychologists. As the numbers of clinical psychologists grew within the American Psychological Association, the tension grew between the clinical psychologists, who wanted the Association to service its professional needs, and the experimental psychologists who would keep psychology "pure."

The new clinical psychologist pioneers, fresh with their Ph.D.s, were met on the outside world, as it were, by the medical profession, whose attitude to them was one of petulance or, at best, sufferance. While the medical profession had hardly pursued the clinical psychological venture with vigour, it also resisted the encroachment of the clinical psychologists. There was conflict within institutions for power, prestige, and funds. And the medical profession hindered registration and certification legislation in state legislatures.

The new clinical psychologists were in an awkward position. Because of their association with the academy they had received a credential by which, at the very least, they could be called "doctor." Their actual training in clinical psychology was often at best marginal—caused not the least by the simple fact that those who taught them were hardly strongly identified with, or experienced in, the clinical enterprise. Their teachers were characteristically experimental psychologists of some type; and under any circumstances the typical socialization of the new clinical psychology Ph.D. entailed acceptance of the scientific super-ego which had developed in the academy over the decades. On confronting the hostility of the medical profession, they tended to drape themselves defensively in their credential, boasting that they had superior research backgrounds and somehow were in contact with some universe that the mere medical practitioner could not hope to aspire to.

The two-step idea of research that they had acquired in their university train-ing occasionally led them to set up research units of one kind of another, for example, in mental hospitals—although most often there was only a remote relationship between these research projects and the kinds of problems which the clinical enterprise entailed.

The fact was that the clinical psychology lacked the kind of empirical, as contrasted with experimental, background which characterizes the development of every other service profession. The kind of empiricism represented in the work of such pioneers as Freud, Binet, Piaget, Rorschach, and others was the object of scorn by the academic teachers of the members of the new profession of clinical psychology. Clinical psychology could sneak some insight and tech-nique from the underground, but it could not accept it openly. And there was little possibility of doing systematic empirical research of the case type. Such research was not honored. Clinical psychologists tended to do experimental research, distinguished only be some accompanying promissory notes suggesting ultimate clinical application. The fact is that to this day, there is relatively little systematic empirical research going on among clinical psychologists. The practice of clinical psychology is characteristically extremely alienated, with very little of the necessary sharing of ideas and observations that the empirical mode needs in order to advance. And there are virtually no funds to bring people together into long sustained teams to work systematically, empirically, and energetically on the solution of clinical problems.

Since the journals were characteristically under the same taboos as the acad-emy, there was relatively little opportunity for appropriate clinical and empirical materials to be reported in print. Indeed, because of the fact that *books* were considerably less under the taboos—the publishers were finding that there was some possibility of sale among the increasing number of clinicians, enough to make at least a reasonable profit—most of the published empirical material has been in the form of books rather than journal articles. The difficulty with this is simply that it is considerably harder, and takes a much more strenuous effort, to write a book than it does to write an article. Furthermore, journals allow a continuing flow of discourse on particular topics, which cannot be done in the same way by books.

I believe that some very significant change is currently possible. One impor-tant change is in the public attitudes to the scientific enterprise. Changes began toward the end of the 60s and continue. By the end of 1969 and the beginning of 1970, the reaction against science had grown quite strong. Government support of the scientific enterprise weakened considerably, reflecting larger trends in the society. The idea that somehow scientific research could solve all problems that beset mankind had grown thin. The public fantasies of indefinitely sustained health, of flying cars, of personal collapsible pocket helicopters, of mechanized robots that would clean house and prepare meals, of inexpensive yet superb prefabricated houses and the like are virtually gone.

It was becoming evident that the pay-off from science, together with the two-step approach, was less than expected. The returns were not commensurate with the huge amounts of money that had been spent. Chemistry has produced very little in the way of new products which would have any great advantages over the old. The multiplication of frivolous plastic products on the market has not enhanced the public image of the chemist. Indeed, the word "plastic" itself has come to mean "inauthentic" in the common language. Physics has produced little of great consequence except in aerospace. Exuberance over the moon-landings was considerably dampened by the awareness of the wretched performance of science on planet Earth. The advances in quality control have not led to improved quality of products. Rather, they have been used to produce shabby products just at the margin of market acceptability and of timed obsolescence. Whereas huge sums of money had been spent in connection with military research, the war in Vietnam was not won with distinction, and the public became aware of such odious things as napalm, defoliants, and poison gases. The association of the scientific enterprise with the military establishment became conspicuous to those who would hope for better solutions to human problems than military ones in the next centuries. The scientist is viewed more and more in the image of Dr. Strangelove. The promise of science as the creator of varieties of new employment opportunities has hardly been realized. Organized labor sees science as wiping out jobs. Science has not produced a reliable and safe contraceptive method. The unwitting use of thalidomide that produced deformed babies severely reduced the prestige of medical research. There are daily reports of dangers in common products created by and not prevented by scientists. Research in dentistry has accomplished little in connection with the prevention of cavities—flourided toothpaste notwithstanding. Computer developments led to the production of information systems that threaten the privacy of individual citizens in a way as to undermine the possibilities of democracy. The scientific evidence in connection with the effect of cigarette-smoking presented to Congress —with scientists arguing among themselves—left Congress without the benefit of clear advice, and left the image of the scientist as an "objective" observer quite tarnished. The neglect of science in connection with pollution has been notorious. The "rhetoric of imminent breakthrough," which scientists have become skilled in using, is met with increasing cynicism. There is boredom with reading about the imminent breakthroughs in cancer research, which appear in the newspapers with inexorable regularity. The promise of energy from the atom has not been realized in the more than 30 years and billions of dollars in research funds since Hiroshima and Nagasaki, while the threat of total destruction from atomic energy continues to be very real.

It appears to me that this disenchantment with science provides an opportunity for psychology to overcome its historical handicaps and move in the direction of becoming much more authentic than it has ever been before.

In what direction should the science of psychology move? This is intrinsically a difficult question, precisely because it is the aim of science to make discoveries. It is in the nature of science that its future should be unknown. For if the future could be known, then its work would be done. It is not easy to establish guidelines for an enterprise that has surprise itself as its aim. Any indication concerning the future has to be, in the very nature of things, only a discussion of strategy.

I am fully aware of the objection that enough time has not elapsed to be able to fully determine whether the strategy of recent science, the two-step approach, and so on, has been successful. Historians in the future may judge the progress in science of the last quarter of a century much differently than it is currently being judged. And certainly I do not mean to say that the field of experimental psychology should not be continued. Quite the contrary. One of the fundamental strategic lessons that emerges out of the contributions of Darwin is that the increase of variation is an extremely sensible way to meet an unknown future. At the same time, those historical efforts which restricted research in psychology in the universities need to be discouraged. It is the inhibiting influence that has been exerted that is objectionable.

Certainly the strategy of the two-step process has not been conspicuously successful in psychology. Preciously few of the findings from the laboratory which often systematically delete the effect of social norm and of economic and political contexts have been very consequential. Perhaps one of the outstanding failures that might be mentioned is the negligible and sometimes even damaging transfer from the psychology of learning to the field of education. And certainly the various experimental studies in the field of personality have led to little in connection with the understanding of the functioning of human beings in their various paths. There has, however, been no shortage of the "rhetoric of imminent breakthrough" in the field of psychology.

The old motto, "Nothing human is alien to me," would appear to be a good one to keep in mind for the future development of psychology. Instead of engaging in extreme efforts to satisfy a parametric model, and thereby trying to "study the effects of one variable at a time," the human world in its complexity needs to be examined and comprehended. Simple-minded presuppositions do not necessarily clarify nonsimple phenomena. The psychologist needs to overcome his aversion to the study of history, field work, and to look at things in other ways than those that yield fact-modules.

The psychologist needs especially to overcome the psychophobia that has characterized the history of academic psychology in America. The definition of psychology as the study of behavior needs to be replaced with the more classical definition of psychology as the study of thinking, feeling, and willing. Certainly the psychologist should be interested in behavior. However, the critical linkages between thoughts, feeling and wishes, on the one hand, and behavior, on the other, need to be carefully examined, and the strategy of concentrating largely on behavior alone is unlikely to reveal the complex nature of those linkages.

It appears to me that the aim of "prediction and control," which has played such an important role in the culture of psychologists since its early formulation by John B. Watson, simply needs to be abandoned. In the light of the history of psychology, that aim has played its role more as a fantasy of power in lieu of real effectiveness than real effectiveness. The role of that fantasy is analogous to a superman fantasy in a young boy who is actually quite ineffective in making circumstances conform to his will. Methodologically, that aim was converted into models of relationships with subjects of investigation in which the critical feature was *manipulation* of the subject by the experimenter. The experiment tended to become an experiment in the manipulation process. That strategy has not led to findings of distinction, and has furthermore led to a severe injury of the capacity of the psychologist to be useful to society.

Psychology must align itself again with the historical aim of knowledge as serving emancipation. If psychology is to remain useful, it is essential that it make contributions to the understanding of the thinking and feeling and wishing of human beings, and that it work to communicate that understanding to the community at large. For there is a great need in society for such an understanding. Many of the difficulties in the world may be traced to the fact that such an understanding by people of the nature of their own thoughts, feelings, and wishes, and the thoughts, feelings, and wishes of others, is inadequate to the complex problems of a world in which a very large number of people must share the planet at one time. Prediction and control, interpreted in such a manner as to imply manipulation, are simply unworthy aims for a contemporary science of psychology, and are aims that will not and should not elicit the support of the community which science serves.

Let me conclude by saying that my argument is not one for a decreased autonomy, but rather for an increased autonomy for the science of psychology. Historically, while psychology has often allowed itself to exclude larger considerations of its involvement with society at large, it has, in point of fact, been all the more under society's influence, in ways in which it itself has not been aware. At the present time, those same factors that have been influencing its direction are working in such a way as to threaten its very existence—precisely at a time when psychological understanding is critically needed by the community at large. It can no longer, for its own sake as an autonomous science and for the sake of the community which it serves, afford the luxury of innocence that the two-step view of science provided.

THE FORTUNES OF A BASIC DARWINIAN IDEA: CHANCE

Howard E. Gruber

Institute for Cognitive Studies
Rutgers University
Newark, New Jersey 07102

> When we first begin to *believe* anything, what we believe is
> not a single proposition, it is a whole system of proposi-
> tions. (Light dawns gradually over the whole.)
>
> Ludwig Wittgenstein[2]

A scientific theory is a much denser structure than is generally recognized. Almost every component idea is itself an intricate structure; and the whole is a complex of interacting parts. In constructing the theory of evolution through natural selection, Darwin made use of a number of images or metaphors: tree of nature, war, wedges, artificial selection, tangled bank, and contrivance. Each of these has a specific function in illuminating a part of the theory. These images are not merely didactic or communicative devices, they seem to play a role in the actual generation of the theory: there is probably a complex and lively interaction between different levels of experience, such as the conceptual and the imaginal.

From a historical point of view, as one theory is assimilated by another, the earlier is necessarily distorted and only partially represented in the latter. As a consequence of this complexity, although some Darwinian ideas have been assimilated into psychological theories, one basic conception has been neglected. There is in the *Origin of Species* only one diagram. It represents Darwin's idea that in the panorama of nature "organized beings represent a tree *irregularly branched*," as he wrote in a notebook in 1837.[1] This was 15 months before he formulated the theory of evolution through natural selection. Darwin used this metaphor in many theoretically productive ways. Yet this conception of funda-mental irregularity in nature remains foreign to psychology and other social sciences, still dominated by a largely Newtonian world view. Some still-unex-ploited implications of Darwin's metaphor have a bearing on the role of the individual in history and on the virtues of "weak theory."

In discussions of the philosophy of science it has grown commonplace to distinguish between the problem of justification, and the problem of discovery. The latter can be further subdivided into procedural and substantive issues. This leaves us with a tripartite division: how to know if a proposition, once uttered or formulated, is true; how to go about looking for propositions worth considering; and what sort of thing to look for. Within the context of discovery, something has been said about procedural matters. For example, writers in the vein of Peirce and Hanson focus on the method of retroduction; writers in the vein of Polanyi stress intuitive and nonrational aspects of the process of discovery. But sub-stantive matters—what to look for?—have received much less attention. In an older philosophical tradition, discussions of the nature of matter, objects, space, time, life, intellect, morals, humanity, and society were not considered matters for specialists in "other" disciplines, but were part of a widespread exchange among intellectuals. This exchange, when it is active enough, helps maintain a general alertness to the mutual import of specialized inquiries and very general conceptions of nature.

The use by scientists of large metaphors and images plays a key role in such discussions, because it bears at once on the procedural and substantive matters referred to above. Even when expressed in very general form (vague, intuitive, poetic) such images have generative and regulatory power, both governing the search for more explicit formulations and giving rise to them. When the metaphor is invested with more precise form it is transformed: we can call it a "model"; it guides analysis and invites the testing of hypotheses. These hypotheses are neither about the metaphor nor about nature, but about relations between them. The testing of hypotheses has been the glory of methodologists, but it remains a sterile glory so long as little or nothing is said of the primitive roots—both imaginal and ideological—from which testable ideas spring.

Experimental psychologists in recent years have become newly interested in imagery, but mainly at the level of reproductive images: either some specific object is called up before the mind's eye, or some imagined relationship between specified objects serves as a mnemonic device, aiding in the recall of previously presented stimuli. The generative role of imagery in productive and creative thinking, unfortunately, still remains outside this universe of discourse. But generative images of wide scope become a central concern when we wish to understand the psychological processes involved in reflecting on the larger conceptions of humanity, society, and nature which provide the framework for all scientific inquiry.[3]

The present paper is located somewhere within the area of concern for such very general conceptions. More specifically, I want to examine the idea that a fundamental aspect of Charles Darwin's thought has been widely neglected by psychologists because they are still guided by a highly deterministic view of nature, a simplistic view of science, and a Newtonian hope that their own universe of discourse can be shown to display the same underlying order, simplicity, and harmony that Newton claimed for his.

Darwin's thought presents itself in two aspects, quite distinct from each other both in form and in aesthetic tone. On the one hand, there is the beautiful simplicity of the theory of evolution through natural selection. As early as 1838, Darwin could state it in nineteen words expressing the three principles of heredity, variation, and superfecundity, from which, as he saw, natural selection and evolution followed inexorably.[4] On the other hand, there is his fascination with complexity and uncertainty, with nature seen as a multitude of small forces perpetually interacting and changing.

In Darwin's early notebooks and later in his published works,[5] these two tendencies produced five metaphors, all of them necessary to express the whole of his thought. After providing some background material, I will discuss these in some detail. For the moment I want only to introduce the idea that psychologists and other social scientists have been eager to borrow some of Darwin's ideas and imagery, especially the *simplifying* images of war and artificial selection, which seem to divide the world into winners and losers, or responses into successes and failures. But they have largely ignored the *complexifying* part of Darwin's thought.

Once it is recognized that organic nature always and in principle involves a dense web of intimately interacting processes, these tendencies toward simplicity appear in a new light. Of course, some simplicities can always be constructed, and it has been and will remain an important part of scientific work to construct them, or, if you prefer, to wrench them out of nature. In moving beyond such simplicities it is enjoyable first to *contemplate* the richness of the organic world. But it is also our task to search for ways to *conceptualize* nature in its richness, its variety, its complexity, and its interconnectedness.

It will be helpful to bear in mind the following chronology: Darwin was born in 1809 and died in 1882. The voyage of the Beagle, in which he circumnavigated the globe, began in 1831 and ended in 1836. In July of 1837 he began his first notebook on evolution, determined to construct a workable theory and probably believing that he already had the key to it, although this proved not to be the case. In July of 1838, he began his notebooks on man, mind, and materialism. This was an explosive moment for him, for during the same month he also undertook a demanding geological investigation; as Martin Rudwick has recently shown, this was not merely the narrowly specialized research that it seemed to be, but bore directly on Darwin's most general views.[6] On September 25, 1838, Darwin recorded his reading (or re-reading?) of Malthus' *Essay on Population*[7] and his own first excited insight into the theory of evolution through natural selection. I have elsewhere reconstructed the slow growth of Darwin's thinking, leading up to that moment.[8] By November of 1838, Darwin was able to reformulate the theory succinctly in the form of the three principles of heredity, variation, and superfecundity. Twenty years later, in 1858, Alfred Russel Wallace wrote to Darwin of his own discovery of the theory of evolution through natural selection, and joint publication of the two men's discovery was arranged. In 1859, finally, Darwin wrote and published the *Origin of Species*.[9] But he remained silent about his views of man's place in nature until 1871, when he published *The Descent of Man*.[10] *The Expression of Emotions in Man and Animals*[11] followed, in 1872. Four of the five metaphors now to be discussed appeared in Darwin's notebooks by 1839 at the latest.

A PLURALITY OF METAPHORS

Artificial Selection

Darwin was drawn to this subject because of his interest in variation and hybridization. He knew much about plant and animal breeding before September 25, 1838, but it was not until some time after that date that he took explicit note of the similarities between artificial and natural selection. In the *Origin*, he enlarged on this subject early in the book: the analogy between natural and artificial selection was as close as he could come to the application of the experimental method to the study of the process of evolution. By 1859, he could draw on his accumulated experience as a pigeon fancier and on many other strands of knowledge to dramatize the impressive cumulative changes that purposeful human beings could make in other species by selecting for the same trait over many generations. But he was also careful to point out that nature operates selectively not on one or a few favored characteristics but on the whole organism's adaptation to its natural environment, and that it operates over immense reaches of time. Thus, his discussion of the similarities and differences between natural and artificial selection served to highlight the importance of *cumulative* change. Moreover, in the course of that discussion he introduced a topic to which he devoted a separate chapter, the "correlation of growth," i.e., the way in which the evolving organism remains a subtly coordinated system in which changes in one part engender or favor changes in other parts, in order to maintain this coordination.

War

The second human activity that Darwin took as a metaphor for natural selection was war. In this, of course, he was following Malthus, for the first volume of the *Essay on Population* is very largely a catalogue of human warfare and decimation. The key point for Darwin is the superfecundity principle, that population growth tends to outrun resources necessary for survival, and that this necessitates both interspecific and intraspecific struggle. Thus, the metaphor of war served to emphasize the role of *struggle* in the process of evolution. But Darwin's conception of struggle was not the kind that appears in other theories, not a titanic struggle between polar opposites—good and evil, oppressor and oppressed, Thanatos and Eros. For Darwin, struggle meant the total activity of each organism permitting it to survive long enough to reproduce its own kind. In this struggle the race is not only to the strong and the swift, but sometimes to the well-concealed, the prolific, the cooperative, the inventive, the adaptable. Since the theory aimed at explaining the evolutionary adaptation of species rather than that of individuals, social characteristics of organisms could be flexibly taken into account. For example, sexual selection, the struggle between males of a species for possession of the female, is rarely a struggle to the death, since the defeated male is of potential use to the species only if he survives.

Wedges

This is the least known of Darwin's metaphors. It appears in the excited passage in his "transmutation notebook" written on September 25, 1838,[12] and it survives through various preliminary essays into the first edition of the *Origin of Species*, but it was deleted from the later editions, including the most widely read 6th, and last, edition. In Darwin's phrasing, the wedge image has two aspects. First, he speaks of "one hundred thousand wedges." By this he means to emphasize the point that the forces making for evolution are *multitudinous,* arising continuously out of the complex manifold of nature. Secondly, he speaks of these wedges as "splitting the face of nature." This phrase reflects Darwin's awareness of the small but vital difference between a God-ordained, perfectly harmonious order and a world in which small *imperfections* in adaptation constantly arise, serving as the motor of evolutionary change.

Tree

The three metaphors discussed so far all bear directly on the concept of natural selection. The remaining two are more general, reflecting even wider conceptions of nature, providing the substratum necessary to think about evolution. Among all his metaphors, Darwin's image of the tree of nature as an irregularly branching tree certainly deserves pride of place. It appears early in the B-notebook (the first of the transmutation notebooks) and is then quickly redrawn to bring out Darwin's thought more precisely. Over the years, Darwin drew a number of tree diagrams, both trying to perfect it and to penetrate it—to learn what his own imagery could tell him. In a highly formalized version, the tree diagram is the only figure in the *Origin*, and Darwin refers to it over and over, throughout the book.

It is reasonably clear from the sequence of events that when Darwin drew his first tree diagram he was already a convinced evolutionist, and that the diagram expressed his view of a continuously evolving, freshly differentiating organic world. At the same time, he was drawing the tree diagram in order to grapple with a puzzling argument against evolution. If evolutionary change were everywhere continuous, there should be no gaps in the natural order: it should be possible for systematists to construct taxonomies in which there would be no "missing links." So Lamarck had believed, taking as fresh evidence for such continuity every new species brought back by the voyages of conquest and discovery. But others used the many apparent gaps in the system of nature as an argument against evolution; and still others attempted to fashion "perfect" taxonomies in which the absence of any gaps would serve as evidence that the panorama of nature as a whole must be the handiwork of a divine artificer. In the tree diagram, Darwin saw another possibility: to be sure, there must be continuity in nature, but continuity does not necessarily require completeness. Beginning from some primitive form, evolution proceeds along diverging pathways; at every branching point some species that exist are extinguished, and the species that these might have become never can evolve. There is thus a fundamental *incompleteness* in nature: not everything that might have been will be.

Secondly, the tree diagram captures Darwin's profound conviction that nature is *irregular*. Among all those species that might evolve, the ones that do appear arise from happenstance. In some ways Darwin grasped this point long before he grasped the principle of natural selection. Suppose, for example, members of a species migrate to a new habitat and there are isolated from other members of the species by the hazards of geography and of geological change (e.g., a land bridge used for migration can be submerged by the subsidence of the sea bottom, or a wind blows a seed or an insect or humans in a canoe to a place previously unvisited by that species). If they are isolated long enough, and if they adapt to their new milieu, they will form a new variant or race, and eventually, perhaps a new species. Darwin could carry this argument this far very early in his theoretical search, for it does not rest on the idea of natural selection. But the argument contains an important new point. The winds of chance, that produce the necessary isolation of a few individuals in a new habitat, have nothing to do with the intrinsic laws of development of members of that species. In that sense, some critical isolating events are accidents and therefore produce a fundamental *irregularity* in the tree of nature. This chanciness and irregularity, so much at odds with his predecessors' (and most of his contemporaries') search for a regular and harmonious order in nature, was explicit in Darwin's very first drawing of the tree diagram, and in the accompanying commentary.[13]

Finally, of course, the tree diagram is the very image of some at first unspecified selection process. Some species are marked off as continuing, others as becoming extinct. A few months later Darwin saw, not too clearly, that the tree diagram was also a model of exponential growth; if this idea is coupled with some constraints, such as a limit on the number of organisms or of species (i.e., the unit of analysis at work in the phase of the theory in question), a formal principle of selection necessarily follows. By *formal* I simply mean that, although no mechanism is specified, the occurrence of selection follows as a conclusion from the premises.

The Tangled Bank

The last metaphor I will discuss here is the "tangled bank," the image of the intricacy of nature at a moment in time evoked in the celebrated passage with which Darwin concludes the *Origin of Species*. It is difficult to specify the first appearance in Darwin's thought of this idea because it goes so far back. In the thousands of pages of notes he kept during the Beagle voyage, there is little or no trace of any concern for evolution, but there are many examples of his fascination with the ecological relations among species. Of course, the idea informs Gilbert White's *Natural History and Antiquities of Selborne,* [14] a book Darwin knew very early, and William Paley's *Natural Theology, or Evidences of the Existence and Attributes of the Deity Collected from the Appearances of Nature,* [15] which had excited Darwin during his student years at Cambridge. In a sense, then, the image of the tangled bank is the least specifically Darwinian of all the images I have discussed. But this does not mean that it is any the less fundamental in his thinking. We can get a better idea of its role in Darwin's thought if we compare the three authors just referred to. For White, there is no metaphoric use of this idea; it is the whole substance of his work. For Paley and for Darwin, some part of nature (e.g., the beehive, the tangled bank) is likened to the whole; in that sense we have a metaphor. But for Paley and the other natural theologians, the central point is harmony and perfection in nature and the beauty of the contrivances by which the Creator has achieved this order of things. This is certainly what struck the young Darwin. But for Darwin the evolutionist, the image is transmuted: it is the disharmony and imperfection which become the cutting edge of his theory.

It seems to me that Darwin had a very clear grasp of the relations between the two images, the tree and the tangled bank. One image describes events at a moment in time in one corner of the world, with hundreds of species and thousands of individuals complexly interacting with each other, producing a kind of microevolution. Meanwhile, in "another part of the forest," something similar is going on, but other organisms and a whole other set of contingencies are involved. From time to time, organisms from these two domains will come in contact with each other. Even though we may be able to speak of some lawful relations within each domain, these laws give us absolutely no way of knowing at what point in their respective evolutions organisms from the two sets will make contact, or what the outcome will be. In this way the tree of nature becomes *fundamentally* irregular and unpredictable.

For example, we can "predict" that some early mammals, faced with a shortage of food near the ground and an abundance of foliage at higher elevations will either evolve some mechanism for reaching the available food or will perish. But even we can conceive of many mechanisms by which the unexploited food supply might be attained, and nature is far more prodigal than we in its inventiveness. There is nothing in our theory that "predicts" the appearance of giraffes in the world. Likewise for the foliage: we can "predict" that the tall trees will *either* evolve in some way influenced by the fact that no herbivorous mammal has come along to exploit it, *or* that it will evolve in some way affected by the arrival on the scene of the unpredictable giraffe.

In short, we are not talking about predictions at all, but about a point of view that helps us make some sense out of what has happened. The armamentarium of conventional science—creative simplification, hypothesis testing, lawmaking, prediction and control—are tools to help us in this effort. I believe we can use these tools to better advantage if we keep in mind that in many key respects nature is irregular, nonrepeating, unpredictable, incomplete, indeterminate, complex, open ended, and inventive.

DETERMINISM IN PSYCHOLOGY

Unfortunately, our discipline, psychology, is still dominated by a highly deterministic point of view. There is an underlying belief in a potentially omniscient being for whom the course of every droplet in the storm would be knowable, and for whom the appearance of complexity would be understood in every detail as resulting from the operation of a finite set of simple laws. One might add, if we take the actual behavior of our colleagues as evidence, that they are hoping and searching for a small number of such laws. I do not want to cast the argument in the form of a Hobson's Choice between an impossible hyperdeterminism and an obscurantist accidentalism. On some scales we can all be determinists some of the time. But it does seem unfortunate that so much psychological work is directed by this vector toward simplistic determinism and so little toward concerted efforts to conceptualize complexity. In the space available I can only mention briefly some of the major symptoms of this tendency.

1. In the heredity-environment controversy, the debate is still dominated by the view that development and behavior are the resultants of fixed entities with fixed properties. Thus, a certain number of "favorable genes" together with a certain "favorable environment" is supposed to lead to a certain predictable result. In contrast, geneticists insist that the significance of each gene depends *entirely* on its place in the whole genomic configuration and on a developmentally evolving sequence of interactions with the environment. Nevertheless, many psychologists cling to the belief that there are favorable genes predisposing favorable outcomes. In this connection I call your attention to geneticist Lewontin's recent criticism of psychologist's Jensen's misuse of the concept of *norm of reaction*.[16]

2. In discussions of the causes of behavior, the myth is still widespread among psychologists—and even more widely taught—that stimuli "cause" responses. With the emergence of cybernetic ideas, a fundamentally different approach has been freshly elaborated. As Powers recently put it: "Control theory changes our basic conception of human and animal nature, from that of a passive system driven according to the whims of the environment to that of an active system which more often than not drives the environment to conform with its own wishes, desires, intentions, goals, and basic requirements."[17]

In a machine-worshipping world, once the feasibility of goal-guided machines has been admitted, it becomes possible to admit the reality of goal-guided people. But if this is granted, the system of their interactions (i.e., the social process) becomes largely indeterminate: it is the working out of an incalculable number of interactions; more important than their number, the social system is a highly differentiated, structured system in which some individuals are more important than others; even more difficult for a highly deterministic approach, the configuration of the system changes from time to time, so that most "laws" of social behavior prevail only within severely limited boundary conditions. In *The Wealth of Nations*[18] Adam Smith proposed a theory in which he treated each individual as a social atom of equal value with all other atoms, the system operating according to very simple laws so that the net result is an equilibrium condition, similar to the way physical atoms operating according to the gas laws give an elastic container its shape and volume. To our sorrow, we read every day that all social atoms are not equal, and that they are arranged in configurations that give some of them almost unbelievable influence over the shape of human affairs. Although it is not necessarily humanity's brightest dream, Smith's mythical free market might be better than today's reality. For better or worse, however, this reality does mean that some purposeful beings can have a greater effect than others on the course of human events.

3. In developmental psychology all of the most influential theories—Freud, Erikson, Piaget—are cast in the form of single developmental pathways, i.e.,

fixed sequences of stages. No matter how dynamic or interactionist a theory may be in other ways, insofar as it is a single pathway model, it is essentially deterministic.

4. In typological and taxonomic efforts by psychologists, what is most striking is the vector toward simplicity. Whole literatures are founded on simple dichotomies, on six-type taxonomies, or on lists of no more than a few dozen traits. Meanwhile, our colleagues in biology think in terms of 3 million known species and an estimated 10 million extant species, not to speak of all those that have perished. Or they think in terms of many thousands of gene loci, with a growing number of known or suspected alleles at each locus.[19]

There is a relation between simplistic taxonomies and deterministic theories that would be worth exploring. As long as the hope exists of reducing the variety of organisms under discussion to a comfortably compact number of types—roughly similar to the 100-odd elements of physics, or even fewer—a corresponding hope remains plausible. We may find a small set of laws governing the determination of each individual's type and then complete the strategy by using the type to explain behavior. But as the number of types approaches the number of individuals, the value of this strategy fades and it becomes incumbent on us to search for other approaches.

Now you may object that contemporary psychological thinking, rather than being deterministic is highly probablistic. Don't we teach our students that lawful regularities in nature are really statistical aggregates, and don't we insist on the careful use of statistical inference in drawing conclusions about these aggregates? Yes, of course. But the theoretical focus of attention is usually on the mean value or on shifts in mean values caused by some independent variable.

We recognize a kind of probability-in-the small, but we look for regularity-in-the-large. This works well under certain simplified boundary conditions. In physics, the chancy dance of millions of molecules in a gas-filled balloon leads to certain average values for their collisions with the interior surface of the container, and this produces a highly regular and predictable result: a spherical balloon (if thickness is uniform) of a volume dependent on a few known variables. The essential requirements for this kind of regularity are: a closed system, a very large number of identical elements, a very large number of equivalent events (e.g., collisions). In human affairs none of these conditions is ever satisfied, and in living systems in general, only under very narrow ranges of conditions.

In recent research in population genetics, for example, the chanciness of the evolution of living systems seems to go well beyond the Darwinian image of nature that I have been sketching out. It is now widely believed that the number of variants extant in a population at any one time is far greater than called for by neo-darwinian theory—greater perhaps by several orders of magnitude. Genetic drift produces much more variability in the gene pool than had been previously recognized.[20] (Variants of this kind owe their existence to protection from selection pressure; that is, they are not functionally significant; but as circumstances change this immunity fades.) Hence the hope is more remote than ever of further refining our already advanced techniques for neglecting individuality.

5. The disciplines of scientific and intellectual history and the history of technology ought to be closely related to psychology, especially cognitive psychology, since they deal with the way human beings get ideas and elaborate them. In fact, psychologists have not paid much attention to these fields, except

for a few seminal books such as Kuhn's *Structure of Scientific Revolutions*[21] and some case studies emanating from the psychoanalytic tradition. More serious, the main ideas that psychologists have gleaned from these fields are part of the deterministic tradition I have been discussing: emphasis on the *Zeitgeist* and denial of the role of the individual in history. Justified criticism of the "great man theory of history" gives due recognition to the many less-than-great contributors and to the complex network of social processes involved in intellectual work; in so doing we need not dismiss either the individual or the great individual. There are such.

If important inventions were inevitable results of massive social forces, we should expect something simple and fundamental to have been invented and disseminated in every corner of the globe where a high civilization has appeared. Yet the whole American continent, from Alaska to Tierra del Fuego, with Aztec Mexico and Incan Peru included, was innocent of the wheel and the wheeled vehicle. The wheel, like all inventions, is really a synthesis, a bringing together of many component inventions. The unique combination necessary for the wheel was not an inevitable consequence of the existence of a civilization that could well have used it. High civilization, roads, cities, and so on, were not enough to evoke the wheel. A certain rare event, a creative process, was also needed—in this instance, probably the confluence of a number of inventions.

We need to learn to look at such unique events. While, by definition, every unique event occurs only once, there are still a large number of interesting ones occurring all the time. If novelty springs from such events, we need some way of making them part of science, some way of asking: How did this happen? Why is it unique?

Lists of simultaneous and independent discoveries or inventions are often propounded as evidence for the deterministic view of intellectual and technological history. Without questioning the role of impersonal social forces or the occurrence of some such cases, my own work has led me to a certain skepticism. The Darwin-Wallace coincidence is one of the most often-cited examples of independent discovery of a scientific idea. Yet they occurred exactly 20 years apart, they were not identical, and they were obviously not independent; when Wallace developed the idea of evolution through natural selection; it was to Charles Darwin and to Darwin alone that he sent his first sketch of it! (I shall expand on this theme in another paper.)

ALTERNATIVES TO SIMPLISTIC DETERMINISM

If psychologists want to understand just how the individual relates to society, just how the unique creative product is at once unique, accidental, *and* a social product, there is one fundamental task they cannot escape; they must look to the individual. They must examine individual cases thoroughly in all their bewildering complexity and learn how to unravel them without destroying their meaning or their uniqueness.

In several notable papers, Donald Campbell has elaborated the theme of the necessity of chance in creative work. His approach is somewhat different from mine, since he thinks in terms of something like a random generator within the individual, thus "blind variation and selective retention."[22] We need to ask, "blind" with respect to what?" In my view, it is at least plausible that every move the individual makes is sensible, i.e., not-blind, from his own perspective. To be sure, in the sense that the individual is an independent system whose manifold interactions with other independent systems cannot be calculated or determined, we can speak of blindness with respect to the ultimate consequences of any act or variant. But this does not mean that the individual is behaving in a way that could be described as senseless or "locally blind".

Piaget has recently advanced still another approach to this subject.[23] Limitations of space prevent my dealing with it here. Once it is granted that chance plays some role in all innovative systems, there is more than one way to conceive of including it in our considerations.

In the field of artificial intelligence, as computers grow in power and humans in skill, complexity becomes more legitimate, and ways of conceptualizing it more urgently sought. A contemporary example is the idea of "scene analysis" being developed in the Artificial Intelligence Laboratory at Massachusetts Institute of Technology. We are far past the point where "bits" or even "chunks" of information are the units of analysis: many complex images and scenes are stored, and problem-solving requires a system for eliciting active exchanges among them. This is not unlike the arrangement of a recent exhibition at the Museum of Modern Art in New York City: in order to capture the feel of one quarter of Tokyo, Shinjuku, more than a dozen "experience maps" were used, and no one would really suppose that this fascinating array exhausted the domain.

In a very different way, a recent paper by Estes represents a cautious move in the same general direction. Reflecting on the chaotic theoretical situation existing in the study of probability learning, he comments, "Evidently, the different models are capturing different aspects of a complex process, some aspects being more prominent in some situations. One would like to replace the collection of locally successful models with one general theory, but this objective may not be within our capabilities. A more feasible immediate goal may be to try to understand why different models are required to deal with different situations."[24] In spite of this bow to a possible pluralism and complexity, the main effort of Estes' paper is unfortunately to find "the" boundary conditions within which "the" revised model will work.

The scientific implementation of the simplistic-deterministic vision of nature depends on an organization of scientific work into isolated specialties. Within such sub-sub-disciplines, a larger view of nature seems a world well lost, narrow boundary conditions for research can be prescribed, and idealized laws pursued in comfort. It is not surprising that some of the criticism of this fragmentation has taken organizational form in groups such as the Group for Dialectical Psychology and the Social Science History Association. Realistically, however, these are still only rump groups, and the main trends in social science are far from interdisciplinary or dialectical.

No one can pretend to real mastery in every branch of contemporary science and social science. But even ordinary polysensory mortals can keep an ear to the ground and a nose to the wind, and stay in touch with general trends over areas much wider than their own specialties. So doing, it is not hard to accumulate expressions similar to my own dissatisfaction with simplistic determinism. In an address in 1974 on receiving the American Psychological Association's Distinguished Scientific Contribution Award, Lee Cronbach made a plea for observational studies and greater respect for descriptive results as against hypothesis-testing, for exorcising the null hypothesis as too frequently leading to a waste of valuable descriptive data, for sensitivity to weak interactions, for avoiding research designs that conceal even strong interactions, for greater awareness of the boundary conditions within which nomothetic laws prevail, and for some recognition that we are often impotent to specify those boundary conditions. He closed with the following words: "social scientists are rightly proud of the discipline we draw from the natural-science side of our ancestry. Scientific discipline is what we uniquely add to the time-honored ways of studying man. Too narrow an identification with science, however, has fixed our eyes upon an inappropriate goal. The goal of our work . . . is not to amass generalizations atop which a theoretical tower can someday be erected. . . . The special task of the social scientist in each generation is to pin down the contemporary facts. Beyond that, he shares with the humanistic scholar and the artist in the effort to gain insight into contemporary relationships, and to realign the culture's view of man with present realities. To know man as he is is no mean aspiration."[25]

Among other recent expressions of the same restlessness is the vigorous discussion in Marxist circles of the deterministic view of social process that relegates ideology to the "superstructure" and thereby fails to recognize that the human brain and its intellectual products are integral parts of the natural world.

If we press home such changes in our images of nature and of scientific knowledge, how might the actual practice of scientific inquiry be modified? I offer a few suggestions, none of them really new, but perhaps gaining some new force from the above reflections.

1. *"Weak theory."* Learn to live with the reality that the drive for strong and simple theories that make highly deterministic predictions may only lead us down the road to fiasco. Historians of the behavioral sciences could make a real contribution by documenting some of these failures. This might reduce the strength of the system of reinforcements that now regulates so much theoretical work.

2. *Sensitivity to boundary conditions.* Within limits, some deterministic laws are possible. (For example, under very specific stimulus conditions, height in the visual field corresponds to distance from the observer.) Inquiry cannot stop with discovering such laws. We need to go beyond them in two ways: systematically determine the boundary conditions within which the laws operate; not be too bemused or self-satisfied by the laws themselves. We need to understand that our whole activity of detecting lawful relations and their boundary conditions is part of a still larger enterprise, forming and reforming our images of nature.

3. *Interdisciplinarity.* Piaget's reaction to uncertainties of the kind this paper is concerned with has been a whole series of writings, not well enough known, on interdisciplinarity.[26] Each discipline makes assumptions that are not grounded or groundable within its own mode of operation. In principle, it must depend on other disciplines. One need not be a Renaissance person to pay attention to such relationships.

4. *Invention.* Another metaphor runs through all of Darwin's thought, the idea that the curious organs whose functions he loved to work out are "contrivances." As Darwin understood nature, it does not, of course consciously contrive or invent; his use of the term is a metaphoric comparison with the human activity of invention.

I believe it was Einstein who said that we know more than we can explain. By the same token, we can invent things without fully understanding how they work. Indeed, such invention is a far greater part of the scientific process than has been recognized. Without attempting to set up the most universal laws, we can still try to invent new ways of doing things; when we have created a novelty we can try to understand it, and this understanding constitutes something like the conventional idea of scientific knowledge. This is how I appreciate the strategy of some workers in the field of artificial intelligence. In a first approximation, they forswear the goal of understanding the human mind; they are satisfied to invent a machine that carries out some functions similar to those of the mind. Then, by examining what they have done, they may also shed light on the "natural" mind.

Considering invention as a part of science echoes Marx's aphorism: "Previous philosophers have only interpreted the world. The point is to change it."[27] Invention (including, of course, social invention) is a form of world-changing. Changing the world can be construed as an attempt to understand it.

5. *Individuality.* Rather than concentrating so much effort on looking for general laws of human functioning, look for laws of the individual. How does *this* person work? Cognitive psychology, in particular, needs new approaches to understanding each person as a unique system with its own mode of operation. With slight extensions, the same idea applies to the study of particular groups.

6. *Openness.* Give up all forms of the effort to characterize the person as a fixed entity. Become far more sensitive both to the changes that are actualized and to those that are just below the surface. Be more accepting of the role of chance in human growth, and of interactions among loosely coupled systems.

7. *Humility.* Don't change nature too much. We do not know, and in principle cannot know, the effects of what we are doing. It's bigger than all of us . . . . fortunately.

NOTES AND REFERENCES

1. DARWIN'S first notebook on Transmutation of Species (July 1837-February 1838), p. 21. The four notebooks on Transmutation of Species and the two notebooks on Man, Mind, and Materialism are kept in the Manuscript Room of the Cambridge University Library, where I have studied them, The Transmutation Notebooks have been published as "Darwin's Notebooks on Transmutation of Species," Bull. British Museum (Natural History), Historical Series Vol. 2: Nos. 2-6, 1960–1961; Vol. 3: No. 5, 1967, edited by Sir Gavin de Beer with the collaboration of M.J. Rowlands and B.M. Skramovsky.
2. LUDWIG WITTGENSTEIN. 1969. On Certainty. Edited by G.E.M. Anscombe and G.H. von Wright: p. 21e. Harper and Row. New York, N.Y.
3. In an older tradition, however, images of wide scope were not foreign to psychologists. TITCHENER begins an important work with an extended description of his image of science as an incoming tide on a sandy, rock-strewn shore. E.B. TITCHENER. 1909. Lectures on the Experimental Psychology of the Thought-Processes. Macmillan. New York, N.Y.
4. DARWIN'S fourth notebook on Transmutation of Species (October 1838-July 10, 1839, p. 58.
5. For an extended discussion of these notebooks see my essay in H.E. GRUBER, Darwin on Man: A Psychological Study of Scientific Creativity together with Darwin's Early and Unpublished Notebooks, transcribed and annotated by P.H. Barret. 1974. E. P. Dutton, Inc. New York, N.Y.
6. M. RUDWICK. 1974. Darwin and Glen Roy: A "Great Failure" in Scientific Method? Stud. Hist. Phil. Sci. 5(2).
7. T.R.MALTHUS. 1826. An Essay on the Principles of Population. Murray. London, England. 2 vols., 6th edit., 1826. This is the edition that Darwin owned.
8. GRUBER AND BARRETT, *op. cit.*
9. C. DARWIN. 1859. On the Origin of Species. John Murray. London, England.
10. C. DARWIN. 1871. The Descent of Man, and Selection in Relation to Sex. John Murray. London, England.
11. C. DARWIN, The Expression of the Emotions in Man and Animals. 1872 John Murray. London, England.
12. DARWIN'S third notebook on Transmutation of Species (July 15th, 1838-October 2nd, 1838), pp. 134-135.
13. DARWIN'S first notebook on Transmutation of Species, p. 26. The irregularity of the tree of nature, and the grasp of the role of isolating mechanisms are explicit. Also quite evident in the B-notebook is Darwin's treatment of the internal laws of growth

of organisms as something quite separate from the factors leading to environmental changes and sometimes to isolation. Although my aim here is to expound Darwin's thinking, I believe I may go a little beyond him in insisting on the necessity of the connection between irregularity and accident.

14. G. WHITE. 1789. Natural History and Antiquities of Selborne.
15. W. PALEY. 1802. Natural Theology; or, Evidence of the Existence and Attributes of the Deity Collected from the Appearance of Nature. London, England.
16. R.C. LEWONTIN. The fallacy of biological determinism. The Sciences. March/April, 1976, pp. 6-10. See also E. TOBACH, J. GIANUTSOS, H. TOPOFF & C. GROSS. 1974. The Four Horsemen: Racism, Sexism, Militarism, and Social Darwinism. Behavioral Publications. New York, N.Y.
17. W.T. POWERS. 1976. Control theory, purpose, and determinism. Paper presented in a symposium on Relevance and Perspectives of Cybernetics in Psychology. American Psychological Ass. Washington, D.C.
18. A. SMITH. 1776. Inquiry into the Nature and Causes of the Wealth of Nations.
19. See, for example, J.V.NEEL. 1976. The circumstances of human evolution. Johns Hopkins Med. J. 138: 233-244.
20. M. KIMURA. 1976. Population genetics and molecular evolution. Johns Hopkins Med. J. 138: 253-261.
21. T.S. KUHN. 1962. The Structure of Scientific Revolutions. Chicago: Uni. Chicago Press. Chicago, Ill.
22. D.T. CAMPBELL. 1960. Blind variation and selective retention in creative thought as in other knowledge processes. Psychol. Rev. 67: 380-400.
23. J. PIAGET. 1974. Adaptation Vitale et Psychologie de l'Intelligence: Selection Organique et Phenocopie. Hermann, Paris, France.
24. W.K. ESTES. 1976. The Cognitive side of probability learning. Psychological Rev. 83: 37-64.
25. L. J. CRONBACH. 1975. Beyond the two disciplines of scientific psychology. Am. Psychol. 30: 116-127.
26. See, for example, J. PIAGET. 1973. Main Trends in Interdisciplinary Research. George Allen and Unwin. London, England.
27. KARL MARX. Theses on Feuerbach. no. 11. Written in 1945, published in 1888 as an appendix to F. ENGELS, Ludwig Feuerbach and the End of Classical German Philosophy.

DISCUSSION OF PART IV. A.

Rand Evans, *Moderator*

Department of Psychology
University of New Hampshire
Durham, New Hampshire 03824

DR. HENRY CARSON: I retired a little over a year ago, but I formerly taught at the Night Division at Rutgers University in Newark and was a school psychologist on Long Island. I'm working on a biography of Watson and I was interested in what Dave [Bakan] said about Watson's position. I'm aware of Dave's high scholarship, but I would just like to point out that Gustav Bergmann wrote an article in the Psychological Review in 1956 in which he said that second only to Freud, Watson ranked as probably the greatest figure in psychology. I believe it was Dr. Spence, in a short article in the '50s, who said Watson's influence on psychology was comparable to that of Copernicus on astronomy. These are two very great minds in this field, and I was wondering if Dave would give his opinions of these men.

DR. BAKAN: I think that the importance of Watson was that he—in his personality, and his attitudes, and the work that he did, and so on—was a kind of personal expression of these various social forces. I really don't accept the Great Man Theory, but I do think that different people more or less express some of the major social forces at work. I think that Watson does so from an historical point of view, for example. I think you've got to consider Max Meyer and Watson. Max Meyer had actually formulated the psychology from the other one, had formulated a position of behaviorism. Max Meyer, coming from Europe and so on, simply was not the expression of that behaviorism in a way in which John Watson was.

John Watson was *the* new man in the Academy: personality and background, the rural background, the antiintellectualism, the whole bit.

DR. SALZINGER: I was both delighted and interested by your talk. That makes it all the more difficult for me to understand how you can also be so wrong! I can't begin to comment on all of your statements I consider to be wrong. Let me just take a couple. You stated you hope that psychology can overcome its historical handicaps; I must say that doesn't sound to me very much like historical analysis, but rather like an attempt to politicize psychology instead of doing an analysis of what the political effects might be. I think the notion that we ought to give up prediction and control and return to thought, wishes, and feelings is merely an attempt to tell us how to do research in your image. Peculiarly enough, that kind of a suggestion is exactly contrary to your point that you preferred increasing variation in research. I wonder if you would comment on these points.

DR. BAKAN: I don't understand what you said. I'm saying that there is a subject matter of psychology, that it has a vigorous, but financially unsupported life in the underground. They [the psychologists] didn't do it too well, because they didn't have all of the leisure, the luxury, the apparatus, the support, and so on, that the Academy has. I'm saying that it is now the season to get on with doing some psychology and overcoming the psychophobia that has characterized it. I'm not saying let us dismiss the experimental psychologist. I'm not saying we should throw him out. But I am saying that we should do everything we can to increase the variation.

246

Looking at the history of departments of psychology in the United States, it has been a history of extreme efforts to restrict the amount of ideological variation within the departments. One major place where it broke occurred when the Veterans' Administration came along with a little money, and said, "Please broaden." So they did, but with enormous ambivalence.

DR. SALZINGER: Unfortunately, the underground, as you call it, which is now much above ground in the applied field, has no claim for success. I would say it has not achieved anything of significance. Clinical psychologists have not found the cure for schizophrenia, or for manic-depressive psychosis, or even for neurosis, an area on which, presumably, they were working, whereas experimental psychology has achieved some progress in the science of behavior.

DR. BAKAN: Every clinical psychologist who has really been working has been working in a highly alienated condition. I, as a college professor, have research assistants available. I have time available, I get money so that I can go to meetings. Moneys are available for research, if I want it, *et cetera, et cetera.* None of these things available to a college professor is usually available to the practitioner. If you say clinical psychologists have not done well, I would say that there has been a dearth of resources. I think that the academic psychologist has had enormous resources thrown his way, relatively. I think that the clinical psychologist has gotten very, very little. And at this stage, sure, I don't know if anybody has done anything terribly important in curing schizophrenia and so on, in or out of the Academy.

But let me put it another way. If you look at the history of virtually all of the professions, you will find that they have a long-standing, empirical tradition: medicine, law, architecture, road-building, and the like. A long-standing—let's call it a craft tradition, a craft tradition in the sense that theory and practice are not two categories. Modern medicine is as good as it is, not because of what happened in the last few years, but because it comes on the back of a long-standing, empirical thing. The fact of the matter is that the therapy relationship as we know it today, the invention of psychotherapy as a social institution, the invention of the psychotherapy relationship—just took place the other day, and there hasn't been very much experience with it. The experience that we've had with it has been highly alientated, and it hasn't been supported.

UNIDENTIFIED SPEAKER: Before I give my name, I'd like to say that I left psychology sixteen years ago. This is the first psychology meeting I have been to since April of 1961. When I left psychology, I was the National Director of Psychological Research of the Veterans Administration. I would like to say that I agree with everything that was said tonight about what was wrong with psychology, but much that is wrong has not been said. My only regret and criticism is that I do not think that your suggestions tonight will do anything to improve psychology, and I will stay as a Director of Mathematics. My name was Clair Bernier when I was with the Veterans Administration, when I left it in 1960.

DR. BAKAN: Hope springs eternal in the human breast.

DR. MARKS: I would say I would be very much concerned if nobody would respond to the statement you just made, which is that psychotherapy was invented yesterday. I think it's indeed one of the problems that people conceive of it as such and that they view psychotherapy as separate from therapy because it's a kind of specialization that has to do with split of body and mind. Certainly the doctor/patient relationship or the healing relationship beginning with the priest is one that's been with humanity since the beginning of time.

DR. BAKAN: What I mean is that Freudian invention, where one human being, in his professional role, makes it his business to attend to the most intimate aspects of the other person's existence on a regular basis, day after day, week after week, month after month, year after year, is a new invention.

DR. MARKS: I think that most healing relationships are lifelong for the society.

DR. BAKAN: As a professional, vocational, career type of thing, where one person says it is my job to devote myself to the most intimate aspects of your being for 50 minutes every day, week in, week out, two years, three years, five years, as long as it's necessary—that is a new invention. If you can match that in history, I'd be very surprised.

DR. MARKS: No, no, it may already be over.

DR. BAKAN: It may be over too, O.K.

DR. MARKS: There was one other point I brought up in a paper in August, which deals with the whole question of freedom of learning and teaching. And the question I raised in my paper, and I'd like to raise it for you, too, is that if this tradition originated in nineteenth century Germany (which I don't think was really all that free and all that liberal), I just wondered to what extent this permission of freedom of the university was based on the understanding at another level that nothing would be done there that would in any way affect what's really going on.

DR. BAKAN: Of course, of course.

DR. RIEBER: I have one question that was bothering me, although I have the greatest respect for anyone who has the guts to get up and say it the way they really believe it, and you certainly did that. Why did you prescribe, if that's the best word, to go back to thinking, feeling, and willing? What specific value has that? I have some reservations in my own mind about whether we ever left thinking, feeling, and willing, except during a brief period, perhaps a couple of decades. We're certainly back in that ball park today, but I don't see any intrinsic value in it, in and of itself, for us to achieve the values that you hinted at. Certainly there's much more to it than that, and I wondered why you chose those three in the first place.

DR. BAKAN: I choose them because I think they are consequential. I think they matter. I am a psychologist. The area of thought, feeling, and willing is my subject matter. That won't be enough to satisfy us, so let me say some other things.

There are a number of extremely important phenomena that you cannot even begin to come to terms with unless you fully accept the reality of psychological phenomena. The essence of behaviorism is that it denies the reality or significance of thoughts, feelings, and wishes. It either denies or ignores, in favor of behavior. Let's take something real, simple, like two people going to a bank. I use this example when I teach introductory psychology. Two people go into a bank. If you watch them carefully, both behave completely identically: that is, there's no way by which you can discriminate the behavior of Mr. A. from Mr. B.

However, Mr. A. is a nice honest gentleman, and Mr. B. is a forger. The behavior is the same; what is the difference? The difference is in something like intention.

Let's take something else. The prominent things you read about in the newspaper these days— the CIA, Watergate, and the like—all center around a certain psychological phenomenon that has no existence in the behaviorist rhetoric. This is the phenomenon of the secret. A secret can be defined as something that you're thinking, but that you do not manifest in your behavior. That's what a secret is. If it's manifest in your behavior, then it's no secret, because the other guy knows it.

Now in Behaviorism we have a whole psychological approach which has, as its cornerstone, a methodological assumption that says there is no reality to secrets.

Let me give you a third example. Behaviorism cannot distinguish between a lie and an error. Because what differentiates a lie from an error is, again, intention.

DR. RIEBER: I know that at dinner, we both agreed that communication at best was impossible. Nevertheless, let's try to make it a little bit better now. What kind of specific research in thinking, willing, and so on, is going to be the kind of research, either applied or basic, that's going to make the kind of psychology we should have? Let's get very specific and very concrete.

DR. BAKAN: I think that one of the main problems in the contemporary world is just what you said, that people aren't communicating with each other effectively. O.K., then, what is communication? Communication means that somehow you come to think and feel and will what I am thinking and feeling and willing. O.K.? In a certain sense, then, the psychologist should be the expert in communication. If we don't understand each other, we have not succeeded in producing appropriately analogous thoughts in each other's minds.

That failure of the passage, as it were, from my thought to your thought, is what a failure of communication is. But the study of thought and feeling and willing is precisely the domain of the psychologist. If the psychologist could do something about increasing the world's understanding of the nature of thought, feeling, and willing, he would thereby be doing something about increasing the effectiveness of interpersonal communications.

DR. RIEBER: Now we're communicating, but one more question here. Thomas Upham tried it, Dewey tried it, and I daresay some of the behaviorists even tried in their own way. Why did they fail?

DR. BAKAN: That's a long story.

DR. KAY SHAKE: (*Rutgers University, New Brunswick, N.J.*): Dr. Bakan, you're calling for the Academy to welcome what up to now have been the interests of the clinician, and you're saying that up until this point, the clinician has functioned in an underground. Well, during the fifteen years or so of the life of this underground, the past fifteen years have seen a tremendous expansion of the clinician's field of observation. He works with the family, he's involved with children in a much broader sense than ever before. We have bioenergetics. We have Janoff studying the emotional expressiveness, and so on. At this point, the underground, I think, is—

DR. BAKAN: There is a growth at this point of what I'm calling an empirical basis. That's right.

DR. SHAKE: O.K. But I think that the notion of an underground is obsolete. The tremendous activities going on in the outside, in the life of the clinician, his professional life, his scholarly life, make the Academy seem like a very arid place for him to exist in. Now, what does the Academy at this point have to offer clinicians?

DR. BAKAN: Resources. That's what.

DR. SHAKE: But since the clinician expanded so well without the Academy, he either didn't need the resources or he has them.

DR. BAKAN: There are and there have been some really distinguished clinicians.

DR. SHAKE: You mean within the Academy?

DR. BAKAN: No, no, outside the Academy. As you know, there has not been any great effort to get people of that type into academic positions where they could teach. There hasn't been any great enthusiasm for giving chairs of psychology to people who are distinguished in the clinical psychology field.

DR. SHAKE: That's not exactly true, because those people teach in their own created academies in the institutes, these psychoanalytic institutes.

DR. BAKAN: Maybe some, over the last ten years. If you look over the longer history of the Academy, it is different. I know of one very distinguished and great clinician, Sam Beck. He was a colleague when I was at the University of Chicago. That man was kept on at the University of Chicago without a professorship, only as a lecturer, year after year after year, and was retired as a lecturer.

And the reason is obvious. Because nobody could bring himself, within the framework of the University, to grant him more than second-rate status and honor him with a professorship.

DR. SHAKE: I couldn't agree with you more.

DR. BAKAN: There has been real discrimination against clinical psychologists in terms of appointments. I won't even begin to talk about the story of graduate students, selection of clinical graduate students, the weeding out of clinical graduate students, and the like.

DR. DIAMOND: Earlier today I had occasion to quote the words of the definition by Cattell in 1904 of psychology as anything psychologists want to do. That was a very broad definition, and it certainly gave you the right to concentrate your efforts on thinking, feeling, and willing. It would also include the work of modern neurophysiologists, for example. But what I can't understand is why you want to decrease our variability by telling us to concentrate our efforts in the field you like.

DR. BAKAN: I thought I answered that already. Didn't I answer it already?

DR. DIAMOND: No. I think you told us to increase variability, and then you told us to decrease it, and I don't understand how you do those two.

DR. BAKAN: Where did I say decrease it? That's where I lose you. In what did I say, did you hear me say, "Decrease variability?"

DR. DIAMOND: In the concentration on—

DR. BAKAN: I'm not talking about concentration. I never used that word. I am not advocating the reduction of variation.

DR. DIAMOND: Well, do you then welcome the increased variation in the direction of neurophysiological foundations of thinking, feeling, and willing?

DR. BAKAN: God bless them.

DR. DIAMOND: Good.

DR. LAZAR: Along with this increased variability, you still would want us to be applied, to look for applications, correct? I only ask this because I may have missed the point. My question hinges on whether or not you still want to deal with applications.

DR. BAKAN: I want to deal with applications.

DR. LAZAR: You still want to deal with applied things, correct? I think that we all are expected to be phenomenal every day; if not every day, maybe once a week. If psychologists or any science group would come up with a breakthrough this month, they would want to know what we're going to do next month.

And I wonder if we can ever feed this kind of society, if we could ever cope with it. I wanted you to comment on that.

DR. BAKAN: Maybe what I'm going to say is not quite an answer to your question. Some years ago I was teaching a course in educational psychology and I was using Cronbach's textbook. Cronbach, in point of fact, recites a good deal of the literature from the psychology of learning; the book seems to be a book based on the psychology of learning. And then you examine the book more closely, and you say, "Let's pick out the really astute observations in this book," where he is really saying something that seems to be informing you. Having identified the informative passages in the book, ask yourself a second question: Where does the information come from? Does it come from the body of literature that Cronbach is citing, or does it come from Cronbach's mother-wit, his vast experience, and his own imaginative intelligence?

The answer to me comes through loud and clear. The reason why that book is a good book is because Cronbach happens to be a very, very bright guy. And in a sense, he is citing these studies, but he isn't really using them. They are not informing him. I said in my paper, and let me say again, I think that perhaps one of the best examples of the bad condition of psychology is the relationship between that one field, where there has probably been more work done in America than any other, the psychology of learning, and the field of education. There's a report, a provisional report, in Ontario, called the Holt Dennis Report, which contains a whole set of recommendations for the revision of the school system. There is one paragraph in that whole book that alludes to this body of experimental literature. All that paragraph says is that the authors, in attempting to outline a new program in education, found little of value for the purposes of the report.

Greg Kimble, who knows the whole field of the psychology of learning very well, once told me that he estimates that there must be something in the order of 100,000 studies in the field of psychology of learning. Yet the payoff for education has been slim. Charles Curran, at the Loyola University, Chicago, a priest who took his Ph.D. with Carl Rogers, was interested in the question of language learning. He did a little investigation. He sat around with people and talked. He came up with a rather interesting idea. The interesting idea is that when you try, if you're an adult, to learn a new language, what happens to you in learning the new language is that you are placed in a position where there is a rearousal of infantile emotions, an infantile mood, from the time when you lived in a world where people spoke a language that you didn't understand, that the rearousal of this infantile mood works to inhibit the learning of French.

O.K. So then he goes and he takes two groups, and he says to one group, look, you are going to feel infantilized, *et cetera, et cetera*. He spends some time preparing the student for the experience of the infantilization in the French class. Of course, one group learns French better than the other. Now Curran's observation is of such a nature that all of the studies of proactive and retroactive inhibition of primary and secondary, and so on, would never have yielded.

It certainly doesn't emerge in the 100,000 studies in the psychology of learning. Why? Because that psychology of learning literature is heavily under the influence of this behavioristic tradition that I'm talking about.

DR. LAZAR: I asked whether society would appreciate our progress, and I'm gathering that you're saying we haven't made any, so there's no way of even guessing.

DR. BAKAN: There's a part of me that says the following: Why don't we just forget the whole thing, because psychology is the most dangerous science, anyway. I'm so glad that Richard Nixon wasn't a good psychologist.

DR. TWENEY: I liked your emphasis on Darwinian variability as a way of characterizing the area, but there's an aspect of that that you didn't comment on, which actually constitutes one of the Academy's often-stated defenses against this kind of exclusion, and that is the idea that the process of variability in science operates by taking ideas, testing them, and rejecting the bad ones.

That clinical psychology, and Freudian psychology in particular, has not presented the Academy with ideas that can meet this kind of test, and I wonder if you'd comment on that.

DR. BAKAN: I'm not at all persuaded that the history of ideas is one in which the Darwinian progressive evolution takes place at all. Socrates was before the Middle Ages.

DR. TWENEY: Isn't that implied by your use of variation, though, that same model?

DR. BAKAN: Probably, except that actually, the place to look is John Stuart Mill, *On Liberty*. That's one of my favorite books, and essentially what John Stuart Mill argues there is for liberty in the social sphere as the mechanism for the promotion of variation.

DR. SKINNER: I've been connected with American psychology for 48 years, which takes me about half-way back to the beginning, and I fail to see myself in what we've been told tonight. I have never been aware of any political, social, academic, or other pressure on my research, on my publications, on my speech. Although I've done things that have had commercial value, I have never done them because of that; I've seen my work applied, but I've not done it because of its applications.

I've had contact with psychiatrists, because I worked with psychotics at a very early stage, and with clinical psychologists. I've worked in education. (I didn't come up to this microphone until Dr. Bakan began talking about the irrelevance of learning theory to education.) I have gone into fields that have aroused a good deal of political discussion. There has been a good deal of animated controversy about my work, but I have never felt any kind of pressure to change what I was doing or saying, nor do I feel that criticism has had much of an effect on me. (I avoid that, usually, by not reading my critics.)

When it comes to learning theory, I agree that the 100,000 articles cited by Greg Kimble, minus several hundred by operant conditioners, have not been relevant. I made that point in one of the first papers I published about programmed instruction. But I have seen laboratory work extended to education, not necessarily because the people who extended it were bright, but because they had something to go on—something that had been demonstrated in the laboratory.

The reason that we have not seen good psychological theory used in education is quite clear. I recently visited a learning center in one of Boston's much-disturbed schools. It is a room in which children who have been pretty much discarded as unteachable are learning to read and do arithmetic, at least at the normal rate if not one and one-half times the normal rate. The children like this room; when the school is vandalized, the room is never touched. They are learning something which is very basic and which is usually badly taught.

I understand that New York public schools will now accept the ability to read a want-ad as proof that a child has learned to read. At that level, students have not learned to *enjoy* reading at all. In the learning center I mentioned, they learn, and they learn very rapidly. Why are such centers not more widely used? There are hundreds of them in the country, but they still encounter difficulties. The reason is that the educational establishment, the philosphers of education, believe that the subject of psychology is thinking, feeling, and wishing.

DR. BAKAN: I'm just running through my mind the various points Fred made, and I'm tryin to ask myself which of the points that he made I should respond to. Let me respond to the argument of positive application, which you gave where you say there exists a learning theory, a whole body of research in the laboratory, which we'll call L, and that L, when applied to a practical situation, has produced positive results. Then you say go from the positive results, P, back to the value and validity of L. So we have: L implies P, and P is true, and now we go back and say, since P is true, L is true.

I've just voiced the classical fallacy of going from the affirmation of the consequent to the affirmation of an antecedent. Some years ago, I read a magnificent paper by one B. F. Skinner on superstitition, which indicated that a superstition is created on the basis of partial reinforcement. When something works sometimes, it has a tendency to develop a superstition. I grant you that you can cite any number of instances where the kind of operant work that you're talking about works, sometimes. But if it doesn't work all the time and invariably, then the possibility that we are dealing with a superstition opens itself.

MAX GARFINKEL (*University of Montreal, Montreal, Can.*): Two different comments that are related. The first is to try to distinguish in my mind between the ideology of psychology as a science and the methodology of psychology as a science. I have the feeling that you sort of switched halfway from one to the other, and I was wondering if your real premise is against the ideology of psychology and you ended up talking against the methodology. Now, I recognize they're related, but I think it's important to keep that distinction very clear.

DR. BAKAN: Thank you for asking that question, because it gives me an opportunity to say something I need to clarify. Yes, it's important to distinguish between ideology and methodology. I came to consider ideology through the examination of methodology. Finding that the methodology—well, one particular instance, for example, is wanting, I look for the reasons in ideology. Consider the use of the test of significance in psychological research, which I examined closely and found to be totally absurd in most social science applications. It is one of the most mischievous devices ever developed. It operates against the investigator's learning anything if the study is to base its results on a test of significance. So I say to myself, psychologists aren't dummies. They're smart. But if they're smart, how come they do such stupid things?

The answer is that their trouble lies not in their heads, but in their hearts, and in their wills. And that's what I've been trying to answer. I'm saying that psychologists who rely on the test of significance regularly and routinely cannot be that stupid. If they're not stupid, then there must be another source of the error. That source is the cultural context in which they live and grow.

DR. JOSEPH ZUBIN: May I ask just one question? I was touched by your appeal for appointing good clinicians to the faculties of universities. I'm reminded of the story they tell of Wagner Von Jauregg, when he came back from winning the Nobel Prize and found the clinicians in his clinic bending over a case of psychoanalysis. So he said to them, "Gentlemen, you too may win the Nobel Prize; if not for science, maybe for literature . . ." Now, that's not to denigrate the Nobel Prize for literature, but it seems to me you have to draw a distinction between research of the kind that follows the conventional approach to verification, experimentation, controls, and statistical tests of significant differences, and the literary approach, which Shakespeare was so good at, and which humanists are good at.

DR. BAKAN: My impulse is to say—and on this I think that the Operant Group is really quite immune, because they have understood the difficulties associated with aggregates—but I would challenge you. Let's say—I don't know what the figures are—but let's say that 40 or 50% of the conventional studies that you're talking about base conclusions on the results of the test of significance.

I challenge you to give me one important discovery or finding based on the test of significance. The test of significance is intrinsically fallacious. Not the least, it cannot satisfy the most elementary criterion of replication, because the test of significance basically gives you two alternatives. You can either reject the null hypothesis, or else the experiment is inconclusive. Those are your two alternatives. If you want to replicate a test-of-significance study, you can either again reject the null hypothesis or come up with "inconclusive." You cannot, within the logic of the test of significance, ever really replicate, really reject, a piece, a presumptive finding which has already been reported in literature. I challenge anybody to point to anything terribly meaningful that has emerged in the literature from these "normative studies."

You know, if the aim of science is to make discoveries, I simply turn to you and I say, "O.K., what discoveries are there? What are the discoveries of psychology in the last 50 or 60 years?" What would you tell me?

DR. J. ZUBIN: What about intermittent reinforcement?

DR. BAKAN: What about it? Would you give me the proposition? What's the proposition? Intermittent reinforcement, what?

DR. ZUBIN: The importance of tests of significance is based on the fact that studies that do not test the significance of their results against chance occurrence can often be misleading. The test of significance separates the results which are worthy of further consideration from those which can be explained by chance. For example, that the effect of intermittent reinforcement is stronger than continuous reinforcement is a fact which has been established by demonstrating that the differences between these two results are not due to chance.

UNIDENTIFIED SPEAKER: I'd just like to return to my previous point. I really think you are showing prejudices against some of the variations within the field of psychology, and it doesn't become you because it doesn't fit the design you gave us.

DR. BAKAN: I'm not the commissar.

DR. MITCHEL ASH: There's been much discussion about the various present-oriented ideological concerns you've raised in your speech. I'd like to direct a question now to the historical, as it were, underpinnings of those concerns as you've expressed them—not to really disagree with them in a terribly fundamental way, but in a sense to suggest that the situation might be a little more complicated than you pictured it in your talk.

DR. BAKAN: I agree with you before you even start. Go ahead.

DR. ASH: I'm certain you do, but let me express two possible areas of complication and see if you can comment on them for us. First of all, the distinction that you raised between underground and—I guess-overground, or underground and establishment. You've suggested that much of the underground is Freudian and clinical in character. But in your discussion of post-World War II struggles within the hospital, as it were, between the clinicians and the medical psychologists or psychiatrists, you don't mention in what sense the medical people are an overground.

The reason why I ask the question is that I've been told, at least or it's been contended, that this medical overground was also Freudian and that the ideas of Freud, at least by the 1950s had proven singularly adaptable to the rebellious clinical psychologists that you referred to and to the establishment of psychiatry. I was wondering what comment you'd have on that before I ask the second question.

DR. BAKAN: I honestly don't think it's true. That is, I think that the impact of psychoanalysis on psychiatry has not been that extensive. Very recently, yes, it's been growing. I'm trying to think of some statistics. I can't do it, but I have seen tables of it. Not as extensive as you might think. I can't pull a table out of my head.

DR. ASH: O.K. I just wanted to raise that as a question. The second question I wanted to ask related to the same dichotomy between underground and establishment, but in another way.

DR. BAKAN: Excuse me, let me make one observation. Characteristically, the psychoanalytic psychiatrists have been bunched: you know, New York, mostly Boston, to some degree, Washington, Los Angeles, San Francisco, and you've had it. A handful in Chicago. Most of them are in private practice, not in any place where they are likely to run at loggerheads with psychologists such as in V.A. hospitals and the like. But for those, for the rest of the psychiatrists and the kind of psychiatrists that psychologists came in contact with, they were not really heavily informed by psychoanalysis.

DR. ASH: Along a slightly different area of concern, there has been in recent years some sort of rebellious movement that thought of itself as an underground, but that we thought was rebelling against both behaviorism and Freud, and I'm referring specifically to humanistic psychology, a so-called third force. Many of these people are not outside the Academy at all, but have rather tried to form an alliance with people who are in the Academy, people who are outside the Academy, for the further benefit of their own particular ideology. I'm not offering a comment either for or against humanistic psychology, I'm just asking you to fit it into the picture.

DR. BAKAN: The answer is yes, and I have difficulty in seeing the contemporary situation with as much clarity as I can the past. That's what we're always doomed with. I might make one observation, though, and that is that the humanistic psychologists in the Academy who have made this union are not very large in number. I mean, for example, you can see it in terms of, say the number of people in the Division of Humanistic Psychology within the APA, which is relatively small compared to the number of people in the Association of Humanistic Psychology. You just take the numbers in one and the numbers in the other. One is a handful, and the other is massive. So that we assume that people in the APA group would tend more to be associated with the Academy. There isn't that much in the way of academic association with the humanistic movement. Just by those numbers.

MR. DAVID MANN: I'm a first year Ph.D. student in Clinical Psychology at Rutgers. The question I have is this. It appears to me that thinking, willing, and feeling have been around in psychology for a long time, and they've been expressed in different forms within different theoretical networks. What have been different have been the data sets that have been applied and the types of substrates that have been postulated to describe the activities of the organism. I'd like to know what specific data sets you are suggesting and what substrate for activities of the organism would lead to the thinking in this area.

DR. BAKAN: I'll give you my latest thinking on that. The best formulation of what I consider to be the significant data of psychology is that which is expressible in a narrative. If I want to understand something about Mary on Tuesday, then I do what every real expert in prediction and control does, and that is to try to develop a history, try to find out the story of it, develop a dossier, a history, a narrative. One of the things that I've come to understand lately is that we characteristically collect data in such a way that we leave the narrative out, and take only the instantaneous. For instance, if you can do a correlational study, you take two measures today on the individual, say measure X and measure Y on Mary, and on Sam, and on Peter, and so on. X and Y are at an instant. You have separated the wheat from the chaff, but you've left the wheat and you've taken the chaff in the way you gather data.

The information, the critical information, is information that is contained in a narrative, and you've left that out of your data. You've left that in the substance, but you've not put that into the data, and you're not analyzing it. One of the reasons why we have done so very poorly in the world of psychology is that indeed we have not done much in the way of using the narrative, the history, the case record, as a data base. Today, if I were going out and doing a piece of research on any problem, I would be after the case history, as a data base, as much as possible.

DISCUSSION OF PART IV. B.

Ethel Tobach, *Moderator*

Department of Animal Behavior
American Museum of Natural History
New York, New York 10024

MR. BILL WAGRON: I am just wondering if in contrasting your initial statements to your later statements, you aren't confusing Darwin's inter- and intra-species differences? You talked about regularity interspecies, but as I understand his writings, he expects regularity within a species.

DR. GRUBER: Well, he is very impressed with reproductive processes producing offspring that are very much like their parents, and of course you can read that either way; "very much like" means not exactly alike. And he wrote also of organs which are beautifully adapted to their functions but not perfectly adapted. In the 1870s, when he wrote the "Descent of Man," the eye, the human eye, gave him very great trouble, because it seems such a perfect optical instrument. Then, the very next year, Helmholtz wrote his famous essay on the imperfections of the eye as an optical instrument, in which he goes on at some length and as the really qualified world expert on the subject, to show how, if you were really an instrument designer, you would never make an eye like that. Darwin received a copy of that paper and in his margin notes you can see that he cheered. So I think that even if you speak within a species, Darwin was thinking of similarity and adaptation, but not of identity and perfection. Of course, he was influenced by the tradition of natural theology. One of the writers to whom he owes a great debt is William Paley. Darwin was in love with the beautiful contrivances, the inventions of nature and their near perfection.

DR. SALZINGER: I am going to try to make this sound like a question, but I am really perplexed. I don't normally take notes but something made me do it, and the list of things and people that you rejected were: Miller, Osgood, The Single Developmental Pathways, Freud, Erickson, and Piaget, Probability in the Small and the Normal Curve. But you apparently embraced the Great-Man theory of history, presumably also the Great-Woman theory of history, but what do you *really* think is happening in science?

DR. GRUBER: What I think is happening in psychology is that there is a persistent tendency toward searching out highly deterministic simplistic schemes for explaining a world of nature which is in principle nondeterministic, nonrepeating, and enormously and beautifully complex. As I tried to say earlier, each of these different points of view that I referred to.has its own richness and complexity when you really look at it, but it seems to me that they get debased and borrowed, as we borrow from each other in our harried, busy, academic life: the vector is toward enormous and unfruitful oversimplification.

DR. W. I. ELLIS: You mentioned that one of the cardinal points of Darwin's theory is the continuity of evolution, including man in that scheme of evolution. Of course, this is one of the justifications, the classic justifications, for much of comparative psychology but there are those who see the discontinuity, cultural, linguistic, symbolic, manipulative, discontinuities between the animals, lower animals and man as much more important in the psychology of the human being

257

than the continuity. How, in your view, given Darwin's writings and your own thinking, are we to balance the principle of continuity with certain discontinuities?

DR. GRUBER: I think, as we are talking about Darwin, Darwin was much more impressed with the idea of continuity. Of course, it fitted the needs of his work. In particular, with regard to psychological issues, he could not allow that the human soul, or anything soul-like—aesthetic impulses, the higher emotions, love, great feats of human rationality—were exempt from the process of evolution. He would not concede that there was some sort of evolutionary process that applied all the way up to humans, but then it stopped and an act of special creation occurred, and humans were exempt from the evolutionary process. That is what he was struggling against, and you have to see Darwin's own way of balancing out the problem that you refer to and put very well. You have to see things in the light of the argument that he was involved in. To him it was very important to find that the worm, the earthworm—to which he devoted a whole book, although not all to its behavior—behaved almost as though it could think. Perhaps you can find places where Darwin talks about discontinuities, our species as being special and as having gone further and all that, but the main emphasis in Darwin is surely on continuity. Maybe if he had lived in another climate of argument, he might have struck another balance.

DR. JAYNES: I am very much interested in the nature of, role of, metaphors in scientific thoughts, and so I would like to say how fascinating I found what you were saying. My question is quite specific about the role of this irregularly branching tree. There have been several studies, I think, about how Darwin came to change through the successive six or so editions of his book, how he changed his emphasis so that there is an increase in the Lamarckism as you go to the final editions. My question is whether or not the metaphor, the irregularly branching tree which seemed to be at the very beginning of his thoughts, became less emphasized, and this may be one of the reasons why, as you pointed out, this has not been recognized in Darwin's thoughts.

DR. GRUBER: I don't know. I think there is such a fundamental difference between Darwin's use of the so-called Lamarckian idea of acquired characteristics and Lamarck's use of it. For one thing, Lamarck's image of the panorama of nature is not an irregularly branching tree or any other sort of tree; it's a ladder, and movement up the ladder represents increase on a scale of perfection. Acquired characteristics are accidents. The idea of accident was important to Lamarck. These are deviations from the straight line up the ladder. What defines the ladder is the metaphysical law of progress. To maintain continuity in the organic world, one must add something else to that notion. Lamarck believed in spontaneous generation: the simplest form, the monad, was beginning over and over again, so that this same ladder was happening repeatedly. For Larmarck, inheritance of acquired characteristics does not explain evolution, it explains the accidents, the deviations from the ladder. It's really a fundamental misreading of Lamarck to put so much emphasis on the inheritance of acquired characteristics. And for Darwin, too, inheritance of acquired characteristics would never have explained evolution because he understood very well, he was quite explicit about the point, that a characteristic that can be acquired through the empiristic action of the environment can just as well be disacquired. The action of the environment is reversible. What appears in one generation can be taken away in another generation. That's why you need a theory that includes the operation of isolating mechanisms of all sorts—geographic, sexual, behavioral and so on—coupled with selection, to produce a branching in the tree which becomes *irreversible*. When

Darwin speculated about acquired characteristics, it was out of a certain embarrassment. After all, for his theory he needed to believe in heredity, and he needed to believe in variations, and he did not know the causes of either. He was obviously on dangerous ground, as long as he could say nothing very useful about these genetical questions of heredity and variation. *The Origin of Species* starts out with what is really its weakest chapter; from the very beginning he tries to say something on this subject and then admits that he doesn't have very much to say. I think it is true that he conceded something, that he put a little more emphasis on the "Lamarckian" idea later on, but it didn't make any fundamental difference to the structure of his argument.

Now, I don't know whether that helps to account for the fact that the image of nature as fundamentally irregular, and all that, is so often lost sight of by behavioral scientists. Of course, this is not the case with people in the field of population biology or in evolution itself. I think they believe the pictures that they print in their books; they are very deeply imbued with this image. I was referring to our own discipline as having lost sight of that aspect of Darwinian thinking.

DR. KEISHECK: Dr. Gruber, considering your thoughts about the way in which psychologists may distort natural phenomena descriptively and by oversimplifying, could you elaborate on that and also on some suggestions about what kinds of problems you think psychologists ought to be working on and what kinds of methods they ought to be using?

DR. GRUBER: I don't have a prescription for what everybody else ought to do, except to honor this complexity each in his or her own way. For myself, the road I have chosen, having started as an experimental psychologist, is to devote a great deal of my life to the study of one case, and I have never come anywhere near exhausting its complexity. Now I am working on a second case, Jean Piaget, but not in the hopes of arriving at an inductive generalization based on an N of two which will be more secure than a generalization based on an N of one. The justification for my studying a second case is the hope of understanding different aspects of the creative process. What I have also been doing in these last years is combining the approach of a detailed case study with experimental or quasi-experimental approaches and studies that arise out of the case. I take issue, not in a very large way, with one point that Dr. Bakan made in his paper. If you remember, he described individuals developing through time, providing the potential material for the narrative which he considered to be the all-important thing that we should turn our attention to. Bakan criticized psychologists for taking out of the narrative one slice of time. He was criticizing an ahistorical approach to psychology which forgets the individual, who can only be considered as developing in time; he put a great deal of emphasis, and I thought very effectively, on the narrative. Where I part company with him is that I think it is possible, and not only possible but vital, to detect issues that can be studied with the precision that comes to us through the accumulation of many instances. This need not be done only experimentally. There are other ways of accumulating many instances and studying a process as it systematically varies in ways that would be prohibitively costly if we relied only on the case-study method. In this way we can focus on a particular issue, for example, secret-keeping behavior. Darwin obviously kept a secret for many years, the secret of his theory of evolution. But we have almost no psychology of secret-keeping behavior. It's an interesting subject that can be studied without looking at an entire case study. We can find other methods of studying that problem, and likewise with other issues. One that I have been very much concerned with, have done a certain amount of real experimental

research on, is what I call "taxonomic behavior" as distinct from concept formation and the relatively simple sorting experiments that psychologists do. What
do people do when they are faced with an interestingly complex array of different sorts of things and they undertake the task of creating a system to organize
these different types? In spite of an enormous literature on concept formation,
the literature on what might be properly called taxonomic behavior is amazingly
poor. Now, that's a subject that lends itself beautifully to the laboratory, and to
developmental studies. Of course, the Geneva school of psychology has done a
certain amount of that, but with extremely simple types of materials that don't
key in well with the problems of richness and complexity that I have been stressing here. Such issues, discoverable in the case, can be taken out of their context
of the life history and looked at in another way. This is the combination of
approaches that I find promising. I am sure there are other ways of dealing with
the same general issue that I am raising; I am not proposing one way as some
sort of gospel, the new methodology.

DR. BRIEL: I wanted to comment in respect to Darwinism and then ask
some questions, but really the events of modern biology in the past 10 or 15
years in relation to Darwinism are most significant in that the materialistic substrate of the prophecies which Darwin described is known; that is to say, the
genetic code and modern molecular biology. Now, it seems to me that if one
doesn't speak about that, one runs the risk of using the word, the complexity,
or the term of the complexity and the richness of nature in a somewhat formal-
istic sense. In another sense you can say that the exact opposite is true. That is
to say, the genetic code and the structure of proteins and so on are quite the
same for bacteria as they are for every other species we know.

DR. GRUBER: I don't really know if I am a good enough biologist to comment on that. I don't want to lean on an article in The New York Times, but
just two days ago it reported on a group of physicists talking about the possibility
that the same picture of underlying or fundamental complexity that I was describing for biology might actually apply to fundamental issues in physics. I don't
think the last word could possibly be in yet on molecular biology. I did think
about that very question as you quite properly put it, and I agree with you that
it's a serious problem for the position that I am presenting tonight, and for the
moment I would let my case rest on a relatively simple point: After a couple of
hundred years of honoring complexity and discovering millions of species and
thousands of gene loci in one rather simple organism—with all that clearly in
mind and with theories of evolution and genetics that took account of all this
complexity—we finally arrived at a point where molecular biology could make
the great strides that it has made. When psychology has taken an honest look at
its organism and done its natural history well, and seen it in all its richness and
complexity and moved through a similar historical pathway, perhaps it may
reach a point where it may have its molecular biology. A very distinguished psychologist (whose name I won't mention; he is a good friend of mine, and you
would all know his name, but I should speak for myself), and I argue about this
point. I say 100 years and he says 500 years. I don't know. What's your guess?

DR. TOBACH: Could I interfere for just one moment, because my own
personal bias in science is in the direction that I think Dr. Gruber was going. I think
there are two things about what you are saying that need to be enlarged upon or
brought together, so to speak. One is, is it true that as knowledge progresses
and we come up with principles and generalizations that organize a lot of material,
that suddenly many things fall into place and seem to become simpler? I think

that's what he is talking about. He is talking about Darwin and what Darwin did, and what Fleming and Franklin did when they contributed to our understanding of the genetic code: they provided explanations and new organizations of knowledge about how genetic material gets passed on, which seemed to simplify phenomena. However, I think that the second point is the other part of the dialectic of the increase of knowledge; as you come up with a generalization, or a law, or a principle, you begin to go back and redo much of your thinking. You find that that principle opens up brand new vistas and brand new problems that you didn't even know before. For example, if you pick up a textbook in genetics published in 1950-1962, the relationship between RNA and DNA seems very clear; it's all out there in a diagram. If you pick up the latest journal of the proceedings of the National Academy of Science, you will find that two thirds of the genetics papers are dealing with new-found differences and problems of the relationship between DNA and RNA which we never dreamed of before. Certainly it is difficult to talk about complexity in a generalized way, because there are different kinds of complexities. On the biochemical level, it is really much more complex than we ever thought it was going to be. For this and other reasons, knowing about the code does not make it simpler to deal with Darwin and the evolution of behavior.

DR. GRUBER: I don't want to end up disagreeing with you too much, though, because I am talking about an image of nature, and I don't think that one image of nature suffices as a guide for a scientific life; I think we need a number of images. Darwin needed a number of metaphors to capture the idea of natural selection. The wish for simplicity and harmony and understanding at the level that you are talking about is a positive thing; it's an important part of science not to be scorned, but not to be left alone. It should be coupled with this other kind of image, the one that I have been stressing tonight.

DR. NESTER: This is an overall reaction to the last two days of presentations. In much of your talk and in the talks of other speakers, people have used male-gender pronouns as if these pronouns represented all scientists. Why do you think so learned a society as the organizers of this conference seems to be reactionary in inviting more men than women as speakers?

DR. GRUBER: Do you mean why there were almost no women on the program?

DR. NESTER: There are few women as chairs. The speakers kept referring to scientists as men, except for a few people in the audience mentioning a great-woman theory; I would put it a "great-person theory," but the speakers keep resorting to sexist language. The speakers—not all of them, but many—seem not to incorporate political changes that are going on. In this afternoon's presentation, one of the people who had the distinction of being analyzed by Freud also had the distinction of not being aware of changes in views about homosexuality. Why is there no more integration of political views with science?

DR. GRUBER: I really can't answer that. I could just say that I had noticed the scarcity of women on the program and was concerned about it. I don't know what to do about the pronoun question, the "he or she" question. I think it's a serious one, and we all need lots of education about it. It's good that you did what you just did.

DR. DIAMOND: It is bad, but it's not as bad as it's been made out to be. A few moments ago Dr. Gruber spoke about one matter that recalled to my mind Dr. Henle's mention of the principle of invariance because it was a direct parallel to it. Dr. Henle did make a very distinguished presentation the first morning. I do believe from something I've heard that another very fine woman historian of psychology was invited to participate, but because of other activities that she is involved in, she was not able to be here. We are making slow progress, but it is progress.

DR. TOBACH: Well, since we are all interested in seeing things changed, I guess we all want to change but at a different pace, since we are not all the same. That helps in some way.

DR. RIEBER: There were several women who could not come to the conference because of circumstances beyond their control: Dr. Anna Freud, Dr. Barbara Ross, and Dr. Marilyn Marshall, and, I believe, several others. I am not talking about those who are speakers here, but if you look carefully at who was available, you would find that we missed very few indeed.

DR. TOBACH: Can I put this on the record, since we are talking about American roots of psychology in the United States, and the question has been raised about variation in the sex of the participants. I must confess that I like to look in old books, and I was looking at the first book that Margaret Floyd Washburn wrote because I thought it might have something to do with what we were talking about tonight. For those of us in the audience who are interested in history, Darwin and psychology and what happened in the United States, that book is a subject of very great interest, as is the story of her career as a comparative psychologist and as a member of the psychological profession. One of the things that she talked about at great length in the introduction to her textbook is the question of Darwin's thinking about the continuity between different species of animals, including people, and her very strong and forthright statement about Morgan and what his contribution was in this respect. I think it takes a whole conference to get involved in these other issues as well; it's certainly worthwhile talking about it at some point.

UNIDENTIFIED SPEAKER: At the Eastern Psychological Association in '74 we had a symposium on Christine Franklin, Mary Calkins, and Margaret Osburn and on nineteenth century American women psychologists, and there are quite a few more biographical studies coming out shortly.

DR. GRUBER: It pays to go to psychological meetings as well as to Academy meetings. I would like to mention that it's well to keep in mind, for better or worse, that people develop unevenly in many matters, including these. Darwin, for example, I think deserves what egalitarian people today would consider a clean bill of health on the race question, but his remarks about the equality of women are really somewhat dubious. Although he was not by any means extreme in that regard for his time, and we should make corrections for the historical moment, he would get about a B minus, compared with John Stuart Mill, who was an ardent feminist and deserves an A plus. It was possible then to be more advanced than Darwin was on this question, yet on other matters he was out front, so unevenness of political development is perhaps another example of what I have been talking about all evening.

UNIDENTIFIED SPEAKER: Getting back to the topic of your talk, Dr. Gruber, I expected that you would have much to say about the kinds of thinking that seem to be developing in psychology coming out of the Wilson "Sociobiology" and works of that type. I wonder if you could speak about that. I would like to get your thinking, at least in a little more detail, before the evening ends on that issue.

DR. GRUBER: I was trying to make one central point and obviously ran out of time, anyway, and so I avoided a number of issues that I could have spoken on. I do feel that the rush toward an easy acceptance of the genetic determination of complex social behavior reflects historical currents in American life, in

Western society generally. Other speakers at these meetings have addressed themselves to the subject in a variety of ways. It's one thing to say that altruism, for example, is an adaptive characteristic of a species; it's another thing to say that it's genetically determined. On the first point, adaptive, there's no question. On the second point, to me it's extremely doubtful.

WILLIAM THORNTON, AN EIGHTEENTH CENTURY AMERICAN PSYCHOLINGUIST: BACKGROUND AND INFLUENCE

Jeffrey Wollock

Section on the History of Psychiatry and the Behavioral Sciences
Cornell Medical College
New York, New York 10021

Dr. William Thornton is chiefly remembered as a gifted self-taught architect who drew up the original designs for the United States Capitol building, a man who served for over a quarter of a century as the nation's first superintendent of patents, an early abolitionist, a partner with John Fitch in the development of this country's first functional steamboat, one of the earliest residents of Washington, D.C., and a friend of Jefferson, Rittenhouse, Washington, the Madisons, and other notable figures.

But Thornton was also the author of a treatise on phonetics and orthography entitled *Cadmus*; of an essay on teaching the deaf to speak; and of a vocabulary of the language of the Miami Indians. Although the immediate influence of these works was limited, to be sure, their significance grows when seen against a historical background. Thornton's main concerns were phonology, phonetic orthography, primary reading instruction, teaching of speech to the deaf, and ethnolinguistics. I hope I may therefore be pardoned the anachronism of calling him a psycholinguist. I mean only that he applied himself, at an early date, to subjects now included among the tools and materials of psycholinguistics. Thornton's political and philosophical outlook will also be worth some notice.

Space permits only the briefest biographical outline. Thornton was born on May 20, 1759, of Scottish parents, in a Quaker community on Jost Van Dyke (one of the Virgin Islands). He was educated in England, and studied medicine at the University of Edinburgh (1781-84). He took his M.D. at Aberdeen but never practiced. After first returning to the Caribbean, he arrived in the United States in 1787, and the following year, in Wilmington, Delaware, he became an American citizen. He married in 1790, and three years later, after George Washington approved Thornton's designs for the Capitol, the couple moved to the new federal city. In May 1802 Jefferson appointed Thornton clerk in the State Department in charge of patents, a position he held until his death, at Washington, March 28, 1828. He was survived by Mrs. Thornton, but left no descendents.[1,2]

The title of Thornton's first linguistic paper gives a general idea of its content: *Cadmus, or, a treatise on the elements of written language, illustrating, by a philosophical division of speech, the power of each character, thereby mutually fixing the orthography and orthoepy*. Appended to this is a short "Essay on the mode of teaching the deaf, or surd and consequently dumb, to speak."[3]

Cadmus was the legendary Phoenician king who first taught the alphabet to the Greeks. In proposing a new phonetic alphabet, Thornton takes on the role of an American Cadmus. He makes it immediately clear that what he intends is not an adjunct or tool, but a *replacement*, of standard orthography. *Ipso facto, Cadmus* is a political as well as a philosophical statement; and hence its sometimes aggressive tone.

Because the English language is not "properly written," says Thornton, children have great difficulty learning to read;* and foreigners find it impossible to learn English pronunciation without a teacher.† Furthermore, with hundreds of "savage" languages still untamed by writing, there is need of a standardized alphabet capable of exactly recording native pronunciation. A universal literacy taught according to this system would destroy all nonstandard dialects. And finally, its adoption must aid the American publishing industry in its competition with the British, since foreigners would certainly prefer to know how to pronounce what they are reading.

Next Thornton gives his new alphabet (TABLE 1), followed by a physiological description of all the "simple sounds"—roughly corresponding to what we now call phonemes—of English. He concludes with miscellaneous topics such as the possibility of the construction of a universal language, the origin of language, and new punctuation marks.

The "Essay on the mode of teaching the deaf" is a plan for a practical application of the ideas put forth in *Cadmus*. Thornton saw that his phonetic alphabet, by visually reinforcing the various patterns of motion and disposition of the speech organs, would be a great aid in teaching the deaf.

He begins by suggesting that the deaf child be taught together with a hearing child of his own age. The teacher is to show the formation of each sound with great exaggeration. "The pupil will try to imitate it. He will no doubt make a sound of some sort . . . if that sound be contained in the language you mean to teach him, point immediately to the letter which you find is the symbol, and repeat it so often, that he can neither forget it, nor have any idea of the sound without the symbol, nor of that symbol without the sound." He will learn to distinguish between voiced and unvoiced sounds by feeling the teacher's throat. If he should at any time hit upon the wrong sound, the teacher must point to the symbol for the sound thus erroneously obtained, and go on as if that had been the one intended. Sounds and symbols already learned should be constantly drilled.

Depending upon the age of the child, different methods of directing the speech organs may be tried; he may perhaps feel the teacher's mouth, or the teacher may form the child's mouth to the correct pattern; a mirror should always be handy. Thornton also discusses the difficulty of lip-reading, which is principally that many sounds are produced by similar or invisible articulations. Yet he believes that with assiduous practice the deaf child can learn to pick up sufficient information from those organs which are visible, to make up for those which are

---

*A memorandum in one of Thornton's notebooks (Library of Congress) refers to a note in an unspecifed edition of Madame de Genlis, *Veillées du Château* (1784), "respecting a system of teaching children to read in a very short time, the work called *Quadrille des Enfans, ou Système Nouveau de Lecture*," by an Abbé Berthaud. This book, first published in 1743, had gone into at least seven editions by 1820. The only copy I know of in this country was, unfortunately, inaccessible to me. There is no indication of whether Thornton ever actually saw the book.

†In one of his notebooks Thornton would later record an anecdote respecting Montesquieu, who "after long studying the English language in his closet, hazarded articulating a few words of it, to which when he had frequently repeated them to some indulgent native, he received for answer, 'Beg pardon, sir, but I don't understand French.' " (Quarterly Rev., Boston edit., May 1820, p. 189.)

TABLE 1

CADMUS.

The Characters.

Common		nasal	flopt · sibilant	short
ꓷꓷΛƐIOU YZRLJVꟾW	MNꟽ GBD ꟾꟾƟS	KPꚌ ӨH		
Vowels			Aspirates	

ꬱꓷaeiouyzrljv·w ꝺ mnꟽ gbd ꟾꟾꙅs ꝅpt өh

The following characters are particularly recommended.

ꓷꓷΛꓛIOUYZRLJVꟾꙍm n ꟽꝹꞇpꝼꞃꝺꙅꓘPꚌӨH ·

	Pronounced like,					as in herd,
ꬱ				e		herd,
ꭎ	- - -			a	- - -	law
a	- - -			a	- -	rat
e	- - -			e	- - -	red
i	- - -			i	- -	fit
o	- - -			o	- - -	fog
u	- - -			o	- -	fool
y	- - -			y	- - -	ye
z	- - -			z	- -	zeal
r	- - -			r	- -	red
l	- - -			l	- -	let
j	- - -			g	- -	judge
v	- - -			v	- -	vaft
ꝺ	- - -			th	- -	that
w	- - -			w	- -	wolf
m	- - -			m	- -	met
n	- - -			n	- -	nap
ꟽ	- - -			ng	- -	king
g	- - -			g.	- -	get
b	- - -			b	- -	bat
d	- - -			d	- -	dim
ſ	- - -			ſh	- -	ſhip
f	- - -			f	- -	fit
ꙅ	- - -			th	- -	thin
ꝺ	- - -			ſ	- -	ſet
k	- - -			k	- -	kiſs
p	- - -			p	- -	pen
t	- - -			t	- -	ten
ө	- - -			wh	- -	when
h	- - -			h	- -	hat

not, much as a good stenographer can read his transcriptions despite the lack or similarity of many symbols. Thornton, incidentally, used shorthand himself in his notebooks.

If this new orthography be generally adopted, or at least used in texts for the deaf, the child will simultaneously learn to speak, to understand others, to read, to write, and according to other parts of the method, to draw and to obtain a knowledge of things. Thornton deplores the lack of a truly *philosophic* pronouncing dictionary, and criticizes Sheridan (1780)[4] and his predecessor Kenrick (1773)[5] for indicating many sounds by combinations of letters, or using a single letter for more than one sound. Under his own system "reading would offer an eternal source of improvement in pronunciation, not only to the deaf, but to all."

In conclusion, Thornton affirms his confidence in the value of his method "from the short trials I have made;" though he admits that the sign method is more easily learned. But "speech would be so useful, that it would certainly more than repay the trouble of obtaining it; especially as it would be a mode of facilitating every other requirement."

When Thornton returned from Tortola to Philadelphia in November 1792 he lost no time in submitting *Cadmus* to the American Philosophical Society, in competition for the annual Magellanic gold medal. It was referred to a committee for examination, who reported "that they have perused it, and found it to be a very ingenious and learned performance, proposing many improvements in the science of communicating ideas by visible signs. They are of the opinion that it is perhaps not to be expected that many of these improvements will suddenly be adopted; it may, nevertheless, have the best tendency to introduce gradually, greater perfection in speaking and writing the English language. And, that such encouragement as the Society may think proper to give the Author, will be judiciously bestowed." The medal was awarded and *Cadmus* was duly published in the Society's *Transactions* and in a separate edition.[6,3]

Attempts at a phonetic spelling for English were nothing new even in Thornton's day. As early as 1569 John Hart had published *An Orthographie*, using a purely phonetic system with symbols for five vowels and twenty-one consonants.[7] Others are found in William Bullokar, *A Book at Large* (1580), Alexander Gill, *Logonomia Anglica* (1619), and Charles Butler, *The English Grammar* (1633).[8,9] Thornton knew of Bullokar and Gill, but had not seen their work.

Systematic speech instruction for the deaf likewise already had a long history, going back at least to the time of Pedro Ponce de León (ca. 1520-1584), who taught his pupils not only Spanish and Latin, but sometimes even Italian and Greek. Note, however, that the orthographies of these languages are all much more nearly phonetic than the English. Another Spaniard, Pablo Bonet (d. 1629) based his method on the association of printed letters and sounds.[10]

The more direct ancestry of Thornton's *Cadmus* and "Essay on the Deaf" can be seen in the activities of a number of founding members of the British Royal Society in the second half of the seventeenth century, and certain others well known to them. It is not surprising to find that this powerful intellectual movement, which championed atomism and the mechanical philosophy, should have fostered the reduction of language to its *atoms*, or simple ideas and sounds, the fixing of symbolic notations to them, and a careful investigation of the *mechanics* of vocal production. Space permits no more than the mention of their names: William Holder, Francis Mercury Van Helmont, Bishop John Wilkins (whose *Essay toward a Real Character* Thornton knew), Francis Lodowyck, and the Scot George Dalgarno; all of whom (with the possible exception of Lodowyck) developed methods for teaching the deaf.[11,12]

The immediate antecedents of Cadmus are found in the British "Elocutionary Movement," which began about 1750. At this time, with increasing nationalism spurring the development and standardization of vernacular languages, natural philosophers began to propose new applications of the research done in the previous century. The elocutionists derived their principles, rules, and systems by using the methods of natural philosophy to observe and record actual speech. Out of this they built a program of training in persuasive delivery, producing graduates who knew how to exert mass public influence through Parliament, podium and pulpit.[13-15]

Now one of the most important areas of elocution is correct pronunciation (orthoëpy), and a method of indicating it by writing (orthography). Pronouncing dictionaries had already been attempted by Kenrick and Sheridan, but Thornton and other Americans believed it could be done in a more scientific manner.‡ Furthermore, the United States, unlike Britain, was committed to the idea of mass education, which meant that *reading* would become a public concern as schools were set up to instruct the children of all the people. Finally, as a new and in many ways artificial nation, the United States was thought to be especially in need of a standardized speech, which would promote uniformity, if not unity. Hence we find that *Cadmus* is only one of a number of American orthographic proposals of the time; others are Benjamin Franklin's "Scheme for a New Alphabet and Reformed Mode of Spelling" (written 1768, published 1779);[16] Noah Webster's "Essay on the necessity, advantages and practicability of reforming the mode of spelling, and of rendering the orthography of words correspondent to the pronunciation" (1789);[17] James Ewing's *The Columbian Alphabet, Being an Attempt to New Model the English Alphabet, in such a Manner as to Mark Every Simple Sound by an Appropriate Character* ... (1798); and Thomas Embree's *Orthography Corrected; or, A plan proposed for improving the English Language by uniting Orthography with Pronunciation* ... (1813).

With the exception of Embree's, which had not yet appeared, all of these were mentioned by Peter Duponceau, the dean of American linguists, in his annotations, written about 1808, to the article "Alphabet" in the American edition of the *New Edinburgh Encyclopaedia*,[18] one of the best known reference works of the time.[19]

In *Cadmus*, Thornton wrote, "All the world have to lament that not only the circumnavigators of different nations, but even of the same nation, who make vocabularies of the languages they hear, are so little acquainted with the philosophy of speech, as never to write them alike: indeed the same person cannot read in his second voyage, but with difficulty, what he wrote in the preceding one, with a pronunciation intelligible to a native ..." (Transactions, p. 265)[3] The vocabulary of the Miami Indian language seems to have been a trial application of the new alphabet toward solving this problem. Its intrinsic value as a vocabulary could not have been great, because it nearly duplicated one taken by Count Volney four years earlier. Now this French traveler-philosopher-linguist was a good friend of Thornton's, and stayed at his house whenever he was in Washington.§ Volney had been able to get his long-hoped-for specimen of an American Indian language when William Wells and his father-in-law, Little Turtle, a chief of the Miamis in Indiana, arrived at Philadelphia in the winter of 1797-98. Wells, captured and adopted by Little Turtle at age 13, was fluent in English

---

‡This would also apply, *mutatis mutandis*, to John Walker's great pronouncing dictionary, although Thornton does not seem to have known of the work, which appeared only a year before *Cadmus*, in 1791.

§One of these visits took place in May 1796 (p. 169),[2] another in July 1797.[20] There are many letters from Volney to Thornton extant among the Thornton papers, Library of Congress.

and Miami.¶ Volney spent nine or ten evenings in January-February 1798 taking
down the vocabulary, and it was published in 1803 in an orthography based on
French.[22] Little Turtle and Wells frequently appeared in American cities after
this, and Thornton's 288-word vocabulary was taken at Washington, January 11,
1802, "in part from Little Turtle, but principally from Capt. Wells."[23] It is the
earliest ethnolinguistic sample I know of written in an artificial phonetic alphabet.
Some of the English sounds do not appear in Miami, and Thornton had to invent
a new sign, a crossed h (ħ) for the sound now written [x], like the German gut-
tural ch.

Thornton must have presented this manuscript to Thomas Jefferson, since the
words "communicated by Mr. Jefferson" appear on the title page. The records
of the Philosophical Society confirm this,‖ and it is understandable, for Jefferson had long been interested in Thornton's linguistic work, as we learn from a
letter of June 11, 1793: "Thomas Jefferson, with his compliments to Dr. Thornton returns him many thanks . . . for his dissertation on the elements of language
which he had read in manuscript with great satisfaction, but shall do . . . with
more in print." (p. 159)[2]** Even more to the point, Jefferson spent some thirty
years in collecting Indian vocabularies, eventually bringing together a master-list
of about 250 English words with their equivalents in as many as fifty Indian
languages. He got the idea from a similar massive project carried out in the 1780s
by order of Catherine the Great of Russia.†† Unfortunately, the bulk of Jefferson's work was lost in 1809 when a thief broke into the trunk in which it was
being transported from Washington to Monticello, and dumped it into the river.
A small part was recovered and sent to the Philosophical Society.[26, 27] Despite
this loss, the project had served as a major stimulus to the organized study of
American Indian languages.‡‡

Nor was Jefferson the only ethnologist who admired *Cadmus*. The great
naturalist-explorer Baron Alexander von Humboldt wrote Thornton from Philadelphia, June 20, 1804 (in French): "At Lancaster I read . . . your *Cadmus* . . .
full of new and ingenious ideas. The celebrated Darwin has recently (1804)
treated this same subject of letters and sounds in his poem The Temple of Nature
. . . but your system is quite a bit simpler than his. HUMBOLDT." (p. 170)[2] § §

The erudite Peter Duponceau, later President of the American Philosophical
Society, was another student of Indian languages who had read *Cadmus*, according to his annotation in the *New Edinburgh Encyclopaedia*,¶ ¶ These notes were
later amplified in a monograph, *English Phonology* (1817).[29] At the end of this
work Duponceau makes certain recommendations for a phonetic alphabet: it
should be composed neither of characters in common use, nor of entirely new
signs; perhaps the lower-case Greek with needed additions from the Cyrillic. But

---

¶ According to an estimate, there were in 1961 somewhere between 10 and 100 speakers
of Miami, all in Indiana, most over 50 years of age.[21]

‖ A catalogue of MS works on the Indians and their languages, presented to the Philosophical Society, indicates that copies of both Volney's and Thornton's Miami vocabularies
were presented by Jefferson.[24]

** A note acknowledging receipt of *Cadmus*, dated June 8, 1793, was sent to Thornton
by George Washington, but there is no indication whether he actually read it. (p. 159)[2]

†† *Sravininmel'nye slovar'vsyokh yazykov i naryochili*, etc. The vocabularies were given in
the Cyrillic alphabet with pronunciation guide for foreigners.[25]

‡‡ See a review of the History of American Indian Linguistics by Hoijer.[47]

§ § The references is to Erasmus Darwin, *The Temple of Nature*, additional note XV,
"Analysis of Articulate Sounds" (Baltimore: Bonsal & Niles, 1804), pp. 123-129.

¶ ¶ A MS copybook of Duponceau, labeled "Indian Dialects" (Am. Phil. Soc. Libr., 497
Ind.) contains a Miami vocabulary, not in Thornton's orthography, but in that which
Thornton referred to as "German orthography" (probably that of Rev. John Heckewelder).[28]

this alphabet, whatever the precise form, is "to be used only as an instrument by which to compare, fix and ascertain the pronunciation of words and as a key to pronouncing dictionaries . . . I am very far from wishing to see such an alphabet introduced into common use, to the destruction of our literature, and perhaps, ultimately, the entire corruption of our language." (p. 30) This is poles apart from Thornton's democratic spirit of reform.

When John Pickering, the leading authority of his time on American Indian languages, came to write his *Essay on a Uniform Orthography for the Indian Languages of North America* (1820), he closely followed his good friend Duponceau's guidelines. His alphabet, employing Roman characters with continental values, was designed for practical use in the field, and was arranged in common alphabetical order rather than according to the organic formation of the sounds, like Thornton's. "It never was my plan," says Pickering, "to give a universal alphabet on strict philosophical principles, but merely a practical one, to be applied to the Indian languages of North America." Even before his book was printed, Pickering's system had been adopted by missionaries as the basis of the orthography of Hawaiian.[30, 31]

Count Volney also kept up his interest in phonetics and orthography, and produced *The European Alphabet applied to the Languages of Asia* in 1818.[32] He explains in the preface to this work that his attention to the problem went back to 1795, but it was not until his stay in the United States (1795-98), at which time he had become acquainted with "the treasures of the British literature in Oriental studies," that he had conceived of the possibility of establishing a single system for all the languages. The fact that Volney was addressing these remarks to the Royal Asiatick Society of Calcutta partially accounts for his flattering reference to British publications, in particular the "Dissertation on the Orthography of Asiatick Words in Roman Letters," by Sir William Jones.[33] Evidently Volney did not think it necessary to mention that while in America he had been the frequent guest of a Dr. Thornton, who had written at length upon this very subject but a short time previous. Yet it would be strange indeed if Volney had not read *Cadmus*; stranger still if he had not at least discussed linguistics with Thornton.

As an orthographic reform, *Cadmus* obviously had no more effect than any of the other attempts. It is remarkable, what with the unprecedented innovations in all walks of life over the last two centuries, to which English-speaking countries have so largely contributed, that our orthography, one of the things most constantly in use, has scarcely changed at all. Certainly there has been no lack of attempts. Our eighteenth century American reformers point in the same direction as the English John Thelwall and the Scottish Rev. James Gilchrist, who, reacting to the inequities of the industrial revolution, committed themselves to the democratization of society through the democratization of education. They were all the direct forerunners of the many utopian "phonographic" movements which sprang forth in the late 1830s.|||| The best known of these was led by Isaac Pitman, and it had great influence in this country through his brother Benn Pitman. Its chief legacy, of course, is the Pitman phonetic shorthand, but these movements embraced a whole panoply of revolutionary ideas such as vegetarianism, phrenology, pacifism, and communal living.[9, 15, 34]

In the academic world, the phonetic alphabet, as a necessary tool in the study of language, was gradually perfected. Pitman played an important part here as

|||| As equally of the opinions expressed by George Bernard Shaw in *Pygmalion* (1912).

well, as did Henry Sweet, with his Broad Romic, which became the basis of the International Phonetic Alphabet adopted in 1888. Its development was delayed no doubt pending improvements in transportation and communication which would make possible an international convention of scholars. And its success rested on the separation of this idea from questions of spelling reform in individual countries.

Later work in linguistics has shown the lack of a phonetic, or, more accurately, a phonemic spelling or alphabet, to be only a small part, and not the most important part, of the problem of beginning reading. The act of reading consists in recognizing language signals expressed in patterns of graphic shapes, as skillfully as these same signals are recognized when expressed in auditory patterns. No matter what alphabet is used, this remains the basic difficulty of learning to read.

In 1852 the Pitman-Ellis phonetic alphabet was introduced in 119 public and five private schools in Massachusetts, and in Syracuse, New York in 1858. According to George Farnham, " . . . for a time it was thought that the true method of teaching children to read had been discovered. After a trial of five years, however, it was seen that while pupils learned to read by this method in much less time than usual, and attained a high state of excellence in articulation, their reading was as mechanical as before, and few of them became good spellers. The two systems of analysis, phonic and graphic, had so little in common that permanent confusion was produced in the mind.[35] ***

Thornton's contribution has been most clearly recognized in the field of deaf education. The oral method nurtured in the bosom of the Royal Society was further developed by a later Fellow of that Society, Henry Baker, who set up the first real school for the deaf in Britain in the early eighteenth century. The next important teacher was Thomas Braidwood, who opened a school at Edinburgh in 1760, and moved it to London in 1783.[11, 36] So many pupils were sent there from America that eventually John Braidwood, a grandson well versed in the secret family method, arrived in the United States, to become in 1812 the first regular teacher of the oral method in this country, in Virginia. Perhaps "regular" is not the right word, for although his efforts met with considerable success, John Braidwood had an unfortunate passion for gambling and liquor, which interrupted his teaching and landed him in prison more than once. Rev. John Kirkpatrick, a later associate, was the first native-born American to teach the oral method. After a final break with Braidwood in March 1818, Kirkpatrick carried on alone; but all trace of him is lost after 1819.[37]

Meanwhile the Rev. Thomas Gallaudet had traveled to Europe in 1815 to study methods of teaching the deaf. But because he received no cooperation from the Braidwoods in London, and every bit of courtesy and assistance from the Abbé Sicard in Paris, who used the sign method exclusively, this became the basis of all American instruction for some time to come. Thus, ironically, members of the Braidwood family on both sides of the Atlantic were directly responsible for the disappearance of oral teaching in the United States. This goes far to explain Thornton's lack of influence. His own life does the rest. Thornton was a polymath, and never took the time to promote or refine his method. He was a volcano of ideas: once thrown out, they were on their own.

***Shades of the new math, the new reading, and the other "experimental programs" in education. I wonder whether the people who dream these things up stop to consider that usually what is needed is not a new method, but a more truthful view of the role of education in society; and also that experiments, very often, *do not work*. And when they don't, whole generations are deprived of basic education.

It was only when Melville Bell, coming directly out of the Pitman-Ellis movement, developed his *visible speech*,††† and his brother Alexander Graham Bell began teaching the deaf by means of visible speech at Boston in 1871, that the oral method was revived here. And once Graham Bell began his careful researches into the history of the art, recognition of Thornton was not long in coming: "To Dr. William Thornton," writes Bell in 1900, "we are indebted for the first work upon the education of the deaf, actually written and published in America . . . . Thornton saw very clearly that one great obstacle to the acquisition of speech by the deaf lay in the unphonetic character of our spelling. . . . The Volta Bureau has in contemplation the republication of Thornton's works, so as to render them more accessible to students. They certainly have not received that attention from practical teachers of the deaf that their importance demands."[38] The Essay, at least, was reprinted in a journal in 1917.[39]

Dr. Tweney will have more to say about Thornton's position in the historical development of American psycholinguistics in the 19th century. § § § But I would like now to tie together the various strands of Thornton's writings on language: primary reading instruction, social reform, deaf education, and ethnolinguistics, by referring to that favorite image of Lockean psychology, the *tabula rasa,* or blank slate.

Tabula rasa symbolizes a typically modern approach to problems, of which its specific meaning in psychological theory is but one expression. Wipe the slate clean: another way of saying it is, destroy whatever is left and start over. But particularly attractive to the Enlightenment mind is the situation in which a blank slate can be found, or at least imagined so, in nature, ready made: The child, and through him, the next generation of society; the deaf man who knows nothing of speech; the unwritten language and the "primitive" who speaks it. Thus John Eliot, the seventeenth-century "Apostle to the Indians" and first to translate the Bible into an American language: "My scope is, to write and imprint no other but Scripture principles in the *abrasa tabula scraped board* of these naked people, that they may be in all their principles a choice people unto the Lord alone . . . "[40] A lovely idea, but one, unfortunately, bearing little relation to reality; and it is no coincidence that the Massachusetts tribes he refers to were virtually extinct within a few generations. What happens is that the scientist is so eager to test his theory, the teacher his method, the missionary to save a soul, that it is very often of secondary concern to them whether the slate is really blank or not, while the true nature of such writings as may already be on it hardly concerns them at all. For if they took the trouble to examine it they might find that their new plans were neither needed nor wanted.¶ ¶ ¶

I mention this in connection with one of the most remarkable phonetician-orthographers of his or any other time, George Guess, known as Sequoyah. In 1813 one of our spelling reformers, Thomas Embree, wrote: " . . . such uncivilized nations as now lack the use of letters, as they become peaceable and civilized . . . may be benefitted by having a correct mode of writing first propagated among them . . . And herein our boasted superiority will be degraded by savage civilization, if we continue in our old habit."[42]

†††Visible speech is a graphic system that schematically depicts the actions of the speech organs; it is capable of expressing any sound made by the human voice, even sneezing, snoring, and grunting.

§ § §This annal.

¶ ¶ ¶An exception, striking by its very abnormality, is "the experience of certain nineteenth-century Russian priests who discovered a tribe on the islands of the Bering Sea leading a life so nearly in accord with the Gospel of Christ that the missionaries confessed they had better be left alone."[41]

Strangely enough, he was soon proved right, for while scholars were pondering the best way to represent the simple sounds of English, Sequoyah, an Indian of the civilized Cherokee tribe, applied himself to the same task in respect of his native language (the only language he ever knew). In the year 1809, in Northern Alabama, during the course of a discussion with some other Indians regarding the white man's "talking leaves," Sequoyah expressed the belief that it was neither a divine gift, nor magic, nor imposture, but that the marks on paper stood for words, and that he could invent a way to do the same thing. It took him twelve years, but by 1821, he had a nearly phonetic syllabary of 86 characters. His method had been the same as the elocutionists'. He went to all public gatherings, listening carefully to speeches and conversations. Eventually an English book came his way, and although he could not read it, he set about adapting the letters to his own use, modifying some of them and inventing new forms. What happened next has no parallel in history. Not a schoolhouse was built and not a teacher was hired, but within a few months the syllabary had spread spontaneously to every corner of the Cherokee country. It generally took a native speaker three or four *days* to learn to read, seldom more than a week. A short time later the tribe had obtained a printing press and type, and started a newspaper.[43] ‖‖‖

In the beginning of 1825 John Pickering was at work on a Chereokee grammar, following his own *Essay on Orthography*, with three additional characters. As soon as he heard of Sequoyah's syllabary, he gave up the project, despite the fact that 48 pages had already been printed. (p. 334, 337)[31] Yet the American Missionary Board doggedly continued to insist on the Pickering orthography for years to come, despite the opposition of the Indians and even some of the missionaries. As Sheehan puts it: "An apparently workable system of Indian writing encroached on the exclusivity of English as the necessary precondition for civilized life. Many philanthropists, consequently, kept a distinct reserve in their reaction to Sequoyah's invention." (p. 139)[26]

And just as worldly piety was beginning its transformation into pious worldliness, and we begin to hear from more and more so-called "citizens of the world" about the blessings of Western civilization, so the religious missionary was beginning to change into the political missionary. Only thus can we understand Count Volney's astonishing rhapsody (in the preface to his *European Alphabet*):

> It is not sufficient to have projected a universal alphabet, it is necessary to put it to use . . . our best European books, translated by able interpreters, must be transcribed and printed in this form as well. An outmoded prejudice vainly extols Oriental literature: but good taste and reason attest that no fund of solid instruction nor of positive science exists in its productions: here history is but a recitation of fables, poetry but hyperboles, philosophy but sophisms, medicine but recipes, metaphysics but absurdities; here natural history, physics, chemistry and higher mathematics are scarcely more than names. The spirit of a European can only shrink and waste itself in such a school; it is up to the orientals, Gentlemen, to attend the school of the modern West. The day when the men of Europe shall translate their ideas into the Asian languages with facility, they shall acquire all over this region a decided superiority over the natives in every walk of life: the latter, astonished to hear their languages spoken more purely, read more fluently, written and understood more quickly by strangers than by themselves, will want

‖‖‖Sequoyah's syllabary is not perfectly phonemic, particularly with regard to consonant clusters. It is, however, quite well adapted to the language, is still taught in most of the 59 Oklahoma Cherokee-speaking churches, and is known by a large portion of adults. Total number of Cherokee speakers is well over 10,000.[44]

to know the mechanical instrument of this singular phenomenon: they will end by discussing, by studying our new European alphabet; the older generation will reject it; the younger will adopt it; it will create a healthy schism, and from that moment a great and fortunate intellectual revolution will commence for Asia, a revolution alone capable of regenerating her. (pp. xiv-xvi)[32]

Now, for all the difference between an American farmer and an Indian Brahmin, how far is this from Thornton's idea? "If the orthography of the language were to be corrected, the pronunciation of the scholar, would, by reading alone, be perfectly attained by the peasant and the foreigner; destroying thus, *in the most effectual manner,* all vulgar and local dialects." (His emphasis; p. 279)[3] We talk a lot about the right of property. I suppose a materialistic society does not understand the most important of all, immaterial properties, such as the right of a man to his own culture and his own language, even if it happens to be a bit less convenient to the state.****

It is certain that orthography has great political and psychological overtones. In the late twenties of this century, for example, the Soviets converted the orthographies of all their Asian languages to Roman characters; they had a change of heart in the late thirties and converted them again, this time to Cyrillic.[45] Many of these languages had been written for centuries in Arabic or Mongolian script. It had been possible then for an educated Tadjik, for instance, to correspond with an Afghan or a Persian in a mutually intelligible literary language.[46] The same story of Western expansionism and intellectual shallowness lies behind these seemingly minor changes. Nothing could more effectively cut a culture off from its own history and traditions, while at the same time rendering it defenseless against propaganda and more intellectual-sounding verbiage published in the new alphabet. All this Count Volney well understood.

Now, from the evangelistic point of view, the effort to teach the deaf was a mission no less than, and in precisely the same sense as the bringing of the Bible to the heathen and the illiterate. Hence the epithet applied to Gallaudet: "*missionary* to the deaf." Add the Constitution and the newspaper to the Scriptures, and you have Thornton's position: as Romans 10:17 says, "faith cometh by hearing, and hearing by the word of God." But in fact, the teaching of the deaf *really does* correspond, at least as far as speech is concerned, to the model of the *tabula rasa*. Once the deaf pupil acquires enough speech to see its efficacy, he has a continual incentive to learn. Speech really is natural to man, even if there is no natural reason why a Cherokee ought to turn white, and the deaf child's acquisition of speech only puts him more in touch with his own culture, a world of which he is already a part, but understands very imperfectly.

There are two areas in particular, then, that link Thornton's work most closely with modern psycholinguistics. First, his part in the development of techniques for the accurate recording of unwritten languages, prerequisite to their comparison, classification, semantic and structural analysis; and second, the technique of teaching the deaf to speak, with special emphasis on the relationship between sound, sight, and meaning (the psychology of reading). These are some of the most important tools and materials available to the psycholinguist.

****This is by no means to suggest that folk and street dialects should be given their own written forms. I very much support the idea of a standard written language. Dialects ought to be left to themselves, however.

REFERENCES

1. DICTIONARY OF AMERICAN BIOGRAPHY. Thornton, William.
2. CLARK, A. C. 1915. Doctor and Mrs. William Thornton. Columbia Hist. Soc. Records 18: 144-208.
3. THORNTON, W. 1793. Cadmus. R. Aitken & Son. Philadelphia, Pa. Also in Trans. Amer. Philos. Soc. 3: 262-319.
4. SHERIDAN, T. 1780. A Complete Dictionary of the English Language . . . London.
5. KENRICK, W. 1773. A New Dictionary of the English Language. London.
6. EARLY PROCEEDINGS OF THE AMER. PHILOS. SOC. PHILADELPHIA, PA. 1884.: 209-210.
7. DANIELSSON, B. 1955. John Hart's Works. Almquist & Wiksell. Stockholm.
8. BAUGH. A. C. 1935. A History of the English Language :485-493. Appleton-Century-Crofts, New York, N.Y.
9. ABERCROMBIE, D. 1965. Forgotten phoneticians. In [his] Studies in Phonetics and Linguistics. Oxford Univ. Press. London :45-75.
10. HODGSON, K. W. 1953. The Deaf and Their Problems. Watts & Co. London.
11. MULLETT, C. F. 1971. 'An Arte to Make the Dumbe to Speake, the Deafe to Heare': a Seventeenth-Century Goal. J. Hist. Med. & Allied Sci. 26(2): 123-149.
12. SALMON, V. 1972. The Works of Francis Lodowyck. Longmans. London.
13. FRITZ, C. A. 1930. From Sheridan to Rush: The beginnings of English elocution. Q. J. Speech 16: 75-88.
14. HABERMAN, F. W. 1954. English sources of American elocution. In History of Speech Education in America. K. R. Wallace, Ed.: 105-126. New York, N.Y.
15. HABERMAN, F. W. 1961. John Thelwall: His life, his school, and his theory of education. In Historical Studies of Rhetoric and Rhetoricians. R. F. Howes, Ed. :189-197. Cornell Univ. Press. Ithaca, N.Y.
16. WISE, C. M. 1948. Benjamin Franklin as a Phonetician. Speech Monographs. 15(1): 99-120.
17. FRIEDMAN, L. J. 1975. Inventors of the Promised Land. Random House. New York, N.Y.: 30-40.
18. WHITING & WATSON'S American Edition of the New Edinburgh Encyclopaedia conducted by David Brewster. 1832. Vol. 1: 539-540. New York, N.Y. Earlier editions were published at Philadelphia, Pa. in 1808 and 1813.
19. WALSH, S. P. 1968. Anglo-American General Encyclopaedias; an Historical Bibliography: 41-42. R. R. Bowker Co. New York, N.Y.
20. CHINARD, G. 1923. Volney et l'Amérique :87-89. Johns Hopkins Univ. Press. Baltimore, Md.
21. CHAFE, W. L. 1961. Estimates regarding the present speakers of N.A. Indian languages. Int. J. Amer. Ling. 28(3): 167.
22. VOLNEY, C. P. C. comte de. 1803. Tableau du Climat et du Sol des Etats-Unis d' Amérique. Paris. Vol. 2: 427-431: 525-532.
23. THORNTON, W. 1802. Ms. Amer. Philos. Soc. Library. Philadelphia, Pa.
24. Amer. Philos. Soc. Trans. Hist. & Lit. Comm. 1819. 1: xlix.
25. ADELUNG, F. 1815. Catherinens der Grossen Verdienste um die Vergleichende Sprachenkunde. St. Petersburg: 65.
26. SHEEHAN, B. W. 1973. Seeds of Extinction; Jeffersonian Philanthropy and the American Indian. 55. Univ. North Carolina. Chapel Hill, N.C.
27. WISSLER, C. 1942. The American Indian and the American philosophical Society. Proc. Amer. Philos. Soc. 86(1): 192.
28. HECKEWELDER, J. & P. S. DUPONCEAU. 1819. Correspondence. Trans. Hist. & Lit. Comm. Amer. Philos. Soc. 1: 351-448.
29. DUPONCEAU, P. S. 1817. English Phonology, or An Essay towards an Analysis and Description of the Component Sounds of the English Language. Philadelphia, Pa. Reviewed in Analectic Magazine. 1819: 16-39.
30. WISE, C. M. & W. HERVEY. 1952. The Evolution of Hawaiian Orthography. Q. J. Speech. 38: 314-315.
31. PICKERING, M.O. 1887. The Life of John Pickering: 321-322. Boston, Mass.
32. VOLNEY, C. F. C. comte de 1818. L'Alfabet Européen Applique aux Langues Asiatiques. Didot. Paris.
33. JONES, Sir W. 1788. Transactions of the Asiatick Society. 1: 1-56 Also in The Works of Sir William Jones. 1807. Vol. 3: 253-318. London.
34. ABERCROMBIE, D. 1965. Isaac Pitman. In [his] Studies in Phonetics and Linguistics. Oxford U. P. London: 92-119.

35. FRIES, C. C. 1963. Linguistics and Reading: 240-241. Holt, Rinehart & Winston.
     New York, N.Y.
36. BEST, H. 1943. Deafness and the Deaf: 381. Macmillan. New York, N.Y.
37. BELL, A. G. 1900. Historical notes concerning the teaching of speech to the deaf.
     Ch. 6. Volta Review 2(5): 489-510.
38. BELL, A. G. 1900. Historical notes, etc. Ch. 3. Volta Review 2(2): 113-115.
39. BELL, M. H. G. 1917. Dr. William Thornton and his essay on teaching the deaf.
     Columbia Hist. Soc. Records 20: 225-236.
40. MACLEAR, J. F. 1975. New England and the Fifth Monarchy: The Quest for the
     Millennium in Early American Puritanism. Wm. & Mary Q. 32: 223-260.
41. HANKE, L. U. 1959. Aristotle and the American Indian: 26. Indiana Univ. Press.
     Bloomington, Ind.
42. EMBREE, T. 1813. Orthography Corrected: iv. D. Heartt. Philadelphia, Pa.
43. DAVIS, J. B. 1930. The life and work of Sequoyah. Chronicles of Oklahoma 8: 159-
     162.
44. WALKER, W. 1967. Review of J. Frederick & A. G. Kilpatrick, The Shadow of
     Sequoyah. Int. J. Amer. Ling. 33(1): 82-84.
45. GILYAREVSKY, R. S. & V. S. GRIVNIN. 1970. Languages Identification Guide.
     Nauka, Central Dept. of Oriental Lit.: passim. Moscow.
46. CASTAGNÉ, J. 1928. Le mouvement de latinisation dans les républiques soviétiques
     musulmanes et les pays voisins. Rev. des Etudes Islamiques 2: 559-595.
47. HOIJER, H. 1976. History of American Indian linguistics. *In* Native Languages of the
     Americas. T. A. Sebeok, Ed. 1: 3-22. Plenum Press. New York, N.Y.

AMERICAN PSYCHOLINGUISTICS
IN THE NINETEENTH CENTURY

Ryan D. Tweney

Department of Psychology
Bowling Green State University
Bowling Green, Ohio 43403

Although recent years have seen much effort devoted to the understanding of American psychology in the period prior to publication of William James' (1890) *Principles of Psychology*,[13] it is still too early to feel comfortable with the level of historical understanding that has been achieved. One reason for this lies in the fact that most studies to date have dealt with individual figures or with the development of a particular theoretical position. Research of this sort is valuable and necessary, but it is also necessary to trace particular theories, ideas, and issues over long periods of time and in the work of a number of individuals. In this way, it will eventually be possible to relate the work of particular individuals to the intellectual history of the period and to determine the impact of a particular individual, group, or set of ideas on subsequent history. I would like to attempt an inquiry of this sort by describing some of the characteristics of early American thought on the nature of language and on the relation of language to mind. I have not tried to be exhaustive or to prepare anything like a definitive account. Further, most of the work described here was produced during the first half of the nineteenth century. In spite of these limitations, I think it is possible to identify some of the most salient characteristics of psycholinguistic inquiry during the period in question.

I have chosen a small group of men who devoted a large amount of effort to the problem of language, and I will try to bring out those themes and concerns which characterize each. The selection of figures is, of course, somewhat arbitrary. Yet each one will highlight some characteristic that I believe to be reasonably general. Each is something like an "ideal type" in the characteristic chosen for analysis, and each could be related to other, similar figures.

Does it make sense to speak of "American psycholinguistics" during this period? Certainly the term psycholinguistics was never used. Yet a fair amount of inquiry was devoted to the problem of language and to attempts to understand its relation to the operations of mind. In this sense, American mental philosophy shared an interest with contemporary European thought, as well as a dominant concern of eighteenth century inquiry on mind.[11, 19] In particular, the question of how words could represent ideas, the importance of which emerged clearly in Locke's *Essay Concerning Human Understanding*,[21] served to structure much of the inquiry on language in English language philosophy during the eighteenth and nineteenth centuries. This was especially true in America where, as we shall see, Locke's concern with language was retained (even if his specific analysis was radically simplified). Today, this question would be seen as one involving theories of psychological semantics[17, 22] whereas recent psycholinguistic research has focused as much on the combinatorial properties of language, with a strong tendency to construct semantic theories consistent with syntactic models. For this reason, we cannot apply a modern yardstick to the earlier period. If we do, the work simply looks naïve.

Even so, genuine questions were involved, and some of the work turned up some surprising and delightful insights into the nature of language. Even where this was not the case, however, it is important to understand how language was conceptualized and which of its characteristics was considered important for psychology.

THE ROLE OF LANGUAGE IN PSYCHOLOGICAL THEORY

Let us begin with two figures whose principal goal was the construction of comprehensive psychological systems. Thomas C. Upham (1799-1872), who is well known for his 1840 *Elements of Mental Philosophy*,[33] was not specifically interested in questions concerning language. He is, however, very much within the realist tradition which runs from Locke through Reid and Stewart and, thence, to a number of American mental philosophers. As such, he was aware of the importance of language for an understanding of man's cognitive functioning. Yet his analysis tends to be disappointing when measured against that of his British predecessors. For Locke, for instance, the emergence of abstract ideas was tied to linguistic operations in that names served as a kind of tangible handle around which the attributes of an abstract concept could be constructed (cf. Locke,[21] Book III, and the accounts of Noyes[22] and Kelemen[17]). Dugald Stewart extended the analysis even further by showing that combinations of words within sentences could produce specific, new meanings of either a concrete or an abstract sort.[28, 32] Upham must have been aware of these analyses, so it is surprising that he made no use of them. The account of abstract ideas in Chapters 12 and 13 of Volume 1 of the 1840 work takes no notice of the important connection to language. Abstraction is instead explained as the result of the mind's "original tendency or susceptibility, by means of which, whenever we perceive different objects together, we are instantly without the intervention of any other mental process, sensible of their relation in certain respects"[33] (p. 190). Upham follows this with a brief discussion of the Nominalist/Realist controversy, providing a long quote from Thomas Brown that does not speak to the issue of the role of language as such. One gets the feeling that Upham ducked the issue.

Volume II of the same work contains a long "Appendix on Language," which is no more satisfactory. Upham there addresses himself to the problem of the origin of language, approaching the issue in good eighteenth century fashion. The existence of "natural signs" and gestural languages precedes oral languages; oral languages evolve from cries and shouts and gradually became more complex; writing systems evolve very late; and, as a consequence of the evolutionary history of language, national characteristics leave their mark on the forms of speech. All of the arguments are derivative (Condillac being cited frequently), examples are few, and, in general, the account is below par for this otherwise well thought-out, careful text.

A substantially different impression is produced by another American work also written in 1840, Frederick A. Rauch's *Psychology, or, A view of the human soul; Including anthropology*.[23] Rauch (1806-1841) was the president of Marshall College in Pennsylvania and the author of the first American book to bear the word "Psychology" in the title.[25] Educated in Germany, Rauch was one of the first proponents of Hegelianism in American mental philosophy. His book is heavily influenced by Hegel, by Kant, and by other representatives of the German academic tradition, though he acknowledges also a strong debt to Locke, Reid, and Stewart. For this reason, Townsend[31] has characterized him as a "Hegelian Realist." Rauch's analysis, like Upham's, centers language within psychology. Unlike Upham's however, his treatment of language is strikingly sophisticated by modern standards. This is so largely because he relied extensively on Humboldt's theory of language, one of the first statements of the systemic nature of language. Since much of contemporary linguistic and psycholinguistic theory fits neatly into a Humboldtian framework, it is relatively easy to appreciate Rauch's treatment (cf. Blumenthal[3] and Chomsky[6]). But close reading reveals some interesting peculiarities.

The problem of the origin of language concerns Rauch, as it did Upham. Rauch's analysis unites the power of reason with the power of language—they are different manifestations of the same mental capability. Man could not, therefore, have invented language. On the other hand, God could not simply have endowed man with language, since this is not compatible with the identity of language and true reason. It follows that "God gave man a power, that in developing itself, would necessarily with itself develop language"[23] (p. 256). Why is there such a diversity of languages, if each manifests a universal reason? Because "Reason, though essentially one in its laws and nature, is nevertheless, modified by its connection with body, the constitution, and through it with climate, as has been seen in Anthropology [i.e., earlier in the book]"[23] (p. 257).

Rauch presents a curious argument in favor of a notion of sound symbolism. British empiricism, and most of the American mental philosophers, had emphasized the arbitrary relationship between the sound of words and the things represented by words. Rauch postulates an intrinsic relationship between the two, citing the physicist E. F. F. Chladni's discovery of the unique resonance pattern produced on a metal plate made to vibrate by a violin bow drawn across the edge. In an analogous fashion, each thing in the world has a characteristic sound, which is imitated by the sound of its name: "Words are either more or less correct, more or less happy imitations of the sounds that are peculiar to the phenomena indicated by them, and as everything expresses its nature by single sounds, according to which man names it, man in his language expresses the true Being of all that exists"[23] (p. 262). A similar kind of universality underlies grammatical processes—both the elementary parts of speech (nouns, verbs, adjectives, etc.)—and the general nature of sentences are common to all languages, although this idea is, unfortunately, not pursued in detail.

Rauch's account recognized also that a complete theory of language needed to be based upon a "processing model" of sentence analysis. This recognition emerges in his account of memory: "That activity, which finds for every general conception or thought the appropriate word, and recognizes in every word the conception it contains"[23] (p. 268). This activity occurs instantaneously, during the production and understanding of language. Certainly this is one of the earliest recognitions of the importance of what we would now call semantic encoding processes.

TREATISES ON LANGUAGE

So far, we have looked at works that were primarily intended as comprehensive systems of psychology and that considered language as only one topic among many. There were, however, several attempts to develop more comprehensive theories of language and language use. The earliest and most notable of these is William Thornton's (1759-1828) *Cadmus; or, a treatise on the elements of written language* . . . (1793).[29] Since Thornton has been considered at length by Wollock in this conference, it is not necessary to present a detailed analysis. It is, however, worth examining Thornton's concern with the problem of a universal language, a fairly common preoccupation during the period we are considering.

Thornton had read the work of John Wilkins, the seventeenth century British clergyman who attempted to devise a completely systematic "philosophical language," a kind of linguistic code that would cut nature at nature's joints, so to speak.[35] The attempt failed, and we now know that no such language is possible because there is no clear way in which nature can be segmented into the requisite sharply defined categories. Yet Wilkins was an important figure in nineteenth century American thought. There were many attempts to form such a language,[26] and a number of European attempts were imported and described in various publications by American proponents.[20] In a sense, the prevalence of such systems reflects the relative naïvete of the American tradition in language. Wilkins is conceptually, as well as chronologically, a pre-Lockean figure in that Locke's analysis of language can be used to show the impossibility of Wilkins' endeavor. The continuing American susceptibility to such schemes thus reflects the same inadequate appreciation of Locke that we saw in Upham.

It would not do to leave the matter there, however; Thornton's work did not result in a universal language, but he did contribute to the development of an alphabet useful in instructing the deaf to speak (a result of his attempts to devise a universal alphabet) and, more generally, to the development of an understanding of the role of the vocal articulators in speech. This, too, is a traditional theme during the period in question and can be seen especially in the work of James Rush (1786-1869), whose 1827 *Philosophy of the Human Voice*[27] presented a unique analysis of speech using musical notation—a scheme that permitted some excellent description of intonational phenomena. The phonological concern culminates with the work of Alexander Melville Bell (1819-1905) on phonology,[1] and that of his son, Alexander Graham Bell (1847-1922), on deaf education.[4] It is interesting to note that the elder Bell was also interested in the universal language problem, though in a more sophisticated sense. In a pamphlet published in 1888,[2] he advocated the use of English as a world language. His argument was based on pragmatic considerations, not on the need for a philosophical "real character." Bell was thus able to avoid the oversimplifications of Thornton's position while preserving the impulse toward universality.

William Samuel Cardell's (1780-1828) *Essay on Language* was published in 1825.[5] The book is a brief grammatical treatise of little orginality. It is worth considering here because Cardell exemplifies a unique kind of American praticality that emerges in a number of the works produced in this period. Cardell's goal was to describe language in terms of general principles, to show the underlying simplicity of those principles, and to describe them in a way that would make a useful, learnable whole. He brings to the task an interesting kind of skepticism: "As far as possible the regions of mere conjecture will be avoided. To Lord Monboddo and the learned Dr. Wilkins may be left the fine-wrought theories, respecting the first name which an untutored savage would give to bread; or what a language might be made by a nation of philosophers, taking it from its elements. These are suppositions which can never be brought to the test of experiment"[5] (p. 6). Cardell is more interested in practical questions, in questions that can be answered, and, in particular, to "the intimate connexion between ideas and words"[5] (p. 3). While his skepticism leads him to reject the major contemporary European works on language, he cites Dugald Stewart favorably, quoting from Stewart's 1810 *Philosophical Essays*.[28] Cardell's position is clearly realist and clearly centered in educational goals.

In spite of a good beginning, however, Cardell's book is too brief to be of much use. It is filled with promising beginnings that are never fulfilled. For example, consider the following passage: "One of the great defects of many writers on grammar, seems to be the want of proper distinction between the effect which words may have, by their relation and use in a sentence, and that which results only from the specific import of the single word. The classification of the different parts of speech depends, not on the *absolute meaning* of words, but their *manner of meaning*"[5] (p. 41). And that is all he provides for us on this topic; the implied analysis is never pursued.

Whereas Cardell must be considered a realist along with Upham, Charles Kraitsir (1804-1860) worked along lines that resemble the effort of Frederick Rauch. Kraitsir's 1852 *Glossology*[18] shares, with Cardell, a distrust of the way language is being taught in the schools. Yet Kraitsir derives his inspiration from Humboldt and from the scientific tradition of German physiology. Kraitsir, a physician, refers at one point to "my teacher Blumenbach"[18] (p. 30), the great physiologist who argued that the different races of man represented varieties of the same species. Kraitsir applies a similar notion to speech. The correct approach to an understanding of language will lead to recognition of "the germs of one common speech"[18] (p. 20). Kraitsir's description of the unity of mind, voice, and object is strikingly like that of Rauch, as are the references to Humboldt. Kraitsir's treatise is distinguished by a strident attack on rote methods of spelling instruction and by perhaps the most amazing prose style found during this period. Speaking of spelling instruction, for instance, he says, "Not hecatombs, but millions of English children fall holocausts to the idol of falsehood, enthroned on the teacher's desk"[18] (p. 23). Obviously, Kraitsir had none of Cardell's admirable enthusiasm for simplicity and clarity!

An interesting semantic theory is presented in the *Essay on Language* of Rowland Gibson Hazard (1801-1888). This work was first published pseudonymously in 1835[8] but was reissued a number of times, notably in 1856[9] and in 1889.[10] Hazard contrasted the "language of ideality" with the "language of abstraction." The former was closely related to images and sensations in a way that could be fully attained only in poetry. Abstraction, which was necessary for rational discourse, actually represented something derived and very different from reality. The language of ideality keeps the perception of objects at the forefront of consciousness, whereas the language of abstraction focuses on terms that are divorced from the objects of perception. In rational discourse, constraints of a cold, logical, unfeeling sort were used to eliminate the more direct, more valid "process of ideality," by which he seems to mean something like the succession of images and associations found in the stream of consciousness. Hazard sought a way to represent the stream of consciousness in words and devalued everything else.

Hazard concluded from his analysis that the language of ideality was better suited for serious inquiry. In particular, when poetry was more advanced and better able to capture the underlying "process of ideality," then a true science of mind would become possible. It should even be possible to eliminate the language of abstraction altogether. If the faculty of attention is sufficiently disciplined, then it should be possible to direct attention "only to those characteristics which belong to all the species"[10] (p. 46), and the use of terms can be dispensed with. Intellectual inquiry will be more efficient because it will then be immediate rather than mediate: "In the processes of ideality, the mind deals with the actual existences of the material or intellectual world, which present themselves with all their natural and widespread associations. In verbal reasoning it deals with words, and the limited, arbitrary associations, which form their definitions"[10] (p. 91). It is interesting to note that the call for a more poetic discourse was answered, at least in part, by the emergence of a kind of stream-of-consciousness technique in novels like *The Rise of Silas Lapham* by William Dean Howells.[12]

Hazard should, I think, be located within the realist tradition, in spite of the unique conclusions he has drawn from his analysis. The process of ideality is very similar to the notion of "primitive perception" developed by the Scottish philosopher Thomas Reid. The distrust of language is Lockean, though the conclusion differs. Thus, in spite of his romanticism, in spite of the call for a more poetic discourse—which sounds like the very antithesis of realism—Hazard's approach and his assumptions place him firmly within the emerging American realism.[7, 31]

ALEXANDER BRYAN JOHNSON (1786-1867)

I have reserved a separate section for Johnson because he produced the most original, most sophisticated, and most complete analysis of language to appear during the nineteenth century. Born in England, Johnson emigrated to the United States in 1801, settling in Utica, New York. Entering the banking profession, he was quite successful and is remembered for his books and pamphlets on economics and on political questions. He was also avocationally interested in philosophy, publishing a number of books on language, mental philosophy, and theology.

Johnson's philosophical work received very little notice during his day (see Rynin's Introduction,[15] pp. 1-23), although he is quoted very favorably in a work by Edward Johnson published in London in 1842.[16] A. B. Johnson was "rediscovered" by Stillman Drake in 1938 and his work on language has since been the topic of considerable interest among philosophers. An excellent critical edition of Johnson's major work, the 1836 *Treatise on Language*,[14] has been published under the editorship of David Rynin.[15] Rynin also provides a useful critique of Johnson's system, comparing it to that of Wittgenstein. Finally, a centennial conference was held in 1967 in Utica, and the papers delivered at that conference have also been published.[30]

Of the thinkers we have discussed, Johnson is the only one who thoroughly and systematically developed a theory of language. There is little that is derivative in his work, in contrast to the work of, say, Cardell, although his citations indicate that he was familiar with Locke, Hume, Reid, Stewart, and Thomas Brown, as well as with contemporary physical science. Johnson was not a realist, however, but a nominalist or, better, an operationalist. He foreshadows the developments in analytical philosophy of the early twentieth century (see Rynin[15] and the paper by Max Black[30]). More to the point, his analysis of language led him to a view of science that was nearly identical to that adopted by American behaviorism in its later stages.

Johnson's theory is based on the proposition that the use of words in philosophical and scientific analysis has led to an enormous amount of absurd discussion, since words and the things they represent are so frequently confused. As a result, "We make language the expositor of nature, instead of making nature the expositor of language"[15] (p. 59). The correct view, says Johnson, is to realize that everything we know is based on sense experience, on "sights and feels," and that words are meaningful only insofar as they are based on these elementary experiences.

This straightforward empirical view is sternly applied to a large number of issues, with some interesting results. Thus, "Two men, who assent to the same general proposition, may possess very diverse meanings . . . . If I assert that George is good, you may assent. Under this verbal identity, I may refer to actions of George that are unknown to you; and you may refer to actions unknown to me"[15] (p. 91). Thus, words can acquire a kind of dangerous independence from reality without the fact of that independence being apparent. The same thing can happen in reasoning: "Words, divested of signification, may still be employed in all the processes of logick. Zeno's paradox respecting motion is an example of the inanity to which we may arrive by the . . . misuse of language . . . It affirms, that whilst Achilles passes over this millionth part of a mile, the tortoise moves on the hundred millionth part of a mile. This is a name without any corresponding existence in nature, hence the sophistry and quibble. The last step [in the argument] is absurd, not from any defect of logick, but because the words are become divested of signification"[15] (pp. 99-100).

Johnson's quarrel is not with logic as such: "When a logician tells me the conclusion to which he is arrived by any process of argumentation, I seldom care to investigate his arguments. I assume that he will not make a false deduction, any more than the tradesman will make a false addition. The part which requires examination is the logician's premises"[15] (p. 190). The premises of an argument are where the relationship to sensible signification (or the lack of it) are to be located. The point is extended to theories, leading to an interesting early recognition of the role of hypothetical constructs in science: "A theoretical agent is something which is only supposed to exist"[15] (p. 226). Further, "If we keep in view this distinction between theoretical agents and the realities of nature, we shall at once discover the absurdity of continuing the employment of theoretical agents beyond the uses which they subserve to science"[15] (p. 227). Johnson had thus achieved a strikingly modern, instrumentalist view of the nature of science. He correctly saw the importance of disconfirmation in science: "When a theory, in some of its results, conflicts with our experience, the theory is usually abandoned"[15] (p. 235). Similarly, he saw the importance of testability as one of the criteria of a good theory: "The wise and the simple, the learned and the ignorant, propound questions without knowing what will constitute a solution; and investgate nature without knowing when to be satisfied"[15] (p. 238).

This criterion, and the necessity of sensible signification, leads to an expression of pessimism about the possibility of psychological theories: "How does memory perform its operations? Before we answer the question, we should ascertain whether the answer must be a theory or a revelation of nature. If the answer is to be a revelation of nature, the mute developments of our experience yield the only correct answer. Words can refer us to these developments; but the moment they attempt more than such a reference, we are theorizing . . . Locke . . . speaks of memory as an agent that runs about the brain in search of faded impressions; like a lackey in search of a mislaid umbrella. The analogies . . . evince the usual unacquaintance with the distinction which exists between an inquiry after a theory, and inquiry after the realities of nature"[15] (pp. 261-262). The reference in the above to the "mute developments of our experience" is reminiscent of Hazard's infatuation with poetic expression. Such expressions would be subject to the same criticisms applicable to any other use of language and would not, for Johnson, solve the problem.

Finally, I would like to call attention to Johnson's way of dealing with sentences. Following his consideration of theories, he generalizes the point by applying the same considerations to questions in ordinary discourse. "A question which the senses cannot answer is insignificant"[15] (p. 242). Further, "It is insignificant because we can frame no question that will not, in its terms, relate to sensible information; and secondly, because we possess no means of knowing any thing of the external universe but what our senses reveal"[15] (p. 251). While no formal account is pursued, it is clear that Johnson is here touching on the nature of presuppositions and the role of presuppositions on the interpretation of sentences. It is true, as Rynin remarks in a critical essay[15] (p. 387), that Johnson did not pursue a sentence-level theory. It is unfair, however, to state that he ignored the problem, since it is so clearly implicated in the above passages.

Limitations of space prohibit more than a very brief sketch of Johnson's system. He is in many respects a nominalist, although the starting point of his analysis lies in the realist conceptions of Reid and Stewart. It should be apparent that the work has a modern ring and that there is nothing half-hearted or incomplete about Johnson's pursuit of the implications of his theoretical system. In fact, the analysis strikes the modern reader as so compelling that one wonders why it had so little influence during its day. There are no followers of A. B. Johnson in nineteenth century America, and it is tempting to attribute this to the very sophistication that makes his work attractive today.

CONCLUSION

In the introduction, a question was raised about the usefulness of referring to "American psycholinguistics" during the previous century. I would like to pose the question again and to reconsider this issue, by way of summary.

Two broad perspectives were manifest in the works surveyed. One, which oriented itself around realist conceptualizations, emphasized the connection between language and objects or between language and mental events. Adherents of this view tended to mistrust theory (Cardell, Johnson) and sometimes oversimplified the issues (Upham, Hazard). Further, none of this group manifested much awareness of the central role of sentences in language. Cardell never developed his system far enough and Johnson, though he did take up the problem of propositional meaning and of questions, failed to see the central role of combinatory processes in language. Hazard and Upham ignored the issue altogether. We can, therefore, consider this group to have developed only the beginnings of a true psychology of language.

The second perspective is seen in the works of Rauch and Kraitsir. They are more aware of the European tradition of language studies, and both provide a Humboldtian conception of the systemics of language. Rauch was not primarily interested in language, however, while Kraitsir was so concerned with educational reform that systematic treatment was given only to word-level processes. Again, only the beginnings of a psycholinguistics can be identified.

The phonological tradition exemplified by Thornton, Rush, and the Bells is certainly credible as part of a science of language. But this is a specialized, though important, area of psycholinguistics. Furthermore, the interest in phonological processes was driven by the nonpsychological and generally naïve impetus toward universal language schemes, as well as by purely practical concerns. It did not have much to do with a desire to understand the nature of language as such.

On the whole, then, we must characterize the period as one relatively lacking in good accounts of language. The occasional flashes of insight, and especially the outstanding achievements of Johnson, contrast sharply with the prevailing superficiality of the remaining work. In any case, such insights were not followed up.

Even so, there clearly was a characteristically "American" approach to the problem of language, and it is tempting to extrapolate it into the early years of the twentieth century. In fact, the same lack of concern with combinatorial processes can be seen in behaviorist accounts of language (e.g., Watson[34]) as was manifest in, say, Cardell. Just as Johnson's operationism clearly foreshadows behaviorist formulations of the nature of theory, many of the thinkers I have discussed foreshadow the kind of semantic theory that would come to be characteristic of behaviorist accounts. Here, as in other domains of the history of psychology, it may turn out that the unique American approach originated on these shores long before William James returned in 1883 with news of the fantastic progress being made by the European laboratories.

REFERENCES

1. BELL, A. M. 1867. Visible Speech: The Science of Universal Alphabetics; or Self-interpreting Physiological Letters, for the Writing of all Languages in One Alphabet. Inaugural edit. Simpkin, Marshall and Co. London, England.
2. BELL, A. M. 1888. World-English; The Universal Language. N.D.C. Hodges. New York, N.Y.
3. BLUMENTHAL, A. L. 1970. Language and Psychology: Historical Aspects of Psycholinguistics. John Wiley & Sons. New York, N.Y.
4. BRUCE, R. W. 1973. Alexander Graham Bell and the Conquest of Solitude. Little, Brown and Co. Boston, Mass.
5. CARDELL, W. S. 1825. Essay on Language, as Connected with the Faculties of the Mind, and as Applied to Things in Nature and Art. Charles Wiley. New York, N.Y.
6. CHOMSKY, N. 1966. Cartesian Linguistics: A Chapter in the History of Rationalist Thought. Harper & Row. New York, N.Y.
7. FAY, J. W. 1939. American Psychology Before William James. Rutgers University Press. New Brunswick, N.J.
8. HAZARD, R.G. 1835. Language; Its Connexion with the Present Condition and Future Prospects of Man. By a Heteroscian. Marshall, Brown, & Co. Providence, R.I.
9. HAZARD, R. G. 1857. Essay on Language, and Other Papers. E. P. Peabody, Ed. Phillips, Sampson & Co. Boston, Mass.
10. HAZARD, R. G. 1889. Essay on Language and Other Essays and Addresses. C. Hazard, Ed. Houghton, Mifflin & Co. Boston, Mass.
11. HOWELL, W. S. 1971. Eighteenth-Century British Logic and Rhetoric. Princeton University Press. Princeton, N.J.
12. HOWELLS, W. D. 1885. The Rise of Silas Lapham. Ticknor & Co. Boston, Mass.
13. JAMES, W. 1890. The Principles of Psychology. 2 vols. Henry Holt & Co. New York, N.Y.
14. JOHNSON, A. B. 1836. A Treatise on Language: or The Relation Which Words Bear to Things, In Four Parts. Harper & Brothers. New York, N.Y.
15. JOHNSON, A. B. 1947. A Treatise on Language. D. Rynin, Ed. University of California Press. Berkeley, Calif.
16. JOHNSON, E. 1842. Nuces Philosophicae; Or, The Philosophy of Things as Developed from the Study of the Philosophy of Words. Simpkin, Marshall & Co. London.
17. KELEMEN, J. 1976. Language Sciences 40: 16-24.
18. KRAITSIR, C. 1852. Glossology: Being a Treatise on the Nature of Language and on the Language of Nature. Author. New York, N.Y.
19. KUEHNER, P. 1944. Theories on the Origin and Formation of Language in the Eighteenth Century in France. Doctoral dissertation. University of Pennsylvania. Philadelphia, Penn.
20. LINDERFELT, K. A. 1888. Volapük, An Easy Method of Acquiring the Universal Language Constructed by J. M. Schleyer. C. N. Caspar. Milwaukee, Wisc.
21. LOCKE, J. 1690. An Essay Concerning Humane Understanding. For Thomas Basset. London.
22. NOYES, H. 1976. John Locke's Theory of Language. Paper presented at the 84th Annual Convention of American Psychological Association. Washington, D.C.
23. RAUCH, F. A. 1846. Psychology, or, A View of the Human Soul; Including Anthropology, Adapted for the Use of Colleges. 4th edit. M. W. Dodd. New York, N.Y.
24. RILEY, W. 1915. American Thought: From Puritanism to Pragmatism and Beyond. Henry Holt & Co. New York, N.Y.
25. ROBACK, A. A. 1952. History of American Psychology. Library Publishers. New York, N.Y.
26. RUGGLES, J. 1829. A Universal Language, Formed on Philosophical and Analogical Principles; Having Claims Founded on the Clearness of its Combinations—The Simplicity of its Construction—The Uniformity and Invariableness of its Rules—and, Especially, The Facility and Speed With Which it can be Acquired, of Being Universally Adopted by the Civilized World. M'Calla & Davis. Cincinnati, Ohio.
27. RUSH, J. 1900. The Philosophy of the Human Voice: Embracing its Physiological

History; Together with a Set of Principles, By Which Criticism in the Art of Elocution May Be Rendered Intelligible, And Instruction, Definite and Comprehensive.
To which is Added a Brief Analysis of Song and Recitative. The Library Co. of Philadelphia. Philadelphia, Pa.

28. STEWART, D. 1810. Philosophical Essays. George Ramsay & Co. Edinburgh, Scotland.
29. THORNTON, W. 1793. Cadmus; or, A Treatise on the Elements of Written Language,
Illustrating By a Philosophical Division of Speech, the Power of Each Character,
Thereby Mutually Fixing the Orthography and Orthoepy—With an Essay on the
Mode of Teaching the Surd or Deaf, and Consequently Dumb, to Speak. R. Aitken
& Son. Philadelphia, Pa.
30. TODD, C. L. & R. T. BLACKWOOD, Eds. 1969. Language and Value. Proceedings of
the Centennial Conference on the Life and Works of Alexander Bryan Johnson.
Greenwood Publishing Corp. New York, N.Y.
31. TOWNSEND, H. G. 1934. Philosophical Ideas in the United States. American Book
Co. New York, N.Y.
32. TWENEY, R. D. 1974. Dugald Stewart's "Psycholinguistics." Paper presented at the
82nd Annual Convention of American Psychological Association. New Orleans, La.
33. UPHAM, T. C. 1841. Elements of Mental Philosophy, Embracing the Two Departments
of the Intellect and the Sensibilities. 2 vols. Harper & Brothers. New York, N.Y.
34. WATSON, J. B. 1914. Behavior: An Introduction to Comparative Psychology. Henry
Holt & Co. New York, N.Y.
35. WILKINS, J. 1668. An Essay Towards a Real Character, and a Philosophical Language.
For S. Gellibrand & J. Martyn. London, England.

ON CARTESIAN LINGUISTICS

John Sullivan

New York University
New York, New York 10003

University of Utah
Salt Lake City, Utah 84112

THE CONTROVERSY OVER CARTESIAN LINGUISTICS

The central doctrine of Cartesian linguistics is that the general features of grammatical structure are common to all languages and reflect certain fundamental properties of the mind. It is this assumption which led the philosophical grammarians to concentrate on *grammaire générale* rather than *grammaire particulière* . . . the study of universal conditions that prescribe the form of any human language is "*grammaire générale.*" Such universal conditions are not learned; rather they provide the organizing principles that make language learning possible, that must exist if data are to lead to knowledge. By attributing such principles to the mind as an innate property, it becomes possible to account for the quite obvious fact that the speaker of a language knows a great deal that he has not learned.

> Noam Chomsky
> *Cartesian Linguistics,* pp. 59-60.

Professor Chomsky has significantly set back the history of linguistics. . . . I do not see that anything at all useful can be salvaged from Chomsky's version of the history. That version is fundamentally false from beginning to end. . . .

> Hans Aarsleff, "The History of
> Linguistics and Professor Chomsky,"
> In *Language,* Vol. 46, No. 3, 1970.

I prefer to think that Chomsky's rendering of continental European rationalism is "fundamentally true."

> Father John W.M. Verhaar, S.J.,
> "Philosophy and Linguistic Theory,"
> *Language Sciences,* 1971.

If historically there had been a Cartesian linguistics, with major exceptions, it probably would have been something similar to what Chomsky proposes.

> John Sullivan, 1974

Both Descartes and Chomsky share a magnificent set of talents, one of which is the capacity for strong statements of opinions counter to contemporary scientific and philosophical paradigms. The result is that both had a talent for being embroiled in controversies. Throughout his life Descartes was dogged with controversies, and thirteen years after his death the *Congrégation de l'Index* (on November 20, 1663) condemned his *Meditations.* Similarly, Chomsky has a flair for polemics, and his *Cartesian Linguistics* has precipitated a mild controversy about the facts and interpretations of seventeenth century philosophy, linguistics, and by implication, cognitive psychology in the general rationalistic and empiricistic traditions. The above quotations indicate the basic Chomsky interpretation of Cartesian linguistics, a strong negative reaction by Hans Aarsleff, a moderating comment by Father John W. M. Verhaar, and my general evaluation of the issues involved.

In this paper I shall try to indicate the sense in which Cartesian linguistics is in the rationalistic tradition. This will require a minor qualification of Chomsky's interpretations of Descartes' theory of mind. I shall try also to show that to account in general for linguistics, Descartes, in rejecting as central a radical empiricistic doctrine and a middle-position Aristotelian epistemology, took a Platonic alternative which he later qualified.

CHOMSKY'S DISCLAIMERS

Cartesian Linguistics is a Whig* history. Chomsky's general disclaimer is as follows:

> I will limit myself here to something less ambitious [than a history of linguistics], namely, a preliminary and fragmentary sketch of some of the leading ideas of Cartesian linguistics with no explicit analysis of its relation to current work that seeks to clarify and develop these ideas. . . . (p. 2)

> Questions of current interest will, however, determine the general form of this sketch; that is, I will make no attempt to characterize Cartesian linguistics as it saw itself, but rather will concentrate on the development of ideas that have reemerged, quite independently, in current work . . . (p. 2)

> This will be something of a composite portrait. There is no single individual who can be shown, on textual grounds, to have held all the views that will be sketched . . . (p. 2)

He further notes that (1) some of the Cartesian linguistics are rooted in earlier work, (2) that several of the active contributors to the linguistic tradition would have considered themselves antagonistic to the Cartesian doctrine, and (3) that Descartes said little about language and his few remarks are subject to various interpretations. Chomsky remarks further:

> Still, it seems to me that there is, in the period under review here, a coherent and fruitful development of a body of ideas and conclusions regarding the nature of language in association with a certain theory of mind and that this development can be regarded as an outgrowth of the Cartesian revolution. (pp. 2-3)

METHOD OF THIS PAPER

Two levels of analysis in the controversy over Cartesian linguistics and Cartesian philosophy in general may be distinguished: discussions of outer and of inner dialectics. The outer dialectics are sociocultural level conflicts which are the context of the inner or intellectual-philosophical dialectics. An old adage applied to this type of analysis is that the outer dialectic without the inner dialectic has no fruit; the inner dialectic without the outer dialectic has no root.

The discussion of the Cartesian inner dialectics is an illustration of the notion

---

*"Whig" history is a term applied by the distinguished British historian H. Butterfield to refer to the type of history written by the Whig historians of the early nineteenth century. These historians were progressive, Protestant, and concerned with the development of individual liberty, and tended to write history as exhibiting progress toward these tendencies. Their versions of history were preambles to their particular contemporary views. Thus the phrase "Whig history" is used to refer to that type of history written in terms of present perspectives instead of the perspectives of the actors of the particular historical period under examination.

of a method of structural history.* This method is simply a structural analysis as propaedeutic to the history of science and philosophy followed by a search for relevant documents.

The methodological justification of this type of history is that the historian needs a clear sense of the intellectual issues involved in the history of philosophy or science, so that while pursuing his scholarly researches, he will be sensitized to relevant data on crucial theoretical problems.† This prescription applied to Cartesian linguistics results in a general assay of Descartes' theory of mind and its implications for a theory of the creative use of language. With these considerations in mind, a close reading of his works, particularly his correspondence, follows. The stress on the correspondence is made because, as Chomsky notes, Descartes did not explicitly devote much attention to the problems of language. Most of the comments he made about language were in the context of discussions of other issues and were thus secondary points. Fortunately, I was able to find a letter that I judge to be excellent evidence for my structural analysis of Descartes' theory of mind (third period) as it could be applied to a theory of language.

While the procedure of doing an analysis and then looking for a relevant passage, finding one, and then interpreting it as evidence for the worth of the analysis looks circular, in fact, it is not. The original evidence for the structural analysis is not the letter which is then used as evidence for the analysis. Rather, the structural analysis is based upon historically presented ontological assumptions rooted in classical Greek philosophy that were modified by seventeenth century thinkers. These ontological positions constituted the philosophical matrix out of which developed the inner dialectics of the seventeenth century. The letter I shall produce has the character of confirmatory evidence for the structural analysis and is not the source of the analysis. The pragmatic justification of such historical method is best made by showing the method in use and displaying its outcomes.

The outer dialectic can be considered metaphysicoreligious, whereas the inner dialectic is strictly metaphysicoscientific and involves specifics of the theory of mind, method, and theory of knowledge. By contrast, the outer dialectic, with its broad philosophicoreligious scope, involves three species of rationalism: religious rationalism, metaphysical rationalism, and scientific rationalism.‡ All of

---

*"Structural" history is a type of history that consists of an analysis of the structure of ideas of a particular person or a succession of persons. The phrase was used by Gustav Bergmann in his *Philosophy of Science* to distinguish the type of writing he did as compared with the description of the social milieu and the examination and comparisons of texts. In structural history the relations and orders of ideas are stressed. A classical example of the type would be a comparison of Plato's and Freud's theories of mind. After such a structural analysis of similarities and differences, then the historians may examine Freud's library, diaries, and correspondence to estimate the influence of Plato on Freud.

†A difficulty with structural history is that the positions generated by the analyses might reflect contemporary views rather than the views of the historical issues as seen by the participants. A possible solution to this problem is to conduct the structural analysis in terms of the issues as they were presented to the participants. In the case of the Cartesian philosophy, the issues in religion, metaphysics, and experimental philosophy (science) were related to the classical philosophical positions of Democritean-Epicurean materialism, Aristotelianism, and Platonism.

‡"Rationalism" is a term which does not have a precise referent as either an epistemological doctrine or as intellectual movement. In this sense it is like the term "romanticism" in literature or "existentialism" in contemporary philosophy. In the French intellectual tradition, a distinction has been made between rationalism in religion, in metaphysics, and in science. This type of scheme obviously follows Comte's notion of the development of

these doctrines distinguish between an empirical phenomenalism and a metaphysical realism. In the inner dialectic we distinguish a concept rationalism of Descartes and a judgment rationalism of Kant.*

THE OUTER DIALECTIC

René Descartes entered the Jesuit College of La Flèche in 1606 at the age of ten. The college had been founded two years previosuly by the Jesuit Order of the Catholic Church. The religious wars of the preceding period had ruined the hope of a united Christianity. As part of a Counter-Reformation reaction, the Church decided to establish a college at La Flèche to help restore the authority of "la scholastique peripateticienne."† At that time the curriculum consisted of the first six years in the humanities and the last three in philosophy. The three-year philosophical curriculum consisted of three parts: (1) morals and logic, (2) mathematics and physics, and (3) metaphysics. During the last three years it was then the custom of students to remain with one instructor. Father Fournet (died January 10, 1638; the *Discours* was published in 1637), Descartes' teacher during this period corresponded with Descartes until his (Fournet's) death.‡

Descartes' various contributions have fared badly in the criticisms of contemporary critics who do not share his religious views and who neglect to place him in the outer dialectics of his own period. On the one hand, the question is how such an acute thinker in mathematics and science could be so loose in welding his particular form of theology with seventeenth century science. Sympathetic critics who tend toward Platonism in philosophy, or with strong religious commitments, on the other hand, tend to marvel at the consistency of the method of research, the theory of mind, the general conception of science, and the theology. Critical views of Descartes seem ultimately to be strongly determined by the acceptance of nonacceptance of religious assumptions of the Platonic type. In evaluating Descartes' religious rationalism, one must remember that he was trained to defend a conservative religious position and that his task was the development of a new cosmology in which both science and religion could be accommodated. Obviously, early Jesuitical training and vigilant Jesuiti-

---

western intellectual tradition. One of the characteristics of Descartes is that his Platonic doubts about the evidence of the senses was not carried over into doubts about the efficacy of reasoning in detecting the structure of reality. His major accomplishment is that he proposed a highly developed metaphysical doctrine that was consistent in religion, philosophy, and science.

*In philosophy a distinction is sometimes made between the rationalism of Descartes, concerned as it was with innate ideas and hostile to Aristotelian syllogisms, and the rationalism of Kant, who looked upon concepts and judgments as having related structures (for every concept there was a particular type of judgment) and who believed Aristotelian logic to be a pattern of thought. The major distinction in terms of the external dialectic was that Kant was a century and a country away from the Catholic theologians whose intense conflicts and interests so troubled Descartes with the result that Kant was sympathetic to Aristotelianism, but took it upon himself in the *Critique of Pure Reason* to construct an organon consistent with eighteenth century physics.

†I have taken much delight in reading Leon Brunschvicg's little book *Descartes*. While much of my structural schematization of Descartes comes from the ontological grid system I place on his work, my sense of the external dialectics has been greatly influenced by Brunschvicg's perceptive remarks.

‡The sociointellectual matrix of Descartes' work can be readily seen in the rather full correspondence published by Vrin and collected and annotated by Adam and Tannery. It will be seen there that a large part of his correspondence was with the clergy.

cal surveillance were strong constraints in the development of his system of philosophy.*

The basic problem of religious thinkers of the seventeenth century was that the growth of mathematics and science was eroding the traditional Aristotelian conceptions of science which, in the Thomistic tradition, had been closely integrated with religious cosmology. The decline of the Aristotelian system brought with it a strong challenge to the theological conceptions closely woven into it. The basic thrust of Descartes' work, while securing the existence of God and the immortality of the soul, was to provide an alternate conception of physics (mechanism over the whole domain), mathematics (geometry by means of algebra and reference systems), and logic (abandonment of syllogistic reasoning for the four-phase scientific method stressing (1) systematic doubt, (2) analysis into elements, (3) synthesis out of elements, and (4) construction of lists to check the adequacy of accounts of phenomena).

THE INNER DIALECTIC

The inner dialectic is between Platonic, Aristotelian, and Democritean-Epicurean theories of knowledge, mind, method, and, ultimately, mathematics and physics. I shall stress this inner dialectic first in terms of Platonism and Aristotelianism and then in terms of a conception of the development of Descartes' theory of mind. TABLE 1 gives the major ontological positions of the inner dialectics.

THE ONTOLOGICAL ALTERNATIVES

How one sets up a category system (grid system) for the analysis of the thought of any particular period is, of course, a matter of level generality of the outcomes one expects. Since the time of Descartes, largely due to his influence, philosophy has gone into what has been called the "epistemological turn." This makes the problem of knowledge central. More specifically, the problem generated by the rise of science has been: How is knowledge of the world possible when the basic data are the sense data of the observing scientist? There are many

---

*Descartes had good reasons to fear the power of the Jesuits and at the same time to be emotionally identified with them as a result of his education. The Edict of Nantes of Henry IV, promulgated in April 1598, gave to his Protestant subjects a measure of religious liberty (among other freedoms they could conduct services five leagues from Paris, as distinguished from being restrained to ten or more leagues from the city). The point is that the Edict was strongly opposed by the Roman Catholic clergy in general and the Jesuits in particular. In 1685 it was revoked and then followed by the great persecution and migrations of the Huguenots. As a result of an essentially metaphysical dispute, as distinguished from a purely scientific issue, on the existence of a plurality of worlds, in 1600 Giordano Bruno was condemned to death as a heretic. In 1616 the Congregation of the Holy Office delivered a report that the proposition "the sun is the centre of the world and altogether devoid of local motion" was "foolish and absurd philosophically and formally heretical, in an much as it expressly contradicts the doctrines of Holy Scripture in many places . . ." (Quoted in A.C. Crombie, Vol. 2, *Medieval and Early Modern Science*, p. 211). This decree was the major basis of Galileo's condemnation. On hearing of Galileo's arrest, Descartes wrote to Mersenne, "Now I would like to point out to you that all the things that I explained in my Treatise (*Le Monde*), among which was this opinion about the movement of the Earth, depend so much upon the other that it is enough to know that one of them is false, to know that all the reasons which I used are invalid; and although I thought that they were based on very certain and evident demonstrations, I would not wish for anything in the world to maintain them against the authority of the Church." (Quoted in A.C. Crombie, Vol. 2, *Medieval and Early Modern Science*, p. 217.)

TABLE 1

FIVE CLASSICAL ONTOLOGIES IN PHILOSOPHIES OF MIND
(WHAT EXISTS? WITH WHAT ARE WE DIRECTLY ACQUAINTED?)

I. Physical Events and Processes	II. Sensory Phenomena	III. Relations	IV. Mental Acts	V. Forms, Ideas GOD

I. The world is conceived of as composed of only physical objects and processes. One can distinguish naïve formulations of the principle in which physical objects and processes are seen only in terms of simple (Newtonian) mechanics. And Descartes, Chomsky, and the Gestalters never tire of stressing the limits of mechanical explanation. A sophisticated contemporary physicalism may include causal mechanisms of natural selection for biology, nuclear principles of the shell model of the atom in physics and chemistry, "smart" molecules in biochemistry, etc.

II. That we have direct acquaintance only with sensory phenomena and all else is a construction is a claim of the phenomenologists.

III. That relations exist and that some relations, particularly in human perception and human performance, influence the properties of the components is a gestalt position.

IV. Experience is of particular events and may or may not be passive; knowledge is an intellectual construction (a mental act) and is of classes. Mental acts (1) form concepts from an amorphous set of sensations, (2) make judgments (AEIO propositions), and (3) reason with judgments (syllogisms). With the distinctions between concepts, judgments, and reasoning, a "concept rationalism" and a "judgment rationalism" may be distinguished. "Concept rationalism" as associated with Cartesianism while "judgment rationalism" is a later product associated with Kantianism.

V. Primary existence is a characteristic of forms (squareness) of which we are cognitively aware. These ideas are innate in us. Physical objects participate in these forms but are not a complete realization of them any more than that a statue by Praxiteles is a complete realization of his ideal of beauty. When objective properties are referred to the term *form* is used. When forms have existence cognitively the term *ideas* is used. The notion of God as an existent falls into these ontological categories, particularly since the notion of God represents a perfection of all his properties.

variations proposed as solutions to this problem, and these constitute the problems of epistemology. The view taken here, however, is that what one proposes as an epistemological formulation has basic ontological assumptions. These ontological assumptions are logically prior to and determine epistemological positions. The ontological positions presented in TABLE 1 were all present in classical Greek thought.*

*The minor qualification to this statement is the existence of relations and the implications of this ontological assumption were not clearly perceived until the end of the nineteenth century. As the result of work both in the foundations of mathematics and phenomenology, Bertrand Russell and William James stressed the independent existence of relations. The psychological analog to this development is to be found in Gestalt psychology; the physical analogue is in the general field of electrical phenomena and atomic physics.

It should be clear that ontologies set limits on epistemologies. If there are no mental acts, for instance, then relations between experiences must occur by some strictly deterministic process like a principle of reinforcement or a law of association. If forms do not exist, and are not innate, then there must be some process in mental acts or some sequences of experiences from which abstract terms like the forms can be generated. An important part of the dialectics about cognitive processes is to show that (1) a nonmental act position can account for all the data of thought phenomena or to show that (2) in principle, the explanation of thought (or speech) phenomena cannot be reduced to or explained by noncognitive models of mental processes.

It is to be noted that these cosmologies in TABLE 1 are even today the substructure of the major psychological systematic theories. The first position, that of scientific materialism of either the physiological or Skinnerian type, has as a task the dialectical refutation of the claims of the other ontologies (that phenomena, even if they exist, are not causally associated with behavior, that mental phenomena such as cognitive acts are explained as constructions

In terms of the ontologies presented, Descartes was engaged in three dialectics. First he rejected a Democritean materialism espoused by Pierre Gassendi (1592-1655) in physics, and Thomas Hobbes (1588-1679) in philosophy. Then he attacked a teleological biology of the prevailing Aristotelian type by sharply distinguishing between mental and physical states and holding that mechanism held over the domain of physical states. Finally, he proposed a highly intellectualized scheme that attempted to be consistent over the problems of religion, mathematics, philosophy, and the sciences. As Brunschvicg notes, this was an intellectual venture that was continued with great clarity by Leibniz.† The essential inner dialectic was how much explanatory weight and what functions can be apportioned to external sensations, innate ideas and reasoning powers. But, as I have previously maintained, how one solves this problem depends upon prior ontological assumptions.

THE STRESS ON MECHANISM ‡

The seventeenth century roots of the mechanism and vitalism controversy are clearly in Descartes' dualism between the mental and the physical, or as he put

---

from processes which do not exhibit any other than physical properties, that innate ideas are explainable by learning and memory). The second position is that of the phenomenologists and the existentialists. The third position, as mentioned above, is a Gestalt position. The fourth position is central to the Freudian notion of a mind that acts. The taxonomy of the mental acts is given by the "mechanisms." The fifth position, that of innate forms, is in Chomsky's interpretation "innate principles" of grammatical processing.

†In 1660 Leibniz, according to Brunschvicg,[5] devoted himself to the task of developing an intellectual system that would simultaneously be an alternative to a mechanistic materialism in physics, teleology in biology, and empiricism in philosophy. In this orientation his work is a variation within the Cartesian tradition.

‡The general topic of mechanism has a long history. It really should be placed in the seventeenth century and have as its dialectical opposite a classical science strongly influenced by the teleology of the Aristotelian system. There was, of course, a classical influence of Platonism on science, but it was largely in mathematics and geometry and resulted in the subordination of experience (and experiment) to a philosophical investigation of the nature of forms. As an alternative to Aristotelianism the capacity of mechanistic explanation seemed to intoxicate thinkers of the late seventeenth century. Because of the successes of the Newtonian physics, the development of the mathematics by Fermat, Descartes, Leibniz, and Newton which supported the physical theories and made their confirmation possible, the world seemed to be one large machine. The decline of mechanism has been a topic of many recent books on the "new physics." Both molecular and relativity physics have confined the Newtonian "world machine" into a restricted range of phenomena. The supporting philosophical concepts of the Newtonian system, substance and cause, have been dispensed with, and probability functions and matrix manipulations have been substituted for the old differential equations and scalar mathematics. Determinism, however, has not been abandoned, only given probability formulations. Limits of knowledge have been drawn more narrowly, for we have learned to live without a theological quest for certainty in our scientific activities (these are delta-epsilon arguments in calculus).

At any event, there seems to be a Princeton general critique of mechanism, and Descartes. The outstanding general, and excellent, analysis of mechanism was W. Kohler's *The Task of Gestalt Psychology* (Princeton University Press, 1969), a series of lectures given in 1966. Julian Jaynes in *Animate Motion in the 17th Century*, published in *Historical Conceptions of Psychology* (Henle, Jaynes, Sullivan, 1973) presents an interesting psychological construction of the source in Descartes' life of the notion of mechanism and the reactions of contemporary biologists to the Cartesian proposals. I abstract his comments as follows:

"[Descartes] a maternally deprived 18 year old suffered . . . several breakdowns . . . hid himself away in Saint Germain for two years . . . [whose] . . . only recreation available were visits to the royal gardens . . . in which there were complicated statues that moved, danced, or even spoke.

"These images . . . perhaps stayed at the very depths of Descartes' thinking. He seems to

it, between substances which exist temporally but are unextended and characterized by consciousness and those substances which are extended. In the Aristotelian scheme of things the world was divided up into objects which are be-souled (animate) and lacking in soul (inanimate). The objective manifestation of this distinction was the capacity of the object to be self-moving or only moved by the application of an external force. Thus within the Aristotelian scheme all of the plant and animal kingdom was viewed as having psyches. There was a vegative psyche which had the properties of nutrition and reproduction. In the animal psyche there were in addition to the vegative functions, those of sensation, movement, passive memory, and imagination. Only man had all of these functions and, in addition, the function of reasoning.

The thrust against Aristotelian theory of mind was to extend the concept of mechanism throughout the physical and biological domain, man as thinker excepted. The Cartesian extention of mechanism broadly across both what we would call today the physical and biological sciences was a bold stroke that fired the imagination of scientists of the succeeding centuries. Its peculiarly attractive feature was the simplicity of the cosmology it proposed, as distinguished from the overripe *post hoc* patching of Aristotelian science by the scholastic tradition. The Cartesian view had the added advantage that it was consistent with a platonic hierarchy of reality. In the Cartesian hierarchy all physical processes (as distinguished from mental rather than as distinguished from biological) are reducible to mechanics, and mechanics is easily reducible to an exemplification of mathematics, and mathematics itself can be reduced to a set of simple, indubitable, innate ideas, and this conception of innate ideas led to a theory of mind as passive, which led to the conception of God as the creative source of innate ideas and man as the instrument of his will. Thus mechanism led to the conception of a world machine designed by God in the manner of Timaeus's Demiurge (*Timaeus*, 54-56), who creates the universe out of proportions of fire, air, water, and earth, and these primary bodies out of triangles arranged to make various solid forms, e.g. cube, tetrahedron, pyramid.

In Cartesianism it was important to exempt mind from this general mechanistic account, although the mind thus exempted was only a passive agent of God's will. The grounds for the exclusion of the cognitive processes from the mechanistic conception of the world was developed by an argument that involved a theoretical couple: machines and mind. Mind was looked upon as a universal instrument that can respond in many different ways to diverse situations, but the notion of the machine was that it only responded in a narrow range of responses and only when the appropriate organ was stimulated. Speech is another differentia between humans and machines.

---

view the entire physical world as though it were modeled in the Francinis' [the constructors of the statues] work. It was nothing but a vast machine. Just as in the Queen's gardens, there was no spontaneity at any point. He loathed animism. He loved statues." (pp. 169-170)

Jaynes further points out: "Archaic for its own day, the errors of Descartes' physiology were pointed out one by one as they appeared. The year following the publication of *Traite de l'Homme*, N. Steno (1638-1686) the young Danish theologican and physiologist, found himself 'obliged to point out . . . the vast differences between Descartes' imaginary machine, and the real machine of the human body'; he showed that the pineal gland existed in animals as well as in man (as had been known before), and in no case had the rich nerve supply which the Cartesian theory demanded." (p. 173)

Although *Traite de l'Homme* was probably written in the early 1630s, it was the second part (Chapter 28) of the withheld *Le Monde*. It was published separately in Leyden in 1662 as *Renatus Des Cartes De Homine* by a Florent Schuyl. Clerselier published on April 12, 1664 *L'Homme de René Descartes*.

Hans Aarsleff, Chomsky's vociferous critic, is also from Princeton.

In *Discours V** Descartes discusses the difference between animals and men. The first distinction is that, as Chomsky notes (*Cartesian Linguistics*, 3-4), animals do not use language grammatically. The second distinction relates to the statues of the Francinis and animals, both; namely, that they respond only under the appropriate stimulation of their particular organs, and their actions are directly related, one might in later terminology say, "instinctively" or "by mediation of reflexes," to the organs originally stimulated. By contrast, humans have the capacity to use reason, the universal instrument, which in many different situations results in appropriate action. Important here is the close relation of speech and reason, as Chomsky continually stresses. The problem is that when the actual discussion gets around to the nature of mind and cognitive processes and the relations of speech, particularly grammatical speech, to these, then the properties given to both reason and mind are hardly sufficient to account for the creative use of language.

*Section V in the *Discours* reads as follows:
    Et je m'étais ici particulièrement arrêté à faire voir que, s'il y avait de telles machines, qui eussent les organes et la figure d'un singe, ou de quelque autre animal sans raison, nous n'aurions aucun moyen pour reconnaître qu'elles ne seraient pas en tout de même nature que ces animaux; au lieu que, s'il y en avait qui eussent la ressemblance de nos corps et imitassent autant nos actions que moralement il serait possible, nous aurions toujours deux moyens très certains pour reconnaître qu'elles ne seraient point pour cela de vrais hommes. Dont le premier est que jamais elles ne pourraient user de paroles, ni d'autres signes en les composant, comme nous faisons pour déclarer aux autres nos pensées. Car on peut bien concevoir qu'une machine soit tellement faite qu'elle profère des paroles, et même qu'elle en profère quelquesunes à propos des actions corporelles qui causeront quelque changement en ses organes: comme, si on la touche en quelque endroit, qu'elle demande ce qu'on lui veut dire; si en un autre, qu'elle crie qu'on lui fait mal, et choses semblables; mais non pas qu'elle les arrange diversement, pour répondre au sens de tout ce qui se dira en sa présence, ainsi que les hommes les plus hébétés peuvent faire. Et le second est que, bien qu'elles fissent plusieurs choses aussi bien, ou peut-être mieux qu'aucun de nous, elles manqueraient infailliblement en quelques autres, par lesquelles on découvrirait qu'elles n'agiraient pas par connaissance, mais seulement par la disposition de leurs organes. Car, au lieu que la raison est un instrument universel, qui peut servir en toutes sortes de rencontres, ces organes ont besoin de quelque particulière disposition pour chaque action particulière; d'où vient qu'il est moralement impossible qu'il y en ait assez de divers en une machine pour la faire agir en toutes les occurrences de la vie, de même facon que notre raison nous fait agir. (pp. 628-629) Éditions Garnier Frères.
Translation:
    And I pause here particularly in order to observe that if there were such machines which had the organs and the face of a monkey, or some other animal lacking reason, we would not have any means of discriminating if they would not be in all ways of the same nature as these animals; instead, if there were some [machines] that resembled our bodies and moreover imitated our actions, which conceivably might be possible, we would always have two excellent means in order to recognize that they were not true humans. The first of which is that they would never be able to use words or signs grammatically as we do in order to express our thoughts. For one can well conceive that a machine could be made so that it uttered words and even that it uttered some appropriate for those bodily actions which caused some change in its organs; for instance, if we touched it in some place, that it ask us what we mean; in another, that cries out that we are hurting it, and similar things; but not that it arrange them [the utterances] differently in order to respond sensibly to all which will be said in its presence, as even the most weak-minded of men can do. And the second is that, although they do several things very well, or perhaps better than some of us, they would lack infallibly in some other things, from which one would discover that they do not act by knowledge but by solely by the disposition of their organs. In contrast to reason, which is an universal instrument which is able to serve in a variety of situations, these organs need some particular disposition for each particular action; therefore, it follows that there are not enough variations in a machine in order to make it act in all circumstances of life in the same way that our reason causes us to act.

THE STRESS ON INNATE IDEAS

The central feature of Platonic realism is that there exist forms that are the ultimate constituents of the world, which are, by essence, simple (elementary) as distinguished from being composites. By virtue of the property of being simple they are unchanging, and in the case of the psyche, which is a form, immortal. Change, which is a constant characteristic of physical objects, is looked upon as the composition or decomposition of composites from simples. The simplicity requirement of the forms also put some constraints on the characteristics of definitions and knowledge of the forms. Forms, since they are simple, had only one essence, and being known at all, were known in their entirety.* The existence of forms, apart from objects which are embodiments of them, is the characteristic feature of Platonic realism. Physical objects "participated" in the forms and were a constantly changing and imperfect realization of them.

The separate existence of the forms, and that physical objects are only imperfect realizations of them, led to the problem of how the forms are knowable. Sense perception is deceptive on three counts: (1) the objects that are sensed are imperfect realizations of the forms: (2) these objects are, moreover, constantly changing; and (3) bodily states interfere with sensations such that, for example, wine tastes sour to the sick man. Yet that the forms exist there is no doubt, and that they are knowable is also not denied. The existence of geometric forms and the technical capability of reducing complex objects into their simple components (the area of any polygon can be found to be the sum of the areas of triangles of which it can be shown to be composed) is the informing image, the basic pattern of analysis, and construction of objects in the world.

To account for the knowledge of the forms, Plato, as was his creative style, created a mythic model, a likely story, corresponding to the elementary ideas. These ideas are in the psyche as a result of prior experience of the psyche in another existence, for the psyche is immortal and only temporarily lodged in the body of an individual. In this other existence, where all forms exist, the psyche had contact (presumably perceptual) with the forms, and thus they entered the psyche. In becoming an individual at birth, which is the process of attachment of the psyche to a physical body, the psyche has the ideas innate in it.

Innate ideas come into use in ways that are standard conceptions even today. A sensation is presented to mind and it is then compared with a mental duplicate, an innate idea. If the sensation is complex—say a cat is presented—the sensation may be compared with a previously acquired empirical concept of "catness," which is composed of the elementary ideas. If the sensation is not pure and there are not empirical concepts with which to compare it, then the sensation is analyzed down into its elementary components. These elementary components are the innate ideas. Cognitive functions are (1) essentially comparisons of simple sensations with these innate ideas; (2) an analysis of complex sensations into simple ones and then comparison with innate ideas; and (3) then the construction by small, logical, intuitively certain, steps of composite concepts, which may be compared with sensations. These mental processes are an internalization of the famous four steps of the *Discours*. Such schemata are used to render cognitively intelligible the stream of sensations presented to the individual.

---

*The phrase "in being known at all is known in its entirety" is one of those frequently used by N.K. Smith to describe Descartes' (also Plato's) conception of the knowledge of the simple, or innate ideas. This schematization is the source of the celebrated Cartesian stress on intuition. When knowledge and perception are structured in terms of the elementary innate ideas, they are beyond reasonable doubt.

Perhaps the doctrine of innate ideas and how they function in the Platonic Cartesian system can be better discriminated by presenting briefly the Aristotelian branch of the dialectic on the nature of mind and the constituents of the world. Aristotle's realism is a naive realism of physical objects as distinguished from the Platonic realism of concepts and forms. For Aristotle, primary existence was given to physical objects. These objects may be conceived to be composed of form and matter immanent in them, but neither the form nor the matter can exist independently of the physical objects. The form is known cognitively, as in the Platonic scheme, but instead of being an innate idea it is constructed by an act of mind as a generalization from the experience of a number of similar individual objects (particulars). Knowledge for the Aristotelians is of the universal concepts and their relations (class names and their relations) which have been generated from particular instances.

In the Platonic scheme there is a basic stock of forms, as there is only a small set of basic geometric forms, and the world is constructed as combinations of these elementary components. This method and model of the world has strong appeal to mathematicians. The Aristotelian conception appeals more to those who look upon mind and reason as constructing models of the world from experience. Where theological issues are involved, Aristotelianism has the weakness that reasoning of men compels belief on the basis of experience as distinguished from the conception that experience itself is intelligible only on the basis of God-granted innate ideas and by means of His grace. The God of the Platonists is the source of our actions and beliefs, that of the Aristotelians is only coherent with our other cognitions. In the Platonic-Cartesian system of thought, only God is creative in generating innate ideas. Humans are only ingenious in their combinations of or analyses of perceptions into innate ideas.

THE DEVELOPMENT OF DESCARTES' THEORY OF MIND

To talk about Plato's or Freud's or Descartes' theory of mind leads to disaster, unless it is recognized that over their careers there was a progressive development of their thought. It is true that there is a Plantonistic, a Cartesian, and a Freudian theory of mind that has some historical warrant, in the sense that there has been a general interpretation of their central ideas. But unless care is taken to appreciate the development of their thought, one finds paradoxes in their work and the frequent comment that Plato or Freud or Descartes is not really a Platonist, or a Freudian, or a Cartesian, respectively. I shall schematize stages in the development of Descartes' theory of mind and characterize the third period as the historical Cartesianism. I shall then present a hitherto untranslated letter from his correspondence which indicates the features of this theory which I mention. I shall then indicate that Descartes backed away from this position and, in doing so, moved from a classical Platonism toward an Aristotelian formulation of mind.

First Period (1610-1619). This first period is characterized by the Aristotelianism Descartes learned while at the college at La Flèche. It is the background against which he revolted, although from the contemporary perspective the revolt, as far as theory of the human mind was concerned, was only partial. That is to say that the revolt against classical mathematics and physics was more sweeping than the modifications of the theory of the human mind. For instance, men were by nature or essense all endowed with the capacity to reason. The crisis he went through and its aftermath in which he thought that he was chosen or privileged to have access to the structure of the world is symbolized in the two dramatic dreams he had in 1619.* These made a significant transformation of his intellectual orientation, so that these events signaled the end of a phase and the beginning of another stage of his development.

Second Period (1619-1628). This stage I conceive of as the development of an alternative to the Aristotelian procedures of science by an application to scientific problems of mathematical methodology. The break from the Aristotelian-scholastic tradition is achieved with the completion of (but not published) *Regulae ad Directionem Ingenii* (Rules for the Direction of the Mind). In agreement with most scholars, I believe that this was worked out during the period of 1627 and the first half of 1628. The point of attack, interestingly enough, was the development of an alternative method to the *Organon* of Aristotle. The *Regulae* is the predecessor to the more famous *Discours de la Méthode* in which the break with Aristotelian methodology is finally consummated. Innate ideas are not mentioned in the *Regulae*, nor is the assumption that physical entities reflected in sensations are rendered intelligible by means of a mental duplicate. I follow N.K. Smith's interpretation of this period by holding, as does he, that there is a reliance on (1) the Self as aware of itself as thinking, doubting, affirming, desiring. For Descartes nothing can be more immediately present to the Self than itself. In addition (2) the Self is its earthbound life is an embodied self, is no less immediately aware of the physical patterns which external objects, by way of their actions on the sense-organs, imprints on the brain.†

Third Period (1629-1646). The difficulties of the formulation of the second state are repaired in the third stage. The problem is what warrant we have for the interpretation that the sensations and thoughts we have constitute knowledge and refer to objects in the outside world. How does one escape from a subjectivity that ultimately leads to solipsism and skepticism? The answer seems to be to adopt the notion of innate ideas, God-given, with which we compare sensations and from which we construct our conceptions of the external world. And the God who gives us these innate ideas is a good God who could not, by his nature, deceive us.

This period in Descartes' development is what came to be known as Cartesianism, at least as far as a theory of mind is concerned. It is of some interest that the seeds of this period can be seen in the second half of the year, in 1629, in correspondence with Mersenne on the problems of language. To clarify what is

---

*Descartes' dreams are presented by N.K. Smith (pp. 33-39). This is a translation from Baillet's *Vie de Descartes* (1691), Book II, Chapter i, pp. 81-86.

†Combined with the dreams, a critical incident while he was still a youth strongly influenced the career of Descartes. In November 1628, soon after arriving in Paris, he went to a meeting at the house of the Papal Nunico to hear a talk by a Sieur de Chandoux, who was to expound his views of philosophy. These turned out to be an attack against Scholastic Philosophy which powerfully influenced the audience, Descartes excepted. Descartes was prevailed upon to give his reaction to the presentation and, with appropriate compliments to Chandoux, proceeded to attack his position mainly on the grounds that it substituted one merely probable position for another. What were needed were better grounds than the probable. He demonstrated the difficulties of the merely probable reasoning by showing that a generally agreed-upon true proposition by this reasoning could be looked upon as false, and a false one given grounds for belief. He, himself, claimed that he could develop by an application of the methods of mathematics a set of philosophical doctrines that were clear and certain. The audience was quick to agree with him. Cardinal de Bérulle, who was present and much impressed, later met with Descartes and told him in effect that since God had given him such a fine mind, he ought to use it to good ends, namely, in the development of the philosophy that he had indicated. This injunction from the Cardinal coincided with his own tendencies, and he decided to withdraw from society, to protect his liberty, and to go to some place where the weather was cool (Paris summers being too hot) and where he would be unknown. He left then for Holland for the life of a recluse devoted to study.

involved epistemologically, the issue is what legitimates knowledge about the external world. To the Platonist, reality, since it is compounded of elementary forms, is knowable directly through the innate idea counterparts of these forms and compounds of these ideas. To the rationalist there is direct insight into the structure of the world and the coherence of the structure with the indubitability of the initial assumptions and the strict logical development legitimates the knowledge of the world. By contrast, to the empiricist constant recourse to experience as the source of ideas and confirming instances in experience legitimate claims to knowledge. As an example of how the system worked in *Meditations III*, the following is remarked by Descartes:

> I find present to me two completely diverse ideas of the Sun; the one, in which the Sun appears to me as extremely small, is, it would seem, derived from the senses, and to be counted as belonging to the class of adventitious ideas, the other, in which the Sun is taken to be many times larger than the whole Earth, has been arrived at by way of astronomical reasonings, *that is to say, elicited from certain notions innate in me, or formed by me in some other manner.* Certainly, these two ideas of the Sun cannot both resemble the same Sun; and reason constrains me to believe that the one which seems to have emanated from it in a direct manner is the more unlike.

> N.K. Smith, *New Studies in the Philosophy of Descartes* (London: Russell and Russell, 1963), p. 236. N.K. Smith translation. (Italics mine. J.J.S.)

Fourth Period (1647-1650). While the grounds for postulating a fourth stage rest upon a rather flimsy evidence, if we can accept that there was strong evidence for a third stage, then there is certainly a retreat from this position into a more generalized rationalistic position. What is involved is the definite deemphasis on innate ideas and a reliance on the powers of reasoning itself to generate these ideas. This particular doctrine is not a minor shift, for since it involves a shift from doctrines of innate ideas which give limited creative powers to the individual to one on which reason itself generates its major ideas, it is a major concession to the Aristotelians and a retreat from Platonism. The following quotation is the evidence for the fourth stage.

> I have never either said or judged that the mind has need of innate ideas which are anything different from its faculty of thinking . . . in the same manner in which we say that generosity is innate in some families and in other families certain diseases, such as gout or gavel. In so speaking I am not saying that the infants or those families suffer from these diseases in the womb of the mother, but that they are born with a certain disposition or faculty of contracting them.

> *Notae in Programma*, Adams and Tannery *Oeuvres*, Vol. 8, pp. 357-8. N.K. Smith translation.

EVIDENCE FOR THE THIRD PERIOD PLATONISTIC THEORY OF LINGUISTICS

As mentioned above, classically Cartesianism has been identified with what we have schematized as the third stage of Descartes' development of a theory of mind. The following letter occurred in the beginning of this stage, and, strangely has not figured in the discussions of Cartesian linguistics. I quote the letter extensively to show how it is an exemplification of the application of the Platonic presuppositions to a theory of language in general and grammar in particular.

This letter is number 15 in Volume 1, *Correspondence,* of the Adam and Tannery *Oeuvres de Descartes* (Paris: Vrin, 1893). It was written by Descartes while he was in Amsterdam and is dated 20 November, 1629. Apparently the letter was in response to a previous one from Père Mersenne, in which he had presented to Descartes six propositions about a language project proposed by a M. Hardy.*

We can infer from the content of Descartes' reply that Hardy had proposed a multilanguage dictionary in which one common term would then represent *l'amour, aymer, amare, philein.* Descartes responded that interesting as this project was, what prevented people from understanding a language is the grammar. There is no doubt, however, that a simplified and regular grammar could be constructed that would make language learning easy. He then adds:

> However, I believe one could add to this invention [conception] to compose the basic words of that language as well as their symbols so that the language could be taught in a very little time and this would be by means of the notion of order, that is to say, to establish an order† between all the thoughts which can enter the human mind in the same way that there is a natural order of numbers. And just as one can learn in one day all the numbers to infinity and to write one with them in an unknown language which yet are an infinity of different words one can do the same for all the other necessary words to express all other things that fall within the purview of the human mind. If this order could be found I have no doubt

*The M. Hardy referred to in this letter has not been identified, to my knowledge, nor has the original letter from Père Mersenne been found. My best guess, however, is that the Hardy referred to in the letter is the mathematician Claude Hardy (1605-1678), who was reputed to have known 36 languages. There is a letter from Descartes in Vol. II of *Correspondence* dated June 1638 to this Hardy giving him some support in a controversy he had with Fermat on some geomaetric properties of a parabola.

†In the platonic intellectual tradition as well as in the general mathematical tradition a sense of intellectual order is of paramount importance. The problem is to determine that which is fundamental from that which is derived. Since the world can be conceptualized as being composite, the problem is to specify the elementary components and how the world is to be analyzed into and further how it is to be constructed out of them. The basic problem is how to start such an analysis. This is the problem of order of ideas. The basic insight is the Platonic notion from *Timeaus* that the objects of the world are really composed of geometric forms. The problem is to do a philosophical analysis similar in outcome to a Fourier analysis of a complex curve.

To show the sense of order generally in Descartes' argument, consider the follow quotation from Alquié.

> Chacun connâit l'importance de la notion d'ordre chex Descartes. Et nul ne saurait nier que Descartes ait toujours présenté sa metáphysique selon un certain ordre qui, au moins dans ses grandes lignes, est la même dans le *Discours,* les *Méditations,* les *Principes:* je doute, je pense, je suis, Dieu est, Dieu garantit mes idées et, par consequent, le science du monde est fondée.

> M.F. Alquiè in Expérience ontologique et déduction systématique dans la constitution de la métphysique de Descartes. *Descartes,* Les Editions de Minuit: Paris, 1957, p. 10.

Translation

> Everybody knows the importance of Descartes of the idea of order. And no one would deny that Descartes always presented his metaphysics in a certain order which, at least in its general aspects is the same in the *Discours,* the *Meditations,* the *Principes:* I doubt, I think, I am, God exists, God guarantees my ideas and, as a consequence, the knowledge of the world is grounded.

whatever that this language would be universally understood for there would be a great number of people who would willingly employ five or six days time in order to be able to be understood by all men. But I do not believe that your author has thought about that simply because nothing in all his propositions attests to it and the invention of this language would depend upon the true philosophy for *it is impossible to decide in any other way all the thoughts of man and to put them in a certain order,* not solely to distinguish them in such a way that they be clear and simple, which is in my opinion the greatest secret that one must unlock in order to acquire true knowledge.

If somebody had well explained which simple ideas in the imagination of man are distinct of which all that he thinks is composed and that this be recognized by everybody I would venture to hope that a universal language very easy to learn, to pronounce, and to write would result. And what is most important is a language which would aid judgment, representing to judgment all things so distinctly that it would be almost impossible for it to be deceived. In contradistinction to this situation the words we use have practically only confused meanings to which the human mind has become accustomed by tradition so that practically man understands nothing perfectly. Now I believe that such a language is possible and that one can find the science on which it depends through which means peasants could better judge the truth of things than philosophers can at present. But I do not hope ever to see that language in use. That would presuppose immense changes in the order of things and it would mean that the whole world were a terrestial paradise, which is only good thinking about in [the domain of] novels. (Italics mine. J.J.S.)*

The underlined sections in the letter to Mersenne indicated the peculiarly

---

*I have used Alquié's translation of the seventeenth century French into modern French in these notes.

Au reste, je trouve qu'on pourrait ajouter à ceci une invention, tant pour composer les mots primitifs de cette langue que pour leurs caractères; en sorte qu'elle pourrait être enseignée en fort peu de temps, et ce par le moyen de l'ordre, c'est-à-dire, établissant un ordre entre toutes les pensées qui peuvent entrer en l'esprit humain, de même qu'il y en a un naturellement établi entre les nombres; et comme on peut apprendre en un jour à nommer tous les nombres jusques à l'infini, et à les écrire en une langue inconnue, qui sont toutefois une infinité de mots différents, qu'on pût faire le même de tous les autres mots nécessaires pour exprimer toutes les autres choses qui tombent en l'esprit des hommes. Si cela était trouvé, je ne doute point que cette langue n'eût binetôt cours parmi le monde; car il y a force gens qui emploieraient volontiers cinq ou six jours de temps pour se pouvoir faire entendre par tous les hommes.

Mais je ne crois pas que votre auteur ait pensé à cela, tant parce qu'il n'y a rien en toutes ses propositions qui le témoigne, que parce que l'invention de cette langue dépend de la vraie Philosophie, car il est impossible autrement de dénombrer toutes les pensées des hommes, et de les mettre par ordre, ni seulement de les distinguer en sorte qu'elles soient claires et simples, qui est à mon avis le plus grand secret qu'on puisse avoir pour acquérir la bonne Science. Et si quelqu'un avait bien expliqué quelles sont les idées simples qui sont en l'imagination des hommes, desquelles se compose tout ce qu'ils pensent, et que cela fût reçu par tout le monde, j'oserais espérer ensuite une langue universelle, fort aisée à apprendre, à prononcer et à écrire, et ce qui est le principal, qui aiderait au jugement, lui représentant si distinctement toutes choses, qu'il lui serait presque impossible de se tromper; au lieu que, tout au rebours, les mots que nous avons n'ont quasi que des significations confuses, auxquelles l'esprit des hommes s'étant accoutumé de longue main, cela est cause qu'il n'entend presque rien parfaitement.

Or je tiens que cette langue est possible, et qu'on peut trouver la Science de qui elle dépend, par le moyen de laquelle les paysans pourraient mieux juger de la vérité des choses, que ne font maintenant les philosophes. Mais n'espérez pas de la voir jamais en usage; cela présuppose de grands changements en l'ordre des choses, et il faudrait que tout le Monde ne fût qu'un paradis terrestre, ce qui n'est bon à proposer que dans le pays des romans.

Oeuvres philosophiques de Descartes,
Edition Garnier, Paris, 1963, pp.
230-232.

Platonic assumptions. The specification of the simple ideas and placing them in an order is the essential problem. Descartes thought that the key to this problem was precisely in the theory and method that he had just worked out. Only the details needed to be specified. It goes without stressing it that we have been waiting for the details of such a proposal since the time of Plato, and that Descartes himself never got beyond thinking of the theoretical possibility.

RETREAT FROM THE DOCTRINE OF INNATE IDEAS

Now we know a conception of the nature of the world is both a function of the structure of the world and the nature of mind, and both of these in turn are a function of the ontological positions one takes as metaphysical presuppositions of science. I have indicated the major alternatives which confronted the thinkers in the various intellectual traditions up to about the turn of this century. The doctrine of innate ideas works with a strong emphasis on perception but yet a distrust of it and a conception of cognitive processes as the consisting of small, step-like inferences, and comparisons of percepts with innate ideas. That mind generates through mental acts its major concepts because of powers unique to it is an ontological posit of the Aristotelians. That the concepts thus generated have their source in experience and are not innate is the main thrust of the British empirical tradition. This tradition after Locke substituted the principle of association for cognitive processes as mechanism by which composite concepts were generated. The crisis that this doctrine led to in the philosophy of Hume resulted in the reconstruction by Kant of a theory of mind in the rationalistic tradition which had innate cognitive powers for giving structure to what was presented to the understanding. The tack taken followed the doctrine of innate powers combined with specific notions of innate ideas. And these innate powers are what was needed to give grammar its flexibility of application. The evolutionary stress on the adaptive modifications and selective survival in the nineteenth century led to the notion that the innate powers reflect not only a philosophical construction but a physiological process. When this phase of development occurred, the issue was clearly no longer one of dispute between methods of philosophically constructing world views but was one of scientific investigation.

CONCLUSIONS

I do not wish to inflate a small point to a strategic issue and declare that anyone who does not see its importance is an idiot. The distinction between innate ideas and innate powers is one that cuts deeply, however, for it goes along with different theories of mind, different ontologies, and thus different conceptions of man and science. The talk about innate ideas was always vague, but there was a ready reference to such elements as points, lines, angles, circles, and triangles as was used in geometry. The world forms were thought to be decomposable to simple geometrical forms, ultimately triangles, whose matter was single stuff on the order of fire, air, water, and earth. This simple stuff became described by Descartes as only having the property of extension. When the theory of mind moved from innate ideas to innate powers, the doctrines which such a theory presumed to explain became harder to test and not so immediately conceivable in terms of an analogy to geometry. These innate ideas, however, found their analogue in Kant's table of categories and the innate powers in his functions of thought in judgment: judgments of quantity, quality, relation, and modality. This is the main line of development of the rationalistic tradition. The transition of the doctrine of innate ideas to one of innate powers can be seen in Descartes and was fully developed by Kant. Running parallel to this development and gaining support from it was the doctrine of grammar generale. The development of the notion of innate powers was needed to explain the creative use of language.

It makes sense in Whig history terms to cast Descartes in a leading role in the empiricism-rationalistic dialectic. It is the Whiggishness of the construction that bothers the historian of psychology. The central thrust of Cartesianism was against Aristotelianism in science, philosophy, and religion and only secondarily against a Democritian materialism. The broad extension of mechanism was a move against Aristotelian teleology in both physics and biology. The doctrine of innate ideas was a move against Aristotelian mental acts which constructed universals from particulars of experience. The doctrine of God being the agent of man's thoughts and actions was a move against the Reformation and Scholastic concept that theology was to be justified on rational grounds rather than God being the condition of rationality.

Chomsky's engagement in contemporary outer and inner dialectics has certain anomalous outcomes when he identifies his position as rooted in Cartesian linguistics. In his outer dialectic he defends almost a radical individualism in which a person is conceived to have rational processes and whose behavior is under volitional control (as does Kant). In his inner dialectic he defends the conception that there are cognitive processes that are different in kind from elementary associative processes. The tie between Chomsky and Descartes is on the secondary point that humans have a special place in nature in which mental processes are exempt from physical (mechanistic) determinism. The modern qualification is that the roots of this special cognitive processing will probably be found in the scientific investigation of physiology rather than being the result of philosophical analysis of cognitive acts. The anomaly is that in outer dialectics Descartes was defending a conservative religious view, but the flight from mechanism ends in innate ideas. What is needed is a flight from mechanism that produces strong cognitive processes. Such a position is Aristotelianism and Kantianism, which is the hard core of the rationalistic theory of mind. This theory of mind is what *Cartesian Linguistics* is all about. The philosophic position supported the growth of *grammaire générale*.

In both inner and outer dialects of the Cartesian period, Chomsky himself could not be counted as a strict Cartesian. Nor, in his late period, was Descartes. But Chomsky is essentially correct in his interpretation of the rationalistic tradition. If there had been a Cartesian linguistics, with a major expection, it would have been something similar to what Chomsky proposes.

REFERENCES

BALZ, A.G.A. 1951. Cartesian Studies. Columbia Univ. Press. New York, N.Y.
BECK, L.J. 1952. The Method of Descartes. Clarendon Press. Oxford, England.
BERGMANN, G. 1956. Philosophy of Science. Univ. of Wisconsin Press. Madison, Wis.
BRUNSCHVICG, LEON. 1937. René Descartes. Les Editions Rieder. Paris, France.
CHOMSKY, NOAM. 1966. Cartesian Linguistics. Harper and Row. New York, N.Y.
CHOMSKY, NOAM. 1968. Language and Mind. Harcourt Brace and World. New York, N.Y.
DE CORDEMOY, GERAUD. 1668, 1974. A Philosophical Discourse Concerning Speech. (Englished out of French, transl. unknown). Printed for the Toyal Society, 1668; reprinted AMS Press, 1974. New York, N.Y.
DESCARTES, RENÉ. 1973. Oeuvres de Descartes. Charles Adam and Paul Tawnery, Eds. Librairie Philosophique J. Vrin. Paris, France.

DESCARTES, RENÉ. 1967. Oeuvres Philosophiques. F. Alquié, Ed. Éditions Garnier. Paris, France.
DESCARTES, RENÉ. 1952. Descarte's Philosophical Writings. N.K. Smith, Ed. & trans. London, England.
EWERT, ALFRED. 1933. The French Language. Faber and Faber. London, England.
LANSON, G. & TRUFFRAU, P. 1953. Manuel Illustre de la Litterature Francaise. Hachette. Paris, France.
LYONS, JOHN. 1970. Noam Chomsky. Viking Press. New York, N.Y.
SMITH, N.K. 1963. New Studies in the Philosophy of Descartes. Russell & Russell. London, England.

CHRONOLOGY OF EVENTS IN
DESCARTES' LIFE

* from *Descartes* by Anscombe and Geach
(Nelson, 1954).

1596	Descartes born at La Haye, in Touraine (March 31).
1606	Enters the Jesuit college of La Flèche.
1611	Hears of Galileo's having discovered the satellites of Jupiter.
1614	Leaves La Flèche.
1616	Takes his degree in law at Poitiers.
1618	Goes to Holland to serve in the army under Prince Maurice of Nassau. Makes the acquaintance of Beeckman at Breda.
1619	Leaves Holland. Attends the Emperor Ferdinand's coronation. Joins the Duke of Bavaria's forces. There flashes upon him the idea of extending the method of analytical geometry to other studies (Nov. 10).
1622	Returns to France.
1623-25	Travels in Italy.
1625-28	After returning to France, stays sometimes in the country and sometimes in Paris.
1628	Composes the *Rules for the Guidance of the Mind*. Leaves for Franeker, Holland, in the autumn.
1630	Moves to Amsterdam. Matriculates at Leyden University.
1632	Moves to Deventer.
1633	Returns to Amsterdam. Learns of Galileo's condemnation by the Inquisition.
1634	Suppresses his treatise on *The World*.
1635	His natural daughter is christened. Moves to Utrecht.
1636	Moves to Leyden.
1637	The *Discourse on Method* is published (in June). Moves to Santport.
1640	Returns to Leyden. Bereaved of his father and his daughter.
1641	Moves to Endegeest. The *Meditations* are published (in August).
1641-43	Quarrels between Descartes and Voëtius, Rector of Utrecht University.
1642	Utrecht University officially decides in favour of the old philosophy.
1643	Frequently visits Princess Elizabeth of Bohemia. Moves to Egmond-op-den-Hoef. Judgment is pronounced against him by the Utrecht magistrates.
1644	Visits France (May to November). The *Principles of Philosophy* are published (in July). On his return to Holland, takes up permanent residence at Egmond-Binnen near Alkmaar, till he leaves Holland in 1649.
1645	After receiving a letter from Descartes, the Utrecht magistrates forbid printed discussion of the new philosophy.
1647	His trouble with Leyden University. Visits France in the summer, and talks with Pascal. Is Awarded (but does not receive) a pension from the King of France.
1648	Again visits France, but leaves hurriedly upon the outbreak of the Fronde rebellion.

1649   Leaves Holland for Sweden at the invitation of Queen Christian.
        Publishes the *Treatise on the Passions* (November).
1650   Dies at Stockholm on February 11.

THE SAPIR-WHORF HYPOTHESIS IN
HISTORICAL PERSPECTIVE

James H. Stam

Department of Philosophy and Religion
Upsala College
East Orange, New Jersey 07017

What is now commonly called the "principle of linguistic relativity" asserts a correlation between language and thinking either with regard to the specifics, the structure, the categories, or some other generalities of each; and in its stronger form it postulates that in some way the language of any given culture is the causal determinant of the patterns of thinking in that culture. It is now best known from the works of Edward Sapir, Professor of Anthropology and Linguistics in the Universities of Pennsylvania, Chicago, and Yale, and Benjamin Lee Whorf, a fire-prevention engineer in Hartford by profession and a linguist by passionate avocation. The pertinent works were composed mainly during the 1930s and the hypothesis reached a broader audience through publication of collected essays by both men during the 1950s. It was then that the position received more extensive discussion, criticism, and evaluation by anthropologists, linguists, psychologists, and philosophers. Similar hypotheses have been recurrent in the history of the philosophy of language since the eighteenth century. It is my purpose to see what some of these previous attempts can tell us about the nature of the alleged correlation: the problems it is meant to illuminate and the errors it is intended to dispel. I will first summarize the hypothesis in the formulations of Sapir and Whorf and roughly sketch the historical links whereby it traveled from eighteenth-century Königsberg to twentieth century Connecticut.

The best statement of the principle by Sapir is from a paper delivered in 1928, "The Status of Linguistics as a Science."

> Language is a guide to 'social reality'. . . . It powerfully conditions all our thinking about social problems and processes. Human beings do not live in the objective world alone, nor alone in the world of social activity as ordinarily understood, but are very much at the mercy of the particular language which has become the medium of expression for their society. It is quite an illusion to imagine that one adjusts to reality essentially without the use of language and that language is merely an incidental means of solving specific problems of communication or reflection The fact of the matter is that the 'real world' is to a large extent unconsciously built up on the language habits of the group. No two languages are ever sufficiently similar to be considered as representing the same social reality. The worlds in which different societies live are distinct worlds, not merely the same world with different labels attached.[1]

Note a few things about this paragraph. First, a causal relationship of some kind is clearly suggested: Language *conditions* our thinking; we are *at its mercy*; and so on. Second, whereas the phrases "social reality" and "real world" are put into quotation marks, the *distinct worlds* to which language is related is not. Finally, the correlation asserted is at this point very general indeed.

Sapir continues:

> The understanding of a simple poem, for instance, involves not merely an under-

standing of the single words in their average significance, but a full comprehension of the whole life of the community as it is mirrored in the words, or as it is suggested by their overtones. Even comparatively simple acts of perception are very much more at the mercy of the social patterns called words than we might suppose. If one draws some dozen lines, for instance, of different shapes, one perceives them as divisible into such categories as 'straight,' 'crooked,' 'curved,' 'zigzag' because of the classificatory suggestiveness of the linguistic terms themselves. We see and hear and otherwise experience very largely as we do because the language habits of our community predispose certain choices of interpretation.[2]

Applications of the principle are here more specific, but are of very different sorts. In the first example, the meaning of the parts—the words of a poem—is said to derive from the whole of a language and the whole of a culture. Only in the last example is a correlation of part to part proposed, that between word and figure identification.

A few paragraphs later, it is to the general correlation that Sapir returns: "We may suspect that linguistics is destined to have a very special value for configurative psychology ('Gestalt psychology'), for, of all forms of culture, it seems that language is that one which develops its fundamental patterns with relatively the most complete detachment from other types of cultural patterning. Linguistics may thus hope to become something of a guide to the understanding of the 'psychological geography' of culture in the large."[3] Sapir writes this in the context of differentiating functional and symbolic activities, wherein he approaches without ever quite formulating the distinction sometimes made between sign and symbol. Although the passage is not fully clear, it is evident that Sapir sees as the distinctive character of human language its ability to transcend functional and one-to-one relationships.

Whorf was more specific than Sapir in his attempts to apply the principle to contrasts between American Indian languages and Standard Average European— as he called everything from Italian to English—but his formulations are also much more varied. He was apparently groping for a philosophical terminology adequate to his meaning and in general does not display any broad or thorough acquaintance with modern philosophical literature. In the array of phrases he employs, however, a definite pattern emerges. Language, says Whorf, involves a "connection of ideas,"[4] a "segmentation of nature,"[5] an "organization, classification, or arrangement of experience,"[6] "a 'geometry' of form principles characteristic of each language."[7] Underlying every language is a "metaphysics,"[8] an "idea-map of language."[9] Grammar must analyze "covert as well as overt structure and meaning," because language and thinking both involve covert as well as overt categories and classes, cryptotypes as well as phenotypes.[10] Thus the purpose of "scientific grammar" must be a "deep analysis into relations."[11] The correlation of language and thought is in several places said to be unconscious: " . . . the forms of a person's thoughts are controlled by inexorable laws of pattern of which he is unconscious. These patterns are the unperceived systematizations of his own language. . . . "[12] "The phenomena of a language are to its own speakers largely of a background character and so are outside the critical consciousness and control of the speaker."[13] Throughout there is an emphasis upon pattern. What is needed, writes Whorf, is a "Gestalt technique" to show how "different languages differently 'segment' the same situation or experience."[14] Basic to language is a "configurative or pattern aspect,"[15] "a systematic synthetic use of pattern,"[16] "a sway of pattern over reference."[17]

What emerges from these varied and often loose formulations is that Whorf's point concerns the relationship of something general in language to something general in thought; only incidentally and in hesitant application does it concern the correspondence between any linguistic particular and any particular perception or conception.[18] Whorf may have lacked either the rigor or the philosophical nomenclature to make these generalities more lucid, but it was such that he was driving at. This is consistent with the applications Whorf himself did undertake, which involved such things as the awareness of time, the awareness of agency, and the like. And it is consistent with his more direct formulation of the linguistic relativity principle itself.

> . . . the background linguistic system (in other words, the grammar) of each language is not merely a reproducing instrument for voicing ideas but rather is itself the shaper of ideas, the program and guide for the individual's mental activity, for his analysis of impressions, for his synthesis of his mental stock in trade. . . . We dissect nature along lines laid down by our native languages. The categories and types that we isolate from the world of phenomena we do not find there because they stare every observer in the face; on the contrary, the world is presented in a kaleidoscopic flux of impressions which has to be organized by our minds—and this means largely by the linguistic systems in our minds. . . . We are thus introduced to a new principle of relativity, which holds that all observers are not led by the same physical evidence to the same picture of the universe, unless their lingistic backgrounds are similar, or can in some way be calibrated.[19]

Or elsewhere: "Users of markedly different grammars are pointed by their grammars toward different types of observations and different evaluations of externally similar acts of observation, and hence are not equivalent as observers but must arrive at somewhat different views of the world. . . . The participants of a given world view are not aware of the idiomatic nature of the channels in which their talking and thinking run. . . . "[20] We here find the same pattern of vocabulary: the *picture* of the universe, *view* of the world, *channels* of our thinking.

Let us then turn to the historical background of the hypothesis. Ignoring Vico, whose influence outside of Italy remains a somewhat misty question, we can locate the beginnings of the line leading to the Sapir-Whorf formulation in Germany during the 1760s and 1770s, particularly in the wirtings of Johann Georg Hamann and Johann Gottfried Herder. To his contemporaries, the obscure Hamann represented an outspoken protest against the Enlightenment in both its rationalist and empiricist versions. Although he is a most difficult writer to paraphrase or even to quote properly, his objections as they relate to language can be summarized. Hamann ridiculed universal grammarians among the rationalists for their attempt to isolate the abstracting function of language and force its compliance with the rational and logically discursive faculties of the mind. Universal grammar, Hamann felt, tells us more about formal logic than it does about speech, and least of all does it explain the foundations of language. In an enticing epigram Hamann wrote that "poetry is the mother-tongue of the human race."[21] Primitive poetry—which at this time referred primarily to Homer and the Old Testament—was written in a sensuous, metaphorical, sometimes ecstatic language, more allied to music and dance than to syllogistics, expressive of a different scale of human values and a distinct outlook on the world and on human existence. In such poesy Hamann found a kind of primordial wisdom embedded more deeply in the human psyche than the axioms of mathematicians or the innate ideas of metaphysicians. The empiricists did, to be sure, draw parallels between stages of language and states of mind, and thinkers like Condillac and Turgot projected this psychological development as the pattern for the historical progression of the human race.[22] But for them, too, abstract reasoning was the implicit goal of this evolution: as the individual becomes more rational with maturity, so human language ages into a mechanism more efficient, more clarified, more scientific. Hamann and Herder insisted that language is not a mechanism at all and that its metamorphoses consitute differences, not improvements. Their contrast of ancient with modern languages involved an appreciation of "primitive" mentality and culture, a protest against modernist ethnocentricity, no less than did Whorf's comparisons of Hopi or Shawnee with Standard Average European.

Hamann and Herder took a phrase which had been used casually in the English and French literature, "the genius of language," and made of it something more systematic. Each language, indeed each stage in the growth of language, has its own peculiar genius, a *Sprachgeist* corresponding to the *Volksgeist*.[23] Since each language has its own genius, each must be understood on its own terms, "from the inside," so to speak, as an integral whole representing a comprehensive world-view. The political implication is clear: Herder's insistence that each national character has its own integrity expressed in its language is a dissent from the then-prevailing cosmopolitanism and Francophile cultural imperialism. Underlying this theme is the notion that language must be understood in organistic rather than mechanistic terms and the rejection of any functionalist explanation of language as a tool: language is not applied to a separable reality or expressive of a separate thought process, but inextricably connected with the delineation of that reality and the shaping of such thought. This motif is continued in German romantic thinkers, in Humboldt, in Steinthal, and evident in the pages of Sapir and Whorf themselves. For example, Whorf: "We are inclined to think of language simply as a technique of expression, and not to realize that language first of all is a classification and arrangement of the stream of sensory experience which results in a certain world-order. . . . "[24]

Similar themes abound in the writings of Wilhelm von Humboldt, though with an important Kantian ingredient. "One must not consider language as though it were a dead product," Humboldt wrote, "but far more as a producing."[25] "Language itself is not a work (*érgon*), but an activity (*enérgeia*).[26] Humboldt repeatedly emphasized the active, formative character of language: "The mutual dependence of thought and word the one upon the other makes it clear that languages are not in fact means for the presentation of a truth already recognized, but rather for the discovery of a truth previously unknown. Their diversity is not one of sounds and signs, but a diversity of the world-views themselves."[27] Subjectively considered, language is the mediation between one individual and the other individuals in his community and nation on the one hand, between the individual and the external world on the other. The various languages of different peoples, in turn, are the mediation between those peoples and universal humanity on the one hand and universal reason on the other. Within these parameters every language places its speakers within a charmed circle, which simultaneously presents a view of the world and limits the horizons of that same view.[28]

The line from Humboldt to Sapir and Whorf is reasonably clear. Humboldt's philosophy of language was taken up by dozens of German authors during the nineteenth century, most eminent among them Haymann Steinthal and Max Müller.[29] Steinthal edited Humboldt's posthumous works, and although he tergiversated on many issues and came under the sway of Herbartian psychology, the ethno- and psycholinguistic questions, in the literal sense of those terms, always remained in the forefront of his concerns.[30] Although Max Müller has now fallen under a nearly universal ill-repute, in his own day he was, after his emigration to Oxford, unrivaled in the English-speaking world as a popularizer of trends in linguistics and the philosophy of language.[31] In addition, references to Humboldt and his predecessors are scattered throughout general works on language—in English and widely read—by A. H. Sayce, Abel Hovelacque, and Dwight Whitney.[32] In 1885 Daniel G. Brinton translated and explicated one of Humboldt's articles.[33] Accessibility in English was not that important, however, since both Sapir and his teacher, Franz Boas, were German-born. The latter knew Steinthal personally while still a student and had an extensive acquaintance with the tradition under discussion.[34] In his introductory volume to the *Handbook of American Indian Languages*, Boas argued against Brinton and against the "Hypothesis of Original Correlation of [Physical] Type, Language, and Culture";[35] but it should be said that Sapir and Whorf also rejected superficial correlations such as those Boas there considered.[36] Sapir did his undergraduate and early graduate work in Germanistics at Columbia before turning to anthropological studies under Boas. An early article about Herder's *Prize Essay Concerning the Origin of Language* also discussed Hamann and Humboldt.[37] Whorf arrived at his formulations more independently: It was relatively late that he came into close contact with Sapir and became somewhat more aware of the historical background for his own hypothesis.

I should make three general points regarding this historical sketch. First of all, it is incomplete, and especially so with regard to a French tradition going back to the seventeenth century and including what is now referred to—for better or worse—as "Cartesian linguistics." So long as we leave the hypothesis in the vague terms of a correlation between language and thought, this can be found as well in the writings of an avowed Cartesian like Cordemoy, or in the *Port-Royal Grammar* or *Logic*, or in the sundry *Grammaires raisonnées*. Two generalizations show the contrast between these and the works of the "German tradition."[38] First, these French works do not emphasize the ways in which the correlation is specific to individual cultures and their languages. The specifically cultural understanding of the relationship between language and thought was in the main a German contribution. Secondly, in these French works language is generally taken to be the mirror or reflection of thought, whereas among the Germans language and language-making are themselves formative factors in thought and in the thinking process. However much Sapir and Whorf may have hedged on this causative factor, something of it seems to be an essential ingredient in the linguistic relativity principle.

Second, this rough history presents us with an apparent anomaly. Critics of the Sapir-Whorf hypothesis have drawn, at least in part, upon the very same tradition and especially on Humboldt. To take a recent example: In *After Babel* George Steiner contrasts the tradition we are here discussing (for which he shows great sympathy) with the universalism of Chomsky and his antecedents.[39] Yet Chomsky, quite properly, considers some of the same thinkers among his own philosophical forbears: His admiration for Humboldt, for example, is as much in evidence as is his distance from the Sapir-Whorf hypothesis.[40]

Finally, when the linguistic relativity principle is placed in historical perspective, the less appropriate to it seem the various psychological experiments and other devices designed since the 1950s to test its validity. These experiments have involved null hypotheses, color-recognition tests, object associations based on figure versus color, and the like.[41] Even though the framers of some of these experiments were well aware of this and other problems involved, by necessity their tests looked toward a matching of verbal particulars with perceptual particulars, of physical stimuli with linguistic responses.[42] But such particulars are rather incidental to the intent of the hypothesis as we have seen it, and so too is overt behavior.[43] Just as Whorf distinguished overt and covert categories, phenotypes and cryptotypes, so Herder concerned himself with "inner language" and Humboldt with the "inner form of language."[44] Experimental tests, perhaps by necessity, measure overt behavior. If, however, the principle of linguistic relativity is not really about overt verbal behavior, then tests of such behavior can constitute neither its confirmation nor its refutation.

Our historical material can shed some light upon these last two points. It is crucial to clarify what is and was meant by the terms "thought" and "reality" as they are said to correlate with language. There was already an attempt to grapple with the first of these during the 1760s. In 1759 Johann David Michaelis received the prize of the Berlin Academy of Sciences in its essay contest concerning the topic: "What is the reciprocal influence of the opinions of a people upon its language and of language upon its opinions?"[45] Michaelis documented such influences and distinguished the deleterious from the beneficial varieties thereof, suggesting ways to overcome the harmful influences. The academy's topic seems directly to pose the question of what we now call the "linguistic relativity principle." Despite its coronation, Michaelis's prize essay received a cool reception from Hamann and from Moses Mendelssohn, and both of their reviews are specifically critical of the way in which the question had been formulated in the first place.

Mendelssohn pointed to both a circularity and an inconsistency built into the question as phrased. There is circularity insofar as it is assumed that linguistic evidence can be used to document the linguistic influence upon opinions—a point repeated in numerous commentators on Sapir and Whorf. There is inconsistency inasmuch as the theme proposed assumes that language does indeed limit and direct our thinking; but if that is in fact the case, then, says Mendelssohn, we are not in a position to see how language limits and directs it, for we are caught under the spell that we are trying to investigate. "As little as the eyes in their natural state can clearly perceive the instrument of sight, the light rays, perhaps just so little can the soul investigate language, the instrument of its thoughts, back to its origin."[46] If language limits our thinking, then we are unconscious of that fact; but "the limitations of language are no longer limitations, as soon as we recognize them as such."[47] Both Michaelis and the academy itself failed to make a fundamental distinction between that sort of unphilosophical thinking or opinion which is but dimly aware of the language it is employing and that more reflective kind of thinking—seen often enough in the works of philosophers, poets, mystics, and others—which consciously expresses its awareness of the limits of language and which wrestles with those very limitations. Even with philosophy so loosely defined as it is here, if a distinction is to be allowed between philosophical and nonphilosophical thinking, the relationship between language and thought would have to be investigated differently in the respective cases.

Hamann's review of Michaelis's prize essay is more outspoken, though it is replete with the enigmas and tropes so typical of Hamann's style. Hamann also demanded a clarification of the topic itself.[48] In particular, "the meaning of the word *opinions* (*Meynungen*) is ambiguous, since the same are sometimes equated with truths and sometimes taken as the opposite of truths."[49] Hamann refers to Plato's explanation of opinion (*dóxa*) as unexamined thinking and as the median stage between ignorance and knowledge. Opinion, for Plato, represents a type of limited thinking—thinking without really thinking about it—which is cave-bound, sense-bound, city- or culture-bound, and in these regards also specifically language-bound; i.e., it is tied up with and down to the limitations of a particular language. But it is Plato's point that such thinking is the antithesis of philosophy, that it is not genuine thinking. Hamann himself makes somewhat more complicated distinctions along these lines,[50] but the point is clear: The correlation of language and thought is only as good as the clarity of our explanation of the kind of thought we are talking about. It may be that the philosopher, in the end, is also unable to escape from his own linguistic cage, but the meaning of this would be something quite different from the linguistic imprisonment of non-philosophers—and again "philosopher" and "nonphilosopher" are used here in the broadest sense.

After the publication of Kant's *Critique of Pure Reason* in 1781, Hamann and Herder both began to work on metacritiques. Because of the interrelated text history of Hamann's brief and Herder's lengthy work,[51] I will here treat the two as one and emphasize their common charges against Kant. Their attack centers around two broad points: 1) Kant's adherence to a discredited faculty psychology; 2) Kant's failure to understand the role of language. In earlier treatises Herder had argued against any psychology that isolates the different faculties of the mind from one another, as though they performed separable operations.[52] Hamann particularly protested such an isolation of reason and, he felt, the consequent idolatry practiced with respect to the abstracted faculty.[53] Instead, Herder maintained, the psychologist must try to explain the total disposition of all the faculties, the specifically human element in the operation of each. Only when we emphasize the relatedness of all these operations do we begin to understand thinking *as a whole* and see what is human about human thinking.

A great bulk of Hamann's and Herder's criticisms concern language. They both accuse Kant of a misuse of language, of a forced style and vocabulary, which alone permit his conclusions.[54] More important, Kant failed to take account of language and the role it plays in the shaping of perceptions, the formation of judgments, and the construction of ideas. This neglect leaves Kant open to a charge which would be devastating to the arguments of the *Critique*, namely that the *a priori* forms of perception and of judgment and the ideas of reason themselves are all linguistically derived categories.[55]

Despite the metacritical attacks on Kant by Hamann and Herder, there is something common to their respective views of reality. That agreement is as important to an understanding of the language-thought correlation as are the differences. None of them takes reality to be something that is a given independently of human consciousness. All three reject the model of objectivity, or the separation of subject and object, implied in Galilean physics and Cartesian metaphysics. The example of Kant makes clear, however, that this does not involve a dismissal of science or of empirical evidence; nor does it entail relativism in the accepted Protagorean sense.[56] Rather, "subjective mind" and "objective reality" must be understood in their reciprocal interrelationship and interactivity. For Kant, reality is not a *Gegebenes,* but an *Aufgegebenes:* not simply given, but given as a task; not set down, but offered up; not a *datum*, but a constructive project.

The same points are equally important for Humboldt. Cassirer has amply documented the decisive influence that Kant had upon Humboldt's philosophy of language.[57] According to Kant, the objects of cognition are first constituted as objects in the act of cognition and in particular through the synthetic judgments of the understanding. Humboldt sought to complete the Kantian philosophy and rectify Kant's own neglect of language by assigning this synthetic function to the formative (*bildende*) powers of language itself, and in turn by relating this to the nature of language as *enérgeia* and to the nature of man as *Streben* (aspiration) and *Geisteskraft* ("spiritual or mental power," roughly translated). Any evaluation of Humboldt's philosophy of language would require a more thorough and careful presentation than this one, but my point is quite simple: The correlation between language and thought proposed by Humboldt, Herder, and Hamann must be understood in the context of this sort of an expansion of objective reality.[58] It is the failure to so so which, I believe, accounts both for the anomaly to which I have alluded earlier and for the inappropriateness of experimental tests of the Sapir-Whorf hypothesis to the hypothesis itself.

The title of Whorf's selected essays, *Language, Thought, and Reality*, serves as a short-hand version of the "linguistic relativity principle" itself. When we place that principle in historical perspective, we find that earlier thinkers tried more carefully to distinguish just what should be meant by "thought" and by "reality" in such an equation. Both Sapir and Whorf, as well as some of their critics and supporters, tried to specify which linguistic elements they thought pertinent to the correlation: lexation or grammar, phonetic or semantic components, even surface or deep structure; but they are more careless when they speak of thought and of reality.[59] I suggest that either the demonstration or the refutation of the hypothesis requires greater clarity about its terms. Otherwise we will as easily be entrapped by the magic spell of our respective methods, as this tradition claims that we can become enwebbed in the magic circle of our language.

NOTES AND REFERENCES

1. EDWARD SAPIR. 1968[1949]. The status of linguistics as a science. *In* Selected Writings of Edward Sapir in Language, Culture and Personality. David G. Mandelbaum, Ed. : 162 Berkeley-Los Angeles, University of California Press, Berkeley, Calif.
2. Ibid.
3. Ibid. pp. 164-165.
4. BENJAMIN LEE WHORF. 1956. On the connection of ideas. *In* Language, Thought, and Reality: Selected Writings of Benjamin Lee Whorf. John B. Carroll, Ed. : 35-39. M. I. T. Press, Cambridge, Mass. The "connection of ideas" is here distinguished from the "association of ideas."
5. "Segmentation of nature is an aspect of grammar . . . . We cut up and organize the spread and flow of events as we do, largely because, through our mother tongue, we are parties to an agreement to do so, not because nature itself is segmented in exactly that way for all to see." WHORF, Language and Logic, ibid., p. 240. "We cut nature up, organize it into concepts, and ascribe significances as we do, largely because we are parties to an agreement to organize it in this way—an agreement that holds throughout our speech community and is codified in the patterns of our language." WHORF. Science and linguistics, ibid., p. 213.
6. WHORF. The punctual and segmentative aspects of verbs in Hopi, ibid., p. 55.
7. WHORF. Language, mind, and reality, ibid., p. 257.
8. WHORF. An American Indian model of the universe, ibid., p. 59.
9. WHORF. Aztec linguistics. Quoted by Carroll in Introduction, ibid., p. 25.
10. WHORF. A Linguistic consideration of thinking in primitive communities, ibid., p. 79. Cf. Grammatical categories, ibid., pp. 88-89, 93; Discussion of Hopi linguistics, ibid., p. 105.
11. Ibid., p. 68.
12. WHORF. Language, mind, and reality, ibid., p. 252. "We all, unknowingly, project the linguistic relationships of a particular language upon the universe, and SEE them there. . . ." Ibid., p. 262.
13. WHORF. Science and linguistics, ibid., p. 211.
14. WHORF, Gestalt technique of stem composition in Shawnee, ibid., pp., 160, 162.
15. WHORF. Language, mind, and reality, ibid., p. 250.
16. WHORF, Languages and logic, ibid., p. 237.
17. WHORF, Language, mind, and reality, ibid., p. 261.
18. Whorf's early interest in linguistics was stimulated by a reading of Antoine Fabre d'Olivet (1768-1825), whose La langue hébraïque restituée (1815-1816), attributed an inherent meaning to each Hebrew letter, a clear part-to-part relationship. Cf.

Carroll, Introduction, ibid., pp. 8-9. Yet Whorf's own interpretation of Fabre d'Olivet deemphasizes this. Cf. A linguistic consideration of thinking in primitive communities, ibid., pp. 74-75.

19. WHORF. Science and linguistics, ibid., pp. 212-214.

20. WHORF. Linguistics as an exact science, ibid., pp. 221-222.

21. JOHANN GEORG HAMANN. 1949-1957. Aesthetica in nuce: Eine Rhapsodie in Kabbalistischer Prose, Kreuzzüge des Philologen. In Sämtliche Werke. Josef Nadler, Ed. Vol. II: 197. Verlag Herder. Vienna, Austria. On the general points of this section, cf. JAMES H. STAM, 1976. Inquiries into the origin of language: The fate of a question. In Studies in Language. ed. Noam Chomsky and Morris Halle, Eds. : 65-72, 109-164. Harper & Row. New York, N.Y. Cf. also JAMES C. O'FLAHERTY. 1952. Unity and Language: A Study in the Philosophy of Johann George Hamann. University of North Carolina Studies in the Germanic Languages and Literatures, No. 6. University of North Carolina Press. Chapel Hill, N. C. RUDOLF UNGER. 1905. Hamanns Sprachtheorie im Zusammenhange seines Denkens: Grundlegung zu einer Würdigung der geistesgeschichtlichen Stellung des Magus in Norden. Munich, Germany.

22. Cf. Etienne Bonnot de Condillac. 1974. An essay on the origin of human knowledge. James H. Stam, introduction. In Language, Man and Society: Foundations of the Behavioral Sciences, R. W. Rieber, Ed. AMS Press. New York, N.Y. cf. also STAM. Op. cit., pp. 45-54.

23. Cf., for example, HAMANN. Versuch über eine akademische Frage. Kreuzzüge des Philologen, op. cit., vol. II, pp. 122-123. The theme and these particular expressions run throughout Herder's writings from the earliest to the late period. Cf. ERNST CASSIRER, The Philosophy of Symbolic Forms, trans. Ralph Manheim (Yale University Press. New Haven, Conn. 1953), vol. I, pp. 143-155.

24. WHORF. The Punctual and Segmentative Aspects of Verbs in Hopi, op. cit., p. 55.

25. WILHELM VON HUMBOLDT. 1903-1918. Ueber die Verschiedenheit des menschlichen Sprachbaues und ihren Einfluss auf die geistige Entwicklung des Menschengeschlechts. In Gesammelte Schriften, Albert Leitzmann, Ed. vol. VII, p. 44. Königlich Preussische Akademie der Wissenschaften. Berlin, Germany.

26. Ibid., p. 46.

27. HUMBOLDT. Ueber das vergleichende Sprachstudium in Beziehung auf die verschiedenen Epochen der Sprachentwicklung, ibid., Vol. IV, p. 27.

28. Cf. ibid., p. 22.

29. In Germany this line continues into the twentieth century in the works of WALTER PORZIG, ERNST CASSIRER, JOST TRIER, and LEO WEISGERBER. Cf. ROBERT L. MILLER. 1968. The Linguistic Relativity Principle and Humboldtian Ethnolinguistics, Janua linguarum, Series minor, no. 67. Mouton. The Hague, the Netherlands. cf. HELMUT GRIPPER. 1972. Gibt es ein sprachliches Relativitatsprinzip? Untersuchungen zur Sapir-Whorf-Hypothese, Conditio humana: Ergebnisse aus den Wissenschaften vom Menschen, T. V. Uexküll and I. Grubrich-Simitis, Eds. S. Fischer Verlag, Stuttgart, Germany; cf. LEONHARD JOST. 1960. Sprache als Werk und wirkende Kraft: Ein Beitrag zur Geschichte und Kritik der energetischen Sprachauffassung seit Wilhelm vom Humboldt. Sprache und Dichtung, Neue Folge. Vol. 6. Verlag Paul Haupt. Bern, Switzerland.

30. Themes from HUMBOLDT appear in nearly all of STEINTHAL'S work, but cf. especially, Die Sprachwissenschaft Wilhelm von Humboldts und die Hegel'sche Philosophie (Berlin 1848); Der Ursprung der Sprache im Zusammenhange mit den letzten Fragen alles Wissens (Berlin 1851); Grammatik, Logik und Psychologie: Ihre Principien und ihr Verhältniss zu einander (Berlin 1855); Einleitung in die Psychologie und Sprachwissenschaft (Berlin 1871).

31. Cf. FRIEDRICH MAX MÜLLER. Lectures on the Science of Language (New York 1866), 2 vols; The Science of Thought (New York 1887), 2 vols.

32. Cf. A. H. SAYCE, Introduction to the Science of Langauge (London 1880), 2 vols.; ABEL HOVELACQUE, The Science of Language: Linguistics, Philology, Etymology, trans. A. H. Keane (London-Philadelphia 1877); WILLIAM DWIGHT WHITNEY. Language and the Study of Language (New York 1867).

33. Cf. DANIEL G. BRINTON. 1885. The Philosophic Grammar of American Languages, as Set Forth by William von Humboldt, with the Translation of an Unpublished Memoir by him on the American Verb. Proc. Am. Philos. Soc. XXII: 332-352.

34. Cf., on this and other points, ROGER LANGHAM BROWN. 1967. Wilhelm von Humboldt's Conception of Linguistic Relativity, Janua linguarum, Series minor, No. 65: 13-16. Mouton, The Hague, The Netherlands.

35. Cf. FRANZ BOAS. 1911. Introduction. In Handbook of American Indian Languages Franz Boas, Ed. vol. I: 11-14; cf. also pp. 64-73. Government Printing Office. Washington, D.C.

36. Cf. SAPIR. Language, op. cit., pp. 26-27; cf. WHORF. A Linguistic Consideration of Thinking in Primitive Communities, op. cit., pp. 65-73, 77-79.

37. Cf. SAPIR. 1907. Herder's "Ursprung der Sprache." Modern Philology V(1): 109-142. The article was based on Sapir's M. A. thesis at Columbia Univ. (1905): Herder's Prize Essay, "Ueber den Ursprung der Sprache," and its Place in the Discussion of the Origin of Language.

38. Cf. GUY HARNOIS. 1928. Les Théories du langage en France de 1660 à 1821: 29-42; cf. PIERRE JULIARD, Philosophies of Language in Eighteenth-Century France. 1970. Janua linguarum, Series minor, No. 18: 45-58. Mouton. The Hague, The Netherlands.

39. Cf. GEORGE STEINER. 1975. After Babel: Aspects of Language and Translation: Oxford University Press. 73-109. Oxford, England.

40. Cf. NOAM CHOMSKY. 1964. Current Issues in Linguistic Theory Janua linguarum, Series minor No. 38: 17-21. Mouton. The Hague, The Netherlands. Cartesian Linguistics: A Chapter in the History of Rationalist Thought, Studies in Language. 1966. Noam Chomsky and Morris Halle, Eds. : 19-30, 57-65. Harper & Row. New York, N.Y.

41. Cf. the reviews of problems, research, and literature in ROGER BROWN. 1958. Words and Things: 229-263. Glencoe, Ill., Free Press. Glencoe, Ill. JOSEPH DE VITO. 1970. The Psychology of Speech and Language: An Introduction to Psycholinguistics : 199-206. Random House. New York, N.Y.; A. RICHARD DIEBOLD, JR. 1965. A Survey of Psycholinguistic Research, 1954-1964. Psycholinguistics: A Survey of Theory and Research Problems. Charles E. Osgood and Thomas A. Sebeok, Eds.: 258-263, 276-291. Indiana Univ. Press. Bloomington, Ind.; DAN I. SLOBIN. 1974. Psycholinguistics : 120-133. Scott, Foresman & Co. Glenview, Ill.

42. Cf. ERIC H. LENNEBERG: "Suppose, for example, that we subject English speakers to a set of physical stimuli and record their linguistic responses." The comment was made in a discussion session, The Strategy of Research in the Interrelations of Language and Other Aspects of Culture. 1954. Language in Culture: Proceedings of a Conference on the Interrelations of Language and Other Aspects of Culture. Harry Hoijer, Ed.: 266-267. University of Chicago Press. Chicago, Ill. Of particular importance from this volume are the papers (and relevant discussion) of JOSEPH H. GREENBERG, FRANKLIN FEARING, HARRY HOIJER, and CHARLES F. HOCKETT. For further discussion of research and verification possibilities, cf. Anthropology Today: An Encyclopedic Inventory (1953. A. L. Kroeber, Ed. University of Chicago Press. Chicago, Ill.), especially Hoijer's paper, The Relation of Language to Culture, pp. 554-573; cf. also An Appraisal of Anthropology Today. 1953 Sol Tax, Loren C. Eiseley, Irving Rouse, and Carl F. Voegelin, Eds.: 273-298; University of Chicago Press. Chicago, Ill. cf. also the papers by FLOYD G. LOUNSBURY, MAX BLACK, HARVEY PITKIN, and SARA RUDDICK In Language and Philosophy: A Symposium. 1969. Sidney Hook, Ed. New York Univ. Press. New York, N.Y.; University of London Press. London, England.

43. Although Whorf used the term "behavior" often enough, consider his comments on behaviorism in On Psychology, op. cit., pp. 40-42. Cf. 36, above.

44. Cf. WALTER PORZIG. 1923. Der Begriff der inneren Sprachform. Indogermanische Forschungen XLI: 150-169; LEO WEISGERBER. 1926. Das Problem der inneren Sprachform und seine Bedeutung für die deutsche Sprache. Germanisch-Romanische Monatsschrift XIV: 241-256; BRIGIT BENES. 1958. Wilhelm von Hunboldt, Jacob Grimm, August Schleicher: Ein Vergleich ihrer Sprachauffassung. 3-28. Winterthur, Verlag P. G. Keller. Winterthur. SIEGFRIED J. SCHMIDT. 1968. Sprache und Denken als sprachphilosophisches Problem von Locke bis Wittgenstein: 36-77. Martinus Nijhoff, The Hague, The Netherlands. pp. 36-77. On the significance of the notion of inner form for Whorf, cf. JOHN T. WATERMAN. 1957. Benjamin Lee Whorf and Linguistic Field Theory. Southwestern J. Anthropol. XIII: 201-211; cf. also HAROLD BASILIUS. 1952. Neo-Humboldtian Ethnolinguistics. Word VIII: pp. 95-105.

45. Cf. JOHANN DAVID MICHAELIS. 1973. A Dissertation on the Influence of Opinions on Language, and of Language on Opinions. Intro., James H. Stam, Language, Man and Society: Foundations of the Behavioral Sciences. R. W. Rieber, Ed. AMS Press. New York, N.Y. Cf. STAM, op. cit., pp. 104-109.

46. MOSES MENDELSSOHN, 1759. Briefe, die neueste Literatur betreffend. 72nd Letter. Vol. IV: 365-366. Stettin. Berlin, Germany.

47. Ibid., p. 370.

48. "In my opinion it would be easier to survey the discussion of the question concerning the reciprocal influence of opinions and language, if the topic itself were explained before plunging into solutions to it." HAMANN, Versuch ÜBER eine akademische Frage, op. cit., p. 121.

49. Ibid.

50. Cf. ibid., pp. 122-125.
51. Both HAMANN and HERDER conceived metacritiques after reading KANT'S Critique and discussed their common ideas in correspondence. Herder received and kept a copy of HAMANN'S unpublished manuscript, Metakritik über den Purismum der Vernunft, after the latter's death in 1788. In 1799 Herder published his own Meta-critique of the Critique of Pure Reason in two volumes and in 1800 his Kalligone, a metacritical response to Kant's Critique of Judgment. F. T. RINK, an avid Kantian, thereupon accused HERDER of plagiarism and published HAMANN'S piece as his evidence. Cf. Rink. 1800. Mancherley zur Geschichte der metacritischen Invasion: Nebst einem Fragment einer ältern Metakritik und einigen Aufsätzen, die Kantische Philosophie betreffend. Königsberg, Germany. Cf. BERNHARD SUPHAN. Einleitung zu Band XXI. XXII. Herders Sämmtliche Werke (Berlin 1877-1913), vol. XXI: v-xxv; cf. ROBERT T. CLARK. 1955 Herder: His Life and Thought: 396-412. Univ. California Press. Berkeley, Cal.
52. HERDER'S two most important works on this theme are Abhandlung über den Ursprung der Sprache (1770) and Vom Erkennen und Empfinden der menschlichen Seele (1778).
53. Cf. W. M. ALEXANDER. 1966. Johann Georg Hamann: Metacritic of Kant. J. History of Ideas XXVII 137-149; WALTER LEIBRECHT. 1966. God and Man in the Thought of Hamann. Trans., James H. Stam and Martin H. Bertram: 161-171; Fortress Press. Philadelphia, Pa. cf. RUDOLF UNGER. 1925. Hamann und die Aufklärung: Studien zur Vorgeschichte des romantischen Geistes im 18. Jahrhundert. 2nd edit. Halle an der Salle. Max Niemeyer.
54. Cf. HERDER'S preface to the Metakritik: "It is not presumptuous to contradict presumptions. To oppose a vain dialectic, which . . . would impose its word-schemes on us as the completed, most elevated results of all thinking, and to cleanse such misused language of its rubbish . . .: this is not presumption, but a duty. Whoever through artifice spoils a nation's language—no matter the acumen with which it is done—he has corrupted and injured the instrument of its reason." Op. cit., p. 12. The criticism of Kant's language begins with the very title, Kritik der reinen Vernunft: cf. ibid., pp. 17-19.
55. If true, incidentally, the charge would not as such entail that those categories are "relative," nor would it even mean that they could not be a priori in some modified sense; but it would mean that neither those categories nor reason as such is autonomous.
56. To a certain extent the label "linguistic relativity" misses the point. On one interpretation Kant was a subjectivist, but he certainly was not a relativist. No more so was Hamann, and neither in the end was Herder. And a concern with "linguistic universals" runs throughout the writings of Humboldt.
57. Cf. ERNST CASSIRER, Die Kantischen Elemente in Wilhelm von Humboldts Sprachphilosophie. 1923. Festschrift für Paul Hensel: 105-127 Greiz, Ohag: The Philosophy of Symbolic Forms. op. cit., pp. 155-163; Structuralism in Modern Linguistics, Word I (1945), pp. 99-120. On p. 116 of the last essay Cassirer paraphrases verses of Goethe to summarize Humboldt:
    All languages are alike, and none is just like the other;
    Thus the chorus points toward a hidden law.
    Cf. also WILHELM STREITBERG. 1909. Kant und die Sprachwissenschaft: Eine historische Skizze. Indogermanische Forschungen XXVI 382-422.
58. In An American Indian Model of the Universe, WHORF himself seems to be attacking Kant when he criticizes our "supposed . . . intuitions of time and space" (op. cit., p. 57), and when he asserts: "The metaphysics underlying our own language, thinking, and modern culture . . . imposes upon the universe two grand COSMIC FORMS, space and time" (p. 59). "Intuition" here was the popular but dubious translation of KANT'S Anschauung. In general, the passage shows unawareness of the points I have tried to make here with respect to Kant.
59. In some ways our best clue is the fact that Sapir and Whorf usually put the words "reality" and "objective world" in quotation marks except when speaking of a social reality; but that is rough, indirect, and insufficient explanation. The twentieth century German thinkers referred to in Ref. 29 are less lax in this regard. Perhaps the vocabulary already employed by Hamann, Herder, and Humboldt—Weltbild, Weltansicht, Weltanschauung and the like—is better suited to express the hypothesis by emphasizing the general and "pattern aspect" of the correlation.

DISCUSSION

Michael Wertheimer, *Moderator*

Department of Psychology
University of Colorado
Boulder, Colorado 80302

DR. WERTHEIMER: It is a pleasure to welcome you to our session entitled "Historial Aspects of the Psychology of Language and Cognition," those incredibly complex but not uniquely human processes that have fascinated humanity since antiquity. The psychology of cognition, of course, is intimately tied to the session on the psychology of self (see Part III). I was reminded then that Wolfgang Köhler in a seminar on Systematic Psychology in the mid-1940s, recounted an ingenious experiment done, if I remember correctly, late in the last or early in the present century by the Frenchman Eduard Claparède in an effort to localize the phenomenal self in space.

He asked subjects to indicate where various points in space around them were located, either in front or in back, above or below, or to the right or to the left. For instance, this is above and to the right and in front. This is directly above, this is where? And so on. By triangulation he came up with a place a little behind the eyes, roughly the same place at which dogs look when they look at you and that people look at when they make eye contact. This location corresponds—which leads indirectly into one of our papers, the one by John Sullivan—this locus, the phenomenal self, corresponds almost perfectly with the pineal gland.

Dr. Arthur Blumenthal reminded us in his *Language and Psychology: Historical Aspects of Psycholinguistics*, that psycholinguistic work represented the culmination of a major tradition in nineteenth century linguistics, namely that begun by Humboldt. This is the same tradition recently renewed by Noam Chomsky and his colleagues in America." Wundt insisted that three problems that were a major focus of his *Völkerpsychologie*—language, myth, and custom, are extremely closely interrelated, being always bound together through social life. Wilhelm von Humboldt had hinted that language mirrors the Vorstellungswelt or the conceptual scheme of its speakers, possibly a forerunner of the Sapir-Whorf notion. Wundt reiterated the common sense position that there is ordinarily in mind a complete idea of what is said *before* a sentence is formulated, and examined how the anticipatory total idea finally yields the sentence, what not long ago might have been called the process of going from deep structure to surface structure. Even Humboldt, more than half a century before Wundt had emphasized the creative aspect of language use. "Language makes *infinite* use of *finite* means." Such a recognition of what are now sometimes called linguistic universals was already on the intellectual scene in the eighteenth century. For instance, James Beattie, in his *The Theory of Language* published in London in 1788, referred to things that all languages have in common or that are necessary to every language, and proposed that we already have a science called universal or philosophical grammar to deal with such things. Some sixty years earlier, César Chesneau de Marsais in *Les véritables principes de la grammaire*, 1729, had written that there are in grammar certain observations that hold for all languages, and that it is these observations which constitute what is called "general grammar." He refers to the articulation of sounds, to the letters that symbolize the sounds, to the nature of words and the different ways in which they can be arranged or have endings added to them so as to convey meaning.

I can't resist augmenting these opening remarks, some of which, incidentally, have been paraphrased from Noam Chomsky's *Aspects of the Theory of Syntax*, 1965, or my crude translations of French writers whom Chomsky quotes in French, by adding just a little more on word order and related matters.

Lancelot, back in 1660, observed that aside from poetry of figurative speech, the sequence of words follows a "natural order" which conforms to the "natural expression of our thoughts." The great encyclopedist, Denis Diderot, wrote in 1751 that "whatever the order of terms in an ancient or modern language, the writer's mind has followed the didactic order of French syntax. . . . We say things in French in the way the mind is forced to consider them, irrespective of what language they are written in. . . . Our every-day language has over others the advantage of utility on top of agreeableness. . . . French is appropriate for the sciences, while Greek, Latin, Italian and English are more suited to literature." Moreover, "good sense would choose the French language; but imagination and the passions would prefer ancient languages, or those of our neighbors. . . . We have to speak French in polite society and in schools of philosophy, and Greek, Latin, English from the pulpit or in the theater. Our [French] language would be that of truth itself, if ever it were to return to the earth, and Greek, Latin and the others would be the languages of fables and lies. French is made to instruct, clarify and convince. Greek, Latin, Italian, English are for propaganda, for emotion and for deception. Speak Greek, Latin, Italian to people at large, but speak French to a sage."

DR. OTTO MARX, *Discussant (Boston University, Boston, Mass.)*: I will restrict myself and say something about the two papers that I had the pleasure to read, Dr. Tweney's and Dr. Stamm's, and share with you some of my concepts. Let me start at the end, which is always a good way, with Dr. Stamm's very beautifully phrased—I cannot say it quite as nicely—idea that we are all caught up within our language and within our own way, and within our own culture, our own kind. I would say that perhaps one of the differences between the nineteenth and the twentieth centuries is that we have become fully aware that we are caught in this particular way, and therefore I would say I also see the circularity that Moses Mendelson saw, but I am less concerned with it. Straight-line thinking is good for short distances, as are the rules that we have, but if we travel at any great length we know it's part of a circle, and if we travel far it's going to be in a circle, or else we take off on a tangent.

With regard to Dr. Tweney's paper, I think it indicates that there is a transition in historiography from dealing with people to trying to do what Willem Van Hoorn suggested, which is to move to movements and masses, while Dr. Tweney suggested that he will view a period, a time, an attitude, an approach. Characteristic of that, indeed he gave us basically great men, if you will, but to what extent is this wish to deal with masses and movements our preoccupation because we are impressed in our own time by the insignificance of the individual? Perhaps in early nineteenth century America it was fine to be an individual and perfectly adequate, especially because people shared presuppositions with each other and therefore could communicate so much better. With regard to historiography, let me say that I think that in both papers, both authors had the sense and the courtesy to their readers to inform them of their goals. I think they were less clear in describing the methods they would use to pursue these goals, and perhaps, most importantly, share with us their idea as to what evidence would be sufficient in their opinion to make the point they were trying to prove.

That is a big problem, especially if you have attended this meeting; you see that there are all kinds of provisions of historiography that come together in this meeting, and we all presume that we know each other's method and approach, but I don't think we really do.

DR. HAROLD VETTER, *Discussant, (University of South Florida, Tampa, Fla.):* I have come away from the conference with three very distinct impressions. The first is that if a tricentennial conference on language in cognition reports that on April 30 the Sapir-Whorf Hypothesis was finally interred, I think it will also record that Prof. Stamm drove the final nail in the coffin, which may leave some people disappointed but may leave others feeling that it's high time, because the Sapir-Whorf Hypothesis has been for psycholinguists and linguists something in the nature of the search for the alkahest or the philosopher's stone in alchemy.

The second impression is that we have in the past couple of centuries, with incredible frequency, reinvented the wheel. In the absence of the development of some consistent methodology, it seems that intuition and insight, however brilliant, aren't enough to provide any real continuity, and third, in his presidential address a number of years ago in the Linguistic Society of America, Fred Hocket said that we only get the kind of immortality we bestow on others, and psychology in rediscovering its own history, I think, has made a tremendous move toward the establishment of its own immortality.

DR. RIEBER, *Discussant*: I would just like to make a few remarks about Ryan Tweney's paper and Jeff Wollock's paper. I think Ryan raised an interesting question for which I would like to speculate an hypothesis, namely, why wasn't Johnson's Theory on Language, as sophisticated as it was, recognized as something very important in his time? One way to approach this would be to ask the question: Which theories of language during the nineteenth century were popular and accepted within the scientific community, and why were they popular? The answer seems to be that only those theories of language which were a by-product of the larger theory of the mind were popular during the nineteenth century. The major concern was a systematic explanation of how the mind functions. Theories of language were, of course, important to nineteenth century scholars, but for the most part they were dependent upon how well they fit into the larger framework of mental and moral philosophy. There are many variables that determine whether or not a particular theory becomes popular. For example, James Rush had both a theory of mind and language but still did not get very much recognition. The major reason for this was that his basic philosophical approach was critical of the establishment and its goals. He also published his work on the mind at a time (Civil War period) when the circumstances were working against him rather than for him. For example, Upham had published his system of the three-part division of the mind thirty years before Rush.

Thornton never published any theory of mind or any real psychological treatise. There are manuscripts, however, fascinating manuscripts talking about animal mind, sleep, and dreams, and human factors related to such. These manuscripts were never published. The first book that Thornton published was his *Cadmus*, a book primarily concerned with the application of scientific knowledge. This was very important to the building of the nation, as Mr. Wollock pointed out, I believe this to be significant in the development of American psychology because the main concern at that time was with the application of knowledge. James Rush is a good example. He published his *Philosophy of the Voice* first (1827), which was his application, and he didn't publish his treatise on the *Mind* (1865) until a few years before he died.

DR. WERTHEIMER: Do any members of the panel want to raise any questions with each other, or comment?

MR. WOLLOCK: A small point, very briefly: Ryan Tweney noted that Bishop Wilkins' universal language was in some respects a retrograde influence in the nineteenth century. I just want to mention some important practical applications developed in Roget's *Thesaurus* (because that comes straight out of Wilkins' idea), which first appeared in 1852; and also in Melvil Dewey's Decimal System of Classification, begun in 1876; these are tremendous influences that we work with constantly.

DR. TWENEY: I just want to say that I didn't mean to imply in reply to what Jeff just said, that Bishop Wilkins was entirely a negative influence, only that Wilkins' idea, when applied to the relation between ideas and thinking, is simply not as powerful and not as sophisticated as the analysis that comes out of Locke. In this regard, let me turn to something Dr. Rieber said and attempt to answer, at least tentatively, the implied question about what really was important in the nineteenth century, if Johnson wasn't. The answer that I tried to suggest is that there was a characteristic and typical approach to language of which Johnson's work is simply one instance. There is recognition that the problem of reference was important but very little serious thought given to exactly how, that's what I meant when I said that the tradition is naïve. I think Wollock's paper points to what was truly important in the nineteenth century with regard to language, and that is the practical applications that flow from it, spelling reform, dictionary construction, the recording of Indian languages, and so on and so on, and these, of course, must be part of any complete account of what went on with regard to language in the nineteenth century.

DR. MARX: Perhaps not everyone knows, but James Rush was the son of Benjamin Rush, and perhaps it is not surprising that he waited a long time to publish his writings on the mind. Benjamin Rush did not publish on the mind until just before he died. The other son of Benjamin Rush was quite insane all his life, so perhaps it's useful to have certain respect before one tackles the mind and doesn't necessarily have all the answers right at the beginning as one begins to use it.

DR. RIEBER: Rush, James Rush, said that it was impossible because of a lack of technology to investigate the mind the way he would like. He thought that there was a crude technological way to investigate the voice, and because the only technology he had to investigate the mind was the natural history approach to the study of the mind, he'd better live damned long before he could do it, and that's what he intended to do, to live as long as he could, continue to observe everything he could, corroborate all of his original hunches, which he did, and write it up before he died, and that he says quite explictly in his book on the mind.

Part VI. Psychological Systems: Past, Present, and Future

HENRY A. MURRAY

R. W. Rieber

*Department of Psychology
John Jay College of Criminal Justice
City University of New York
New York, New York 10019*

Our first speaker is Dr. Henry A. Murray. If a future historian of psychology should one day look back on the development of our profession—and certainly he would have to go through the annals of The New York Academy of Sciences to see what happened during this last decade—he might discover that certain psychologists had been making much of their attempts to flip the lid off a chimpanzee's id. I dare say he will find that research rather uneventful, but his disappointment may be eased when he reaches the moment in 1951 when Dr. Murray analyzed a whale.*

Henry Alexander Murray was born in New York City on May 13, 1893. He was graduated from Harvard University in 1915 with a degree in history, and from Columbia Medical School in 1919. Returning the following year to Harvard, he divided his time between research and an instructorship in physiology. After two years' surgical internship at the Presbyterian Hospital, New York, he became assistant and then associate member of the Rockefeller Institute for Medical Research. A year's leave (1924-25) was spent at Trinity College, Cambridge, England, carrying out studies that resulted in a Ph.D. degree in Biochemistry (1927). During this year abroad he became interested in medical psychology, and after analytic work with Jung in Zurich and study in psychiatric clinics in New York he joined Morton Prince in founding the Harvard Psychological Clinic.

Upon Prince's retirement in 1928, Dr. Murray became director of the clinic and assistant professor of abnormal psychology. Collaborative researches and experiments in the field of personality resulted in the classic *Explorations in Personality* (1938). He helped found the Boston Psychoanalytic Institute, where he completed the training he had interrupted when he left Harvard to serve in the Medical Corps as Major and then Lieutenant Colonel, assigned to the office of Strategic Services. At the war's end he received the Legion of Merit for his work in organizing and directing assessment procedures and researchers for the OSS in Britain, France, China, and the United States. Another result of this work was the book *Assessment of Men.*

His studies of Herman Melville, begun in 1925, culminated in the publication of an edition of Melville's *Pierre*, to which he added a discussion of the psychology of creative writing. The following year he returned to Harvard as professor of psychology in the newly formed Department of Social Relations, and as Emeritus in 1962. Dr. Murray's best known achievement is perhaps the Thematic Apperception Test, a personality assessment test still widely used. He also did research on religion, myth, fantasies, dreams, sentiments, and fear.

*I.e., In Nomine Diaboli, New England Quart. 24: 435-452, a paper on Melville's *Moby Dick*.

Dr. Murray has served on the Board of the Asian Institute and the Advisory Board, Educational Testing Service; as Assistant Editor of *Psychosomatic Medicine;* and on the Board of the Frances G. Wickes Foundation. He is a member of the American Academy of Arts and Sciences, American Association for the Advancement of Science, American Psychological Association, American Psychoanalytic Society, Soc. Franc. de Psychologie and the Melville Society. A volume of essays written by admiring colleagues and edited by Robert W. White was presented to him on his seventieth birthday. We warmly welcome Dr. Murray.

INDISPENSABLES FOR THE MAKING, TESTING, AND REMAKING OF A PERSONOLOGICAL SYSTEM

Henry A. Murray

Department of Psychology
Harvard University
Cambridge, Massachusetts 02138

To reduce the probability of an eruption of disastrous semantic misunderstandings, it seems best to state at the outset what meanings are being ascribed to each of the critical terms in this discourse. "Personology" has proved, in my experience, to be a neater and (with its adjectival form) a more pliable term than the sprawling, cumbersome "psychology of personality." "Personology" has been advocated in order to avoid the cultish practice of using a word that refers to a particular theorist rather than to a definable field of interest. Freud's "psychoanalysis is my creation" was a scarcely excusable scientific heresy. "Personology" is for everyone for free.[1] Next in order is "personality,"* which is the most comprehensive term we have in psychology, including, as it does, the entire system of subsystems (of situational dispositions: structures and functions) as they undergo their serial transformations through the fullest span: from birth to death. At this point its chief meaning is that of domain of scientific concern from which nothing psychological is excluded on principle. Then we come to "system," which may be today's most fashionable scientific word.[2,3] It is applicable from the smallest to the largest definable unit of reality—from an atom to the solar system. Its use points to the fact that one is dealing—*not* with a single, singular, solitary, isolated entity—a solid material particle—, or *not* with a mere aggregate of independent entities—a randomly behaving rabble—not a list, not an inventory; but an assemblage of interdependent units.

Its meaning is exemplified in this paper by three of its uses.[4] In my title the term refers to a conceptual system—a coherent, self-consistent assemblage of abstract concepts and postulates, in terms of which any event in the life of a person should be representable and explainable. In contrast to this system of abstractions we may want to refer to the living system, as James G. Miller names it[5]—the ongoing, concrete organization of psychological states and processes in the head of a given individual. Finally, we have an assessment system—an organi-

---

Referent of the term "personality." Some psychologists find no use at all for this term; they would vote for its extinction. Others use it to refer to something that a person (particularly a psychologist, psychiatrist, biographer, etc.) says about the nature of another person (subject, applicant for a position, patient, historical character, etc.). This usage is unfortunate, since experience has taught us that ·the statements that are made by different people (say psychologists and psychiatrists), especially if they belong to different schools of thought, about the nature of this or that individual, are likely to be significantly different; and so, if "personality" is taken to mean a *representation* of a person's nature, we shall have to admit that an individual has as many personalities as there have been representors of his nature, that in choosing his psychiatrist he is choosing his personality, and that if no psychologist has attempted to represent his nature, he has no personality at all; all of which is nonsense. From this we gather that a representation is one thing, and the nature (personality) that it is designed to represent is another thing; the first can be located in the sentences of the representor, but where can the second be located? In the brain, of course. No reputable psychologist of this era denies that. Consequently, all the more or less enduring constituents of personality are invisible and problematical. Their presence and activity must be inferred on the basis of what *is* visible or audible.

zation of procedures: interviews, questionnaires, projective tests, situational
tests, and much else, all aimed at revealing significant subsystems and their
properties—variables of the personalities to be assessed.

Here I shall have to modify my original intention and leave out two large
sections of my discourse, and the main substance of my paper will consist of
outlining the *assessment system*,[6] which, in this form, includes the composition
of the *conceptual system*.[7]

I will present an abstract of the series of personological procedures that compose the *assessment system* with which I am familiar and which I am keen to
advocate to others. I have participated in six executions of this series of procedures in collaboration with a varying number of other personologists (from about
six to twelve). In four cases, three years were devoted to carrying out the program (twelve years in all), and it will be these last four series which I shall have
in mind while writing the following brief outline. To offer a hint or two regarding the operation of the need-drive concept on the intellectual level, I shall
assume that the members of each staff experienced the lack of a suitable conceptual scheme to guide a number of related researches they had in mind in
the domain of personality theory, and that it was the existence of this felt lack
which prompted them to collaborate in the composition of a workable personological system. Usually, a number of other, more personal and self-centered
wants and drives are aidfully involved in the advancement of this shared, impersonal, cultural enterprise.

1) The collaborative *composition of a provisional conceptual/theoretical
system*[8] is, in my terminology, the aim and product of the first of the series of
five *concrete*, macro-subsystems of cooperating intellects (each subsystem consisting of the interacting mentational processes (sub-sub-systems) of the participating psychologists) which constitute the total system of procedures. The aim
and product of each of the four succeeding, concrete, macro-subsystems may be
briefly defined as follows: 2) the differentiated and integrated *application* of
this provisional theoretical system to the examination—by the *multiform method*
(a variety of procedures, administered by a variety of psychologists to educe
(draw out) a variety of functionings)—of each of a series of individual subjects;
3) the *composition*, based on all the data obtained by these procedures, of a
partial, hypothetical formulation of the personality of each subject which was
designed to represent the mutual relations of its more important component
properties; 4) the cooperative *evaluation* of each of these formulations (and
hence of the provisional theoretical system in terms of which the formulation
was composed) according to its success in sufficiently representing, relating, and
explaining each of the various, important, recorded manifestations of the personality in question (a kind of compound feed-back process consisting of positive
and negative reinforcements emitted by the evaluators); and 5) the cooperative,
adaptive *reconstruction of the provisional theoretical system* (together with its
modes of application) in ways that would correct so far as possible its demonstrated insufficiencies. These five successive, concrete, macro-subsystems of
cooperating psychologists, each with his own (meso) system of participating
mental and verbal processes—attending, transmitting and receiving, rejecting,
accepting, justifying, differentiating, defining, classifying, composing, integrating,
etc.—these five interdependent, macro-temporal subsystems taken as a series
constitute the total *concrete* system of science-making in the domain of personality which was approximately exemplified by each of the six staffs with
which I have had the privilege of working. It may be more simply described as
the ongoing program of performance of numerous specialists (each executing a

different experiment or administering a different assessment procedure on the same population of subjects) complemented by a few generalists whose task was to explain the individual differences in each experiment or test, in terms of an invented formulation of the organized components of the individual's whole nature. Naturally, I have had to omit from my account of this entire theoretical-system-making process many consequential factors, such as the all-important solitary creative processes of individual psychologists and the competitions, oppositions, and disputes among members of the staff, all of them essential components of the whole operation.

Criteria for the Evaluation of a Personological System. On the basis of multiple experiences of the sort I have described, I am proposing as the best, overall criterion of the effectiveness of a personological system as well as of the personologist who makes use of it: 1) his/her power with its use to compose an hypothetical formulation (a macro-model) of the nature of each of a large number of very dissimilar persons during any short span of his or her life's cycle (in childhood, adolescence, adulthood, or senescence), in terms of which formulation the more important, critical, and recurrent situational experiences, activities, and effects (successful and unsuccessful) of that person (during the given span) may be sufficiently represented, related, and explained (and possibily, in some cases, predicted or produced); and also 2) the personologist's power with its use to conceptualize and to explain the important changes of that person's nature that occur from any one to any other shorter or longer span of its historic course from birth to death. The overall utility of a conceptual theoretical system, as estimated in these ways, depends on a number of factors, or attributes of the system, in terms of which attributes, or subcriteria, more differentiated judgments of its value can be made, before or after putting the system to a series of pragmatic tests (the overall criterion). These interdependent sub-criteria are as follows: 1) *conceptual equipment*: what proportion of the basic concepts that are necessary to the sufficient representation of a wide variety of conditions and events and of their determinants are included in the system? 2) *definitional and operational precision*: what proportion of the included concepts are adequately defined by means of specific criteria and operations (procedures) to be used in the identification and possibly in the measurement of their referents? 3) *scope and span of application*: what proportion of the most important species of transactions (proceedings, episodes), and what proportion of the most important states or conditions of the personality engaged in these transactions, and what proportion of the time spans, or stages, of the life cycle, and of the species of transitions from one span to another is the system designed to represent and to explain conceptually? 4) *congruity of application*: what desirable degree of precise and/or complete correspondence with the observed facts is attainable by the system when the relevant parts of it are utilized to represent and to explain each of those species of phenomena to which the system was designed to apply? 5) *conceptual coherence*: to what extent is the system conceptually or propositionally consistent? and to what extent is it capable of representing the internal dynamic relationships of the various situational states, activities, and effects (the concrete systems and subsystems of processional achievements) that were manifested by the personality in action? and 6) *theoretical plentitude*: how many promising or partially verified special theories productive of further research are included in the system?

I have enumerated these criteria to serve as a rough definition of the distant target, as I see it, of personological endeavors, of the ideal against which to measure contemporary intellectual productions. Judged by these indices, no existing personological system could be given a high rating, a high rating being far beyond the limits of realistic expectation and even of what is profitable at this early stage of methodological and theoretical development. An unsuitable high ambition in some of these respects would constitute an almost lethal degree of scientism in this domain of investigation. Anyhow, it can be said that the criteria give no quarter to any hopes of representing a personality in a few sentences or paragraphs, or by a *list* of single variables, such as rated traits. The criteria favor the view that a personality is a more or less organized system of components, but it gives no quarter to those theorists who stress organizations, structures, or systems without specifying, in each particiular case, the nature and number of the components that are involved, and in what way they are structured or organized, or they interact as a system. Finally, it gives no quarter to those who talk about "personality" in an environmental vacuum, or in the abstract without regard to its concrete manifestations.

REFERENCES

1. MURRAY, H.A. *et. al.* 1938. Explorations in Personality. Oxford Press. Boston, Mass.
2. VON BERTALANFFY, L. 1950 The theory of open systems in physics and biology. *Science* **III**.
3. VON BERTALANFFY, L. 1951. metabolic types and growth types. American Naturalist 85, 111.
4. HALL, A.D. & R.E. FAGEN. 1965. Definition of system. *In* General Systems. L. VON BERTALANFFY and A. RAPOPORT, Eds. Vol. 1.
5. LASZLO, E. 1972. The Systems View of the World. Braziller. New York, N.Y.
6. MURRAY, H.A. *et al.* 1948. Assessment of men. Winston, Holt and Rhinehart. New York, N.Y.
7. MURRAY, H.A. 1965. Studies of stressful disputation *In* Personality Theory Sources and Research. Gardner Lindsey and Calvin S. Hall, Eds. John Wiley & Sons, Inc. New York, N.Y.
8. MURRAY, H.A. 1968. Components of an evolving personological system. Personality: Contemporary Viewpoints II. *In* International Encyclopedia of the Social Sciences. Crowell, Collier, and Macmillan, Inc. New York, N.Y.

PUBLICATIONS

Henry A. Murray

Articles

1. The development of the cardiac loop in the rabbit, with especial reference to the bulbo-ventricular septum. *Amer. J. Anatomy*, 1919, 26, 29-39.
2. Two unusual cases of melanocarcinoma. *Proc. of the New York Pathological Soc.*, 1919, XIX, 28-37.
3. Groton and adaptation, *Grotonian*, 1919, 31, 402-419.
4. With A. L. Barach. Tetany in a case of sprue. *J. of the A.M.A.*, 1920, 74, 786-788.
5. With G. King. A new blood coagulometer. *J. of the A.M.A.*, 1920.
6. With F. C. McLean and L. J. Henderson. The variable acidity of hemoglobin and the distribution of chlorides in the blood. *Proc. Soc. Exper. Biol. & Med.*, 1919-20, XVII, 180.
7. With A. B. Hastings and C. D. Murray. Certain chemical changes in the blood after pyloric obstruction in dogs. *J. of Biol. Chem.*, 1921, XLVI, 223-232.
8. With A. B. Hastings. Observations on parathyroidectomized dogs. *J. of Biol. Chem.*, 1921, XLVI, 233-256.
9. The bicarbonate and chloride content of the blood in certain cases of persistent vomiting. *Proc. Soc. Exper. Biol. & Med.*, 1922, XIX, 273-275.
10. With A. R. Felty. Observations on dogs with experimental pyloric obstruction. The acid-base equilibrium, chlorides, non-protein nitrogen, and urea of the blood. *J. of Biol. Chem.*, LVII, 573-585.
11. The chemical pathology of pyloric occlusion in relation to tetany. *Arch. of Surgery*, 1923, 7, 166-196.
12. Physiological ontogeny, A. chicken embryos. II. catabolism. Chemical changes in

fertile eggs during incubation. Selection of standard conditions. *J. gen Physiol.*, 1925, IX, 1-37.

13. Physiological ontogeny, A. chicken embryos. III. Weight and growth rate as functions of age. *J. gen. Physiol.*, 1925, IX, 39-48.

14. With A. E. Cohn. Physiological ontogeny, A. chicken embryos. IV. The negative acceleration of growth with age as demonstrated by tissue cultures. *J. exper. Med.*, 1925, XLII, 275-290.

15. Physiological ontogeny, A. chicken embryos. VII. The concentration of the organic constituents and the calorific value as functions of age. *J. gen. Physiol.*, 1926, IX, 405-432.

16. Physiological ontogeny, A. chicken embryos. VIII. Acceleration of integration and differentiation during the embryonic period. *J. gen. Physiol.*, 1926, IX, 603-619.

17. Physiological ontogeny, A. chicken embryos. IX. The iodine reaction for the quantitative determination of gluthathione in the tissues as a function of age. *J. gen. Physiol.*, 1926, IX, 621-624.

18. Physiological ontogeny, A. chicken embryos. X. The temperature characteristic for the contraction rate of isolated fragments of embryonic heart muscle. *J. gen. Physiol.*, 1926, IX, 781-788.

19. Physiological ontogeny, A. chicken embryos. XI. The pH; chloride, carbonic acid, and protein concentrations in the tissues as functions of age. *J. gen. Physiol.*, 1926, IX, 789-803.

20. Physiological ontogeny, A. chicken embryos. XII. The metabolism as a function of age. *J. gen. Physiol.*, 1926, X, 337-343.

21. With A. E. Cohn. Physiological ontogeny. I. The present status of the problem. *Quart. rev. Biol.*, 1927. II, 469-493.

22. What to read in Psychology. *The Independent*, 1927, 118, 134.

23. A case of pinealoma with symptoms suggestive of compulsion neurosis. *Arch. neurol. Psychiat.*, 1928, 19, 932-945.

24. Abnormal psychology at Harvard. *Harvard Crimson*, 1929, Jan. 12.

25. With H. Barry, Jr. and D. W. KacKinnon. Hypnotizability as a personality trait. *Hum. Biol.*, 1931, 3, 1-36.

26. The effect of fear upon estimates of the maliciousness of other personalities. *Psychol.*, 1933, 4, 310-329.

27. With H. A. Wolff and C. E. Smith. The psychology of humor. *J. abnorm. soc. Psychol.*, 1934, 28, 341-365.

28. The psychology of humor. II. Mirth responses to disparagement jokes as a manifestation of an aggressive disposition. *J. abnorm. soc. Psychol.*, 1934, 29, 66-81.

29. With C. D. Morgan. A method of investigating fantasies. *Arch. neurol. Psychiat.*, 1935, 34, 289-306. Reprinted in *Measuring human motivation*, (Eds) R.C. Birney, R.C. Teenan, D. van Nostrand Co., Princeton, N. J.

30. Psychology and the university. *Arch. neurol. Psychiat.*, 1935, 34, 803-807.

31. The Harvard Psychological Clinic. *Harv. Alumni Bull.*, 1935, Oct. 25, 1-8.

31a Techniques for systematic investigation of fantasy. *J. Psychol.*, 1936, *3*, 115-143.

32. Facts which support the concept of need or drive. *J. Psychol.*, 1936, 3, 115-143.

33. Some concepts for a psychology of personality. *J. gen. Psychol.*, 1936, 15, 240-268.

34. With D. R. Wheeler. A note on the possible clairvoyance of dreams. *J. Psychol.*, 1936, 3, 309-313.

35. With R. Wolf. An experiment in judging personalities. *J. Psychol.*, 1936, 3, 345-365.

36. Visceral manifestations of personality. *J. abnorm. soc. Psychol.*, 1937, 32, 161-184.

37. What should psychologists do about psychoanalysis. *J. abnorm. soc. Psychol.*, 1940, 35, 150-175.

38. Personality and creative imagination. *English Institute Manual*, 1942, (New York: Columbia Univer. Pr., 1943) 139-162.

39. With M. Stein. Note on the selection of combat officers. *Psychosom. Med.*, 1943, 5, 386-391.

40. Assessment of the whole person. *Proc. Meeting Military Psychologists and Psychiatrists*, Univer. Maryland Pr., 1945.

41. With D. W. MacKinnon. Assessment of OSS personnel. *J. consult. Psychol.*, 1946, 10, 76-80.

42. Proposals for research in clinical psychology. *Amer. J. Orthopsychiat.*, 1947, 17, 203-210.

43. Time for a positive morality. *Surv. Graphic*, 1947, 36, 195.

44. America's mission. *Surv. Graphic*, 1948, 37, 411-415.

45. Research planning: a few proposals. *Culture and Personality*, (Ed) S.S. Sargent and M. W. Smith. *Proc. Interdisciplin. Conf.* (Nov. 1947), Viking Fund, 1949.

46. Uses of the TAT. *Amer. J. Psychiat.*, 1951, 107, 577-581.
47. Toward a classification of interactions. In T. Parsons, E. A. Shils, E. C. Tolman et al. *Toward a general theory of action*, Harv. Univer. Pr., 1951.
48. World concord as a goal for the social scientist. *Proc. Internat. Congress Psychol.*, Stockholm, 1951.
49. In nomine diaboli. *The New England Quart.*, 1951, XXIV, 435-452. Reprinted in *Moby-Dick Centennial Essays* (Ed.) Melville Society, 1953, also *Discussions of Moby-Dick* (Ed) M. R. Stern, Boston, 1960, and *Melville, a collection of critical essays*, (Ed.) R. Chase, New York: Prentice-Hall, 1962. and *Theories of Personality*, (Eds.) G. Lindzey & E.S. Hall, John Wiley & Sons, Inc., N.Y.: 1965, pp. 153-161. *Psychology Today*, 1968, Vol. 2, *4*, 64-69.
50. Some basic psychological assumptions and conceptions, *Dialectica*, 1951, 5, 266-292.
51. Science in two societies. *The Contemporary Scene*, A symposium, Metropolitan Museum of Art, New York, 1954.
52. Versions of man. In *Man's right to knowledge*, 2nd series, Present Knowledge and New Direction Columbia Univer. Pr., N.Y.: 1955. (An international symposium presented in honor of the 200th anniversary of Columbia Univer., 1754-1954.) Pub. by Herbert Muschel, Box 800, Grand Central, N.Y. 17, N.Y.
53. American Icarus. In (Eds.) A. Burton and R. E. Harris, *Clinical Studies of personality*, Vol. 2, New York, Harper, 1955. Reprinted in *Theories of Personality*, (Eds.) G. Lindzey, C.S. Hall, N.Y.: John Wiley & Sons, 1965, pp. 162-175.
54. With A. Davids. Preliminary appraisal of an auditory projective technique for studying personality and cognition. *Amer. J. Orthopsychiat.*, 1955, 25, 543-554.
55. Creative evolution, or a deity imprisoned in the past? *The Christian Reg.*, 1956, 135, 10ff. (abbreviated version of No. 64)
56. Theoretical basis for projective techniques. *Proc. Internat. Congress for Psychol.*, Brussels, 1957.
57. Drive, time, strategy, measurement, and our way of life. In (Ed.) G. Lindzey, *Assessment of human motives*. New York: Rinehart, 1958.
58. Notes on the Icarus syndrome. *Folia psychiatrica, neurologica, et neurochirugica Neelandica*. 1958, 61, 204-208.
59. Individuality: The meaning and content of individuality in contemporary America. *Daedalus*, 1958, 87, 25-47. Reprinted in *The American Style*, New York, 1958; and in (Ed.) H. M. Ruitenbeck, *Varieties of modern social theory*, New York, 1963.
60. Vicissitudes of creativity. In (Ed.) H. H. Anderson, *Creativity and its cultivation*. New York: Harper, 1959.
61. Preparations for the scaffold of a comprehensive system. In (Ed.) S. Koch, *Psychology: a study of science*. Vol. 3, New York: McGraw-Hill, 1959.
62. With H. Cantril and M. May. Some glimpses of Soviet psychology. *Amer. Psychologist*, 1959, 14, 303-307.
63. Beyond yesterday's idealisms. Phi Beta Kappa Oration, Harvard Chapter, 1959, printed in *Views from the circle: seventy-five years of Groton School*, 1960, 371-382; also in (Ed.) C. Brinton, *The fate of man*, New York: Braziller, 1961; also in *Man thinking*, by the United Chapters of Phi Beta Kappa, Cornell Univer Pr.; some of it (entitled *A mythology for grownups* in *Saturday Rev.* Jan. 23, 1960.
64. Two versions of man. In (Ed.) H. Shapley, *Science ponders religion*. New York: Appleton-Century-Crofts, 1960.
65. Historical trends in personality research. In (Eds.) H. P. David and J. C. Brengelmann, *Perspectives in personality research*. New York: Springer, 1960.
66. The possible nature of a "mythology" to come. In *Myth and mythmaking*, New York: George Braziller, 1960.
67. Unprecedented evolutions. *Daedalus*, 1961, 90, 547-570. Reprinted in (Eds.) H. Hoagland and R. W. Burhoe, *Evolution and man's progress,* Columbia Univer. Pr., New York, 1962.
68. Commentary on the case of El. *J. proj. Tech.*, 1961, 25, 404-411.
69. Prospect for psychology. *Internat. Congress of Applied Psychology*, Copenhagen, 1961. Reprinted in *Science*, 1962, 136, 483-488.
70. Definitions of Myth. In (Ed.) Ohmann, R.M. *The Making of Myth*. N.Y.: G.P. Putnam's Sons, 1962.
71. The personality and career of Satan. *J. soc. Issues*, XVIII, 1962, 28, 36-54.
72. Studies of stressful interpersonal disputations. *Amer. Psychologist*, 1963, 18, 28-36. Reprinted in *Theories of Personality*, (Eds.) G. Lindzey & C.S. Hall, N.Y.: John Wiley & Sons, Inc. 1965, pp. 176-184.
73. Bartleby and I. In (Ed.) Howard P. Vincent, *Bartleby the Scrivener*. Ohio: The Kent State Univer. Press, 1966, p. 3-24.

74. Dead to the world: Or the passions of Herman Melville. In E.S. Shneidman (Ed.) *Essays in self-destruction*. New York: Science House, 1967.
75. Autobiography. In *History of Psychology in Autobiography*. Vol. V., pp. 285-310 (Eds.) E.G. Boring, G. Lindzey, Appleton-Century-Crofts, N.Y., 1967.
76. Symposium on Morality. *American Scholar*, Summer, 1965.
77. Personality: II Contemporary viewpoints. Components of an evolving personological system. In D. Sills (Ed) *International Encyclopedia of Social Science*. New York: Macmillan & Free Press, 1968, *12*, 5-13.
78. A conversation with Henry A. Murray. (Mary H. Hall, interviewer). *Psychology Today*, 1968, Vol. 2, *4*, 56-63.
79. Sundry thoughts on imagination. Paper presented at the meeting of the Society for Projective Techniques, APA convention, San Francisco, September, 1968.

Monographs

With C. D. Morgan. A clinical study of sentiments. *Genet, psychol. Monogr.*, 1945, 32, 3-311.

Books

With Staff. *Exploration in personality*. New York: Oxford Univer. Pr., 1938.
With Staff. *Assessment of men*. New York: Rinehart, 1948.
With C. Kluckhohn (Eds.). *Personality in nature, society, and culture*. New York: Alfred A. Knopf, 1950.
With C. Kluckhohn and D. M. Schneider (Eds.). *Personality in nature, society, and culture*. (2nd ed.) New York: Alfred A. Knopf, 1953.
(Ed,) *Myth and mythmaking*. New York: George Braziller, 1960.

Prefaces, Introductions, Forewords

1. Introduction, *Contemporary psychopathology*, S. S. Tonkins, Cambridge, Mass.: Harvard Univer. Pr., 1943.
2. Introduction, *Clinical studies in personality*, Vol. I, A. Burton & R. E. Harris. New York: Harper & Bros., 1947.
3. Introduction with footnotes (Ed.) *Pierre or the ambiguities*, H. Melville, New York: Farrar, Straus, Hendricks House, 1949.
4. Foreword, *An introduction to projective techniques*, H. H. Anderson & Gladys Anderson. New York: Prentice-Hall, 1951.
5. Foreword, *Thematic test analysis*, E. S. Schneidman. New York: Grune & Stratton, 1951.
6. Introduction, *Clinical studies of personality*, Vol. II, A. Burton & R. E. Harris New York: Harper, 1955.
7. Introduction, *Methods in personality assessment*, G. G. Stern, M. I. Stein, & B. S. Bloom. Glencoe, Ill.: Free Press, 1956.
8. Foreword, *Man made plain*, R. N. Wilson. Cleveland: Howard Allen, 1958.
9. Introduction, issue "Myth and mythmaking," *Daedalus*, Boston: American Academy of Arts and Sciences, 1959.
10. Foreword, *The inner world of choice*. Frances G. Wickes, New York: Harper & Row, 1963.
11. Prelude, *Melville and Hawthorne in the Berkshires—A symposium, Melville Annual 1966*, H.P. Vincent (Ed.), Kent State University Press, 1968.
12. Introduction, *Experiencing others*. Franz From, Copenhagen, Denmark, 1971.

Tests and Manuals

With Staff. *Thematic Apperception Test*. Cambridge, Mass,: Harvard Univer. Pr., 1943.
Thematic appreception test. *Military Clinical Psychology*, 1951. TM8-242-AFM160, 45, 54-71.

Reviews

1. *Timon of America, Herman Melville*, by Lewis Mumford. New York: Harcourt, Brace & Co., 1929. Reviewed in *Hound and Horn*, 1929, 430.
2. *Herman Melville*, by Lewis Mumford. New York: Harcourt, Brace & Co., 1929. Reviewed in *New England Quart.*, 1929, 523.
3. *Mrs. Eddy: the biography of a virginal mind*. by Edwin Franden Daken. New York: Charles Scribner's Sons, 1929. Reviewed in *New England Quart.*, 1929, 341.

4. *Pierre, or the ambiguities*, by Herman Melville. New York: Alfred A. Knopf, 1930. Reviewed in *New England Quart.*, 1930, 333.
5. *The conquest of happiness*. by Bertrand Russell, Horace Liveright. Reviewed in *Altantic Monthly*, 1930, 12.
6. *Civilization and its discontents*. by Sigmund Freud. Cape and Smith. Reviewed in *Atlantic Monthly*, 1930, 14.
7. *Not to eat, not for love*. by George Weller. New York: Harrison Smith & Robert Haas, 1933. Reviewed in *Harvard Crimson*, 1933, also in *Harvard Alumni Bull.*—"A novel about Harvard," 1933, 729-730.
9. *Private worlds*. by Phyllis Bottome. Boston: Houghton Mifflin Company, 1934. Reviewed in *The J. Rev. of Literature*, Cambridge, Mass., April 21, 1934.
10. *The inner world of man*. by Frances G. Wickes. New York: Farrar & Rinehart, 1938. Reviewed in *The New York Times Book Review*, Dec. 4, 1938.
11. *Psychological foundations of personality*. by Louis P. Thorpe. New York: McGraw-Hill Book Co., 1938. Reviewed in *Amer. J. Psychol.*, 1939, 53, 493-94.
12. *Fulcra of conflict: a new approach to personality measurement*. by Douglas Spencer. New York: World Book Co., 1939. Reviewed in *Amer. J. Psychol.*, 1940, 53, 161-162.
13. *Personality and problems of adjustment*. by Kimball Young. New York: F. S. Crofts & Co., 1940.
14. *Mind explorers*. by John K. Winkler & Walter Bromberg. New York: Reynal & Hitchcock, 1940. Reviewed in *The New York Times Book Review*, Jan. 21, 1940.
15. *Counseling and psychotherapy*. by Carl R. Rogers. Boston: Houghton Mifflin Co., 1942.
16. *Studies in personality*. by Lewis M. Terman. New York: McGraw-Hill, 1942. *Book Reviews*, edited by George L. Dreezer, Cornell Univer. Reviewed in *Amer. J. Psychol.*, 1943, 56, 307-308.
17. *Personality: a biosocial approach to origins and structure*. by Gardner Murphy. New York: Harper, 1947. Reviewed in *Surv. Graphic*, March, 1948.
18. *The trying-out of Moby-Dick*. by Howard P. Vincent. Boston: Houghton-Mifflin Co. 1949. Reviewed in *The New England Quart*, 527-530.
19. *Herman Melville, a biography*. by Leon Howard. Los Angeles: Univer. California Pr., 1951.
20. *Melville's early life and Redburn*. by William H. Gilman. New York: New York Univer. Pr., 1951.
21. *Dynamic psychiatry*. by Franz Alexander & Helen Ross. Chicago: Univer. of Chicago Pr., 1952. Reviewed in *Psychol. Bull.*, 1953, 50, 304-306.
22. *Freud: the mind of the moralist*. by Philip Rieff. New York: Viking Pr., 1959. Reviewed in *Amer. Sociolog. Rev.*, 299-300.
23. *Anthropology and the classics*. by Clyde Kluckhohn. Providence, R.I.: Brown Univer. Pr., 1961. Reviewed in *Amer. Anthropologist*, 1963, 65, 139-140.
24. *The psychology of Jung, a critical interpretation*. by Avis M. Dry. New York: Wiley, 1961. Reviewed in *Contemp. Psychol.*, Dec. 1963, 468-469.
25. The Freudian Hawthorne. *The Sins of the Fathers: Hawthorne's Psychological Themes*. by Frederick C. Crews. Fair Lawn, N.J.: Oxford Univer. Press, 1966. Reviewed in *The American Scholar*, Vol. 36, 2, Spring, 1967, pp. 308-312, Reprinted in *Psychiatry & Social Science Review*, May 1967, Vol. 1, 5, pp. 11-13.
26. *Tolstoy*. by Henri Troyat, Doubleday. Reviewed in *The American Scholar* Summer, 1968, p. 536.

Sketches, Obituaries

1. Dr. Morton Price, a founder of psychopathology. *Harvard Alumni Bull.*, 1930, Jan. 23, 490-495.
2. William Herman, published in *Boston Transcript*, about 1935.
3,4. Alfred E. Cohn, 2 unpublished addresses.
5. Sigmund Freud, 1856-1939. *Amer. J. Psychol.*, 1940, 53, 134-138.
6. Conrad Aiken, poet of creative dissolution. *Wake*, 1952, 11, 95-106.
7. Frank Wigglesworth. Published in *40th Anniversary Report* of Harvard Class of 1915.
8. Morton Prince, sketch of his life and work. *J. abnorm. soc. Psychol.*, 1956, 52, 291-295.
9,10. Clyde Kluckhohn, a) Memorial service, Oct., 1960. b) Minute on his life and services, read at a meeting of the Harvard Faculty, 1961.
11. Carl G. Jung. Address at Memorial Meeting in New York, Dec., 1962.
12. Felix Frandfurther, the humanity of this man. In Festschrift composed in his honor, 1964.

13. Leaves of green memories. Verses in celebration of the authors of *The Study of Lives* and other students of lives who attended the dinner at the Hotel Barclay, Philadelphia, Aug. 28, 1963 (privately printed).
14. Josephine Lee Murray 1894-1962. Radcliffe Quarterly, Feb. 1965, p. 9.
15. Ernest W. Hocking, 1967. Unpublished.
16. Edward Craighill Handy, Sept. 1967. Unpublished.
17. Frances G. Wickes: 1875-1967 a memorial meeting, Oct. 25, 1967, New York: Privately printed by the Ram Press, N.Y., 1968.

GENETIC EPISTEMOLOGY AND
DEVELOPMENTAL PSYCHOLOGY

Bärbel Inhelder

Department of Psychology
University of Geneva
1211 Geneva, Switzerland

The genesis of knowledge, the productivity of the human mind, and its ceaseless inventions and discoveries have always been the central theme of Piaget's theoretical and experimental work in epistemology and psychology. His conceptual approach to these great problems has led to a highly consistent system, which nevertheless is in constant evolution. Growth in the biological sense, with both conservation and transformation of structures, is also the main characteristic of the human mind, and figures prominently in Piaget's theory. Piaget himself seems to have wanted to make this perfectly clear: the subject he chose for this year's research at the International Center for Genetic Epistemology is how the child comes to envisage an ever-wider range of possibilities while simultaneously building up a concept of what is logically necessary.

Although Piaget's publications are widely disseminated, many psychologists find his work difficult to understand. This is partly due, I believe, to the interdisciplinary character of most of Piaget's research; he sets out to solve epistemological problems experimentally by combining the developmental approach with critical studies of the history of science and by using models based on logic, mathematics, and biological cybernetics. This multidimensional approach leads to a remarkably broad perspective of the laws and mechanisms of cognitive development; yet psychology proper has for Piaget always been a by-product of his genetic epistemology, as was stressed by the American Psychology Association when its annual award went to Jean Piaget.

EARLY WORKS AND INFLUENCES

Since this symposium is concerned with the historical background of contemporary psychology, I should like first of all to sketch the initial steps that gradually led Piaget forward; he himself, by the way, maintains that he has never tried to build up a system, but has merely attempted to coordinate the results and interpretations of his many pieces of research, to explain certain key notions, to discern their epistemological significance, and to open up new directions for research.

Piaget took a Ph.D. in zoology and, as he is wont to remark, his only degrees in psychology are honorary. His first steps in psychology and epistemology were undoubtedly influenced by Immanuel Kant and, more directly, by Leon Brunschvicg, James Marc Baldwin, and Pierre Janet, who, like Freud, was a pupil of Charcot. "The children studied by Piaget are young Immanuel Kants and Piaget himself is a young Immanuel Kant grown old," as the Swiss philosopher Jean-Claude Piguet remarked. Writing many volumes on the development of the categories of space, time, and causality, and on number and logic, Piaget chose his problems outside the traditional fields of experimental psychology. He does not use an *a priori* interpretative framework: in line with the biological methods and concepts of his malacological studies, he reaches a kind of dynamic, one might say biological, Kantism, and sees the mechanisms by which knowledge is constructed in an epigenetic perspective; the structures inherent in the subject are considered to be the result of progressive constructions due to the interaction of endogenous regulatory mechanisms and the impact of variations in the environment.

Brunschvicg's influence on Piaget was exerted principally through the former's critical relativism and his historicocritical method of analysis of the laws of evolution and revolution that characterize the progress of mathematics and physics. Since every scientist is first a child who has to discover once more the fundamental concepts of reason, Piaget studied the origins of knowledge in children. Yet, his aim was not to establish a direct parallel between cognitive development and the course of scientific thought, but to look for common mechanisms. Despite the structural differences between the elementary stages of child thought and the higher levels of human reason, many common functional mechanisms have been brought to light.

A number of Piaget's ideas and interests have sprung from Baldwin's work. Baldwin's theoretical project of founding a "genetic logic" has, in a sense, found experimental actualization in Piaget's research. Moreover, Baldwin's insistence on the social factor in the construction of reason is reflected in Piaget's early work, where the notion of progressive decentration starting from a lack of differentiation between the young child's own point of view and that of others is elaborated, and in which the role of cooperation with their peers in the constitution of logical norms and autonomous morality is stressed. Even in his recent botanical work, in which he is concerned with organic selection, Piaget's findings are once again in agreement with the "Baldwin effect."

The constructivist hypothesis that is gradually refined and enriched in many of Piaget's work finds its clearest expression in the notion of stages in cognitive development. The concept of stages can be traced back to Janet's influence. Janet, while studying what he called "illness of belief" (hysteria and psychasthenia), which he considered to be a disintegration of the synthesis of mental energy, conceived a system of hierarchical stages in mental development. His frequent discussions with his friend Baldwin may well have roused Janet's interest in the development of intelligence in children, the origins of which he placed before the beginning of language.

At first, the concept of stages was used by Piaget as a useful heuristic with which to account for the successive, qualitatively different forms of a construction process; later, the developmental stages define equilibrium states in a continuous process of cognitive structurations whose formation is ordered so that each construction having attained a state of relative equilibrium opens up new possibilities, each step in the process being necessary for the subsequent one.

This conception of stages—which in essence is biological—paralleled embryological and epigenetic processes that have been variously accounted for by concepts such as competence, chreodes, homeorhesis, and so on.

SENSORIMOTOR DEVELOPMENT

Piaget's[1,2] studies on the sensorimotor origins of intelligence were a first example of a synthesis between epistemology and constructivist psychology with biological foundations. Some thirty years later, this first approach was further developed within the framework of modern biology in his work "Biology and

Knowledge."[3] Recently, Piaget published a new volume on the same subject, "Adaptation Vitale et psychologie de l'intelligence,"[26] which aims to show the existence of a functional continuity between organic and psychological structures, the latter being considered as a special case of biological adaptation; psychological structures show the same kind of reciprocal relationship between assimilation and accommodation as organic structures do, but going further since they can generate new structures.

During the preverbal, sensorimotor period, a certain logic of actions, but without any extension, is built up and lays the foundations for later development of logic and of knowledge of reality. The infant who perceives and manipulates objects does not simply establish associations: because the objects are integrated into his actions, the infant recognizes them and can generalize from one action-situation to another. The fundamental psychological fact is, in this view, assimilation: assimilation between action schemes and objects, but also between different action-schemes that become coordinated and thus prepare what later will be logical operations.[5] The infant establishes correspondences; from the point of view of "putting into," a small box and a little ball are equivalent, since they can both be put into a large box, and he will repeatedly carry out this action, first with the small box, then with the little ball; the infant also notes differences in properties—the same little box and small ball are different, since he can put his finger inside the one but not inside the other, and he will repeatedly poke his finger into the ball and then put it inside the box. Primitive "intersections" are discovered: certain objects (a ball, a round pencil) can be pushed so that they roll along by themselves; others (a small ruler, a spoon) can be stuck into a lump of clay; and, surprise, the pencil can be both an object to be rolled and an object to be a stuck into something else.

Reciprocal assimilations of such nascent systems of action introduce a certain consistency into the immediate concrete universe of the child and lead to the more complex constructions that presage the culmination of the sensorimotor period, such as the capacity of spatial orientation (for the one-year-old, within his immediate environment) according to a system that Poincaré called the "group of displacements" and that, according to him, plays a part in all effective actions. Piaget has shown how this capacity is constructed during the first year or so of the baby's life, in close connection with the construction of the first cognitive invariant, object-permanency, and with the development of sensorimotor intelligence. Thus, the first fundamental forms of knowledge are constructed before the appearance of language and Piaget showed the important part played by the interaction between the infant and his environment. This research, which was published as early as 1936 and 1937, aroused great interest among Freudians such as David Rapaport, Peter Wolff, Thérèse Gouin Decarie, and Sybille Escalona.

FROM SENSORIMOTOR INTELLIGENCE TO THE OPERATIONS OF THOUGHT

At some time during the second year of life, this first logic of actions with its principle of invariants and structures of movement in space is fully constructed and a new stage begins. The growth of the child's representational capacities—the symbolic function—makes for a restructuration of what has been acquired at the level of effective actions. Progressively, the child acquires concepts of conservation of numerical and physical quantities,[6] and the development of these concepts goes together with that of concrete operations. Operations are defined as interiorized actions that are reversible, so that any transformation can be either cancelled by its inverse or compensated reciprocal transformation.

Following the sensorimotor period and before the first operator equilibrium is reached, the child's way of reasoning assumes a form that Piaget[7] called "semilogical" or "half-logical," and whose one-way mappings will be transformed by reversibility. The one-way mappings conserve the directional property of the real actions out of which they grew; they are an important step toward concrete operations, but the inverse correspondences have to be established before the first level of equilibrium of thought can be attained. In the well-known problem of the quantity of clay* contained in a lump of play-dough before and after its shape has been altered, the younger child already has mentally established one correspondence: when one rolls out the dough, it becomes longer. He also establishes the inverse relation: when one compresses the dough and rolls it into a ball, it becomes shorter. However, these two correspondences (or functions, as Piaget calls them) remain at first separate; only later does each correspondence become completed by a covariance: when the dough is rolled into a sausage, it becomes thinner; when it is rolled back into a ball, it becomes fatter. As long as the child's thought remains unidirectional, conservation of quantity has no logical necessity. Once the operatory system is functioning, covariations become compensations, and conservation, instead of being only qualitative, becomes quantitative. Qualitative properties are, indeed,[8] in a sense conserved much earlier; the child distinguishes between permanent and nonpermanent qualities of objects, but, though he asserts that "it's still the same play-dough," this does not mean that its quantity did not change.

At each level of organization there is thus harmony between the various systems (action-logic, semilogic, and operatory logic) and their invariant properties (object permanency, qualitative identity, and quantitative conservation). These systems have been formalized by Piaget, and such a structural analysis generates hypotheses about and suggests parallels between behavior patterns that at first might appear to be totally independent. The research on learning,[9] for example, was based on such hypotheses and demonstrated reciprocal interaction between operatory systems by showing that training in conservation concepts greatly improved concepts of class inclusion and vice versa.

CAUSALITY

The studies just mentioned are mainly concerned with the way the child constructs a certain consistency in his own thoughts, a development we may consider as being fundamentally logicomathematical. But simultaneously the child also constructs a coherence between what he thinks and what actually happens in reality, and this development provides the bases for his causal explanatory thought.

Piaget[10] devoted one of his early works to the child's concept of causality, and since then causality has been investigated in numerous experimental studies at the Center of Genetic Epistemology.[11] Recurring themes of these studies are the child's understanding of mechanical links when movement is transmitted from one object to another.[12] In general, the results of the experiments point to a parallelism between logicomathematical operations and the understanding of causal phenomena in that the subject "attributes" to the behavior of the objects

---

*The conservation principle was first discussed by Piaget at the Tercentenary Celebration of Harvard University in 1936.[25]

the operations he elaborates in his logical thinking. Before the child understands transmission, he describes what he seems to observe in the following way: the marble that's rolling down hits the first marble, then skips in and out of the others and continues its trajectory. This is the only explanation he can find for the fact that three marbles remain motionless and only the first one is propelled. Such transmission of movement is understood at the same time that the concept of transitivity is reached in logicomathematical problems. This "attribution" (in mathematical terms) to the objects of the subject's own operations means that objects themselves become operators. From this point of view, the concept of causality, like the operations themselves, involves a compensatory relationship between transformations and conservations.

Nevertheless, the development of the capacity of causal explanation is not simply a repetition of what happens during the construction of logicomathematical operations: the latter are the result of free constructions by the subject, whereas the former depend on the properties of objects and their interactions. These object properties, and the fact that they may resist whatever the child wants to do with them, call for a very different mental effort, which is the main source of the child's discoveries about the physical world.

Other studies were concerned with the child's understanding of probability and chance (or randomness), time and space, measurement, and so on. The experimental situations were mostly chosen because of their epistemological meaning; in all of them it was possible to follow the way the child gradually builds up a coherent system of structures that permit him to deal with many problems of different kinds.

REFLEXIVE ABSTRACTION AND CONSTRUCTIVE GENERALIZATION

How does the child build up these structures, and, especially, how, around the age of 11 or 12, does he attain a logical structure that goes beyond that of classes and relations, beyond the double-entry matrices of the concrete operations period? Piaget[13] calls the mechanism by which this is achieved "reflexive abstraction." Such abstraction takes place when the subject derives from his actions and operations certain principles that lead to a new organization when he is confronted with a new problem. For example, at the level of concrete operations, the child is already capable of substituting one criterium for another (shifting), and of conserving the whole in whatever way it has been divided into parts (Inhelder and Piaget, 1964). This is a manifestation of what has been called "vicariance". Subsequently, by reflexive abstraction, this concept leads to the idea of a division of one and the same totality into all its possible parts. Through this abstraction, which is accompanied by a constructive generalization, the subject reaches the logicomathematical concept of the set of all subsets. The different links between the parts form a combinatory system, one of the most fundamental structures of formal operations.[14]

We have said that reflexive abstraction is always accompanied by constructive generalizations. Just as we have to distinguish two kinds of abstraction, empirical abstraction bearing on objects and their properties, and reflexive abstraction bearing on the actions of the subject, two kinds of generalizations have also to be distinguished; one simply extends an already existing concept and involves no more than a verification of the transition from some to all. Whereas the other can indeed be called constructive, since it introduces new combinations or operations on operations (such as combinatory systems and the set of all subsets).

At a lower level an example of constructive generalization[13] is the following. The child is given ten sticks of different lengths correctly seriated, and is asked:

"How many sticks are there that are bigger than this tiny one?" The child easily shows the smallest stick and correctly counts the others. Then the experimenter shows the biggest stick and asks, "And how many are smaller than this one?" The five-to-six-year-old will then count the sticks again, whereas one or two years later he will laugh and immediately answer, "Nine also, of course," Such constructive generalization is the main mechanism of progress in mathematics, and it is striking that it should already be present in the child.

The relationship between reflexive abstraction and constructive generalization is necessarily a very close one; each abstraction leads sooner or later to constructive generalizations, and each generalization is based on reflexive abstractions.

EQUILIBRATION

Piaget's quest for a model to account for the continuity between biological and psychological adaptation goes back to his very first research, when he was still an adolescent, and may be thought of as the "red thread" that runs through his entire work, reappearing with particular clarity each time he discusses his equilibrium theory. His latest thoughts on equilibrium[4] can be summed up as follows.

Three forms of equilibration can be distinguished. The simplest form, the first to appear during development, is that between assimilation and accommodation. Already in the sensorimotor period, an action scheme applied to new objects becomes differentiated as a function of the object's properties. An equilibrium is reached so that the action scheme is conserved and at the same time adapted to the object's properties. If these properties are unexpected and interesting, the equilibration can lead to the formation of a subscheme, or even of a new scheme, which in turn needs to be equilibrated. These functional mechanisms are at work at all levels.

A second form of equilibration takes place between the subsystems of the system of operations the subject is elaborating, for example, between numerical and spatial measurement systems in problems of quantification where both these subsystems play a part. Since such subsystems generally develop at different rates, conflicts may appear, and equilibration will necessitate a distinction between what is common to both subsystems on the one hand and their specific properties on the other. In one of the learning situations,[9] for example, the children had to build what we called "roads" out of bits of wood, so that their "road" was of the same length as the experimenter's. The child was given bits of wood that were five-sevenths of the length of the bits the experimenter worked with, a fact that they could and did indeed observe in one of the situations where the experimenter put five bits into a straight line and the child was asked to construct his road directly underneath. This problem raises no difficulties. When, however, the experimenter built his road (of five bits of wood) in a zig-zag, and the children were asked to build theirs immediately below, they made the endpoints coincide with those of the experimenter's road, thus building a line that was far shorter than the model. When they were asked to build a road of equal length to the zig-zag model not directly below, but somewhere on the other side of the table, they no longer used the "not-going-beyond principle," but used a numerical equivalence idea; they counted the experimenter's bits of wood, five, and used five of their own bits. Going back to the proximity situation, in which four bits of wood constitute a line that does not go beyond the experimenter's, a conflict appears: five is the answer based on numerical evaluation, four is the answer based on the topological correspondence (the "not-going-beyond principle"). The awareness of this conflict often led to curious compromise solutions, such as breaking one piece into two pieces without bypassing the endpoints of the configuration, and later on to correct solutions after a certain number of training sessions.

Piaget distinguishes further that a third form of equilibration is based on the second, but leads to the construction of a new total system; the process of differentiation of new subsystems demands a procedure that allows their integration into a new totality and thus constitutes a third form of equilibration.

Superficially, it would seem that equilibration implies a simple balance between opposing forces: the differentiation that threatens the unity of the whole and the integration that endangers the necessary distinctions. But more profoundly, the particularity of cognitive equilibrium is to ensure that the total structure is continuously enriched by the differentiations and that, reciprocally, these differentiations increase with the variations of the intrinsic properties of the total structure.

In other words, cognitive equilibration has the characteristic of being what Piaget calls "majorante," that is to say, augmentative; in other words, the various disequilibria do not lead to a simple reequilibration in the sense of a return to a former equilibrium state, but to a new and more powerful form of equilibrium that incorporates more numerous internal dependencies and logical implications. From this point of view, disequilibria acquire a functional importance, which is best examplified by Piaget's work on contradiction.

CONTRADICTION

For Piaget, the periods of disequilibrium should not be explained by pointing to contradictions the subject feels in his logical reasoning; rather, the subject's inconsistencies and contradictions should point to a psychological source of such disequilibria. The problem of contradiction[15, 16] is closely related to another question: why are there so many initial disequilibria, since it might have been expected that subjects at any level of development, however elementary, are capable, without contradictions, of mastering problems that do not go beyond an appropriate level of complexity? It turns out that the psychological source of many inconsistencies and contradictions is to be sought in a simple and general phenomenon: the difficulty of compensating affirmations (or positive factors) by negations (or negative factors). The young child is essentially focused on the effect he wants to achieve through his actions, and is likely to lose sight of the situation he started from. In number conservation situations, for example, the young child feels that something has somehow been added at the end of the transformation, but he does not understand that what has been added must in some way have been subtracted from the initial state.[17] In all mathematical and logical problems, the child "succumbs" to this primacy of positive factors over negative ones, which accounts for the lack of reversibility of thought in these areas. The same phenomenon appears also in different situations: for example, the young child understands quickly what is meant by a full glass, or an almost full or a half-full glass, but has much more difficulty with expressions such as half-empty, almost empty, and so on. Very young children will not accept that a glass can at the same time be half full and half empty; for them, this is a contradictory statement. The fact is doubly instructive for the psychologist. On the one hand, it reaffirms the hypothesis of the primacy of positive factors over negative ones, and on the other hand it shows the importance of what for the adult are pseudocontradictions, such as are encountered in seriation tasks, where for children of a certain level, if B is bigger than A, B cannot at the same time be smaller than C.

EPISTEMOLOGY

Piaget's psychology cannot be separated from his epistemology. His epistemological theory may be called constructivist (and Piaget[18, 19] himself qualifies it thus) in the sense that knowledge is neither preformed in the object (empiricism) nor in the subject (nativism), but results from progressive construction. The two main considerations that lead to the rejection of empiricism are the following.

1. Acts of knowledge are never simply based on associations, but always on assimilation, i.e., on the integration of present data into already existing structures.

2. If the first point is conceded, development can no longer be an accumulation of pieces of learning, and learning must depend on the laws of development and the competence of the subject, according to his cognitive level, as has been shown in our research on learning and the development of cognition.[9] In other words, knowledge is never a simple copy of reality, but always results from a restructuration of reality through the activities of the subject (on this point Piaget agrees with von Foerster's position concerning the cognitive relationships between subject and object).

To say that knowledge depends on the activities of the subject does not mean that knowledge is innate, since it is precisely the activities of the subject that constantly create new structures and new forms of organization. If knowledge were innate, logical necessity should be present before, rather than after, the subject masters certain constructions. This appears not to be the case. The simplest example is that of the concept of transitivity ($A < C$ if $A < B$ and $B < C$), which is reached at the end of the operatory construction of seriation and is not understood at the level of empirical success in seriating sticks of different lengths.

T. Bower[20] and others, it is true, have shown the existence of certain innate reactions, such as perceptive constancies. But between this early behavior and analogous behavior patterns that arise some months later, there is a necessary reconstruction and no direct continuity as would be supposed by a generalized nativism. Each new stage in cognitive development is characterized by new creations that, in turn, open up new possibilities. When the structure is comparatively weak, the new possibilities are comparatively few, but the more powerful the structure, the greater the number of new possibilities. This principle is illustrated not only by the child's cognitive development, but also by the history of mathematics and physics. Piaget[21] is at present working with the physicist and historian of science Rolando Garcia in order to elucidate the mechanisms that account for both the psychogenetic structuration of intelligence and the historical development of scientific thought.

The constructivist aspect of cognitive development is also manifest in the mechanisms of how subjects become aware of their own action or thought patterns. For most authors, and particularly for Freud, awareness does not go beyond the uncovering of realities that already existed in the subject's unconscious. According to Piaget,[22] awareness always implies a conceptualization and therefore supposes a reconstruction that transforms whatever remained unconscious in action into new realities of a conceptual nature.

Piaget's work in genetic epistemology revealed a striking parallelism between the psychogenesis of concepts and the development of theories in mathematics and physics. The levels of abstraction as well as the types of concepts are obviously quite different among children and among scientists. Yet one finds surprising analogies between children's ways of explaining natural phenomena and the thinking about mechanics in Antiquity and the Middle Ages, especially when comparing the answers of children concerning the "explanations" with specific passages in Buridan or Oresme, the great masters of the XIVth century. These analogies, however, may be considered as bearing on content of knowledge rather than on mechanisms of concept building. Parallels concerning mechanisms of progress are far more important. These mechanisms characterize not only the *stages* of development, but furthermore—and this is perhaps more important—the transition from one stage to the next.

For example, in the history of geometry before our century, one may consider three stages characterized by (a) the geometry of the Greeks and its evolution up to the end of the XVIIIth century; (b) the projective geometry (Poncelet, Chasles); (c) the "global" conception of geometry introduced by Klein. The development of descriptive geometry by Descartes and Fermat, and of calculus, provided the instruments for the transition from (a) to (b); and group theory for the transition from (b) to (c). Here one finds a similarity with the stages described by Piaget in children as "intrafigural," "interfigural," and "transfigural." The epistemological analysis of these differences shows profound reasons for this parallelism and has demonstrated, beyond expectation, the fertility of psychogenetic research for understanding the evolution of science.

This epistemological theory opened up many new directions in research. In Geneva, colleagues drew upon Piaget's work in pursuing studies in related fields —psycholinguistics, cybernetics, psychopathology of thought, and other fields— as well as in extending the scope of developmental psychology itself.

Until recently, studies in cognitive psychology were mainly concerned with the structural aspects of knowledge and the different modes of apprehending reality, and aimed at an analysis of the subject's cognitive potentialities at different periods of development. Research on learning led toward the study of the dynamic processes that make for the transition from one level of thought to the next. A better understanding of these processes drew attention to the important role played by the different strategies by which the subjects seek to generalize their newly acquired reasoning patterns. The latest research in Geneva[23] is thus concerned with these processes of strategies in children: how does the child come to invent procedures that he thinks will help him to solve a problem, and what kind of relationship exists between his inventions and his "theories in action" or his implicit system of dealing with reality?[24] (Karmiloff and Inhelder 1975). These are among the fundamental questions we are dealing with at the moment.

For Piaget, psychology may be a mere by-product of his work in epistemology, especially of his constructivist theory of knowledge; but for his colleagues, collaborators, and admirers this by-product constitutes an extraordinarily rich source of inspiration.

ACKNOWLEDGMENT

I wish to express my gratitude to M. and H. Sinclair for their generous help in translating the manuscript.

REFERENCES

1. PIAGET, J. 1952. The Origins of Intelligence in Children. International University Press. New York, N.Y. (First French edition 1936.)

2. PIAGET, J. 1954. The Child's Construction of Reality. New York, Basic Books. New York, N.Y. (First French edition 1937.)
3. PIAGET, J. 1971. Biology and Knowledge (An Essay on the Relations between Organic Regulations and Cognitive processes). Edinburgh University Press. (First French edition 1967.) Edinburgh, Scotland.
4. PIAGET, J. 1975. L'équilibration des structures cognitives (probléme central du développement). Etudes d'Epistémologie génétique. Vol. **XXXIII**. PUF. Paris, France.
5. MORENO, L., N. RAYNA, H. SINCLAIR, M. STAMBAK & M. VERBA, 1976. Les bébés et la logique. Les Cahiers du CRESAS no. 14. Paris.
6. PIAGET, J. & B. INHELDER. 1974. The Child's Constructions of Quantities (Conservation and Atomism). Routledge and Kegan Paul. London, England. (First French edit. 1941.)
7. PLAGET, J. et al. 1968. Epistémologie et psychologie de la fonction. Etudes d'Epistémologie génétique Vol. **XXIII**. PUF. Paris, France.
8. PIAGET, J. et al. 1968. On the Development of Memory and Identity. Heinz Werner Lectures, Series 2. Clark University Press. Worcester, Mass.
9. INHELDER, B., H. SINCLAIR & M. BOVET. 1974. Learning and the Development of Cognition. Harvard University Press. Cambridge, Mass. (French edit. 1974.)
10. PIAGET, J. 1930. The child's conception of physical causality. Harcourt Brace. New York, N.Y. (First French edition 1927.)
11. PIAGET, J. & R. GARCIA. 1974. Understanding Causality. Norton. New York, N.Y. (French edit. 1971.)
12. PIAGET, J., A. SZEMINSKA & E. FERREIRO. 1972. La transmission médiate du mouvement. In La Transmission des Mouvements. Piaget et al. Etudes d'Epistémologie génétique. Vol. **XXVII**. PUF. Paris, France.
13. PIAGET, J. et al. Recherches sur l'abstraction réfléchissante (1. Relations logico-arithmétiques). Etudes d'Epistémologie génétique. Vol. **XXXIV**. PUF. Paris, France. In press.
14. INHELDER, B. & J. PIAGET. 1964. The early growth of logic in the child (classification and seriation). Harper. New York, N.Y. (First French edit. 1959.)
15. PIAGET, J. 1974. Recherches sur la contradiction. I. Les différentes formes de la contradiction. Etudes d'Epistémologie génétique. Vol. **XXXI**. PUF. Paris, France.
16. PIAGET, J. 1974. Recherches sur la contradiction. 2. Les relations entre affirmations et négations. Etudes d'Epistémologie génétique. Vol. **XXXII**. PUF. Paris, France.
17. INHELDER, B. et al. 1975. Relations entre les conservations d'ensembles d'éléments discrets et celles de quantités continues. Année Psychol. **75**: 23-60.
18. PIAGET, J. 1970. Genetic Epistemology. Woodbridges Lectures no. 9 Columbia University Press. New York, N.Y.
19. PIAGET, J. 1972. The principle of genetic epistemology. Routledge and Kegan Paul. London, England.
20. BOWER, T. 1974. Development in Infancy. Freeman. San Francisco, Calif.
21. PIAGET, J. & R. GARCIA. Mécanismes communs entre la psychogénése et l'histoire des sciences. In preparation.
22. PIAGET, J. et al. 1976. The Grasp of Consciousness. Harvard Univ. Press. Cambridge, Mass. (First French edition, 1974.)
23. INHELDER, B. et al. 1976. Des structures cognitives aux procédures de découverte. Arch. Psychologie (Geneva) **XLIV**. (171): 57-72.
24. KARMILOFF, A. & B. INHELDER. 1975. "If you want to get ahead, get a theory." Cognition 3(3): 195-212.
25. PIAGET, J. 1937. Principal factors determining intellectual evolution from childhood to adult life. In Factors Determining Human Behavior. Cambridge, Mass. Harvard Univ. Press. Cambridge, Mass. Harvard tercentenary publications 32-48.
26. PIAGET, J. 1974. Adaptation vitale et psychologie de l'intelligence (sélection organique et phénocopie). Hermann. Paris, France.

IN TRIBUTE TO PIAGET: A LOOK AT HIS SCIENTIFIC IMPACT IN THE UNITED STATES*

Gilbert Voyat

Department of Psychology
The City University of New York
New York, New York 10031

Although it is not an easy task in such a small compass, I want to try to convey here some idea of Jean Piaget's remarkably rich and prolific contribution and something of the vitality of the "Centre International d'Epistémologie Génétique"; to draw attention to the extensive and wide-ranging work of the Faculty of Psychology and Educational Sciences; to mention, if only summarily, the essential research carried out by Piaget's close collaborators, notably Bärbel Inhelder; and, above all, to offer some account of the influence of the thinking and writing of the Geneva school upon present-day American psychology.

In the first place, it must be borne in mind that aside from the spread of the influence of the Geneva school, the mainstream of American experimental psychology is still largely circumscribed by a behaviorist ideology. This ideology continues to offer stout and often sophisticated resistance to any theoretical approach based on an interactionist epistemology, and indeed to any theory at all that puts the emphasis on the idea of structure.

Secondly, we must remember the interesting fact that this dominant orientation of American psychology is more susceptible to the constraints imposed by a pragmatic and quasiutilitarian conception of psychology and pedagogy than is psychology as taught in the majority of European universities.

In fact, the "American" approach, founded on the notion of transcendence and governed by the perspective of constant and rapid individual improvements, still colors the main concerns of most researchers and educational theorists—a fact that never ceases to amuse Piaget himself. By the same token, meanwhile, many American psychologists and educators treat the Piagetian idea of a dynamic synthesis, sustained thanks to an equilibrium among horizontal extensions of thinking within the framework of progressive restructurings, as part of the "Genevan enigma."

The problem is not, however, that the concept of equilibration has failed to find articulate proponents in the United States. Nor is it—even less so, in fact— that this concept has not been accorded recognition as a basic notion of operational theory on a par with the concepts of assimilation, accomodation, schema, operation, and internalization. Operational theory is both easily accessible and intensively studied in North America. Twelve years after the publication of *Piaget Rediscovered*,[1] an event that marked a rebirth of interest in the Geneva school in the United States, there is scarcely a manual of child psychology that does not offer an extensive account of the Piagetian approach. There is not one volume of the journal *Child Development*, to take a case in point, that does not contain recapitulations, extensions, or refinements of the Genevan experiments.

In short, it is not a dearth of publicity from which the Geneva school suffers.

*A French version of this paper was adapted for the *Bulletin the Psychologie de l'Université de Paris*, Tome XXX, 1976-1977. Special Issue in honor of Jean Piaget.

The truth is that the school constitutes a manifest problem of accommodation for the behaviorist tendency—a fact of which the consequences are of the utmost importance if we wish to understand the impact of Piaget's school on American psychology as a whole. The influence exerted by Piagetian notions is best viewed as affected by two main factors. The first is an educational practice which—though no doubt open to the lessons of a wide spectrum of experience—remains captive to an approach the prime concern of which is the acceleration of development. The second factor is a theoretical psychological frame of reference of which the true goal is to further at all costs the pedagogical approach just described.

In confronting these limiting factors the Piagetians are not alone; psychoanalysis and its offshoots have to battle similar constraints. Behavior modification techniques—behavior modification therapy, for instance—find more grace in the eyes of many Americans, because of their immediate results, than approaches calling for reflexive abstractions or introspection from subjects in whom insight may take as many years to acquire—perhaps even more—than the construction and mastery of concrete or formal thinking. Thus, many people cannot conceive of the time taken for a child to construct an operational universe without thinking in terms of those holy cows of American educationalists, the "three R's" of reading, writing, and arithmetic.

Ideologically speaking, both psychoanalysis and operational theory have an important standing in the U.S., yet they exist in parallel with each other and remain, in a peculiar sense, outside the behaviorist stream, which appears to furnish the aptest response to what are perceived as the immediate needs of education.

So far as the Geneva school is concerned, one of the reasons for this state of affairs is the stress Piaget lays on the individual's autonomous activity and on the essential role of factors of assimilation in cognitive development. The contradiction that Piaget's thesis enshrines in the view of most American psychologists and educationalists resides in the very assumptions on which his argument is based. For Piaget sets out to discover, analyze, and explain the way in which the child *constructs reality*, whereas the American "common sense" approach persists in thinking that this development can be precipitated and directed by the appropriate external manipulation, by the correct "programming."

It is within this context of cross-purposes that we should approach the question of the influence of the Geneva school in America. For despite the contradiction between the two perspectives, the bald assertion that the mainstream of American psychology has undergone no far-reaching changes as a result of Piaget's ideas is far from the mark.

OPERATIONAL THEORY AND THE MAINSTREAM OF AMERICAN EXPERIMENTAL PSYCHOLOGY

Among the many and various products of this first kind of interaction we may conveniently start by considering those which fall under the head of a systematic operationalization of the concepts and experimental method of the Geneva school. This kind of interaction often boils down to an American attempt to integrate Piaget's thinking into the behaviorist approach. This may be observed principally in two spheres. The first is the conceptual and theoretical sphere epitomized by Berlyne's book[2] and by the work of Beilin.[3] Ironically enough, Berlyne sees Piaget as a neobehaviorist, whereas Beilin calls him a neomaturationist. This confusion is a typical expression of the difficulty Americans have in understanding not only the idea of interaction but also, and most importantly, the concept of new constructions as the outcome of internal regulations.

The second area in which this type of interaction may be seen is experimental and empirical; here the work of the Geneva school is operationalized, reproduced, or modified within the framework of an experimental approach in which conceptual advance is governed more by statistical considerations than by the findings produced by observation of the child's thought processes.

Aside from misunderstandings of a semantic kind and those produced by the need for experimental adaptation, this first type of interaction brings out a real contradiction in the way in which the object of experimental psychology is conceived of by the Genevans on the one hand and by the Americans on the other. Even though behaviorism and operational theory may not necessarily be incompatible, and even though the discovery of a good deal of common ground between them has given rise to much useful and productive work, a great difficulty remains, a difficulty related to the very foundation of Piaget's thesis and not to problems of methodological or conceptual adaptation.

The dialectical opposition that we run into here arises in part from the presence of two distinct methodological conceptions. Piaget, who in this respect follows in the footsteps of Binet, always takes care to adapt his conceptual and experimental strategy to the requirements of the problems that he has set himself. Behaviorism, however, adapts its problems to the methods it has at its disposition. According to the first conception, Piaget's, the method to be followed is a function of the question being asked; according to the second approach, the behaviorist approach, the methodological framework defines the hypotheses put forward and the problems to be solved.

In addition, it is hard to find any common measure between, say, the data produced by administering a five-minute questionnaire to a hundred children and that obtained by conducting a hundred-minute experiment with just five children. Yet the differences between the results sought by the clinical or genetic method on the one hand and the classical behaviorist approach on the other are precisely of this order.

A second type of interaction between the Geneva school and the dominant tendency of American psychology is constituted by attempts to standardize the Genevan concepts and experimental methods. Piaget has concentrated most of his efforts on the study of the development of the "epistemic" subject, and in consequence he has set out to give an account of the genesis of operational structures unaffected by sex, social class, or cultural differences (structural invariants in his view being more important than individual variations of this kind). For many Americans, however, such variables are of prime importance and must not be relegated to the status of secondary determinants in this way. These opponents of the Piagetian outlook consider the notion of an invariant development of operational structures to be highly abstract, arguing that it evokes an abstract mechanism for which norms and functional differences should be established.

Such considerations aside, there is no disputing the usefulness of quantitative studies of intellectual operations, or of the collection of psychometric data after the fashion of authors such as Pinard and Laurendeau[4] and Beth Stephens[5]—to mention only two examples. Such data may not necessarily be indispensable to operational theory, but their implications are important because in this context "the constraints imposed by the empirical method invariably predominate over the properly clinical method of research."† The establishment of behavioral norms as typical for specific age groups calls *de facto* for the use of experimental

---

†Cf. J. Piaget, Foreword to G. Voyat, *Piaget Systematized*. Teachers College Press, Columbia University. In press.

techniques in which the systematic control of variables is indispensable. Also relevant in this connection are the very solid results generated by cross-cultural studies. Like the work just mentioned, this kind of research helps to clarify the problem of the relationship between given ages and given acquisitional stages and to verify the criteria governing the integration of successive structures.

Generally speaking, efforts of this type often end up by identifying the idea of operational evaluation with that of psychological testing (a favorite American pastime!), or even by substituting one for the other.

The dialectic involved in this second type of interaction embodies a subtle but real reversal of Piaget's intentions, which were never to treat intelligence as a progressive accretion of specific reactions, but rather to analyze it as an overall structure.

Where there is no basic incompatibility between operational theory on the one hand and psychometry, standardization, or empirical verification on the other, these interactions raise valuable problems whose resolution opens up many new areas. What is more, they allow us to see clearly that operational theory has shown itself well able to endure the confrontation with behaviorism, benefiting greatly from the behaviorists' empirical contributions and adapting itself readily to their findings.

OPERATIONAL THEORY, CLINICAL PSYCHOLOGY AND EDUCATION

There are two other areas of interaction, still within the psychological field, which it is worth our looking at. The first is interaction between the Geneva school and clinical psychology, and the second is interaction between the Geneva school and American education.

First of all, it should be pointed out that clinical psychology, just like developmental psychology, occupies a rather special position in the United States. Classical experimental psychologists, though ready to grant both of these fields the status of disciplines and viable forms of knowledge in their own right, remain skeptical as to their meeting the criteria of scientific rigor. So far as operational theory is concerned, this attitude attests to a misunderstanding—perhaps even a total incomprehension—with regard not only to the empirical nature of the data gathered by the Piagetian approach, but also to the operational method of dealing with this data.

The problem becomes very clear if we compare the methodology of the Skinnerian with that of a Chomsky. On the one hand, both Skinner and Chomsky assert that their theses are verifiable, Skinner's by empirical means, Chomsky's by deductive reasoning. On the other hand, Skinner needs a horde of subjects, whereas Chomsky needs none at all. Operational theory may be said to occupy a middle position between the two poles of Skinner and Chomsky. It must rely on the deductive procedure in the formalization of structures, yet the fact is that this procedure is every bit as scientific as the experiments whose results it is designed to deal with.

Apart from this methodological affinity, the interplay between American clinical psychology and operational theory has produced a plethora of results that may best be divided up under two main headings. The first of these covers theoretical contributions, e.g. comparative studies of psychoanalysis and operational theory like those of P. Wolff.[6] The second category takes in experimental contributions in this area, and here a variety of syndromes and a large group of psychopathological data have been clearly defined, thanks to the use of operational tasks. See especially the work of Escalona[7] and of Anthony.[8]

In fact, this area of interaction has been very fruitful indeed, and it is worth noting that one reason for this is that both operational theory and clinical psychology lay much stress on the idea of process and on the modalities of cognitive and/or affective organization. On the other hand, the dialectic that develops here is also important, because once again it depends on a sort of subtle distortion of Piaget's original aims. Operational theory seeks to explain the normal development of cognitive structures. Basically, it takes normality as its starting point and constructs its conception of cognitive development on this foundation. By contrast, clinical psychology sets out from the opposite pole, drawing inferences from its observation of the abnormal and sometimes—as in the case of Freud—developing a theory on this basis. It is quite clear, however, that operational theory constitutes an indispensable tool, and this not only methodologically speaking. As a matter of fact, it is the concept of structure that has elevated clinical psychology to its present essential position, because it is this concept which makes it possible to analyze the link and the transitional process between normal and abnormal thought. To take just one illustration of this, Rapaport's[9] attempt to work out a psychoanalytic theory of thinking relies heavily on the notion of structure.

In sum, clinical psychology has taken very much into account the concepts developed by operational theory, recognizing their importance and the vital need for them in any thorough interpretation of personality development.

Interaction between the Geneva school and American pedagogy, affected as it is by the factors already mentioned, has been going through a very interesting development. One reason for this, no doubt, is that education and educational theory are intimately bound up with questions of social class and socioeconomic level. In the United States, as elsewhere, education is also a *political* reality. And it is precisely in this aspect that it is a sensitive issue.

The present situation of Piaget's influence on education in the United States is characterized by the publication of an ever-increasing flood of popular works like the one by Mary Ann Pulaski;[10] by a number of books and articles intended to encourage an experimental teaching genuinely based on operational theory, an example here being the collection *Piaget in the Classroom*;[11] and, perhaps most strikingly, by a vast movement of educationalists broadly favoring the Piagetian approach.

The intensity and breadth of the interest aroused in America by the findings of the Geneva school are truly remarkable. A host of individual teachers and the many "new schools" (sometimes called "Piaget schools") all claim to base their educational epistemology on operational theory. One might well ask how such enthusiasm is possible when the mainstream of American pedagogy is still in thrall to a militant and vigilant behaviorism. Part of the answer to this question is that the demands which American education has to meet on the pragmatic level tend to maintain the system in a state of permanent instability. Another point worth mentioning is the complementarity and resemblance between Piaget's approach and Dewey's, which continues to underpin a dissenting tradition in educational thinking in America.

There is another reason, too, why American pedagogy has opened its doors to operational theory, and this is quite simply that an increasing number of educationalists find in this theory exactly what they are looking for, namely, a theoretical framework and the knowledge needed for the organization of their projected applications. In this connection the following anecdote may be of interest. In 1975 Piaget paid a return visit to our teaching project in Harlem (the Children's Art Carnival), where every cognitive intervention is based on observations by psychoeducational teams.[12] His way of gauging the results of these attempts to apply psychopedagogical lessons was to look for changes in the behavior of the teachers he had first seen at work three years earlier; what he noticed was a new pedagogical understanding indicating that the teachers had assimilated the essential concepts of cognitive development.

Thus it is not inconceivable that a teaching practice based on an appropriate application of operational theory will one day make its contribution to the reorganization of the American educational system. Meanwhile, it is worth reminding ourselves of the existence in the United States of numerous pilot projects whose organizers explicitly cite Piaget's theory as their basic frame of reference. The American Jean Piaget Society has as many educators as psychologists among its members, while another association, "Piaget Theory and the Helping Profession," has just concluded its sixth annual symposium in California. All this testifies to an overwhelming effervescence in this area, accompanied, as is inevitable, by all the problems of the rapid popularization and hurried application of a theory as complex as Piaget's.

It is clear also that this type of interaction has no true internal dynamic of its own. No unifying tendency is visible here save for the explicit invocation of Piaget's thought, and what we see is actually a large number of distinct trends with no predominant orientation emerging for the time being.

OPERATIONAL THEORY AND EPISTEMOLOGY

Of all the areas of knowledge that Piaget has affected in the United States, that of genetic epistemology occupies the clearest, the best differentiated, and, in a sense, the most important position.

For one thing, structuralism as a method of analysis has undergone a thoroughgoing renovation, thanks to Piaget's influence, while at the same time the epistemology underpinning this method has enlisted the support of a select group of proponents in the United States.

Aside from Piaget's own efforts to disseminate genetic epistemology in North America, notably by delivering the Woodbridge Lectures at Columbia University,[13] which he devoted entirely to this area, and aside too from work dealing with the epistemology of operational theory itself,[14] genetic epistemology has given rise to two kinds of interaction. The first occurs on a theoretical plane and is exemplified by the anthology *Cognitive Development and Epistemology*,[15] seven of whose fifteen contributors belong to philosophy departments. The second type is a result of the profound kinship between operational theory and cybernetics. As Papert and Voyat[16] note, ". . . it is people concerned with the resolution of specific problems arising from the operation of cybernetic machines who are the most urgently in need of a theory of knowledge." (p. 92). In this context we should note that work on artificial intelligence bears the deep imprint of Piaget's influence and has borrowed whatever it needed from both genetic epistemology and operational theory. Actually, the conceptual link with cybernetics was also established thanks to the concepts of regulation and self-regulation —i.e., the intrinsic conceptual components of the notion of structure.

THEORY OF KNOWLEDGE AND BIOLOGY

In the last reckoning it is perhaps the interaction between the theory of knowledge and biology that best reveals both the problems and the achievements of Piaget's influence in the United States. It is worth our looking at some of the reasons for this, because it will help us form an overall view of the enormous impact of the Geneva school in America.

Taken in conjunction with the suspicion of "disguised Lamarckism" that it tends to arouse in its biological context, the notion that "one of the most general processes in the development of cognitive structures consists in the replacement of exogenous knowledge by endogenous reconstructions" (Piaget,[17] p. 193) causes problems for many students, biologists included.

Though such ideas are far removed from the traditional framework of classical American psychology, there is some willingness to accept the conception of cognitive structures conceived as the outcome of internalized acts and of active manipulation of the physical environment. And structuralism, equilibration, and the idea of contradictions are not completely unacceptable, either. But when it comes to the thesis that exogenous knowledge is liable to be superseded by endogenous reconstructions the defenders of the classical approach tend to run out of patience.

Apart from his questioning of Darwinian assumptions, Piaget's hypothesis regarding the generality of the process of phenocopy[18] is also very troublesome for many. And it must be admitted that the mechanisms of regulations are more difficult to grasp in a psychobiological context than in the more circumscribed sphere of cognitive development considered alone.

This brings us to what would seem to be a fundamental obstacle for operational theory in its interaction with the various tendencies of American psychology and pedagogy. The fact is that the concept of interaction is the one that remains the most mysterious to the American way of thinking. It is paradoxical to discover that this most vital element in operational theory, in tandem with the notion of equilibration as an essential mechanism in cognitive development, remains the most alien of concepts for those schooled in the classical tradition of American psychology.

The problem arises not because of the overall structures that Piaget evokes to account for modes of organization, nor because of his interpretations of the notions of equilibration, creativity, or opening on to the possible; nor yet because of the type of misunderstanding to which his analytical approach sometimes gives rise. Rather, the difficulty is due to the intrinsic complexity of the development of knowledge itself.

This complexity leaves its mark on every form of interaction between the Geneva school and the different trends in American research, and it will doubtless continue to do so. Since its "rediscovery" in 1964, Piaget's theory, while certainly remaining true to itself, has undergone modification as a result of both internal revisionism and outside pressures. But it is also true that Piaget's ideas have contributed to the profound modification of the dominant conceptual paradigm of American educational psychology. Although this modification does not as yet amount to a qualitative or structural transformation of the paradigm, it is no longer inconceivable that the Genevan influence may one day precipitate such a radical change.

This prospect confirms our belief in the fecundity and originality of the Piagetian approach and strengthens our conviction that its influence is destined to increase in the future.

REFERENCES

1. DUCKWORTH, E. 1964. Piaget Rediscovered. *In* Piaget Rediscovered (a report of the Conference on Cognitive Studies and Curriculum Development). R.E. Ripple and V. N. Rockcastle, Eds. Cornell University School of Education. Ithaca, N.Y.

2. BERLYNE, D. E. 1965. Structure and Direction in Thinking. John Wiley and Sons. New York, N.Y.
3. BEILIN, H. 1969. Stimulus and cognitive transformation in conservation. *In* Studies in Cognitive Development: Essays in Honor of Jean Piaget. D. Elkind and J. H. Flavell, Eds.: 409-437. Oxford University Press. New York, N.Y.
4. PINARD, A. & M. LAURENDEAU. 1962. Causal thinking in the child. International University Press. Montréal, Canada.
5. STEPHENS, B. *et al.* 1974. Symposium: developmental gains in the reasoning, moral judgment, and moral conduct of retarded and nonretarded persons. Am. J. Mental Deficiency 79: 113-161.
6. WOLFF, P. 1960. The developmental psychologies of Jean Piaget and psychoanalysis. International Universities Press. New York, N.Y.
7. ESCALONA, S. 1968. The Roots of Individuality. Aldine. Chicago, Ill.
8. ANTHONY, E. J. 1956. The significance of Jean Piaget for child psychiatry. Brit. J. Med. Psychol. 29: 20-34.
9. RAPAPORT, D. 1960. Psychoanalysis as a developmental psychology. *In* Gill, M. (ed.): The collected papers of David Rapaport. 1967. M. Gill, Ed. Basic Books. New York, N.Y.
10. PULASKI, M. A. 1971. Understanding Piaget. Harper and Row. New York, N.Y.
11. SCHWEBEL, M. & J. RAPH, EDS. 1973. Piaget in the classroom. Basic Books. New York, N.Y.
12. VOYAT, G. 1975. Open education and the embodiment of thinking, reading and writing. ADE Bulletin (Special Carnegie Sponsored issue) no. 6.
13. PIAGET, J. 1970. Genetic Epistemology. (Trans. by E. Duckworth.) Woodbridge Lectures. Columbia University Press. New York, N.Y.
14. GRUBER, H. & J. VONECHE. The Essential Piaget. Basic Books. New York, N.Y. In press.
15. MISCHEL, T. ED. 1971. Cognitive Development and Epistemology. Academic Press. New York, N.Y.
16. PAPERT, S. & G. VOYAT. 1968. A propos du perceptron: qui a besoin de l'epistémologie. Vol XXII Etudes d'Epistémologie Génétique. Presses Universitaires de France. Paris, France.
17. PIAGET, J. 1975. From noise to order: the psychological development of knowledge and phenocopy in biology. Urban Rev. 8(3): 209-218.
18. PIAGET, J. 1974. Adaptation Vitale et Psychologie de l'Intelligence. Selection organique et phénocopie. Hermann. Paris, France.

SOME RECENT RESEARCH AND ITS LINK WITH A NEW THEORY OF GROUPINGS AND CONSERVATIONS BASED ON COMMUTABILITY*

Jean Piaget

University of Geneva
Geneva, Switzerland

I would like first to express my regret at not having been able to attend this session of the New York Academy of Sciences devoted to psychological systems, but I am very happy that Bärbel Inhelder was able to take my place, especially as she is not coauthor but the sole author of another paper in this volume.

Perhaps I may be permitted to add a few words concerning our current research before presenting a new theory of grouping and conservation. At the International Center for Genetic Epistemology we are at present dealing with what we call the opening up of new possibilities, that is to say, the way in which an action, an operation, or a structure acquired by the child generates new possibilities.

To give an example of our experiments, we place the child in the following types of situations. We give him, for instance, a piece of cardboard and three blocks, and he is asked to arrange these blocks in all possible ways without specification whether in regular, irregular, or random fashion. In another type of experiment we give the child a square sheet of paper and ask him to cut it up in all possible ways. Will the child produce only diagonals or medians or will he find other ways? Or again, we show the child a half-hidden object and ask him to guess its complete shape or to suggest what possible ways he can think of to complete the visible portion.

There are, of course, many variations, and among young children from four to six years of age we find little variation. They find five to ten possibilities, then claim that nothing more can be done.

Between seven and eleven we find a progressive increase of new possibilities and around eleven to twelve years of age the child, after two or three tries, immediately tells us that the number of possibilities is infinite and gives us justifications as to why. There is thus an increase with age of the number of possibilities perceived. Our fundamental thesis is that possibilities are not predetermined. It is in effect a contradiction in terms to talk of a totality of all possibilities. The concept of a totality of all possibilities is antinomic, because the whole is itself one possibility among others, and because every possibility generates new ones. There is something here which transcends all preformation. There is an authentic creativity which plays a fundamental role in my conception of equilibration: the "possible" is the moment of reequilibration between one form of equilibrium and the next.

Another avenue of research pursued at the Center for Epistemology, the result of which are still to be published, concerns what in mathematics are called correspondences or morphisms. Correspondences and morphisms had not been studied until recently. Previously, we had placed a great emphasis on

*Translated by Gilbert Voyat of The Graduate School and University Center of the City University of New York, in collaboration with Donald Nicholson-Smith. The French version will appear in the *Bulletin de Psychologie de l'Université de Paris*, special issue in honor of Paul Fraisse.

operations as transformations of a given object, whereas correspondences and morphisms are essentially comparisons, comparisons that do not transform objects to be compared but that extract common forms from them or analogies between them.

As an example, we may take the case of family relationships. We confront the child with a series of identical dolls marked with arrows representing relations such as grandfather, uncle, nephew, cousin, brother, and so forth. Let us suppose that A is the grandfather of B. For A there exists a number of taxonomical relationships with all other members of the family, and the child will name them. A is the father of C, the cousin of D, and so on. Let us now take B, who is A's grandson. For B there is also a whole series of relationships with other family members. The child is asked to state the reciprocal relationships, taking into account the points of view of both A and B; i.e., the grandfather and the son, where these two are to be taken together and compared with other members of the family such as a brother or a cousin. There is a system of correspondences here between two relational systems that the child is asked to establish. This is easy for the close relationships and becomes more and more complex and interesting to study when subjects reach eleven to twelve years of age.

This research on correspondences and morphisms has shown us, in regard to our previous research on operations and transformations, that the groundwork for any operation or transformation is laid by correspondences. One needs to understand the correspondence between an initial and a final state to understand what the transformation is that leads from one state to the next. Once the operations are completed, once the operational structures are built, correspondences become a function of the operational structures. They no longer prepare the operations but become their deductible consequences.

We have a number of completed studies that will soon be published, and here we can present only a small sample; these are only a few examples of the research presently under way in Geneva.

Inasmuch as this new research on possibilities had to be integrated with our earlier work on operations, we had to review its status on the basis of the results obtained. This enabled us to work out a new theory of groupings and conservations based on commutability. In addition, thanks to our new findings, it became possible to refine our grouping theory by introducing two kinds of fresh formalizations, one of them being logistic in character and the other categorical. Some account of this development follows.

NEW FORMULATIONS REGARDING THE STRUCTURE OF GROUPINGS AND CONSERVATIONS

In seeking to describe the earliest operational structures built by the child (classifications, seriations, etc.), we have used the term "grouping"[1] to refer to a model that has generated little enthusiasm from logicians and mathematicians because of its unavoidable limitations (step-by-step composition, disjoint sets) and consequent "lack of elegance." Our defense, however, was that no matter how primitive its use is between the ages of seven and eleven (and thus before the construction of "complete networks" or "integrated wholes"), "grouping" evoked a structure which from Linné to the present has provided an adequate basis for all zoological and botanical classifications (which are also never more than semilattices).

Just recently, however, two logicians and mathematicians have taken an interest in this problem and managed to give the concept of grouping a respectable status. One of them, H. Vermus, has supplied a complete axiomatization.[2] He bases himself on four very simple axioms: 1) The asymmetry of the binary predicate linking y to x as its "immediate sucessor;" 2) the unicity of this sucessor; 3) the "contiguous junction" that gives rise to the immediate successor z from two contiguous elements x and y; and 4) the existence and the unicity of the (dichotomous) "subtraction" of one element from its successor.

The other mathematician, E. Whittman, taking the aximoatization produced by Vermus as his starting point, has shown that the "grouping" constitutes a special "category" in the sense in which this term is used by his mentor S. McLane. McLane inverted this notion of "categories" with Eilenberg, and he has endorsed Wittman's remarks. We have no need to recapitulate Wittman's account here, but since a "category" in this sense is a system of "morphisms" (i.e. correspondences in which the structure is conserved), it is worth while from the psychologist's point of view to isolate a few of these morphisms in order to see that the grouping is not just a system of operations (and hence transformations) but that it also embodies a set of correspondences (and hence of comparisons).

Classifications

In the first place, these include a system of "superjective and injective applications."[3] It should be remembered that the application of an initial set E to a final set E' must be exhaustive to the left ("all" of the X's of E) and univocal to the right (on the X's of E').

We have superjection if each element of E' receives "at least 1 x" of E and injection if the x's in E' receive only "at most one x" of E thus 1 or 0. Furthermore, we have bijection (isomorphisms) if each x of E corresponds to only one x of E' and vice versa. This said, suppose that we have in a given classification a set $B1$ made up of subsets $A1$, $A2$, etc., and a given number of individuals x to be classified, each possessing the property $b1$ intrinsic to $B1$, but also the differential properties $a1$, $a2$, etc., specific to $A1$, $A2$, etc.: we will then have superjections of these individuals into the A sets. Similarly these sets are superjected into $B1$ (though not into $B2$, $B3$, etc. which are superjected along with $B1$ into $C1$), and so on. As regards the inclusion $A1 < B1$, it is an injection of the individuals with the properties $a1b1$ into the group of terms of $B1$ with $b1$ properties where they join only those possessing in addition $a1$ properties without correspondence to the other $B1$: we are thus dealing with the same individuals $a1b1$. However, on the one hand they constitute the set $A1$, and on the other hand they also belong to $B1$.

This injective application is important because its reciprocal (i.e. subjection of $B1$'s into $A1$ to the extent that these $B1$'s do not all correspond to the $A1$'s.) is a necessity for the quantification of the inclusion ($B1 > A1$ where $A1 < B1$). We know that when confronted with a collection B of 10 flowers of which 6 are daisies (=A) and 4 other flowers (=A'), young subjects understand clearly that all the A's are B's just as all the A' are. On the other hand, when they are asked whether there are "more flowers B or more daisies A" they reply that "there are more of A." Thus in this situation they simply compare the A's with the other flowers a' and proceed as though once they have separated the A's from the B's in their minds, isomorphisms must exist between the B' and the A''s; in terms of correspondences, this means that what causes the problem is the reciprocal of the injection which we are calling "superjection," inasmuch as it is an incomplete correspondence (without application.) But if these various superjective and injective correspondences are cotransformational in that they are bound up with the operations of union and enclosure, the fact remains that they are determined by an extralogical qualitative content, whence the factual necessity (as distinct from a normative necessity) to proceed by means of contiguous links; the union of any two sets of individuals, e.g. worms and elephants, can only give rise to correspondences of such generality that the resulting set remains open to a large number of other factors and is thus not a "natural" set. By contrast, the union of elephants and hippopotamuses would give rise to more correspondences in terms of comprehension and thus to a more circumscribed and hence "natural" set. In addition, such cotransformational correspondences may follow or precede the transformations. In such cases unions are constituted only on the basis of similarities established at the outset.

In a systematic classification in the form of a more or less leafy tree, where any two branches at some distance from one another do not give rise by themselves to the construction of a basic set and so do not correspond to one another in this way, we still have a precise bijection between two areas of the classification: whether we are concerned with worms or elephants, a "species" from a zoological point of view (type 1) is part of a "genus" (type 2). A "genus" is part of a "family" (type 3). A family is part of an "order" (type 4). An "order" is part of a "class" and a "class" is part of a branch (type 6). It is clear, therefore, that if we leave aside the content, the forms involved in groupings are linked by well-defined morphisms, the recognition of which is facilitated here by the fact that the different "types" of classes have been given generic names. But even without such denomination it is always possible (and this from an early moment in development) to establish correspondences between one class and another, so long as the hierarchy of types is respected.

But there is more to be said. Zoological classification only concerns itself with taxonomical distinctions and has no nomenclature for relations. It would be quite possible, however, to give names and definitions to the different relationships between classes. One might, for instance, compare members of a species A to "brothers" and unite them in a single genus B analogous to their "fathers"; thus the "brother B' of the father B" would be comparable to an "uncle" and his "sons" to their "cousins," and so on. It is quite clear that such relations, although they are not named, are comparable to those shown in a genealogical tree (with no marriages indicated): they give rise to unlimited combinations for n generations along with kinship relations to the nth degree; and along with compositions of superjections, injections, and bijections working in conformity with the principles described above but being restricted to their forms alone. We have recently been studying such family relations perceived by children from 4/5 to 12/15 years of age, using as experimental materials small identical dolls distinguished only by groups of arrows to indicate the various sorts of correspondence (see above). We found that whereas subjects of seven to ten years of age are restricted to a limited number of relations, subjects in the eleven-to-twelve age range produce remarkable compositions even without recourse to a tree figure.

Vicarious Relationships

If $B = A1 + A'1$, we say that there is a vicarious relationship where B is subdivided in addition as follows: $B = A2 + A'2$ or $A2\ A'$ and $A1\ A'2$. In this case we have:

1) Superjection of the elements of B into $A1$ and $A'1$;
2) an analoguous superjection of B into $A2$ and $A'2$;
3) a correspondence between these superjections in three senses: a) the same

operation is involved as when the two unions $A1 + A'2$ and $A2 + A'2$ are equal to B. b) In these last two cases we have $B - A = A'$ whether A is $A1$ or $A2$ and c) its complementary relationship in which B may be either $A'1$ or $A'2$;

4) most importantly an injection of $A2$ into $A'1$ and from $A1$ into $A'2$: these two injections correspond to one another whether they are reciprocal or symmetrical;

5) lastly, a vicarious relationship between $A1 + A'1$ and $A2 + A'2$ which is reversible.

It would seem justifiable therefore to speak here of morphisms that conserve the structure, especially in view of the fact that one can proceed after the fashion $B = A3 + A'3$ in random manner by means of free transformations. We can conclude that the vicarious relationships represent an automorphism. This is to be expected, because the classificatory system constitutes a category if we include in it the entire treelike classification and not only a linear sequence of enclosures $A + A' = B$; $B + B' = C$, etc., and if we restrict ourselves to forms and pay no attention to content.

It should be noticed, however, that this category comprises only compositions between morphisms of the same status (despite the overlapping between classes of increasing rank), and excludes morphisms of a higher order. When it comes, more specifically, to vicarious relationships among such relationships themselves, it is clear that we are approaching the realm of "integrated wholes," and this has been well pointed up by some recent work. Such relationships do not consist merely in the generalization of the form $A + A'$ into the form $A2 + A'2$, $A3 + A'3$, etc., but they also entail a change in the form itself through pairing: $(A1 + A2) = (A'1 + A'2)$, etc.

Seriations

a) Each element, except the last, possesses a successor which is "greater," "darker," "further away," etc.

b) Each element except the first possesses a predecessor.

c) For every " " relationship there is a corresponding x "$>$" relationship, in terms both of bijection and symmetry.

d) The first term and all its successors are equal to the last term and all its predecessors (cf. $A1 + A'1 = A2 + A'2$) by virtue of the vicarious relationship between the terms which derive from the reciprocity between "$<$ and $>$".

e) For each term X or Y we have S (successors); $X + P$ (predecessors); $X = SY + PY = \epsilon$ ($<$ or $>$) = the number of elements less one. In other words, for any X or Y we have: $n (> X) + n' (< X) = n (> Y) + n' (< Y) = \epsilon$ of the relations.

f) One instance of this vicarious relationship, (a relationship facilitated by the fact that the various relations $<$ or $>$ bear distinguishing names), is that of linear seriation of direct family ascent and descent: "A is the father of B who is the grandfather of D" = "A is the grandfather of C who is the father of D" = "A is (in both cases) the great grandfather of D." In this instance the reciprocal injection of $A > B$ into $A > C$ and of $C > D$ into $B > D$ is of the same nature at that of $A1$ into $A'2$ and of $A2$ into $A'1$ in a vicarious relationship between sets. As for the correspondence $n (> X) + n' (< X) = n (> Y) = n' (< Y)$, it is the one used by the operational subject when, in seeking to construct a seriation, he looks at successive elements in search of an element

E which is both the smallest of all those remaining $(E < S)$ yet greater than those already arranged. $(E > P)$. He thus proceeds by means of a double superjection into E of $E's$ successors $(S > E)$ and predecessors. $(P < E)$. This occasions a continued vicarious relationship in that E is at all times the new element that must be found and thus each time partakes in a new fashion of the same aggregate "$<$ and $>$."

It is apparent that seriation, like systems of classification, constitutes a category and that it is accompanied by automorphisms when the vicarious relationships and compositions are involved in the form of recurrence, transitivity and reciprocity which are characteristic of seriated relationships.

Conservations

In a recent article[4] we proposed a new interpretation of conservations starting from the assumption that the subject arrives at these when two conditions are met: 1) a change in the form of an object or collection is understood as being the result of simple changes in the position of the components; 2) in any change what is added at the terminal point has been removed or substracted at the starting point ("commutability"). It follows that the categorial tools of conservation are founded on commutability and vicarious relationships, for the first expresses the identity of a component despite displacements while the second expresses the invariance of the whole irrespective of internal rearrangements. In order to obtain morphisms, therefore, rearrangements and displacements have to be combined.

Let A be a displaced part during a change in the form of an object or collection B and let A' be the parts which remain immobile. Let aA be an A in its initial position and bA the same A at its final position. Let u be a union with a particular area between A and A', and w a union with another area in a different location from A'. We thus have: (1) $(aA1\ u\ A'1 = A'1\ w\ bA1)\ (=)\ (aA2\ u\ A'2 = A'2\ w\ bA2)\ (=)\ (aA3\ u\ A'3 = A'3\ w\ bA3)\ (=)$ etc. $= B$.

The whole object B is thus conserved through all of the equivalences ($=$ or $(=)$) in that the A' parts remain in place and the A parts merely change their position. But it will readily be seen that two morphisms are combined here both of which are acquisitions of the operational stage of grouping (around seven to eight years of age):

1) First we have the correspondence between the aA and the bA inasmuch as we are dealing with the same parts that have simply been displaced and not with any quantitative increase due to a new disposition of the parts, as is supposed by preoperational subjects who fail to see that an addition in bA entails a subtraction in aA. (This morphism of identity thus expresses commutability).

2) We come next to isomorphism which holds between these types of commutability ($aA1 = bA1$) and those we encounter as a result of different rearrangements (between $A2$ and $A'2$; $A3$ and $A'3$, etc.)—in short, as a result of their composition with vicarious relationships. The superjections of the A's and A' into B's which are specific to the vicarious relationship are thus generalized in random fashion. As to the reciprocal injection of $A1$ into $A'2$'s and of $A2$'s into $A'1$, this means simply that if a mobile part A has become attached to an invariant part A', a portion of this has in turn been displaced, which is an obvious development once commutability has been understood. Yet this poses no problem to a five-to six-year-old subject provided that the experimenter avoids merely pushing the A's and is careful to lift them from one position and place them in

the other. On the other hand, where no clearcut rearrangement goes on, and the form is modified only by stretching, for example, the discovery, at a later age, of the invariance of the whole (prompted by the statements "nothing here has been added or taken away"), is apparently based on commutability alone. The fact is that, although the displaced elements are not delimited in number, the subject discovers that $(aA \text{ u } A' = A' \text{ w } bA)$ by means of a morphism of compensation: in other words, what the object loses in one dimension (diameter) is made up for in another (length). But whereas a displacement with commutability does not as yet amount to a change involving segmentation of the whole, and consists merely in a new disposition of the parts (since both A's and A''s remain stable), the equivalence maintained in the results of several rearrangements (i.e. the "$< = >$" located outside the parentheses in our equation above) constitute an authentic vicarious relationship in that the A's and the A''s undergo modifications (in $A1$, $A2$, $A3$, etc.), and in that we have $A1 + A'1 = A2 + A'2$, etc. Since these various transformations become free in this way, we may conclude that the total system formalized above does indeed embody an automorphism, so constituting a category on a par with groupings of classifications or seriations; as a matter of fact it is a necessary correlate of such groupings in that it is at once a precondition and a consequnce of them. On the other hand, in the absence of morphisms of the nth degree it can only constitute a category of a primitive order. For to link changes through rearrangements (commutability) by means of vicarious relationships which express the invariance of the results is merely to compose morphisms of the same order: such morphisms relate to connections "among" themselves without ever giving rise to new structures constructed "upon" themselves, as would be the case with an "integrated whole" determined by all of its component parts or with a group of permutations taking into account all possible substitutions. But the problem now inevitably arises of how we can characterize morphisms of the same order in the face of different forms such as commutabilities and vicarious relationship. As far as grouping operations are concerned, the answer is that these deal with concrete material objects and not with their forms (though they may have forms of their own). A combinatorial system, for its part, is designed to tackle all the forms capable of structuring a single content. Yet, there is still the question of the recursiveness peculiar to our formula, for it is inevitable, diachronically speaking, that a displaced part $A1$ or $A2$, etc., will undergo a formal change as a result of displacements, and that its subparts $\alpha1$ or $\alpha2$, etc. will themselves engender, with their own changes of location, commutabilities and vicarious relationships which may be expressed for $A1$, etc., as follows: (2) $(a \alpha 1 \text{ u } \alpha' = \text{w b } \alpha 1) + (a \alpha 2 \text{ u } \alpha' 2) = (a \alpha 2 \text{ u } \alpha' \alpha 2 = \alpha' 2 \text{ w ba } 2) = \text{etc.} \ldots = A1$.

Note that what has changed between formula (1) and (2) is the scale of the content (parts A, subparts $\alpha > $ sub-subpart, etc.), and not that of the form: whereas for the permutation of n elements we have neither more nor less than n possible seriations, we have no means of knowing how many equations (2) correspond to equations (1). This implies that equation (1) is not an operation upon an operation but simply an operation that may be repeated, in terms of content, at various levels. Thus we could immediately dispense with A, and thus with the equation (1), by dividing the whole (B) into parts of inferior order α (cf. equation (2)).

In conclusion, we may say that the "groupings" and conservations we have discussed here do not consist solely in operational systems (or transformations), but also in correspondences. Yet if these correspondences pave the way for such operational systems (comparisons arise before unions, etc.) it is also the case that they can be derived from them subsequently, by means of necessary deductions once the operations have been organized into structures of well-regulated compositions.

REFERENCES

1. PIAGET, J. 1949. Traité de Logique. Essai de Logistique opératoire. Librarie Armand Colin. Paris, France.
2. WERMUS, H. 1973. Une axiomatisation des groupements. Archives de Psychologie 1973. 42(163).
3. DIENDONNE, J. 1965. Fondements de l'analyse Moderne. Gauthier-Villars. Paris, France.
4. PIAGET, J. *et al.* 1975. Relation entre les conservation d'ensembles d'élements discrets et celles de quantités continues. Année Psychologique 75: 23-60.

BOOKS BY JEAN PIAGET IN THE PIAGET SOCIETY LIBRARY*

Piaget, Jean. Biologie et Connaissance, Essai sur les Relations Entre les Relations Entre les Régulations Organiques et les Processus Cognitifs. Paris: Gallimard, 1967. 433 p.

The Child and Reality: Problems of Genetic Psychology. Transl. by A. Rosin. N.Y.: Grossman Pubs., 1973. 182 p.

With Bärbel Inhelder and Alina Szeminska. The Child's Conception of Geometry. Transl. by E. A. Lunzer. London: Routledge and Kegan Paul, 1960. 411 p.

The Child's Conception of Movement and Speed. Transl. by G. Holloway and M. Mackenzie. N.Y.: Basic Books, 1970. 306 p.

The Child's Concept of Number. Transl. by C. Gattegno and F. M. Hodgson. London: Routledge, K.P., 1952, 248 p.

The Child's Conception of Physical Causality. Trans. by M. Gabain. London: Routledge K.P., 1930, 1970. 309 p.

With Bärbel Inhelder. The Child's Conception of Space. Transl. by F. J. Langdon and J. L. Lunzer. London: Routledge, K.P., 1956. 490 p.

The Child's Conception of Time. Transl. by A. J. Pomerans. N.Y.: Basic Books, 1970, c. 1969. 285 p.

The Child's Conception of the World. Transl. by J. and A. Tomlinson. London: Routledge, K.P., 1967. 397 p.

La Construction du Réel Chez l'Enfant, Neuchâtel: Delachaux et Niestlé, 1967, 342 p.

The Construction of Reality in the Child. Transl. by M. Cook. N.Y.: Basic Books, 1954. 386 p.

Avec le Concours de 4 Collabs. Le Dévelopement de la Notion de Temps Chez l'Enfant. 2° ed. Paris: Presses Univ. de France, 1946, 1973. 298 p.

Avec Bärbel Inhelder. Le Dévelopement des Quantites Physiques Chez l'Enfant: Conservation et Atomisme 3° ed. Neuchâtel D. et N., 1968. 344 p.

Avec Hermine Siaclair, Vinh Bang, et. al. Épistémologie et Psychologie de l'Identité. Paris: Presses Univ. de France, 1968, 211 p.

L'Epistémologie Génétique. Paris: Presses Univ. de France, 1970. 126 p.

Avec Jean-Blaise Grize, Alina Azeminska et Vinh Bang. Epistémologie et Psychologie de la Fonction. Paris: Press Univ. de Fr., 1968, 239 p.

Essai sur les Transformations des Operations Logiques; Les 256 Operations Ternaires de la Logique Bicalente des Propositions. (l éd) Paris: Pressed Univ. de Fr., 1952, 239 p.

Études Sociologiques. (2 ed.) Genève: Librarie Droz, 1967, 202 p.

Avec Bärbel Inhelder. Expériences sur la Construction Projective de la Ligne Droits chez les Enfants de Deux à Huit Ans. Neuchâtel: D. et N., 1947, 17 p.

Avec R. Garcia. Les Explications Causales. (1 éd.) Paris: Presses Univ. de Fr., 1971, 190 p.

La Formation du Symbole chez l'Enfant: Imitations, Jeu et Rêve, Image et Représentation. (4 éd.) Neuchatel: D et N, 1968, 310 p.

Avec. B. Inhelder. La Genèse de L'Idée de Hasard chez l'Enfant. (1 éd.) Paris: Presses Univ. de Fr., 1951, 265 p.

Avec Alina Szeminska, et. al. La Genèse du Nombre chez l'Enfant. (4 éd.) Neuchatel: D et N., 1967, 308 p.

Genetic Epistemology. Transl. by E. Duckworth. N.Y.: Columbia Univ. Press, 1970, 84 p. (Woodbridge Lectures—1968)

*Courtesy of the Jean Piaget Society, Paley Library, Temple University, Philadelphia, Pa. 19122.

Avec B. Inhelder et A. Szeminska. La Gémétrie Spontanée de l'Enfant. (1 éd.) Paris: Presses Univ. de Fr., 1948, 514 p.

Le Langage et la Pensée chez l'Enfant. (7 éd.) Neuchâtel: D. et N., 1968, 213 p.

The Language and Thought of the Child. Pref. by E. Claparede. (3 ed.) Transl. by M. Gabain. N.Y.: Humanities Press, 1959, 288 p.

Avec B. Inhelder, et. al. L'Image Mentale chez l'Enfant: Étude sur le Dévelopement des Représentation Imagées. Paris: Presses Univ. de Fr., 1966, 463 p.

Insights and Illusions of Philosophy. Transl. by W. Mays. (1 ed.) N.Y.: World Pub. Co., 1971, 232 p.

Introduction a l'Épistémologie Génétique. (1 éd.) Paris; Presses Univ. de Fr., 1950.

Judgment and Reasoning in the Child. N.Y.: Harcourt Brace and Co., 1928, 260 p. Transl. by M. Gabain.

Le Judgement et le Raisonnement chez l'Enfant. Neuchâtel: D. et N., 1967, 204 p.

Le Jugement Moral chex l'Enfant. (3 éd.) Paris: Presses Univ. de Fr., 1969, 334 p.

Logique et Connaissance Scientifiques. Volume publié sous la direction de J. Piaget. Paris: Gallimard, 1967, 1346 p.

Logic and Psychology. Transl. by W. Mays. and F. Whitehead. Introd. by W. Mays., Manchester, Eng.: Manchester Univ., 1965, 48 p.

Les Méchanismes Perceptifs: Modéles Probabilistes, Analyse Génétique, Relations avec l'Intelligence. (1 éd.) Paris: Presses Univ. de France, 1961, 457 p.

The Mechanisms of Perception. Transl. by G. N. Seagrim. N.Y.: Basic Books, 1969, 384 p.

Avec B. Inhelder et H. Sinclair-De Zwart. Mémoire et Intelligence. Paris: Presses Univ. de Fr., 1968, 488 p.

With B. Inhelder and H. Sinclair de Zwart. Memory and Intelligence. Transl. by A. J. Pomerans. N.Y.: Basic Books, 1973, 414 p.

The Moral Judgment of the Child. Transl. by M. Gabain. London: Routledge and K.P., 1932, 1968, 418 p.

La Naissance de l'Intelligence Chez l'Enfant. (6 éd.) Neuchâtel: D. et N., 1968, 370 p.

Les Notions de Mouvement et de Vitesse chez l'Enfant. Paris: Presses Univ. de Fr., 1946, 1972, 284 p.

On the Development of Memory and Identity. Transl. by E. Duckworth. Worcester, Mass.: Clark Univ. Press, 1968, 42 p. (Heinz Warner Lectures–1967)

The Origins of Intelligence in Children. Transl. by M. Cook. N.Y. : Internat'l Univs. Press, 1952, 419 p.

Piaget's Researches into Mathematical Concepts: A Collection of Articles from "Mathematics Teaching", now out of print. London: 1963, 24 p.

La Psychologie de l'Intelligence. Paris: A. Colin, 1967, 192 p.

Psychologie et Épistémologie. Paris: Éditions Gonthier, 1970, 187 p.

Psychology and Epistemology. Transl. by A. Rosin. N.Y. : Grossman Pubs, 1971, 166 p.

Psychologie et Pédagogie, Paris: Denoël, 1969, 264 p.

The Psychology of Intelligence. Transl. by M. Piercy and D. E. Berlyne, London: Routledge and K.P., 1950, 1971, 182 p.

With B. Inhelder. The Psychology of the Child. Transl. by H. Weaver. N.Y. : Basic Books, 1969, 173 p.

Sagesse et Illusions de la Philosophie (1 éd.) Paris; Presses Univ. de Fr., 1965, 288 p. (2 éd.) Augmentée d'une Postface, 1968, 309 p.

Science of Education and the Psychology of the Child. Transl. by D. Coltman. N.Y.: Orion Press, 1970, 186 p.

Six Études de Psychologie. Paris, Genève: Gonthier, 1964, 190 p.

Six Psychological Studies. With an Introd. by David Elkind. Transl. by A. Tenzer. N.Y.: Vintage Books, 1967, 1968, 169 p.

Le Structuralisme. (5 éd.) Paris: Presses Univ. de Fr., 1972, 125 p.

Structuralism. Trans. by C. Maschler. N.Y.: Basic Books, 1970, 153 p.

Avec Joan Bliss, et. al. La Transmission des Mouvements. (1 éd.) Paris: Presses Univ. de Fr., 1972, 241 p.

To Understand is to Invent: The Future of Education. Transl. by G. A. Roberts. N.Y.: Grossman Pubs., 1973, 148 p.

With R. Garcia. Understanding Causality. Transl. by D. and M. Miles. N.Y. :Norton, 1974, 192 p.

WORKS OF JEAN PIAGET*

I.   OEUVRES DE JEAN PIAGET

1. Collection livres (1)   1974

La genèse de l'idée de hasard chez l'enfant.

> Par Jean Piaget et Bärbel Inhelder.
> -Paris, Presses Universitaires de France, 2e éd. 1974,
> 229 p. (Bibliothèque de philosophie contemporaine.
> Psychologie et sociologie).

Recherches sur la contradiction. I. Les différentes formes de
la contradiction.

> Par Jean Piaget avec la collaboration de J. P. Bronckart
> A. Bullinger, A. Cattin, J. J. Ducret, A. Henriques, C. Kamii,
> A. Munari, I. Papandropoulou, S. Parrat-Dayan, M. Robert
> et T. Vergopoulo.
> -Paris, Presses Universitaires de France, 1974, 147 p.
> (Etudes d'Epistémologie Génétique, 31).

Recherches sur la contradiction. II. Les relations entre affirmations
et négations.

> Par Jean Piaget avec 'la collaboration de A. Blanchet,
> G. Cellerier, C. Dami, M. Gainotti-Amann, Ch. Gilliéron,
> A. Henriques, M. Labarthe, J. de Lannoy, R. Maier,
> D. Maurice, J. Montangero, O. Mosimann, C. Othenin-
> Girard, S. Uzan et T. Vergopoulo.
> -Paris, Presses Universitaires de France, 1974, 178 p.
> (Etudes d'Epistémologie Génétique, 32).

Réussir et comprendre.

> Par Jean Piaget avec la collaboration de M. Amann,
> C-L. Bonnet, M-F. Graven, A. Henriques, M. Labarthe,
> R. Maier, A. Moreau, C. Othenin-Girard, C. Stratz,
> S. Uzan et T. Vergopoulo.
> -Paris, Presses Universitaires de France, 1974, 255 p.
> (Psychologie d'aujourd'hui).

(1) classés par date de parution ou de réédition et par ordre
     alphabétique des titres.

*Reproduced by courtesy of the Foundation of the Archives of Jean Piaget, University of Geneva, Geneva, Switzerland, from the complete bibliography in Catalogue des Archives, published in 1975 by G. K. Hall, Boston, Mass. 02111.

1975

L'équilibration des structures cognitives. Problème central du développement.
    -Paris, Presses Universitaires de France, 1975, 188 p.
    (Etudes d'Epistémologie Génétique, 33).
Les mécanismes perceptifs. Modèles probabilistes, analyse génétique,
relations avec l'intelligence.
                -Paris, Presses Universitaires de France, 2e éd. 1975.
                (Psychologie d'aujourd'hui).

Motivation, émotion et personnalité.
                Par Joseph Nuttin, Paul Fraisse et Richard Meili.
                -Paris, Presses Universitaires de France,
                3e éd. 1975, 288 p.
                (Traité de Psychologie Expérimentale, 5).

La naissance de l'intelligence chez l'enfant.
                -Neuchâtel & Paris, Delachaux & Niestlé, 8e éd. 1975.
                (Actualités pédagogiques et psychologiques).

La perception.
                Par Jean Piaget, Paul Fraisse, Eliane Vurpillot
                et Robert Frances.
                -Paris, Presses Universitaires de France,
                3e éd. 1975, 255 p.
                (Traité de Psychologie Expérimentale, 6).

La psychologie de l'enfant.
                Par Jean Piaget et Bärbel Inhelder.
                -Paris, Presses Universitaires de France, 6e éd. 1975.
                (Que sais-je ? 369).

1976

Le langage et la pensée chez l'enfant.
                Par Jean Piaget et collaborateurs.
                Préf. : E. Claparède. -Neuchâtel & Paris, Delachaux &
                Niestlé, 9e éd. 1976.
                (Actualités pédagogiques et psychologiques).

La représentation du monde chez l'enfant.
                Par Jean Piaget et collaborateurs.
                -Paris, Presses Universitaires de France, 5e éd. 1976.
                (Bibliothèque de philosophie contemporaine).

2. Collection livres traduits   (1)   1972

Traité de psychologie expérimentale, en espagnol :
Tratado de psicologia experimental.

        Ed.: Paul Fraisse et Jean Piaget.
        -Buenos Aires, Paidos, 1972-1974. Vol. 1-9; chap. 1-34.

Oeuvres choisies, en italien :
Dal bambino all'adolescente. La costruzione del pensiero.

        Par Jean Piaget. Passi scelti a cura di O. Andreani
        Dentici e G. Gorla.
        -Firenze, La Nuova Italia, 2e éd. 1972.
        (Problemi di psicologia, 17).

Traité de psychologie expérimentale, en italien :
Trattato di psicologia sperimentale.

        Ed. : Paul Fraisse et Jean Piaget.
        Trad.: Carla Costantini.
        -Torino, Einaudi, 1972-1975. Vol. 1-9; chap. 1-34.

                1973

Psychologie et pédagogie, en danois :
Psykologi og paedagogik.

        Par Jean Piaget. Trad.: Knud Kielgast.
        -København, Hans Reitzel, 2e éd. 1973.

Psychologie et pédagogie, en espagnol :
Psicologia y pedagogia.

        Par Jean Piaget. Trad.: F. J. Fernandez Buey.
        -Barcelona, Ariel, 4e éd. 1973.

Sagesse et illusions de la philosophie, en italien :
Saggezza e illusioni della filosofia. Caratteri e limiti del conoscere filosofico.

        Par Jean Piaget. Trad.: Alberto Munari.
        -Torino, Einaudi, 3e éd. 1973.

Le développement des quantités physiques chez l'enfant, en japonais :
Ryo no hattatsu shinri gaku.

        Par Jean Piaget et Bärbel Inhelder.
        Trad.: Takehisa Takizawa et Hiroshi Ginbayashi.
        -Tokyo, Kokudosha, 5e réimpr. 1973.

(1) Classés par date de parution ou de réédition, par ordre alphabétique
     des langues et par ordre alphabétique des titres.

1973

La genèse du nombre chez l'enfant , en japonais :
Kazu no hattatsu shinri gaku.

> Par Jean Piaget et Alina Szeminska.
> Trad.: Kei Toyama, Hiroshi Ginbayashi et T. Takizawa.
> -Tokyo, Kokudosha, 10e réimpr. 1973.

La psychologie de l'enfant, en japonais :
Atarashii jido shinri gaku.

> Par Jean Piaget et Bärbel Inhelder.
> Trad.: Kanji Hatano, Tetsuo Suga et Hiroshi Sugo.
> -Tokyo, Hakusuisha, 6e réimpr. 1973.

La psychologie de l'intelligence, en norvégien :
Intelligensens psykologi.

> Par Jean Piaget.
> -Oslo, Cappelen, 1973, 182 p. (Cappelens almabøker).

L'épistémologie génétique, en portugais :
A epistemologia genética.

> Par Jean Piaget. Trad.: Nathanael C. Caixeiro.
> -Petropolis, Editora Vozes, 2e éd. 1973.

1974

Le jugement et le raisonnement chez l'enfant, en allemand :
Urteil und Denkprozess des Kindes.

> Par Jean Piaget. Préf.: Harm Paschen.
> Trad.: Herbert Christ. Réd.: Harm Paschen.
> -Düsseldorf, Pädagogischer Verlag Schwann, 2e éd. 1974.
> (Sprache und Lernen, 9).

Mémoire et intelligence, en allemand :
Gedächtnis und Intelligenz.

> Par Jean Piaget et Bärbel Inhelder. Trad.: Luc Bernard.
> -Olten & Freiburg i. Br., Walter-Verlag, 1974, 503 p.

Psychologie et pédagogie, en allemand :
Psychologie und Pädagogik. Dans : Theorien und Methoden der modernen
Erziehung.

> Par Jean Piaget. Trad.: Wolfgang Teuschl.
> -Frankfurt a. M., Fischer Taschenbuch Verlag, 1974, 278 p.
> p. 9-149; Bücher des Wissens, 6263.

1974

Six études de psychologie, en allemand:
Sechs psychologische Studien. Dans: Theorien und Methoden der modernen Erziehung.

> Par Jean Piaget. Trad.: Wolfgang Teuschl.
> -Frankfurt a.M., Fischer Taschenbuch Verlag, 1974, 278 p., p. 153-277; Bücher des Wissens, 6263.

Biologie et connaissance, en anglais:
Biology and knowledge. An essay on the relations between organic regulations and cognitive processes.

> Par Jean Piaget. Trad.: Beatrix Walsh.
> -Chicago, University of Chicago Press, 2e éd. 1974.

Le développement des quantités physiques chez l'enfant, en anglais:
The child's construction of quantities. Conservation and atomism.

> Par Jean Piaget et Bärbel Inhelder. Trad.: Arnold J. Pomerans.
> -London, Routledge & Kegan Paul, 1974, 285 p.
> -New York, Basic Books, 1974, 285 p.

Les explications causales, en anglais:
Understanding causality.

> Par Jean Piaget avec la collaboration de Rolando Garcia.
> Trad.: Donald et Marguerite Miles.
> -New York, Norton, 1974, 192 p.

La psychologie de l'enfant, en arabe :
La science psychologique de l'enfant.

> Par Jean Piaget.
> -Liban, Editions Arabes, 1974, 126 p. (Que sais-je?)

Le structuralisme, en castillant:
El estructuralismo.

> Par Jean Piaget. Trad.: J. Garcia-Bosch et Damia de Bas.
> -Barcelona, Oikos-Tau, 1974, 167 p. (Coleccion Mini-Tau, 12).

La formation du symbole chez l'enfant, en italien :
La formazione del simbolo nel bambino. Imitazione, gioco e sogno. Immagine e rappresentazione.

> Par Jean Piaget. Trad.: Elena Piazza.
> -Firenze, La Nuova Italia, 2e éd. 1974 (Problemi di psicologia, 33).

L'image mentale chez l'enfant, en italien:
L'immagine mentale nel bambino.

> Par Jean Piaget et Bärbel Inhelder. Trad.: Itala Brusa.
> -Firenze, La Nuova Italia, 1974, 560 p.

1974

Oeuvres choisies, en italien :
Lo sviluppo e l'educazione dell'intelligenza.

> Par Jean Piaget. Antologia di scritti a cura di Roberto
> Maragliano.
> -Torino, Loescher, 1974, 219 p. (Scienze dell'educazione 1).

Psychologie et épistémologie, en italien:
Psicologia ed epistemologia.

> Par Jean Piaget. Introd. (p. VII-XII), notes et trad. :
> Piero Simondo.
> -Torino, Loescher, 2e éd. 1974, 170 p. (Testi di
> filosofia, pedagogia e didattica. Nuova serie: Attualità
> pedagogiche).

Le structuralisme, en italien:
Lo strutturalismo.

> Par Jean Piaget. Introd. (p. 7-34) et trad. : Andrea
> Bonomi.
> -Milano, Il Saggiatore di Alberto Mondadori, 5e éd. 1974,
> (I gabbiani, nuova serie 76).

Apprentissage et connaissance, en portugais :
Aprendizagem e conhecimento.

> Par Jean Piaget et Pierre Greco. Trad. : Equipe da
> Livraria Freitas Bastos.
> -Rio de Janeiro, Freitas Bastos, 1974, 238 p.
> (Biblioteca Pedagogica).

Epistémologie génétique et recherche psychologique, en portugais:
Epistemologia genetica e pesquisa psicologica.

> Par Jean Piaget, Evert W. Beth et Wolfe Mays.
> Trad. : Equipe da Livraria Freitas Bastos.
> -Rio de Janeiro, Freitas Bastos, 1974, 153 p.

Où va l'éducation ?, en portugais:
Para onde vai e educaçao?

> Par Jean Piaget. Trad. : Ivette Braga.
> -Rio de Janeiro, José Olympio, 2e éd. 1974, 89 p.

La psychologie de l'enfant, en portugais:
A psicologia da criança.

> Par Jean Piaget et Bärbel Inhelder. Trad. : Octavio
> Mendes Cajado.
> -Sao Paulo, Difusao Europeia do Livro, 3e éd. 1974,
> 137 p. (Saber Actual, 16).

Etudes sociologiques, l'article: "L'explication en sociologie", en suédois :
Sociologiska förklaringar. Den sociologiska förklaringen.

> Par Jean Piaget. Introd. et trad. : Joachim Israel.
> -Lund, Studenten Litteratur, 1974, 91 p.

1975

Adaptation vitale et psychologie de l'intelligence. Sélection organique et phénocopie, en allemand :
Biologische Anpassung und Psychologie der Intelligenz.

> Par Jean Piaget. Trad.: Luc Bernard.
> -Stuttgart, Ernst Klett Verlag, 1975, 118 p.
> (Konzepte der Humanwissenschaften).

La construction du réel chez l'enfant , en allemand:
Der Aufbau der Wirklichkeit beim Kinde.

> Par Jean Piaget. Trad.: Johann-Ulrich Sandberger et
> Christiane Thirion. Introd.: Hans Aebli.
> -Stuttgart, Klett, 2e éd. 1975 (Gesammelte Werke 2 -
> Studienausgabe).

Le développement des quantités physiques chez l'enfant, en allemand:
Die Entwicklung der physikalischen Mengenbegriffe beim Kinde.
Erhaltung und Atomismus.

> Par Jean Piaget et Bärbel Inhelder. Introd.: Hans Aebli.
> Trad.: Hermann Karl Weinert et Jörg Uwe Sandberger.
> -Stuttgart, Klett, 2e éd. 1975 (Gesammelte Werke 4-
> Studienausgabe).

La formation du symbole chez l'enfant, en allemand:
Nachahmung, Spiel und Traum. Die Entwicklung der Symbolfunktion beim Kinde.

> Par Jean Piaget. Introd.: Hans Aebli; trad.: Leo
> Montada.
> -Stuttgart, Klett, 2e éd. 1975 (Gesammelte Werke 5-
> Studienausgabe)

La genèse du nombre chez l'enfant, en allemand:
Die Entwicklung des Zahlbegriffs beim Kinde.

> Par Jean Piaget et Alina Szeminska. Introd.: Hans
> Aebli; trad.: Hermann Karl Weinert.
> -Stuttgart, Klett, 4e éd. 1975 (Gesammelte Werke 3-
> Studienausgabe).

La géométrie spontanée de l'enfant, en allemand:
Die natürliche Geometrie des Kindes.

> Par Jean Piaget, Bärbel Inhelder et Alina Szeminska.
> Introd.: Hans Aebli; trad.: Rosemarie Heipcke.
> -Stuttgart, Klett, 2e éd. 1975 (Gesammelte Werke 7-
> Studienausgabe).

Introduction à l'épistémologie génétique. Tome 1: La pensée mathématique, en allemand:
Die Entwicklung des Erkennens. 1. Das mathematische Denken.

> Par Jean Piaget. Avec préface de l'auteur à l'édition
> allemande. Introd.: Hans Aebli; trad.: Fritz Kubli.
> -Stuttgart, Klett, 2e éd. 1975 (Gesammelte Werke 8-
> Studienausgabe).

1975

Introduction à l'épistémologie génétique. Tome 2: La pensée physique,
en <u>allemand:</u>
Die Entwicklung des Erkennens. 2. Das physikalische Denken.

> Par Jean Piaget. Trad.: Fritz Kubli.
> -Stuttgart, Klett, 2e éd. 1975 (Gesammelte Werke 9-
> Studienausgabe).

Introduction à l'épistémologie génétique. Tome 3: La pensée biologique,
la pensée psychologique et la pensée sociologique, en allemand:
Die Entwicklung des Erkennens. 3. Das biologische Denken; das psychologische Denken; das soziologische Denken

> Par Jean Piaget. Préf. et trad.: Fritz Kubli.
> -Stuttgart, Klett, 2e éd. 1975 (Gesammelte Werke 10-
> Studienausgabe).

La naissance de l'intelligence chez l'enfant, en allemand:
Das Erwachen der Intelligenz beim Kinde.

> Par Jean Piaget. Introd.: Hans Aebli; trad.: Bernhard
> Seiler.
> -Stuttgart, Klett, 2e éd. 1975 (Gesammelte Werke 1.-
> Studienausgabe).

La représentation de l'espace chez l'enfant, en allemand:
Die Entwicklung des räumlichen Denkens beim Kinde.

> Par Jean Piaget et Bärbel Inhelder. Introd.: Hans Aebli;
> trad.: Rosemarie Heipcke.
> -Stuttgart, Klett, 2e éd. 1975 (Gesammelte Werke 6-
> Studienausgabe).

Jean Piaget dans Main trends of research in the social and human sciences,
part I, introduction: the place of the sciences of man in the system of
sciences, en <u>danois:</u>
De humanistiske videnskaber. Problematik og placering.

> Par Jean Piaget. Trad.: Nina Lautrup-Larsen.
> -København, Hans Reitzel, 1975, 122 p.

La composition des forces et le problème des vecteurs, en <u>espagnol</u> :
La composicion de las fuerzas y el problema de los vectores.

> Par Jean Piaget con la colaboracion de Joan Bliss,
> Monique Chollet-Levret, Catherine Dami, Pierre
> Mounoud, Madelon Robert, Colette Rossel-Simonet,
> Vinh-Bang. Trad.: A. Corazon.
> -Madrid, Morata, 1975, 191 p.

La formation du symbole chez l'enfant, en espagnol:
La formacion del simbolo en el nino. Imitacion, jugeo y sueno; imagen
y representacion.

> Par Jean Piaget. Trad.: José Gutiérrez.
> -Mexico & Buenos Aires, Fondo de Cultura economica,
> 3e réimpr. 1975 (Biblioteca de psicologia y psicõanalisis).

1975

La construction du réel chez l'enfant, en italien:
La costruzione del reale nel bambino.

> Par Jean Piaget. Introd. et trad.: Gioia Gorla.
> -Firenze, La Nuova Italia, 2e éd. 1975 (Problemi di
> psicologia , 34).

Le développement des quantités physiques chez l'enfant, en italien:
Lo sviluppo delle quantità fisiche nel bambino. Conservazione e atomismo.

> Par Jean Piaget et Bärbel Inhelder. Trad.: Itala Brusa.
> -Firenze, La Nuova Italia, 2e éd. 1975 (Problemi di
> psicologia, 29).

Les mécanismes perceptifs, en italien:
I mecanismi percettivi.

> Par Jean Piaget. Trad.: Lucia Zanuttini.
> -Firenze, Giunti-Barbera, 1975, 445 p.

La prise de conscience , en italien:
La presa di coscienza.

> Par Jean Piaget avec la collaboration de A. Blanchet,
> J.-P. Bronckart, N. Burdet, A. Cattin, C. Dami,
> I. et M. Fluckiger , C. Gillièron, A. Henriques,
> D. Liambey, O. de Marcellus, A. Munari, M. Robert,
> A.-M. Zutter. Trad.: Silvia Stefani.
> -Milano, Etas Libri, 1975, 201 p . (Uomo e Società).

Introduction à l'épistémologie génétique, I. La pensée mathématique,
en japonais:
Hasseiteki Ninshikiron Josetsu. Tome I. Sugakushiso.

> Pa Jean Piaget. Trad.: Shintaro Tanabe.
> -Tokyo, Sanseido, 1975, 466 p.

Problèmes de psychologie génétique, en portugais:
Problemas de psicologia genetica.

> Par Jean Piaget. Trad.: Fernanda Flores.
> -Lisboa, Publicaçoes Dom Quixote, 2e éd. 1975
> (Universidade moderna, 34).

Six études de psychologie en portugais: (2e traduction)
Seis estudos de psicologia.

> Par Jean Piaget. Trad.: Nina Constante Pereira.
> -Lisboa, Publicaçoes Dom Quixotte, 3e éd. 1975
> (Colecçao universidade moderna, 39).

1976

Oeuvres choisies , en espagnol:
El mecanismo del desarrollo mental.

> Par Jean Piaget. Edicion preparada por Juan A. Delval.
> -Madrid, Editora Nacional, 1976, 177 p.

La naissance de l'intelligence chez l'enfant, en portugais:
O nascimento da inteligencia na criança.

> Par Jean Piaget. Trad.: Alvaro Cabral.
> -Rio de Janeiro, Zahar, 2e éd. 1976 (Biblioteca de ciencias
> da educaçao).

3. Collection articles   (1)   1936

La genèse des principes de conservation dans la physique de l'enfant.

> Annuaire de l'instruction publique en Suisse ,
> Lausanne (etc.), Librairie Payot, 1936, 27, p. 31-44.

1954

L'éducation artistique et la psychologie de l'enfant.

> Dans: Art et éducation, Recueil d'essais.
> Ed.: Edwin Ziegfeld (Paris, Unesco, 1954), p. 22-23.

1973

Jean Piaget. L'Express va plus loin avec Jean Piaget.

> L'Express va plus loin avec ces theoriciens, Paris,
> Laffont, 1973, p. 97-126.

Fondements scientifiques pour l'éducation de demain.

> Nouvelle publication dans: Education et développement,
> Paris, 82, 1973, p. 6-22;
>
> et dans: Schweizer Erziehungs-Rundschau , St-Gallen,
> 45, 1972, p. 273-276 et 46, 1973, p. 33-36.

Die Entwicklung des Zahlbegriffs beim Kind.

> Dans: Psychologie der Zahl. Ed.: Anita Riess
> (München, Kindler Taschenbücher, 1973), p. 146-154.
> Repris de Jean Piaget et Alina Szeminska, Die
> Entwicklung des Zahlbegriffs beim Kind. -Stuttgart,
> Klett, 1965, p. 15-20.

(1) classés par date de parution et suivant l'ordre de réception aux Archives.

1973

Jean Piaget: Piaget sau destinele psihologiei. Interviuri.

Dans: Mircea Herivan. Meridiane pedagogice. Interviuri cu personalitati ale invatamintului, (Bucuresti, Editura Didactica si Pedagogica, 1973, 347 p.), p. 154-166.

Bref témoignage. Hommage à Lucien Goldmann.

Revue de l'Institut de Sociologie, Bruxelles (1973), 3-4, p. 545-547.
Ce texte a été repris dans: Lucien Goldmann et la sociologie de la littérature. Hommage à Lucien Goldmann (Bruxelles, Editions de l'Université de Bruxelles, 1975), p. 53-55.

Piaget takes a teacher's look. A dialogue between Jean Piaget and Eleonor Duckworth.

Learning, the magazine for creative teaching, october 1973, p. 22-27.

How children form mathematical concepts, en allemand:
Wie Kinder mathematische Begriffe bilden.

Trad.: Hellgard Rauh. Dans: Pädagogische Psychologie, Bd. 1: Entwicklung und Sozialisation. Funk-Kolleg Grundlagentexte. Ed.: C. F. Graumann et H. Heckhausen (Frankfurt a. M., Fischer, 1973; Fischer Taschenbuch, 6113), p. 53-62.

Genetic epistemology.

Nouvelle publication dans: Readings in human development 1973-1974 (Guilford, Dushkin Publishing Group, 1973), p. 41-48.

1974

Foreword.

In: Learning and the development of cognition. Par Bärbel Inhelder, Hermine Sinclair et Magali Bovet. Trad.: Susan Wedgwood. (Cambridge, Harvard University Press, 1974), p. IX-XIV.

A propos de la généralisation.

Dans: Gymnase cantonal de Neuchâtel. 1873-1973. Edité par le Gymnase de Neuchâtel (Neuchâtel, Attinger, 1974), p. 211-222.

1974

Les idées de Claparède sur l'intelligence.

> R. suisse Psychol. pure appl., Berne, 33, (1974) p. 274-278.
> Participation à la table ronde de psychologie, le 16
> novembre 1973 à Genève, pour la célébration du centenaire
> de la naissance d'Edouard Claparède à l'Ecole de
> Psychologie et des Sciences de l'Education.

The future of developmental child psychology.

> Journal of Youth and Adolescence, New York, 3 (1974)
> 2, p. 87-93.
> Lecture delivered at First International Kittay Award,
> on June 1st, 1973, in New York City.

Autobiographie, en espagnol·
Autobiografia.

> Dans: Jean Piaget y las ciencas sociales. Par G. Busino,
> L. Goldmann, G. Cellerier, J.B. Grize, H. Sinclair,
> R. Girod, R. Holmes, J. Piaget et B. Inhelder.
> Introd. (p. 9-20)· Miguel A. Quintanilla sur: Las ideas
> sociologicas de Jean Piaget; trad.: Miguel A. Quintanilla
> (Salamanca, Ediciones Sigueme, 1974), p. 147-181.

Piaget, Jean, en italien:
Piaget, Jean.

> In: Scienzati e technologi contemporanei. Vol. 2. Da
> Samuel K. Hoffman & Wendell M. Stanley. (Milano,
> Arnoldo Mondadori Editore, 1974), p. 352-354.

A conversation with Jean Piaget and Bärbel Inhelder by Elisabeth Hall,
en allemand:
Gespräch mit Jean Piaget und Bärbel Inhelder. Warum Kinder lernen.

> Psychologie heute, Weinheim und Basel, 1 (1974) Heft 1,
> September, p. 13-17, 72-74 (Piaget), p. 74-77 (Inhelder).

1975

L'intelligence selon Alfred Binet.

> Bulletin de la Société Alfred Binet et Théodore Simon,
> Psychologie de l'enfant et pédagogie expérimentale, 75
> (1975) 544, p. 106-119.
> Texte de la conférence prononcée le 13 novembre 1974
> à Lyon à l'occasion du 75e anniversaire de la Société.

Solubilité, miscibilité et flottaison.

> Par Jean Piaget et J. F. Chatillon. Archives de psychologie,
> 43 (1975) 169, p. 27-46.

1975

L'appareil de Rosenfeld et Hein pour l'étude des effets indépendants d'un même processus causal.

> Par Jean Piaget et Catherine Dami. Archives de psychologie 43 (1975) 169 ,p. 105-114.

Relations entre les conservations d'ensembles d'éléments discrets et celles de quantités continues.

> Par Bärbel Inhelder, Alex Blanchet, Anne Sinclair et Jean Piaget. Année Psychologique , 75 (1975) p. 23-60.

Foreword.

> In: William Douglas Wall. Constructive education for children . (London/ Paris, Harrap /The Unesco Press, 1975) p. XI-XII.

Introduction générale au dialogue connaissance scientifique et philosophie.

> Dans: Connaissance scientifique et philosophie. Colloque organisé les 16 et 17 mai 1973 par l'Académie Royale des Sciences, des Lettres et des Beaux-Arts de Belgique. (Gembloux, Belgique, Duculot, 1975), p. 13-38.

Préface.

> Dans: Monique Pinol-Douriez. La construction de l'espace (Neuchâtel/ Paris, Delachaux et Niestlé, 1975), p. 5-7.

From noise to order: the psychological development of knowledge and phenocopy in biology.

> The urban review . Issues and ideas in public education, New York, 8 (1975) 3, p. 209-218.
> Excerpt from The essential Piaget, edited by Howard E. Gruber and Jacques Vonèche (Basic Books, in press).

L'éducation artistique et la psychologie de l'enfant, en anglais:
Art education and child psychology.

> Art and the integrated day, New York, 1 (1975) 1.

Le structuralisme, en anglais:
Structuralism.

> Humanitas . Journal of the institute of man, Pittsburgh, 11 (1975), p. 313-327.

1976

Le mécanisme du développement mental, en espagnol:
El mecanismo del desarrolo mental.

> Dans: Jean Piaget. El mecanismo del desarrollo mental. Editado y traducido por Juan A. Delval. (Madrid, Editora Nacional, 1976), p. 17-133.

B.F. SKINNER

Kurt Salzinger

Biometrics Research Unit
New York State Psychiatric Institute
New York, New York 10032

Polytechnic Institute of New York
Brooklyn, New York 11201

The idea of introducing a man of B.F. Skinner's caliber and fame is simultaneously presumptuous, difficult, and terrifying. It is presumptuous because there is so little one can say about a man of fame that the audience might not already know better than the introducer, and which that man as speaker will not make so much more obvious by speaking himself. It is difficult because reviewing such a man's life well requires too long a time and then still courts danger in failing to emphasize those things which are most significant. It is terrifying to introduce such a man because it is both presumptuous and difficult, as I have already said, and because it is added to the usual terror any introducer feels because he/she knows that the speaker will, after all, have the last word.

Now these are the difficulties that I share with my fellow introducers today. The special problem with the introduction of B.F. Skinner stems from his unusual view of the business of taking credit for one's accomplishments. At the end of his delightful lecture on "having" a poem, he points out "has had" his lecture, much in the way of a hen having had her egg. He says, "If I deserve any credit at all, it is simply for having served as a place in which certain processes could take place."* A little earlier in the same lecture, he says: "Only a person who truly initiates his behavior can claim that he is free to do so and that he deserves credit for any achievement. If the environment is the initiating force, he is not free, and the environment must get the credit."† It is, therefore, quite clear that the one thing I may not do in this introduction is exactly the one thing that is expected in an introduction in this society. I thought about this problem for a while and finally came up with the following solution. I decided that I would praise Skinner's environment and genes. Thus, although I have not had the opportunity to read his autobiography, I am quite convinced of the wisdom of his parents who raised him, and of the excellence of the genetic stock that they passed down to him. I am impressed by the schools that taught him and by the country that allowed him to flourish (I thought I would throw that in, since this is a bicentennial conference), by the erudition of the books that were made available to him for perusal and the experimental apparatus and the conditions that called forth their construction, incidentally, by him, by the people who have supported his work, and by those who have argued vehemently against him and his work, and by the publishers who have seen fit to allow his books and papers to see the light of day. Thus the conditions were just right, so that those of us who have been influenced by the products of his interaction with the environment could be the locus of those derivative experiments and findings that carry on the behavior theory tradition that his environment began.

*Skinner, B.F. 1972 Cumulative Record. Third edit.: 355.
†p. 352.

As to the business of whether those of us who convinced Dr. Skinner to appear before you today ought to get credit for doing so, you have to search our own environment first, and that at last brings us back to B.F. Skinner, since, were it not for that environment with which B.F. Skinner provided us, we would not have thought of inviting him and he would not be here. Thus, although I cannot praise him for his achievements, I can do so for providing us with the requisite environment for asking him to appear here before you.

Finally, as to what we mean to achieve by having B.F. Skinner before us here today: It is to engender new behavior in you, the audience, through reexamination of the past of one man who has contributed so much (it's hard to avoid doing this) to our present. In that same lecture from which I have been quoting, Dr. Skinner says: "The task is not to think of new forms of behavior but to create an environment in which they are likely to occur."‡ Ladies and gentlemen, I present you such an environment, Dr. B.F. Skinner.

‡p. 355.

THE EXPERIMENTAL ANALYSIS OF OPERANT BEHAVIOR

B. F. Skinner

Department of Psychology and Social Relations
Harvard University
Cambridge, Massachusetts 02138

I was drawn to psychology and particularly to behaviorism by some papers which Bertrand Russell published in the *Dial* in the 1920s and which led me to his book *Philosophy*[1] (called in England *An Outline of Philosophy*), the first section of which contains a much more sophisticated discussion of several epistemological issues raised by behaviorism than anything of John B. Watson's. Naturally, I turned to Watson himself, but at the time only to his popular *Behaviorism*.[2] I bought Pavlov's *Conditioned Relfexes*[3] shortly after it appeared, and when I came to Harvard for graduate study in psychology, I took a course that covered not only conditioned reflexes but the postural and locomotor reflexes of Magnus and the spinal reflexes reported in Sherrington's *Integrative Action of the Nervous System*.[4] The course was taught by Hudson Hoagland in the Department of General Physiology, the head of which, W. J. Crozier, had worked with Jacques Loeb and was studying tropisms. I continued to prefer the reflex to the tropism, but I accepted Loeb's and Crozier's dedication to the organism as a whole and the latter's contempt for medical school "organ physiology." Nevertheless, in the Department of Physiology at the Medical School I later worked with Hallowell Davis and with Alexander Forbes, who had been in England with Adrian and was using Sherrington's torsion-wire myograph to study the reflex control of movement.

By the end of my first year at Harvard I was analyzing the behavior of an "organism as a whole" under soundproofed conditions like those described by Pavlov. In one experiment I quietly released a rat into a small dark tunnel from which it could emerge into a well-lighted space, and with moving pen on a moving strip of paper I recorded its exploratory progress as well as its retreat into the tunnel when I made a slight noise. Some of my rats had babies, and in their early squirmings I thought I saw some of the postural reflexes stereoscopically illustrated in Magnus' *Körperstellung*,[5] and I began to study them. I mounted a light platform on tight wires and amplified its forward-and-backward movement with an arm writing on a smoked drum. I could put a small rat on the platform and record the tremor of its leg muscles or the sudden forward leap when I pulled it gently by the tail.

I decided to do something of the sort with an adult rat. I built a very light runway about eight feet long, the lengthwise vibration of which I could also amplify and record on a smoked drum, and I induced a rat to run along it by giving it food at the end. When it was halfway along, I would make a slight noise and record the way in which it came to a sudden stop by the effect on the runway. I planned to watch changes as the rat adapted to the noise; possibly I could condition another stimulus to elicit the same response. My records looked a little like those made by a torsion-wire myograph, but they reported the behavior of the organism as a whole.

This was all pretty much in the tradition of reflex physiology, but quite by accident something happened that dramatically changed the direction of my research. In my apparatus the rat went down a back alley to the other end of the apparatus before making its recorded run, and I noticed that it did not immediately start to do so after being fed. I began to time the delays and found that they changed in an orderly way. Here was a *process*, something like the processes of conditioning and extinction in Pavlov's work, where the details of the act of running, like those of salivation, were not the most important thing.

I have described elsewhere[6] the series of steps through which I simplified my apparatus until the rat simply pushed open the door of a small bin to get a piece of food. Under controlled conditions and with pellets of food that took some time to chew, I found that the rate of eating was a function of the quantity of food already eaten. The title of my first experimental paper, "On the Conditions of Elicitation of Certain Eating Reflexes," shows that I was still applying the concept of the reflex to the behavior of the organism as a whole.

Pushing open a door was conditioned behavior, but in order to study the process of conditioning, I needed a more clearly defined act. I chose pushing down a horizontal bar mounted as a lever. When the rat pressed the lever, a pellet of food was released into a tray. The arrangement was, of course, close to that with which Thorndike had demonstrated his Law of Effect, and in my first paper I called my apparatus a "problem box," but the results were quite different. Thorndike's cat learned by dropping out unsuccessful bits of behavior until little or nothing remained but the successful response. Nothing of the sort happened in my experiment. Pavlov's emphasis on the control of conditions led me to take certain steps to avoid disturbing my rat. I gave it plenty of time to recover from being put into the apparatus by enclosing it first in a special compartment from which I later quietly released it. I left it in the apparatus a long time so that it could become thoroughly accustomed to being there, and I repeatedly operated the food dispenser until the rat was no longer disturbed by the noise and ate as soon as food appeared. All this was done when the lever was resting in its lowest position and hence before pressing it could be conditioned. The effect was to remove all the unsuccessful behavior which had composed the learning process in Thorndike's experiment. Many of my rats began to respond at a high rate as soon as they had depressed the lever and obtained only one piece of food.

Conditioning was certainly not the mere survival of a successful response; it was an increase in the rate of responding, or in what I called reflex strength. Thorndike had said that the cat's successful behavior was "stamped in," but his evidence was an increasing priority over other behavior that was being "stamped out." The difference in interpretation became clearer when I disconnected the food dispenser and found that the behavior underwent extinction. As R. L. Woodworth[8] later pointed out, Thorndike never investigated the extinction of problem-box behavior.

Though rate of responding was not one of Sherrington's measures of reflex strength, it emerged as the most important one in my experiment. Its significance was clarified by the fact that I recorded the rat's behavior in a cumulative curve; one could read the rate directly at the slope of the curve and see at a glance how it changed over a considerable period of time. Rate proved to be a particularly useful measure when I turned from the acquisition of behavior to its maintenance, in the study of schedules of intermittent reinforcement. Theoretically, it was important because it was relevant to the central question: what is the probability that an organism will engage in a particular form of behavior at a particular time?

I was nevertheless slow in appreciating the importance of the concept of strength of response. For example, I did not immediately shift from "condition" to "reinforce," although the latter term emphasizes the strengthening of behavior.

I did not use "reinforce" at all in my first report of the arrangement of lever and food dispenser, and my first designation for intermittent reinforcement was "periodic reconditioning."

Strength or probability of response fitted comfortably into the formulation of a science of behavior proposed in my thesis. Russell was again responsible for a central point. Somewhere he had said that "reflex" in psychology had the same status as "force" in physics. I knew what that meant because I had read Ernst Mach's *Science of Mechanics*,[9] the works of Henri Poincaré on scientific method, and Bridgman's *Logic of Modern Physics*.[10] My thesis was an operational analysis of the reflex. I insisted that the word should be defined simply as an observed correlation of stimulus and response. Sherrington's synapse was a mere inference that could not be used to explain the facts from which it was inferred. Thus, a stimulus might grow less and less effective as a response was repeatedly elicited, but it did not explain anything to attribute this to "reflex fatigue." Eventually the physiologist would discover a change in the nervous system, but so far as the behavioral facts were concerned, the only identifiable explanation was the repeated elicitation. In my thesis[11] I asserted that in the intact organism "conditioning, 'emotion,' and 'drive' so far as they concern behavior were essentially to be regarded as changes in reflex strength," and I offered my experiments on "drive" and conditioning as examples.

One needed to refer not only to a stimulus and a response but to conditions that changed the relation between them. I called these conditions "third variables," and represented matters with a simple equation:

$$R = f(S, A)$$

where A represented any condition affecting reflex strength, such as the deprivation with which I identified "drive" in the experimental part of my thesis.

The summer after I got my degree, Edward C. Tolman was teaching at Harvard, and I saw a great deal of him. I expounded my operational position at length and the relevance of third variables in determining reflex strength. Tolman's book *Purposive Behavior in Animals and Men*[12] was then in press, and in it he speaks of "independent variables" but only as such things as genetic endowment or an initiating physiological state. Three years later he published a paper[13] containing the equation

$$B = f(S, H, T, P)$$

in which B stood for behavior, as my R stood for response, S for "the environmental stimulus set up" (my S), H for heredity, T for "specific past training" (my "conditioning"), and P for "a releasing internal condition of appetite or aversion" (my "drive"). Woodworth later pointed out that these equations were similar. There was, however, an important difference: what I had called a "third variable" Tolman called "intervening." For me the observable operations in conditioning, drive, and emotion lay *outside* the organism, but Tolman put them inside, as replacements for, if not simply redefinitions of, mental processes, and that is where they still are in cognitive psychology today. Ironically, the arrangement is much closer than mine to the traditional reflex arc.

Although rate of responding, in the absence of identifiable stimulation, had no parallel in Sherrington or Pavlov, I continued to talk about reflexes. I assumed that some features of the lever were functioning as stimuli that elicited the response of pressing the lever. But I was unhappy about this, and I began to look more closely at the role of the stimulus. I reinforced pressing the lever when a light was on but not when it was off, and found that in the dark the behavior underwent extinction. Turning on the light then appeared to elicit the response, but the history behind that effect could not be ignored. The light was not *eliciting* the behavior; it was functioning as a variable affecting its rate, and it derived its power to do so from the differential reinforcement with which it had been correlated.

In the summer of 1934 I submitted two papers for publication in separate efforts to revise the concept of the reflex. In "The Generic Nature of Stimulus and Response"[14] I argued that neither a stimulus nor a response could be isolated by surgical or other means and that the best clue to a useful unit was the orderliness of the changes in its strength as a function of "third variables." In "Two Types of Conditioned Reflex and a Pseudo-type"[15] I distinguished between Pavlovian and what I would later call operant conditioning. Quite apart from any internal process, a clear difference could be pointed out in the contingent relations among stimuli, responses, and reinforcement.

I was forced to look more closely at the role of the stimulus when Konorski and Miller[16] replied to the latter paper by describing an experiment they had performed in the late twenties which they felt anticipated my own. They had shocked the paw of a dog and given it food when it flexed its leg. Eventually the leg flexed even though the paw was not shocked. I replied that true reflexes seldom have the kinds of consequences that lead to operant conditioning. Shock may be one way of inducing a hungry dog to flex its leg so that the response can be reinforced with food, but it is an unusual one, and an eliciting stimulus can in fact seldom be identified. (As to priority, Thorndike was, of course, ahead of us all by more than a quarter of a century.)

In my reply[17] I used the term "operant" for the first time and applied "respondent" to the Pavlovian case. It would have been the right time to abandon "reflex," but I was still strongly under the control of Sherrington, Magnus, and Pavlov, and I continued to hold to the term doggedly when I wrote *The Behavior of Organisms* (1938).[18] It took me several years to break free of my own stimulus control in the field of operant behavior. From this point on, however, I was clearly no longer a stimulus-response psychologist.

The lack of an identifiable eliciting stimulus in operant behavior raises a practical problem: we must wait for behavior to appear before we can reinforce it. We thus start with much less control than in respondent conditioning. Moreover, there is a great deal of complex behavior for which we shall certainly wait in vain, since it will never occur spontaneously. In human behavior there are many ways of "priming" an operant response (that is, evoking it for the first time in order to reinforce it), and one of them is also available in lower organisms: complex behavior can be "shaped" through a series of successive approximations. To reinforce pressing a lever with great force, for example, we cannot simply wait for a very forceful response, but we can differentially reinforce the more forceful of the responses that do occur, with the result that the mean force increases.

I used a similar programming of contingencies of reinforcement to shape complex topography in a demonstration (reported in *The Behavior of Organisms*) in which a rat pulled a chain to release a marble, picked up the marble, carried it across the cage, and dropped it into a tube. The terminal behavior was shaped by a succession of slight changes in the apparatus. Later my colleagues and I discovered that we could avoid the time-consuming process of altering the apparatus by constructing programmed contingencies while reinforcing directly by hand.

I soon tried the procedure on a human subject—our nine-month old daughter. I was holding her on my lap one evening when I turned on a table lamp beside the chair. She looked up and smiled, and I decided to see whether I could use the light as a reinforcer. I waited for a slight movement of her left hand and turned on the light for a moment. Almost immediately she moved her hand again, and again I reinforced. I began to wait for bigger movements, and within a short time she was lifting her arm in a wide arc—"to turn on the light."

I was writing *Walden Two*[19] at the time, and the book is often cited as an essay in behavioral engineering, but I believe it contains no example of the explicit use of a contrived reinforcer. The community functions through positive reinforcement, but the contingencies are in the natural and social environments. They have been carefully designed, but there is no continuing intervention by a reinforcing agent. The only contrived contingencies are Pavlovian: children are "desensitized" to frustration and other destructive emotions by being exposed to situations of carefully graded intensity.

I began to analyze the contingencies of reinforcement to be found in existing cultures in an undergraduate course at Harvard in the spring of 1949. *Science and Human Behavior* (1953)[20] was written as a text for that course, and in it I considered practices in such fields as government, religion, economics, education, psychotherapy, self-control, and social behavior—and all from an operant point of view.

Practical demonstrations soon followed. A graduate student at Indiana, Paul Fuller, had reinforced arm-raising in a twenty-year old human organism that had never before "shown any sign of intelligence," and in 1953 I set up a small laboratory to study operant behavior in a few backward patients in a mental hospital. Ogden R. Lindsley took over that project and found that psychotics could be brought under the control of contingencies of reinforcement if the contingencies were clear-cut and carefully programmed. Ayllon, Azrin, and many others subsequently used operant conditioning in both management and therapy to improve the lives of psychotic and retarded people.

At the University of Pittsburgh in the spring of 1954 I gave a paper called "The Science of Learning and the Art of Teaching"[21] and demonstrated a machine designed to teach arithmetic, using an instructional program. A year or two later I designed the teaching machines that were used in my undergraduate course at Harvard, and my colleague, James G. Holland, and I wrote the programmed materials eventually published as *The Analysis of Behavior* (1961).[22] The subsequent history of programmed instruction and, on a broader scale, of what has come to be called applied behavior analysis or behavior modification is too well known to need further review here.

Meanwhile, the experimental analysis of operant behavior was expanding rapidly as many new laboratories were set up. Charles B. Ferster and I enjoyed a very profitable five-year collaboration. Many of our experiments were designed to discover whether the performance characteristic of a schedule could be explained by the conditions prevailing at the moment of reinforcement, including the recent history of responding, but administrative exigencies drew our collaboration to a close before we had reached a sound formulation, and we settled for the publication of a kind of atlas showing characteristic performances under a wide range of schedules (*Schedules of Reinforcement*[23]). The subsequent development of the field can be traced in the *Journal of the Experimental Analysis of Behavior*, which was founded in 1958.

Several special themes have threaded their way through this history, and some of them call for comment.

Verbal Behavior

I began to explore the subject in the middle thirties. The greater part of a manuscript was written with the help of a Guggenheim Fellowship in 1944-45, from which the William James Lectures at Harvard in 1947 were taken. A sabbatical term in the spring of 1955 enabled me to finish most of a book, which appeared in 1957 as *Verbal Behavior*.[24] It will, I believe, prove to be my most important work. It has not been understood by linguists or psycholinguists, in part because it requires a technical understanding of an operant analysis, but in part because linguists and psycholinguists are primarily concerned with the listener—with what words mean to those who hear them, and with what kinds of sentences are judged grammatical or ungrammatical. The very concept of communication—whether of ideas, meanings, or information—emphasizes transmission to a *listener*. So far as I am concerned, however, very little of the behavior of the listener is worth distinguishing as verbal.

In *Verbal Behavior*, verbal operants are classified by reference to the contingencies of reinforcement maintained by a verbal community. The classification is an alternative to the "moods" of the grammarian and the "intentions" of the cognitive psychologist. When these verbal operants come together under multiple causation, the effect may be productive if it contributes, say, to style and wit, but destructive if it leads to distortion and fragmentation. Speakers manipulate their own verbal behavior in order to control or qualify the responses of listeners, and grammar and syntax are "autoclitic" techniques of this sort, as are many other practices in sustained composition. A technology of verbal self-management emerges that is useful both in "discovering what one has to say" and in restricting the range of controlling variables—emphasizing, for example, the kinds of variable (characteristic of logic and science) most likely to lead to effective practical action or the kinds found to be more productive of poetry or fiction.

The Nervous System

My thesis was a sort of declaration of independence from the nervous system, and I restated the position in *The Behavior of Organisms*. It is not, I think, antiphysiological. Various physiological states and processes intervene between the operations performed upon an organism and the resulting behavior. They can be studied with appropriate techniques and there is no question of their importance. A science of behavior has its own facts, however, and they are too often obscured when they are converted into hasty inferences about the nervous system. I would still say, as I said in *The Behavior of Organisms*, that no physiological fact has told us anything about behavior that we did not already know, though we have been told a great deal about the relations between the two fields. The helpful relation is the other way round: a behavioral analysis defines the task of the physiologist. Operant theory and practice now have an important place in the physiological laboratory.

Psychopharmacology

At Minnesota, W. T. Heron and I studied the effects of a few familiar drugs on operant behavior, and in the early fifties, Dr. Peter Dews of the Department of Pharmacology at the Harvard Medical School became associated with my laboratory and coworkers. At about the same time many of the ethical drug companies set up operant laboratories, some of which contributed to the present armamentarium of behavior-modifying drugs. Operant techniques are now widely used in the field, as well as in the study of drug addiction and related medical problems.

Ethology

Ethologists often assert that their work is neglected by behaviorists, but Watson's first experiments were ethological, and so were mine. The process of operant conditioning itself is part of the genetic equipment of the organism, and I have argued that reinforcers are effective, not because they reduce current drives (a widely held view), but because susceptibilities to reinforcement have had survival value. Species-specific behavior may disrupt operant behavior, but the reverse is also true.

In *Science and Human Behavior* I pointed out that contingencies of survival in natural selection resembled contingencies of reinforcement in operant conditioning. Both involve selection by consequences, a process which, in a work in progress, I argue to be particularly relevant to the question of whether human behavior can indeed take the future into accout. Phylogenic contingencies that could have shaped and maintained, say, imitative behavior resemble the contingencies of reinforcement that shape similar behavior in the individual, but one repertoire does not evolve from the other. An experiment on imprinting has shown how an operant analysis may clarify field observations and correct conclusions drawn from them: the young duckling does not inherit the behavior of *following* its mother or an imprinted object; it acquires the behavior because of an innate susceptibility to reinforcement from being close.

A Theory of Knowledge

I came to behaviorism, as I have said, because of its bearing on epistemology, and I have not been disappointed. I am, of course, a radical rather than a methodological behaviorist. I do not believe that there is a world of mentation or subjective experience that is being, or must be, ignored. One feels various states and processes within one's body, but these are collateral products of one's genetic and personal histories. No creative or initiating function is to be assigned to them. Introspection does not permit us to make any substantial contribution to physiology, because "we do not have nerves going to the right places." Cognitive psychologists make the mistake of internalizing environmental contingencies —as in speaking of the storage of sensory contacts with the environment in the form of memories that are retrieved and responded to again at some later date. There is a sense in which one *knows* the world, but one does not *possess* knowledge; one behaves because of one's exposure to a complex and subtle genetic and environmental history. As I argued in a final chapter in *Verbal Behavior*, thinking is simply behaving and may be analyzed as such. In *About Behaviorism* I attempted to make a comprehensive statement of the behaviorist's position as I understood it forty-six years after I first entered the field.

Designing a Culture

Walden Two was an early essay in the design of a culture. It was fiction, but I described a supporting science and technology in *Science and Human Behavior*. I was made aware of a basic issue when *Walden Two* was immediately attacked as a threat to freedom. Its protagonist was said to have manipulated the lives of people and to have made an unwarranted use of his own value system. I discussed the issue in a paper called "Freedom and the Control of Men" in 1955[26] and in a debate with Carol Rogers in 1956.[27] The control of behavior became especially critical with the rise of an applied behavioral analysis in the 1960s, and I returned to the issue in *Beyond Freedom and Dignity* in 1971.[28] Unfortunately, that title led many people to believe that I was opposed to freedom and dignity. I did, indeed, argue that people are not in any scientific sense free or responsible for their achievements, but I was concerned with identifying and promoting the conditions under which they *feel* free and worthy. I had no quarrel with the historical struggle to free people from aversive control or from punitive restrictions on the pursuit of happiness, and I proposed that that struggle be continued by shifting to practices that employed positive reinforcement, but I argued that certain aspects of the traditional concepts stood in the way. For example, to make sure that individuals receive credit for their actions, certain punitive practices have actually been perpetuated. I believe that a scientific formulation of human behavior can help us maximize feelings of freedom and dignity.

There is a further goal: what lies beyond freedom and dignity is the survival of the species, and the issues I first discussed in *Walden Two* have become much more pressing as the threat of a catastrophic future becomes clearer. Unfortunately, we move only slowly toward effective action. A question commonly asked is this; when shall we have the behavioral science we need to solve our problems? I believe that the real question is this: when shall we be able to use the behavioral science we already have? More and better science would be helpful, but far more effective decisions would be made in every field of human affairs if those who made them were aware of what we already know.

REFERENCES

1. RUSSELL, BERTRAND. 1927. Philosophy. W.W. Norton Company. New York, N.Y.
2. WATSON, JOHN B. 1924. Behaviorism. W.W. Norton Company. New York, N.Y.
3. PAVLOV, I.P. 1927. Conditioned Reflexes. Oxford University Press. Oxford, England.
4. SHERRINGTON, CHARLES S. 1906. Integrative Action of the Nervous System. Yale University Press. New Haven, Conn.
5. MAGNUS, R. 19524. Körperstellung. Springer. Berlin, Germany.
6. SKINNER, B.F. 1956. A case history in scientific method. American Psychologist 11:221-233. (Reprinted in Reference 7.)
7. SKINNER, B.F. 1972. Cumulative Record. Third edit. Appleton-Century-Crofts. New York, N.Y.
8. WOODWARD, ROBERT S. 1931. Contemporary Schools of Psychology. Ronald Press. New York, N.Y.
9. MACH, ERNST. 1893. The Science of Mechanics. Open Court. Chicago, Ill.
10. BRIDGMAN, PERCY W. 1928. The Logic of Modern Physics. MacMillan. New York, N.Y.
11. SKINNER, B.F. 1931. The concept of the reflex in the description of behavior. Doctoral thesis. Harvard University Library. Cambridge, Mass. (Part One reprinted in Reference 7.)
12. TOLMAN, EDWARD C. 1932. Purposive Behavior in Animals and Men. Century. New York, N.Y.
13. TOLMAN, EDWARD C. 1935. Psychology versus immediate experience. Philosophy of Science 2: 356-380.
14. SKINNER, B.F. 1935. The generic nature of stimulus and response. J. Gen. Psychol. 12: 40-65. (Reprinted in Reference 7.)
15. SKINNER, B.F. 1935. Two types of conditioned reflex and a pseudo-type. J. Gen. Psychol. 12: 66-77. (Reprinted in Reference 7.)
16. KONORSKI, J. & S. MILLER. 1937. On two types of conditioned reflex. J. Gen. Psychol. 16: 264-272.
17. SKINNER, B.F. 1937. Two types of conditioned reflex: a reply to Konorski and Miller. J. Gen. Psychol. 16: 272-279.
18. SKINNER, B.F. 1938. The Behavior of Organisms. Appleton-Century. New York, N.Y.
19. SKINNER, B.F. 1948. Walden Two. MacMillan. New York, N.Y.
20. SKINNER, B.F. 1953. Science and Human Behavior. MacMillan. New York, N.Y.

21. SKINNER, B.F. 1954. The science of learning and the art of teaching. *In* Current Trends in Psychology and the Behavioral Sciences. University of Pittsburgh Press. Pittsburgh, Pa. Reprinted in Skinner, B.F. 1968. The Technology of Teaching. Appleton-Century-Crofts. New York, N.Y.
22. HOLLAND, J. G. & B.F. SKINNER. 1961. The Analysis of Behavior. McGraw-Hill. New York, N.Y.
23. FERSTER, C. B. & B.F. SKINNER. 1957. Schedules of Reinforcement. Appleton-Century-Crofts. New York, N.Y.
24. SKINNER, B.F. 1957. Verbal Behavior. Appleton-Century-Crofts. New York, N.Y.
25. SKINNER, B.F. 1974. About Behaviorism. Alfred A. Knopf. New York, N.Y.
26. SKINNER, B.F. Freedom and the control of men. American Scholar. Winter 1955-1956.
27. SKINNER, B.F. & C. R. ROGERS. 1956. Some issues concerning the control of human behavior. Science 124: 1057-1066.
28. SKINNER, B.F. 1971. Beyond Freedom and Dignity. Aldred A. Knopf. New York, N.Y.

PUBLICATIONS

B.F. Skinner

Papers

1. The progressive increase in the geotropic response of the ant *Aphaenogaster*. Journal of General Psychology, 1930, 4, 102-112. (with T.C. Barnes)
2. On the inheritance of maze behavior. Journal of General Psychology, 1930, 4, 342-346.
3. On the conditions of elicitation of certain eating reflexes. Proceedings of National Academy of Sciences, 1930, 16, 433-438.
4. The concept of the reflex in the description of behavior. Journal of General Psychology, 1931, 5, 427-458.
5. A paradoxical color effect. Journal of General Psychology, 1932, 7, 481-482.
6. Drive and reflex strength I. Journal of General Psychology, 1932, 6, 22-37.
7. Drive and reflex strength II. Journal of General Psychology, 1932, 6, 38-48.
8. On the rate of formation of a conditioned reflex. Journal of General Psychology, 1932, 7, 274-286.
9. The rate of establishment of a discrimination. Journal of General Psychology, 1933, 9, 302-350.
10. On the rate of extinction of a conditioned reflex. Journal of General Psychology, 1933, 8, 114-129.
11. The measurement of "spontaneous activity." Journal of General Psychology, 1933, 9, 3-24.
12. "Resistance to extinction" in the process of conditioning. Journal of General Psychology, 1933, 9, 420-429.
13. The abolishment of a discrimination. Proceedings of National Academy of Sciences, 1933, 19, 825-828.
14. Some conditions affecting intensity and . . . American Journal of Physiology, 1933, 106, 721-737. (with E.F. Lambert and A. Forbes)
15. Has Gertrude Stein a secret? Atlantic Monthly, January 1934, 50-55.
16. The extinction of chained reflexes. Proceedings of National Academy of Sciences, 1934, 20, 234-237.
17. A discrimination without previous conditioning. Proceedings of National Academy of Sciences, 1934, 20, 532-536.
18. The generic nature of the concepts of stimulus and response. Journal of General Psychology, 1935, 12, 40-65.
19. Two types of conditioned reflex and a pseudo type. Journal of General Psychology, 1935, 12, 66-77.
20. A discrimination based upon a change in the properties of a stimulus. Journal of General Psychology, 1935, 12, 313-336.
21. A failure to obtain "disinhibition." Journal of General Psychology, 1936, 14, 127-135.
22. The reinforcing effect of a differentiating stimulus. Journal of General Psychology, 1936, 14, 263-278.
23. The effect on the amount of conditioning of an interval of time before reinforcement. Journal of General Psychology, 1936, 14, 279-295.

24. Thirst as an arbitrary drive. Journal of General Psychology, 1936, **15**, 205-210.
25. The verbal summator and a method for the study of latent speech. Journal of Psychology, 1936, **2**, 71-107.
26. Conditioning and extinction and their relation to drive. Journal of General Psychology, 1936, **14**, 296-317.
27. Two types of conditioned reflex: A reply to Konorski and Miller. Journal of General Psychology, 1937, **16**, 272-279.
28. Changes in hunger during starvation. Psychological Record, 1937, **1**, 51-60. (with W.T. Heron)
29. The distribution of associated words. Psychological Record, 1937, **1**, 71-76.
30. Effects of caffeine and benzedrine upon conditioning and extinction. Psychological Record, 1937, **1**, 340-346. (with W.T. Heron)
31. An apparatus for the study of animal behavior. Psychological Record, 1939, **3**, 166-176. (with W.T. Heron)
32. Some factors influencing the distribution of associated words. Psychological Record, 1939, **3**, 178-184. (with W.T. Heron)
33. The alliteration in Shakespeare's sonnets: A study in literary behavior. Psychological Record, 1939, **3**, 186-192.
34. The psychology of design. Art Education Today. B. Boas (editor). New York: Columbia Press, pp. 1-6, (1937).
35. The rate of extinction in maze-bright and maze-dull rats. Psychological Record, 1940, **4**, 11-18. (with W.T. Heron)
36. A method of maintaining an arbitrary degree of hunger. Journal of Comparative Psychology, 1940, **30**, 139-145.
37. A quantitative estimate of certain types of sound-patterning in poetry. American Journal of Psychology, 1941, **54**, 64-79.
38. Some quantitative properties of anxiety. Journal of Experimental Psychology, 1941, **29**, 390-400. (with W.K. Estes)
39. The processes involved in the repeated guessing of alternatives. Journal of Experimental Psychology, 1942, **30**, 495-503.
40. Reply to Dr. Yacorzynski. Journal of Experimental Psychology, 1943, **32**, 93-94.
41. The operational analysis of psychological terms. Psychological Review, 1945, **52**, 270-277.
42. Baby in a box. Ladies Home Journal, October 1945.
43. An automatic shocking-grid apparatus for continuous use. Journal of Comparative and Physiological Psychology, 1947, **40**, 305-307.
44. 'Superstition' in the pigeon. Journal of Experimental Psychology, 1948, **38**, 168-172.
45. Are theories of learning necessary? Psychological Review, 1950, **57**, 193-216.
46. Human use of human beings. Psychological Bulletin, 1951, **48**, 241.
47. How to teach animals. Scientific American, 1951, **185**, 26-29.
48. The experimental analysis of behavior. Proceedings and papers of the 13th International Congress of Psychology, 1951.
49. Some contributions of an experimental analysis of behavior. American Psychologist, 1953, **8**, 69-78.
50. The science of learning and the art of teaching. Harvard Educational Review, 1954, **24**, 86-97.
51. A new method for the experimental analysis of the behavior of psychotic patients. Journal of New Mental Diseases, 1954, **120**, 403-406.
52. Critique of psychoanalytic concepts and theories. Scientific Monthly, 1954, **79**, 300-305.
53. What is psychotic behavior? Theory and Treatment of the Psychoses, (Dedication of Renard Hospital, St. Louis), 1955, 77-99.
54. The control of human behavior. Transactions of the New York Academy of Sciences, 1955, **17**, 547-551.
55. Freedom and the control of men. American Scholar, 1955-56, **25**, 47-65.
56. A case history in scientific method. American Psychologist, 1956, **2**, 221-233.
57. Some issues concerning the control of human behavior. Science, 1956, **124**, 1057-1066. (with C.R. Rogers)
58. The experimental analysis of behavior. American Scholar, 1957, **45**, 343-371.
59. A second type of superstition in the pigeon. American Journal of Psychology, 1957, **70**, 308-311. (with W. H. Morse)
60. Concurrent activity under fixed-interval reinforcement. Journal of Comparative and Physiological Psychology, 1957, **50**, 279-281. (with W.H. Morse)
61. Diagramming schedules of reinforcement. Journal of Experimental Analysis of Behavior, 1958, **1**, 67-68.

62. Some factors involved in the stimulus control of operant behavior. Journal of Experimental Analysis of Behavior, 1958, 1, 103-107. (with W.H. Morse)
63. Reinforcement today. American Psychologist, 1958, 13, 94-99.
64. Teaching machines. Science, 1958, 128, 969-977.
65. Fixed-interval reinforcement of running in a wheel. Journal of Experimental Analysis of Behavior, 1958, 1, 371-379. (with W.H. Morse)
66. Sustained performance during very long experimental sessions. Journal of Experimental Analysis of Behavior, 1958, 1, 235-244.
67. John Broadus Watson, behaviorist. Science, 1959, 129, 197-198.
68. Pigeons in a pelican. American Psychologist, 1960, 15, 28-37.
69. The design of cultures. Daedalus, Summer 1961, 534-546.
70. Why we need teaching machines. Harvard Educational Review, 1961, 31, 377-398.
71. Technique for reinforcing either of two organisms with a single food magazine. Journal of Experimental Analysis of Behavior, 1962, 5, 58. (with G.S. Reynolds)
72. Operandum. Journal of Experimental Analysis of Behavior, 1962, 5, 224.
73. Squirrel in the yard. Harvard Alumni Bulletin, May 1962.
74. Two "synthetic social relations." Journal of Experimental Analysis of Behavior, 1962, 5, 531-533.
75. Conditioned and unconditioned aggression in pigeons. Journal of Experimental Analysis of Behavior, 1963, 6, 73-74. (with G.S. Reynolds and A.C. Catania)
76. Behaviorism at fifty. Science, 1963, 140, 951-958.
77. Operant behavior. American Psychologist, 1963, 503-515.
78. Reply to Thouless. Australian Journal of Psychology, 1963, 15, 92-93.
79. A Christmas caramel, or, a plum from the hasty pudding. Worm Runner's Digest, August 1963, 2, 42-46.
80. Reflections on a decade of teaching machines. Teachers College Record, 1963, 65, 168-177.
81. New methods and new aims in teaching. New Scientist, May 20, 1964.
82. "Man." Proceedings of the American Philosophical Society, 1964, 108, 482-485.
83. The technology of teaching. Proceedings of the Royal Society, 1965, 162, 427-443.
84. Stimulus generalization in an operant: a historical note. Edited by D.I. Mostofsky in Stimulus Generalization, California: Stanford University Press, 1965, 193-209.
85. Why teachers fail. Saturday Review, October 16, 1965.
86. The phylogeny and ontogeny of behavior. Science, 1966, 153, 1205-1213.
87. An operant analysis of problem-solving. Edited by B. Kleinmuntz in Problem Solving: Research, Method and Theory, New York: Wiley, 1966.
88. Conditioning responses by reward and punishment. Royal Institution of Great Britain, Lecture Summary, 1966, 41, 48-51.
89. Contingencies of reinforcement in the design of a culture. Behavioral Science, 1966, 11, 159-166.
90. What is the experimental analysis of behavior? Journal of the Experimental Analysis of Behavior, 1966, 9, 213-218.
91. Some responses to the stimulus "Pavlov". Conditional Reflex, 1966, 1, 74-78.
92. Visions of utopia. The Listener, January 5, 1967.
93. Utopia through the control of human behavior. The Listener, January 12, 1967.
94. The problem of consciousness—a debate. Philosophy and Phenomenological Research —a quarterly Journal, 1967, 3, 325-337.
95. The science of human behavior. Twenty-five Years at RCA Laboratories 1942-1967, 92-102.
96. Utopia and human behavior. Humanist, July-August 1967.
97. Teaching science in high school. Science, 1968, 159, 704-710.
98. Edwin Garrigues Boring. Year Book of the American Philosophical Society, 1968, 111-115.
99. The design of experimental communities. International Encyclopedia of the Social Sciences, 1968, 271-275.
100. Contingency management in the classroom. Education, 1969, 90, 93-100.
101. The machine that is man. Psychology Today, April 1969, 2.
102. Creating the creative artist. On the Future of Art, New York: Viking Press, 1970.
103. Humanistic behaviorism. The Humanist, May/June 1971.
104. Autoshaping, Science, 1971, 173, 752.
105. A behavioral analysis of value judgments. The Biopsychology of Development, 1971, 543-551.
106. Why are the behavioral sciences not more effective? The Listener, September 30, 1971.

107. Some relations between behavior modification and basic research. Modificacion de la Conducta. Edited by Bijou, Ribes, 1972.
108. On "having" a poem. Saturday Review of the Arts, July 1972.
109. Humanism and behaviorism. The Humanist, July/August 1972.
110. Freedom and dignity revisited. New York Times, August 11, 1972.
111. The freedom to have a future. The 1972 Sol Feinstone Lecture, Syracuse University, 1973.
112. Compassion and ethics in the care of the retardate. Jos. P. Kennedy, Jr. Foundation for Mental Retardation. (Not published)
113. Reflections on meaning and structure. From I.A. Richards Essays in His Honor, Oxford University Press, 1973, 199-209.
114. Some implications of making education more efficient; 72nd Yearbook of the National Society for the Study of Education, 1973, Chap. XIV, 446-456.
115. Are we free to have a future? Impact, 1973, 3, 6-12.
116. Walden (one) and walden two. Thoreau Society Bulletin, One hundred twenty-two, Winter 1973.
117. The free and happy student. New York University Education Quarterly, IV, Winter 1973, 2-6.
118. Designing higher education. Daedalus, 1974, 196-202.
119. The steep and thorny way to a science of behavior. American Psychologist, 1975, 30, 42-49.
120. The shaping of phylogenic behavior. Acta Neurobiol. Exp., 1975, 35, 409-415.
121. The ethics of helping people. Criminal Law Bulletin, 1975, 11, 623-636.
122. Farewell, my lovely! Journal of Experimental Analysis of Behavior, 1976, 25, 218.

Books

Behavior of Organisms. 1938. New York: Appleton-Century.
Walden Two. 1948. New York: Macmillan.
Science and Human Behavior. 1953. New York: Macmillan.
Verbal Behavior. 1957. New York: Appleton-Century-Crofts.
Schedules of Reinforcement. (with Charles F. Ferster) 1957. New York: Appleton-Century-Crofts.
Cumulative Record. 1959. New York: Appleton-Century-Crofts. (Enlarged Edition 1961; Third Edition 1972.)
The Analysis of Behavior. (With James G. Holland) 1961. New York: McGraw-Hill.
The Technology of Teaching. 1968. New York: Appleton-Century-Crofts.
Contingencies of Reinforcement. 1969. New York: Appleton-Century-Crofts.
Beyond Freedom and Dignity. 1971. New York: Alfred A. Knopf, Inc.
About Behaviorism. 1974. New York: Alfred A. Knopf, Inc.
Particulars of My Life. 1976. New York: Alfred A. Knopf, Inc.

DISCUSSION

Robert W. Rieber, Kurt Salzinger, and Gilbert Voyat, *Moderators*

DR. INHELDER: (In response to an inaudable question): One of my points was that the theory of self-regulating mechanism or equilibrium of compensations is one of the main factors. Contradiction is one symptom of the fact of bringing these regulatory mechanisms into play.

Awareness of contradiction, as I tried to say, is the cue for the observer that the growing mind is in a state of disequilibrium, that he cannot bring all the parts together in an overwhelming scheme, and has to produce new subschemes to deal with.

QUESTION: Since this is a very historic occasion, with Dr. Skinner and Dr. Inhelder on the same panel, I would like to ask them both a question, and that is, do you think there is any chance of resolving the conflicts between your two points of view into one broad theory?

DR. SKINNER: I think the situation stands as follows. Last night Dr. Bakan paid operant conditioning a very great compliment. He said that it worked *some of the time*. Nothing else he mentioned last night seemed to work any of the time. I will accept that. Let's say that an operant analysis works half the time. I am willing to leave the other half to Dr. Piaget.

DR. INHELDER: I also want to make the point that Skinner and Piaget are asking different questions. I think it's incorrect to speak of contradictory theories. Rather, they complement each other. In Geneva, we are mostly interested in the process of development and how changes occur through development; therefore, we are asking questions regarding transition mechanisms, as well as studying the epistemological relationship between subject and object, in the course of growing knowledge.

[Editor's Note: The common denominator of Skinner and Piaget's points of view is without doubt their biological perspective, which implies the activity of the organism or of the "epistemic" subject. Both are principally interested in behavioral changes and are asking the question of the role and the mechanisms that can be attributed to the environmental factors of selection. R. W. R.]

DR. SKINNER: I accept that. I think that we must always wait for the child or the organism to give us the answer. We had a saying around my laboratory that the rat is always right. When graduate students plan experiments and they don't come out right, they feel that something is wrong with their animals, but of course something must have been wrong with their plans or their procedures. It's a very difficult point to learn, but we have to learn it. After all, it is the subject matter that will finally tell us the story. We are asking questions in different ways. It would be nice if the answers suddenly applied to both our questions.

DR. RIEBER: I think that makes it clear that the golden fleece is surely not for sale here this afternoon.

QUESTION: In developing the T.A.T., to what extent were you influenced by Jung's method of dream elaboration, where he asks the patient to focus on a particular aspect, a particular scene from the dream, and create a story around that scene from the dream; because I have read that you were at one time analyzed by Dr. Jung. Is that correct?

DR. MURRAY: I don't think I got any influence in that way. Only now for the first time have I heard of that way of analyzing dreams. I think it came from the theory of projection tested in earlier experiments that we did with children who gave different estimates of the malevolence of others—as judged from photographs—when they (the children) were in a state of fright. Fright was engendered by participation in a game called "Murder."

DR. SIDNEY LANDAU: Dr. Skinner, given your views that we ought to promote the illusion of freedom and responsibility, isn't your continued statement that we in fact have no freedom, and therefore no responsibility, subversive of that idea.

DR. SKINNER: I don't want to promote an illusion; I want to promote the feeling of freedom and dignity. I want to put people under contingencies of reinforcement such that when they feel their bodies and report what they feel, they will say "I feel free," or will say they are doing what they *want* to do, rather than what they *have* to do. There is no illusion; there are simply different types of contingencies. I think a world in which people work for things rather than to avoid things is a better world. It makes more use of genetic endowment, there are fewer by-products, and so on.

DR. LANDAU: Well, but if people understood the behavioral grounds of the actions, how could they possibly feel that they had the responsibility to act as they wish?

DR. SKINNER: What is important is not their feelings but the contingencies under which they are acting. If you want to change human behavior, then change the contingencies rather than the feelings. You can't actually get at the feelings except by changing the contingencies, anyway. That would be the case with felt states like responsibility or belief or confidence. I don't want to change people's feelings, but I do want to use contingencies under which they will have the kinds of feelings that are important to them. I want to induce them to subscribe to a way of life in which environmental contingencies generate the bodily conditions felt as freedom.

DR. SALZINGER: I wonder if I may ask a question. Despite the fact that there has just been an armistice declared between Piaget and Skinner, I wonder if I can ask Dr. Inhelder about a reaction that I seem to have whenever I see Piagetian experiments and whether that is a conflict or whether that too is simply another way of looking at things and it's all right. Whenever I hear the statement that at one "stage" the child pays attention to, say, the horizontal length of bars, and at another stage, the child behaves in a way that can be called "counting," I wonder if that isn't at least explained as well as by the behavior theory explanation that the child is at this point being reinforced for paying attention to one aspect of the bar and at another time to another aspect of the stimulus.

DR. INHELDER: I think the child is really trying to make his own estimates and the way of making these estimates is not the same on the different levels of his development. As it is switching rapidly from one type of estimate to another, it brings them into connection; there are, of course, situations where experimental design facilitates this bringing together of different kinds of estimates, and activates the "prise de conscience" of possible conflict. This grasp of consciousness of conflicting new problems which the child tries to overcome brings about new judgments.

DR. SALZINGER: But is that learning? Isn't that simply learning? In other words, you could produce that conflict in me by making the instructions sufficiently complicated that I wouldn't quite know which it is that you want me to do. Am I supposed to match the pattern, the number, or the horizontal length, or maybe even the thickness of the lines which also vary?

DR. RIEBER: Since the armistice has just been signed, perhaps it is a little too early to add the inevitable differences that will come out.

DR. VOYAT: Still, if I may, I would like to ask a question of Dr. Skinner, namely, the conditions under which correct contingencies can be defined. Are they only external to the subject definitions, or is the idea of an internal structuration for the understanding of correct contingency inherently part of your definition of what a correct contingency is?

DR. SKINNER: The body of a person stimulates that person. The sense organs in use, however, evolved at a time when people were not verbal organisms and had no intellectual life. They simply report movement of the skeleton musculature and events in the viscera important for the internal economy and the execution of action. What we should like to have are nerves running to those centers in the brain which are involved in the kinds of activities that you are talking about. The motivational activities in the brain stem have no connection with them because we have had no chance to evolve a suitable nervous system. Introspection has been too recent a thing in human history. Perhaps in a million years we could evolve a new nervous system that would be in contact with all the important parts of the brain. At the moment we do not have nerves going to the right places; hence we don't know what's going on.

What we learn about our own body is obviously important, but we talk about it inaccurately. You observe a child eating rapidly, and you say "Oh, you must be hungry." If the child is getting internal stimulation as well, then later on he will say "I am hungry" in response to nothing but the internal stimulation. But the precision depends upon the correlation between internal and external events.

DR. S. ANDERSON (New York State Psychiatric Institute): I have a question for Dr. Skinner. I am afraid I am one of those psycholinguists who is chastised for being much too attentive to the behavior of the listener, perhaps at the expense of granting to Dr. Skinner's theory of verbal behavior less credit than it deserves. But I would like to propose that the listener can be usefully regarded, especially in terms of human communication, as a reinforcement schedule. The listener is indeed a reinforcer of a very elaborate sort, such that each one of us, when he acquires language, acquires the ability to feed signals to this mysterious listener, in such a way that once a signal has been received, the listener can appropriately reinforce it as verbal input, whether it be *mand, tact,* or whatever. Now, taking the viewpoint that the input is a sentence, must not the operations of generative grammar be taken seriously as constituting some of the formal properties of this listener reinforcement schedule, from the viewpoint of verbal behavior itself?

DR. SKINNER: Now I am sorry I have given so much ground to Piaget and Inhelder, because I must take a bit of it back. I think I am handling the cognitive aspects of verbal behavior in my book. I see no reason to add anything to account for that subject matter. I still think that when you are preoccupied with what the listener does in responding to so-called sentences that are often generated by simply moving words around, you are wasting a great deal of time. These are often "sentences" that no one could ever conceivably emit upon any occasion. You make up sentences that no one could possibly say, and you spend a great deal of time trying to figure out why they don't mean anything. It's obvious why they don't mean anything if nobody could possibly say them. You can make up some of the famous paradoxes this way. Someone says, "This sentence is false," and, believe it or not, for 2,500 years philosophers have tried to find out what's wrong. Nobody could possibly emit that sentence as verbal behavior. There is no sentence to be called false until it has been said.

DR. ANDERSON: Well, by this account, that sentence has been much reinforced. Behaviorally, why cannot philosophers, like rats, always be right?

DR. SKINNER: I know they have emitted their sentences for very good reasons, but the reasons do not contribute to the future of the analysis of verbal behavior. I don't mean that what everybody says is right, because there are reasons for saying it.

EPILOGUE:
SITZFLEISCH, THE ZEITGEIST,
AND THE HINDSIGHTGEIST

Kurt Salzinger

Biometrics Research Unit
New York State Psychiatric Institute
New York, New York 10032

Polytechnic Institute of New York
Brooklyn, New York 11201

Ambrose Bierce bitterly defined the historian as "A broad-gauge gossip," and many psychologists, taking his definition seriously, have taught the history of psychology in precisely this way. Suffice it to say that this conference has amply demonstrated how wrong that definition is. Unfortunately, my own background in the history of psychology comes from that time when history was viewed as a collection of hazy, unverifiable guesses about what in human behavior might have caused some particular experimental psychologist to have tried which particular experiment. In those days, we viewed history only as error from which we were, if smart enough, privileged to profit. To find the error of a previous scientist's ways was the highest kind of mental activity, even for the behaviorist.

In the course of my teaching career, I stumbled into a Department of Social Sciences that includes, among the subjects that it teaches, both history and psychology, thus forcing me to learn some history just to communicate with my colleagues, and so I like to think that I am not altogether as ignorant of this subject matter as I used to be. Nevertheless, I cannot point to any publication directly bearing on the subject matter of the history of psychology in my *vita*. True enough, I did, a couple of years ago[1] introduce a day-long meeting on the history of psychology, and for that purpose I did analyze somewhat the contents of some then recent issues of the *Journal of the History of the Behavioral Sciences*, but there are those who have not viewed that presentation entirely as a scholarly work of the first rank. Therefore, to overcome my inferiority complex in this area, I decided to use the occasion at last to prepare a scholarly piece of research in the history of psychology.

I have learned, by this time, that a true historian does not rely on mere published material to discover the contributions of, for example, some particular psychologist, but that he/she must make every effort to find in the personal effects of the significant figure being studied the unpublished, not to speak of the unpublishable, papers, and perhaps most important, to find those unpublished materials never meant to be seen by the public at all. Since this is a bicentennial conference, I realized that I must find a person—unhappily, I must report I investigated the life of a man, not a woman, but that undoubtedly reflects those times rather than the capability of women in those days—living around two hundred years ago who might have been influenced by the writers of the Declaration of Independence, who was perhaps active in government, and, most important of all, who had not been studied by anyone else before. I am happy to report that I found a person having at least some of these qualifications. Although I am not totally at liberty to divulge all of my sources, I can say that all were reliably checked by having at least two sources for every fact stated in this paper. What's more, I expect to be able to write a book on the material that I found. The tentative title is *The First, Middle and Final Days of Dr. Wilhelm Urpsyche.*

As you probably guessed from the name, our hero is of German extraction. The significance of that will come out of our discussion as we go on. I employed a recently discovered technique of using the impressions made on vases by the voices of the potters as they worked. Suffice it to say here that we replayed some of the vases that Dr. Urpsyche, an accomplished psychoceramicist, was known to have thrown; that is to say, to have made himself. The fidelity of these vases is not very good, but with the aid of some amplification equipment borrowed from the Haskins Laboratory, we have deduced a definite German accent in whatever the hell he could have been saying when he threw his pots. I hesitate to report what one observer has been insisting he heard, because this is the only instance of one source for a statement of fact. But it is interesting enough for us to speculate about, so I am including it here. The reported statement is: "Stop with the water already." The possible significance of this statement is such as to require no further comment.

But to return to the life of Dr. Wilhelm Urpsyche. As close as I could determine, he was born in the year 1746. He was 30 years of age at the time of the signing of the Declaration of Independence. I wish I could say that his birthday coincided with the day of the signing, but since I was unable to find his exact birthday, I am unable to do so. The only evidence I could find for any awareness of the fathers of our country was a statement by Urpsyche to the effect that any man who invented as many things as Jefferson did, had to be lazy.

Those of you who are interested in the methodology of obtaining original material might wish to hear how I came upon it. The tale of the finding of the records is actually quite brief. They were left on my doorstep in a carefully wrapped package measuring four feet wide, by four feet long, by six feet high. I decided to unwrap it, given the fact that it otherwise would have been impossible for any of us in my family to get out the door. Now that I have told you how I acquired my data, I am not sure how I can advise you to make use of this method. As already indicated, I obtained confirmation of all the most exciting details of Dr. Urpsyche's life from at least one other source. Unfortunately, I am not at liberty to divulge the name of the Medium. She insisted that we always work in the dark, a condition not unknown to some historians, and which is what finally convinced me of her authenticity. She brought me into communication with the various compatriots of Dr. Urpsyche, and I shall have occasion to refer to those contacts later.

I might just point out to the students in the audience how fortunate it is that I know German, since despite the fact that Dr. Urpsyche worked exclusively in the United States, he wrote all of his papers and books in German. After he wrote them, they had to be translated into English in order to be read by his colleagues. You must know languages, if you are going to do any significant work in the history of psychology.

The circumstance of Dr. Urpsyche's writing all of his work in German may well account for the fact that there is so little mention of him in our history of psychology books. It was one of the factors that held my work up very badly in communicating with the colleagues of Dr. Urpsyche through the Medium: They all insisted that I translate long excerpts of Dr. Urpsyche's work for them; most of them had had only an inkling of his writings when they were all alive, having got to know his work based only on his infrequent lectures at a small college just outside Boston, called, they tell me, Saint Catastrophe. I have not, so far, been able to verify the name, although it does seem appropriate for an increasing number of schools. The school apparently did come to an untimely end sometime in the third quarter of the eighteenth century, according to my immaterial informants.

The informants were able to explain the existence of the large number of documents on this psychologist. According to them, he was always very conscious of what would happen after he died, and apparently he wanted to make sure that if ever there was an historian of psychology desirous of reconstructing his life and works, he, Dr. Urpsyche, would make it as easy as possible.

What makes the collection of notes and diaries from Dr. Urpsyche so valuable is that in his last few years he became obsessed with the idea of getting all of his thoughts down on paper. In order that he not lose anything, he refused to communicate with people at all unless they agreed to write down whatever they wanted of him and were willing to put up with having to wait for him to write down whatever he wanted to say in response.

As a result of his copious notekeeping and the writing down of all of his conversations, I had quite a time separating the significant from the mundane. Just to give you one example, I can't begin to tell you the number of times I came across the notation, "Please pass the salt," although I am having a graduate student get a precise count for me. On the basis of a preliminary analysis, I can say that the response of asking for salt clearly outnumbers the response for asking for molasses. In about three months we should have precise figures on this matter.

The matter of asking for the salt to be passed as often as he did, by the way, may have some significance in that his colleagues described him to me as being a man who would take the then-current theories of behavior with more than a grain of salt. He used to put it, one of my incorporeal informants reported, "Zu viel verstehen heisst zu viel verdrehen." (Too much understanding means too much confusing.) The richness of information available on his behavior at home, so to say, provides us with a storehouse of insights into his behavior in the laboratory. The data we have on Dr. Urpsyche's private life might well bring within our reach the possibility of finally responding to the recent onslaught of psychohistories whose only validation is in the minds of their authors; we might look upon Dr. Urpsyche's historical analysis as a kind of Urpsychohistory.

Dr. Urpsyche's writings were legion, although, as already explained, his publications were rather slow in coming, since he wrote everything in German. Then, in characteristic fashion, having once finished a particular piece of work, he lost interest, refusing to return to it in order to translate it. The Hessian soldiers he employed to do the translation of his work at the time of the Revolution unfortunately did not live long enough to do the kind of thorough job he found acceptable, and in some cases whole manuscripts were actually lost on the battlefield.

Of the book-length manuscripts that came to me in that large package of artifacts, I found first of all the book that apparently was instrumental in getting Dr. Urpsyche his first job at a university. The book was called *Mach Schnell*; it was the only book that was actually completely translated into English, but somehow it didn't get any publisher sufficiently interested to put it into print. Students apparently passed the book around from one to another, as can be gleaned from the various gratuitous remarks that are to be found on the margins of its pages. Suffice it to say that the student caliber of that day is quite comparable to that of today. The title, *Mach Schnell*, as you no doubt know, means Do It Quickly. It was Dr. Urpsyche's treatise on reaction time, was well liked among his colleagues, and apparently was also what got him elected to the status of

Honorary Fellow in the International Society of Schnell Machen, so named after his book of similar title. He was just about putting the finishing touches on a second book, *Mach Schneller*, when he was elected president of that organization.

In his later years, when he completely disowned his earlier work and published his countertreatise, *Mach Langsam*, Do It Slowly, he was actually read out of that organization. We know how badly he felt about his colleagues' fair-weather friendship from the notes we see of conversations he had with his wife, Langsam. She kept asking, "Why is it important to do things quickly, Wilhelm?" and he kept retorting, "I know, I know, I will try to make it langsam, Langsam."* Once again we see the importance of having available private conversations to shed light on the critical interactions that must take place in all scientists between their scientific and their private behaviors.

The last paper that I found written by Urpsyche was unfinished. It begins with the words, "Nun steh ich da, ich armer Tor"—Here I stand, poor fool I am —. This is also the only paper in which he had a coauthor, a certain Dr. Faust. Dr. Faust left a note not to forget to thank Gretchen (no last name is given) for all her help in making this paper possible.

There are some other tidbits of Dr. Wilhelm Urpsyche's life that I have learned over the past few months in communication with my incorporeal informants. Dr. Urpsyche had a sense of humor. After particularly bad results on an examination that he gave his students, he was wont to say: "If God had really wanted people to think, he would have given them brains." This remark, oft repeated, eventually turned into, "Maybe God really didn't want people to think."

I have also looked a little into Dr. Urpsyche's childhood, his toilet-training regime, sleeping arrangements, opportunities to witness the primal scene, and such, but have so far found nothing of significance in that area beyond the fact that Dr. Urpsyche's family lived in one room, which contained one bed (quite large by reputation, although the exact dimensions were not available), and no toilet facilities. Apparently, all the toilet training was done at a neighbor's house some two and one-half miles away. I am quite sure that none of these peculiar circumstances of early life have any bearing on Dr. Urpsyche's later—shall we say —unique sexual orientations. But I expect to continue to mine this large mound of information for a while longer and to report on these results on a later occasion.

Before I end my paper, I should explain its title. The Zeitgeist hardly needs any explanation at all; it refers to the fact that the time has finally come when historians of psychology can freely talk about its history and do so in a professional way, my presentation notwithstanding. The Sitzfleisch concept refers to the fact that the bottom line of writing history is remaining in one place for a long time. Finally, the Hindsightgeist reminds us all to be modest in our historical analyses, for our wisdom comes from viewing things that have already taken

---

*The remarkable coincidence of Dr. Urpsyche's wife's name, Langsam, and the meaning of the German word *langsam*—namely, slow—is in fact just that, a remarkable coincidence. The fact of the repeated occurrence of the word Mach in all the book titles so far treated, and the fact of Dr. Urpsyche's son's name being Ernst—as in Ernst Mach—are also, as far as I could determine from looking over the Mach papers, to be ascribed to coincidence. No historian can afford to read meaning into every observed coincidence of events lest he/she commit the fallacy of misplaced literalism.[2] Ernst Mach never mentioned Urpsyche, which is not to say that he did not know of his existence, but certainly we have no proof that he did. Also, we have no evidence that Ernst Mach changed his name to Ernst Mach, which might be one way in which Urpsyche might have influenced Mach. Finally, although not directly pertinent to the point in question, Ernst Urpsyche (Dr. Urpsyche's son) died in an accident during a boat race (Mach Schnell?). His boat capsized and his body was never found.

place. To make even more significant contributions, we must try to spell out the lessons of foresight, namely how to do it better the next time around.

REFERENCES

1. SALZINGER, K. 1976. What's in a title? Ann. N.Y. Acad. Sci. **270**: 1-5.
2. FISCHER, D. H. 1970. Historians' fallacies. Harper & Row. New York, N.Y.